CAREER DEVELOPMENT INTERVENTIONS IN THE 21ST CENTURY

FOURTH EDITION

SPENCER G. NILES
Pennsylvania State University

JOANN HARRIS-BOWLSBEY
Kuder, Inc., Adel, Iowa

PEARSON

Boston   Columbus   Indianapolis   New York   San Francisco   Upper Saddle River
Amsterdam   Cape Town   Dubai   London   Madrid   Milan   Munich   Paris   Montreal   Toronto
Delhi   Mexico City   São Paulo   Sydney   Hong Kong   Seoul   Singapore   Taipei   Tokyo

Vice President and Editorial Director: Jeffery W. Johnston
Senior Acquisitions Editor: Meredith D. Fossel
Associate Editor: Anne Whittaker
Editorial Assistant: Andrea Hall
Vice President, Director of Marketing: Margaret Waples
Marketing Manager: Christopher Barry
Senior Managing Editor: Pamela D. Bennett
Project Manager: Kerry Rubadue
Senior Operations Supervisor: Matthew Ottenweller
Senior Art Director: Diane Lorenzo

Text Designer: S4Carlisle Publishing Services
Cover Designer: Karen Noferi
Cover Image: Shutterstock
Media Project Manager: Rebecca Norsic
Full-Service Project Management: S4Carlisle Publishing Services
Composition: S4Carlisle Publishing Services
Printer/Binder: Courier/Westford
Cover Printer: Courier/Westford
Text Font: Sabon LT Std

Credits and acknowledgments borrowed from other sources and reproduced, with permission, in this textbook appear on the appropriate page within the text.

Library of Congress Cataloging-in-Publication Data

Niles, Spencer G.
   Career development interventions in the 21st century/Spencer G. Niles, JoAnn
Harris-Bowlsbey.—4th ed.
      p. cm.
   Includes index.
   ISBN-13: 978-0-13-265859-1
   ISBN-10: 0-13-265859-3
   1. Career development.   2. Career development—Case studies.   I. Harris-Bowlsbey, JoAnn.   II. Title.
   HF5381.N547 2013
   650.14—dc23

                                                                                      2011047148

10 9 8 7 6 5 4 3 2 1

www.pearsonhighered.com

ISBN 10:   0-13-265859-3
ISBN 13: 978-0-13-265859-1

PREFACE

We have taught career courses to students in numerous universities in the United States as well as in Canada, Japan, Denmark, Portugal, England, Turkey, Australia, United Arab Emirates, and Spain, to mention just a few. Wherever students are interested in learning about career development theory and practice, we are eager to go! In each instance, however, not only are we teaching students about career development interventions, but students also teach us. The idea for this book began in response to student requests (pleas) for a career development textbook that was readable, useful, and interesting. These are high but reasonable expectations, which have served as our guiding principles as we composed the chapters of this book.

NEW TO THIS EDITION

In addition to consistently updating this textbook to reflect the most cutting-edge research, trends, and pedagogy, we have made the following changes to this edition:

- Discussions of the impact of globalization, contemporary issues, and the financial crisis of the 21st century on career development have been incorporated into Chapter 1.
- The research and work of additional critical theorists, including Anne Roe, Mark Savickas, and Jim Bright have been integrated.
- Additional sections on culturally competent career assessment and Lesbian/Gay/Bisexual/Transgender Questioning Identity Models have been included.
- New technology sections cover Web-based career guidance systems and the use of social networking for career guidance and job-seeking purposes.
- New in-text student assignments and activities have been provided to encourage application and practice of the theoretical concepts presented in each chapter. These assignments and activities make use of advanced systems such as the Kuder® Career Planning System and challenge the student to use this resource as a basis for further study.
- Additionally, many of these student assignments are based upon new video content created for this edition. These videos include outstanding examples of how leading career development experts conduct career counseling with diverse career counseling clients. The clients are real clients with genuine career concerns. The career counseling sessions were not scripted in any way. The career counselors had very little, and in some cases, no information about their clients prior to their career counseling sessions. The sessions are also not edited. Thus, the videos offer a realistic view of how nationally-recognized career counseling experts conduct career counseling. Some of the videos also contain interviews with leading career development theorists and/or representatives of the leading theories who were

close collaborators with the theorists they represent. These videos are designed to show how theory translates to practice. Videos featuring David Reile, Carol Dahir, Michael Hall, Mark Savickas, Barbara Suddarth, and Janet Lenz can be accessed through the Video and Resource Library on the **MyCounselingLab**™ website. (See below for more information about **MyCounselingLab**™).

- Use of this book provides access to no-fee use of *Kuder Navigator,* an industry-leading, Web-based career planning system that provides outstanding resources for helping secondary school students develop their educational and career plans.
- To make this book more accessible and applicable, every chapter now includes a case study. Our goal is to help readers connect chapter content to the lives of the people represented in the cases. Although the cases are, for the most part, fictional, they reflect the career concerns of people with whom we have worked as career counselors in schools, in community settings, and in higher education. Thus, we are indebted to our clients as well as our students for teaching us about the career development process. We seek to share these experiences with the readers of this book.

Another goal of this text is to convey to our readers the deep respect and long-term commitment we have for career development theory and practice. We emphasize this goal in Chapter 1. As we note in the book, few things are more personal than career choice, and we were cognizant of this fact as we wrote each chapter. Making career decisions involves deciding how we will spend one of the most precious commodities we have—our time on Earth. We realize that these decisions are often difficult and overwhelming. Thus, we draw upon the work of our colleagues in the field to present readers with state-of-the-art career theory and practice. However, the current situation evolved from the past contributions of many leaders in the field. We acknowledge their important foundational contributions in Chapter 1.

Although we cover a wide variety of theoretical perspectives in the book (especially in Chapters 2 and 3), we emphasize that careers develop over time. A decision point in one's career development is just that: a point in time at which one makes decisions based on previous and current career development experiences. Although knowing how to help people at these important points in their career development is crucial, career practitioners can also intervene proactively in the lives of children, adolescents, and adults in ways that facilitate positive career development prior to the occurrence of career crises. Being able to provide assistance in both instances is critical.

We are especially concerned that career development theory and practice be inclusive. Constructing culturally inclusive career development interventions should be standard practice within the field. Unfortunately, this has not traditionally been the case. In part because of their historical context, career theories and practices focused primarily on the career experiences of European American middle-class males. Although we devote a chapter to providing culturally competent career development interventions (Chapter 4), throughout the book we also address the need for inclusive career interventions. Our case studies highlight the career experiences of clients from diverse backgrounds. We think both approaches (having a single chapter devoted to the topic and infusing diversity throughout the book) are needed to begin to more adequately address the career development needs of all people. We are also excited about the career counseling videos we produced for this edition as they provide excellent examples of career counseling with diverse clients.

The need to provide clients with culturally sensitive career interventions provides an important foundation for discussing career counseling interventions in Chapter 8 and career assessment approaches in Chapter 5. The career counseling process and outcomes information provided here reflect the most recent work within the field. We also provide career information, resources, and Web site references (Chapters 6 and 7) that represent important aspects of the career development process. We highlight the essential considerations in designing and implementing career development programs in Chapter 9. We also emphasize in Chapter 9 the importance of engaging in the ongoing evaluation of career services. This is important for improving service delivery. However, when resources are limited, as they are in many situations, the need for both accountability and the ability to demonstrate effectiveness is great. Finally, we highlight developmental approaches to providing career assistance in the schools, community settings, and higher education in Chapters 10 through 13.

Of course, the desire to engage in ethical practice is also a standard in the field. However, there are many challenges confronting career practitioners. Web-based services such as career counseling and career assessment, the possibility of dual relationships, and theories with deeply rooted value sets present challenges to practitioners as they engage in ethical practice. Thus, we address many of these current ethical challenges in Chapter 14. This is the first, and still one of the few, career development textbooks with a chapter devoted to ethical practice.

To make the book even more useful to readers, we use a framework developed by the National Career Development Association (NCDA). Specifically, we use the NCDA's career counseling competencies and the CACREP Standards to guide us in the identification of chapter topics. These competencies and standards appear in the appendices at the end of the book and at the following Web addresses:

associationdatabase.com/aws/NCDA/pt/sd/news_article/37798/_self/layout_ccmsearch/true

cacrep.org

Please note that printed on the inside front cover is a grid identifying the chapters that are most relevant to each competency category and Council for Accreditation of Counseling and Related Educational Programs (CACREP) standard. For those focused on career interventions in K–12 settings, we also incorporate the National Career Development Guidelines into Chapters 10 (elementary school) and 11 (middle and high school).

We hope that we have accomplished the goals that motivated us to write this book. We also hope that we have fulfilled our students' expectations. In teaching our career courses, we consider it high praise when students tell us that they have a new respect and appreciation for career development interventions as a result of the class experience. This is what we hope occurs with this book. We invite readers to send us their feedback directly (sgniles@psu.edu). We are committed to improving the book in any way that we can. Your comments will guide us in the revisions that we make. We are also happy to speak (either in person or virtually) to classes that are using our text. Simply contact us with such requests and we will arrange for a time to make this happen. Finally, we wish you the very best as you embark on an exciting adventure with regard to your ongoing professional development.

MyCounselingLab™

Help your students bridge the gap between theory and practice with MyCounselingLab™. MyCounselingLab™ connects your course content to video- and case-based real world scenarios, and provides:

- Assignments & Activities assess students' understanding of key concepts and skill development. Hints and feedback provide scaffolding and reinforce key concepts.
- Building Counseling Skills exercises offer opportunities for students to develop and practice skills critical to their success as professional helpers. Suggested responses are available to instructors, making grading easy.
- Multiple-Choice Quizzes help students gauge their understanding of important topics and prepare for success on licensure examinations.

Access to MyCounselingLab™ can be packaged with this textbook or purchased standalone. To find out how to package student access to this website and gain access as an Instructor, go to www.MyCounselingLab.com, email us at counseling@pearson.com, or contact your Pearson sales representative.

ACKNOWLEDGMENTS

I am grateful for and humbled by the support and love I have received from my family members and mentors. My mother, Pauline, taught me at an early age about the importance of Donald Super's life-space theory segment as she balanced work and family demands as a single parent in the 1960s and 1970s. She was a pioneer who lived with grace and dignity—despite substantial challenges presented both to professional women and to single parents.

My family members have challenged statements of self-doubt and have tolerated my long work hours for many years. My children, Jenny and Jonathan, teach me about love each day and help to make me a better person. I am fortunate to have the opportunity to watch as their careers unfold. I am particularly thrilled that my daughter, Jenny, is soon to graduate from the school counseling program at Wake Forest University. Jenny contributed activities for the school counseling chapters in this book. I hope that she and her counterparts at all counselor education training programs find this book to be helpful to them in their work.

My professional mentors and cherished friends have guided me through multiple career development tasks. Edwin L. Herr was the first to provide support and guidance, and he has continued to do so for more than 25 years. He embodies the best of what a mentor should represent. I will forever be indebted to Ed for his personal and professional assistance. Mark L. Savickas and Donald E. Super have also provided guidance, and I am honored that, at various times in my career, they have cared.

Finally, I have been honored to coauthor this book with JoAnn Harris-Bowlsbey. She is extremely knowledgeable, wise, gracious, and kind. I look forward to future editions and opportunities to work together.

Spencer G. Niles

Like Spencer, my life was molded by a mother who was a single parent and who worked incredibly hard to ensure that I had a level of education and access that she never enjoyed. She taught me the principles of faith, responsibility, commitment, and service. I want to acknowledge her role in laying the foundation that made my present life and contributions possible.

My most valued professional mentor was Donald E. Super, who was kind enough to share his writings and thoughts with me for 30 years. I have personally enjoyed the fullness of his career rainbow in my life. Nancy Schlossberg and David Tiedeman also contributed mightily to my conception of the process of career development and have enriched the well from which the content of this book flows.

My professional contributions would not have been possible without the ongoing support of my late husband, Stan. For the 33 years of our marriage, he placed a very high priority on my career and helped all that he could—editing, proofreading, doing home chores—to nourish it, never pressuring for more of my time. Finally, my ongoing friendship with and respect for Spencer Niles deepens as we experience the authorship of this book and other professional pursuits together.

JoAnn Harris-Bowlsbey

We both appreciate the dedicated assistance and support provided by Meredith Fossel and Kerry Rubadue at Pearson.

We wish to thank those who reviewed the third edition and made suggestions for improvement that we have incorporated into this fourth edition of the book: Rebecca M. Dedmond, George Washington University; Kimberly J. Desmond, Indiana University of PA; Al Levin, California State University, Sacramento; A.J. Metz, University of Utah; and Daniel Philip, University of North Florida.

Brief Contents

CONTENTS

1

Introduction to Career Development Interventions

Like it or not, work (our job) becomes and remains one of the most omnipresent parts of our lives. In many ways it defines who we are. And let's face it, it's the essential element in which to provide ourselves with the basic needs of day-to-day living, such as food, shelter, and transportation. In time, as our careers progress, they can provide more: quality leisure time, a pool in the backyard, investments for our children's education. Every day we get up and go to work. There's no getting out of it, so it's imperative to choose a field or endeavor that will enrich our lives. It adds a certain quality not only to our personal worlds but also to the world around us, not with great bursts of genius, but rather with a slow, steady infusion of our knowledge and skills.

Regarding the many complexities of work, I believe one of the most important aspects of any job is the finished product. Whether we are contractors building a house, doctors repairing a heart, or teachers educating a student, from the very onset we need to focus on the finished product and take pride in the process that achieves that finished product. We should never settle for anything less than our best effort, because it matters. It matters to the homeowner, the patient, and the student, and it most certainly should matter to us. Pride in our work, our accomplishments, and the diligence we put into them can and will make all the difference in the world.

David H.
Contractor

Work is something that I do because I have to. If I won the lottery, I wouldn't work. As a single parent of two young children, I have to be responsible. I do it for them. Can work be "meaningful"? I hope to experience that some day. Right now, it's how my family and I get by—that's the most important thing and most days it's not fun.

Ann D.
Food service worker

My work means everything to me (well, almost everything). As an oncologist, I am dedicated to my work and my patients. I feel a tremendous responsibility to be the best physician that I can be. I also feel a responsibility to be the best I can be as a representative of my family and the African American community. I have dedicated much of my life to this activity. It is what gives me meaning and purpose. I feel fortunate to do the work that I do.

Camille S.
Physician

MyCounselingLab™

Visit the **MyCounselingLab**™ site for *Career Development Interventions in the 21st Century,* Fourth Edition to enhance your understanding of chapter concepts. You'll have the opportunity to practice your skills through video- and case-based Assignments and Activities as well as Building Counseling Skills units, and to prepare for your certification exam with Practice for Certification quizzes.

As Stephanie and her classmates discussed their new lives as master's degree students in counselor education, their attention turned toward their class in career development. They wondered why they needed to take this course. José confidently declared that he had no interest in providing career counseling and that he was not likely ever to need to know much about the topics they would cover in the career development course. Jonathan agreed and stated that he found the prospect of giving people tests to be rather boring. Beth was clear that she was headed toward private practice as a licensed professional counselor and that she would probably just refer clients with career concerns to other practitioners interested in that sort of work. Chandra did not agree, but her peers seemed so clearly negative about this class that she was reluctant to say so. She had witnessed the influence that work had on her family, and she knew it was an important topic to understand. Her father had been laid off from his job as an engineer when the company he worked for moved overseas. Her family had struggled to make ends meet as Chandra's father searched for new employment. Her mother struggled to keep her full-time job while also taking care of Chandra and her two younger brothers. When her father was forced to settle for a job that provided far less than his previous one in terms of pay, challenge, and satisfaction, she watched as he became more depressed and as the tension between her parents increased. Even her brothers were behaving differently and getting into more trouble at school. Chandra worried about her family and she knew that their future was being influenced significantly by her parents' career development. Chandra saw connections between work and life through the experience of her own family, and she hoped that the career development course would help her understand how to help people in similar situations.

David H., Ann D., and Camille S. each communicate the diverse values, purposes, and goals that people attach to work. When they can, many people view work as an outlet for self-expression and a vehicle for creating meaning and purpose in life. Other people work to provide for their families and, often due to circumstances beyond their control, approach work as a means to an end. Some, like Camille, view work as an individual responsibility connected to her cultural identity and cultural group. Many others struggle simply to find work. The unemployment rate in the United States in April 2011 was 9% compared to 4.4% in April of 2001 (Bureau of Labor Statistics, 2011). An unemployment rate of 9% equates to more than 13 million people without a means to earn a living in one of the wealthiest countries in the world. Unfortunately, Chandra's experience is not unusual today. Adults struggle to cope with their careers in uncertain times. Adolescents feel the pressure to succeed but are often unclear as to how their daily experiences in high school connect to their future educational and career opportunities. Children are constantly exposed to occupational stereotypes that influence their perceptions of what future opportunities are open to them. Thus, it is no surprise that the need to provide career assistance exists in every setting in which counselors work. Counselors in school, higher education, and community settings will, to varying degrees and at various times, encounter clients confronting career development issues. For example, the American School Counselor Association identifies career development as one of three key areas essential to the work of school counselors. Survey results examining the concerns expressed by students in higher education consistently identify the need for career planning assistance as the most dominant area of concern that students experience. Employers downsize frequently, making career issues a constant concern for adult workers.

Despite the prevalence of career issues confronting people in contemporary society, many students in counseling and related educational programs are similar to José, Jonathan, and Beth in that they react less than enthusiastically to enrolling in the required "career information" course (Heppner, O'Brien, Hinkelman, & Flores, 1996). Perhaps some students imagine course requirements as forcing them to memorize sections of occupational information books or spending hours learning how to administer and interpret tests to advise clients as to what occupations they should choose. Perhaps they view career development interventions as separate from more general counseling interventions, with the skills requirements of the former involving information dissemination, advising, and test administration, and the skills of the latter involving more "sophisticated" therapeutic techniques. Maybe they envision career development interventions that resemble mechanistic processes in which the counselor acts in directive ways and takes complete responsibility for career intervention outcomes. Or, perhaps, like Beth, they view career development interventions as irrelevant to their future work as counselors. Whatever the reasons for the lack of enthusiasm many students feel toward courses related to career development, we challenge such views and assumptions.

We believe (and we think that Chandra would agree!) that competent career practitioners must possess expertise in a broad and challenging array of counseling-related competencies. The knowledge and skills required for providing career assistance effectively encompass and go beyond those required in more general counseling (Blustein & Spengler, 1995; Crites, 1981; Gysbers, Heppner, & Johnston, 2003; Herr, Cramer, & Niles, 2004; Liptak, 2001). For example, the career counseling competencies identified by the National Career Development Association (NCDA) (2003a) indicate that career counselors need knowledge and skills in career development theory; individual and group counseling; individual/group assessment; career information/resources; program promotion, management, and implementation; career coaching/consultation; multicultural counseling; supervision; ethical/legal issues; and using technology effectively in the career intervention process. These skill areas obviously extend far beyond those limited to career advising and test administration!

Moreover, the topics related to career development interventions are exciting and challenging. In many ways, career development interventions connect with recent emphases in psychology on optimal human functioning, maximizing happiness, and fulfilling human potential (Hartung, 2002; Niles, Amundson, & Neault, 2011; Savickas, 2009). Essentially, career practitioners seek to help their clients increase their life satisfaction. At their core, career development interventions focus on helping people consider how they will develop and use their talents as they live their lives. Career development practitioners in the 21st century seek to empower people to construct meaning out of their unique life experiences and then translate that derived meaning into appropriate occupational and other life-role choices. Translating life experiences into career choices requires people to possess a relatively high level of self-awareness. Accordingly, career practitioners strive to provide interventions that help their clients clarify and articulate their self-concepts. These interventions can include formal, standardized assessments as well as informal, nonstandardized assessment activities that actively and creatively engage clients in the career intervention process (Amundson, 2009). Because sorting through career concerns and engaging in career planning are complex processes, competent career practice requires counselors to be skilled at developing effective working alliances with their clients (Anderson & Niles, 2000; Multon, Heppner, Gysbers, Zook, & Ellis-Kalton, 2001; Perrone, 2005). Career practitioners meet their clients at the intersection of what has been and what might be in their clients' lives. When career counselors work collaboratively and innovatively with their clients to construct a clear career direction, both the client and the counselor experience the intervention process as exciting and positive (Anderson & Niles).

We also realize that multiple challenges confront career practitioners in the career intervention process. Career decision making is rarely a simple task and, therefore, good career counseling is never mechanistic and routine. When we consider the fact that decisions about work are made within a life context that intertwines with other life roles and responsibilities, the complex and often stressful nature of career decision making becomes clear (Perrone, Webb, & Blalock, 2005). What might, on the surface, seem to be a relatively straightforward process of making a decision about work can quickly become overwhelming, frustrating, and complicated when important factors such as family expectations, limited occupational opportunities, financial limitations, and multiple life-role commitments are considered (Vondracek, Lerner, & Schulenberg, 1986). Clearly,

Chandra had already learned this fact as a result of her parents' career development experiences. The opening quote from Ann D. also reinforces the complexity of career challenges.

Given the complexity of career decision making, there should be little surprise that many clients seeking career counseling experience substantial levels of psychological distress (Multon et al., 2001; Niles & Anderson, 1993). Obviously, career counselors must address their clients' distress as they also help them clarify their values, skills, life-role salience, interests, and motivations. When clients also experience low self-esteem, weak self-efficacy, and little hope that the future can be more satisfying than the past, the career counselor's task becomes even more challenging (Lent, Brown, & Hackett, 2002). Clients coping with such issues require more assistance in resolving their career dilemmas than a test battery can provide. Given this fact, it is not surprising that career counseling clients describe the support and the experience of an effective therapeutic alliance with their career counselors as one of the most helpful aspects of their career counseling experience (Anderson & Niles, 2000; Multon et al., 2001). Obviously, skills found to be essential counseling skills (e.g., establishing rapport, reflective listening, expressing empathic understanding) are also essential career counseling skills.

Working collaboratively and effectively with clients also requires career practitioners to possess multicultural competencies at an advanced level (Leong, 1995). For instance, clients operating from a collectivistic orientation engage in the career planning process in important ways that differ from clients operating from an individualistic orientation (Hartung, Speight, & Lewis, 1996). Working with the client's cultural context is essential to providing effective career assistance. For example, Kim, Li, and Liang (2002) found that career counselors focusing on the expression of emotion were perceived as having greater cross-cultural competence than were counselors focusing on the expression of cognition when working with Asian American college students with high adherence to Asian values. Leong (2002) found acculturation to be positively related to job satisfaction and negatively related to occupational stress and strain. Gomez and colleagues (2001) found that Latina career development is strongly influenced by sociopolitical, cultural, contextual, and personal variables. Specifically, factors such as socioeconomic status, family, cultural identity, and the existence of a support network all helped to shape the course of career development for the Latinas participating in the Gomez et al. study. Madonna, Miville, Warren, Gainor, and Lewis-Coles (2006) highlight the importance of understanding the client's religious orientation within the career development experience. Paul (2008) describes the use of a constructive-developmental approach to career counseling that incorporates a client's sexual identity into the career counseling process. Pepper and Lorah (2008) discuss the importance of workplace considerations and career concerns for transsexual individuals. The client's constellation of cultural/contextual variables clearly matters in the career intervention process. Thus, similar to general counseling interventions, the career development intervention process is a dynamic, complex, and challenging one that requires career practitioners to draw upon multicultural counseling skills to effectively help their clients move forward in their career development (and, like general counseling, all career counseling is also multicultural counseling).

Tips from the Field

Because there are few things more personal than a career choice, it is important to remember that good career counselors are, first, good counselors.

Additionally, indications are that the career development process will become more, rather than less, complex in the near future. Change, transition, and instability dominate the career development landscape. For example, the Bureau of Labor Statistics (2004) reports that one in four workers has been with his or her current employer for less than a year. This level of transition involves costs to companies and to society as new workers must be trained, and transitioning workers often require social benefits such as unemployment insurance and Temporary Assistance to Needy Families as they experience periods of unemployment between jobs.

In addition to decreased longevity with a single employer, workers today are operating within a globalized economy. Thomas Friedman described this phenomenon, in his book titled *The World is Flat: A Brief History of the 21st Century*. Friedman notes that technological advances have created a more level economic playing field with previously disadvantaged countries rising in knowledge and wealth to rival that of the United States and other world powers. Computer and communications technologies, previously a stronghold of developed countries, have been accessed and mastered by countries such as China and India, making these nations more economically competitive. This leveling or "flattening" of access and opportunity has had a major impact on the nature of work throughout the world. For one thing, it has accelerated economic globalization or the economic interdependence of national economies so that what happens economically in one country has an impact on the economy of another country. The global unemployment rates of the past several years provide clear evidence of this fact.

Another impact of economic globalization is the outsourcing of jobs from the United States to other countries. When viewed in the most positive light, reallocation of jobs from America to a foreign country raises that country's economy and standard of living, and consequently, the demand for American goods and services. The company that outsources the work enjoys the benefit of lower costs because the wages in developing countries are lower than those of developed countries. Workers in the developing countries have greater employment opportunities and developing countries get access to the latest technology. Because globalization also results in increased competition, companies are forced to lower the prices of their products, thereby resulting in benefits to the consumer. In Friedman's view, these developments will continue until world economies are lateral, that is, show a flat line. A flat world means we are mutually economically dependent and in more communication with each other.

To compete effectively in a "flat" world, Friedman proposes the following as being necessary for 21st-century workers. First, there is the need to be constantly engaged in learning. It is essential that workers learn new ways of doing old things as well as new ways of doing new things. Second, it is essential to develop a sense of passion for, and curiosity about, life. Passion and curiosity are powerful forces that bring energy, innovation, and new ideas to the workplace. Third, the capacity to work collaboratively is a requisite skill for addressing the complex challenges in the 21st century. Interpersonal skills contribute to someone being viewed as a valued team member who contributes positively to any workplace challenge. Finally, being able to balance analytical thinking with creativity provides a valuable perspective to solving problems that companies encounter. Friedman's list of effective career self-management skills for the 21st century can be expanded to include (a) the capacity to cope with change and tolerate ambiguity, (b) the ability to acquire and use occupational information effectively, (c) the ability to adjust quickly to changing work demands, and (d) the skills to use technology effectively. Developing these capacities with specific job content skills will enable workers to stay current in today's global economy.

Before leaving our discussion of globalization, however, it is important for us to note that the globalization scenario is not altogether positive. There are substantial and undeniable negative outcomes of a flattening world. For example, workers in manufacturing and white-collar jobs have fewer employment opportunities in nations where this work has been outsourced to other countries. Those employed as programmers, editors, engineers, and accountants represent examples of workers who have experienced fewer opportunities in developed countries due to the outsourcing of their work to developing countries. Globalization has also led to the increased exploitation of workers in developing countries. A report by the Untied Nations (2000) indicates that globalization has increased inequality and discrimination while also widening the economic gap between the "haves" and the "have-nots." Safety standards are often ignored to produce goods less expensively. It is also the case that many developing countries do not have child labor laws and, in such countries, child workers are often placed in inhumane working conditions. Many companies have established factories in countries that are lacking in environmental regulations and that take advantage of this lack by discharging pollutants into the soil and nearby waterways. There has also been an increase in human trafficking related to globalization. Finally, the UN report notes that multinational companies have become increasing influential in political decisions impacting legislation and public policies that often benefit companies but not those who work within them.

Clearly, globalization presents a mixture of positive benefits for us to enjoy and negative outcomes for us to address. The list of negative outcomes listed above can be added to the long-existing income disparities between men and women; differences in income levels and employment opportunities between White and nonwhite workers; economic disparities and employment discrimination between those who are abled and differently disabled; disparities between those who have access to quality education and the opportunities that education provides and those for whom those opportunities are currently closed; employment discrimination experienced by sexual minorities; and unfortunately, the list goes on. Such issues highlight the relevance of social justice and advocacy for career development practitioners. In fact, we contend that being able to engage effectively in social justice and advocacy has become essential for competent career practitioners in the 21st century.

Among other things, engaging in social justice and advocacy requires career development practitioners to learn about legislation and public policies that support workers and provide for the provision of career development services (e.g., the Workforce Investment Act, the Americans with Disabilities Act) across the life span. Related to this, Friedman identifies the need for legislation that makes it easier to switch jobs by making retirement benefits and health insurance less dependent on one's employer and by providing insurance that would partly cover a possible drop in income when changing jobs. Friedman also believes there should be more inspiration for youth to be scientists, engineers, and mathematicians due to a decrease in the percentage of these professionals. Such recommendations provide implicit support for infusing career development language into the reauthorization of the next iteration of the Elementary and Secondary Education Act (most recently referred to as No Child Left Behind). Knowing how to impact policy and legislation thus becomes an important skill for career development practitioners. Being a multiculturally competent career practitioner is also an essential component of providing effective career interventions. Throughout this book we highlight these skills and connect them to more traditional career development interventions. We also emphasize the point that due to the fact that children, adolescents, and adults are all required to cope successfully with career development tasks to manage their careers effectively, all counselors must be skilled at providing career interventions and must understand the career development process, regardless of their work setting (Niles & Pate, 1989).

THE MEANING OF WORK ACROSS TIME

Obviously, understanding the career development process and being able to provide holistic, comprehensive, and systematic career development interventions across the life span requires career practitioners to appreciate the role that work plays in people's lives. There is substantial evidence indicating that the meaning of work for people across the globe is changing in the 21st century (e.g., Ardichvili & Kuchinke, 2009; Borchert & Landherr, 2009; Ferrar, Nota, Soresi, Blustein, Murphy, & Kenna, 2009). Unfortunately, the shifts occurring in work patterns are not necessarily positive for workers in the United States. For example, most workers in industrialized countries now enjoy the benefits of substantial periods of paid annual leave (typically about three weeks per year) and paid parental leave. Currently, 134 countries have laws establishing a maximum length to the work week. The exception to these trends is the United States. Williams and Boushey (2010) report that there is no legally mandated annual leave, no federal law requiring paid sick days, and there is no national paid parental leave benefit in the United States. According to the International Labour Organization, Americans work 137 more hours per year than Japanese workers, 260 more hours per year than British workers, and 499 more hours per year than French workers. Workers in the United States seem to cling tightly to the centrality of work in their lives. Currently, 85.8% of men and 66.5% of all women in the United States work more than 40 hours per week. So it should come as no surprise that Americans report sharply higher levels of work-family conflict than do citizens of other industrialized countries. Fully 90% of American mothers and 95% of American fathers report work-family conflict (Williams & Boushey).

By standards that existed in the 1800s, when the average American worked 70 hours per week, the centrality of work in the identities of many Americans has arguably lessened, but by current standards the data indicate that work continues to dominate the identities of many Americans. This is not surprising given that the work you choose influences the persons with whom you will associate for a major portion of your daily life; it also affects how much vacation you take and when it will occur, the types of continuing education and training that you will engage in, the type of supervision you will have, the degree of autonomy you will experience, and the lifestyle you will enjoy. Thus, it is no surprise that one of the first questions people ask each other when first meeting is, "What do you do?" Although on the surface this is a rather open question and people could respond by describing a wide variety of life activities, they seldom do. There is the implicit (if not explicit) understanding that the query relates to what one does to earn a living. Such interactions reinforce the contention that in a fluid industrial society, occupation is one of the principal determinants of social status (Super, 1976). Such interactions also support Sigmund Freud's statement that "work is the individual's link to reality." For better or worse, our choice of work colors the perceptual lens through which others often view us and through which we often view ourselves. No doubt we make differing assumptions about people who tell us they are neurosurgeons as compared with those who tell us they are employed at a local fast-food restaurant. In the United States, occupational title tends to be used, correctly or incorrectly, to identify a person more than does any other single characteristic.

It is important to note, however, that in some countries, and at different periods of history, one's choice of work was not as closely connected to one's identity as it is today. Other characteristics, such as one's surname or residence, provided a primary means for self-identification. How is it that work has become such a core component of one's identity? Obviously, in primitive societies work was taken for granted. One worked to survive. In the classical societies, work was viewed as a curse insofar as it involved manual labor as opposed to intellectual labor. (It is interesting to note that the Greek word for "work" has the same root as the word for "sorrow.") The early Christians viewed work as providing the opportunity to help those less fortunate by sharing the fruits of one's labor. The notion that "idleness was akin to sinfulness" also emerged from early Christianity and was maintained throughout the Middle Ages, with the growing idea that work was appropriate for all people as a means of spiritual purification. The Reformation brought little change to this attitude, except for the influence of Martin Luther and John Calvin. Luther viewed work as a form of serving God. Whatever type of work a person engaged in, if it was performed to the best of one's ability, then it had equal spiritual value with all other forms of work.

A more dramatic shift in the meaning of work resulted from the theological perspective espoused by John Calvin and his followers. John Calvin built on earlier traditions that viewed work as the will of God by adding the idea that the results of work (i.e., profits) should be used to finance new ventures for additional profit and, in turn, for additional investment. Additionally, Calvin's doctrine of predestination (i.e., that one's fate after life is predetermined) led his followers to search for visible signs in this life that one was predestined for eternal life. Success in work came to be viewed as a visible sign that one was predestined for eternal life. This view of work resulted in the notion that one was obligated to God to achieve the highest possible and most rewarding occupation. As a result, striving for upward mobility became morally justified. This coincided with the belief that God rewards those who devote time and effort to work. Thus, the Reformation brought about a view of work labeled as the "Protestant work ethic." The value attached to hard work, the need for all persons to work, and the justification of profit emerging from Calvinism would eventually form the basis of modern capitalism and industrialism. The values associated with the Protestant work ethic also served as the basis for the 19th-century view of work labeled by Savickas (1993) as the "vocational ethic." This ethic valued independent effort, self-sufficiency, frugality, self-discipline, and humility and was brought to the United States by the Puritans.

The meaning of work continued to evolve as the United States industrialized and increased its reliance on mechanically generated energy. The determination of a person's status became a question not only of how hard one worked, but also a question of the type of work in which one engaged. In essence, *occupation* replaced *work* as a means of determining one's status. Savickas (1993) noted that this shift in the nature of work occurred on the brink of the 20th century because, at this point in history, individuals turned their vocational efforts to organizing craftspeople into companies and forming large cities built around industries. The rugged individualism reflected in self-employment on farms and in small, craft-oriented businesses was replaced for many people with the challenge of working for a company and moving up the corporate ladder. Because people working for companies found little reinforcement for independence, self-sufficiency, and self-management, a new work ethic emerged as the United States entered the 20th century. Maccoby and Terzi (1981) described this new ethic in the nature of work in the 20th century as the "career" ethic. The career ethic could be described as challenging workers to "find their fit and don't quit." That is, successful careers became defined as work that led to having long tenures within the same company, and successful career paths were those reflecting an upward climb through the organizational ranks. Today, it seems clear that this largely male, White, middle- and upper-socioeconomic class model provides, at best, a minimally useful description of the careers most people experience.

Recent developments in the nature of work bring into question the viability of the career ethic (McCortney & Engels, 2003). For example, many of the organizations served by the career ethic are downsizing in unprecedented numbers. Many workers have found that computers are performing the work tasks they once did. Many employers view workers as expendable commodities. Those workers who have been downsized are often left feeling betrayed, anxious, and insecure about the future (Savickas, 1993). After working long hours and/or relocating to new communities to maintain their employment, many workers are becoming less willing to sacrifice everything for their employers when their employers are so willing to sacrifice them. Survivors of downsizing realize that their situations are anything but secure and their anxieties manifest themselves in longer working hours and more alienation at home (McCortney & Engels).

Additionally, companies are flattening their organizational structures, resulting in fewer career ladders to climb. The elimination of vertical hierarchies brings into question the definition of a "successful" career. Hall and his associates (1996) argue that changes occurring in the structure of employment opportunities portend a future in which "people's careers will increasingly become a succession of 'ministages' of exploration-trial-mastery-exit, as they move in and out of various product areas, technologies, functions, organizations and other work environments" (p. 33). These shifts have led some people to suggest that "work has ended" and the "career has died" (Bridges, 1994; Rifkin, 1995). The tragic echoes of September 11, 2001, and the more recent global economic downturn resulting in high unemployment rates still reverberate throughout the world, influencing politics, economics, international relations and, by logical extension, work. We are still sorting through the ways in which these events will shape people's approach to work. McCortney and Engels (2003) note that "it is essential to consider whether the current concept of the work ethic can be accurately, uniformly applied to all individuals in the 'salad bowl' of the United States today" (p. 135). As we noted previously, due to globalization, this question can be applied regardless of the nation in which one works. Thus, the dust has yet to settle regarding the emerging meanings that people attach to their work activity in the 21st century.

What is clear is that, collectively, these changes in work ethics highlight the fact that career development occurs within a context of constant economic, social, cultural, technological, political, global, and historical change. These changes also underscore the fact that career development, like human development, is an evolutionary process. However, unlike biological expressions of development—which are ontogenetic and, therefore, fairly predictable—career development is a process that is dynamic, interactive, contextual, relational, and often unpredictable.

LINKING WORK WITH WORTH

It also seems clear that, despite historical changes in the meaning people attach to work, and whether it is viewed as a blessing or a curse, work continues to play a central role in our lives. The centrality of work in people's lives was evident in a speech made 30 years ago by then-U.S. Secretary of Education Terrence Bell:

> Work in America is the means by which a person is tested as well as identified. It is the way in which a youngster becomes an adult. Work shapes the thoughts and life of the worker. Changing the way one earns a living can effect a change in atmosphere and lifestyle. For most of us in adult life, being without work is not living. (Riegle, 1982, p. 114)

These are strong words. If they were an accurate reflection of the meaning attached to work during the latter half of the past century, it is not likely that the meaning people attach to work has changed dramatically in the past 30 years. The fact that work maintains its standing as a central role in the lives of many has also been supported empirically (Brief & Nord, 1990; Mannheim, 1993). More recently, Doherty (2009) found that work played a central role in the lives of his study participants, specifically noting that work provided social interactions, which fulfill social and personal needs and a sense of personal identity and meaning. The results supporting the primacy of work in people's lives in the Doherty study were uniform across workplaces and occupations.

Moreover, this phenomenon is not limited to the United States—results from cross-national studies suggest that many people in other countries view work as being more important than leisure, community, and even religion

(Ardichvili & Kuchinke, 2009; Borchert & Landherr, 2009). Harpaz (1999) found that in several multinational studies work was second in importance only to family activities. Not only do we continue to place an extremely high value on work, but people in the United States also tend to use psychological definitions of work. For example, Super (1976) defined work as:

> The systematic pursuit of an objective valued by oneself (even if only for survival) and desired by others; directed and consecutive, it requires expenditure of effort. It may be compensated (paid work) or uncompensated (volunteer work or an avocation). The objective may be intrinsic enjoyment of work itself, the structure given to life by the work role, the economic support which work makes possible, or the type of leisure that it facilitates. (p. 12)

Super's psychologically oriented definition of work places the perceptions and motivations relative to work within the individual's actions and ability to develop one's career. Such definitions reflect the largely American view toward work, which emphasizes individual control in career development (e.g., motivation, discipline, perseverance, goal-directedness) and deemphasizes the role that sociological/contextual variables (e.g., the opportunity structure, the economy, socioeconomic status) play in shaping one's career. Thus, if a person has a "successful career," we tend to make a number of very positive attributions to the person who is a "success" (regardless of whether we actually know the person). The corresponding assumption is that the "unsuccessful" person is inferior. Our denial of the sociological factors influencing the pattern of one's career development, and the centrality of work in our culture, become problematic for many of us because we link work with self-worth (Shanahan & Porfeli, 2002; Subich, 2001). Obviously, if our sense of self-worth is substantially dependent upon how we feel about our work contributions, then our self-esteem can unravel fairly quickly if our work situations go awry (Herr, Cramer, & Niles, 2004). If you have ever felt undecided about your career choice; if you have ever been fired from a job, or worked in a job that was extremely dissatisfying; and/or if you have been unable to find a job, or lived with anyone experiencing any of these events, then you probably have a good sense of the negative emotions that often surface in negative work-related situations.

Linking work with self-worth also becomes problematic when we develop unrealistic expectations for work. For example, O'Toole (1981) suggests that "when it is said that work should be meaningful, what is meant is that it should contribute to the self-esteem, to the sense of self-fulfillment, through the mastering of one's self and one's environment, and to the sense that one is valued by society" (p. 15). Although these are clearly desirable experiences, issues such as dehumanizing work conditions, unemployment, prejudicial hiring practices, downsizing, and mismatches between people and their jobs lead to the conclusion that for many people, work is anything but meaningful (Warnath, 1975). Denying contextual factors influencing career situations can lead people to engage in excessive self-blame when work experiences are negative for reasons beyond their control.

Research conducted by O'Toole (1981) indicates that not only do many workers experience negative work situations and job dissatisfaction, but also they do not know how to improve their situations. A poll conducted by the National Career

Development Association NCDA (1989) revealed that a significant percentage of Americans (39%) did not have a career plan, and an even larger percentage of Americans (69%) did not know how to make informed career choices. Obviously, many adults have information and skill deficits related to career planning and career self-management. Many people have also had limited opportunities to engage in systematic self-exploration for career development, and they are unclear about their training and educational needs. Results from the same poll indicated that almost half of all U.S. workers experience job-related stress and think that their skills are being underutilized in their jobs. Although a similar, more recent survey has yet to be conducted, it seems reasonable to suggest that such experiences have persisted and, perhaps, become exacerbated given the current levels of unemployment globally. If these are the experiences of many, and if we link work with self-worth, then it seems reasonable to suggest that the need for competent career practitioners in contemporary society is substantial and urgent.

Unfortunately, there is a pattern of difficulty in managing career tasks that can be tracked developmentally. For example, Mortimer, Zimmer-Gembeck, Holmes, and Shanahan (2002) provide evidence that many adolescents do not receive assistance in acquiring the skills required for managing their career development effectively. Drawing upon results from 69 interviews (43 women, 26 men) of participants in the Youth Development Project ($n = 1000$), which is a longitudinal study of work through adolescence and early adulthood, these researchers report that study participants experienced few formal mechanisms for helping them locate suitable work as they moved into postsecondary school experiences. The lack of institutional support for young people as they make the school-to-work transition is perplexing, given the centrality of work in people's lives. Mortimer and her colleagues contend that "more systematic efforts are needed to provide vocational information to youth in high schools" (p. 463), and that effort should be made to connect students with the schools and occupations in which they express an interest. Having actual experiences with potential occupations is important in differentiating between satisfied and dissatisfied entrants to the labor force, as well as those whose interest and jobs are congruent. "For youth who lack vocational direction, shifting schools and jobs can entail substantial economic, personal, and social costs" (Mortimer et al., p. 463).

Herr (1989) agrees, noting that high levels of career uncertainty and occupational dissatisfaction are positively correlated with high levels of psychological and physical distress. High levels of unemployment have been associated with increased rates of chemical dependency, interpersonal violence, suicide, criminal activity, and admissions to psychiatric facilities (Herr et al., 2004; Kalton, 2001; Liem & Rayman, 1982). Difficult career situations often translate to difficult life situations. Fritzche and Parrish (2005) cite research supporting the "spillover hypothesis," which suggests that feelings in one area of life affect feelings in other areas of living. Clearly, the ripple effects occurring when career situations go awry can be dramatic and tragic. Moreover, all counselors, regardless of their work settings, will encounter these ripple effects either directly (by working with a client experiencing career difficulties) or indirectly (by working with a family member of a person experiencing career difficulties).

PROVIDING SYSTEMATIC CAREER DEVELOPMENT INTERVENTIONS

It is clear that the need to provide systematic assistance to individuals attempting to deal more effectively with the influence of work in their lives is tremendous. The young, the elderly, the unemployed, the underemployed, the displaced homemaker, the displaced worker; and members of diverse racial, ethnic, and socioeconomic groups are each confronted with work-related issues that have significant implications for their lives. How well they are able to cope with these issues may be the difference between living a life that is meaningful and productive and one that is largely void of meaning and satisfaction.

Counselors provide career assistance to their clients in a number of ways. For example, counselors in high school, postsecondary, and community settings can teach clients the types of skills (e.g., self-assessment, job search, and career information acquisition) that are necessary for effective career planning and career decision making. Counselors in all settings can also help their students/clients to realize that decisions about work influence one's total life. Correspondingly, counselors can help clients develop realistic expectations for what work can provide in terms of personal satisfaction. When work is lacking in personal satisfaction, meaningful participation in other life roles helps to offset this lack of satisfaction. Given the extreme emphasis we place on intra-individual variables in career development, a major task confronting counselors involves helping people to realize that self-worth is not defined by one's work situation. Self-worth relates more to how one lives rather than where one works. These are important lessons that counselors in school, postsecondary, and community settings can teach and reinforce in their students/clients.

More specifically, to help people manage their career development effectively in the 21st century, career counselors help their clients or students learn how to do the following:

1. How to use both rational and intuitive approaches in career decision making
2. How to be clear about the importance attached to each life role and the values one seeks to express through participating in the roles of life
3. How to cope with ambiguity, change, and transition
4. How to develop and maintain self-awareness, especially in the areas of interests, values, motivation, and aptitudes
5. How to develop and maintain occupational and career awareness
6. How to develop and keep one's occupationally relevant skills and knowledge current
7. How to access and participate in lifelong learning opportunities
8. Search for jobs effectively, even when one is not looking for a job
9. Provide and receive career mentoring
10. Develop and maintain skills in multicultural awareness and communication

Skills related to each of these learning areas must be placed in a developmental context so that counselors working with children, adolescents, and/or adults can provide appropriate career interventions. When counselors provide systematic career development interventions that help people acquire these skills, they are effectively responding to former labor secretary Elaine L. Chao's point that "To succeed in the 21st century, our nation must be prepared to adapt to changes in our economy—in how we work, where we work, and how we balance our professional and family lives. We cannot simply react to changes. We must anticipate them, thus helping all workers to have as fulfilling and financially rewarding careers as they aspire to have" (dol.gov/).

DEFINITION OF TERMS

Career development interventions are shaped, in part, by how we define our terms. A major issue within the area of career development interventions is the misuse of terminology among career practitioners as well as clients. For example, it is not uncommon for professional counselors to use the terms *career* and *work* interchangeably. It is also not unusual to hear professionals talk about "doing career development" as if career development were an intervention rather than the object of an intervention. Similarly, counselors often confuse the terms *career guidance* and *career counseling*. This lack of precision confuses practitioners, students, and clients and, therefore, is a barrier to advancing the efficacy of career development interventions. When language lacks precision, the implication is that terminology does not matter. However, words have power in that career development practitioners are "engaged in a verbal profession in which words and symbols frequently become the content of the interactions they have with clients" (Herr, 1997, p. 241). Thus, the need exists for greater clarity and specificity with regard to the key terms related to career development interventions. Such specificity enhances the credibility of our profession and provides a common ground for devising, implementing, and evaluating career development interventions. In this book, we define key terms as explained in the following paragraphs.

Career

Rather than limiting the definition of career to work, we advocate viewing *career* as a lifestyle concept. Accordingly, we concur with Super's (1976) view of career as the course of events constituting a life, and Herr et al.'s (2004) notion of career as the total constellation of roles played over the course of a lifetime. These definitions are broader than the one offered by Sears (1982), which defines career as the totality of work one does in a lifetime. Broader definitions highlight the multiple life roles people play and acknowledge differences across people regarding life-role salience generally and the importance of work in people's lives in particular (Richardson, 1993). For example, broad definitions of career apply to those locating work in the life role of homemaker or in volunteer activities.

Career Development

Career development refers to the lifelong psychological and behavioral processes as well as contextual influences shaping one's career over the life span. As such, career development involves the person's creation of a career pattern, decision-making style, integration of life roles, values expression, and life-role self-concepts (Herr et al., 2004).

Career Development Interventions

Career development interventions, defined broadly, involve any activities that empower people to cope effectively with career development tasks (Spokane, 1991). For example, activities that help people develop self-awareness, develop occupational awareness, learn decision-making skills, acquire job-search skills, adjust to occupational choices after they have been implemented, and cope with job stress can each be labeled as career development interventions. Specifically, these activities include individual and group career counseling, career development programs, career education, computer-assisted career development programs, and computer information delivery systems, as well as other forms of delivering career information to clients.

Career Counseling

Career counseling involves a formal relationship in which a professional counselor assists a client or group of clients to cope more effectively with career concerns (e.g., making a career choice, coping with career transitions, coping with job-related stress, or job searching). Typically, career counselors seek to establish rapport with their clients, assess their clients' career concerns, establish goals for the career counseling relationship, intervene in ways that help clients cope more effectively with career concerns, evaluate clients' progress, and, depending on clients' progress, either offer additional interventions or terminate career counseling.

Career Education

Career education is the systematic attempt to influence the career development of students and adults through various types of educational strategies, including providing occupational information, infusing career-related concepts into the academic curriculum, offering various worksite-based experiences, and offering career planning courses (Isaacson & Brown, 2000).

Career Development Programs

Career development programs can be defined as "a systematic program of counselor-coordinated information and experiences designed to facilitate individual career development" (Herr & Cramer, 1996, p. 33). These programs typically contain goals, objectives, activities, and methods for evaluating the effectiveness of the activities in achieving the goals.

IMPORTANT EVENTS IN THE HISTORY OF CAREER DEVELOPMENT INTERVENTIONS

The rise of career development interventions accelerated in the late 1800s as the national economy in the United States shifted from one based primarily in agriculture to one that was grounded in the industrial and manufacturing processes. This economic shift brought with it new sets of occupational opportunities. These new occupational opportunities connected to industrial and manufacturing activities created new dilemmas for workers in the United States. Particularly, workers were confronted with the new challenge of identifying and accessing the new jobs emerging in the United States. Moreover, the emerging jobs were often located in urban areas of the country, requiring many workers to move from rural areas to the growing cities. These trends were accompanied by increasing numbers of immigrants seeking new lives and opportunities in the United States (Herr, 2001).

Thus it is not surprising that in the early part of the 20th century, emphasis was placed on helping people to identify appropriate occupational options and make vocational choices. The time frame was limited as career guidance for vocational decision making emphasized the act of making a choice and viewed the decision-making process as a single, point-in-time event. In his brief history of career counseling in the United States, Pope (2000) notes that this early period in the evolution of career development interventions continued until 1920 and was characterized by an emphasis on job-placement services.

The early emphasis on job placement, in part, reflected the prevailing White, lower-, and middle-class, male linear model of career development that dominated the field until recent times. Put simply, this view involved choosing an occupation early in one's career (usually upon leaving secondary or postsecondary school) and then staying in one's chosen occupation until retirement. To help people cope with vocational decision-making tasks, practitioners used objectivistic methodologies, usually in the form of standardized aptitude and interest tests.

Important advances regarding the development and use of aptitude and interest tests were identified and articulated in books such as *Aptitude Testing*, authored by Clark Hull and published in 1928; *Aptitudes and Aptitude Testing*, authored by Walter Bingham and published in 1937; and *Vocational Interests of Men and Women*, authored by E. K. Strong and published in 1943. For most of the 20th century, the process of matching people to jobs based on the person's characteristics or traits and the requirements of occupations was the dominant approach to helping people identify appropriate occupational options.

FRANK PARSONS

Thus, early approaches to career development interventions reflected an emphasis on testing clients, providing them with occupational information, and advising them as to which occupational choices seemed to offer a reasonable chance for experiencing occupational success. This approach evolved from the work of Frank Parsons. An engineer by training and a social reformer by personal commitment, in the early 1900s, Parsons merged his training and commitment to outline a systematic process of occupational decision making, which he referred to as "true reasoning." Zytowski (2001) noted that Parsons delivered a lecture in 1906, titled "The Ideal City," to the Economic Club of Boston. In this lecture, Parsons discussed the need for young people to receive assistance in the choice of a vocation. The lecture generated interest and requests by recent high school graduates for personal meetings with Parsons. From these activities, Parsons generated his systematic approach to vocational guidance. This approach was described in detail in Parsons' book *Choosing a Vocation* (1909). In this book, published one year after his death, Parsons discussed various principles and techniques that he found useful in helping the adolescents with whom he worked, first at the Breadwinners' College at the Civic Service House, a settlement house in Boston, and then at the Boston Vocation Bureau. Specifically, Parsons noted the following principles pertaining to vocational counseling:

1. It is better to choose a vocation than merely to hunt for a job.
2. No one should choose a vocation without careful self-analysis, thorough, honest, and under guidance.
3. The youth should have a large survey of the field of vocations and not simply drop into the convenient or accidental position.
4. Expert advice, or the advice of men who have made a careful study of men [*sic*] and vocations and of the conditions of success, must be better and safer for a young man than the absence of it.
5. Putting it down on paper seems a simple matter, but it is one of supreme importance in study. (Parsons, 1909, p. viii)

These principles provided the basis for the techniques Parsons relied on to help young people achieve the goal of "choosing a vocation." Parsons advocated activities such as reading biographies, observing workers in their settings, and reading existing occupational descriptions. These techniques were incorporated into the "Parsonian approach," which consisted of three steps or requirements for helping someone make an occupational choice:

1. Develop a clear understanding of yourself, aptitudes, abilities, interests, resources, limitations, and other qualities.
2. Develop knowledge of the requirements and conditions of success, advantages and disadvantages, compensation, opportunities, and prospects in different lines of work.
3. Use "true reasoning" on the relations of these two groups of facts. (Parsons, 1909, p. 5)

Step one requires self-investigation and self-revelation, when possible assisted by a career counselor. The second step relies upon accurate and comprehensive occupational information. Because during Parsons' time it was uncommon for occupational information to meet these two requirements, Parsons developed occupational materials that described occupations in great detail (e.g., compensation, task requirements, work settings). The third step, "true reasoning," relied upon the person's capacity (with the help of a counselor) to integrate information acquired from steps one and two into a career decision. A task that while, on the surface appears rather straightforward, in practice proved to be rather challenging.

Parsons developed his model against a background of social (e.g., rapid urbanization, child labor, immigration), economic (e.g., the rise of industrialism and the growing division of labor), and scientific (e.g., the emergence of human and behavioral sciences) changes that were occurring in the United States. These changes resulted in the need to place workers in jobs requiring specific skills and aptitudes, to help young people develop career plans, and to protect young people from child abuse in the labor force. Parsons' approach also fit nicely with the dominant scientific thinking of the 20th century, which emphasized positivism and objective methodology. That is, the Parsonian model encouraged practitioners to objectify interests, values, and abilities through the use of standardized assessment to guide people in identifying where they fit within the occupational structure.

The three requirements of the Parsonian approach formed the basic elements of what evolved first into the *matching model* and subsequently into the *trait-and-factor* approach to career development interventions, which is located within the *person-environment* tradition of psychology. These elements are essentially self-knowledge, occupational knowledge, and decision-making skills.

The basic assumptions of the person-environment approaches are:

1. As a result of one's self-characteristics, each worker is best fitted for a specific type of work.
2. Groups of workers in different occupations have different self-characteristics.
3. Occupational choice is a single, point-in-time event.
4. Career development is mostly a cognitive process relying on rational decision making.
5. Occupational adjustment depends on the degree of agreement between worker characteristics and work demands.

The matching model sought to address the challenges inherent in step three of Parsons' model. An initial solution to the challenge of matching persons to environments was the use the practice of "clinical matching," in which expert clinical judgments were made to ascertain the person's chances of success within an occupational field based on the use of a "psychograph." The psychograph, developed by Viteles in 1932, was a graphic representation of a person's relevant characteristics (e.g., abilities, trainings, specific vocational skills) and numerical ratings of the person's strengths as they relate to each characteristic (e.g., on a scale of 1–10). Job psychographs were also developed with similar ratings for the relevant characteristics required for successful performance in that job. Comparisons between the psychograph and job psychographs were made to determine the person's "goodness of match" for the occupation.

The trait-and-factor approach then emerged with an emphasis on the identification of a person's relevant traits or characteristics, usually through the use of standardized tests or inventories. The same approach is used in describing occupational factors or requirements (i.e., occupations are profiled according to the degree to which they require certain traits such as aptitudes). Then the individual's profile of traits is matched with the factors or requirements of specific occupations. The goal of this type of matching is to identify the degree of fit between the person and an occupation.

When conducting trait-and-factor career counseling, Williamson (1939) advocated a six-step process:

1. Analysis
2. Synthesis
3. Diagnosis
4. Prognosis
5. Counseling
6. Follow-up

In this model, the counselor collects clinical (using interview techniques) and statistical (often using standardized assessment) data and then synthesizes these data to draw inferences about the client's strengths and weaknesses. These inferences help to clarify the client's presenting problem and to identify probable causes. For Williamson (1939), the client's presenting problems can be diagnosed as: (a) no choice, (b) uncertain choice, (c) unwise choice, or (d) a discrepancy between interests and aptitudes. Once the client's problem is diagnosed, the counselor offers a prognosis that includes alternative courses of action or alternative adjustments and the associated degree of success the client is likely to encounter with each alternative. Counseling in Williamson's model involves "helping the client marshal and organize personal and other resources to achieve optimal adjustment either now or in the future" (Isaacson, 1985, p. 82). Finally, the counselor conducts a follow-up by checking later with the client to ascertain the effectiveness of the counseling and whether any further assistance is required.

In classic trait-and-factor approaches, the counselor is active and directive while the client is a relatively passive participant in the process. It is the counselor's responsibility to take the lead in the collection, integration, and organization of client data. Moreover, the counselor uses these data in conjunction with occupational information to help the client identify a plan of action.

The Theory of Work Adjustment (TWA), developed by Rene Dawis and Lloyd Lofquist at the University of Minnesota in the 1960s, is an excellent example of a theory within the person-environment tradition (Dawis, 1996). TWA addresses the "correspondence between the individual (abilities and needs) and the environment (ability requirements and reinforcer system)" (Dawis, England, & Lofquist, 1964, p. 11). Thus, TWA focuses on person and environment interactions and posits "the person and environment attempt to maintain correspondence with each other" (Dawis, 1996, p. 81). Both the worker and the work environment have needs and requirements, respectively, that must be satisfied. Adjustment to work is achieved when the person and environment are coresponsive to each other's requirements. Such correspondence is not always achieved, however. The degree to which the worker is willing to tolerate discorrespondence defines the worker's flexibility. Work environments also demonstrate varying degrees of flexibility. The worker's tenure in a specific job is influenced by the worker's satisfactoriness (defined as the work environment's degree of satisfaction with the worker), satisfaction (defined as the degree to which the work environment provides the worker with sufficient and appropriate reinforcers), and the work environment's perseverance (Dawis et al., 1964). Thus, there are four possible states that relate to the person's work experience: the person experiences satisfaction with work and the person's work performance is satisfactory; the person experiences satisfaction with work but the person's work performance is unsatisfactory; the person experiences dissatisfaction with work but the person's work performance is satisfactory; and the person is dissatisfied with work and the person's performance is unsatisfactory (Dawis, 2005). The first condition (satisfied and satisfactory) theoretically leads to maintaining the person's employment, while the latter three conditions theoretically will result in behavior to change the situation (adjustment behavior) (Dawis). Although research results pertaining to TWA constructs have been generally supportive, unfortunately, TWA has failed to generate sufficient research activity, and few empirical tests of TWA have been published within the past 15 years (Swanson & Gore, 2000).

Dawis (2002) also describes a more generalized TWA in his Person-Environment Correspondence (PEC) theory. A basic assumption of PEC theory is persons (P) interact with environments (E). Both P and E are active and reactive. Moreover, both P and E have requirements and expectations that P and E interactions will result in fulfilling these requirements. For example, a counselor (P) working within a counseling environment (E) expects to have the opportunity to help others by using her counseling skills. Likewise, the counseling environment (E) expects the counselor (P) to perform competently and successfully as a counselor. To the degree that such expectations are met successfully, the result is satisfaction on the part of P and E and the corresponding behavior is maintained. When expectations are not met successfully, then dissatisfaction occurs and adjustment is required on the part of P and/or E. Adjustment is pursued until satisfaction occurs or until P or E gives up. A good fit, or correspondence, occurs when the person's capabilities fulfill the environment's requirements. A bad fit, or discorrespondence, occurs when the person's capabilities are not able to fulfill the environment's requirements.

Although the level of sophistication regarding the techniques currently used in person-environment approaches such as TWA and the more general PEC is much greater than the techniques advocated originally by Parsons, Parsons' contributions to the field remain significant. In his book *History of Vocational Guidance,* John Brewer (1942) listed Parsons' contributions to the field as follows:

1. He paved the way for vocational guidance in the schools and colleges by advocating their role in it and offering methods they could use.
2. He began the training of counselors.
3. He used all of the scientific tools available to him at the time.
4. He developed "steps" to be followed in the vocational progress of the individual.
5. He organized the work of the Vocation Bureau in a way that laid the groundwork for groups to model in schools, colleges, and other agencies.
6. He recognized the importance of his work and secured for it the appropriate publicity, financial support, and endorsements from influential educators, employers, and other public figures.
7. He laid the groundwork leading to the continuance and expansion of the vocational guidance movement by involving friends and associates in it and preparing the manuscript for *Choosing a Vocation.* (p. 27)

However, Parsons was not the only significant contributor to early advances in vocational counseling. For example, the testing movement exemplified through the work of James Cattell, Alfred Binet, and Walter Bingham was also a primary force in the growth of career development interventions and helped to operationalize Parsons' emphasis on self-understanding.

Influential publications, organizations, and legislation also emerged in the early part of the 20th century. For example, *The Vocational Guidance Newsletter* was first published by Boston's Vocation Bureau in 1911 (which opened in 1908 with Parsons as its first director and vocational counselor); the National Vocational Guidance Association (NVGA) was founded in Grand Rapids, Michigan, in 1913; the U.S. Department of Labor was organized in 1913; the *Vocational Guidance Bulletin* was first published in 1915 by NVGA; the Vocational Rehabilitation Act became law in 1918; and Harry D. Kitson of Teachers College authored the book *The Psychology of Adjustment,* published in 1925.

In 1931 the Minnesota Employment Stabilization Research Institute was established. Among the Institute's conclusions from its research studies was the principle that improved guidance services were needed to create a more stable labor force and to foster an economic recovery from the Great Depression. The U.S. Employment Service was created in 1933 by the Wagner-Peyser Act. In 1939 the U.S. Employment Service published the first edition of the *Dictionary of Occupational Titles,* in which 18,000 occupations were titled, coded, and defined.

In the early 1940s, personnel testing and placement activities were greatly expanded as a result of World War II (the G.I. Bill was enacted in 1944). An excellent example of the advances being made in testing at this time is provided in E. K. Strong, Jr.'s publication, *Vocational Interests of Men and Women,* in which he documents nearly 20 years of interest-measurement research. Also during World War II, women entered the workforce in unprecedented numbers, with many finding successful employment in manual and technical jobs that were previously held exclusively by men.

At the same time that testing and placement activities were being expanded, Carl Rogers' book *Counseling and Psychotherapy* (1942) was published. In this book, Rogers highlighted the importance of attending to clients' verbalized feelings: "Among the significant developments which resulted were a revamping of the older cognitive concept of the client in vocational guidance to include the dynamics of affective and motivational behavior, the increased emphasis on self-acceptance and self-understanding as goals of vocational counseling" (Borow, 1964, p. 57).

Another significant influence in the evolution of career development interventions occurred in 1951 when Donald E. Super launched the Career Pattern Study, one of the first longitudinal studies of career development. In his excellent historical review, Borow (1964) noted that Super, more than anyone else, helped shift the focus of career development interventions from a "static, single-choice-at-a-point-in-time concept" (p. 60) focused on vocational choice toward a model that conceptualized career development as an ongoing process involving the congruent implementation of the person's self-concept in a compatible occupational role. Super was primarily responsible for changing the definition of vocational guidance from "the process of assisting an individual to choose an occupation, prepare for it, enter upon it, and progress in it" to

> [t]he process of helping a person to develop and accept an integrated and adequate picture of himself [*sic*] and of his role in the world of work, to test this concept against reality, and to convert it into reality, with satisfaction to himself and to society. (Super, 1951, p. 89)

Additionally, Super's multidisciplinary approach to studying career development incorporated contributions from economics and sociology while placing career behavior in the context of human development.

The 1940s and 1950s also saw the emergence of a number of professional organizations related to career development. In 1947, the American Psychological Association (APA) created organizational divisions resulting in the establishment of Division 17, which from 1947 to 1952 was known as the Division of Counseling and Guidance but was later renamed Counseling Psychology. Since its creation, this division has served as the primary APA division for psychologists interested in career development interventions. More recently, a special interest group within Division 17 has formed to focus more directly on the topic of career development theory and practice.

The merging of the NVGA, the American College Personnel Association, the National Association of Guidance Supervisors and Counselor Trainers, and the Student Personnel Association for Teacher Education resulted in the formation of the American Personnel and Guidance Association in 1951. The American School Counselor Association was formed in 1953, and its primary focus was the provision of career services to young people. Finally, in 1957, the American Personnel and Guidance Association created the American Board on Professional Standards in Vocational Counseling, the functions of which "were to evaluate and certify qualified vocational counseling agencies and to foster the maintenance of high professional standards, including standards of ethical practice" (Borow, 1964, p. 62).

However, the primary organization for professional career counselors has been the NVGA (which changed its name to the National Career Development Association [NCDA] in 1985). From its inception, the NVGA (NCDA) has been dedicated to improving the quality of services provided by career development practitioners. As early as 1920, the NVGA (NCDA) established a code of principles to guide practitioners in the delivery of career-related services. In 1981 the NVGA Board of Directors approved the first policy statement for the roles and competencies of career counselors. This statement has been updated several times since then (most recently in 2003). The most recent competencies are listed in Figure 1.1. This statement reflects a broad range of general counseling skills and specific career-related competencies. The competencies reflect the belief of NVGA/NCDA that professional career counselors are professionally trained counselors with additional and specialized training related to career development. In addition, the competencies reflect the importance of providing a wide range of career development interventions to meet the needs of diverse client populations. An excellent history of the NVGA/NCDA is presented in *The Career Development Quarterly,* Volume 36, No. 4, 1988.

In the 1960s, the field experienced tremendous growth in the area of theory generation, with behavioral, developmental, and psychoanalytical theories of career development emerging during this time period. At the same time, the number of career assessment instruments also grew dramatically (see Kapes & Whitfield, 2002). Concurrently, the use of computer-assisted career guidance and information-delivery systems in the provision of career services, primarily in secondary schools and higher education settings, emerged during this time period (Bowlsbey, Dikel, & Sampson, 2002).

During the 1970s, career education emerged as a federal priority, highlighting the importance of providing career development interventions to young people and adults. "The term 'career education' also symbolized the need to address systematically a range of conditions that were changing the relationship between education and work, particularly with regard to preparing students to understand the linkages between educational opportunities and the subsequent implications of these in work choice and work adjustment" (Herr & Cramer, 1996, p. 34). Recent efforts in the 1990s by school-to-work transition proponents focused on imparting the

continued on page 28

These competency statements are for those professionals interested and trained in the field of career counseling. For the purpose of these statements, career counseling is defined as the process of assisting individuals in the development of a life career with focus on the definition of the worker role and how that role interacts with other life roles.

Professional competency statements provide guidance for the minimum competencies necessary to perform effectively a particular occupation or job within a particular field. Professional career counselors (master's degree or higher) or persons in career development positions must demonstrate the knowledge and skills for a specialty in career counseling that the generalist counselor might not possess. Skills and knowledge are represented by designated competency areas, which have been developed by professional career counselors and counselor educators. The Career Counseling Competency Statements can serve as a guide for career counseling training programs or as a checklist for persons wanting to acquire or enhance their skills in career counseling.

Minimum Competencies

In order to work as a professional engaged in career counseling, the individual must demonstrate minimum competencies in 11 designated areas. These 11 areas are: Career Development Theory, Individual and Group Counseling Skills, Individual/Group Assessment, Information/Resources, Program Management and Implementation, Consultation, Diverse Populations, Supervision, Ethical/Legal Issues, Research/Evaluation, and Technology. These areas and their respective performance indicators are defined as follows:

Career Counseling Competencies and Performance Indicators

Career Development Theory

Theory base and knowledge considered essential for professionals engaging in career counseling and development. Demonstration of knowledge of:

1. Counseling theories and associated techniques
2. Theories and models of career development
3. Individual differences related to gender, sexual orientation, race, ethnicity, and physical and mental capacities
4. Theoretical models for career development and associated counseling and information-delivery techniques and resources
5. Human growth and development throughout the life span
6. Role relationships which facilitate life-work planning
7. Information, techniques, and models related to career planning and placement

Individual and Group Counseling Skills

Individual and group counseling competencies considered essential to effective career counseling. Demonstration of ability to:

1. Establish and maintain productive personal relationships with individuals
2. Establish and maintain a productive group climate
3. Collaborate with clients in identifying personal goals
4. Identify and select techniques appropriate to client or group goals and client needs, psychological states, and developmental tasks
5. Identify and understand clients' personal characteristics related to career
6. Identify and understand social contextual conditions affecting clients' careers
7. Identify and understand familial, subcultural, and cultural structures and functions as they are related to clients' careers
8. Identify and understand clients' career decision-making processes
9. Identify and understand clients' attitudes toward work and workers
10. Identify and understand clients' biases toward work and workers based on gender, race, and cultural stereotypes

11. Challenge and encourage clients to take action to prepare for and initiate role transitions by:
    - locating sources of relevant information and experience
    - obtaining and interpreting information and experiences
    - acquiring skills needed to make role transitions
12. Assist the client to acquire a set of employability and job-search skills
13. Support and challenge clients to examine life-work roles, including the balance of work, leisure, family, and community in their careers

Individual/Group Assessment

Individual/group assessment skills considered essential for professionals engaging in career counseling. Demonstration of ability to:

1. Assess personal characteristics such as aptitude, achievement, interests, values, and personality traits.
2. Assess leisure interests, learning style, life roles, self-concept, career maturity, vocational identity, career indecision, work environment preference (e.g., work satisfaction), and other related lifestyle/development issues
3. Assess conditions of the work environment (such as tasks, expectations, norms, and qualities of the physical and social settings)
4. Evaluate and select valid and reliable instruments appropriate to the client's gender, sexual orientation, race, ethnicity, and physical and mental capacities.
5. Use computer-delivered assessment measures effectively and appropriately
6. Select assessment techniques appropriate for group administration and those appropriate for individual administration
7. Administer, score, and report findings from career assessment instruments appropriately
8. Interpret data from assessment instruments and present the results to clients and to others
9. Assist the client and others designated by the client to interpret data from assessment instruments
10. Write an accurate report of assessment results

Information/Resources

Information/resource base and knowledge essential for professionals engaging in career counseling. Demonstration of knowledge of:

1. Education, training, and employment trends; labor market information and resources that provide information about job tasks, functions, salaries, requirements and future outlooks related to broad occupational fields and individual occupations
2. Resources and skills that clients utilize in life-work planning and management
3. Community/professional resources available to assist clients in career planning, including job search
4. Changing roles of women and men and the implications that this has for education, family, and leisure
5. Methods of good use of computer-based career information delivery systems (CIDS) and computer-assisted career guidance systems (CACGS) to assist with career planning

Program Promotion, Management, and Implementation

Knowledge and skills necessary to develop, plan, implement, and manage comprehensive career development programs in a variety of settings. Demonstration of knowledge of:

1. Designs that can be used in the organization of career development programs
2. Needs assessment and evaluation techniques and practices
3. Organizational theories, including diagnosis, behavior, planning, organizational communication, and management useful in implementing and administering career development programs

Figure 1.1 *Continued*

4. Methods of forecasting, budgeting, planning, costing, policy analysis, resource allocation, and quality control
5. Leadership theories and approaches for evaluation and feedback, organizational change, decision making, and conflict resolution
6. Professional standards and criteria for career development programs
7. Societal trends and state and federal legislation that influence the development and implementation of career development programs

Demonstration of ability to:

8. Implement individual and group programs in career development for specified populations
9. Train others about the appropriate use of computer-based systems for career information and planning
10. Plan, organize, and manage a comprehensive career resource center
11. Implement career development programs in collaboration with others
12. Identify and evaluate staff competencies
13. Mount a marketing and public relations campaign on behalf of career development activities and services

Coaching, Consultation, and Performance Improvement

Knowledge and skills considered essential in relating to individuals and organizations that impact the career counseling and development process. Demonstration of ability to:

1. Use consultation theories, strategies, and models
2. Establish and maintain a productive consultative relationship with people who can influence a client's career
3. Help the general public and legislators to understand the importance of career counseling, career development, and life-work planning
4. Impact public policy as it relates to career development and workforce planning
5. Analyze future organizational needs and current level of employee skills and develop performance improvement training
6. Mentor and coach employees

Diverse Populations

Knowledge and skills considered essential in relating to diverse populations that impact career counseling and development processes. Demonstration of ability to:

1. Identify development models and multicultural counseling competencies
2. Identify development needs unique to various diverse populations, including those of different gender, sexual orientation, ethnic group, race, and physical or mental capacity
3. Define career development programs to accommodate needs unique to various diverse populations
4. Find appropriate methods or resources to communicate with limited-English-proficient individuals
5. Identify alternative approaches to meet career planning needs for individuals of various diverse populations
6. Identify community resources and establish linkages to assist clients with specific needs
7. Assist other staff members, professionals, and community members in understanding the unique needs/characteristics of diverse populations with regard to career exploration, employment expectations, and economic/social issues
8. Advocate for the career development and employment of diverse populations
9. Design and deliver career development programs and materials to hard-to-reach populations

Supervision

Knowledge and skills considered essential in critically evaluating counselor or career development facilitator performance, maintaining and improving professional skills. Demonstration of:

1. Ability to recognize own limitations as a career counselor and to seek supervision or refer clients when appropriate
2. Ability to utilize supervision on a regular basis to maintain and improve counselor skills
3. Ability to consult with supervisors and colleagues regarding client and counseling issues and issues related to one's own professional development as a career counselor

4. Knowledge of supervision models and theories
5. Ability to provide effective supervision to career counselors and career development facilitators at different levels of experience
6. Ability to provide effective supervision to career development facilitators at different levels of experience by:

- knowledge of their roles, competencies, and ethical standards
- determining their competence in each of the areas included in their certification
- further training them in competencies, including interpretation of assessment instruments
- monitoring and mentoring their activities in support of the professional career counselor and scheduling regular consultations for the purpose of reviewing their activities

Ethical/Legal Issues

Information base and knowledge essential for the ethical and legal practice of career counseling. Demonstration of knowledge of:

1. Adherence to ethical codes and standards relevant to the profession of career counseling (e.g., National Board of Certified Counselors [NBCC], NCDA, and American Counseling Association [ACA])
2. Current ethical and legal issues which affect the practice of career counseling with all populations
3. Current ethical/legal issues with regard to the use of computer-assisted career guidance systems
4. Ethical standards relating to consultation issues
5. State and federal statutes relating to client confidentiality

Research/Evaluation

Knowledge and skills considered essential to understanding and conducting research and evaluation in career counseling and development. Demonstration of ability to:

1. Write a research proposal
2. Use types of research and research designs appropriate to career counseling and development research
3. Convey research findings related to the effectiveness of career counseling programs
4. Design, conduct, and use the results of evaluation programs
5. Design evaluation programs which take into account the need of various diverse populations, including persons of both genders, differing sexual orientations, different ethnic and racial backgrounds, and differing physical and mental capacities
6. Apply appropriate statistical procedures to career development research

Technology

Knowledge and skills considered essential in using technology to assist individuals with career planning. Demonstration of knowledge of:

1. Various computer-based guidance and information systems as well as services available on the Internet
2. Standards by which such systems and services are evaluated
3. Ways in which to use computer-based systems and Internet services to assist individuals with career planning that are consistent with ethical standards
4. Characteristics of clients which make them profit more or less from use of technology-driven systems
5. Methods to evaluate and select a system to meet local needs

Figure 1.1

Introduction to career counseling competency statements.
Source: Revised by the NCDA Board of Directors, July, 2003. © 2003 National Career Development Association. Retrieved August 19, 2011, from http://www.ncda.org.

knowledge, skills, and attitudes essential for effective workforce participation that closely resemble the ideas of career education efforts initiated in the 1970s (Lent & Worthington, 1999).

Another critically important development in recent years has been the increased attention to addressing the career development needs of diverse client populations (Lee & Richardson, 1991). Research related to career development theory and practice has gone beyond addressing the career development of White, middle-class men. Issues of gender, class, sexual orientation, and cultural bias in career development theories and practices have been exposed, resulting in greater attention to how such variables factor into the career development process and bringing into focus the importance of including the cultural context in career development theories and interventions (Chung, 2001; Leong & Hartung, 2000; Pope, 2000). Models of identity development as they relate to areas such as gender, race, sexual orientation, and disability status are increasingly being integrated into career development theory and practice (Pope, 2000). Career treatment outcome studies are also beginning to move beyond the traditional college student samples to examine career intervention effects with more diverse populations (Luzzo, 2000).

Interestingly, acknowledging the multiple ways in which the societal context artificially limits career development for many people has led commentators to remind career theorists and practitioners of the importance of addressing social justice in career development interventions in the 21st century (Blustein, 2006; Chope, 2006; Herr & Niles, 1998; O'Brien, 2001). Lee (1989) agrees, stating that career counselors must act as "career development advocates for disenfranchised clients by actively challenging long-standing traditions that stand in the way of equity in the workplace" (p. 219). Indeed, striving for social justice through career interventions commenced with the work of Frank Parsons and, therefore, is an important theme throughout the history of the career development field. In this regard, Herr and Niles note:

> . . . for most of the last 100 years, whether or not it has been explicit, counseling and, in particular, career counseling and career guidance have become sociopolitical instruments, identified by legislation at the federal level, to deal with emerging social concerns such as equity and excellence in educational and occupational opportunities, unemployment, human capital development, persons with disabilities, child abuse, AIDS, teenage pregnancy, substance abuse, career decision making relative to the preparation for entrance into emerging skilled occupations, and the identification and encouragement of students with high academic potential to enter higher education in science and mathematics. (p. 121)

Recapturing the spirit of social justice by acting as agents of social change to maximize the career development opportunities available to all members of our society is emerging as an essential aspect of career interventions for many career practitioners today (see Blustein, 2006).

Conducting career interventions for social action requires counselors to provide multifaceted career interventions and to expand their roles beyond traditional individual career counseling practice. Career counseling for social action begins with career counselors possessing the multicultural competencies (i.e., knowledge, skills, and attitudes) necessary for understanding how the environments their clients occupy interact to influence the interpretations and meanings clients attach to work and occupational opportunities. Multicultural competencies serve as the foundation for identifying social action strategies aimed at facilitating career development.

Career practitioners engaged in social action also use community resources to provide clients with access to information and opportunities (e.g., employment offices, "one-stop career shops," support groups). Learning about career resources that are available in the community facilitates appropriate referrals and increases the probability that clients will receive the services they need. Therefore, career counselors engaging in social action play the role of facilitator by providing information, referrals, and encouragement to clients (Enright, Conyers, & Szymanski, 1996). To play this role effectively, career counselors are required to maintain files of useful resources, including names of potential mentors representing a diversity of backgrounds (e.g., African American, Asian American, individuals with disabilities, gay and lesbian men and women), information on accommodations for disabled individuals with different functional limitations, names of employers willing to provide opportunities for job shadowing and internship experiences, and names of individuals willing to participate in informational interviewing experiences (Enright et al., p. 111).

Having a thorough knowledge of career resources available in the community also allows counselors to identify areas in which services are lacking. In these instances, counselors once again take on a strong advocacy role and seek to rectify service deficiencies in their communities (Lee, 1989).

Advocacy is also important when clients' career concerns are the result of external factors such as large-scale downsizing, wage stagnation, and salary inequities experienced by women, persons of color, and persons with disabilities. More often than many care to acknowledge, workers struggle to earn a living. On average, women must work 66 weeks to earn what men earn in 52 weeks (Armendariz, 1997). The inequities experienced by persons with disabilities are even greater. According to Uchitelle and Kleinfeld (1996), in the past 20 years, nearly 75% of all households in the United States have experienced a job loss either directly or indirectly (i.e., they have a friend or relative who has lost a job). Those in the dwindling minority of persons not experiencing an encounter with job loss are also acutely aware of the tenuous nature of job security and experience high levels of guilt, fear, and anxiety.

In each of these instances, career counselors concerned with social action address not only the career concerns of individual clients, but also the career concerns of the community at large (Cahill & Martland, 1996). This is accomplished by integrating individual career counseling skills with community counseling skills. Integrating career counseling and community counseling strategies is especially critical in rural communities in which economic restructuring can threaten the very existence of the community. Cahill and Martland argue that community career counseling builds on the strength of individual career counseling and offers assistance to people in their struggle to maintain their communities as they create opportunities for career development. Thus, in addition to individual career counseling skills, career practitioners need skills in facilitating group problem solving and consensus building, and an understanding of social and economic factors that affect careers in contemporary society. Finally, Ludwikowski, Vogel, and Armstrong (2009) point out the importance of career interventions that engage potential clients via their social networks. The use of social media as a vehicle for communicating the importance of career assistance and for normalizing the use of career counseling resources may help to reduce the stigma that some experience related to seeking counseling of any sort.

Essentially, career counselors who instill hope in their clients and empower them to manage their careers are multiculturally competent, they act as facilitators of information and referrals, they advocate for their clients when employment practices and community traditions stand in the way of equity in the workplace, and they integrate individual career counseling skills with community counseling skills to assist people in their struggle to maintain their communities and create opportunities for career development (Blustein, 2006; Chope, 2006). Only time will tell if the recent attention related to addressing social justice issues in career development interventions will blossom into a more common and prominent role for career practitioners. It seems reasonable to expect this to occur given the high rates of global unemployment and growing economic disparities between the "haves" and "have-nots."

FUTURE TRENDS IN CAREER DEVELOPMENT INTERVENTIONS

Bingham and Ward (1994) note that "if vocational counseling was born from the changing demographics and economic needs of this century, then clearly career counseling will need to change in response to the changing needs of the coming century" (p. 168). Indeed, the rapid changes occurring in the world of work that are influenced by technological developments, the emergence of an interdependent global economy, and an increasingly diverse workforce reinforce the need for career development theory and practice to be revised to meet the career development tasks confronting people in the 21st century. The evidence is clear that people, both young and old, are struggling to cope more effectively with these tasks. Research results also indicate clearly that when an individual's career situations go awry, the effects are far-reaching and often negative, for both the person and society (Herr, 1989).

We are confronted daily with news reports citing statistics about high levels of global unemployment, corporate downsizing, and a jobless economic recovery. These statistics provide examples of the fact that the social contract between employer and employee is gone. Other evidence that the nature of work is changing is found in the number of companies now offering day care and parental leave; increases in the numbers of families requiring dual earners; and increases in the numbers of people working at home. These themes reflect the strong intertwining of work and family roles. Thus, career theories, career interventions, and career development professionals must respond to these evolutionary shifts occurring in the nature of work. Moreover, career development interventions must be embedded in assumptions that reflect the shifts we are experiencing in work (e.g., that adults change occupations many times over the course of their lives, that lifelong learning is essential to maintaining one's marketability, that life roles interact, that rapid changes in the world of work are a constant, and that everyone must become skilled at interacting with diverse coworkers). In 2003, Herr contended that the demand for career assistance would expand due to rising unemployment rates and an increase in part-time work. His prediction is now a reality.

How we intervene in the lives of the people we serve is guided by our understanding of how these contextual shifts influence what is required for people to move forward in their careers. The emerging career concerns people experience in contemporary society point to the need for career counselors to continue their historical tradition of responding to current concerns with current interventions. Precious little appears in the professional literature proposing future directions for career counseling. Because the discourse barely exists, the direction remains unclear. Thus, career counseling's identity status resembles that of a career counseling client who lacks vocational identity and clearly articulated goals (Niles, 2003).

Savickas (1993) discusses his interpretation of what is required to move the profession forward. Specifically, he notes that in the 21st century, career development professionals will shift from supporting the 20th-century notion of careerism to fostering self-affirmation in their clients. Career counselors, Savickas contends, will teach people to be more critical of authority. People will need to be encouraged to make a commitment to their culture and community and learn how to develop and express their values in the real world. Rather than providing clients with predefined services in a sort of "one size fits all" approach, career counselors will collaborate with their clients to help them interpret and shape their career development. Rather than emphasizing a singular truth and objectivity, career counselors will move toward appreciating multiple realities, perspectivity, and relationships in their work with clients (Savickas). In the emerging scenario it seems clear that a primary task of career practitioners involves clarifying (rather than assuming) how they can be *useful* to their clients. Achieving this basic and essential understanding requires career practitioners to be skilled at providing culturally appropriate career interventions.

In addition to the Savickas (1993) article, a special issue of *The Career Development Quarterly* (September 2003) stands as one of the few examples in the literature in which future directions for career counseling are identified. Building upon these contributions, we identify several ways in which career development professionals can construct career interventions that respond to clients' career concerns in the 21st century.

MOVE TO VIEWING CAREER DECISIONS AS VALUES-BASED DECISIONS

Career decisions are essentially values-based decisions. Some values will figure prominently in a future scenario and others will be left behind, subordinated, or perhaps even distorted in a career transition. Indeed, career decisions entail determining what is to prevail and what is to be sacrificed (Cochran, 1997). Without the promise of gain and the threat of loss, there is no decision to make. One could just follow a "perfect" possibility that was presumably all positive. Yet, in an ordinary decision, one must evaluate to decide. It can be argued that these evaluations are primarily values-based and that the way one evaluates defines the person one is to become and the life one is to live. Our identity is defined by these fundamental evaluations. Thus, helping clients clarify and articulate their values will become even more important in providing career development interventions in the 21st century. Career practitioners can empower clients to make choices that implement their declared values through serving as counselor, coach, and advocate for their clients.

MOVE BEYOND OBJECTIVE ASSESSMENT

An increased emphasis on values clarification reflects the fact that today, perhaps more than ever, it should be clear that providing clients with information about themselves and the world-of-work (through objective assessment) is necessary, but not sufficient, for empowering people to manage their careers effectively. To be sure, having information about how one's interests compare with others and where one stands on the normal curve is helpful in the process of identifying viable career options. However, most people do not think of themselves as locations on a normal curve. Rather, they focus on the process of trying to make meaning out of their life experiences. Certain life experiences capture more attention in this regard than others do. Most likely, the experiences that capture the most attention are those that have been the most painful. A painful or negative experience creates a yearning for its opposite, which becomes an ideal toward which to strive (Watkins & Savickas, 1990). In this sense, one's early life preoccupations provide the direction for what later in life can become one's occupation. Our life experiences provide the crucial backdrop against which we sort through our values, interests, and skills and then try to connect them to career options. Career development interventions in the 21st century must be directed toward helping people clarify and articulate the meaning they seek to express in their career activities.

MOVE TO COUNSELING-BASED CAREER ASSISTANCE

Implicit in what we have discussed thus far is that "personal" and "career" concerns are inextricably intertwined. Research by Niles and Anderson (1995) indicates that many adults in career counseling are coping with concerns related to uncertainty, ambiguity, self-efficacy, and personal, as well as occupational, information deficits. Career counseling clients also report valuing the relationship dimension of the career counseling experience, and they often take advantage of the opportunity to discuss general concerns in the career counseling process (Anderson & Niles, 2000). Accordingly, many researchers now conclude that there are few things more personal than a career choice and that the overlap between career and general concerns is substantial (Anderson & Niles, 1995; Krumboltz, 1993; Savickas, 2010; Subich, 1993). Career development practitioners can respond to this overlap by offering counseling-based career assistance.

Career practitioners offering counseling-based career assistance do not view their clients as the problem and the counselor as the solution (Savickas, 1993). Rather, they seek to empower clients to articulate their experiences and construct their own lives. Savickas noted that career counselors operating from this perspective function as collaborators in the career counseling process and pay special attention to the relationship within career counseling (Anderson & Niles, 2000). Moreover, Savickas

(2010) contends that all career counseling involves helping clients res̶ they experience in career decision making by increasing the client's: (1) co̶ work, (2) sense of control over his or her career, (3) curiosity about oppor̶ and (4) confidence to make a choice (p. 1843). We agree with Savickas but ex̶ his recommendations to increasing the client's confidence not only make a choic̶ but to implement and adjust to the choice made. We also view it as necessary that clients become curious about themselves as well as their opportunities. Career coun-selors can share their own sense of curiosity about the client's situation to foster and model a sense of curiosity within the client. Functioning effectively in these ways also requires career development practitioners to possess multicultural counseling skills.

MOVE TO A STRONGER EMPHASIS ON MULTICULTURAL CAREER DEVELOPMENT THEORIES AND INTERVENTIONS

Concern about meeting the career development needs of culturally diverse clients has been a significant issue in the literature since the early 1980s (Sue et al., 1982). This issue becomes even more critical given the increasing diversity within society and the workforce (Parmer & Rush, 2003). Career development interventions must address the "effects of social and economic barriers such as economic hard-ship, immigration disruption, and racial discrimination on the career behavior of ethnic minority individuals" (Leong, 1995, p. 550). Certainly, Leong's list can be expanded to include persons with disabilities and persons who are gay, lesbian, transgendered, or questioning (Hershenson, 2005). Moreover, career practitioners must be aware of the worldviews embedded in their interventions and offer as-sistance that is congruent with the client's worldview (Fouad & Byars-Winston, 2005). Byars-Winston and Fouad (2006) recommend that career counselors ac-tively engage in self-reflective processes throughout the course of career counseling to increase their capacity to examine the impact of their personal cultural contexts on their work with their clients (p. 188). Thus, providing multicultural career development interventions requires counselors to be culturally aware, sensitive to their own values, and sensitive to how their cultural assumptions may affect their clients. Pope-Davis and Dings (1995) noted that multiculturally competent counselors must also:

> . . . consider factors such as the impact of the sociopolitical system on people of color in the United States, have knowledge and information about particular cultural groups, and be able to generate a wide range of appropriate verbal/nonverbal responses to client needs. (p. 288)

These statements are in contrast to many career theories and practices that have limited relevance for clients who do not adhere to Eurocentric worldviews empha-sizing individualistic and self-actualizing perspectives regarding career behavior (Byars-Winston & Fouad, 2006; Hershenson, 2005; Leong, 1995). Such statements also reinforce the importance of context in career development. Blustein (1994) defined context as "that group of settings that influence developmental progress, en-compassing contemporary and distal familial, social, and economic circumstances"

iversity in clients and client concerns makes it clear that context must be
. in the construction and implementation of career development interven-
.ct otherwise is to risk providing "culturally encapsulated" (Wrenn, 1962)
;istance.

SING ON MULTIPLE LIFE ROLES

orating context into career development interventions also requires career
tioners to acknowledge that the metaphor of the "boxes of life" does not
.t life as many people live it. Life is not lived in compartmentalized life-role
..._s." For some people, work provides a focus for personality organization, but
for other people, work may be more peripheral. To understand a person's career, it
is important to understand the person's web of life roles. How a person structures
the basic roles of living into a life organizes and channels the person's engagement
in society (Super, Savickas, & Super, 1996). Theories and interventions that are
not sensitive to this basic fact address a life situation that does not exist. Life roles
interact and influence each other so that the same job holds different meanings for
two individuals who live in different contexts. Because people seek to express specific values in each of the life roles they play, career development practitioners must
encourage their clients to clarify and articulate the values they seek to express in the
life roles that are important to them. Once clarified and articulated, clients can be
encouraged to identify outlets for values expression within each of their salient life
roles (Super, 1980). The increasing sense of work-family conflict reported by both
men and women (Williams & Boushey, 2010) reinforces the need for career interventions addressing the person's life structure. Career development interventions
in the 21st century will need to address the totality of career concerns that people
experience so they can be empowered not only to make a good living, but also to
live a good life.

MOVE TO INCORPORATING SOCIAL JUSTICE AND ADVOCACY INTO CAREER DEVELOPMENT INTERVENTIONS

The NCDA Career Counseling Competencies (2003b) identify the need for career
counselors to engage in advocacy for social justice. For example, the following competencies are noted:

- Identify community resources and establish linkages to assist clients with specific
  needs.
- Assist other staff members, professionals, and community members in understanding the unique needs/characteristics of diverse populations with regard to
  career exploration, employment expectations, and economic/social issues.
- Advocate for the career development and employment of diverse populations.
- Design and deliver career development programs and materials to hard-to-reach
  populations.

S

Such competencies require career counselors to move beyond individual and group counseling interventions to advocate for their current and potential clients. Toporek (2006) also emphasizes the role of career counselors as social change agents and advocates. Toporek and Liu (2001) define advocacy as "action taken by counseling professionals to facilitate the removal of external and institutional barriers to clients' well-being" (p. 387). Toporek and Liu also note that advocacy involves career counselor actions ranging from empowerment to social action. The former tends to occur in individual and group-level interventions. The latter often involves engaging in the political process via a variety of actions such as writing letters to the editor of a newspaper, meeting with congressional representatives, conferring with lobbyists, collaborating with other groups with similar interests to generate more political capital in order to influence the legislative process, and conducting strikes and/or demonstrations. For example, when it was revealed that a popular restaurant chain engaged in discriminatory practices toward sexual minorities, a number of human rights groups conducted protests located at a number of that chain's restaurant locations. The negative publicity related to these protests led to an eventual change in the restaurant's practices. Similar actions and congressional testimonies have led to increased workplace safety standards, legislation protecting persons with disabilities, nondiscriminatory practices in hiring racial/ethnic minorities, and so on. It seems clear that the negative effects of globalization on workers worldwide indicate that career practitioners have much work to do in the social justice arena. Incorporating social justice and advocacy into career development interventions raises the collective consciousness of career issues and can serve to engage participants from educational, political, and other societal arenas in the process of creating more just conditions for all workers.

MyCounselingLab™

Go to Topic 1: *Introduction to Career Counseling* in the **MyCounselingLab™** site (www.MyCounselingLab.com) for *Career Development Interventions in the 21st Century*, Fourth Edition, where you can:

- Find learning outcomes for *Introduction to Career Counseling* along with the national standards that connect to these outcomes.
- Complete Assignments and Activities that can help you more deeply understand the chapter content.

- Apply and practice your understanding of the core skills identified in the chapter with the Building Counseling Skills unit.
- Prepare yourself for professional certification with a Practice for Certification quiz.
- Connect to videos through the Video and Resource Library.

Summary

Careers are person-specific and are created by the choices we make throughout our lives. Careers emerge from the constant interplay between the person and the environment. They include activities engaged in prior to entering the workforce and after formal activity as a worker has been completed. Careers are personal and encompass the total constellation of life roles that we play. Thus, managing our careers effectively also involves integrating the roles of life effectively. In a very real sense, careers are the manifestations of our attempts at making sense out of our life experiences. The career development process is, in essence, a spiritual journey reflecting our choices concerning how we will spend our time on Earth. Professional counselors must be mindful of these facts as they attempt to intervene in the lives of their clients and assist them in their journeys. We hope that if Stephanie and her classmates were to read this book, they would agree.

Case Study

Carlos presents for career counseling at an urban career center. At his initial appointment he states that he heard that career counselors do testing on interests and that he would like to take this type of test "to find out what he should do for the rest of his life." He notes that he decided to pursue career counseling now because his partner had been "nagging" him to get some help.

Carlos reported that he had been in the navy for the past 21 years. He joined the navy after graduating from high school because there were no jobs in the rural community in the southwestern United States, where he grew up. He spent the majority of his naval career on ships and submarines where his expertise was in radar and sonar maintenance, and where he managed crews of 15–50 personnel. He enjoyed his maintenance work but stated that, at times, being a supervisor was "very frustrating." Often he thought it was just easier to do the work himself rather than to rely on others to get the job done. When he was not chosen for a higher rank, he decided to retire from naval service.

After leaving the navy, Carlos began looking for employment as a "manager," but after eight months of job searching, he has received no offers of employment. Although income from his retirement and his wife's part-time employment have been sufficient to meet the mortgage and basic utility bills, Carlos has borrowed heavily to meet other expenses and he and his spouse are rapidly depleting the savings intended for the education of their children. They have two sons, ages 16 and 18, and one daughter, age 12.

Carlos reported that lately he had been feeling tired most of the time. Even his hobbies—gardening and horticulture that have fascinated him since his boyhood days—are not satisfying now. He confesses that he has been drinking rather heavily for the past month and that there are some days when he just stays at home in his bathrobe watching television. He hopes that the results of an interest test will help him "get back on track."

How do you think you would work with Carlos if you were his career counselor? Would you give him the interest assessment he seeks? Would you refer him to a "personal" counselor? What additional information would you seek from Carlos if you were to become his career counselor?

Student Activities

1. What are your assumptions about career development interventions? Rate them on a scale of 1 (boring) to 10 (exciting). Discuss your reasons for your rating.

2. Have you ever received career counseling? What happened? What was helpful? What was not helpful?

3. Consider your own motivation for working. Do you think you "work to live" or do you "live to work?" What are the pros and cons of each approach to work?

4. Review the history of career development interventions. Identify two ways in which cultural/historical events have influenced career development interventions.

5. Identify the most important life roles for you. How do your life roles interact with each other? What is your most important life role at this point in your life? What values do you try to express in your most important life role?

References

Amundson, N. E. (2009). *Active engagement: Enhancing the career counseling process* (3rd ed.). Vancouver, Canada: Ergon Press.

Anderson, W. P., & Niles, S. G. (1995). Career and personal concerns expressed by career counseling clients. *Career Development Quarterly, 43,* 240–245.

Anderson, W. P., Jr., & Niles, S. G. (2000). Important events in career counseling: Client and counselor descriptions. *Career Development Quarterly, 48,* 251–263.

Ardichvili, A., & Kuchinke, K. (2009). International perspectives on the meanings of work and working: Current research and theory. *Advances in Development Human Resources, 11,* 155–167.

Armendariz, Y. (1997, April 11). Today women's pay catches up to men's. *El Paso Times,* p. C1.

Bingham, W. V. (1937). *Aptitudes and aptitude testing.* New York: Harper & Brothers.

Bingham, R. P., & Ward, C. M. (1994). Career counseling with ethnic minority women. In W. B. Walsh & S. H. Osipow (Eds.), *Career counseling for women* (pp. 165–196). Hillsdale, NJ: Erlbaum.

Blustein, D. L. (1994). "Who am I?" The question of self and identity in career development. In M. L. Savickas & R. W. Lent (Eds.), *Convergence in career development theories: Implications for science and practice* (pp. 139–154). Palo Alto, CA: Consulting Psychologists Press.

Blustein, D. L. (2006). *The psychology of working: A new perspective for career development, counseling, and public policy.* New York: Routledge.

Blustein, D. L., & Spengler, P. M. (1995). *Personal adjustment: Career counseling and psychotherapy.* In W. B. Walsh & S. H. Osipow (Eds.), *Handbook of vocational psychology: Theory, research, and practice* (2nd ed., pp. 295–330). Mahwah, NJ: Lawrence Erlbaum Associates.

Borchert, M., & Landherr, G. (2009). The changing meanings of work in Germany. *Advances in Developing Human Resources, 11,* 204–217.

Borow, H. (Ed.). (1964). *Man in a world at work.* Boston: Houghton Mifflin.

Bowlsbey, J. H., Dikel, M. R., & Sampson, J. P. (2002). *The Internet: A tool for career planning* (2nd ed.). Tulsa, OK: National Career Development Association.

Brewer, J. M. (1942). *History of vocational guidance.* New York: Harper.

Bridges, W. (1994). *Jobshift: How to prosper in a workplace without jobs.* Reading, MA: Addison-Wesley.

Brief, A., & Nord, W. (1990). Work and meaning: Definitions and interpretations. In A. Brief & W. Nord (Eds.), *The meaning of occupational work* (pp. 21–45). Lexington, MA: Lexington.

Brown, D. & Minor, C. W. (1989). *Working in America: A Status Report on Planning and*

Problems. Washington, DC: National Career Development Association.

Bureau of Labor Statistics. (2004, August 25). *Number of jobs held, labor market activity, and earnings among younger baby boomers: Recent results from a longitudinal study*. Washington, DC: United States Department of Labor.

Bureau of Labor Statistics. (2011). Retrieved July 14, 2011, from http://www.bls.gov/.

Byars-Winston, A., & Fouad, N. (2006). Metacognition and multicultural competence: Expanding the culturally appropriate career counseling model. *The Career Development Quarterly, 54*, 187–201.

Cahill, M., & Martland, S. (1996). Community career counseling for rural transition. *Canadian Journal of Counseling, 30*, 155–164.

Chope, R. C. (2006). Family matters: The influence of the family in career decision making. Austin, TX: Pro-Ed.

Chung, Y. B. (2001). Work discrimination and coping strategies: Conceptual frameworks for counseling lesbian, gay, and bisexual clients. *The Career Development Quarterly, 50*, 33–44.

Cochran, L. (1997). *Career counseling: A narrative approach*. Thousand Oaks, CA: Sage.

Crites, J. O. (1981). *Career counseling: Models, methods, and materials*. New York: McGraw-Hill.

Dawis, R. (2002). Person-environment correspondence theory. In D. Brown and Associates, *Career choice and development* (4th ed., pp. 427–464). San Francisco: Jossey-Bass.

Dawis, R. V. (1996). The theory of work adjustment and person-environment correspondence counseling. In D. Brown, L. Brooks, & Associates (Eds.), *Career choice development* (3rd ed., pp. 75–120). San Francisco: Jossey-Bass.

Dawis, R. V. (2005). The Minnesota theory of work adjustment in career development and counseling. In S. D. Brown & R. W. Lent (Eds.), *Career development and counseling: Putting theory and research to work* (pp. 3–23). Hoboken, NJ: John Wiley & Sons.

Dawis, R. V., England, G. W., & Lofquist, L. H. (1964). A theory of work adjustment. *Minnesota Studies in Vocational Rehabilitation, No. XV*, 1–27.

Doherty, M. (2009). When the working day is through: The end of work as identity? *Work, Employment, & Society, 23*, 84–101.

Enright, M., Conyers, L., & Szymanski, E. M. (1996). Career and career-related educational concerns of college students with disabilities. *Journal of Counseling & Development, 74*, 103–114.

Ferrar, L., Nota, L., Soresi, S., Blustein, D., Murphy, K., & Kenna, A. (2009). Construction of work among adolescents in transition. *Journal of Career Assessment, 17*, 99–115.

Fouad, N. A., & Byars-Winston, A. M. (2005). Cultural context of career choice: Meta-Analysis of race/ethnicity differences. *The Career Development Quarterly, 53*, 223–233.

Friedman, T. H. (2005) *The World is Flat: A Brief History of the 21st Century*. New York: Farrar, Straus, and Giroux.

Fritzche, B. A., & Parrish, T. J. (2005). Theory and research on job satisfaction. In S. D Brown & R. W. Lent (Eds.), *Career development and counseling: Putting theory and research to work* (pp. 180–202). Hoboken, NJ: Wiley.

Gomez, M. J., Fassinger, R. E., Prosser, J., Cooke, K., Mejia, B., & Luna, J. (2001). Voces abriendo caminos (Voices forging paths): A qualitative study of the career development of notable Latinas. *Journal of Counseling Psychology, 48*, 286–300.

Gysbers, N. C., Heppner, M. J., & Johnston, J. A. (2003). *Career counseling: Process, issues, and techniques* (2nd ed.). Boston: Allyn & Bacon.

Hall, D. T. & Associates. (1996). *The career is dead—long live the career: A relational approach to careers*. San Francisco: Jossey-Bass.

Harpaz, I. (1999). The transformation of work values. *Israel Monthly Review, 122*, 46–50.

Hartung, P. J. (2002). Development through work and play. *Journal of Vocational Behavior, 61*, 424–438.

Hartung, P. J., Speight, J. D., & Lewis, D. M. (1996). Individualism-collectivism and the vocational behavior of majority culture college students. *The Career Development Quarterly, 45*, 87–96.

Heppner, M. J., O'Brien, K. M., Hinkelman, J. M., & Flores, L. Y. (1996). Training counseling psychologists in career development: Are we our own worst enemies? *The Counseling Psychologist, 24*, 105–125.

Herr, E. L. (1989). Career development and mental health. *Journal of Career Development, 16*, 5–18.

Herr, E. L. (1997). Super's life-span, life-space approach and its outlook for refinement. *The Career Development Quarterly, 45*, 238–246.

Herr, E. L. (2001). Career development and its practice: A historical perspective. *The Career Development Quarterly, 49,* 196–211.

Herr, E. L. (2003). The future of career counseling as an instrument of public policy. *The Career Development Quarterly, 52,* 8–17.

Herr, E. L., & Cramer, S. H. (1996). *Career guidance and counseling through the lifespan: Systemic approaches* (5th ed.). New York: HarperCollins.

Herr, E. L., Cramer, S. H., & Niles, S. G. (2004). *Career guidance and counseling through the lifespan: Systemic approaches* (6th ed.). Boston: Allyn & Bacon.

Herr, E. L., & Niles, S. G. (1998). Career: Social action in behalf of purpose, productivity, and hope. In C. Lee & G. R. Walz (Eds.), *Social action: A mandate for counselors* (pp. 117–156). Alexandria, VA: American Counseling Association.

Hershenson, D. B. (2005). INCOME: A culturally inclusive and disability-sensitive framework for organizing career development concepts and interventions. *The Career Development Quarterly, 54,* 11–23.

Hull, C. L. (1928). *Aptitude testing.* Yonkers, NY: World Book Company.

Isaacson, L. E. (1985). *Basics of career counseling.* Boston: Allyn & Bacon.

Isaacson, L. E., & Brown, D. (2000). *Career information, career counseling, and career development.* Boston: Allyn & Bacon.

Kalton, C. A. (2001). Client psychological distress: An important factor in career counseling. *The Career Development Quarterly, 49,* 324–335.

Kapes, J. T., & Whitfield, E. A. (2002). *A counselor's guide to career assessment instruments* (4th ed.). Alexandria, VA: National Career Development Association.

Kim, B. S. K., Li, L. C., & Liang, C. T. H. (2002). Effects of Asian American client adherence to Asian cultural values, session goal, and counselor emphasis of client expression on career counseling process. *Journal of Counseling Psychology, 49,* 3–13.

Krumboltz, J. D. (1993). Integrating career and personal counseling. *The Career Development Quarterly, 42,* 143–148.

Lee, C. C. (1989). Needed: A career development advocate. *The Career Development Quarterly, 37,* 218–220.

Lee, C. C., & Richardson, B. L. (Eds.). (1991). *Multicultural issues in counseling: New approaches to diversity.* Alexandria, VA: American Counseling Association.

Lent, R. W., Brown, S. D., & Hackett, G. (2002). Social cognitive career theory. In D. Brown & Associates (Eds.), *Career choice and development* (4th ed., pp. 255–311). San Francisco: Jossey-Bass.

Lent, R. W., & Worthington, R. L. (1999). Applying career development theories to the school-to-work transition process. *The Career Development Quarterly, 47,* 291–296.

Leong, F. T. L. (1995). *Career development and vocational behavior of racial and ethnic minorities.* Mahwah, NJ: Lawrence Erlbaum Associates.

Leong, F. T. L. (2002). Challenges for career counseling in Asia: Variations in cultural accommodation. *The Career Development Quarterly, 50,* 277–284.

Leong, F. T. L., & Hartung, P. J. (2000). Adapting to the changing multicultural context of career. In A. Collin & R. A. Young (Eds.), *The future of career* (pp. 212–227). Cambridge, England: Cambridge University Press.

Leong, S. A. (1995). Career development and counseling: A multicultural perspective. In J. G. Ponterotto, J. M. Casas, L. A. Suzuki, & C. M. Alexander. *Handbook of multicultural counseling* (pp. 549–566). Thousand Oaks, CA: Sage.

Liem, R., & Rayman, P. (1982). Health and social costs of unemployment. *American Psychologist, 37,* 1116–1123.

Liptak, J. J. (2001). *Treatment planning in career counseling.* Belmont, CA: Brooks/Cole.

Ludwikowski, W., Vogel, D., & Armstrong, P. (2009). Attitudes toward career counseling: The role of public and self-stigma. *Journal of Counseling Psychology, 56,* 408–416.

Luzzo, D. A. (2000). *Career counseling of college students: An empirical guide to strategies that work.* Washington, DC: American Psychological Association.

Maccoby, M., & Terzi, K. (1981). What happened to the work ethic? In J. O'Toole, J. L. Scheiber, & L. C. Wood (Eds.), *Working, changes, and choices* (pp. 162–171). New York: Human Sciences Press.

Madonna, M. G., Miville, M. L., Warren, M. K., Gainor, K. A., & Lewis-Coles, M. E. L. (2006). Religion, spirituality, and career development in African American college students: A qualitative inquiry. *The Career Development Quarterly, 54,* 227–241.

Mannheim, B. (1993). Gender and the effects of demographics status and work values on work centrality. *Work and Occupations, 20,* 3–22.

McCortney, A. L., & Engels, D. W. (2003). Revisiting the work ethic in America. *The Career Development Quarterly, 52,* 132–140.

Mortimer, J. T., Zimmer-Gembeck, T., Holmes, M., & Shanahan, M. J. (2002). The process of occupational decision making: Patterns during the transition to adulthood. *Journal of Vocational Behavior, 61,* 439–465.

Multon, K. D., Heppner, M. J., Gysbers, N. C., Zook, C., & Ellis-Kalton, C. A. (2001). Client psychological distress: An important factor in career counseling. *The Career Development Quarterly, 49,* 324–335.

National Career Development Association. (2003a). *The professional practice of career counseling and consultation: A resource document.* Tulsa, OK: Author.

National Career Development Association. (2003b). *Career counseling competencies.* Tulsa, OK: Author.

Niles, S. G. (2003). Career counselors confront critical crossroads: A vision of the future. *The Career Development Quarterly, 52,* 70–77.

Niles, S. G., Admundson, N. E., & Neault, R. A. (2011). *Career flow: A hope-centered approach to career development.* Columbus, OH: Merrill Prentice Hall.

Niles, S. G., & Anderson, W. P. (1993). Career development and adjustment: The relation between concerns and stress. *Journal of Employment Counseling, 30,* 79–87.

Niles, S. G., & Anderson, W. P. (1995). A content analysis of career and personal concerns expressed by career counseling clients. *Educational and Vocational Guidance Bulletin, 57,* 59–62.

Niles, S. G., & Pate, P. H., Jr. (1989). Competency and training issues related to the integration of career counseling and mental health counseling. *Journal of Career Development, 16,* 63–71.

O'Brien, K. M. (2001). The legacy of Parsons: Career counselors and vocational psychologists as agents of social change. *The Career Development Quarterly, 50,* 66–76.

O'Toole, J. (1981). Work in America. In J. O'Toole, J. L. Schiber, & L. C. Wood (Eds.), *Working:*

Changes and choices (pp. 12–17). New York: Human Sciences Press.

Parmer, T., & Rush, L. C. (2003). The next decade in career counseling: Cocoon maintenance or metamorphosis? *The Career Development Quarterly, 52,* 26–34.

Parsons, F. (1909). *Choosing a vocation.* Boston: Houghton Mifflin.

Paul, P. (2008). Applying a constructive-developmental approach to issues of sexual orientation and religion in career counseling. *The Career Development Quarterly, 56,* 344–352.

Pepper, S., & Lorah, P. (2008). Career issues and workplace considerations for the transsexual community: Bridging a gap of knowledge for career counselors and mental health care provides. *The Career Development Quarterly, 56,* 330–343.

Perrone, K. M. (2005). Work-family interface for same-sex dual-earner couples: Implications for counselors. *Career Development Quarterly, 53,* 317–325.

Perrone, K. M., Webb, L. K., Blalock, R. H. (2005). The effects of role congruence and role conflict on work, marital and life satisfaction. *Journal of Career Development, 31,* 225–238.

Pope, M. (2000). A brief history of career counseling in the United States. *The Career Development Quarterly, 48,* 194–211.

Pope-Davis, D. B., & Dings, J. G. (1995). The assessment of multicultural counseling competencies. In J. G. Ponterotto & J. M. Casas (Eds.), *Handbook of multicultural counseling* (pp. 287–311). Thousand Oaks, CA: Sage.

Richardson, M. S. (1993). Work in people's lives: A new location for counseling psychology. *Journal of Counseling Psychology, 40,* 425–433.

Riegle, D. W., Jr. (1982). Psychological and social effects of unemployment. *American Psychologist, 21,* 113–115.

Rifkin, J. (1995). *The end of work.* New York: Putnam.

Rogers, C. R. (1942). *Counseling and psychotherapy: Newer concepts in practice.* Boston: Houghton Mifflin.

Savickas, M. L. (1993). Predictive validity criteria for career development measures. *Journal of Career Assessment, 1,* 93–104.

Savickas, M. L. (2009). Career studies as self-making and life designing. *Career Research & Development, 24,* 15–17.

Savickas, M. L. (2010). Vocational counseling. In I. B. Weiner & W. E. Craighead (Eds.), *Corsini's encyclopedia of psychology* (4th ed., pp. 1841–1844). Hoboken, NJ: John Wiley & Sons.

Sears, S. (1982). A definition of career guidance terms. A National Vocational Guidance Association perspective. *The Vocational Guidance Quarterly, 31,* 137–143.

Shanahan, M. J., & Porfeli, E. (2002). Integrating the life course and life-span: Formulating research questions with dual points of entry. *Journal of Vocational Behavior, 61,* 398–406.

Spokane, A. R. (1991). *Career interventions.* Upper Saddle River, NJ: Prentice Hall.

Strong, E. K., Jr. (1943). *Vocational interests of men and women.* Stanford, CA: Stanford University Press.

Subich, L. M. (1993). How personal is career counseling? *The Career Development Quarterly, 42,* 129–131.

Subich, L. M. (2001). Introduction: Special section on contextual factors in career services delivery. *The Career Development Quarterly, 50,* 20.

Sue, D. W., Bernier, Y., Durran, A., Feinberg, L., Pedersen, P., Smith, E. J., & Nuttall, E. V. (1982). Position paper: Cross-cultural counseling competencies. *The Counseling Psychologist, 10*(2), 45–52.

Super, D. E. (1951). Vocational adjustment: Implementing a self-concept. *Occupations, 51,* 88–92.

Super, D. E. (1976). *Career education and the meaning of work.* Washington, DC: Office of Education.

Super, D. E. (1980). A life-span, life-space approach to career development. *Journal of Vocational Behavior, 16,* 282–298.

Super, D. E., Savickas, M. L., and Super, C. M. (1996). The Life-Span, Life-Space Approach to Careers. In D. Brown, L. Brooks and Associates (Eds.), *Career Choice Development: Applying Contemporary Theories to Practice* (3d ed., pp. 121–178). San Francisco: Jossey–Bass.

Swanson, J. L., & Gore, P. A., Jr. (2000). Advances in vocational psychology theory and research. In S. D. Brown & R. W. Lent (Eds.), *Handbook of counseling psychology* (3rd. ed., pp. 233–269). New York: Wiley.

Toporek, R. L. (2006). An integrative approach for competence: Career counseling, social justice advocacy and the multicultural counseling competencies. *Career Planning and Adult Development Journal, 4,* 34–50.

Toporek, R. L., & Liu, W. M. (2001). Advocacy in counseling: Addressing race, class, and gender oppression. In D. B. Pope-Davis & H. L. K. Coleman (Eds.), *The intersection of race, class, and gender in multicultural counseling* (pp. 285–413). Thousand Oaks, CA: Sage.

Uchitelle, L., & Kleinfield, N. R. (1996, March 3). On the battlefield of business, millions of casualties. *The New York Times,* Section 1, p. 1ff.

United Nations (2000). The Global Compact. New York: Author.

Viteles, M. S. (1932). *Industrial psychology.* New York: Norton.

Vondracek, F. W., Lerner, R. M., & Schulenberg, J. E. (1986). *Career development: A life-span developmental approach.* Hillsdale, NJ: Erlbaum.

Warnath, L. F. (1975). Vocational theories: Directions to nowhere. *Personnel and Guidance Journal, 53,* 422–428.

Watkins, C. E., Jr., & Savickas, M. L. (1990). Psychodynamic career counseling. In W. B. Walsh & S. H. Osipow (Eds.), *Career counseling: Contemporary topics in vocational psychology* (pp. 79–116). Hillsdale, NJ: Erlbaum.

Williams, J. C., & Boushey, H. (2010). *The three faces or work-family conflict: The poor, the professionals and the missing middle.* Washington, DC: The Center for American Progress.

Williamson, E. G. (1939). *How to counsel students.* New York: McGraw-Hill.

Wrenn, C. G. (1962). The culturally encapsulated counselor. *Harvard Educational Review, 32,* 444–449.

Zytowski, D. G. (2001). Frank Parsons and the progressive movement. *The Career Development Quarterly, 50,* 57–65.

2

Understanding and Applying Theories of Career Development

Don't Let Theories Boggle Your Mind.

It is easy to be intimated by the word, theory' The real world is an extremely complicated place. Human beings and their behavior are so complex that no one understands completely why people think, feel, and act as they do. A theory is just an explanation—an oversimplified explanation of what is going on.

A theory is like a road map. Suppose you have a road map of California and you want to drive from San Francisco to Los Angeles. You see a red line marked "101" stretching between the two cities on the map. Aha, you think, I'll drive down that red highway 101. But when you get to the highway, you see it is black asphalt. Why does the map show it to be red? The map lies! Why does the map lie? Because the map-maker wants to make it easier for you to see the path. You drive down the highway and see office buildings, gardens, and swimming pools, but none of them are indicated on the map. The map not only distorts reality—it omits zillions of details. Why? Because all those details would make it too complicated to find the best route between two cities.

In the same way, a theory attempts to explain a complex situation by overemphasizing and distorting the importance of certain variables while ignoring completely other variables that the theory-maker considers irrelevant. Theories are oversimplifications just as road maps are oversimplifications. Yet road maps are very useful for certain purposes—even with all of their faults. Similarly, theories can be useful—even with their faults.

A theory is just one way of oversimplifying a complex situation so that it is easier for you to see the big picture. That picture is not reality itself—just one theory-maker's version of it.

John D. Krumboltz
Stanford University

MyCounselingLab™

Visit the **MyCounselingLab**™ site for *Career Development Interventions in the 21st Century*, Fourth Edition to enhance your understanding of chapter concepts. You'll have the opportunity to practice your skills through video- and case-based Assignments and Activities as well as Building Counseling Skills units, and to prepare for your certification exam with Practice for Certification quizzes.

Juanita is a 17-year-old Latina student in the eighth grade in a predominantly White, middle-class neighborhood. She is "normal" in intelligence but reports that she dislikes school. She associates with a group of girls who are often in trouble with the police. It is your impression, however, that these friendships are superficial. Recently, some of the girls in her circle of friends were arrested for drug possession (marijuana). Juanita is not hostile or disrespectful. However, she routinely hands schoolwork in late, if at all. Her parents have asked you to help her "make a good career choice."

In most classes, Juanita is apathetic, but she enjoys art class (especially painting) and being in the school band (she plays the flute). She dislikes math classes. Juanita has two younger sisters, ages 12 and 14. Her mother is employed as a teacher's aide in a local elementary school and her father is employed as a car salesperson in a local dealership. Juanita's current plans are to finish high school but she has not made plans for what she will do beyond that point. She stated that she "might like to be in a rock band." She agrees to meet with you to discuss her career plans.

CAREER DEVELOPMENT THEORIES

As you read about career development theories, we encourage you to keep John Krumboltz's comments in mind and to reflect upon how effectively each of the theories addresses Juanita's career concerns. You will notice that career development theories differ in their coverage of the career development process versus career decision-making content. Savickas (2002) notes that theories emphasize either "individual differences" related to occupations (viewed as describing how people can find their fit within the occupational structure) or "individual development" related to careers (viewed as how people express career behavior across time). For example, developmental theories (e.g., Super, Gottfredson) highlight the expression of career behavior over time. Person-environment theories (e.g., Work Adjustment Theory, Holland) address the essential ingredients (i.e., occupational and self-information) for choosing an occupation. One of the major reasons for studying the various approaches to career theory rather than concentrating on only one emphasis, whatever that emphasis may be, is the fact that no one theory is sufficient to explain the totality of individual or group career behavior. As Super (1992) observed, the question of "which theory is better" is specious because the theories complement each other in addressing various facets of the complexity of career behavior. In this sense, each theory adds to the comprehensiveness of insight about career behavior that now exists. As John Krumboltz notes above, theories are useful, even with their limitations. We encourage you to become familiar with the extensive research literature regarding career theories and to use that information plus your own experience to determine ways in which career development theories help you in your work with your students or clients.

In reflecting upon career development theories, Richardson (1993) states that "the theoretical and research literature in vocational psychology career development is notably oriented toward the White middle class. Moreover, there is almost no acknowledgement that poor and lower class populations, regardless of race or ethnicity, are almost totally absent from the literature" (p. 426). Tinsley (1994) counters that a substantial body of research over the years has not provided support for sex or economic-level differences. Tinsley expresses concern that "there is a tendency to dismiss general models that have applicability to both sexes and all economic class levels as limited in applicability only to White, middle-class men" (p. 109). These varying views, offered by leading scholars in the field, require serious consideration and thoughtful reflection. Most would agree, however, that the need for expanding our understanding of the career development experiences of persons of color, women, sexual minorities, persons with disabilities, and the less affluent members of our society remains an important task for the field. Thus, we encourage you to consider the following questions as you read the theories presented in Chapters 2 and 3:

1. How well do the theories describe the career development process for members of diverse groups?
2. How well do the theories describe the career development process in general?
3. How well do the theories describe the factors involved in making a career choice?
4. How well do the theories inform the practice of career counseling?
5. To what degree is there empirical support for the theories?
6. What gaps can you identify within the theories presented?

Because no one theory is likely to "do it all," we think it is important to identify the strengths and limitations of each theory. Doing so will allow you to draw upon the best the field has to offer. For those interested in career development research, identifying the gaps will also provide useful information for potentially fruitful research pursuits.

There are many ways to present career theories. Often, theories are presented in chronological order, beginning with the work of Frank Parsons and proceeding to the most recent theories. Other times they are grouped by categories (e.g., psychological, developmental, trait-factor; objective vs. subjective). In determining how to organize the career theories, we attempted to present them in a fashion that we thought made sense as practitioners.

Tips from the Field

Theories seldom explain the whole story, but good theories guide you as you gather information and fill in the gaps to paint a more complete picture of a student's or client's career development experience.

The work of Parsons and later trait-factor theorists was discussed in the previous chapter, largely because these models are intimately intertwined with the historical roots of career development interventions. The work of contributors such as Parsons, Williamson, and Dawis and Lofquist highlights the importance of considering the interactions between the person's traits and factors in the work environment in career decision making. Building upon our discussion of Parsons' model and trait-factor approaches (e.g., TWA) presented in Chapter 1, we begin the current chapter with Donald Super's theory for several reasons. First, Super's theory provides a useful framework for conceptualizing career development over the life span. His theory also acknowledges the various personal (e.g., needs, values, abilities) and situational (e.g., peer groups, family, labor market) determinants that influence career development. Super's theory places work within the context of multiple roles played in life. Finally, his theory addresses helping people to clarify, articulate, and implement their life-role self-concepts. Thus, Super's theory provides a useful, overarching framework for viewing career development processes.

To expand on the influence of personal and situational influences on career development, we briefly discuss Anne Roe's career theory and then describe Linda Gottfredson's theory. Roe's theory points to the importance of early life experiences in career development. Gottfredson's theory addresses the fact that sex-role stereotyping influences the career aspirations of men and women (Gottfredson, 1996, 2002). Her theory offers a developmental and sociological perspective of career development. The theory is focused primarily on the career development process as it relates to the types of compromises people make in formulating their occupational aspirations.

We then discuss Holland's theory, which has generated more research than any other career theory. Arguably, Holland's typology provides the most useful framework for understanding and predicting individual behavior (i.e., job satisfaction, job performance, and occupational stability) within work environments. Through the use of assessment instruments, Holland applies his typology to help individuals clarify and implement their vocational identities (Spokane, Luchetta, & Richwine, 2002).

There are times, however, when "faulty" or irrational thinking impedes individuals in their career development. The cumulative effect of a variety of learning experiences can result in varying degrees of functionality among individuals with regard to their ability to make effective career decisions. For example, when individuals receive adequate support and are exposed to effective role models, they often develop interests and skills leading to satisfying career options. Conversely, when such support is lacking or individuals are misinformed, they often disregard appropriate options because they lack confidence or they adhere to beliefs (e.g., "I must decide now what I will do for the rest of my life") that keep them "stuck" in their career development. In the latter cases, individuals need assistance in developing beliefs that are more useful in making effective career decisions. In these instances, the work of John Krumboltz provides a useful framework for helping practitioners to foster career development in their clients. We discuss this theory in the final section of this chapter. In Chapter 3, we focus attention on emerging theories of career development that hold promise for providing effective descriptions of career development processes and practices. Table 2.1 summarizes the theories discussed in Chapters 2 and 3.

Table 2.1
Brief Overview of Career Theories

Theory	Theorists	Orientation	Key Constructs	Research Support	Multicultural Emphasis
Work Adjustment	Rene Dawis, Lloyd Lofquist	Trait-factor Career choice/adjustment	Satisfaction Satisfactoriness Person-in-an environment Correspondence	Moderate	Low
Life-Span, Life-Space	Donald Super	Developmental	Life span Career stages Career development tasks Life space Self-concept Career maturity Career adaptability	High	Moderate
Personality Theory of Career Choice	Anne Roe	Personality Theory/Psychodynamic	Early childhood experiences Needs hierarchies Field/level	Low	Low
Circumscription, Compromise, and Self-Creation	Linda Gottfredson	Developmental/sociological Career choice/development	Circumscription Compromise	Low	High
Vocational Personalities and Work Environments	John Holland	Trait-factor Career choice	Congruence Consistency Differentiation Vocational identity	High	Low
Learning Theory of Career Counseling	John Krumboltz	Social learning Career choice development	Learning experience Self-observation generalizations Worldview generalizations Task approach skills, actions Planned happenstance	Moderate	High
Social Cognitive Career Theory	Robert Lent, Steven Brown, Gail Hackett	Social cognitive career choice development	Self-efficacy Outcome expectations Personal goals Triadic reciprocal model	Moderate	High

Theory	Theorist(s)	Perspective	Key Concepts		
Cognitive Information Processing Approach	Gary Peterson, James Sampson Jr., Robert Reardon, Janet Lentz	Cognitive career choice	Pyramid of information processing CASVE cycle Executive processing domain Career thoughts inventory	Moderate	Moderate
Career Construction Theory	Mark Savickas	Differential, developmental, and dynamic perspective of careers	Vocational personality Life themes Career Adaptability Career Style Interview	Moderate	High
Integrative Life Planning	L. Sunny Hansen	Contextual career choice/adjustment	Social justice Social change Connectedness Diversity Spirituality Integrative life planning inventory	Low	High
Postmodern	Richard Young, Ladislav Valach, Audrey Collin	Action-theory	Context Joint action Career project Interpretation Functional steps	Low	High
	Vance Peavey	Constructivist	Meaning-making	Low	High
	Larry Cochran	Narrative	Career problem Life history Future narrative	Low	High
Chaos Theory of Careers	Robert Pryor and Jim Bright	Self-organization and change; phenomenalist	Attractors Patterns Patterns and Fractals	Moderate	Low

SUPER'S LIFE-SPAN, LIFE-SPACE THEORY

The leading developmental approach is Donald Super's "life-span, life-space" theory (Super, 1990; Super, Savickas, & Super, 1996). The life-span, life-space theory evolved over a 40-year time period, as Super and his colleagues worked to elaborate and refine the various aspects of the theory (Super et al., 1996). Although Super's theory is primarily developmental in nature, he labeled it as a "differential-developmental-social-phenomenological career theory" (Super, 1969). This label communicates Super's efforts at synthesizing and extending extant developmental and career theories. Super understood that describing a process as complex as career development requires synthesizing the work of scholars from various disciplines (e.g., psychology and sociology). For example, Super synthesized work by Buehler (1933), Havighurst (1951), Kelly (1955), Miller & Form (1951), and Rogers (1951) in conceptualizing various aspects of his theory of career development.

Super extended career theories by addressing shortcomings he perceived in the theories proposed by his predecessors and his contemporaries. For example, Super's contemporaries, Ginzberg, Ginsburg, Axelrad, and Herma (1951), proposed a career theory asserting that career choice is a developmental process (rather than a single decision) in which compromises are made between the individual's wishes and occupational possibilities. They viewed the developmental process as spanning three stages: (a) fantasy (birth to age 11), (b) tentative (age 11 to 17), and (c) realistic (age 17 to early twenties). They theorized that four factors (individual values, emotional factors, the amount and kind of education, and the effect of reality through environmental pressures) converged to shape the individual's career decisions.

Super argued that the theory proposed by Ginzberg and his associates was deficient in that it (a) did not take into account research related to the role of interests in career decision making, (b) failed to operationally describe "choice," (c) made a sharp distinction between choice and adjustment, and (d) lacked a clear articulation of the process of compromise as it relates to career choice. Responding to conditions such as these, Super developed his "differential-developmental-social-phenomenological career theory."

Rather than developing a unified theory, however, Super developed his theory segmentally. In fact, Super noted that in one sense "there is no 'Super's theory'; there is just the assemblage of theories that I have sought to synthesize. In another sense, the synthesis is a theory" (1990, p. 199). The result is really a "segmental theory" describing three key aspects of career development: (a) life span, (b) life space, and (c) self-concept. The theory culminates in an intervention model labeled as the Career Development Assessment and Counseling (C-DAC) model (Super, Osborne, Walsh, Brown, & Niles, 1992). We provide an updated version of the C-DAC model in this chapter. The C-DAC model translates the three theory segments into career practice to help people articulate their career concerns, examine their life-role salience, and clarify their self-concepts.

Life-span, life-space theory builds upon key assumptions proposed by Super (1953, 1933, 1990; Super & Bachrach, 1957). These assumptions contend that people differ in their important self-characteristics and self-concepts; that their respective self-characteristics make them eligible for a number of occupations; that each occupation requires specific worker traits but that these requirements are flexible enough to allow for a variety of persons within specific occupations; and that self-concepts evolve over time, making choice and adjustment continuous processes for everyone. Further assumptions are that the change process for each person can be described by specific life stages (growth, exploration, establishment, maintenance, and decline or disengagement); that a person's occupational level and career pattern are influenced by contextual (e.g., family, socioeconomic status, educational opportunities, community) and personal (e.g., skills, personality, needs, values, interests) factors; and that people's readiness to cope with the career development tasks (career maturity) they encounter is influenced by the their degree of success in coping with previous tasks encountered in earlier stages of career development.

The life-span, life-space theory also builds on other factors, such as the notion that a person's career development can be facilitated by providing developmentally appropriate career interventions across the life span; career choice involves developing and implementing one's self-concepts and reflects a synthesizing and compromising process as the person develops and interacts with, as well as learns from, his or her environment; that life satisfaction is dependent upon finding life-role opportunities that are consistent with a person's important self-characteristics; and that it is important for each person to structure life-role involvements that reflect his or her preferences, values, and life-role self-concepts.

The propositions incorporate statements from diverse theoretical perspectives (e.g., trait-and-factor, developmental, social learning, and psychodynamic), thus supporting Super's contention that his theory is more than a developmental one. Super's propositions also introduce some relatively novel concepts into the career development literature. Specifically, Super expanded career development concepts by encouraging the field to consider the notion that there is intraoccupational variability among workers, that multiple life-role development is important to consider in career development, and that self-concepts evolve over time, making choice and adjustment a continuous process. Thus, when Super's propositions are placed in historical context, they provide the impetus for shifting the paradigm within the field from one that focuses on "vocation" to one that focuses on "career"; from one that focuses exclusively on the content of career choice to one that highlights the process of career development over the life span.

Life Span

Although career development, like physical development, is a lifelong process, it is unlike physical development in that career development is not ontogenetic. Rather, careers develop within the context of psychosocial development and societal expectations and against the backdrop of the occupational opportunity structure. Early in life, career development is relatively homogeneous and age related. Most young people are enrolled in educational institutions that require them to make decisions at specific grade levels (e.g., students in eighth grade must select a curriculum of study for high school, students leaving high school must make choices about what they will do when their secondary-school experience ends). Thus, in childhood and adolescence the term *career maturity* is used in relationship to career decision-making readiness. Career development in adulthood, however, is heterogeneous and not as directly connected to age. Adult careers develop in response to the challenges presented by changing occupational opportunities and evolving patterns of life-role participation. Thus, adults may recycle through various career development stages and tasks, depending on their situations in life. Because career development in adulthood is heterogeneous, the term *career adaptability* (rather than *career maturity*) is used when referring to an adult person's career decision-making readiness. The term *career adaptability* reflects the fact that "as adults cope with their changing work and working conditions, adults make an impact on their environments and their environments make an impact on them" (Niles, Anderson, & Goodnough, 1998, p. 273). Just as the self-concept evolves over time, making choosing and adjusting continuous processes, educational and work environments also change over time, making choosing and adjusting continuous requirements. Complacency becomes the enemy of effective career self-management. In this sense, career adaptability parallels Piaget's model of adaptation based on the two processes of assimilation and accommodation. Career adaptability also supports the view that adults are "responsible agents acting within dynamic environmental settings" to find ways to effectively manage their career development (Super & Knasel, 1981, p. 199). Others (e.g., Savickas, 2005) have elaborated upon Super's use of the career adaptability construct.

Although Super originally applied "adaptability" to adult career development, it seems reasonable to suggest that the term *career adaptability* can also be applied to children and adolescents. Despite their relative homogeneity in career development when compared with adults, young people experience differences in their readiness to cope with career development tasks. Some young people encounter environmental obstacles (e.g., poverty, racism, sexism) that influence their career development in less-than-positive ways. Some young people are provided with environmental experiences (e.g., the opportunity to enroll in outstanding schools, opportunities to engage in multiple recreational and co-curricular school activities) that foster career development. Differences in contextual "affordances" (Vondracek, Lerner, & Schulenberg, 1986) have implications for career development. Thus, *career adaptability* seems a more fitting term for young people than does *career maturity*. Savickas (1997) agrees and states that "career adaptability should replace career maturity as the critical construct in the developmental perspective" (p. 247). We concur with Savickas' recommendation.

In describing the process of career development over the life span, Super drew on the research of Buehler (1933), Miller and Form (1951), and Havighurst (1953). Super conceptualized career as "the life course of a person encountering a series of developmental tasks and attempting to handle them in such a way as to become the kind of person he or she wants to become" (Super, 1990, pp. 225–226). Super identified the series of developmental tasks that are typically encountered and related them to stages and substages of career development. The stages of career development, in their typical sequence, are growth (childhood), exploration (adolescence), establishment (early adulthood), maintenance (middle adulthood), and disengagement (late adulthood).

GROWTH.   Children ages 4 to 13 are confronted with the career development tasks of developing a beginning sense of self and a basic understanding of the world-of-work. In so doing, children progress through the substages of fantasy, interest, and capacity. They progress through these substages by using their innate sense of curiosity, first to engage in occupational fantasies, and then, through exploring their environment (e.g., home, school, parental, and peer relationships). Their curiosity leads them to acquire information about work and about their own interests and capacities. When things go well, children begin to develop a sense of mastery and control over their environment and in their ability to make decisions. Moving through the growth stage, children begin to realize the importance of planning for the future and that their behavior in the present influences their future lives. Moreover, they are increasingly able to use what they have learned about themselves and work to explore the viability of various educational and occupational opportunities.

EXPLORATION. Using self and occupational information, and their heightened sense of awareness that the present influences the future, adolescents ages 14 to 24 turn to planning for the future. Within the career development domain, future planning involves addressing the tasks of crystallizing and specifying occupational preferences. Once a preference is specified, people turn to implementing an occupational choice. These tasks occur within the substages of tentative, transition, and trial (with little commitment), respectively.

Crystallizing an occupational preference requires people to clarify the type of work they would enjoy. The process of crystallization builds upon the occupational and self-information acquired during the growth stage. Using this information, people focus on acquiring more in-depth occupational information to explore the degree to which specific occupations may allow for self-concept implementation. Thus, accurate self-understanding is essential for identifying appropriate occupational preferences.

The process of specifying occupational preferences requires the ability to make decisions by choosing from among the occupations being considered. The process of implementing varies, depending on what choice has been specified. Some choices require further training and education in order to gain entry into an occupation. Other choices provide the opportunity for direct entry into an occupation. Regardless of the choice, implementing requires taking action toward getting started in one's chosen occupational field.

ESTABLISHMENT. Getting established in a career generally occurs from about age 25 to age 45. The career development tasks associated with this stage are stabilizing, consolidating, and advancing. Stabilizing begins immediately after entering an occupation as one evaluates whether the occupational preference one has implemented provides adequate opportunity for self-concept expression. Specifically, one must assess the organizational culture and determine whether he or she possesses the skills and interests necessary to succeed in the occupation he or she has entered.

As one becomes more stabilized in an occupation, he or she turns attention away from questioning whether the choice was a good one and begins to focus on becoming a dependable producer and developing a positive reputation in the occupation (i.e., consolidating). Focusing on becoming a dependable producer often leads to the opportunity to move into a position of higher pay and responsibility (i.e., advancing). The reputation for successful performance one sought to develop is now achieved.

It is important to note, however, that at any time in this process a person may decide that the occupational choice he or she made is no longer a good one. If this occurs, recycling to exploration occurs so that a more appropriate occupational choice can be crystallized, specified, and implemented.

MAINTENANCE.   During maintenance (approximately ages 45 to 65), workers encounter the career development tasks of holding, updating, and innovating. Many people are confronted with the choice of either keeping up with the advancements in their field to maintain or improve their level of performance or opting for a change in occupational fields. In the latter instance, workers must recycle through exploration- and establishment-stage tasks. In the former (i.e., holding), workers turn their attention to updating their skills and applying new skills in innovative ways within their current occupations. Those who decide to stay in their current occupations but not to update their skills often become poor performers and stagnate in their work (i.e., they become "stuck" at the holding task). In these instances, career interventions addressing career renewal are required. Those who update and innovate often become excellent mentors to less experienced workers.

DISENGAGEMENT.   At some point toward the end of the maintenance stage, often as physical capacities begin to decline, interest in work activities begins to wane. Workers become more concerned with planning for retirement living. Thus, the disengagement stage involves the career development tasks of deceleration, retirement planning, and retirement living. As workers begin decelerating from their work activities (currently at about age 65), they tend to become concerned about their lifestyles and activities in retirement. Often, these concerns contain physical, spiritual, and financial considerations.

Although career development stage theory originally represented a more linear version of career development, Super readily acknowledged that recycling through career stages and tasks occurs with frequency throughout one's life, thereby suggesting a process that *could* be linear in nature, but in all likelihood will not be for most people. We suggest a further refining of stage theory. Specifically, we make two recommendations regarding using Super's stage theory in career counseling. First, we suggest that career practitioners understand that people can be concerned with multiple career development tasks and multiple stages simultaneously. Second, we recommend that career practitioners conceptualize stages in a fashion that is similar to the notion of "status." Regarding the former, it is not hard to imagine, for example, that people can be concerned about deciding what they will do next in their careers (i.e., exploration) while also being concerned about whether they will have the resources to survive financially in retirement (i.e., disengagement). Such a person is likely to explore more narrowly than another person who may only be concerned with exploration stage tasks. We think that understanding the constellation of career concerns a client or student experiences at any point in time provides important information regarding the sort of support and resources the client will find useful. Viewing the client's constellation of career concerns from the perspective of status moves away from linear notions of career stage theory and helps reinforce the point that career tasks present themselves to persons in ways that are not always restricted by chronological age. Thus, Super's stages and tasks provide important information regarding the potential array of career concerns, or societal expectations, that a person may be attempting to cope with at any point in his or her life. Understanding the life span segment of Super's theory in this way will foster a greater understanding of a person's career development experience.

Life Space

While workers are busy earning a living, they are also busy living a life (Super et al., 1996). The "simultaneous combination of life roles we play constitutes the lifestyle; their sequential combination structures the life space and constitutes the life cycle. The total structure is the career pattern" (Super, 1980, p. 288). Life roles interact so that the same job holds different meanings for two individuals who live in different situations. For example, the meaning and purpose your professor finds in his or her job is influenced by previous roles your professor has played in life (e.g., child, student, worker in previous occupations) as well as the current roles your professor is playing (e.g., partner, parent, child, homemaker, sibling, friend). Because of the life roles each professor plays, your professor's dedication to work, and the way in which he or she defines the work role, may differ from someone else's who is also a professor.

The salience people attach to the constellation of life roles they play defines what Super referred to as the "life structure." The life-space segment of Super's theory acknowledges that people differ in the degree of importance they attach to work. Unfortunately, as we mentioned in Chapter 1, many people link work with self-worth in such a way that devalues the various life roles that have so much to contribute to one's sense of self-esteem and self-efficacy (not to mention to society). Many models of career counseling have disregarded the effects of life-role interactions and the fact that effective participation in multiple life roles allows for maximal opportunities for values expression.

Super noted that people tend to play nine major roles throughout their lives. In approximate chronological order these roles are: (1) son or daughter, (2) student, (3) leisurite, (4) citizen, (5) worker, (6) spouse (or partner), (7) homemaker, (8) parent, and (9) pensioner. The individual's career comprises the total constellation of life roles engaged in over the course of a lifetime (Super, 1980, p. 284). Life roles are generally played out in specific theaters. These theaters are: (1) the home, (2) the school, (3) the workplace, and (4) the community.

Effective life-role participation is very difficult to achieve. Conflicting life-role demands make effective life-role participation feel like a "moving target." At various times, priority must be given to specific life roles. Sometimes deciding which role takes priority is relatively easy (e.g., giving priority to one's job when there are low demands from one's children) and sometimes not (e.g., when the demands from job and family are concurrently high). At times, life roles typically played in one theater spill over into another theater and create conflict (Eagle, Miles, & Icenogle, 1997; Loscocco, 1997; Perrone, 2005). For example, when work spills over from the workplace to the home, the roles of worker, partner, and parent become enmeshed and insufficient attention is paid to each role. Thus, life roles interact in ways that can be extensive or minimal: supportive, supplementary, compensatory, or neutral. Life is best when the life roles we play nurture each other and offer opportunities for us to express our values. Life is stressful when the life roles we play are at odds with each other and provide little opportunity for us to express what we value.

Thus, it is not surprising that many career counseling clients present with concerns related to life-structure issues. That is, many of them are seeking assistance in coping more effectively with changing life-role demands. For such clients, career interventions that address only one life role—work—are inadequate. Super's theory embraces this fact by focusing on how clients structure the basic roles of work, play, friendship, and family into a life that is satisfying (Super et al., 1996).

Self-Concepts

Super defined self-concept as a "picture of the self in some role, situation, or position, performing some set of functions, or in some web of relationships" (1963, p. 18). Super (1980) uses the Archway Model and the Life-Career Rainbow to depict the various personal (e.g., aptitudes, values, needs) and situational (e.g., the family, the community, the economy, society) determinants that shape the constellation of life roles that individuals play over the course of a life span and that interact to influence the development of the person's self-concepts. In these models, Super delineates both the longitudinal processes of career development as well as the more situation-specific content of career decision making. Career decisions reflect our attempts at translating our self-understanding (i.e., our self-concepts) into career terms (Super, 1984).

Self-concepts contain both objective and subjective elements. Objectively, we develop self-understanding by comparing ourselves with others (e.g., "I am like accountants in that I am good with numbers" or "I am in the 95th percentile on mechanical ability"). Subjectively, we develop understanding through focusing on our uniqueness emerging out of the life stories we construct. Our life stories represent our efforts at constructing meaning from our life experiences. There is relative homogeneity in our objective career experience (e.g., almost everyone reading this book is focused on acquiring the occupational title of counselor or counseling psychologist). There is tremendous heterogeneity in our subjective career experience (e.g., everyone reading this book has a unique history of personal experience that has led him or her to the place of wanting to work within the helping professions). We use our objective and subjective understanding to identify appropriate career goals. Such understanding guides us as we make choices about the degree and the nature of our life-role participation. Because self-concepts continue to develop over time, the need to make choices and the process of adjusting to the choices implemented represent lifelong tasks.

Applying Super's Theory

Toward the end of his career, Super increasingly focused on translating his theory into practice (Super et al., 1992). As noted, Super labeled his approach the Career Development Assessment and Counseling (C-DAC) model. Like other theorists (e.g., Holland, Krumboltz), Super translated his theory into practice, in part, through the systematic application of career assessment instruments emanating from each of his theory segments. Although these assessment instruments are key elements in the C-DAC model, they are not required for addressing Super's theory segments in career counseling. (It is important to note that many of the C-DAC assessment instruments are available for no cost at vocopher.com.)

The primary emphasis of the C-DAC model (and the traditional focus of career counseling) is on helping clients cope with concerns arising within the exploration stage of the life-span theory segment (Super, 1957; Super et al., 1996). Many people associate exploration only with adolescents who are at the preimplementation stage of career development; however, exploration continues throughout life: "Exploration has come to be expected not only in adults who are changing career direction, but also in adults who are responding to the demands of progressing in the career they have chosen and in which they wish to remain" (Phillips, 1982, p. 130).

Persons encountering the exploration stage for the first time focus on clarifying their values, skills, and interests, and connecting these attributes to initial occupational options. Formal standardized assessments can be very useful in providing initial career explorers with foundational self-information required for coping effectively with exploration stage tasks. However, persons recycling through the exploration stage use exploratory behavior to resolve a wide variety of career issues (Niles et al., 1998). For example, some people use exploratory behavior to maintain their current positions while they focus on retirement living. Others use exploration to start over in new occupations, whereas still others use exploratory behavior to become more innovative in their current positions. As we noted earlier, it is not uncommon for people to experience career concerns across multiple career stages concurrently. It is important to note, therefore, that understanding the full range of a client's career concerns provides important information regarding the career tasks with which the client is attempting to cope. Although exploration always involves learning more about our situation, or ourselves, what needs to be learned depends on our developmental status and salient life roles (Super, 1983). Career development rarely occurs in a linear fashion. Thus, identifying each client's constellation of developmental task concerns is an important first step in constructing appropriate career interventions.

For example, Juanita (presented at the beginning of the chapter) is confronting the career development tasks of crystallizing and specifying occupational preferences for the first time (i.e., she is an "initial career explorer"). To cope effectively with the exploration-stage tasks, Juanita will need to acquire much more self-information (e.g., values, interests, and abilities) and information about the world-of-work. She may also need to learn about the career decision-making process (i.e., how good career decisions are made). Then she will need assistance in translating the information she acquires into a career plan. That is, she must be able to make concrete connections between this information and her future career. It is hoped that in the process of developing a career plan, Juanita will also be able to make connections between her school activities and her future, thereby becoming more motivated at school. As Juanita crystallizes her occupational self-concept, she will need to reality-test her tentative choices. Activities such as role playing, participating in school clubs, job shadowing, volunteering, and part-time employment will be useful to her in increasing her self-knowledge and occupational information.

To measure concern with life-span career development stages and tasks with adult clients, Super and his colleagues developed the Adult Career Concerns Inventory (ACCI) (Super, Thompson, & Lindeman, 1988). The ACCI measures planfulness or concern for the developmental tasks of the four career stages of exploration, establishment, maintenance, and disengagement posited in life-span, life-space theory (Super et al., 1988). Each career stage includes three tasks, which respondents rate in terms of level of concern using a 5-point Likert-type scale ranging from 1 (*no concern*) to 5 (*great concern*) with the associated task. For example, the exploration stage consists of the tasks of crystallization, specification, and implementation. The tasks for each of the stages are arranged in 5-item substages, resulting in a total of 60 items. Summing each set of three-task substage scores yields a total score for the corresponding career stage.

The ACCI is useful at the onset of career counseling to identify clients' developmental task concerns and for identifying the exploratory resources that may be of most use in helping clients cope effectively with their career concerns. For example, clients concerned with the task of updating can be encouraged to attend meetings and seminars on new methods in their fields, to visit places where they can see new developments in their fields, to conduct information interviews with knowledgeable people, and to take refresher training (items 36 to 40, respectively, on the Updating Scale of the ACCI). Counselors can use ACCI scores to identify the client's career development status regarding the constellation of career concerns with which the client is attempting to cope.

Some clients, however, may be unable to make career choices due to the fact that they lack the resources necessary for choosing (e.g., adolescents may be lacking career maturity and adults may be lacking career adaptability). Individuals who are not ready to make good career choices need to (a) develop positive attitudes toward career exploration and planning, (b) learn how to gather information about themselves and occupational options, and (c) learn how to make career decisions.

The Career Development Inventory (CDI) (Thompson, Lindeman, Super, Jordaan, & Myers, 1984) assesses whether high school and college students are ready to make career decisions. Specifically, the CDI assesses career planning, career exploration, world-of-work information, and knowledge of career decision-making principles. Scores indicate the client's degree of readiness for career decision making. CDI scores can be used to answer questions such as: Does the respondent know how to make career decisions? Is the respondent aware of the need to make career plans? Does the respondent possess both general information about the world-of-work and specific information about the preferred occupation? Does the respondent know how to make use of exploratory resources for gathering information relevant to the career decision-making process?

High scores on the CDI scales indicate affirmative answers to these questions (i.e., that the client has been involved in making career plans, possesses occupational information, has used exploratory resources effectively, and knows how to make decisions). In such instances, clients are often able to proceed with career decision making.

Low scores on CDI scales indicate deficiencies that must be remediated prior to proceeding with career decision making. For example, a low CDI score suggests that the client is not aware of the need to make a career choice and is not involved in planning for the future. Low scores related to occupational information indicate the need to become more aware of occupational requirements and tasks. Using the CDI with Juanita will help identify specific areas in which she may need assistance in becoming ready to make career decisions (i.e., in developing career maturity).

The next step in applying the C-DAC model involves determining the priority clients attach to the life roles they play. This step in the C-DAC model distinguishes Super's approach from most other career counseling models because it helps clients understand how they "structure the basic roles of work, play, friendship, and family into a life" (Savickas, 1993, p. 211).

Achieving this understanding involves exploring the importance, or salience, clients attach to their life roles. It also means realizing that the problems clients present in career counseling cannot be precisely categorized as reflecting either "personal" or "career" concerns. Because few issues are more personal than those related to career choice and adjustment, it is not surprising that career and noncareer concerns overlap substantially (Betz & Corning, 1993; Krumboltz, 1993; Subich, 1993; Super, 1993). Research supports this perspective by indicating that clients seeking career counseling often experience high levels of psychological stress and discuss concerns related to nonwork roles throughout the duration of the career counseling process (Anderson & Niles, 1995; Lucas, 1993; Niles & Anderson, 1993). Such findings point to the importance of attending to the emotional issues clients encounter as they cope with problems emerging in the context of their unique life structures.

Counselors can encourage clients to examine the personal meaning they attach to the life roles they play by asking questions such as: How do you spend your time during a typical week? How important are the different roles of life to you? What do you like about participating in each of the life roles you play? What life roles do you think will be important to you in the future? What do you hope to accomplish in each of the life roles that will be important to you in the future? What life roles do members of your family play? What do your family members expect you to accomplish in each of the life roles? What helpful (and not so helpful) lessons have you learned about playing each life role? Questions such as these would be important to discuss with Juanita to help her consider what life roles will be important to her in the future and what she can do in the present to begin preparing for those life roles. Asking clients to describe how they spend their time in the course of a typical week and then to consider the values reflected in their weekly activities is also a useful strategy for inviting clients to consider life-structure issues in career counseling. Counselors can also encourage clients to describe how they would like to spend their time at some future point (e.g., five years in the future). The counselor can then encourage the client to engage in planning by identifying specific strategies for increasing the probability that the future life-structure scenario will occur.

Counselors can also use the Salience Inventory (Super & Nevill, 1986) as a starting point for discussing life-role salience. The Salience Inventory measures the relative importance of five life roles (student, worker, citizen, homemaker, and leisurite) on three dimensions, one behavioral and two affective. The behavioral component, Participation, assesses what the individual does or has done recently in each of the life roles. The first affective component, Commitment, requires the inventory-taker to indicate how he or she feels about each of the five life roles. The second affective component, Values Expectations, requires the respondent to indicate the degree to which there will be opportunities now or in the future to express important values in each of the life roles.

Finally, life-role activities can be examined using the "Pie of Life" exercises. In the Pie of Life activity, clients divide a circle into "slices" reflecting the amount of time they spend in various life activities during the course of a typical week. They are then asked to identify the values that they think are reflected in their life pie. After listing the values, the counselor and client then discuss how the client feels about the values exposed in the slices of pie. The counselor focuses on reinforcing the time spent in activities that the client feels good about and explores changes the client can make in Pie of Life slices that do not reflect the client's value structure. The counselor and client can also discuss what the client would like to accomplish in each of the life roles that are important to the client. They can then focus on what the client needs to do to increase the chances of accomplishing the life-role goals identified.

To further guide the self-concept crystallization process, career counselors can use the Values Scale (VS) (Nevill & Super, 1986). The VS measures 21 intrinsic (e.g., creativity, altruism) and extrinsic (e.g., economic rewards) values individuals hope to express in their life roles. Counselors can use the results of the VS to help clients focus their exploration on life roles and occupational options. Thus, the VS can be a useful supplement to measures of interests and abilities for clients attempting to crystallize work and life goals.

With the information provided by the Salience Inventory and the Values Scale, counselors help clients identify the life roles in which they are currently spending most of their time, those to which they are emotionally committed, the values they hope to express in their life roles, and the life roles they expect to be important to them in the future.

With regard to the latter, counselors can help clients construct strategies for preparing for their salient life roles. For example, if the life role of worker is one that Juanita expects to be salient in her future, she can discuss ways to plan and prepare for that role. She can identify present activities that can help her develop her readiness for the role of worker. Special attention can be given to helping Juanita make connections between her current life role as a student and her future as a worker. Information from the Salience Inventory can also be used to encourage Juanita to think proactively about areas of potential role conflict and discuss strategies for coping with excessive demands from multiple life roles.

Contextual Factors Influencing Life-Role Salience

Super's Archway model suggests that life-role self-concepts are shaped by our contexts (i.e., personal and situational determinants). However, many individuals lack an awareness of the ways in which contextual factors (e.g., the dominant culture, culture of origin) interact with identity development to shape life-role salience (Blustein, 1994).

DOMINANT CULTURE.   Often persons simply "inherit" patterns of life-role salience that are passed on from the dominant or popular culture. Such inheritances can be problematic when they are embedded in beliefs based on gender, racial, and other stereotypes. For example, researchers have consistently found gender bias in life-role salience and occupational sex-role stereotyping in portrayals of workers in the popular culture. With regard to the former, Niles and Goodnough (1996) reported in a literature review that researchers have consistently found gender differences in role salience that coincide with traditional sex-role expectations (e.g., women participating more in home and family and expecting more from this life role than men). Women who have high salience for the worker role are placed at an obvious disadvantage in the workforce by such traditional expectations. Also, men limit their opportunities for participating in the home and family when they adhere to traditional expectations for life-role salience. Concerning sex-role stereotyping, Coltrane and Adams (1997) found that women are typically portrayed in popular culture as unemployed or employed in service or clerical occupations, thus perpetuating gender inequality in the workplace. Raising client awareness regarding the influence of the dominant culture on patterns of life-role salience helps clients minimize the influence of racist beliefs and sexist attitudes on their career decision making.

CULTURE OF ORIGIN.   Discussions related to the influence of the dominant culture on life-role salience can also lead to discussions focusing on how clients' cultural backgrounds influence their career development. Counselors and clients can explore how cultures of origin influence the values expressed in life roles (e.g., seeking to express self-actualization in work for the individual from a Eurocentric cultural background or seeking to express cultural identity in work for the individual from an Asian background). When these discussions occur in small groups, they stimulate increased awareness of, and sensitivity to, cultural diversity in life-role salience.

This type of exploration can also lead to exploring the various cultural prescriptions (e.g., Eurocentric men are expected to be "good providers" and upwardly mobile in their occupations) that are generally assigned to specific life roles. In these discussions, counselors can encourage clients to identify how they perceive and interpret the role expectations emanating from their cultures of origin and how these expectations influence their decisions as to whether a particular life role is important. Special attention can be paid to exploring how these expectations influence the client's understanding of the behaviors required for effective role performance (e.g., men who define their parenting role primarily as being a good provider can consider whether this behavior is sufficient for good parenting).

One specific activity for discussing these topics is suggested by Borodovsky and Ponterotto (1994). They have found the family genogram to be a useful tool for exploring the interaction between family background, cultural prescriptions, and career planning. The genogram provides a tool for tracking career decisions across generations and identifying sources of important career beliefs and life themes that people have acquired.

This technique can be expanded to address the same topics for other life roles. That is, by using the genogram, counselors can encourage clients to identify the beliefs and life themes pertaining to specific life roles (e.g., parent, and citizen) that they have acquired from members of their immediate and extended families. Counselors can also use the information provided by clients to contrast the influences on life-role salience emanating from group-oriented cultures with influences from more individualistic cultures. Terms such as "cultural assimilation" and "cultural accommodation" can be introduced in these discussions. The effects of sex-role stereotyping on life-role salience can also be examined in these discussions. The goal of these interventions is to increase client awareness as to the factors influencing their beliefs about the primary roles of life so they can make informed decisions about their future life-role participation.

Although examining life-role participation more holistically is very important, the central concern in career development interventions continues to be helping clients clarify their occupational self-concepts. In the C-DAC model, clients use their understanding of life-role salience as a foundation on which to build as they move forward with clarifying and articulating their vocational identities.

Vocational identities are clarified using two methods: the actuarial method (Super, 1954, 1957) and the developmental method (Super, 1954, 1961). The actuarial method relates to the trait-and-factor approach of using test scores to predict future occupational performance and satisfaction. For instance, Juanita might be given an interest inventory, such as the Strong Interest Inventory (SII) (Harmon, Hansen, Borgen, & Hammer, 1994), to compare her interests with those of people already employed in various occupations. Using the actuarial method, the counselor "acts like an actuary, consults tables, graphs, and formulas seeking the optimal prediction, in probability terms, based on the observed correlations with similar performances of other people" (Jepsen, 1994, p. 45). Juanita's pattern of interests would be related to the patterns of workers within a variety of occupations. The counselor would focus on similar patterns (as starting points for further exploration) and dissimilar patterns (to identify types of occupations Juanita is not likely to find satisfying). Ability tests could be used in the same way. Juanita's abilities can be compared with the abilities required for successful performance in specific occupations. Occupations for which her interests and abilities merge to predict satisfying and successful performance can be identified and focused on for further consideration.

Values inventory results or values card sorts can then be used to guide further exploration. Some occupations might be appropriate for a client's interests and abilities, but they may not provide sufficient opportunities for values expression. For clients like Juanita who are attempting to crystallize occupational preferences, values inventories or values card sorts may be especially helpful supplements to results from measures of interests and abilities (Super et al., 1996).

Using the developmental method (which Super also described as the Thematic-Extrapolation Method), counselors act more like historians (rather than actuaries) by inviting clients to construct autobiographical stories of development. Specifically, clients construct chronologies of what they did in the past. These life histories are then examined for recurrent themes or "threads of continuity" that are used to "make sense of the past, explain the present, and draw a blueprint for the future" (Super et al., 1996, p. 157). Whereas the actuarial method is based on traits (e.g., How do my traits compare with the traits of others? In what occupations do my traits predict success?), the developmental method is based on life patterns (e.g., What patterns are revealed in my life history? Which of these patterns and themes are important to incorporate in my future planning?). Jepsen (1994) has noted that the developmental or thematic-extrapolation method contains three distinct steps:

1. Analyze past behavior and development for recurring themes and underlying trends.
2. Summarize each theme and trend, taking into account the other themes and trends.
3. Project the modified themes and trends into the future by extrapolation. (p. 45)

Encouraging the client to consider his or her life as if it were a book and then asking the client to identify the "chapters of his or her life" is a strategy for identifying recurring life themes and underlying trends. The future can then be described as "chapters that must be lived for the client to feel as if his or her life is complete" and the focus can shift toward identifying future goals and aspirations.

The actuarial and developmental methods can be incorporated into career counseling by using Super's (1957) cyclical model of nondirective and directive methods. Super noted that: "Since vocational development consists of implementing a self-concept, and since self-concepts often need modification before they can be implemented, it is important that the student, client, or patient put his [sic] self-concept into words early in the counseling process. The client needs to do this for himself, to clarify his actual role and his role aspirations; he needs to do it for the counselor, so that the counselor may understand the nature of the vocational problem confronting him" (p. 308). Specifically, Super (1957) described the cycles of career counseling as follows:

1. Nondirective problem exploration and self-concept portrayal (i.e., the client tells his or her story)
2. Directive topic setting, for further exploring (i.e., the counselor and client clarify the career concerns and identify which concerns will be the initial focus of career counseling)
3. Nondirective reflection and clarification of feeling for self-acceptance and insight (i.e., the career counselor uses empathic responding and basic counseling skills to help the client clarify his or her situation, feelings, and thoughts)
4. Directive exploration for factual data from tests, occupational pamphlets, extracurricular experiences, grades, and so forth, for reality testing (i.e., the counselor and client collect relevant information regarding the client's characteristics and potential occupational options; they also identify options for reality testing or "trying out" potential options via job shadowing, occupational information interviewing, volunteering, and externships)
5. Nondirective exploration and working through of attitudes and feelings aroused by reality testing (i.e., the client tries out potential options and then reflects upon the experiences with the counselor, focusing on the client's thoughts and feelings and how the experience may inform the client in terms of next steps)
6. Nondirective consideration of possible actions, for help in decision making (i.e., the client identifies what she or he will do next to move forward in her or his career development). (p. 308)

Essentially, the career counseling model articulated by Super emphasizes helping clients to clarify and articulate their self-concepts and then move toward implementing their self-concepts in appropriate life-role activity. Specific career counseling interventions, such as the C-DAC model and the thematic extrapolation method, can be incorporated into Super's cyclical model (most likely at steps 3–6).

Evaluating Super's Theory

Super's theory continues to stimulate career development research. For example, Lewis, Savickas, and Jones (1996) used the Career Development Inventory (Super, Thompson, Lindeman, Jordaan, & Myers, 1981) to predict success in medical school. Their results supported Super's (1981) contention that having a future orientation and being planful are important ingredients for achieving career maturity and career adaptability.

Reviewing literature pertaining to Super's Work Importance Study led Niles and Goodnough (1996) to three conclusions. First, life-role salience and values must be viewed within specific developmental and cultural contexts. Second, in diverse settings, and with different groups, there are sex differences related to the relative importance of life roles and values. And, third, in order to facilitate their clients' career development, counselors must attend to life-role salience and values issues in career counseling (see also Parasuraman, Purhoit, Godshalk, & Beutell, 1996).

Salomone (1996) provided a historical perspective by tracing the evolution of three key segments of Super's theory over a 40-year period: (a) theoretical propositions, (b) conceptualization of the career stages, and (c) definition of career. Salomone's review led him to several conclusions. First, Super's theoretical propositions have not changed substantially in 40 years. Second, there is the need for more research related to Super's propositions and career stage model. Finally, Salomone noted that Super's contributions represent an unparalleled legacy in developmental career theory. Additionally, Super's theory segments provide a useful framework for helping clients clarify their life-role identities and the values they seek to express in their life roles. Moreover, Super's theory provides a useful framework for researchers investigating the process of life-role identity development.

A number of journal articles provide examples of the systematic application of the C-DAC assessment instrument. For example, articles by Nevill and Kruse (1996) (Values Scale), Nevill and Calvert (1996) (Salience Inventory), Savickas and Hartung (1996) (Career Development Inventory), and Cairo, Kritis, and Myers (1996) (Adult Career Concerns Inventory) provide useful literature reviews, test descriptions, and information concerning the practical application of each assessment in career counseling practice. Hartung et al. (1998) describe strategies for appraising the client's cultural identity in the initial stages of the C-DAC model and offer techniques for considering cultural factors throughout the C-DAC process, thereby making the model more applicable to clients representing diverse contexts.

Commenting on Super's theory and the research it has generated, Osipow and Fitzgerald (1996) noted that Super's theory "has the virtue of building upon aspects of the mainstream of developmental psychology and personality theory and has considerable utility for practice and research" (p. 143). They also noted that "most of the research reported on Super's theory generally supports his model" (p. 143). Borgen (1991) noted that Super's theory "has splendidly stood the test of time" (p. 278). Brown (1996) pointed out that Super's theory "will forever be the segmental legacy of a brilliant thinker" (p. 522). The development of the C-DAC model should provide stronger links between Super's theory and career development intervention research.

ANNE ROE'S PERSONALITY THEORY OF CAREER CHOICE

Anne Roe (1904–1991), a clinical psychologist, initially became interested in career behavior through her research investigating personality factors related to artists' expression of creativity. Roe subsequently expanded her research to eminent scientists. From these investigations, Roe (1956, 1957) suggested that early childhood experiences influence career behavior. As Brown, Lum, and Voyle (1997) emphasize, however, from Roe's perspective the relationship between early childhood experiences and subsequent career behavior is mediated by the "structure of psychological needs that develop due to the pattern of frustrations and satisfactions experienced in childhood" (p. 284). Specifically, the resultant need structure orients persons either toward people or not toward people. Drawing upon Maslow's (1954) needs theory, Roe contended that needs not satisfied become important motivators in the occupational choices people make.

The child-rearing environments to which children are exposed shape early childhood experiences. Roe identified three primary modes of child rearing or environments to which children are exposed: emotional concentration, avoidance, and acceptance. *Emotional concentration* on the child ranges from overprotection to overly demanding behaviors. While physical needs are met, psychological needs may be withheld as parents place conditions on their love and approval. Children exposed to overly protective environments learn that conforming elicits rewards and, thus, a dependence on others for approval and a positive sense of self-esteem is developed. Overly demanding environments result in the development of perfectionist tendencies as children learn to adhere to "all-or-nothing" standards. *Avoidance* of the child, according to Roe, ranges from neglecting the child's physical needs to rejecting the child's emotional needs. *Acceptance of the child* involves environments in which the child's physical and psychological needs are met. Independence and self-reliance are encouraged in either an unconcerned, noninvolved way or an active, supportive one.

Each of these climates affects the satisfaction of the child's needs, which, in turn, subsequently influences the adult's choice of occupational field. For example, adults working in service occupations are oriented toward people and thus were likely exposed to loving, overprotective early childhood environments. Adults in more scientific occupational fields are typically not oriented toward people and therefore were most likely exposed to rejecting and avoidant early childhood environments.

Roe developed an occupational classification system that contains eight fields based on arts and entertainment, and general culture. Service fields are generally more people-oriented occupations such as teaching, counseling, and social work. Business contact occupations involve interpersonal interactions of a persuasive nature, such as sales. Organizational occupations emphasize systems and management. Technology involves occupations such as engineering. Outdoor occupations focus on the application of scientific principles in outdoor occupations such as forest management. Science includes occupations such as chemist and physicist. Arts and entertainment involves occupations related to acting, musical performance, and painting. General culture involves occupations that perpetuate the civilization such as government occupations. People choose occupational fields based on their need structures, which were influenced by the childhood environments that they experienced. The level of one's occupation is influenced by factors such as the person's genetic structure and socioeconomic background.

Evaluating Roe's Theory

Largely due to the retrospective nature of Roe's theory, researchers have been challenged in their attempts to validate the theory's assumptions. Variability in a parent's parental style, variability in each parent's respective parenting style, variability in the early life environments experienced by members of the same occupation, and the inherent challenge in attempting to predict events that are distant in time from their causal influences have all resulted in little empirical support for Roe's theory. When this fact is combined with the reality that Roe's theory focuses on explaining factors underlying career choice and does not offer much relative to career interventions, then it is not hard to understand why this theory has largely faded from the current career development literature. Roe's theory does, however, point to the role of parents and the influence of a person's needs structure in the career development process.

LINDA GOTTFREDSON'S THEORY OF CIRCUMSCRIPTION, COMPROMISE, AND SELF-CREATION

One theory that describes the process leading to the formulation of occupational aspirations in childhood and adolescence is Gottfredson's theory of circumscription, compromise, and self-creation (Gottfredson, 2002, 2005). Gottfredson developed her theory, in part, to address the following question: "Why do children seem to re-create the social inequalities of their elders long before they themselves experience any barriers to pursuing their dreams?" (Gottfredson, 2002, p. 85). She addresses the compromises that people make in their career aspirations, particularly as these compromises relate to sex-typed learning and experiences. Specifically, compromise involves the process of modifying career choices due to limiting factors, such as prestige, sex type, and field of interest (Gottfredson, 1981). Gottfredson's theory emphasizes the view that "career choice is an attempt to place oneself in the broader social order" (1996, p. 181). Thus, she offers a developmental and sociological perspective of career development.

Gottfredson (2002) notes that people distinguish occupations according to the dimensions of: "masculinity-femininity, occupational prestige, and field of work" (p. 88). Gottfredson (2005) further suggests that occupational prestige is positively correlated with the degree of intellectual capacity required for job performance. The person's self-concept interacts with the person's occupational stereotypes when making decisions about the perceived compatibility of different occupations. Compatibility, or the suitability of any occupation, is determined when the individual considers factors such as the perceived gender appropriateness (most important), prestige (second in importance), and, finally, the degree to which the occupation will fulfill the person's preferences and personality needs (last in importance within the compromise process). The "zone of acceptable occupational alternatives" or "social space" (2002, p. 91) represents the person's conclusions as to his or her fit in society. Gottfredson contends that people compromise in their search process because they typically search for an occupational choice that is "good enough," but not necessarily the best possible choice. This is because the best possible choice requires substantially more intensive information gathering related to factors such as values clarification and determining the accessibility of various occupational alternatives than what is required for a choice that is "good enough." People become indecisive when they perceive the options within their social space as undesirable. Occupational satisfaction hinges on the degree to which "the compromise allows one to implement a desired social self, either through the work itself or the lifestyle it allows self and family" (2002, p. 107).

Circumscription involves the process of eliminating unacceptable occupational alternatives based primarily on gender and prestige. Circumscription highlights the fact that young people begin eliminating occupational options from consideration "as soon as they are able to perceive essential distinctions among people and lives" (Gottfredson, 2002, p. 131). The circumscription process is guided by five principles (2002, pp. 94–95). The first principle notes that circumscription is guided by the growing capacity of children to understand and organize complex information about themselves and the world. Children move from magical to abstract thinking as they develop. The second principle reflects the belief that because occupational aspirations are inextricably linked with one's sense of self, occupational preferences reflect attempts to both implement and enhance one's self-concept. The third principle underlying the circumscription process is that children begin to grapple with more complex distinctions among people (e.g., perceptions related to prestige) while they are still in the process of integrating more concrete phenomena (e.g., sex roles) into their self-conceptions. The fourth circumscription principle emphasizes the belief that children progressively eliminate occupational options as their self-conceptions increase in complexity and clarity. At the same time, Gottfredson notes that "people reconsider options they have ruled out as unacceptable in sextype and prestige only when they are prompted to do so by some formative new experience or some notable change in their social environment" (2002, p. 95). Finally, the circumscription process is gradual and typically not immediately obvious despite its strong effect on the individual. These principles operate throughout the stages of cognitive development Gottfredson (1996) delineated to describe the circumscription process.

Stage One: Orientation to Size and Power

The first stage occurs between the ages of 3 and 5 and reflects the onset of object constancy in cognitive development. At this stage, children classify people in simple terms, such as big versus little. Thus, children orient themselves to the size difference between themselves and adults.

Stage Two: Orientation to Sex Roles

This stage occurs between the ages of 6 and 8. During this stage, children become aware of different sex roles between men and women. They think dichotomously (e.g., good-bad, rich-poor) and interpret sex-role stereotypes as behavioral imperatives. Their occupational aspirations also reflect this concern for behaving in ways that are appropriate for one's sex (e.g., certain jobs are for boys and certain jobs are for girls). Thus, it is during this stage that children develop their "tolerable-sextype boundary" (Gottfredson, 2005).

Stage Three: Orientation to Social Valuation

During this stage, which occurs between the ages of 9 and 13, children are able to think more abstractly and they become aware of social class and prestige. Occupations that are not in line with their perceived ability levels and that do not meet with the approval of their social reference group are no longer considered. The elements of social class and ability determine the "tolerable-level boundary," which represents the lower limit of occupations children in this stage are willing to consider (i.e., which occupations are "beneath" them and, therefore, not worthy of their consideration). Children also establish a "tolerable-effort level" based on the upper limit of effort children are willing to exert and the risks children are willing to take in pursuing occupational options (i.e., those occupational goals that are not beyond their ability to achieve). Together, these levels determine the zone of occupations children consider as acceptable (Gottfredson, 1996).

Stage Four: Orientation to the Internal, Unique Self

This stage occurs from age 14 to beyond. During this stage, adolescents become more introspective and self-aware. Now able to engage in more abstract thinking than in previous stages, adolescents begin identifying internally generated goals and self-concepts. As Gottfredson notes, "vocational development erupts into conscious awareness during Stage 4" (2005, p. 81). Adolescents engage in exploring occupational options that are congruent with their emerging sense of self. Thus, this stage represents a shift from the previous stages in that the emphasis turns from eliminating unacceptable options to identifying options that are most preferred and acceptable. It is also during this stage that the process of compromise is introduced. Compromise involves being forced to choose among minimally acceptable occupational options. Specifically, compromise occurs as preferred occupational options are eliminated from further consideration due to factors such as the perceived accessibility of any occupational option. Compromise can be anticipatory (i.e., prior to actual encounters with external barriers) or experiential (i.e., after encountering an external barrier to a preferred option).

Applying Gottfredson's Theory to Practice

Gottfredson (1996) noted that, traditionally, career development interventions occur during stage four when people are attempting to crystallize and clarify their self-concepts. However, Gottfredson's theory highlights the importance of providing career development interventions, often in the form of career education programs, to young people in earlier stages of development. Accordingly, career education programs should focus on exploring the full range of occupational options to promote systematic exploration in career choice (Gottfredson). Clearly, interventions that address occupational sex-role stereotypes and that expose children to options across occupational levels should be cornerstones of such programs. Specifically, Gottfredson posited that career education programs need to be sensitive to students' levels of cognitive development; they need to expose students to a wide range of career options, and help them become aware of the circumscription of alternatives and compromise process.

From Gottfredson's perspective, a major concern to address in individual career counseling is the degree to which clients have engaged in the unnecessary restriction of occupational options. "The problem in compromise is the failure to come to grips with reality, either by ignoring it or failing to deal with it effectively" (Gottfredson, 1996, p. 217). Gottfredson identified criteria to guide counselors attempting to clarify the degree to which their clients may have engaged in the unnecessary restriction of options. For example, she noted that: clients should be able to identify occupational options and the relevant self-characteristics required to perform those occupations; clients should not unnecessarily restrict their occupational options; and they should be aware of obstacles they may encounter in implementing occupational choices.

In examining these criteria with clients, career counselors can explore their clients' tolerable level and effort boundaries, perceptions of barriers, and the contextual factors influencing clients' perceptions of acceptable career options. Gottfredson advocates incorporating discussions of ability more explicitly into the career counseling process. Despite the fact that ability is a strong predictor of career success, it is often not highlighted in career counseling. Gottfredson (2003) contends that avoiding the discussion of ability restricts the usefulness of career counseling. When ability is integrated into the career counseling experience for adolescents, it can also help them to see the importance of school performance and career achievement, thereby increasing their academic motivation and engagement.

Applying Gottfredson's criteria to Juanita's case, it is important that the counselor explore with her what occupational options she has considered thus far (in addition to being in a band). It would also be important to build upon Juanita's strengths and interests. Understanding her interests in artistic endeavors might be a good starting point. In discussing these interests, the counselor can assess whether Juanita has unnecessarily restricted her options. Her counselor can also address questions such as: Is her ability sufficient for a performance career? Is Juanita aware of the obstacles likely to be encountered in pursuing this option? Has Juanita considered additional opportunities for expressing her values, interests, and abilities? What has caused her to eliminate other occupational options from further consideration? The counselor can support and challenge Juanita as she becomes increasingly aware of her emerging sense of self and her attempts to identify congruent options.

Evaluating Gottfredson's Theory

Research related to Gottfredson's theory has not been extensive. Moreover, research activity related to the theory seems to be in decline and existing research results have been equivocal. Much of the research has focused on circumscription related to social class, gender, and intelligence. For example, using a sample of Canadian twelfth-grade students, Hannah and Kahn (1989) found that students from higher social classes held higher aspirations than students from lower social classes. Helwig (2001) conducted two studies testing the applicability of Gottfredson's theory to the career development of children. This longitudinal research followed students from second to twelfth grades. In the first study, Helwig examined the occupational aspirations of children and found support for Gottfredson's theory of circumscription and compromise. Support for Gottfredson's theory was found in the second study as well; Helwig reported that students abandoned fantasy occupational ideals in favor of more realistic occupational aspirations toward the end of their high school education. Other researchers applaud Gottfredson's theoretical emphasis on career development in childhood and gender differences, noting that the theory fills an important gap in the career literature (McLennan & Arthur, 1999).

Empirical results from a study focusing on New Zealand students between the ages of 5 and 14, and conducted by Henderson, Hesketh, and Tuffin (1988), did not support the importance of gender in Gottfredson's stage two (Orientation to Sex Roles). Their findings were supportive of the importance of social class in stage three (Orientation to Social Valuation). A study conducted by Hesketh, Elmslie, and Kaldor (1990) suggested an alternative model of compromise in which interests were more important in career choices than either sex type or prestige, because interests incorporate the latter. Leong and Plake (1990) found that women, more often than men, opted for cross-sex work rather than same-sex work if the former provided them with higher prestige. Blanchard and Lichtenberg (2003) studied Gottfredson's compromise process and found that study participants who were engaged in a moderate or high degree of compromise placed an equal amount of importance on prestige and sex type, thus differing from what the theory purports. The same study participants did, however, place a greater importance on prestige and sex type than they did on interests as they considered factors influencing the compromise process.

More recently, Cochran, Wang, Stevenson, Johnson, and Crews (in press) used data from a longitudinal sample to investigate the relationship between adolescent occupational aspirations and mid-life career success using Gottfredson's theory. The results of this study lend support for the influence of socioeconomic status (SES) and ability in the formation of occupational aspirations. Occupational aspirations, ability, and gender were significantly related to career achievement in later life. These researchers also found that adolescent girls achieved less career success in mid-life than adolescent boys.

In evaluating Gottfredson's theory, Brown (1996) noted "the propositions relating to the factors that lead to circumscription and compromise are too general. The result is that we are left with questions about what actually occurs in the career choice and selection process" (p. 523). Nonetheless, Gottfredson's theory provides many interesting concepts describing boundaries and motivational dimensions related to the formation of occupational aspirations (Herr et al., 2004). Her theory also addresses important gaps within the career-related literature (i.e., career development in childhood and gender differences). Moreover, Gottfredson's (2005) more recent explication of her theory begins to address Brown's critique regarding the need for more specificity related to career development processes. Research studies testing Gottfredson's theory using a longitudinal and cross-sectional design would be particularly useful.

JOHN HOLLAND'S THEORY OF TYPES AND PERSON-ENVIRONMENT INTERACTIONS

Holland's (1959, 1966, 1973, 1985a, 1997) theory belongs to a long tradition of theoretical perspectives seeking to describe individual differences in personality types (e.g., Murray, 1938; Spranger, 1928). Holland's theory has been described as structural-interactive "because it provides an explicit link between various personality characteristics and corresponding job titles and because it organizes the massive data about people and jobs" (Weinrach, 1984, p. 63). The theory is based on four basic assumptions:

1. In our culture, most persons can be categorized as one of six types: realistic, investigative, artistic, social, enterprising, or conventional.
2. There are six kinds of environments: realistic, investigative, artistic, social, enterprising, and conventional.
3. People search for environments that will let them exercise their skills and abilities, express their attitudes and values, and take on agreeable problems and roles.
4. A person's behavior is determined by an interaction between personality and the characteristics of the environment. (Holland, 1973, pp. 2–4)

From these assumptions it is clear that a key to understanding and using Holland's theory is in understanding his typology. A good starting point for this is to consider how personality types develop. To a large degree, "types produce types" (Holland, 1973, p. 11). That is, personality types are both genetically and environmentally based:

> A child's special heredity and experience first lead to preferences for some kinds of activities and aversions to others. Later, these preferences become well-defined interests from which the person gains self-satisfaction as well as reward from others. Still later, the pursuit of these interests leads to the development of more specialized competencies as well as to the neglect of other potential competencies. At the same time, a person's differentiation of interests with age is accompanied by a crystallization of correlated values. These events—an increasing differentiation of preferred activities, interests, competencies, and values—create a characteristic disposition or personality type that is predisposed to exhibit characteristic behavior and to develop characteristic personality traits. (Holland, 1973, p. 12)

Holland contends that, to a large degree, career interests are an expression of the individual's personality (Holland, 1959, 1966, 1973, 1985a, 1992). As Spokane (1996) elaborated, "Interests, however, are complex measures that reflect personality as well as preferences, values, self-efficacy and so on. Types, then, are complex theoretical groupings based upon personality and interests" (p. 40). Personality traits are identified by preferences for leisure activities, school subjects, avocational interests, and work. To varying degrees, each individual resembles one of six basic personality types. The more one resembles any particular personality type, the more likely it is that the person will manifest the behaviors and traits associated with that type (Weinrach, 1984). Following is a discussion of each of the six personality types defined by Holland (1973, pp. 14–18; 1994, pp. 2–3).

The Realistic Type

The realistic personality type prefers activities that entail the explicit, ordered, or systematic manipulation of objects, tools, machines, and animals and has an aversion to educational or therapeutic activities. The realistic person has mechanical abilities but may lack social skills. Realistic types prefer jobs such as automobile mechanic, surveyor, farmer, or electrician. Realistic types are often described as:

conforming, humble, normal, frank, materialistic,

persistent, genuine, modest, practical, hardheaded, natural,

shy, honest, and thrifty.

The Investigative Type

The investigative personality type prefers activities that entail the observational, symbolic, systematic, and creative investigation of physical, biological, and cultural phenomena in order to understand and control such phenomena. Investigative types have an aversion to persuasive, social, and repetitive activities. These tendencies lead to an acquisition of scientific and mathematical competencies and to a deficit in leadership ability. Investigative types prefer jobs such as biologist, chemist, physicist, anthropologist, geologist, or medical technologist. Investigative persons are often described as:

analytical, independent, modest, cautious, intellectual,

pessimistic, complex, introverted, precise, critical,

methodical, rational, curious, and reserved.

The Artistic Type

The artistic personality type prefers ambiguous, free, unsystematized activities that entail the manipulation of physical, verbal, or human materials to create art forms or products. Artistic persons have an aversion to explicit systematic and ordered activities. These tendencies lead to an acquisition of artistic competencies in language, art, music, drama, and writing and to a deficit in clerical- or business-system competencies. Artistic types like jobs such as composer, musician, stage director, writer, interior decorator, or actor/actress. Artistic persons are often described as:

complicated, imaginative, introspective, disorderly,

impractical, intuitive, emotional, impulsive, nonconforming,

expressive, independent, open, idealistic, and original.

The Social Type

The social personality type prefers activities that entail the manipulation of others to inform, train, develop, cure, or enlighten. They have an aversion to explicit, ordered, and systematic activities involving materials, tools, or machines. These tendencies lead to an acquisition of human relations competencies such as interpersonal and educational competencies and to a deficit in mechanical and scientific ability. Social types like jobs such as teacher, religious worker, counselor, clinical psychologist, psychiatric caseworker, or speech therapist. Social persons are often described as:

convincing, idealistic, social, cooperative, kind,

sympathetic, friendly, patient, tactful, generous,

responsible, understanding, helpful, and warm.

The Enterprising Type

The enterprising personality type prefers activities that entail the manipulation of others to attain organizational or economic gain. They have an aversion to observational, symbolic, and systematic activities. These tendencies lead to an acquisition of leadership, interpersonal, and persuasive competencies and to a deficit in scientific ability. Enterprising types like jobs such as salesperson, manager, business executive, television producer, sports promoter, or buyer. Enterprising persons are often described as:

acquisitive, domineering, optimistic, adventurous,

energetic, pleasure-seeking, agreeable, extroverted,

attention-getting, ambitious, impulsive, self-confident,

sociable, and popular.

The Conventional Type

The conventional personality type prefers activities that entail the explicit, ordered, and systematic manipulation of data, such as keeping records, filing materials, reproducing materials, organizing written and numerical data according to a prescribed plan, and operating computers to attain organizational or economic goals. Conventional types have an aversion to ambiguous, free, exploratory, or unsystematized activities. These tendencies lead to an acquisition of clerical, computational, and business system competencies and to a deficit in artistic competencies. Conventional types like jobs such as bookkeeper, stenographer, financial analyst, banker, cost estimator, or tax expert. Conventional persons are often described as:

conforming, inhibited, persistent, conscientious, obedient,

practical, careful, orderly, thrifty, efficient, and

unimaginative.

Holland (1973) used the same six types to describe occupational environments (pp. 29–33). For example, the realistic environment requires the explicit, ordered, or systematic manipulation of objects, tools, machines, and animals. It encourages people to view themselves as having mechanical ability. It rewards people for displaying conventional values and encourages them to see the world in simple, tangible, and traditional terms.

The investigative environment requires the symbolic, systematic, and creative investigation of physical, biological, or cultural phenomena. It encourages scientific competencies and achievements and the perception of the world in complex and unconventional ways. It rewards people for displaying scientific values.

The artistic environment requires participation in ambiguous, free, and unsystematized activities to create art forms or products. It encourages people to view themselves as having artistic abilities and to see themselves as expressive, nonconforming, independent, and intuitive. It rewards people for the display of artistic values.

The social environment requires participation in activities that inform, train, develop, cure or enlighten others. It requires people to see themselves as liking to help others, as being understanding of others, and as seeing the world in flexible ways. It rewards people for the display of social values.

The enterprising environment requires participation in activities that involve the manipulation of others to attain organizational and self-interest goals. It requires people to view themselves as aggressive, popular, self-confident, sociable, and as possessing leadership and speaking ability. It encourages people to view the world in terms of power and status and in stereotyped and simple terms. It rewards people for displaying enterprising goals and values.

The conventional environment requires participation in activities that involve the explicit, ordered, or systematic manipulation of data, such as record keeping, filing materials, and organizing written and numerical data according to a prescribed plan. It requires people to view themselves as conforming, orderly, nonartistic, and as having clerical competencies. It rewards people for perceiving the world in stereotyped and conventional ways.

Congruence

The key construct in Holland's theory is that of congruence. Congruence describes the degree of fit between an individual's personality type and current or prospective work environment. A person is in a congruent work environment when the person's personality type matches the occupational environment (e.g., a social type working as a counselor). Conversely, incongruence occurs when individuals are in environments that do not match their personality types (e.g., a social type working as an auto mechanic). Individuals tend to be more satisfied and perform better in environments that match (or are congruent with) their personality types. Thus, congruence is based on the assumption that "birds of a feather flock together" and that "different types require different environments" (Holland, 1973, p. 4). Also, "environments are characterized by the people who occupy them" (Weinrach, 1984, pp. 63–64). To distinguish "congruence" from Holland's other constructs, students often find it helpful to view the "u" and "e" in "congruence" as representing the fact that congruence refers to the relationship between "you" and the "environment."

Holland uses a hexagonal model to represent the relationships within and between types (Figure 2.1). Concerning the latter, the highest level of congruence exists when there is a direct correspondence between workers' personality types and their work environments (e.g., investigative personality types in investigative work environments). The next highest level of congruence exists when individuals are in work environments that are adjacent to their types on the hexagon (e.g., a realistic personality type in an investigative work environment). The lowest level of congruence exists when individuals are in work environments that are opposite to their personality types on the hexagonal model (e.g., a social type in a realistic work environment). The primary goal of career counseling is helping clients identify and connect with congruent work environments.

Figure 2.1

The relationships among Holland types.

Source: Information from *Holland's Hexagon, ACT Research Report No. 29,* by J. L. Holland, D. R. Whitney, N. S. Cole, and J. M. Richards, Jr., 1969, Iowa City: The American College Testing Program. Copyright © 1969 The American College Testing Program. Reprinted by permission.

Differentiation

To describe people and their work environments, Holland focuses on the three types the person or environment most closely resembles. However, some people and environments are more clearly defined, or differentiated, than others. For example, a person may more predominantly resemble one Holland type and have little resemblance to other types (a high level of differentiation), or a single type may dominate an environment. Other persons or environments may resemble multiple types equally and therefore be relatively undifferentiated or poorly defined. Holland referred to the degree of distinctness among types representing a person's personality profile as "differentiation." Because people who are undifferentiated can have difficulty making career decisions, career interventions are often directed toward helping clients achieve greater differentiation among Holland types.

Consistency

The degree of relatedness within types is referred to as *consistency*. The hexagonal model is useful in illustrating the similarities across types. For example, types located next to each other on the hexagon (e.g., realistic and investigative) have more in common than types that are farther apart (e.g., realistic and social). Higher degrees of consistency within personality types suggest more integration or harmony regarding traits, interests, values, and perceptions than lower degrees of consistency. Holland assumes that consistent persons are more predictable in their behavior and more likely to be higher achievers in their careers than persons who are not consistent. It is important to note, however, that it is not a goal of career counseling to make clients more consistent. Rather, the primary use of consistency in career counseling relates to client awareness. Specifically, it is important for clients with low consistency (e.g., a realistic-social personality type) to be aware of the fact that it may be difficult for them to find an occupational environment that will allow them to express the diverse aspects of their personalities. In such cases it is often necessary for clients to identify avocational activities that provide opportunities for expressing personality types that are not expressed in work. For example, a realistic-social personality type working as a social worker may choose to spend her leisure time in woodworking activities.

Vocational Identity

Vocational identity is defined as the "possession of a clear and stable picture of one's goals, interests, and talent" (Holland, 1985a, p. 5). Vocational identity is an important goal of many career development interventions and is dependent upon acquiring sufficient occupational and self-information.

Applying Holland's Theory

Congruence, differentiation, consistency, and vocational identity are the key theoretical constructs used to link Holland's theory to practice. "All things being equal, an individual with high identity who is congruent, consistent, and differentiated should be more predictable and better adjusted than one who is incongruent, inconsistent, and undifferentiated" (Spokane et al., 2002, p. 385). Assessment instruments developed by Holland and his associates are typically used to measure these constructs, and the results from these measures provide the stimuli for career counseling content.

For example, the Self-Directed Search (SDS) (Holland, 1994) and the Vocational Preference Inventory (VPI) (Holland, 1985b) are used to translate individuals' self-estimates of interests and competencies into Holland types. The SDS consists of an assessment booklet (used to identify the individual's Holland type), an Occupations Finder (two versions are available, each contain a listing of 1,334 occupations classified according to either three-letter Holland codes or presented in alphabetical order), and an interpretive guide titled *You and Your Career*. The latter provides individuals with additional information, activities, and readings related to using Holland's theory in career decision making. The SDS, which is the most widely used interest inventory, is available in different versions based on reading level (SDS Form E), setting (SDS CP, Corporate Version), and language spoken.

The SDS provides a useful starting point and straightforward approach for focusing Juanita's career exploration and information gathering. First, Juanita can use the assessment booklet to identify her three-letter summary code. (Because researchers have found a high error rate in summary code calculations [e.g., Miller, 1997], it is important that counselors take precautions to minimize such errors.) Then Juanita and the career counselor can review her summary code ("ASI" with low differentiation) to explore how her abilities and interests relate to the characteristics of the types her summary code comprises.

It is especially important to discuss with the client his or her summary code when the code lacks consistency. A client with a code of RSA, for example, may have difficulty finding occupations that resemble this code exactly (few jobs require workers to have strong mechanical abilities and strong social skills). Clients who do not understand this fact can experience a sort of "pendulum shifting" in their career choices. That is, a person may opt for a realistic, or R, occupation and find that, for a time, it is satisfactory in that it offers the opportunity for engaging in R tasks and rewards R competencies. Over time, however, the person may begin noticing the absence of social, or S, opportunities in his or her R work. The absence of S opportunities may lead to a growing sense that the R occupation needs to be replaced with one in the S environment. If this occupational change occurs, it may provide satisfaction initially, but, over time, the person may feel that the occupation is too S and not enough R and the pendulum may shift back toward desiring an R occupation.

Helping the client who is low in consistency to become aware of the possible "pendulum shifting" that can occur in occupational decision making is important because, if a congruent occupational environment is not possible, appropriate avocational activities may provide the solution (rather than an ongoing shifting from occupations in one Holland environment to another). In these instances, counselors may use the Leisure Activities Finder (Holmberg, Rosen, & Holland, 1990) to help clients identify opportunities to express important dimensions of their perso~ ties that they may not be able to express in work. For example, the pers~ RSA code may choose to emphasize working with things (R) at wo˙' cook), but spend leisure time in activities emphasizing the social (S) youth group leader for a church). As noted, it is important for career understand that consistency is not a goal of career counseling. Rather, consistency is a construct that helps clients understand who they are and then use this understanding to make effective career decisions.

Clients with codes that lack differentiation (determined by comparing either the client's highest score minus the lowest score among the six types or by examining the numerical difference among the client's three-letter code) often experience a lack of focus in their career direction for a number of reasons. Persons may lack differentiation because: (a) they lack exposure to activities across Holland environments, (b) they have difficulty in decision making, (c) they have multipotentiality, or (d) they are depressed.

Clients lacking in exposure to Holland environments (e.g., young people with little or no work experience, homemakers returning to the labor market after an extended departure) may need help increasing their self-understanding related to interests, abilities, and values. In such instances, counselors may use activities such as values inventories, values card sorts, or skills checklists to foster client understanding of these career decision-making variables. Those persons returning to the labor market after an extended departure may find it particularly useful to engage in an "accomplishments exercise" in which the counselor invites the client to list activities, or accomplishments, about which the client feels especially proud. As the client describes the activity, the counselor encourages the client to list the skills embedded in the successful performance of the activity. After engaging in this discussion for several activities, the counselor and client will have generated a long list of skills the client demonstrated in the successful completion of each activity he or she described. These skills can then be categorized according to Holland type and the counselor and client can review the skills they enjoy using most to identify the Holland type that reflects the client's dominant type. Undifferentiated clients with limited work experiences may also need to take steps such as information interviewing, volunteering, and job shadowing to increase their self-understanding and become more differentiated.

Clients with decision-making difficulties can be taught decision-making skills and then encouraged to retake the SDS and/or to discuss their perceptions as to which Holland types they most closely resemble. As an alternative to retaking the SDS in these instances, the client can engage in a Holland card sort activity in which the client sorts through activities according to the degree to which he or she likes, dislikes, or feels neutral toward each activity. Each group of cards can then be reviewed in light of the Holland types they reflect. During this activity, the counselor can observe how difficult it is for the client to make decisions. After having been taught decision-making skills and after engaging in self-assessment activities and reviewing occupational information, some clients may remain undecided. Indecisive clients may have concerns that result in a "fear of deciding." Clients may be fearful of making choices for a variety of factors. For example, a client may have excessive fears related to failing, succeeding, or disappointing significant others. In these instances, the counselor and client will need to engage in a counseling or therapy-like process to help the client understand his or her fears.

Scores on the SDS that are elevated and undifferentiated may also reflect the fact that, rather than being indecisive or lacking experience, the client is multipotentialed in interests and competencies. This is, in fact, the case for Holland himself, who has elevated and undifferentiated scores across almost all Holland types (Weinrach, 1996)! For clients with elevated and undifferentiated SDS scores, the counselor may find it useful to focus on the client's values as a guide for making occupational decisions. Finally, counselors also need to determine whether clients with low scores for all Holland types are having difficulty with depression or low self-esteem. Given Juanita's difficulties in school and her young age, all of the aforementioned possibilities should be explored in relationship to the low differentiation in her summary code.

With a general understanding of the Holland typology and a specific understanding of their own Holland summary codes, clients are ready to examine the Occupations Finder to locate occupations that resemble their summary codes. Each client focuses on occupations resembling all combinations of his or her summary code (e.g., Juanita would explore occupations in the categories of ASI, SIA, AIS, SAI, IAS, and ISA). Clients then identify specific occupations within these categories that are of interest to them.

Next, counselors encourage clients to take some sort of action (e.g., information interviewing, reading about occupational requirements, job shadowing) to increase their understanding of occupations of interest. Clients can then discuss with their counselors the information they acquire from these activities and narrow their list of occupational options. In these discussions, counselors encourage clients to take additional steps (e.g., volunteering, taking courses related to a particular occupation, job searching) toward implementing tentative occupational choices. In discussing the information the client obtains, the counselor and client also review how each specific option provides opportunities for expressing the types comprising the client's summary code. The overarching goals in this process are to clarify the client's vocational identity and help the client make a congruent career decision.

In addition to the SDS, counselors can use the VPI in helping clients identify their Holland type and connect their summary codes to congruent occupational environments. The VPI (1985b) contains 160 occupational titles, the six type scales, and five supplemental scales (self-control, masculinity, status, infrequency, and acquiescence). To assess vocational identity, counselors can use the instrument entitled *My Vocational Situation* (MVS) (Holland, Gottfredson, & Power, 1980). Specifically, the MVS measures vocational identity and perceived career development barriers. The Vocational Identity scale measures awareness of and the ability to specify one's interests, personality characteristics, strengths, and goals as they relate to career choices. The Occupational Information (OI) scale of the MVS measures the respondent's need for occupational information.

Gottfredson and Holland (1996) have also created an inventory (the Position Classification Inventory [PCI]) for classifying specific work environments using the Holland typology. Prior to the PCI, which uses the workers' judgments to classify the work environment, researchers and counselors relied on conducting an actual census of workers to classify a specific work environment according to the Holland types. Because variability exists across same-type occupations in different work environments, the PCI may be particularly useful in helping clients understand their degree of congruence in a specific job. Miller and Bass (2003) have found the PCI to be useful in classifying work environments in a paper manufacturing plant.

Other inventories also use the Holland typology in reporting assessment results. For example, the Strong Interest Inventory (SII) (Harmon et al., 1994), the Career Assessment Inventory (CAI) (Johannson, 1986), and the Armed Services Vocational Aptitude Battery (ASVAB) (U.S. Department of Defense, 1993) each use Holland's types in reporting assessment results.

Evaluating Holland's Theory

Research emanating from Holland's theory is extensive. In fact, it can be argued that Holland's theory has been subjected to more empirical tests than any other career theory (Spokane & Cruza-Guet, 2005). Gottfredson and Richards (1999) note that a major advantage of Holland's theory is that it provides a parallel way of describing people and environments. In 1996, Holland summarized research findings supporting the use of his typology to explain career certainty, career change, and career satisfaction. From Holland's review it is evident that his theory continues to stimulate much research activity. Generally, this activity focuses on (a) the relations between congruence and important career outcomes, (b) methods for calculating constructs such as congruence, and (c) the application of Holland's theory to diverse populations.

Spokane et al. (2002) summarized the congruence-related research, noting that although research results are somewhat mixed, there is a "modest relationship between person-environment fit and job satisfaction" (p. 400). Spokane, Fouad, and Swanson (2001) argued that most of the congruence-related research, especially in the early years, was correlational in nature and therefore does not reflect the complexity inherent in person-environment interactions. Longitudinal, cross-sectional, and experimental studies are needed to more accurately represent person-environment interactions and to understand the validity of the congruence construct.

Though there are data to support the importance of congruence in vocational satisfaction, research support for the relationship between consistency and differentiation to vocational outcomes has been weak. Perhaps to an even greater degree than what is true for the congruence research, research methodologies employed in these studies have not been sufficiently sophisticated to examine the complex processes related to consistency, differentiation, and relevant occupational outcomes (e.g., satisfaction, stability).

Nonetheless, some interesting studies provide intriguing data related to the validity of Holland's theory. For example, Miller (2002) investigated the degree of change in a male client's three-letter Holland code over a 10-year time span. The client initially took the SDS when he was 16 years old. The client's Holland code remained stable across the 10-year period, thus supporting Holland's contention that personality types measured by the SDS remain stable over time. Lent, Brown, Nota, and Soresi (2003) examined the relationship of interest congruence to the occupational choices of 796 Italian high school students. Lent et al. found that interests were significant predictors of occupational choices for all Holland types.

Oleski and Subich (1996) provided an example of the first type of research in their investigation of adults in the process of changing careers. Studying 42 nontraditional students (mean age 34.4) pursuing a career change, Oleski and Subich found support for Holland's (1985a) basic assumption that people change careers to achieve greater congruence.

Lent and Lopez (1996) investigated the relationship between congruence indices and job satisfaction among adult workers. Although they found partial overlap among methods for calculating congruence in their study, Lent and Lopez noted the need for more research to understand the relations among indices of congruence, methods for coding work environments, and the antecedents to congruence.

Tracey (2008) found that for college students enrolled in a career development class, the RIASEC model was related to better career decision-making outcomes (students considering congruent career options have more career certainty and career decision-making self-efficacy than those who do not adhere to the congruence principle). In a study examining career persisters versus career changers, Donahue (2006) found person-environment congruence to be related to career stability. Perdue, Reardon, and Peterson (2007) also found person-environment congruence to be associated with job satisfaction within a sample of 198 employees working for a multinational communications corporation.

Of course, achieving congruence is, in part, dependent upon the availability of occupations allowing for the expression of one's personality. Downes and Kroeck (1996) hypothesized that there is an overall discrepancy between normative occupational interests and the number of existing positions in the United States. Using normative interest data from the Self-Directed Search and data extracted from the *Monthly Labor Review,* Downes and Kroeck found support for their hypothesis. Specifically, they found a lack of interest for Conventional and Enterprising jobs relative to the number of existing positions. They found the opposite with regard to the remaining Holland categories. For instance, there was excess interest among high school students for Social, Artistic, and Investigative jobs relative to the number of existing positions. Investigative and Realistic jobs represented high-interest areas for the adults in the study. Based on their findings, Downes and Kroeck called for a concerted effort to reshape the interests and skills of the U.S. labor force in order to meet the labor needs of corporations and educational institutions.

Ryan, Tracey, and Rounds (1996) and Rounds and Tracey (1996) studied the generalizability of Holland's (1985a) model of vocational interests across ethnicity, gender, and SES. Ryan, Tracey, and Rounds found similar interest structures in the Caucasian and the African American high school students in their study. Ryan and her colleagues also found no differences in the structure of interests between low- and high-SES groups. A similar result was obtained when comparing low- and high-SES Caucasian groups. However, the low-SES African American group was better fit by Holland's model than the high-SES African American group. Both male and female students fit Holland's model. Thus, Ryan and her colleagues concluded that Holland's model is generalizable across ethnicity, gender, and socioeconomic status as defined in their study. Oliver and Waehler (2005) found support for Holland's typology and their arrangement in circular RIASEC order within a sample of Native Hawaiians.

Mihalik (1996) examined whether clients' types predicted reactions to counselor intentions. Using a sample of undergraduate college students, Mihalik found that clients' vocational interests as measured by the SDS (Holland, 1987) were predictive of client reactions to counselor interventions. For example, participants with high Enterprising scores responded positively to feeling challenged in counseling and participants with high Social scores responded positively to being supported by the counselor.

This very brief sample of research provides an indication of the fact that Holland's theory has generated more research than any other model of career choice. Much of this research supports the theory (Holland, 1996; Spokane, 1985; Spokane et al., 2002). Also, the theory provides a clear link to practice: "The combination of empirical support and practical application accounts for the theory's popularity among the public as well as among professionals" (Spokane, 1996, p. 62). More studies investigating the validity of Holland's method across cultural contexts are needed.

JOHN KRUMBOLTZ'S LEARNING THEORY OF CAREER COUNSELING

Krumboltz and his colleagues (especially Mitchell and Jones) developed a learning theory of career counseling comprising two distinct parts. The first part focuses on explaining the origins of career choice and is labeled as the "social learning theory of career decision making" (SLTCDM) (Mitchell & Krumboltz, 1996). The second part focuses on career counseling and is labeled the "learning theory of career counseling" (LTCC) (Krumboltz & Henderson, 2002; Mitchell & Krumboltz, 1996). Because the SLTCDM identifies the factors influencing the career decisions people make (and is, therefore, subsumed under the LTCC part of the theory) and because the LTCC explains what career counselors can do to help clients make effective career decisions, Mitchell and Krumboltz labeled the entire theory as the LTCC.

LTCC is based on the application of Bandura's (1977, 1986) social learning theory to career decision making. Bandura's theory emphasizes the influence of reinforcement theory, cognitive information processing, and classical behaviorism on human behavior. Social learning theory "assumes that people's personalities and behavioral repertoires can be explained most usefully on the basis of their unique learning experiences while still acknowledging the role played by innate and developmental processes" (Mitchell & Krumboltz, 1996, p. 234). Social learning theory also assumes that "humans are intelligent, problem-solving individuals who strive at all times to understand the reinforcement that surrounds them and who in turn control their environments to suit their own purposes and needs" (Mitchell & Krumboltz, 1984, p. 236). Bandura (1986) described the interaction of environment, self-referent thought, and behavior as the "triadic reciprocal interaction system."

Krumboltz and his colleagues drew upon these theoretical assumptions in developing LTCC. As noted earlier, SLTCDM describes the factors influencing individuals' career decisions and LTCC describes what career counselors can do to help their clients make effective career choices.

SLTCDM

The SLTCDM identifies four factors that influence our career decision making:

1. Genetic endowment and special abilities. Genetic endowments are inherited qualities, such as sex, race, and physical appearance. Special abilities such as intelligence, athletic ability, and musical and artistic talents result from the interaction of genetic factors and exposure to selected environmental events.

2. Environmental conditions and events. Factors in this category are generally outside our control and can involve a wide variety of cultural, social, political, and economic forces. For example, government-sponsored job-training programs, such as the Comprehensive Employment Training Act and the Job Training Partnership Act, can provide opportunities for learning new skills and increasing employability. Technological developments (e.g., computer technologies) create new job opportunities and make others obsolete. Legislation related to welfare, labor laws, and union policies influences job availability and facilitates or restricts job entry. Natural disasters can dramatically influence career opportunities and career paths. Family traditions, as well as neighborhood and community resources, can also significantly affect individuals' career decision making. Job entry requirements can persuade or deter us from considering specific occupational opportunities. Our geographical location can also play a prominent feature in influencing our career choices and the availability of job opportunities (e.g., climatic differences between Maine and Florida result in differences in the availability of some job opportunities; the availability of counseling jobs is greater in the United States than in other countries in which counseling concerns are resolved by spiritual leaders).

3. Instrumental and associative learning experiences. Instrumental learning experiences involve antecedents, behaviors, and consequences. According to Mitchell and Krumboltz (1996):

> Antecedents include the genetic endowments, special abilities, and environmental conditions and events previously discussed as well as the characteristics of a particular task or problem. Behavioral responses include cognitive and emotional responses as well as overt behavior. Consequences include immediate and delayed effects produced by the behavior as well as "self-talk" about those consequences. (p. 238)

To illustrate, consider Jennifer, a master's degree student in counselor education. She is very competent interpersonally (genetic endowment, special abilities, and skills) but feels anxious about enrolling in the required research course. Statistics and research design especially intimidate her. Because the research course is a program requirement, she must take this course (planned environmental condition). The professor in this course, however, is well acquainted with counselor education students and knows that many feel anxious about the program requirement in research. Hence, in teaching the course the professor works hard at praising students for their successes and supporting them when they struggle with course content. In this situation, Jennifer decides to apply herself and work as hard as she can to master the course content (covert and overt action). On her first exam, Jennifer earns a B grade—far better than she ever had imagined (consequences). As a result, she begins to think that, rather than being frightening, research is fun and that she might be able to become a competent researcher (covert reactions to consequences). As the semester goes on, Jennifer begins to tutor her peers who are struggling with this course. In her second year, she serves as a graduate assistant in the research course and enjoys helping students who feel anxious about being able to succeed in the course (impact on significant others).

Associative learning experiences occur when a neutral stimulus is paired with a positive and/or negative stimulus or consequences. For example, Juanita's school counselor encourages her to attend a job fair at her high school because Juanita is undecided about her career options. Juanita agrees to attend the fair. She has no real career options in mind but decides she will "browse" to see what options seem interesting. At the job fair, Juanita encounters a news anchor, who also happens to be Latina, for the local television station. Juanita had never given much thought to jobs in TV journalism (neutral stimulus), but thoroughly enjoys her meeting with the local anchor (positive stimulus). Juanita is even invited to take a tour of the studio and sit in on a live broadcast. After taking the tour and observing the broadcast, Juanita decides to enroll in a formal externship program the high school has established with the television station (positive consequences).

4. Task-approach skills. Juanita will need to use many skills in determining whether journalism is a good career choice for her. For example, she will need to be able to clarify her interests, values, and skills; gather occupational information; and know how to integrate this information in her decision making. In this process, Juanita will need to consider her genetic characteristics, special abilities, and environmental influences (e.g., family support, training opportunities, financial resources, and occupational opportunities). These behaviors are examples of task-approach skills that Juanita must use in making a career choice. Task-approach skills also include the individual's work habits, mental set, emotional responses, cognitive processes, and problem-solving skills. Additionally, if Juanita decides to pursue a career as a television journalist, she will need to develop a wide range of journalistic skills in order to achieve her goal. Thus, task-approach skills influence outcomes and are themselves outcomes.

These four factors influence our beliefs about ourselves (e.g., what we are good at, what our interests are, what we value) and our beliefs about the world (e.g., "hard work always pays off," "all accountants are stuffy," "all counselors value altruism over economic rewards"). Although the interactions of these four factors influence people differently, there are generally four ways in which they can influence our career decision making.

1. Self-observation generalizations. Overt or covert statements evaluating our actual or vicarious performance or self-assessments of our interests and values are defined as self-observation generalizations (Mitchell & Krumboltz, 1996, p. 244). Learning experiences lead us to draw conclusions about ourselves. We compare our performance with the performance of others and to our own performance expectations. We use these comparisons to draw conclusions about our performance capabilities. Conclusions about our interests and values also result from learning experiences. In SLTCDM, interests link learning experiences with specific actions (as when doing well in a research course leads to the decision to participate in research projects and teach others about research). Self-observations about values are, in essence, statements about the desirability of specific outcomes, behaviors, or events (Mitchell & Krumboltz, 1996). For example, the statement that "it is important that my job provides ample time for me to be with my family" is a values-related self-observation generalization about desirable outcomes resulting from previous learning experiences.

2. **Worldview generalizations.** Likewise, generalizations about the nature and functioning of the world (e.g., "It's not what you know, it's who you know," "It is better to try and fail than to not try at all") are formed from learning experiences. The accuracy of worldview generalizations is dependent on the learning experiences shaping such generalizations.

3. **Task-approach skills.** Mitchell and Krumboltz (1996) define these outcomes as "cognitive and performance abilities and emotional predispositions for coping with the environment, interpreting it in relation to self-observation generalizations, and making covert and overt predictions about future events" (p. 246). As noted earlier, task-approach skills influence career decision making and are outcomes of learning experiences that shape individuals' career development. Task-approach skills critical to career development are those involved in decision making, problem solving, goal setting, information gathering, and values clarifying.

4. **Actions.** Learning experiences eventually lead individuals to take actions related to entering a career. These actions can include applying for a job, entering a training program, applying to college, changing jobs, or taking other overt steps to make progress in one's career.

The SLTCDM suggests that career decision making is "influenced by complex environmental (e.g., economic) factors, many of which are beyond the control of any single individual" (Krumboltz, Mitchell, & Gelatt, 1976, p. 75). The theory also underscores "the interaction between innate predispositions and learning experiences within the intra-individual, family, social, educational and cultural context" (Krumboltz & Henderson, 2002, p. 43). Also, based on SLTCDM, Krumboltz (1994) noted that people will prefer an occupation if:

1. They have succeeded at tasks they believe are like tasks performed by members of that occupation.
2. They have observed a valued model being reinforced for activities like those performed by members of that occupation.
3. A valued friend or relative stressed its advantages to them and/or they observed positive words and images being associated with it. (p. 19)

Conversely, Krumboltz noted that people will avoid an occupation if:

1. They have failed at tasks they believe are similar to tasks performed by people in that occupation.
2. They have observed a valued model being punished or ignored for performing activities like those performed by members of that occupation.
3. A valued friend or relative stressed its disadvantages to them and/or they have observed negative words and images being associated with it. (p. 19)

The Learning Theory of Career Counseling

The strength of SLTCDM is that it provides a description of factors influencing career decision making and identifies outcomes resulting from those influential factors. As such, it is a useful theory for understanding career paths retrospectively. The understanding acquired from such a perspective is helpful in making current career decisions and in formulating future career goals.

When career concerns arise, they typically involve one or more of the following: (a) the absence of a goal, or career indecision (Juanita's presenting concern); (b) expressed feeling of concern about high aspirations, or unrealism; and (c) a conflict between equally appropriate alternatives, or multipotentiality (Krumboltz & Thoresen, 1969). Krumboltz developed the learning theory of career counseling (LTCC) to guide counselors in constructing career development interventions to help clients cope more effectively with these career concerns. Specifically, counselors using LTCC help clients to: (a) acquire more accurate self-observation generalizations, (b) acquire more accurate worldview generalizations, (c) learn new task approach skills, and (d) take appropriate career-related actions. LTCC assumes that counselors must be prepared to help their clients cope with four current career-related trends identified by Mitchell and Krumboltz (1996, pp. 250–252).

1. People need to expand their capabilities and interests, not base decisions on existing characteristics only. Interest inventories assess what we know and what we have experienced. To maximize a client's career choice options, counselors must encourage that client to explore new activities, develop new interests, and consider new options based on newly formed interests and capabilities.
2. People need to prepare for changing work tasks, and not assume that occupations will remain stable. Because change is constant, career counselors must help their clients identify new skills to learn and develop strategies for coping with the stress inherent in an ever-changing world of work.
3. People need to be empowered to take action, not merely to be given a diagnosis. For some clients, implementing a career choice is more challenging than making the choice. Many clients need ongoing assistance from their career counselors as they attempt to adjust to the career choice made and implemented.
4. Career counselors need to play a major role in dealing with all career problems, not just career selection. Career-related concerns exist beyond this concern of identifying a career choice. Many clients struggle with the burnout, underemployment, relationships with coworkers, family members' reactions to career choices, and low self-efficacy.

These four trends suggest the importance of providing clients with learning experiences to (a) correct faulty assumptions, (b) learn new skills and interests, (c) identify effective strategies for addressing issues emanating from interactions between work and other life-role activities and concerns, and (d) learn skills for coping with changing work tasks. Career counselors can use assessments to help clients identify what characteristics (e.g., beliefs, skills, values, interests, personality) they have learned and to identify opportunities for learning new characteristics. Thus, the task of the career counselor is to promote client learning and the goal of career counseling is to enhance the ability of clients to create satisfying lives for themselves (Krumboltz, 1996).

Applying LTCC

Krumboltz (1996) divides career development interventions into two categories: (a) developmental/preventive and (b) targeted/remedial. The former includes career education programs, school-to-work initiatives, job club programs, study materials, and simulations. These career development interventions facilitate the acquisition of accurate and occupational self-information and the use of this information in the career decision-making process. Learning through active on-the-job participation (e.g., job shadowing, internships, and worksite observation) is emphasized. It is important to note that although many clients, such as Juanita, could certainly benefit from participating in many of these activities, they must first receive more targeted and remedial career development interventions.

Targeted and remedial career development interventions include goal clarification, cognitive restructuring, cognitive rehearsal, narrative analysis, role playing, desensitization, paradoxical intention, and humor (Krumboltz, 1996, pp. 66–72). LTCC also emphasizes the importance of teaching decision-making skills to clients. Learning how to make career decisions helps clients to resolve current career concerns and equips clients with an important task approach skill for coping with changing work and personal conditions in the future (Krumboltz, 1976). For example, once Juanita has clarified her goals and learns how to make good decisions, she will then be ready to participate in more focused on-the-job activities (e.g., job shadowing, volunteering).

To help counselors identify problematic client beliefs related to each of the career problem categories (i.e., indecision, unrealism, and multipotentiality), Krumboltz (1988) developed the Career Beliefs Inventory (CBI). The CBI is based on the rationale that people make career decisions according to what they believe about themselves and the world-of-work. As Krumboltz wrote in 1994, "If their beliefs are accurate and constructive, they will act in ways that are likely to help them achieve their goals. If their beliefs are inaccurate and self-defeating, they will act in a way that makes sense to them but may not help them achieve their goals" (p. 424). The CBI helps counselors to understand their clients' career beliefs and assumptions. Thus, the instrument is most useful when administered at the beginning of career counseling. The CBI contains 25 scales organized into the following five categories: My Current Career Situation, What Seems Necessary for My Happiness, Factors That Influence My Decisions, Changes I Am Willing to Make, and Efforts I Am Willing to Initiate. These categories are related to mental barriers blocking clients from taking action. As Krumboltz and Henderson (2002) remind us, meaningful journeys, including our career journey, contain obstacles that must be confronted. Some clients allow discouragement and other problematic beliefs to dominate their thinking and thwart efforts to take positive actions. Self-defeating beliefs such as those measured by the CBI must be addressed if the client is to move forward. Counseling strategies such as cognitive restructuring and reframing are useful in helping the client to address these issues.

Related to the notion of career beliefs is the fact that often in career counseling, clients refer to significant events in ways that suggest the client had little to do with the experience. For example, a client may say "I just got lucky" or "I just happened to be in the right place at the right time." Krumboltz and his associates (Mitchell, Levin, & Krumboltz, 1999) recognize that career counseling often involves helping clients understand and take advantage of the chance events they encounter in daily living. In fact, they note that "unplanned events are not only inevitable, they are desirable" (p. 118) and refer to this phenomenon as "planned happenstance." Planned happenstance can be incorporated into career counseling by teaching clients "to generate, recognize, and incorporate chance events into the process of their career development" (Krumboltz & Henderson, 2002, p. 49). Specifically, career counselors can ask their clients questions such as: "How have unplanned events influenced your career in the past? How did you enable each event to influence your career development? How do you feel about encountering unplanned events in your future?" (2002, p. 50). Counselor and client interactions that intentionally address the role of chance in career development help to normalize such occurrences, help clients see their thematic influence upon their career development, and help clients be increasingly open to noticing and acting upon unplanned events in the future. In essence, an internal locus of control and increased sense of personal self-efficacy are fostered.

Mitchell et al. (1999) focus on the skills clients need to develop to take advantage of unplanned events in their career development. They note that developing a sense of curiosity, being persistent, being flexible, maintaining a sense of optimism, and being willing to take risks represent a set of skills that increase the individual's ability to take advantage of unplanned events.

Evaluating Career Development Interventions

Typically, counselors evaluate the success of career development interventions by standards determining whether clients experience a reduction in career indecision. Krumboltz recommends that career counselors consider revising these criteria. For example, counselors using LTCC view indecision as a desirable quality for motivating clients to engage in new learning activities. Hence, Krumboltz recommends reframing "indecision" to "open-mindedness."

Krumboltz also suggests that the goal of achieving congruence between individuals and their work environments is unnecessarily restricting because "birds of a feather" do not always flock together (i.e., there is intra-occupational variability among people). Two very different people can be successful in the same occupation. Krumboltz (1996) also argues that the congruence criterion is less useful today because it is based on stagnant definitions of occupational environments, thereby overlooking changes in work environments: "Heterogeneity, not homogeneity, within occupations is now more highly valued" (p. 73).

In place of these two traditional outcome criteria, Krumboltz recommends focusing on measuring changes in client characteristics such as skills, values, beliefs, interests, and work habits. Counselors can ask themselves whether their career development interventions have stimulated their clients to engage in new learning activities. Process measures can focus on assessing the degree to which clients have made efforts to create more satisfying lives (e.g., Have they engaged in career exploratory or information-seeking behaviors?).

Evaluating LTCC

LTCC is new and relatively untested by research. There is, however, extensive research supporting the general social learning theory (Hackett et al., 1991). Additionally, Krumboltz (1996) cites several studies supporting SLTCDM hypotheses related to the development of educational and occupational preferences, task-approach skills, and action.

A strength of LTCC is that it addresses both environmental and intra-individual variables affecting career development. As such, LTCC is very compatible with Super's Archway model of career development, with LTCC offering a bit more in terms of specific ways in which environmental and personal variables influence career decision making. LTCC also can be used as a framework for understanding the development of interests leading to one's personal modal orientation as described by Holland's theory. Finally, the development of the CBI, and subsequent application of strategies such as cognitive restructuring and reframing, provide useful and important applications of the theory to career development interventions.

MyCounselingLab™

Go to Topic 4: *The Development of Career Behavior and Choice* in the **MyCounselingLab**™ site (www.MyCounselingLab.com) for *Career Development Interventions in the 21st Century*, Fourth Edition, where you can:

- Find learning outcomes for *The Development of Career Behavior and Choice* along with the national standards that connect to these outcomes.

- Complete Assignments and Activities that can help you more deeply understand the chapter content.
- Apply and practice your understanding of the core skills identified in the chapter with the Building Counseling Skills unit.
- Prepare yourself for professional certification with a Practice for Certification quiz.
- Connect to videos through the Video and Resource Library.

Summary

The theories discussed in this chapter form the foundation for how the leading theorists and practitioners have conceptualized the career development process for more than 50 years. There are ways in which these theories converge, but there are many ways in which they do not. They each contribute important perspectives for conceptualizing how careers develop and how career choices are made. Thus there is no one theory that sufficiently addresses all possible factors influencing career development and all client career concerns. This is not surprising given the highly complex nature of career development. However, these theories do provide a solid foundation upon which to expand our thinking

about the career development process and career development interventions. Particular areas ripe for expansion include describing how careers develop for a wider range of people. Most of the early theories of career development were based on the career experience of White males and may lack applicability to women and members of diverse racial, ethnic, socioeconomic, and religious groups. Another area ripe for theory expansion is the process and content of career counseling. Most early theories of career development emphasize the career development process rather than career development interventions. More treatment-outcome studies directed toward determining which interventions are appropriate for which clients with what career concerns are needed.

Nonetheless, the theories discussed in this chapter provide an important stimulus in the evolutionary process of theory development. As these theories continue to evolve and as new theories emerge, it is hoped that theorists will continue the process of providing fuller, more detailed, and more comprehensive descriptions of the career development process that can be used to provide effective career development interventions to a wide range of people. The emerging theories discussed in the next chapter provide evidence of such progress.

Student Activities

1. Review the Holland types. Which types are you most like? How do your activities reflect these types?

2. Review Super's career development tasks. Which tasks are you most concerned with at this point in your life? What resources and support would help you to cope effectively with those tasks?

3. Review Gottfredson's theory. In what ways has sex-role stereotyping impacted on your career?

4. Consider the life role of a worker. What have you learned about this life role from your parents/guardians? What have you learned about this life role from your relatives? In what ways has culture influenced your understanding of the life role of a worker?

5. Review the theory of John Krumboltz. Identify two worldview generalizations that you hold. Identify three self-observations (you might begin this by stating, "I'm the kind of person who . . ." and "One thing I value is . . ." and "I'm really good at . . .").

6. Reflect upon your early life experiences and consider how well Anne Roe's theory describes your career choices.

References

Anderson, W. P., & Niles, S. G. (1995). Career and personal concerns expressed by career counseling clients. *The Career Development Quarterly, 43,* 240–245.

Bandura, A. (1977). *Social learning theory.* Upper Saddle River, NJ: Prentice Hall.

Bandura, A. (1986). *Social foundations of thought and action: A social-cognitive theory.* Upper Saddle River, NJ: Prentice Hall.

Betz, N. E., & Corning, A. F. (1993). The inseparability of "career" and "personal" counseling. *The Career Development Quarterly, 42,* 137–148.

Blanchard, C. A., & Lichtenberg, J. W. (2003). Compromise in career decision making: A test of Gottfredson's theory. *Journal of Vocational Behavior, 62,* 250–271.

Blustein, D. L. (1994). "Who am I?" The question of self and identity in career development. In M. L. Savickas & R. W. Lent (Eds.), *Convergence in career development theories: Implications for science and practice* (pp. 139–154). Palo Alto, CA: Consulting Psychologists Press.

Blustein, D. L., Gill, N. J. K., Kenna, A. C., & Murphy, K. A. (2006). The psychology of working. *Career Planning and Adult Development Journal, 21,* 10–21.

Borgen, F. H. (1991). Megatrends and milestones in vocational behavior: A 20-year counseling psychology perspective. *Journal of Vocational Behavior, 39,* 263–290.

Borodovsky, L., & Ponterotto, J. (1994). A family-based approach to multicultural career development. In P. Pedersen & J. Carey (Eds.), *Multicultural counseling in schools* (pp. 195–206). Boston: Allyn & Bacon.

Brown, D. (1996). Brown's values-based, holistic model of career and life-role choices and satisfaction. In D. Brown, L. Brooks, & Associates

(Eds.), *Career choice and development* (3rd ed., pp. 337–372). San Francisco: Jossey-Bass.

Brown, M. T., Lum, J. L., & Voyle, K. (1997). Roe revisited: A call for the reappraisal of the theory of personality development and career choice. *Journal of Vocational Behavior, 51,* 283–294.

Buehler, C. (1933). *Der menschliche lebenslauf als psychologisches problem.* Leipzig: Hirzel.

Cairo, P. C., Kritis, K. J., & Myers, R. M. (1996). Career assessment and the Adult Career Concerns Inventory. *Journal of Career Assessment, 4,* 189–204.

Cochran, D. B,, Wang, E. W., Stevenson, S. J., Johnson, L. E., & Crews, C. (in press). Adolescent occupational aspirations: Test of Gottfredson's Theory of Circumscription and Compromise. *The Career Development Quarterly.*

Coltrane, S., & Adams, M. (1997). Work-family imagery and gender stereotypes: Television and the reproduction of difference. *Journal of Vocational Behavior, 50,* 323–347.

Donahue, R. (2006). Person-environment congruence in relation to career change and career persistence. *Journal of Vocational Behavior, 68,* 504–515.

Downes, M., & Kroeck, K. G. (1996). Discrepancies between existing jobs and individual interests: An empirical investigation of Holland's model. *Journal of Vocational Behavior, 48,* 107–117.

Eagle, B. W., Miles, E. W., & Icenogle, M. L. (1997). Interrole conflicts and the permeability of work and family domains: Are there gender differences? *Journal of Vocational Behavior, 50,* 168–184.

Ginzberg, E., Ginsburg, S. W., Axelrad, S., & Herma, J. (1951). *Occupational choice: An approach to a general theory.* New York: Columbia University Press.

Gottfredson, L. S. (1981). Circumscription and compromise: A developmental theory of occupational aspirations. *Journal of Counseling Psychology, 28,* 545–579.

Gottfredson, L. S. (1996). A theory of circumscription and compromise. In D. Brown, L. Brooks, & Associates (Eds.), *Career choice and development* (3rd ed., pp. 179–281). San Francisco: Jossey-Bass.

Gottfredson, L. S. (2002). Gottfredson's theory of circumscription, compromise, and self-creation. In D. Brown & Associates (Eds.), *Career choice and development* (4th ed., pp. 85–148). San Francisco: Jossey-Bass.

Gottfredson, L. S. (2003). The challenge and promise of cognitive career assessment. *Journal of Career Assessment, 11,* 115–135.

Gottfredson, L. S. (2005). Applying Gottfredson's theory of circumscription and compromise in career guidance and counseling. In S. D. Brown & R. W. Lent (Eds.), *Career development and counseling: Putting theory and research to work* (pp. 71–100). Hoboken, NJ: Wiley.

Gottfredson, L. S., & Holland, J. L. (1996). *Position classification inventory.* Odessa, FL: PAR.

Gottfredson, L. S., & Richards, J. M. (1999). The meaning and measurement of environments in Holland's theory. *Journal of Vocational Behavior, 42,* 200–211.

Hackett, G., Lent, R., & Greenhaus, J. (1991). Advances in vocational theory and research: A 20-year retrospective. *Journal of Vocational Behavior, 38,* 3–38.

Hannah, J., & Kahn, S. (1989). The relationship of socioeconomic status and gender to the occupational choices of Grade 12 students. *Journal of Vocational Behavior, 34,* 161–178.

Harmon, L. W., Hansen, J. C., Borgen, F. H., & Hammer, A. L. (1994). *Strong Interest Inventory applications and technical guide.* Stanford, CA: Stanford University Press.

Hartung, P. J., Vandiver, B. J., Leong, F. T. L., Pope, M., Niles, S. G., & Farrow, B. (1998). Appraising cultural identity in career development assessment and counseling. *The Career Development Quarterly, 46,* 276–293.

Havighurst, R. J. (1951). Validity of the Chicago Attitude Inventory as a measure of personal adjustment in old age. *Journal of Abnormal and Social Psychology, 46,* 24–29.

Havighurst, R. J. (1953). *Human development and education.* New York: Longmans Green.

Helwig, A. A. (2001). A test of Gottfredson's theory using a ten-year longitudinal study. *Journal of Career Development, 28,* 77–95.

Henderson, S., Hesketh, B., & Tuffin, A. (1988). A test of Gottfredson's theory of circumscription. *Journal of Vocational Behavior, 32,* 37–48.

Herr, E. L., Cramer, S. H., & Niles, S. G. (2004). *Career guidance and counseling through the lifespan: Systematic approaches* (6th ed.). Boston: Allyn & Bacon.

Hesketh, B., Elmslie, S., & Kaldor, W. (1990). Career compromise: An alternative account to Gottfredson's theory. *Journal of Counseling Psychology, 37,* 49–56.

Holland, J. L. (1959). A theory of vocational choice. *Journal of Counseling Psychology, 6,* 35–45.

Holland, J. L. (1966). *The psychology of vocational choice.* Waltham, MA: Blaisdell.

Holland, J. L. (1973). *Making vocational choices: A theory of careers.* Upper Saddle River, NJ: Prentice Hall.

Holland, J. L. (1985a). *Making vocational choices: A theory of vocational personalities and work environments* (2nd ed.). Upper Saddle River, NJ: Prentice Hall.

Holland, J. L. (1985b). Vocational Preference Inventory. Odessa, FL: PAR.

Holland, J. L. (1992). *Making vocational choices* (2nd ed.). Odessa, FL: Psychological Assessment Resources.

Holland, J. L. (1994). Separate but unequal is better. In M. L. Savickas & R. W. Lent (Eds.), *Convergence in career development theories: Implications for science and practice* (pp. 45–51). Palo Alto, CA: CPP Books.

Holland, J. L. (1996). Integrating career theory and practice: The current situation and some potential remedies. In M. L. Savickas & W. B. Walsh (Eds.), *Handbook of career counseling theory and practice* (pp. 1–12). Palo Alto, CA: Davies-Black.

Holland, J. L. (1997). Current status of Holland's theory of careers: Another perspective. *The Career Development Quarterly, 36,* 31–44.

Holland, J. L., Gottfredson, G., & Power, P. (1980). Some diagnostic scales for research in decision-making and personality: Identity, information, and barriers. *Journal of Personality and Social Psychology, 39,* 1191–1200.

Holmberg, K., Rosen, D., & Holland, J. L. (1990). *Leisure activities finder.* Odessa, FL: Psychological Assessment Resources.

Jepsen, D. A. (1994). The thematic-extrapolation method: Incorporating career patterns into career counseling. *The Career Development Quarterly, 43,* 43–53.

Johannson, C. B. (1986). *The Career Assessment Inventory.* Minneapolis, MN: NCS Assessments.

Kelly, G. A. (1955). *The psychology of personal constructs.* New York: Norton.

Krumboltz, J. D. (1976). A social learning theory of career choice. *Counseling Psychologist, 6,* 71–80.

Krumboltz, J. D. (1988). *Career beliefs inventory.* Palo Alto, CA: Consulting Psychologists Press.

Krumboltz, J. D. (1993). Integrating career and personal counseling. *The Career Development Quarterly, 42,* 143–148.

Krumboltz, J. D. (1994). The Career Beliefs Inventory. *Journal of Counseling and Development, 72,* 424–428.

Krumboltz, J. D. (1996). A learning theory of career counseling. In M. Savickas & B. Walsh (Eds.), *Integrating career theory and practice* (pp. 233–280). Palo Alto, CA: CPP Books.

Krumboltz, J. D., & Henderson, S. J. (2002). A learning theory for career counselors. In S. Niles (Ed.), *Adult career development: Concepts, issues, and practices* (pp. 39–56). Tulsa, OK: National Career Development Association.

Krumboltz, J. D., Mitchell, A., & Gelatt, H. G. (1976). Applications of social learning theory of career selection. *Focus on Guidance, 8,* 1–16.

Krumboltz, J. D., & Thoresen, C. E. (1969). *Behavioral counseling: Cases and techniques.* New York: Holt, Rinehart and Winston.

Lent, E. B., & Lopez, F. G. (1996). Congruence from many angles: Relations of multiple congruence indices to job satisfaction among adult workers. *Journal of Vocational Behavior, 49,* 24–37.

Lent, R. W. (2005). A social cognitive view of career development and counseling. In S. D. Brown & R. W. Lent (Eds.), *Career development and counseling: Putting theory and research to work* (pp. 101–130). Hoboken, NJ: Wiley.

Lent, R. W., Brown, S. D., Nota, L., & Soresi, S. (2003). Testing social cognitive interest and choice hypotheses across Holland types in Italian high school students. *Journal of Vocational Behavior, 62,* 101–118.

Leong, S. A., & Plake, T. S. (1990). A choice dilemma approach for examining the relative importance of sex type and prestige preferences in the process of career choice compromise. *Journal of Counseling Psychology, 37,* 399–406.

Lewis, D. M., Savickas, M. L., & Jones, B. J. (1996). Career development predicts medical school success. *Journal of Vocational Behavior, 49,* 86–98.

Loscocco, K. A. (1997). Reactions to blue-collar work: A comparison of men and women. *Work and Occupations, 17,* 152–177.

Lucas, M. S. (1993). A validation of types of career indecision at a counseling center. *Journal of Counseling Psychology, 40,* 440–446.

Maslow, A. H. (1954). *Motivation and personality*. New York: Harper & Row.

McLennan, N. A., & Arthur, N. (1999). Applying the cognitive information processing approach to career problem solving and decision making to women's career development. *Journal of Employment Counseling, 36*, 82–96.

Mihalik, J. R. (1996). Client vocational interests as predictors of client reactions to counselor intentions. *Journal of Counseling and Development, 74*, 416–421.

Miller, D. C., & Form, W. H. (1951). *Industrial sociology*. New York: Harper & Row.

Miller, M. J. (1997). Error rates on two forms on the Self-Directed Search and satisfaction with results. *Journal of Employment Counseling, 34*, 98–103.

Miller, M. J. (2002). A longitudinal examination of a three-letter Holland code. *Journal of Employment Counseling, 39*, 43–48.

Miller, M. J., & Bass, C. (2003). Application of Holland's theory to a nonprofessional occupation. *Journal of Employment Counseling, 40*, 17–23.

Mitchell, L. K., & Krumboltz, J. D. (1984). Social learning approach to career decision making: Krumboltz's theory. In D. Brown, L. Brooks, & Associates (Eds.), *Career choice and development: Applying contemporary theories to practice* (2nd ed., pp. 235–280). San Francisco: Jossey-Bass.

Mitchell, L. K., & Krumboltz, J. D. (1996). Krumboltz's theory of career choice and counseling. In D. Brown, L. Brooks, & Associates (Eds.), *Career choice development* (3rd ed., pp. 233–280). San Francisco: Jossey-Bass.

Mitchell, A., Levin, A., & Krumboltz, J. D. (1999). Planned happenstance: Constructing unexpected career opportunities. *Journal of Counseling and Development, 77*, 115–124.

Murray, H. (1938). *Explorations in personality*. New York: Oxford University Press.

Nevill, D. D., & Calvert, P. D. (1996). Career assessment and the Salience Inventory. *Journal of Career Assessment, 4*, 399–412.

Nevill, D. D., & Kruse, S. J. (1996). Career assessment and the Values Scale. *Journal of Career Assessment, 4*, 383–397.

Nevill, D. D., & Super, D. E. (1986). *The Values Scale: Theory, application, and research manual* (research ed.). Palo Alto, CA: Consulting Psychologists Press.

Niles, S. G., & Anderson, W. P. (1993). Career development and adjustment: The relation between concerns and stress. *Journal of Employment Counseling, 30*, 79–87.

Niles, S. G., Anderson, W. P., & Goodnough, G. (1998). Exploration to foster career development. *The Career Development Quarterly, 46*, 262–275.

Niles, S. G., & Goodnough, G. E. (1996). Life-role salience and values: A review of recent research. *The Career Development Quarterly, 45*, 65–86.

Oleski, D., & Subich, L. M. (1996). Congruence and career change in employed adults. *Journal of Vocational Behavior, 49*, 221–229.

Oliver, K. E., & Waehler, C. A. (2005). Investigating the validity of Holland's (1959, 1997) RIASEC typology among Native Hawaiians. *Journal of Counseling Psychology, 52*, 448–452.

Osipow, S. H., & Fitzgerald, L. F. (1996). *Theories of career development* (4th ed.). Needham, MA: Allyn & Bacon.

Parasuraman, S., Purhoit, Y. S., Godshalk, V. M., & Beutell, N. J. (1996). Work and family variables, entrepreneurial career success, and psychological well-being. *Journal of Vocational Behavior, 48*, 275–300.

Perdue, S., Reardon, R., & Peterson, G. (2007). Person-environment congruence, self-efficacy, and environmental identity in relation to job satisfaction.: A career decision theory perspective. *Journal of Employment Counseling, 44*, 29–39.

Perrone, K. M. (2005). Work-family interface for same sex, dual-earner couples: Implications for counselors. *The Career Development Quarterly, 53*, 317–324.

Phillips, S. D. (1982). Career exploration in adulthood. *Journal of Vocational Behavior, 20*, 129–140.

Richardson, M. S. (1993). Work in people's lives: A location for counseling psychologists. *Journal of Counseling Psychology, 40*, 425–433.

Roe, A. (1956). *The psychology of occupations*. New York: Wiley.

Roe, A. (1957). Early determinants of vocational choice. *Journal of Counseling Psychology, 4*, 212–217.

Rogers, C. R. (1951). *Client-centered therapy, its current practice, implications, and theory*. Boston: Houghton Mifflin.

Rounds, J., & Tracey, T. J. G. (1996). Cross-cultural structural equivalence of RIASEC models and measures. *Journal of Counseling Psychology, 43,* 310–329.

Ryan, J. M., Tracey, T. J. G., & Rounds, J. (1996). Generalizability of Holland's structure of vocational behavior interest across ethnicity, gender, and socioeconomic status. *Journal of Counseling Psychology, 43,* 330–337.

Salomone, P. R. (1996). Tracing Super's theory of vocational development: A 40-year retrospective. *Journal of Career Development, 22,* 167–184.

Savickas, M. L. (1993). Predictive validity criteria for career development measures. *Journal of Career Assessment, 1,* 93–104.

Savickas, M. L. (1997). Career adaptability: An integrative concept for life-span, life-space theory. *The Career Development Quarterly, 45,* 247–259.

Savickas, M. L. (2002). Career construction: A developmental theory of vocational behavior. In D. Brown & Associates (Eds.), *Career choice and development* (4th ed., pp. 149–205). San Francisco: Jossey-Bass.

Savickas, M. L. (2005). The theory and practice of career construction. In S. D. Brown & R. W. Lent (Eds.), *Career development and counseling: Putting theory and research to work* (pp. 42–70). Hoboken, NJ: Wiley.

Savickas, M. L., & Hartung, P. J. (1996). The Career Development Inventory in review: Psychometric and research findings. *Journal of Career Assessment, 4,* 171–188.

Spokane, A. (1985). A review of research on person-environment congruence in Holland's theory of careers. *Journal of Vocational Behavior, 26,* 306–343.

Spokane, A. (1996). Holland's theory. In D. Brown, L. Brook, & Associates (Eds.), *Career choice and development* (3rd ed., pp. 33–74). San Francisco: Jossey-Bass.

Spokane, A. R., & Cruza-Guet, M. C. (2005). Holland's theory of vocational personalities in work environments. In S. D. Brown & R. W. Lent (Eds.), *Career development and counseling: Putting theory and research to work* (pp. 24–41). Hoboken, NJ: Wiley.

Spokane, A. R., Fouad, N., & Swanson, J. (2001). *Culture-centered career intervention. Paper presented at a symposium on career intervention.* (S. Whiston, Chair). San Francisco: American Psychological Association.

Spokane, A., Luchetta, E., & Richwine, M. (2002). Holland's theory of personalities. In D. Brown & Associates (Eds.), *Career choice and development* (4th ed., pp. 373–426). San Francisco: Jossey-Bass.

Spranger, E. (1928). *Types of men: The psychology and ethics of personality* (Paul J. W. Pigors, Trans.). Halle, Germany: Max Niemeyer Verlag.

Subich, L. M. (1993). How personal is career counseling? *The Career Development Quarterly, 42,* 129–131.

Super, D. E. (1953). A theory of vocational development. *American Psychologist, 8,* 185–190.

Super, D. E. (1954). Career patterns as a basis for vocational counseling. *Journal of Counseling Psychology, 1,* 12–20.

Super, D. E. (1957). *The psychology of careers.* New York: Harper & Row.

Super, D. E. (1961). The self concept in vocational development. *Journal of Vocational and Educational Guidance, 8,* 13–29.

Super, D. E. (1969). Vocational development theory: Persons, positions, processes. *The Counseling Psychologist, 1,* 2–9.

Super, D. E. (1980). A life-span, life-space approach to career development. *Journal of Vocational Behavior, 16,* 282–298.

Super, D. E. (1981). Approaches to occupational choice and career development. In A. G. Watts, D. E. Super, & J. M. Kidd (Eds.), *Career development in Britain* (pp. 28–42). Cambridge, England: Hobsons Press.

Super, D. E. (1983). Assessment in career guidance: Toward truly developmental counseling. *Personnel and Guidance Journal, 61,* 555–562.

Super, D. E. (1984). Leisure: What it is and might be. *Journal of Career Development, 11,* 71–80.

Super, D. E. (1990). A life-span, life-space approach to career development. In D. Brown, L. Brook, & Associates (Eds.), *Career choice and development: Applying contemporary theories to practice* (2nd ed., pp. 197–261). San Francisco: Jossey-Bass.

Super, D. E. (1992). Toward a comprehensive theory of career development. In D. Montross & C. Shinkman (Eds.), *Career development: Theory and practice* (pp. 35–64). Springfield, IL: Charles C. Thomas.

Super, D. E. (1993). The two faces of counseling: Or is it three? *The Career Development Quarterly, 42,* 132–136.

Super, D. E., & Bachrach, P. (1957). *Scientific careers and vocational development theory.* New York: Teachers College Press.

Super, D. E., & Knasel, E. G. (1981). Career development in adulthood: Some theoretical problems and a possible solution. *British Journal of Guidance and Counselling, 9,* 194–201.

Super, D. E., & Nevill, D. D. (1986). *The Salience Inventory.* Palo Alto, CA: Consulting Psychologists Press.

Super, D. E., Osborne, W. L., Walsh, D. J., Brown, S. D., & Niles, S. G. (1992). Developmental assessment and counseling: The C-DAC model. *Journal of Counseling and Development, 71,* 74–80.

Super, D. E., Savickas, M. L., & Super, C. (1996). A life-span, life-space approach to career development. In D. Brown, L. Brook, & Associates (Eds.), *Career choice and development* (3rd ed., pp. 121–128). San Francisco: Jossey-Bass.

Super, D. E., Thompson, A. S., & Lindeman, R. H. (1988). *Adult Career Concerns Inventory: Manual for research and exploratory usage in counseling.* Palo Alto, CA: Consulting Psychologists Press.

Super, D. E., Thompson, A. S., Lindeman, R. H., Jordaan, J. P., & Myers, R. A. (1981). *Career Development Inventory.* Palo Alto, CA: Consulting Psychologists Press.

Thompson, A. S., Lindeman, R. H., Super, D. E., Jordaan, J. P., & Myers, R. A. (1984). *Career Development Inventory: Technical manual.* Palo Alto, CA: Consulting Psychologists Press.

Tinsley, H. E. A. (1994). Construct your reality and show us its benefits: Comment on Richardson. *Journal of Counseling Psychology, 40,* 108–111.

Tracey, T. (2008). Adherence to RIASEC structure as a key career decision construct. *Journal of Counseling Psychology, 55,* 146–157.

U. S. Department of Defense. (1993). *Technical supplement to the counselor's manual for the Armed Services Vocational Aptitude Battery.* North Chicago, IL: U. S. Military Entrance Processing Command.

Vondracek, F. W., Lerner, R. M., & Schulenberg, J. E. (1986). *Career development: A life-span developmental approach.* Hillsdale, NJ: Erlbaum.

Weinrach, G. (1984). Determinants of vocational choice: Holland's theory. In D. Brown, L. Brooks, & Associates (Eds.), *Career choice and development: Applying contemporary theories to practice* (3rd ed., pp. 61–93). San Francisco: Jossey-Bass.

Weinrach, S. G. (1996). The psychological and vocational interest patterns of Donald Super and John Holland. *Journal of Counseling and Development, 75,* 5–16.

3

Understanding and Applying Recent Theories of Career Development

Career theory provides a framework through which to view the career situations of individuals. Theory serves as a "road map" to help us understand individuals' career journeys, what factors along the way may have shaped their career development, what barriers and obstacles they may face now and in the future, and how to plot a course for the future. Like a prism, career theory enables us to view careers from many different angles. The constructs and concepts that comprise various theoretical approaches can serve as guides in helping us learn more about the unique characteristics of individuals. Theories can sensitize us to factors that may have negatively impacted a person's career development and strategies for moving forward in a positive direction. Some career theories help us learn about and see the connection between persons and their options, which include work, education, and leisure. Career theories also help us understand how work interacts with the other life roles an individual may pursue. Finally, career theories provide models to further our insight into the career decision-making and problem-solving process. Theories come alive when they move beyond the written page and further inform our work with individuals who are making career choices and exploring career transitions.

Janet G. Lenz, Ph.D., MCC, NCC
President, National Career Development Association (2004–2005)
Assistant Professor Career Center,
Florida State University

MyCounselingLab™

Visit the **MyCounselingLab**™ site for *Career Development Interventions in the 21st Century,* Fourth Edition to enhance your understanding of chapter concepts. You'll have the opportunity to practice your skills through video- and case-based Assignments and Activities as well as Building Counseling Skills units, and to prepare for your certification exam with Practice for Certification quizzes.

Ronald, a 20-year-old African American male, presents for career counseling during the second semester of his sophomore year in college. In his initial appointment he states that he has not given much serious consideration to "life after college" and that he feels "confused" about his career goals. As the starting quarterback for the university's football team, Ronald had always thought he would play professional football. However, an injury and lackluster performance in the past season have left him feeling less confident about his ability to achieve this goal. He reports feeling "overwhelmed" and "doubtful" that he will be able to identify a suitable occupational alternative to professional football.

Ronald has a high grade-point average (3.6 out of 4.0) and has taken a wide variety of courses without declaring a college major. He is very personable and reports interests in math, literature, and music (he has played the piano since elementary school). He is also very involved in community service and is a mentor for two middle school students. From his comments, it is clear that Ronald has high expectations for himself. He now feels very anxious because he is not sure what he wants to do. Both of Ronald's parents are educators. His mother is employed as a high school math teacher, and his father is employed as a high school principal.

RECENT THEORIES

Theories are developed to address important questions that people ask about their career situations. The theories discussed in the previous chapter rose to prominence because they provided effective responses to questions regarding how worker traits can be matched to work requirements (e.g., person-environment theories) and how workers can develop their careers effectively across the life span (e.g., developmental theories). A number of career theories have emerged since the theories discussed in the previous chapter were initially developed. In part, these recent theories tend to be more explicitly attuned to diverse populations and to the complexity involved in career decision making, especially as the latter relates to cognitive processes concerning career choice. As such, the theories we discuss in this chapter may be very relevant for a client such as Ronald.

Specifically, social cognitive career theory developed by Lent, Brown, and Hackett (Lent, Brown, & Hackett, 1996, 2002); the cognitive information processing theory developed by Peterson, Sampson, Reardon, and Lenz (1996), Peterson, Sampson, Lenz, and Reardon (2002), and Sampson, Reardon, Peterson, and Lenz (2004); the career construction model developed by Savickas (2005, 2009); the chaos theory of careers developed by Pryor and Bright (2011); and the integrative life-planning model developed by Hansen (1997) are each excellent examples of theories that have evolved to address cognitive and mean-making processes that people use to manage their careers effectively within a global and mobile society. Theories seeking to help workers manage multiple job changes across their work lives without losing their sense of self and social identity are theories described as "postmodern." Postmodern approaches to career development interventions address the client's "subjective" experiences of career development (Cochran, 1997; Young, Valach, & Collin, 1996). Approaches emphasizing the subjective career highlight the ways in which meaning is made out of life experiences and then translated into a career choice (Carlsen, 1988; Cochran, 1990, 1997; Savickas, 1995).

For the most part, each of these emerging theories draws upon a solid foundation of research support. Emerging career theories reflect two major trends within career theory and practice. One trend is the rising prominence of cognitive theories within the career domain. The second trend is the growing realization that career interventions must fit the client (rather than the other way around), and that clients are active agents in the career construction process. Finally, the theories discussed in this chapter are, for the most part, particularly useful in advancing career development practice.

Tips from the Field

Almost by definition, theories lag behind career experiences in the current context. Try to blend current experience with theories to bridge the gaps between what the theories describe and what your student's or client's current career experiences are. Keep striving to make your career theory and practice relevant for the current context.

LENT, BROWN, AND HACKETT'S SOCIAL COGNITIVE CAREER THEORY

The social cognitive career theory (SCCT) (Brown & Lent, 1996; Lent, 2005; Lent & Brown, 2002; Lent & Brown, 2006; Lent et al., 1996, 2002) provides a conceptual framework for understanding how people develop career-related interests, make (and remake) occupational choices, and achieve career success and stability. SCCT builds upon the assumption that cognitive factors play an important role in career development and career decision making. SCCT is closely linked to Krumboltz's learning theory of career counseling, or LTCC (Mitchell & Krumboltz, 1996). Lent et al. (1996) noted, however, that SCCT differs from Krumboltz's theory in several ways. For example, in comparison to LTCC, SCCT "is more concerned with the specific cognitive mediators through which learning experiences guide career behavior; with the manner in which variables such as interests, abilities, and values interrelate; and with the specific paths by which person and contextual factors influence career outcomes. It also emphasizes the means by which individuals emphasize personal agency" (p. 377). Lent (2005) views SCCT as a model that is complementary to trait-factor and developmental models of career behavior.

SCCT also draws heavily from Albert Bandura's (1986) social cognitive theory. Specifically, SCCT incorporates Bandura's triadic reciprocal model of causality, which assumes that personal attributes, the environment, and overt behaviors "operate as interlocking mechanisms that affect one another bidirectionally" (Lent et al., 1996, p. 379). Within this triadic reciprocal model, SCCT highlights self-efficacy beliefs, outcome expectations, and personal goals. Thus, SCCT also incorporates research, applying self-efficacy theory to the career domain (Hackett & Betz, 1981; Lent & Brown, 2002; Lent & Hackett, 1987).

Bandura defines self-efficacy beliefs as "people's judgments of their capabilities to organize and execute courses of action required to attain designated types of performances" (1986, p. 391). Self-efficacy beliefs are dynamic self-beliefs and are domain specific. Self-efficacy beliefs provide answers to questions pertaining to whether we can perform specific tasks (e.g., Can I make this presentation? Can I pass the statistics exam? Can I learn person-centered counseling skills?). Our beliefs about our abilities play a central role in the career decision-making process. We move toward those occupations requiring capabilities we think we either have or can develop. We move away from those occupations requiring capabilities we think we do not possess or that we cannot develop.

Four sources shape self-efficacy beliefs: (a) personal performance accomplishments, (b) vicarious learning, (c) social persuasion, and (d) physiological states and reactions (Bandura, 1986). The most influential of these sources is the first (personal performance accomplishments). Successful accomplishments result in more positive or stronger domain-specific, self-efficacy beliefs and failures lead to more negative or weaker domain-specific beliefs.

Outcome expectations are beliefs about the outcomes of performing specific behaviors (e.g., What is likely to happen if I apply for an internship at the university counseling center? What job opportunities am I likely to have if I earn a doctoral degree in counseling?). Outcome expectations include our beliefs about "extrinsic reinforcement (receiving tangible rewards for successful performance), self-directed consequences (such as pride in oneself for mastering a challenging task), and outcomes derived from the process of performing a given activity (for instance, absorption in the task itself)" (Lent et al., 1996, p. 381). Outcome expectations influence behavior to a lesser degree than self-efficacy beliefs (e.g., even though I might like to have more job options, I am not likely to enroll in a doctoral program in counseling if I think there is a low probability that I will be successful in this program of study). Thus, outcome expectations are what we imagine will happen if we perform specific behaviors.

Personal goals also influence career behaviors in important ways. Personal goals relate to our determination to engage in certain activities to produce a particular outcome (Bandura, 1986). Goals help to organize and guide our behavior over long periods of time (e.g., I will persist in my research course because it is an important step along the way toward earning my master's degree in counseling and obtaining a job as a counselor).

The relationship among goals, self-efficacy, and outcome expectations is complex and occurs within the framework of Bandura's (1986) triadic reciprocal model of causality (i.e., personal attributes, external environmental factors, and overt behavior). In essence, this model describes how *person inputs* (e.g., predisposition, gender, and race) interact with contextual factors (e.g., culture, geography, family, gender-role socialization) and learning experiences to influence our self-efficacy beliefs and outcome expectations. Self-efficacy beliefs and outcome expectations in turn shape our interests, goals, actions, and, eventually, our attainments. However, these are also influenced by contextual factors (e.g., job opportunities, access to training opportunities, financial resources).

For example, our client Ronald stated that as a young child he was athletically gifted and large for his age (person inputs). Because he lived in the United States and because his father had been an outstanding football player (contextual factors),

Ronald was encouraged to play football at an early age (persuasion). His physical size and talents led to success as a football player (positive reinforcement). He came to believe he was good at this sport (self-efficacy beliefs) and that if he continued playing it, he would continue to do well (outcome expectations). His interest in this activity led him to develop the goal of playing football in college at a major university (personal goal). To achieve this goal, Ronald continued to practice hard and develop his skills as a football player (actions). His family could financially afford to send him to the best football camps where Ronald was able to further develop his skills and to be exposed to football coaches from the best university football programs (proximal contextual factors). Eventually, Ronald was awarded a football scholarship to a major university (performance attainment).

Obviously, Ronald's path may have been very different if he had possessed different person inputs (e.g., lacked athletic ability, been born a girl), had different contextual influences (e.g., been born in Europe), and experienced different learning experiences (e.g., received no support for participating in athletics, performed poorly as a football player). No doubt these differences would have resulted in different efficacy beliefs, outcome expectations, interests, goals, actions, and performance attainments.

Applying SCCT

SCCT is particularly useful in addressing two areas of career concern: performance attainment and persistence at overcoming obstacles. Performance is influenced by ability, self-efficacy, outcome expectations, and goals. Ability affects performance both directly and indirectly through influencing self-efficacy beliefs and outcome expectations. According to Lent and Brown (1996), "Higher self-efficacy and anticipated positive outcomes promote higher goals, which help to mobilize and sustain performance behavior" (p. 318). Problems in career development emerge when individuals prematurely foreclose on occupational options due to inaccurate self-efficacy beliefs, outcome expectations, or both, and when individuals forego further consideration of occupational options due to barriers they perceive as insurmountable (Brown & Lent, 1996).

For example, given Ronald's early and intense commitment to becoming a professional football player, it is possible that he did not fully explore a wide range of occupational possibilities prior to selecting professional football. His recent difficulties as a football player have caused him to realize that he has not explored other career options. In fact, Ronald reports feeling overwhelmed by the prospect of engaging in career exploration. He even questions whether there are occupations that will allow him to experience success and satisfaction. Thus, career development interventions in SCCT are often directed toward self-efficacy beliefs and outcome expectations.

To examine premature foreclosure on occupational options, Brown and Lent (1996) recommend that counselors encourage their clients to discuss those options that they have eliminated from further consideration. Specifically, in discussing occupations of low interest, counselors should analyze the experiences and beliefs upon which their clients' lack of interest is based. Here counselors focus on identifying any inaccuracies in their clients' self-efficacy beliefs and occupational information. Brown and Lent also state, "The basic processes for facilitating interest exploration are, therefore, fairly straightforward and include assessing discrepancies between self-efficacy and demonstrated skill and between outcome expectations and occupational information" (p. 357).

One approach used by Brown and Lent for facilitating interest exploration involves the use of a card sort exercise. In this exercise, clients sort occupations according to (a) those they would choose, (b) those they would not choose, and (c) those they question. Clients are then instructed to focus on the latter two categories by identifying occupations in these categories that they might choose if they thought they had the skills (self-efficacy beliefs), those they might choose if they thought the occupation offered them things they value (outcome expectations), and those they definitely would not choose under any circumstances. Occupations placed in the first two categories (relating to self-efficacy beliefs and outcome expectations) are then examined for accuracy in skill and outcome perceptions.

To analyze obstacles or barriers to their clients' career development, Lent (2005) recommends adapting Janis and Mann's (1977) decisional balance sheet procedure. Their adaptation of this procedure involves asking clients to first list their preferred career option(s) and then to identify the negative consequences they imagine will occur in pursuing any specific option. Negative consequences are explored as possible career-choice-implementation barriers by asking clients (a) to consider the probability of encountering each barrier and (b) to develop strategies for preventing or managing the barriers clients are most likely to encounter.

For example, in career counseling, Ronald noted that he would be interested in becoming a math teacher but was reluctant to do so because teachers have to deal with a lot of "grief from students and parents." He also stated that teachers do not make a salary that is sufficient for raising a family. The counselor suggested to Ronald that much of the "grief" encountered from students represented opportunities to help them deal with difficulties in their lives (Ronald placed a high value on helping others). It was also suggested that teachers can receive skill training to learn how to respond effectively to many student and parent concerns. To explore the issue of salary, the counselor encouraged Ronald to conduct information interviews with teachers in several local school districts (his parents were employed in a district that was known for having below-average teaching salaries). When he learned that there can be significant salary differences between school districts, Ronald began to think that it might be possible to earn a decent wage as a teacher. Ronald also began to identify ways he could eventually increase his salary (e.g., coaching, moving into administration) if he were to become a teacher.

Clients can be helped to modify their self-efficacy beliefs in several ways. When ability is sufficient, but self-efficacy beliefs are low due to factors such as racism and sex-role stereotyping, clients can be exposed to personally relevant, vicarious learning opportunities. For example, a woman who is African American and who possesses ability sufficient for a career in engineering, but has low self-efficacy beliefs, can be exposed to engineers who are also African American and female (Hackett & Byars, 1996). Clients with sufficient ability but low self-efficacy beliefs can also be encouraged to gather ability-related data from friends, teachers, and others to counteract faulty self-efficacy beliefs. Counselors can also work collaboratively with these clients to construct success experiences (e.g., taking specific academic courses, participating in volunteer experiences) to strengthen weak self-efficacy beliefs. In processing these success experiences, counselors can challenge clients when they identify external attributions for their successes and disregard internal, stable causes (i.e., ability) for their successes. Thus, the four sources of self-efficacy can be used as organizing structures for career interventions (Lent, 2005).

Evaluating SCCT

Most research related to SCCT focuses on self-efficacy. In summarizing this literature, Lent et al. (1996) noted support for the following theory-related conclusions: (1) domain-specific measures of self-efficacy are predictive of career-related interests, choice, achievement, persistence, indecision, and career exploratory behavior; (2) intervention, experimental, and path-analytic studies have supported certain hypothesized causal relations between measures of self-efficacy, performance, and interests; and (3) gender differences in academic and career self-efficacy frequently help explain male-female differences in occupational consideration (p. 397).

Additionally, research findings indicate some support for SCCT's theorized relationships among self-efficacy beliefs, outcome expectations, goals, and interests (Lent, Brown, & Hackett, 1994). For example, Choi, Park, Yang, Lee, and Lee (in press) found that career decision-making self-efficacy correlated significantly with self-esteem, vocational identity, and outcome expectations among their study participants. Tang, Pan, and Newmeyer (2008) found career self-efficacy had a mediating effect on the career decision-making process for the 141 high school students participating in their research. Rogers, Creed, and Glendon (2008) surveyed 414 Australian high school students and found that career exploration was related to goals and social support (levels of exploration were highest when goals were clear and social support was strong), highlighting the fact that social cognitive variables are influenced by personal and contextual variables. Gibbons and Borders (2010) used SCCT to study college-related expectations in 272 seventh-grade students. Differences were found between prospective first-generation college students and nonprospective first-generation college students, "with the former group demonstrating lower self-efficacy, higher negative outcome expectations, and more perceived barriers" (p. 194). Self-efficacy directly affected outcome expectations and both variables directly affected the students' strength of educational intentions. Gibbons and Borders suggest, however, that for their population of interest, the SCCT model may need to be revised as the effects of barriers and supports may directly influence outcome expectations rather than being mediated through self-efficacy.

Lent et al. (2001) investigated the applicability of SCCT to educational choices made by college students. They found that contextual barriers and supports indirectly affect educational choices through their influence on self-efficacy and the individual's willingness to convert interests into educational choices. Lindley (2005) found that her study participants had high rates of correspondence between the Holland codes for their career choices and their highest self-efficacy scores for their respective Holland types. Ochs and Roessler (2004) examined the relationship among career self-efficacy, career outcome expectations, and career exploration intentions of 77 special education students and 99 general education students. They found career decision-making self-efficacy and outcome expectations to be significant predictors of career exploratory intentions in both student groups. Nauta, Kahn, Angell, and Cantarelli (2002) investigated the SCCT assumption that changes in self-efficacy precede changes in interests. Using a cross-lagged panel research design and structural equation modeling, they found a reciprocal relationship between self-efficacy and interests but no clear pattern of temporal precedence. Flores and O'Brien (2002) conducted path analyses on data acquired from a sample of 364 Mexican American adolescent women to assess SCCT's propositions related to the influence of contextual and social cognitive variables on career aspiration, career choice prestige, and traditionality of career choice. These researchers found partial support for SCCT as nontraditional career self-efficacy, parental support, barriers, acculturation, and feminist attitudes predicted career choice prestige. Additionally, acculturation, feminist attitudes, and nontraditional career self-efficacy predicted career choice traditionality. Finally, feminist attitudes and parental support predicted career aspiration. Gainor and Lent (1998) examined the relations among SCCT, racial identity, math-related interests, and choice of major within a sample of 164 African American first-year university students. They found that self-efficacy and outcome expectations predicted interests, and interests predicted choice intentions across racial identity attitude levels. Diegelman and Subich (2001) found that raising outcome expectations among college students considering pursuing a degree in psychology resulted in an increased interest in pursuing this degree option for their study participants.

Although more treatment outcome research is needed, several additional studies have demonstrated positive outcomes for SCCT-based interventions used with diverse client groups (e.g., Chartrand & Rose, 1996; Chung, 2002; Hackett & Byars, 1996; Ochs & Roessler, 2004). An additional strength of SCCT is that it addresses both intra-individual and contextual variables in career development. Incorporating these two dimensions increases the applicability of the theory for diverse career development issues and populations. (It is interesting to note that the earliest research extending social cognitive theory to the career domain was conducted by Hackett and Betz [1981] to demonstrate how self-efficacy might be used to explain specific aspects of women's career development.) Finally, Brown & Lent (1996) noted that SCCT is a carefully developed theory that deserves high marks for translating theory into practice. Clearly, SCCT continues to generate a substantial level of interest among researchers suggesting a vibrant future for this recent theory. A recent literature review conducted by Patton and McIlveen (2009) reinforces this point and indicates that SCCT is generating substantial research, especially in comparison to other career theories.

THE COGNITIVE INFORMATION PROCESSING APPROACH

The cognitive information processing (CIP) approach (Peterson et al., 1996; Peterson et al., 2002; Sampson et al., 2004) is rooted in the three-factor Parsonian model for making career choices (i.e., self-understanding, occupational knowledge, and bringing self-understanding and occupational knowledge together to make a choice). The CIP approach extends the Parsonian model, however, by incorporating more recent developments related to how people engage in cognitive information processing.

Peterson and his associates apply what is known about cognitive information processing to career counseling.

There are four assumptions underlying the theory. The first assumption is that career decision making involves the interaction between cognitive and affective process. Second, the capacity for career problem solving depends on the availability of cognitive operations and knowledge. Third, career development is ongoing and knowledge structures continually evolve. And fourth, enhancing information-processing skills is the goal of career counseling (Peterson et al., 2002).

The CIP approach to career intervention includes several dimensions: (1) the pyramid of information processing, (2) CASVE cycle of decision-making skills, and (3) the executive processing domain. First, the approach uses an information-processing pyramid to describe the important domains of cognition involved in a career choice. The first three levels of the pyramid reflect domains that are traditionally included in career theories: self-knowledge (values, interests, skills), occupational knowledge (understanding specific occupations and educational/training opportunities), and decision-making skills (understanding how one typically makes decisions). The fourth domain and top of the pyramid is metacognitions and includes self-talk, self-awareness, and the monitoring and control of cognitions (Sampson, Peterson, Lenz, & Reardon, 1992). Knowledge of self and occupations forms the foundation of the pyramid, and then decision-making skills and metacognitions build upon this foundation.

The second dimension of the CIP approach is labeled the CASVE cycle of career decision-making skills. The CASVE cycle represents a generic model of information-processing skills related to solving career problems and making career decisions. These skills are (a) communication, (b) analysis, (c) synthesis, (d) valuing, and (e) execution (CASVE).

The use of these skills is cyclical beginning with the realization that a gap exists between a real state and an ideal state (e.g., an existing state of career indecision and a more desired state of career decidedness). Becoming aware of such gaps can occur internally through the existence of ego-dystonic emotional states (e.g., depression, anxiety); the occurrence of behaviors such as excessive tardiness, absenteeism, or drug use; or the existence of somatic symptoms (e.g., headaches, loss of appetite). Or, we can become aware of such gaps through external demands (e.g., the need to select a curriculum of study in high school or college, the need to make a decision to accept or reject a job offer). Career problems, therefore, involve cognitive, affective, behavioral, and physiological components. Interpreting these internal and external cues involves *communication*. Specifically, clients must ask themselves two questions: (a) "What am I thinking and feeling about my career choice at this moment?" and (b) "What do I hope to attain as a result of career counseling?" (Peterson et al., 1996, p. 436).

Once we recognize that a gap or career problem exists, we must *analyze* what is required for problem resolution. For example, do we need more information about ourselves (e.g., values, interests) and/or the situation (e.g., my supervisor's expectations, job requirements)? What must we do to acquire the information or resources necessary to cope more effectively with the career problem (e.g., take an interest inventory, conduct an occupational information interview, seek counseling to understand our feelings related to our job situation)?

Synthesis involves two phases: (1) elaboration and (2) crystallization. During elaboration, clients seek to identify as many potential solutions to their career problems as possible (as in brainstorming, the focus is on quantity rather than quality solutions). During crystallization, clients identify those solutions that are consistent with their abilities, interests, or values. The outcome of these two phases that synthesis comprises is a manageable list of alternatives that are acceptable to the client.

Valuing involves examining and prioritizing each of the alternatives generated in light of one's value system, the benefits to be gained and the costs incurred with each alternative, each alternative's impact on significant others and society, and the probability that the alternative will result in a successful outcome (i.e., removing the gap). Once the alternatives have been prioritized, the optimal alternative is identified. The primary question for clients engaged in the process of valuing is, "Which alternative is the best course of action for me, my significant others, and society?" (Peterson et al., 1996, p. 437).

The *execution* phase involves converting the optimal alternative into action. A plan of action is developed to implement the alternative and achieve its goal (e.g., I will enroll in psychology courses, study three hours per day, and take a course to improve my Graduate Record Examination scores in order to achieve my goal of gaining entry into a highly selective counselor education program). Thus, the execution phase requires clients to identify the specific steps necessary to operationalize the solution chosen in the valuing phase. The primary question in execution is "How can I transform my choice into an action plan?" (Peterson et al., 1996, p. 437).

Once the plan has been enacted, clients return to the communication phase to determine whether the alternative was successful in resolving the career problem. Once again, cognitive, affective, behavioral, and physiological states are assessed in evaluating the success of the alternative (e.g., Do I feel less anxious? Am I more content with my career situation? Has my class attendance improved?). If the evaluation is positive then clients move on, but if the evaluation is negative, clients recycle through the CASVE phases with the new information acquired from enacting the first alternative.

A third dimension of the CIP approach is the *executive processing domain*. The function of the executive processing domain is to initiate, coordinate, and monitor the storage of and retrieval of information (Peterson, Sampson, & Reardon, 1991). This domain involves metacognitive skills (Meichenbaum, 1977), such as self-talk, self-awareness, and control. Positive self-talk (e.g., "I am capable of making a good career choice") is required for effective career problem solving. Negative self-talk ("I can't make a good decision") leads to career indecisiveness. Self-awareness is necessary in monitoring and controlling internal and external influences on career decisions. Effective problem solvers and decision makers are aware of their values, beliefs, biases, and feelings. They use this awareness in generating and selecting problem solutions. Control and monitoring are essential for deciphering the information needed to resolve a career problem and for knowing when one is ready to move to the next phase in the CASVE cycle. The "control and monitoring of lower-order functions ensures that an optimal balance is met between impulsivity and compulsivity" (Peterson et al., 1991, p. 39), thereby providing a "quality control mechanism to ensure a complete, orderly, and timely progression through the CASVE cycle" (Peterson et al., 1996, p. 439).

Applying the CIP Approach

The pyramid model can be used as a framework for providing career development interventions. For example, the self-knowledge domain can be addressed through standardized and nonstandardized assessments. The occupational knowledge domain can be addressed by engaging in job-shadowing exercises and by reading about occupational biographies (as when Ronald was encouraged to conduct occupational information interviews). The five steps of the CASVE cycle can be used to teach decision-making skills, and the executing processing domain provides a framework for exploring and challenging clients' dysfunctional metacognitions.

Peterson et al. (1991) have outlined a seven-step sequence for delivering individual, group, and classroom career development interventions. Step one involves conducting an initial interview with the client. During this step, the counselor attempts to understand the context and nature of the client's career problem. The counselor develops an effective working relationship with the client by responding empathically to client statements and by using basic counseling skills (e.g., clarification, summarization, reflection of affect, immediacy, and self-disclosure).

Counselors introduce clients to the pyramid model and the CASVE cycle to clarify client concerns and to provide clients with a model for understanding the career decision-making and problem-solving processes (Sampson et al., 1992). During this step, counselors focus on questions such as "What are the client's perceptions of the extent of development in each of the domains? How does the client typically make career decisions? Which metacognitions, if any, are dysfunctional and need changing? At which phase is the client currently focused?" (Sampson et al., 1992, p. 73).

In Ronald's case, he was feeling stuck because he was not clear about the process typically used in making career decisions. He was also stuck because he believed that there were no occupational options that would be suitable for him (although he had not really engaged in any systematic exploration of occupational options). Moreover, he doubted his ability to make an effective occupational choice. Using the pyramid model to explain the decision process could provide Ronald with a sense of control and structure, thereby lessening his feeling of being "overwhelmed." Establishing an effective working relationship with Ronald and offering him a sense of hope that he could learn the skills necessary for managing his career could also help him to feel more confident and reassured that he could cope effectively with these career development tasks.

Step two involves conducting a preliminary assessment to determine the client's readiness for career decision making. The CIP approach uses the Career Thoughts Inventory (CTI) (Sampson, Peterson, Lenz, Reardon, & Saunders, 1996) to identify clients with dysfunctional career thoughts and, thereby, provide an indication of career development interventions that may be required to address the client's executive processing domain. For example, Ronald may be adhering to beliefs such as "I must be absolutely certain an occupation will be satisfying to me before I can take action," "All teachers are paid poor salaries," or "I must decide now what I want to do for the rest of my life." Adherence to such beliefs will be problematic for Ronald as he engages in career planning. Thus, these beliefs need to be challenged and restructured for him to move forward (Lewis & Gilhousen, 1981).

In step three, counselors and clients work collaboratively to define the career problem(s) and to analyze potential causes of the problem. Here, counselors communicate nonjudgmentally their perceptions of clients' gaps between a real state of career indecision and the desired or ideal state of career decidedness (Cochran, 1997). Clients respond by agreeing with counselors' perceptions or by clarifying and restating the gap they are experiencing.

In step four, counselors and clients continue to collaborate by formulating achievable career problem-solving and decision-making goals. The formulation of goals leads to the development of an individual learning plan in step five. Individual learning plans provide clients with a guide concerning what activities they need to engage in and what resources they need to use to achieve their goals. Although individual learning plans provide a mechanism for monitoring and evaluating client progress, they may also be revised as clients acquire more information about themselves and their career concerns.

Step six in the CIP approach requires clients to execute their individual learning plans. Counselors can provide support, feedback, and assistance to clients as they complete their individual learning plans. Counselors can challenge clients with dysfunctional career thoughts to revise their thinking and then take action to complete their individual learning plans. Finally, during step seven, counselors and clients conduct a summative review of client progress and then generalize new learning to other current and future career problems.

Evaluating CIP

Although research investigating CIP theory is not extensive, the number of studies based on CIP theory is growing. The development of the CTI should serve as a catalyst for CIP researchers investigating theoretical propositions related to the executive processing domain. The workbook accompanying the CTI, titled *Improving Your Career Thoughts: A Workbook for the Career Thoughts Inventory* (Sampson et al., 1996), is an excellent example of the translation of theory into practice. This more recent extension of the CIP approach builds on what one reviewer noted as the major contribution of the theory—the executive processing domain (Helwig, 1992). Brown & Lent (1996) noted that the description of the decision-making process outlined in Peterson et al. (1996) "is perhaps the clearest description of the variables involved in this process yet to emerge" (p. 521). Clemens and Milsom (2008) recommend using CIP with military families coping with transitions to new jobs in the civilian world. Hirshi and Lage (2008) used CIP as the theoretical framework for a career workshop delivered to 334 Swiss seventh-grade students. An evaluation of this workshop revealed that the students significantly increased their career decidedness, career planning, career exploration, and vocational identity. Osborn, Howard, and Leierer (2007) examined the effect of a CIP-based career development course on the dysfunctional thoughts of racially and ethnically diverse college freshmen. Using CTI scores as a springboard to discussing dysfunctional career thinking, Osborn and her associates found that students decreased their dysfunctional career thoughts as they related to career decision-making confusion, commitment anxiety, and external conflict. They also found that neither gender nor race/ethnicity was related to dysfunctional career thoughts. Ecke (2007) did find a significant relationship between a more secure attachment style, as evidenced by less anxiety and less avoidance in response to attachment issues, and lower career-thought dysfunction in a sample of adult Dutch and Belgian immigrants living in California.

Strauser, Lustig, Cogdal, and Uruk (2006) investigated whether trauma symptoms in college students relate to dysfunctional career thoughts, vocational identity, and developmental work personality. Using a sample of 131 students, they found significant relationships between higher levels of trauma (e.g., parental divorce, death of a loved one) and higher levels of dysfunctional career thoughts and lower levels of developmental work personality (i.e., the degree to which an individual has successfully completed the tasks necessary for developing a healthy work personality such as completing one's work on time in school). Among other things, this study highlights the personal-career connection and indicates that career counselors should be aware of post-traumatic stress disorder symptoms.

Strauser, Lustig, and Uruk (2004) examined career thoughts as measured by the CTI by comparing scores between college students with disabilities and students without disabilities. Strauser and his associates found significant differences between individuals with disabilities and college students without disabilities on the CTI total and subscale scores. Specifically, individuals with disabilities had more negative thoughts than their nondisabled counterparts, pointing to the possible usefulness of the CIP model when providing career interventions to university students with disabilities.

Another study conducted by Yanckak, Lease, and Strauser (2005) explored the relationship between career thoughts and vocational identity using study participants diagnosed with cognitive and physical disabilities. Yanckak et al., found significant differences between individuals with cognitive impairments as compared to those with physical disabilities in their Decision-Making Confusion and External Conflict scores on the CTI. Individuals with cognitive impairments had more dysfunctional career thoughts than individuals with physical disabilities. A study conducted by Reed, Reardon, Lenz, and Leierer (2001) examined the effectiveness of a career-planning course based on the CIP approach. Using the CTI, results of this study indicated a significant decrease in negative career thoughts from pretest to posttest. Saunders, Peterson, Sampson, and Reardon (2000) used the CTI to investigate depression and dysfunctional career thinking as components of the state of career indecision among a sample of 215 undergraduate university students. They found a significant positive correlation between dysfunctional career thoughts as measured by the CTI and career indecision and, thus, recommend using the CTI in career counseling to help identify appropriate treatment strategies for clients experiencing career indecision.

Osborn, Peterson, Sampson, and Reardon (2003) used CIP as the theoretical framework for investigating client anticipations prior to using a computer-assisted career guidance system. Clients' most frequent anticipations for computer use included increased career options, enhanced self-knowledge, and strengthened occupational knowledge. Reardon and Wright (1999) describe how the CIP approach can be used in conjunction with Holland's theory to help a 19-year-old college student become aware of negative thought patterns serving as obstacles to choosing a college major. Similarly, McLennan and Arthur (1999) describe how CIP is useful for helping women to cope effectively with structural and individual barriers in their career development.

The fact that the CIP research team (i.e., Peterson, Reardon, Lenz, and Sampson) built their theory upon a solid foundation of research in cognitive psychology, have developed clear definitions of the different dimensions of the theory, and are committed to translating theory into practice suggests a bright future for the CIP approach to career development interventions. Plus, the CIP approach appears to be robust enough to address a wide array of client concerns and client populations (e.g., college students with disabilities).

SAVICKAS' CAREER CONSTRUCTION THEORY

Career construction theory incorporates three perspectives: differential, developmental, and dynamic. It incorporates a differential perspective by addressing what different people prefer to do in their work (Savickas, 2005, 2009). The developmental perspective in career construction theory emphasizes the various ways in which people cope with career development tasks and transitions. The dynamic perspective attends to the dynamics by which people use life themes to develop meaning in their career behavior as they fit work into their lives. As Savickas noted, "career construction theory asserts that individuals construct their careers by imposing meaning on their vocational behavior and occupational experiences . . . *Career* imposes personal meaning on past memories, present experiences, and future aspirations by weaving them into a life theme that patterns the individual's work life" (2005, p. 43). Thus, career counselors using career construction theory replace an individual's assessment scores with an individual's personal stories. Assessment scores focus on the "psychology of possession" while personal stories emphasize a "psychology of use." The assumption here is that it is how you use what you possess relative to abilities, interests, values, personality, and so on, that matters relative to career behavior. A person's subjective career emerges from this active meaning-making process in which experiences are woven into a pattern that portrays a life theme. In career counseling, clients are helped to increase their awareness and understanding of the life projects embedded within their life themes and their life stories. Career construction counseling also helps clients understand the ways in which their life projects revealed in their life themes are important to them and to others.

Within career construction, career-related "traits" such as interests, abilities, values, and so on, are viewed as strategies for adapting to and connecting with the environment. Put another way, they are verbs rather than nouns (Savickas, 2005). Long-practiced traits (like playing football for Ronald) do coalesce into tested styles.

Career adaptability is the third component of career construction theory. Life themes guide personality expression in work but their expression is managed by the career adaptation process (Savickas, 2005). Transitions (e.g., from school to work, from job to job, from job to school) require adaptation, which is characterized by the following behaviors: orientation, exploration, establishment, management, and disengagement (Savickas). These behaviors form the cycle of adaptation. For example, Ronald is considering disengaging from football (his previous career goal) due to his poor performance. He is hoping to find new options to consider as he becomes reoriented to a new direction, which will subsequently involve exploring the nature of potential options, and then, if he chooses a new direction, will require him to manage the new role. Maintaining an adaptive approach to career construction involves: (a) being concerned about the future, (b) increasing personal control over the future, (c) displaying curiosity about exploring future scenarios and considering possible selves, and (d) developing the confidence to pursue identified aspirations (Savickas).

Career construction counseling involves engaging the client in the Career Style Interview (Savickas, 2005). The Career Style Interview (CSI) helps clients clarify and articulate the private meanings they attach to their career behavior. Through the use of questions eliciting client preferences for self-expression within life contexts, career construction counselors help clients remember their pasts in ways that foster the construction of possible futures (Savickas). In addition to asking clients to share three specific early life recollections, career construction counselors using the CSI ask the following questions to stimulate client consideration of their subjective career experience (i.e., meaning making process):

1. Who do you admire? Who would you like to pattern your life after?
   Who did you admire when you were growing up? Why?
   How are you like _____?
   How are you different from _____?
2. Do you read any magazines regularly? Which ones?
   What do you like about these magazines?
   Do you have any favorite television shows?
3. What do you like to do in your free time?
   What are your hobbies?
   What do you enjoy about these hobbies?
4. Do you have a favorite saying or motto?
   Tell me a saying that you remember hearing.
5. What are/were your favorite subjects in school?
   Why?
   What subjects do/did you hate?
   Why?

Responses to these questions are connected to the life themes revealed in the early life recollections to help clients clarify the life projects that guide their career behavior. Rehfuss, Cosio, and Del Corso (2011) investigated counselors' perspectives on using the CSI with clients who had career concerns. Specifically, they asked 34 counselors to describe their experiences with the CSI and to identify the benefits and challenges of the CSI. Results from this study indicated that counselors found the CSI to be a helpful resource in helping clients resolve their career concerns. Specifically, counselors thought that the CSI was useful in helping clients identify their life themes, which they then could use to make meaningful career decisions. Moreover, counselors viewed the CSI as being helpful to clients in increasing self-understanding and developing a sense as to how work could provide opportunities for meaning making. Taber, Hartung, Briddick, Briddick, and Rehfuss (2011) provide a detailed description of how the CSI can be integrated into career counseling to help clients clarify their self-concepts and make their work lives more meaningful.

Evaluating Career Construction Theory

Career construction theory has largely been the result of the work of Mark Savickas. However, Savickas and his colleagues have authored a number of articles in which the theoretical assumptions underlying career construction theory have been described and the usefulness of the Career Style Interview has been analyzed (Rehfuss, Cosio, & Del Corso, 2011; Savickas, 1997, 2005, 2009; Taber, Hartung, Briddick, Briddick, & Rehfuss, 2011). This recent trend is noteworthy and bodes well for the increased relevance of career construction theory in career counseling. More treatment outcome data and research studies directed toward theory validation are needed—especially with regard to diverse client populations. Toward this end, Savickas has formed an international research team to begin this process, and it appears that the theory is gaining greater adoption by career counselors within and beyond the United States.

HANSEN'S INTEGRATIVE LIFE PLANNING

Of all the theories discussed in Chapters 1 and 2, Hansen's integrative life planning model (ILP) (Hansen, 1997) is unique in that, rather than offering a theory that can be translated into individual counseling, Hansen contends that ILP is a new worldview for addressing career development. As such, ILP centrally addresses diversity issues related to ethnicity, race, gender, socioeconomic status, and spirituality. The "integrative" aspect of ILP relates to the emphasis on integrating the mind, body, and spirit. The "life planning" concept acknowledges, in a fashion similar to Super's (1980) life-space theory, that multiple aspects of life are interrelated. "Planning" is included in the title because, despite recent discussions about the value of planning in a time of uncertainty, it connotes a sense of personal agency in the career development process (Hansen, 2002). The ILP framework also draws upon psychology, sociology, economics, multiculturalism, and constructivism and takes a holistic approach by encouraging people to connect various aspects of life. Rather than a life-span model, ILP focuses on adult career development and is based on the following assumptions (Hansen, 2002):

1. Changes in the nature of knowledge support the addition of new ways of knowing to career development theory, research, and practice.
2. Career professionals need to help students, clients, and employees develop skills of integrative thinking—seeing connections in their lives and in their local and global communities.
3. Broader kinds of self-knowledge (beyond interests, abilities, and values) and societal knowledge (beyond occupational and educational information) are critical to an expanded view of career, including multiple roles, identities, and critical life tasks in diverse cultures.
4. Career counseling needs to focus on career professionals as change agents, helping clients to achieve more holistic lives and becoming advocates and agents for positive societal change through the choices they have and decisions they make.

Hansen (1997) uses these four broad assumptions to identify six career development tasks confronting adults today. The six tasks reflect Hansen's emphasis on social justice, social change, connectedness, diversity, and spirituality. For example, the first task is labeled as "finding work that needs doing in changing global contexts." Here Hansen suggests that adults consider focusing on work that will result in a more socially just world (e.g., preserving the environment, understanding and celebrating diversity, advocating for human rights, and exploring spirituality). Similar to early notions of "bad" work and "good" work, Hansen encourages people to identify what they can do to contribute to positive change for social and environmental justice.

The second task Hansen identifies is "weaving our lives into a meaningful whole." This task emphasizes the point that few things are more personal than a career choice (Niles & Pate, 1989). Occupational choices are intertwined with other life-role choices and must be considered both holistically and within the greater context of one's life. This task also suggests that persons must draw upon their subjective experiences in clarifying and articulating their career choices.

Hansen's third task is an extension of the second. Labeled as "connecting family and work," it emphasizes life-role integration and the importance of negotiating roles and relationships (Hansen, 2002). This task also highlights the need to examine gender-role expectations and stereotypes. ILP envisions men and women as partners in the home and in the workplace. Hansen also advocates for valuing self-sufficiency and connectedness within men and women. Although not stated in ILP, one would expect that the same notions of equity in work and in home activities would also be applied to same-sex couples.

"Valuing pluralism and inclusivity" represents the fourth task confronting adults. Hansen notes the importance of celebrating diversity and developing multicultural competencies as critical for work and nonwork activities. Valuing pluralism recognizes the importance of difference and establishes a foundation for celebrating diversity.

Hansen's fifth task relates to "managing personal transitions and organizational change." Given the constancy of change in everyday experience and developing skills, the ability to cope effectively with transition is an essential task of adult development. In fact, Hansen (2002) suggests that transition counseling may be one of the most needed skills in career counseling. Tolerating ambiguity, developing personal flexibility, and being able to draw upon a reservoir of self-awareness and social support all help to negotiate life changes successfully. Finally, incorporating both rational and logical decision-making skills with intuitive orientations that value "positive uncertainty" (Gelatt, 1989) and "planned happenstance" (Mitchell, Levin, & Krumboltz, 1999) is also important for coping effectively with transitions in a time of change, instability, and ambiguity in career development.

The sixth task in ILP is that of "exploring spirituality and life purpose." Spirituality may or may not be defined as religion. Spirituality embraces purpose, meaning, connectedness, and a sense of community. Career choices are, at their best, spiritual in that they are expressions of one's gifts and talents. Career practitioners help their clients consider spiritual issues in career decision making when they explore questions such as: "What does work mean in and for my life?" and "What do I want to mean to others through my work?" People engage in spiritually based career decision making when they examine the degree to which career options foster positive treatment of others, the environment, and themselves. The ILP approach joins Miller-Tiedeman's (1997) Lifecareer Theory and the work of Bloch and Richmond (1998) as a small but growing body of career development literature addressing the important topic of spirituality in career development. Collectively, spiritual approaches to career development emphasize common themes that can be summarized as follows:

1. Career development intertwines with human development. Life cannot be compartmentalized into "silos" of activity; thus, careers should be viewed holistically.
2. Clients should be encouraged to embrace and celebrate their life journeys, rather than judging past experiences negatively. All life experiences provide opportunities for learning and growth.
3. Maintaining an attitude of flexibility and openness fosters development as well as the opportunity to identify new opportunities for growth and learning.
4. Change should be celebrated and embraced rather than feared and avoided.
5. Career development interventions that actively and collaboratively engage the client in career counseling; incorporate intuition as well as reason in decision making; and draw upon subjective assessment activities, imagery, meditation, and positive self-affirmations also engage the spirit in the career development process.

Applying ILP

ILP suggests that career counselors help their clients to understand these six tasks, see the interrelatedness of the various tasks, and prioritize the tasks according to their needs. The specifics of how ILP is applied in career counseling are still being developed. Hansen, Hage, and Kachgal (1999) developed the Integrative Life Planning Inventory to help clients identify where they are in relation to integrative thinking and planning. The assumptions and tasks of ILP also form the basis for career development programs aimed at teaching participants holistic career planning. Currently, ILP seems most useful as a framework for teaching an approach to life planning that emphasizes connectedness, wholeness, and community.

Evaluating ILP

ILP offers a creative approach to life planning. It appears to be a very useful framework from which counselors can encourage clients to consider important life issues in their career decisions. It is one of the few models to include spirituality as an important aspect of the career development process. The topic of spirituality is growing in interest as evidenced by the fact that it was the theme of the National Career Development Association's 2004 conference ("Celebrating the Spirit in Career Development"), and ILP is at the forefront of addressing this important topic. Similar to many recent models, ILP acknowledges the importance of context in career development. Moreover, it embraces social action by encouraging clients to consider the impact of their career choices on others and on the environment. More research of ILP is needed in terms of the model's concepts as well as the ways in which the model can be applied effectively in career development interventions. It is also interesting to note that ILP has much in common with the emerging postmodern approaches to career development interventions and, in many ways, could be placed in this category.

POSTMODERN APPROACHES

Recently, attention has been given to career development theories and interventions "that depart from the positivistic scientific tradition that has dominated social and behavioral science research, in general, and most of the normative career development research, in particular" (Vondracek & Kawasaki, 1995, p. 115). The label of *postmodern* can be used to refer to those approaches (e.g., narrative, contextual, constructivist) that emphasize the importance of understanding our careers as they are lived or, to put it another way, our subjective experience of career development. Postmodernism embraces multicultural perspectives and emphasizes the belief that there is no one fixed truth but rather that we each construct our own realities and truths. In this way, postmodern views include constructivist assumptions. Postmodern approaches also emphasize personal agency in the career construction process. For example, Cochran's (1994) narrative approach contends that career development theories should "provide systematic accounts of how persons become active agents rather than patients or victims of circumstances regarding career. The aim of career counseling is to enhance agency regarding career" (p. 209).

Creating Narratives

The narrative approach represents an example of a postmodern approach that highlights personal agency in career development. Specifically, career counseling from the narrative approach emphasizes understanding and articulating the main character to be lived out in a specific career plot (Cochran, 1997). This type of articulation uses the process of composing a narrative as the primary vehicle for defining the character and plot. Howard (1989) noted that "people tell themselves stories that infuse certain parts of their lives and actions with great meaning and de-emphasize other aspects. But had any of them chosen to tell himself or herself a somewhat different story, the resulting pattern of more-meaningful and less-meaningful aspects of his or her life would have been quite different" (p. 168). By constructing personal career narratives, we can come to see our movement through life more clearly and can understand our specific decisions within a greater life context that has meaning and coherence. Thrift and Amundson (2005, p. 18) contend that "as career counselors come to grips with social justice and the growing inequities with society" they will increasingly move to narrative approaches in career counseling.

Cochran (1997) identified several ways in which narratives help people make meaning out of their life experiences. For example, he notes that narratives help to provide a sense of personal continuity across time (i.e., a beginning, middle, and end). As one becomes aware of how the past has influenced the present, one also can make decisions about the future. As Polkinghorne (1988) noted, a narrative is a "meaning structure that organizes events and human actions into a whole, thereby attributing significance to individual actions and events according to their effect on the whole." Cochran also highlighted the fact that a narrative helps give meaning to the plot of a person's story. Each story contains examples of behaviors and decisions that help to paint a portrait of who the person is relative to engaging in the world. Moreover, the plot contains story lines relative to problems encountered and how those problems either have or have not been resolved. Within each story line, there is a "moral to the story" (e.g., if I work hard and succeed, I learn that hard work pays off and am likely to continue working hard to succeed).

Career counseling from a narrative approach begins with the identification of a career problem. Career problems are defined as gaps between one's current career situation and a desired career future (Cochran, 1985, p. 145). In the narrative sense, the career problem represents the beginning, and the middle relates to the way one is to move from the beginning to an end (Cochran, 1997, p. 36). The career counseling process involves a number of "episodes" that are incorporated into counseling depending on each client's career concerns. For example, first a problem must be elaborated by the client and clarified through interactions between the client and the career counselor. Second, the counselor helps the client compose a life history to elucidate the client's career narrative. Techniques such as constructing a lifeline (Goldman, 1992), the life chapters exercise (Carlsen, 1988), the accomplishments interview (Bolles, 1998), identifying early life-role models (Watkins & Savickas, 1990), and identifying early life recollections (Watkins & Savickas, 1990) facilitate the narrative construction process. The next episode builds upon and extends the narrative by creating a future narrative. Techniques include constructing a lifeline using the life chapters exercise, using guidance material such as the Self-Directed Search (Holland, 1985), using the accomplishments interview, and using guided fantasy. Testing the future narrative against reality becomes the next episode. Through job shadowing, volunteering, gaining internships and externships, conducting occupational information interviews, and working part-time the person is able to acquire data that either support the constructed future narrative or lead to the revision of it based upon the new information the person has acquired. At this point, the person engages in making a choice that translates potentialities into actualities. To facilitate this process, clients can examine their values in light of specific career options via a career grid activity (Neimeyer, 1989), guided fantasy exercises, and life-themes identification (Watkins & Savickas, 1990). As clients crystallize a decision, they may encounter internal and external barriers or obstructions (e.g., Will I succeed? Will the option be satisfying? What will my family think?). They may also need assistance in identifying activities that provide opportunities to connect with their "new stories" constructed earlier in the career counseling process. Opportunities for making connections with new stories are labeled as *actualizations* by Cochran (1997).

Narrative approaches to describing career development and for providing career development interventions highlight the notion that "we are the stories that we live." Career counseling from this perspective provides clients with opportunities to reconstruct a coherent life story. As Peavy (1992) writes, "Stories of self and career can be used by counselor and client to consolidate present self-knowledge and to help guide forward movement into anticipated futures" (p. 219).

The life chapters exercise mentioned earlier is very useful in helping clients construct narratives and in sensitizing them to the subjective experience of career (Cochran, 1997). In this exercise, clients are encouraged to consider their lives as if they were books by dividing their life events into chapters. Clients are asked to give titles to the chapters of their past. They are also invited to identify three important lessons they have learned by living each chapter of their lives. Clients are then asked to look ahead at the rest of their lives and create chapter titles that move from the present on through to death. They are asked to identify the chapters they expect to happen and the chapters they want to make sure happen if their lives are to be complete. In processing this activity, positive chapters are restored and negative chapters are reversed in the future.

Contextualizing Career Development

Evident in our discussion thus far is the fact that postmodern approaches to career development interventions are sensitive to the immediate (e.g., family, cultural heritage, level of acculturation) and distal (e.g., economics, environmental opportunities) contextual factors influencing the meaning-making process for individuals (Blustein, 1994; Vondracek, Lerner, & Schulenberg, 1986; Young, Valach, & Collin, 1996, 2002). Postmodern approaches to career development interventions that identify ways in which contextual factors can be incorporated into the career counseling process are labeled as contextual career theories. Young, Valach, and Collin (1996) noted several assumptions pertaining to contextual career theories:

1. Acts are viewed as purposive and as being directed toward specific goals.
2. Acts are embedded in their context.
3. Change has a prominent role in career development. Because events take shape as people engage in practical action with a particular purpose, analysis and interpretation are always practical. Researchers look at action for a particular purpose.
4. Contextualism rejects a theory of truth based on the correspondence between mental representations and objective reality. (p. 480)

In their contextual theory, Young and his associates view career development as an action system that achieves social meaning through an interaction between individual intention and social context (Young & Collin, 1992). In their view, people construct their careers through action. Action can be organized according to hierarchical, sequential, and parallel dimensions (Young et al., 1996, 2002). Hierarchy relates to the prioritization of career goals into superordinate and subordinate construct categories. Sequence pertains to the sequencing or ordering of actions, and actions can be parallel in that "different actions for different goals can coexist" (1996, p. 484).

Thus, career and action are related constructs through which people make sense out of their lives and through which events in people's lives acquire meaning (Young & Valach, 1996). Of special importance are the goal-directed actions people take in the career construction process. Such actions can be viewed from three perspectives: manifest behavior (i.e., the explicit career-related behavior taken), internal processes (i.e., thoughts and feelings related to the behavior being manifested), and social meaning (i.e., the meaning of the action to self and others). These three perspectives provide a framework both for explaining career development and for explaining career development interventions. Concerning the latter, we can view client–counselor interactions as manifest behaviors; client–counselor thoughts and feelings represent internal processes concerning the behaviors being manifested; and both clients and counselors are embedded in contexts from which they make social meaning concerning the career counseling experience. Thus, career counseling represents a project involving joint action between the counselor and client. Career and action emerge as the counselor and client engage in the career counseling process (Young et al., 2002).

The perspective of manifest behavior, internal processes, and social meaning also provides a framework for the ongoing assessment process within career counseling. For example, clients can participate in career-related actions (e.g., discuss post–high school plans with parents) and identify the thoughts, feelings, and social meaning associated with the career-related action (Young et al., 2002).

Social meaning also figures prominently in the interpretive process associated with career counseling. In discussing interpretation in career counseling, Young and Valach (1996, p. 367) note several assumptions. First, "people interpret their own and others' behavior as actions." Behavior is viewed as intentional and directed toward particular goals. Second, "people interpret ongoing action as part of some superordinate process such as career." Third, "people reinterpret their present action, and possibly their career, thus establishing the relevance of career and similar constructs." Finally, "people not only interpret but also plan their behavior in terms of social meaning." Language and narrative also play an important role in interpretation. As noted earlier, language and narrative help people make sense out of their life events. They are the means by which people construct coherence and continuity out of their past, present, and goal-directed actions. Thus, Young, Valach, and Collin (2002) advise counselors to identify three important elements within a client's story: coherence, continuity, and causality. Coherent stories make sense chronologically. Continuity is revealed in goal-directed behavior. The explanation of how events occurred reveals the causality within the client's story. In focusing on these three dimensions within a client's story the client is placed in the role of active agent in the career construction process.

To help place the client's actions in context, Young and his associates propose three constructs that relate and extend the notion of action: (1) joint action, (2) project, and (3) career (Young et al., 2002). *Joint actions* are any actions that people take together (e.g., having a conversation, engaging in career counseling) and they include manifest behavior, internal processes, and social meaning. A *project* is a superordinate construct that represents goal-oriented actions (e.g., making plans to attend graduate school to pursue a master's degree in counselor education). The *project* is comprised of multiple actions necessary to achieve the goal (e.g., researching various counselor education programs, deciding to which counselor education program to apply, getting the application materials, completing and submitting the application). *Career* is also a superordinate construct that extends over a longer period of time than a project and allows people to construct connections among actions. All actions are comprised of elements (verbal and physical behaviors), functional steps (a series of contiguous behaviors), and goals (the person's general intention). Constructing narratives represents attempts at interpreting meaning in people's actions. To bring important contextual information into the career counseling process, Young and his associates recommend that career counselors use narratives to help clients reconfigure their pasts and futures to make meaningful actions possible.

Constructivist Career Counseling

A theme connecting the narrative approach of Cochran and the contextual theory of Young and his associates is that people are active organizers of their own experiences. People construct meaning through the decisions they make and the actions they take. This theme forms the basic assumption upon which Kelly (1955) developed his theory of personal constructs. Constructs represent personal theories that we develop regarding people and events; they are our perceptions of events and they include the judgments and evaluations we make about others, the world, and ourselves. We use our theories, or personal constructs, to predict future events (e.g., because I value helping others and counseling provides the opportunity to help others, if I become a counselor, then I am likely to experience occupational satisfaction). Constructs with greater predictive validity tend to be more stable than those that are not as useful in predicting events. Our constructs become refined over time, and we revise our perceptions based on life experience.

Peavy (1992) draws upon Kelly's theory in identifying four questions that are important for career counselors to consider in what he labels "constructivist career counseling":

1. How can I form a cooperative alliance with this client? (Relationship factor)
2. How can I encourage the self-helpfulness of this client? (Agency factor)
3. How can I help this client to elaborate and evaluate his or her constructions and meanings germane to this decision? (Meaning-making factor)
4. How can I help this client to reconstruct and negotiate personally meaningful and socially supportable realities? (Negotiation factor) (p. 221)

Herr and Cramer (1996) note that the questions posed by Peavy connect with Cochran's view that "agency in career, the willingness to act, to bring something about, to achieve life goals, should be the prime topic in career theory" (p. 191). This view, in turn, is consistent with Kelly's (1955) personal construct theory. Particularly useful here is Kelly's (1955) notion that personal constructs cohere to form a matrix of meaning or a system of hierarchically organized dimensions that can be adjusted to a range of events (Neimeyer, 1992, p. 164). Personal constructs evolve across time. Life transitions (e.g., marriage, divorce, having children, children leaving home) often stimulate changes in our personal constructs. These assumptions led to the development of several career counseling interventions aimed at exploring and reconstructing the client's unique matrix of meaning.

One such technique is the laddering technique (Hinkle, 1965; Neimeyer, 1992). Neimeyer described the laddering technique as a strategy for helping clients identify their more important (superordinate) and less important (subordinate) constructs. The laddering technique can be initiated in a more open fashion or it can be based on a specific dilemma confronting the client. For example, we could begin the laddering technique by asking our client, Ronald, to identify three occupations he is currently considering. Let's imagine that Ronald identified the occupations of engineer, social worker, and school administrator. We could then ask Ronald to identify any way in which two of the occupations he selected are alike, but different from, the third. Ronald might note that social workers and school administrators help people and that engineers might be helpful but only indirectly. We could then ask Ronald which he would prefer, helping people directly or indirectly. If Ronald noted that his preference was for working directly with people in a helping way, we would then ask Ronald why he preferred helping directly as opposed to indirectly. Ronald might state that it is important to him to see whether he is actually making a difference in people's lives as opposed to not knowing whether he has made a positive impact. The laddering technique would be continued with our asking Ronald why he would prefer each contrast. Laddering is completed when the elicited construct is so obvious that justification is evident and unnecessary.

A more elaborate technique for identifying personal constructs is called the *vocational reptest*. Based on Kelly's (1955) Role Construct Repertory Test, the reptest requires clients to systematically compare and contrast a set of career-related elements (e.g., occupations). This technique can be initiated in a fashion similar to the laddering technique. By considering several occupations at a time, clients identify ways in which two are similar to, but different from, the third. For example, construction worker and landscape architect are similar in that they involve working outdoors and this makes them different from the work of an accountant, which involves working indoors. Another group of three occupations is then presented to the client and the client identifies how two of the occupations are similar to each other and different from the third. The ways in which the client identifies occupations as being similar and different represent the client's personal constructs. The client's personal constructs are used to help the client evaluate occupational options. Once seven to ten personal constructs (e.g., working indoors versus working outdoors) are identified, the client provides ratings for each of the occupations along each of the constructs he or she identified (e.g., using a scale of 1, *strongly dislike*, to 10, *strongly prefer*). Neimeyer (1992) noted that "when completed, the vocational reptest provides a useful window into the unique considerations that each person brings to bear in career decision making, as well as the interrelationship among those considerations" (p. 166).

Vocational card sorts can also be used within constructivist career counseling. For example, the career counselor can provide the client with a stack of cards, each containing an occupational title. The client can be instructed to sort the cards according to occupations they would consider, those that they would not consider, and those that they are uncertain about. Each occupation in the "would consider" and "would not consider" stacks can then be discussed with regard to reasons why the client would or would not consider the occupation. As each reason is discussed, the counselor listens for, and helps the client identify, important constructs the client uses in making decisions about occupational options (e.g., being able to engage in creative self-expression, having autonomy in work, having an occupation that provides job security). The constructs can then be reviewed and summarized.

From the constructivist perspective, career counseling outcomes are considered in terms of their "fruitfulness." Fruitfulness refers to the assumption that counseling should result in a changed outlook or new perspective on some aspect of life (Peavy, 1992). Career development interventions are framed as "experiments" conducted both in-session and out-of-session that are directed toward helping clients think, feel, and act more productively in relation to their career concerns. Peavy noted that experiments can be conducted in the imagination of the client (e.g., guided fantasy), by engaging the client in critical self-reflection (e.g., laddering technique), by engaging the client in simulation or vicarious experiences (e.g., role playing or skill learning), and by engaging the client in real-world experiences (e.g., job shadowing, job interviewing).

Chaos Theory of Careers

Acknowledging the uncertainty and unpredictability of career development in the 21st century, Pryor and Bright (2011) offer a theory that responds to "new realities" such as the speed of communication, the reshaping of organizations, the speed and extent of change, the need for lifelong learning, globalization, the emergence of contingent and contractually based work, and the rapidity of technological innovation. These new realities result in career challenges that are influenced by greater complexity, more chance events, and greater change than people experienced in the last century.

According to Pryor and Bright (2011), the complexity of the factors influencing career development highlights the need to avoid traditional approaches that attempt to explain career behavior in terms of one factor influencing another factor. To illustrate this point, Pryor and Bright note research conducted by Morrison (1994), who found that study participants with similar Holland codes diverged in their career paths over time in ways that were not predictable from descriptions of their Holland types. Pryor and Bright also point to their own research regarding complexity in career development. Specifically, Bright, Pryor, Wilkenfield, and Earl (2005) found that 70% of their research participants reported that their career development was influenced by unplanned events ranging from unplanned meetings, to illness, to messages from God. Given such complexity, it is more reasonable to focus on patterns in career development rather than attempting to use stable and isolated variables to predict career outcomes. Thus, Pryor and Bright view approaches such as Savickas' Career Style Interview to be useful in career counseling. Although Pryor and Bright acknowledge that it is not possible to know fully what influences people or how they will respond in the future to the myriad influences they encounter in life, they suggest that by examining patterns across time, career counselors can help clients identify their emergent patterns of behavior.

The chaos theory of careers also highlights nonlinearity in career development. In nonlinear systems such as career behavior, small or seemingly trivial and unplanned events can have significant career implications. For example, on the day that Ron experienced his injury playing football, it had rained early in the morning. Although the sun was shining at the start of the game, the early morning rain resulted in the field being slightly slick for the game. The lack of sure footing caused Ron to slip during a rather routine run downfield. When he slipped, he also tore ligaments in his knee. Ron never returned to his pre-injury performance level and it was that lackluster performance that led him to question (and consider) his future goals. Had the game started later in the day or, better yet, had it not rained at all, Ron's future might have been very different. In this way, the chaos theory of career development resonates with Krumboltz's planned happenstance concept. In fact, the same recommendations made by Krumboltz for addressing planned happenstance in career counseling can be applied to helping clients cope successfully with nonlinearity as described in chaos theory and discussed by Pryor and Bright (2011).

Pryor and Bright (2011) also incorporate the notion from chaos theory of "attractors" and their influence in career development. They note that systems tend to function in particular ways and that these ways of functioning can be described as attractors. Specifically, Pryor and Bright identify four types of attractors that influence career behavior. Point attractors describe the tendency of a system to move toward a fixed or single point. In career terms this relates to theories that tend to encourage movement toward a single, best occupational option. Trait-factor theorists, for example, might emphasize how a client's assessment results point to the appropriateness of pursuing a particular occupational option or a narrow band of options. Pryor and Bright note that such approaches tend to disregard the role of chance and uncertainty and elevate the predictive validity of assessments in career decision making.

Pendulum attractors describe a system that "functions by regular swings between two places, points, or outcomes" (Pryor & Bright, 2011, p. 42). In career counseling this is evident when clients operate from black or white thinking, perfectionist thinking, and/or right or wrong thinking (e.g., there is only a right choice or a wrong choice). Such clients often experience career indecisiveness as they seek the perfect option that will provide for all their needs and meet all their expectations. Cognitive behavioral interventions that challenge the underlying dynamics influencing pendulum attractors can encourage clients to view options from multiple perspectives (i.e., the gray between the black or white).

Torus attractors describe a system that tends to engage in repetitive behavior over time. Psychologically speaking, torus attractors represent habitual, routine, and predictable thinking and behavior. Change is viewed as a threat. The goal is maintaining control over one's situation. Of course, achieving such control would require the elimination of change in life. Helping clients understand the inevitable failure of such a goal may encourage greater flexibility and openness to embracing the consideration of new strategies for coping with new situations (perhaps while also acknowledging the usefulness of some "old" behaviors in new situations).

Strange attractors appear to be similar to torus attractors in that they involve systems that seem to repeat themselves, yet they never exactly repeat. That is, strange attractors are similar but never identical in their repetition. Meteorologists deal with such systems on a regular basis. They attempt to predict weather by identifying the emergent patterns while also knowing that inevitable variations in such patterns make the accuracy of their predictions limited. On a larger level, however, it is possible to predict seasonal variations in weather within specific locations because there is some level of predictability to the general weather patterns. Thus, strange attractors operate on the "edge of chaos" where there is both predictability and variation, where change and chance are acknowledged realities of life. For example, we can acknowledge that career planning is important for moving in positive career directions and, at the same time, acknowledge that being open to chance events and their influence on our plans is also important.

Evaluating the Chaos Theory of Careers

The chaos theory of career development is an emerging theory that has tremendous potential for addressing the career context of the 21st century. It is a theory that readily acknowledges the impact of change, uncertainty, and complexity in the career development process. It also is a theory that, like career construction theory, connects with spiritual dimensions of career development. That is, it is a theory that is directed toward meaning making, connectedness, purpose, and transcendence in career development (Pryor & Bright, 2011, pp. 146–174). For the potential of this theory to be realized, however, more theory validation research is needed. In addition, making the theory more accessible to career practitioners and more practical for career counseling will be required for greater adoption of this theory in the future.

MyCounselingLab™

Go to Topic 6: *Systematic Planning for Career Guidance and Counseling* in the MyCounselingLab™ site (www.MyCounseling-Lab.com) for *Career Development Interventions in the 21st Century,* Fourth Edition, where you can:

- Find learning outcomes for *Systematic Planning for Career Guidance and Counseling* along with the national standards that connect to these outcomes.

- Complete Assignments and Activities that can help you more deeply understand the chapter content.
- Apply and practice your understanding of the core skills identified in the chapter with the Building Counseling Skills unit.
- Prepare yourself for professional certification with a Practice for Certification quiz.
- Connect to videos through the Video and Resource Library.

Summary

Strengths in Recent Career Theories

The emerging career development theories discussed in this chapter reflect the vitality that exists within the field. Emergent theories maintain vitality within the career field by advancing new notions for career development theory and practice. Moreover, the theories discussed in this chapter fill numerous gaps in the literature. Strengths inherent in the emerging theories include (a) the theoretical propositions espoused are often applicable to diverse client populations, (b) most emerging theories have clear links with practice, and (c) many of the emerging theories incorporate and extend the theory and research base of preexisting theories (e.g., Bandura, 1986; Kelly, 1955; Rokeach, 1973).

Need for More Attention to the Career Experiences of Diverse Populations

Despite increased attention on constructing career theories that are applicable to diverse populations, there is much more work to be done in this regard. Not surprisingly, there is the need for more extensive research in testing the theoretical propositions and the practical applications of emerging career theories. Although the emerging theories generally incorporate a stronger emphasis on culture and context in career development, the need for more research investigating the applicability of the emerging models for diverse population remains. A series of articles published in *The Career Development Quarterly* (September 2001) emphasized the need for career theorists and practitioners to pay greater attention to ways in which contextual factors (culture, gender, sexual orientation, sociopolitical events, etc.) shape career development. More than a decade later, this need still exists.

Historically, career theories and practices in North America have deemphasized the person's context. This is a serious limitation as it restricts our ability to understand a person's career development. Context provides essential data to help us understand the dynamic interactions between the person and the environment that shape a person's career. Without context all we can hope for is to describe a career (e.g., she worked as a physician specializing in oncology; he pursued a major in electrical engineering and secured a position with Florida Power and Light Company upon graduation from college; he moved from job to job with no apparent direction or focus).

Although some career theorists (most often, those in the trait-factor category) seem to ignore the influence of discrimination in career development, other theories (many in the developmental and emerging theories categories) acknowledge the fact that there is not equal access to a full range of occupational opportunities. Understanding the dynamic interaction between the individual and various levels of environments (e.g., family, school, community) in which individual development and career behavior are embedded will deepen our capacity to understand career decisions and pathways.

Clearly, placing a greater emphasis on culture and context in career theory, research, and practice will increase our sensitivity to how factors such as racism, sexism, ageism, classism, and discriminatory behavior toward persons who are gay, lesbian, transgendered, or disabled influence career development by artificially constraining the opportunity structure for millions of people. Increased understanding of these processes should lead to increased effectiveness at counteracting negative effects of environmental influences in career development. This is a goal toward which all within the profession should strive.

Theory Summary and Integration

Although some (e.g., Patton & McMahon, 1999) contend that we are moving toward career theory convergence, others view it differently. It is clear that we have experienced the emergence of a paradigm shift from theories based on logical positivism (e.g., trait-factor) to postmodern perspectives emphasizing subjectivity, perspectivity, and counselor–client collaboration in career development interventions. It also is clear that although no one theory is superior, the field is stronger because of the multiple perspectives currently espoused. For example, Super's theory provides an overarching framework for understanding career development processes; Holland's theory offers a useful vocabulary to help the counselor and client engage in the complex activity of career decision making; Roe and Gottfredson remind us that careers develop from an early age and societal influences shape our thinking about future possibilities (often in negative ways); Krumboltz, Lent, Brown, and Hackett highlight how interactions between the person and the environment create self-beliefs that affect our career decisions; Peterson, Sampson, Lenz, and Reardon offer important descriptions as to how we make career decisions; Savickas highlights how careers are constructed by integrating the subjective dimension of career development in career counseling; Hansen urges us to consider a greater context that includes spirituality and cultural influences; Pryor and Bright encourage us to embrace the "chaos" that permeates 21st-century career development; and the postmodern theorists, such as Young, remind us to never lose sight of the ways in which a person's unique life experiences provide meaning and purpose in career behavior. Each of the theories we have discussed in Chapters 2 and 3 are part of the rich tapestry that career practitioners can draw on systematically to guide their conceptualizations of their clients' career concerns and to inform their decisions regarding appropriate career interventions. Finally, we hope that future research results in even more clearly defined theoretical statements that are applicable to diverse populations and have strong connections with career development interventions.

Thus, the stage has been set for a bright future. Although learning about multiple theoretical perspectives can seem overwhelming at times, it is important to remember that these multiple perspectives also indicate the vitality that exists within the career development field.

We encourage you to not only become more familiar with the theories that we have discussed but also to engage in the task of constructing your own career development theory. Draw on extant theory and reflect on how you think careers develop. Incorporate career development research results into your reflection process. Such personal reflections will be useful to you as a counselor and may even be useful to you in your own career development!

Case Study

Emily—The Case of the Loner

Emily is a 39-year-old, slender Caucasian female who presents herself professionally and is very well groomed. She is the oldest of three children in her family. She attended a suburban community college for two years; however, she did not earn a degree. Emily is currently working as an administrative assistant, which is her first full-time job in 15 years. Emily recently left her husband of 14 years as he would not allow her to work outside of the home or to pursue further education; he felt that he should be her job. She decided to seek career counseling because she thinks she "can be more than a secretary," but she is not sure of the possibilities. She is concerned that any change she makes will stretch her financially.

Emily is currently seeking a divorce from her husband. She stated he does not want a divorce and he is encouraging her to enter counseling with him. She indicated she is "tired of being controlled" even though staying married would resolve her financial issues. She is struggling with the decision surrounding the divorce. Her family is supportive of her but does not have the resources to help her financially.

Emily is confident that her abilities surpass simply keeping house and taking care of her husband. She would like to grow as a person and feels this would be best accomplished by obtaining higher education. She is obviously struggling with her possible divorce and adjusting to the change in lifestyle. As she has not been in the workforce for a number of years, she is not very knowledgeable about the world of work.

She has expressed an interest in the creative fields and stated she has often edited videotapes for herself and her family. She would like to explore educational programs related to this field.

She is battling the negative messages she has been receiving from her husband about the meaninglessness of the position she holds. In her hobbies, she tends to take part in creative activities as well as in physically active activities.

Using one or more of the theories discussed in this chapter, describe Emily's career development. Which theory (or theories) discussed in this chapter would you use to provide Emily with career counseling? What are the limitations of these theories for Emily's situation?

Student Activities

1. Choose one theory from this chapter and write a one-page summary of how you would use this theory to describe the career development of Ronald (described in this chapter).

2. Refer to the MyCounselingLab™ Video and Resource Library and select the video entitled, "21st Century Application of Career Construction Theory with a College Student:

Dr. Mark Savickas." What are the strengths of this approach? What do you view as the limitations of this model? Consider the questions Dr. Savickas posed to his client for yourself. How would you answer them? What do your answers suggest to you about your career goals? How would you describe your life project?

3. Think about one activity in your life right now for which you have very positive outcome expectations (i.e., you expect to be successful). Then, think about one activity in your life for which you have negative outcome expectations. Consider the contrast in your feelings about these two activities. What is your interest level for participating in each of these activities?

4. Complete the values sorting exercise provided in this chapter. Identify your top five values and define them for yourself. Consider the ways in which you express your top values on a daily basis. Ask yourself whether there are ways that you can increase the degree to which you express these values. If there are, then construct

strategies for making this possibility reality.

5. After you have completed #4 above, give the values exercise to a friend. Tell your friend to first identify his or her top ten values, then their top five writing each one of his/her top five values on a separate slip of paper. Next, begin taking a value away one at a time. Each time you take a value away, be sure that your friend defines that value for her- or himself. Writing down the definition is important. Then, discuss the ways in which each of these values is manifested in the person's life. Discuss whether there are possibilities for increasing the degree to which the values can be manifested in the person's life. If there are, brainstorm strategies for making this occur.

6. Refer to the MyCounselingLab™ Video and Resource Library and select the video entitled, "21st Century Application of Holland's Theory with a College Student: Dr. Janet Lenz." In what ways does Dr. Lenz incorporate CIP theory in her work with her client? What are the advantages of integrating this theory with Holland's theory?

References

Bandura, A. (1986). *Social foundations of thought and action: A social cognitive theory.* Upper Saddle River, NJ: Prentice Hall.

Bloch, D. P., & Richmond, L. J. (1998). *Soul work: Finding the work you love, loving the work you have.* Palo Alto, CA: Davies-Black.

Blustein, D. (1994). "Who am I?" The question of self and identity in career development. In M. L. Savickas & R. W. Lent (Eds.), *Convergence in career development theories: Implications for science and practice* (pp. 139–154). Palo Alto, CA: Consulting Psychologists Press.

Bolles, R. N. (1998). *What color is your parachute?* Berkeley, CA: Ten Speed Press.

Bright, J. E. H., Pryor, R. G. L., Wilkenfield, S., & Earl, J. (2005). The role of social context and serendipitous events in career decision making.

International Journal for Educational and Vocational Guidance, 5, 19–36.

Brown, S. D., & Lent, R. W. (1996). A social cognitive framework for career choice counseling. *The Career Development Quarterly, 44,* 354–366.

Carlsen, M. B. (1988). *Making meaning: Therapeutic processes in adult development.* New York: W. W. Norton.

Chartrand, J. M., & Rose, M. L. (1996). Career interventions for at-risk populations: Incorporating social cognitive influences. *The Career Development Quarterly, 44,* 341–353.

Choi, B., Park, H., Yang, E., Less, S., & Lee, Y. (in press). Understanding career decision self-efficacy: A meta-analytic approach. *Journal of Career Development.*

Chung, Y. B. (2002). Career decision-making self-efficacy and career commitment: Gender and ethnic differences among college students. *Journal of Career Development, 28,* 277–284.

Clemens, E., & Milsom, A. (2008). Enlisted service members' transition into the civilian world of work: A cognitive information processing approach. *The Career Development Quarterly, 56,* 246–256.

Cochran, L. (1985). *Position and nature of personhood.* Westport, CT: Greenwood.

Cochran, L. (1994). What is a career problem? *The Career Development Quarterly, 42,* 204–215.

Cochran, L. (1997). *Career counseling: A narrative approach.* Thousand Oaks, CA: Sage.

Cochran, L. R. (1990). Narrative as a paradigm for career research. In K. A. Young & W. E. Borgen (Eds.), *Methodological approaches to the study of careers* (pp. 71–86). New York: Praeger.

Diegelman, N. M., & Subich, L. M. (2001). Academic and vocational interests as a function of outcome expectancies in social cognitive career theory. *Journal of Vocational Behavior, 59,* 394–405.

Ecke, Y. (2007). Attachment style and dysfunctional career thoughts: How attachment style can affect the career counseling process. *The Career Development Quarterly, 55,* 339–350.

Flores, L. Y., & O'Brien, K. M. (2002). The career development of Mexican American adolescent women: A test of social cognitive career theory. *Journal of Counseling Psychology, 49,* 14–27.

Gainor, K.A. & Lent, R.W. (1998). Social cognitive expectations and racial identity attitudes in predicting the math choice of Black college students. *Journal of Counseling Psychology, 45,* 403–413.

Gelatt, H. B. (1989). Positive uncertainty: A new decision-making framework for counseling. *Journal of Counseling Psychology, 36,* 252–256.

Gibbons, M. M., & Borders, L. D. (2010). Prospective first-generation college students: A social-cognitive perspective. *The Career Development Quarterly, 56,* 194–208.

Goldman, L. (1992). Qualitative assessment: An approach for counselors. *Journal of Counseling and Development, 70,* 616–621.

Hackett, G., & Betz, N. (1981). A self-efficacy approach to the career development of women. *Journal of Vocational Behavior, 18,* 326–329.

Hackett, G., & Byars, A. (1996). Social cognitive theory and the career development of African American women. *The Career Development Quarterly, 44,* 322–340.

Hansen, L. S. (1997). *Integrative life planning—Critical tasks for career development and changing life patterns.* San Francisco: Jossey-Bass.

Hansen, L. S. (2002). *Integrative life planning: A holistic theory for career counseling with adults.* In S. G. Niles (Ed.), *Adult career development: Concepts, issues, and practices* (3rd ed., pp. 59–76). Tulsa, OK: National Career Development Association.

Hansen, L. S., Hage, S., & Kachgal, M. (1999). *Integrative life planning inventory.* University of Minnesota, MN: Integrative Life Planning, Counseling and Student Personnel Psychology.

Helwig, A. A. (1992). Book review of career development and services. *Journal of Employment Counseling, 29,* 77–78.

Herr, E. L., & Cramer, S. H. (1996). *Career guidance and counseling through the lifespan* (5th ed.). New York: HarperCollins.

Hinkle, D. (1965). *The change of personal constructs from the viewpoint of a theory of implications.* Unpublished doctoral dissertation, Ohio State University, Columbus, Ohio.

Hirshi, A., & Lage, D. (2008). Increasing the career choice readiness of young adolescents: An evaluation study. *International Journal for Educational and Vocational Guidance, 8,* 95–110.

Holland, J. L. (1985). *Making vocational choices: A theory of vocational personalities and work environments* (2nd ed.). Upper Saddle River, NJ: Prentice Hall.

Howard, G. S. (1989). *A tale of two stories: Excursions into a narrative approach to psychology.* Notre Dame, IN: Academic.

Janis, I. L., & Mann, L. (1977). *Decision-making: A psychological analysis of conflict, choice, and commitment.* New York: Free Press.

Kelly, G. A. (1955). *A theory of personality: The psychology of personal constructs.* New York: Norton.

Lent, R. W. (2005). A social cognitive view of career development and counseling. In S. D. Brown, & R. W. Lent (Eds.), *Career development and counseling: Putting theory and research to work* (pp. 101–127). New York: Wiley.

Lent, R. W., & Brown, S. D. (1996). Social cognitive approach to career development: An overview. *The Career Development Quarterly, 44,* 310–321.

Lent, R. W., & Brown, S. D. (2002). Social cognitive career theory and adult career development. In

S. Niles (Ed.), *Adult career development: Concepts, models, and practices* (3rd ed., pp. 77–98). Tulsa, OK: National Career Development Association.

Lent, R. W., & Brown, S. D. (2006). On conceptualizing and assessing social cognitive constructs in career research: A measurement guide. *Journal of Career Assessment, 14,* 12–35.

Lent, R. W., Brown, S. D., Brenner, B., Chopra, S. B., Davis, T., Talleyrand, R., & Suthakaran, V. (2001). The role of contextual supports and barriers in the choice of math/science educational options: A test of social cognitive hypotheses. *Journal of Counseling Psychology, 48,* 474–483.

Lent, R. W., Brown, S. D., & Hackett, G. (1994). Toward a unifying social cognitive theory of career and academic interests, choice, and performance. *Journal of Vocational Behavior, 45,* 79–122.

Lent, R. W., Brown, S. D., & Hackett, G. (1996). Career development from a social cognitive perspective. In D. Brown, L. Brooks, & Associates (Eds.), *Career choice and development* (3rd ed., pp. 373–416). San Francisco: Jossey-Bass.

Lent, R. W., Brown, S. D., & Hackett, G. (2002). Social cognitive career theory. In D. Brown & Associates (Eds.), *Career choice and development* (4th ed., pp. 255–311). San Francisco: Jossey-Bass.

Lent, R. W., & Hackett, G. (1987). Career self-efficacy: Empirical status and future directions. *Journal of Vocational Behavior, 30,* 347–382.

Lewis, R. A., & Gilhousen, M. R. (1981). Myths of career development: A cognitive approach to vocational counseling. *The Personnel and Guidance Journal, 5,* 296–299.

Lindley, L. D. (2005). Perceived Barriers to Career Development in the Context of Social Cognitive Career Theory. *Journal of Career Assessment, 13,* 271–287.

McLennan, N. A., & Arthur, N. (1999). Applying the cognitive information processing approach to career problem solving and decision making to women's career development. *Journal of Employment Counseling, 36,* 82–96.

Meichenbaum, D. (1977). *Cognitive behavior modification.* New York: Plenum.

Miller-Tiedeman, A. L. (1997). The Lifecareer Process Theory: A healthier choice. In D. P. Bloch & L. J. Richmond (Eds.), *Connection between spirit and work in career development* (pp. 87–114). Palo Alto, CA: Davies-Black.

Mitchell, L. K., & Krumboltz, J. D. (1996). Krumboltz's learning theory of career choice counseling. In D. Brown, L. Brooks, & Associates (Eds.), *Career choice and development* (3rd ed., pp. 233–276). San Francisco: Jossey-Bass.

Mitchell, L. K., Levin, A. S., & Krumboltz, J. D. (1999). Planned happenstance: Constructing unexpected career opportunities. *Journal of Counseling & Development, 77,* 115–124.

Morrison, R. F. (1994). Biodata applications in career development research and practice. In G. S. Stokes, M. D. Mumford, & W. A Owens (Eds.), *Biodata handbook: Theory, research and use of biographical information in selection and performance prediction* (pp. 451–484). Palo Alto, CA: Consulting Psychologists Press.

Nauta, M. M., Kahn, J. H., Angell, J. W., & Cantarelli, E. A. (2002). Identifying the antecedent in the relation between career interests and self-efficacy: Is it one, the other, or both? *Journal of Counseling Psychology, 49,* 290–301.

Neimeyer, G. J. (1989). Personal constructs systems in vocational development and information processing. *Journal of Career Development, 16,* 83–96.

Neimeyer, G. J. (1992). Personal construct and vocational structure: A critique of poor status. In R. A. Neimeyer & G. J. Neimeyer (Eds.), *Advances in personal construct psychology* (pp. 91–120). Greenwich, CT: Jai Press.

Niles, S. G., & Pate, R. H. (1989). Competency and training issues related to the integration of career counseling and mental health counseling. *Journal of Career Development, 16,* 63–71.

Ochs, L. A., & Roessler, R. T. (2004). Predictors of career exploration and intentions: A social cognitive career theory perspective. *Rehabilitation Counseling Bulletin, 47,* 224–233.

Osborn, D. S., Howard, D. K., & Leierer, S. J. (2007). The effect of a career development course on the dysfunctional career thoughts of racially and ethnically diverse college freshmen. *The Career Development Quarterly, 55,* 365–377.

Osborn, D. S., Peterson, G. W., Sampson, J. P., Jr., & Reardon, R. C. (2003). Client anticipations about computer-assisted career guidance system outcomes. *The Career Development Quarterly, 51,* 356–367.

Patton, W., & McMahon, M. (1999). *Career development and systems theory: A new relationship.* Pacific Grove, CA: Brooks/Cole.

Patton, W., & McIlveen, P. (2009). Practice and research in career counseling and development–2008. *The Career Development Quarterly, 58,* 118–161.

Peavy, R. V. (1992). A constructivist model of training for career counselors. *Journal of Career Development, 18,* 215–228.

Peterson, G. W., Lumdsden, J. A., Sampson, J. P., Jr., Reardon, R. C., & Lenz, J. G. (2002). Using a cognitive information processing approach in career counseling with adults. In S. Niles (Ed.), *Adult career development: Concepts, models, and practices* (3rd ed., pp. 99–120). Tulsa, OK: National Career Development Association.

Peterson, G. W., Sampson, J. P., Jr., & Reardon, R. C. (1991). *Career development and services: A cognitive approach.* Pacific Grove, CA: Brooks/Cole.

Peterson, G. W., Sampson, J. P., Jr., Lenz, J. G., & Reardon, R. C. (2002). A cognitive information processing approach to career problem solving and decision making. In D. Brown & Associates (Eds.), *Career choice and development* (4th ed., pp. 312–372). San Francisco: Jossey-Bass.

Peterson, G. W., Sampson, J. P., Jr., Reardon, R. C., & Lenz, J. G. (1996). A cognitive information processing approach. In D. Brown, L. Brooks, & Associates (Eds.), *Career choice and development* (3rd ed., pp. 423–476). San Francisco: Jossey-Bass.

Polkinghorne, D. E. (1988). *Narrative knowing and the human sciences.* Albany: State University of New York Press.

Pryor, R., & Bright, J. (2011). *The chaos theory of careers: A new perspective on working in the twenty-first century.* New York: Routledge.

Reardon, R. C., & Wright, L. K. (1999). The case of Mandy: Applying Holland's theory and cognitive informational processing theory. *The Career Development Quarterly, 47,* 195–203.

Reed, C. A., Reardon, R. C., Lenz, J. G., & Leierer, S. J. (2001). A cognitive career course: From theory to practice. *The Career Development Quarterly, 50,* 158–167.

Rehfuss, M. C., Cosio, S., & Del Corso, J. (2011). Counselors' perspectives on using the career style interview with clients. *The Career Development Quarterly, 59,* 208–218.

Rogers, M. E., Creed, P. A., & Glendon, A. I. (2008). The role of personality in adolescent career planning and exploration: A social cognitive perspective. *Journal of Vocational Behavior, 73,* 132–142.

Rokeach, M. (1973). *The nature of human values.* New York: Free Press.

Sampson, J. P., Jr., Peterson, G. W., Lenz, J. G., & Reardon, R. C. (1992). A cognitive approach to career services: Translating concepts into practice. *The Career Development Quarterly, 41,* 67–74.

Sampson, J. P., Peterson, G. W., Lenz, J. G., Reardon, R. C., & Saunders, D. E. (1996). *The Career Thoughts Inventory (CTI).* Odessa, FL: Psychological Assessment Resources.

Sampson, J. P., Jr., Reardon, R. C., Peterson, G. W., & Lenz, J. G. (2004). *Career counseling and services: A cognitive information processing approach.* Pacific Grove, CA: Brooks/Cole.

Saunders, D. E., Peterson, G. W., Sampson, J. P., Jr., & Reardon, R. C. (2000). Relation of depression and dysfunctional career thinking to career indecision. *Journal of Vocational Behavior, 56,* 288–298.

Savickas, M. L. (1995). Constructivist counseling for career indecision. *The Career Development Quarterly, 43,* 363–373.

Savickas, M. L. (1997). The spirit in career counseling: Fostering self-completion through work. In D. P. Bloch & L. J. Richmond (Eds.), *Connections between spirit and work in career development* (pp. 3–25). Palo Alto, CA: Davies-Black.

Savickas, M. L. (2005). The theory and practice of career construction. In S. D. Brown & R. W. Lent (Eds.), *Career development and counseling* (pp. 42–70). Hoboken, NJ: Wiley.

Savickas, M. L. (2009). Career-style counseling. In T. J. Sweeney (Ed.), *Adlerian counseling and psychotherapy: A practitioners' approach* (5th ed., pp. 183–207). New York: Routledge.

Strauser, D. R., Lustig, D. C., Cogdal, P. A., & Uruk, A. C. (2006). Trauma symptoms: Relationship with career thoughts, vocational identity, and developmental work personality. *The Career Development Quarterly, 54,* 346–360.

Strauser, D. R., Lustig, D. C., & Uruk, A. C. (2004). Differences in career thoughts between individuals with and without disability: Do they really exist? *Journal of Applied Rehabilitation Counseling, 35,* 25–31.

Taber, B. J., Hartung, P. J., Briddick, H., Briddick, W. C., & Rehfuss, M. C. (2011). Career style interview: A contextualized approach to career counseling. *The Career Development Quarterly, 59,* 274–287.

Tang, M., Pan, W., & Newmeyer, M. D. (2008). Factors influencing high school students' career aspirations. *Professional School Counseling, 11,* 285–295.

Thrift, E. & Amundson, N. (2005). Hermeneutic-narrative approach to career counseling: An alternative to postmodernism. *Perspectives in Education, 23,* 9–21.

Vondracek, F. W., & Kawasaki, T. (1995). Toward a comprehensive framework for adult career development theory and intervention. In B. W. Walsh & S. H. Osipow (Eds.), *Handbook of vocational psychology: Theory, research, and practice* (2nd ed., pp. 111–141). Mahwah, NJ: Erlbaum.

Vondracek, F. W., Lerner, R. M., & Schulenberg, J. E. (1986). *Career development: A life-span developmental approach.* Hillsdale, NJ: Erlbaum.

Watkins, C. E., Jr., & Savickas, M. L. (1990). Psychodynamic career counseling. In W. B. Walsh & S. H. Osipow (Eds.), *Career counseling: Contemporary topics in vocational psychology* (pp. 79–116). Hillsdale, NJ: Erlbaum.

Yanckak, K. V., Lease, S. H., & Strauser, D. R. (2005). Relation of disability type and career thoughts to vocational identity. *Rehabilitation Counseling Bulletin, 48,* 130–138.

Young, R. A., & Collin, A. (Eds.). (1992). *Interpreting career: Hermeneutical studies of lives in context.* Westport, CT: Praeger.

Young, R. A., & Valach, L. (1996). Interpretation and action in career counseling. In M. L. Savickas & W. B. Walsh (Eds.), *Handbook of career counseling theory and practice.* Palo Alto, CA: Davies-Black Consulting Psychologist Press.

Young, R. A., Valach, L., & Collin, A. (1996). A contextual explanation of career. In D. Brown, L. Brooks, & Associates (Eds.), *Career choice and development* (3rd ed., pp. 477–508). San Francisco: Jossey-Bass.

Young, R. A., Valach, L., & Collin, A. (2002). A contextualist explanation of career. In D. Brown & Associates (Eds.), *Career choice and development* (4th ed., pp. 206–254). San Francisco: Jossey-Bass.

4

Providing Culturally Competent Career Development Interventions

Though the U.S. population and workforce have become increasingly diverse in culture, in addition to the globalization of economy and business trades, it is essential for career counselors and career development professionals to be multiculturally sensitive and competent. The recent multicultural counseling movement has matured from an exclusive focus on race/ethnicity to the inclusion of all cultural dimensions such as gender, gender identity, sexual orientation, disability, spirituality, religion, age, and social class. We all have multiple identities and our personalities are built on many cultural identities. To become a multiculturally competent counselor requires a lifelong commitment to self-reflection and growth. It is also important to help all people and workers become multiculturally sensitive. Such sensitivity benefits not only oppressed group members, but all people—only when everybody feels respected as a human and cultural being are we able to be free.

Y. Barry Chung
Professor and Chair, Department of Counseling
and Applied Educational Psychology and President,
National Career Development Association (2006–2007)

MyCounselingLab™

Visit the **MyCounselingLab™** site for *Career Development Interventions in the 21st Century,* Fourth Edition to enhance your understanding of chapter concepts. You'll have the opportunity to practice your skills through video- and case-based Assignments and Activities as well as Building Counseling Skills units, and to prepare for your certification exam with Practice for Certification quizzes.

Ju-Shin, a 28-year-old, first-generation Asian American (her parents were from Taiwan) presented for career counseling expressing concern about her current career choice. She was nearing completion of her doctoral degree in counseling. Initially, she planned on becoming a counselor educator. Recently, she was having second thoughts. Ju-Shin reported that, lately, her interest in counseling was fading. She also confided that she had enjoyed her research and statistics courses very much. One of her friends was enrolled in a doctoral program in educational research and Ju-Shin was now wondering if this might be a better choice for her. As she spoke, the counselor noticed that she was very anxious. As the session continued, Ju-Shin expressed a substantial amount of concern over how her parents would react if she were to switch degree programs. In fact, she seemed convinced that her parents would not approve of such a change. The more Ju-Shin discussed her concern, the more reluctant she seemed to consider changing her program of study. Yet, she also continued to note how much she seemed to enjoy her research-oriented courses.

A counselor operating from a traditional trait-factor approach and an individualistic approach to career decision making may be inclined to provide Ju-Shin with a test battery that would offer her more self-information concerning her degree of fit for research-oriented programs of studies and related occupations versus becoming a counselor educator. Once Ju-Shin had relevant information about traits such as interests, skills, and so on, the counselor would encourage her to consider how well her traits fit with the factors required for success in the occupations Ju-Shin was considering.

Although the acquisition of such information would undoubtedly be useful to Ju-Shin, there are other issues surrounding her career dilemma. Ju-Shin's cultural background is based in a group-oriented approach to career decision making, in which she is not alone. Her career decisions play out within the context of her family. It would be critical for Ju-Shin's counselor to explore this contextual factor in career counseling. Ju-Shin's counselor will need to understand how familial expectations interact with other factors (e.g., her interest in research) influencing Ju-Shin's career exploration. It would also be important for the counselor to understand the degree to which cultural stereotypes and discriminatory behavior influence Ju-Shin's views as to what might be possible for her to achieve in her career. Such interactions exist for all clients, and counselors must develop the requisite multicultural knowledge, skills, and awareness for conducting culturally appropriate career counseling.

Ju-Shin demonstrates the fact that cultural variables rest at the core of the career intervention process. To construct culturally appropriate career interventions, counselors need to embrace this fact. Counselors need to be sensitive to the tremendous cultural shifts occurring in society. During the past four decades the United States has been awash in cultural pluralism (Axelson, 1985). According to Lee and Richardson (1991), "The concept of cultural pluralism has received its impetus not only from the great economic, legislative, and civil rights struggles of the 1960s, but, more recently, from changing population demographics." Throughout the 21st century, people of color will experience significant growth in numbers while the White population will decline significantly. According to the U.S. Census Bureau (2010), the Hispanic population between 2000 and 2010 grew by 43%, totaling 50.5 million.

The Asian population also increased by 43% between 2000 and 2010, growing from 10.2 million in 2000 to 14.7 million in 2010. The Black or African American population comprised 13.6% of the total population in the United States in 2010. The White population was the only major racial group to decrease in population from 2000 to 2010, decreasing from 75% to 72% of the population in the United States across that time period. By the year 2050 it is predicted that people of color will represent the numerical majority in the United States (Worthington, Flores, & Navarro, 2005). The influx of new immigrants into the United States will also continue in large numbers (U.S. Census Bureau, 2010). Between 820,000 and 1.2 million immigrants per year entered the United States between 1996 and 2006.

Such changing population demographics provided the impetus for the development of multicultural counseling. Axelson (1985) defined *multicultural counseling* as a helping process that places the emphasis for counseling theory and practice equally on the cultural impression of both the counselor and client. Ivey, D'Andrea, Ivey, & Simek-Morgan (2009) emphasize the important role that cultural background plays in shaping a person's view of reality. Lee and Richardson (1991) suggested that:

> Counseling professionals must consider differences in language, social class, and, most importantly, culture between helper and client. These factors may be potential impediments to effective intervention, and counselors need to work to overcome the barriers such variables might produce in the helping process. (p. 3)

Changing demographics, multiple worldviews, and cultural plurality also influence the career development intervention process. Moreover, the demographic changes experienced in the United States from 2000 to 2010 will continue to shape the composition of the labor force, which increasingly reflects the cultural pluralism existing within society. The 2010–2011 edition of the *Occupational Outlook Handbook* offers projected changes in the labor force, which is comprised of those looking for work and those who are working, for the time period of 2008–2018. These projected changes indicate that among racial groups, Whites are expected to make up a decreasing share of the labor force, while Blacks, Asians, and all other groups will increase. Among ethnic groups, persons of Hispanic origin are projected to increase their share of the labor force from 14.3% to 17.6%, reflecting 33.1% growth. The male labor force is projected to grow by 7.5% from 2008 to 2018, compared with 9.0% for the female labor force. The share of workers ages 16 to 24 is expected to decrease from 14.3% in 2008 to 12.7% by 2018. The primary working-age group, those between 25 and 54 years old, is projected to decline from 67.7% of the labor force in 2008 to 63.5% by 2018. Workers aged 55 years and older, by contrast, are anticipated to increase from 18.1% to 23.9% of the labor force during the same period (Bureau of Labor Statistics, 2010, bls.gov/news.release/empsit.t06.htm).

Despite these developments, there is also ample evidence to suggest that women, people of color, persons with disabilities, gay men, lesbian women, and transgender persons continue to encounter tremendous obstacles in their career development. For example, the wage gap between sexes still plagues the American workforce. Women earn 78 cents on a dollar for every dollar a man earns in a year (Arons, 2008). The gender wage gap has extreme costs for women over the course of their careers. The average female worker loses approximately $434,000 in wages over a 40-year period as a direct result of pay inequities. Out of 23 Organization for Economic Co-operation and Development (OECD) countries, the United States has the seventh-largest gender earnings gap. The gender wage gap in the United States is 21.6%, well above the OECD average of 18.5% (OECD, 2010).

> According to the 2010 Bureau of Labor Statistics (bls.gov/news.release/empsit.nr0.htm), 16.1% of African Americans and 11.8% of Hispanics were unemployed in April of 2011. This contrasts with 8% of Whites being unemployed. Nearly 25% of all teenagers were also unemployed in April of 2011. With regard to postsecondary education, only 30% of African Americans ages 25 to 34, and less than 20% of Latinos in that age group, have an associate's degree or higher while students from the highest income families are almost eight times as likely as those from the lowest income families to earn a bachelor's degree by age 24 (Lewin, 2010).
>
> Given these statistics, it is not surprising that Daire, LaMothe, and Fuller (2007) found that African American college students tend to place greater importance on future income, future status, and making a difference in society as influences in their career decision making than do White college students. Whites tend to be employed in managerial and professional specialty occupations (occupations that tend to have job security, decent salaries, due processes in hiring and firing, etc.). Only 23% of African Americans and 15% of Hispanics are employed in such occupations as compared to 32% of all Whites (Bureau of Labor Statistics, 2010). According to Herr, Cramer, and Niles (2004) "more than half of the employed Hispanic women are either clerical workers or nontransport operatives (dressmakers, assemblers, machine operators, and so on)" (p. 277). The poverty rate of American Indian families is twice the rate (24.2%) of the general population in the United States (U.S. Bureau of Census, 2010). The unemployment rate for American Indians reached 13.6% in 2009. Moreover, occupational desegregation rates tend to be highest in occupations in which men are paid less and in which the number of workers is declining. Men are still 18.7 times more likely than women to be in higher-prestige occupations in science, math, or technology (Farmer, Rotella, Anderson, & Wardrop, 1998). African American as well as Hispanic families earn approximately 60% of the income of White, non-Hispanic families (U.S. Census Bureau, 2010).

Despite legislation aimed at protecting their rights (e.g., Public Law 93-112, the Rehabilitation Act of 1973; Public Law 94-142, the Education for All Handicapped Children Act of 1975; Public Law 95-602, the Rehabilitation, Comprehensive Services, and Developmental Disabilities Amendment of 1978; Public Law 101-476, the Education of the Handicapped Amendments of 1990; Public Law 101-336, the Americans with Disabilities Act of 1990), Americans with disabilities have fared no better. Persons with disabilities experienced an unemployment rate of 14.5% in 2011 (Bureau of Labor Statistics, 2010). The number of Americans reporting some type of disability now approaches 50 million, according to the U. S. Bureau of Census (2010). Post-secondary school employment outcomes for many young people are of concern, to put it mildly. According to the National Council on Disability (2000), 350,000 people between the ages of 18 and 25 receive social security income support (and, therefore, are not employed). Widen the age range to include all adult persons with disabilities and the data are no more positive. Two-thirds of working-age people with disabilities are unemployed, even though the majority of those persons wish to work (Fabian & Liesener, 2005).

Gay, lesbian, and bisexual individuals also experience discriminatory treatment in the labor force. Goleman (1990) suggested that the negative bias toward this group is often more intense than that directed toward any other group. Herr, Cramer, and Niles (2004, p. 278) noted that gay, lesbian, and bisexual persons are essentially barred from certain occupations and find vertical mobility blocked simply because of their sexual orientation. Despite this obvious discrimination, career development theorists and practitioners have been slow to respond (Chung, 2003; Pope & Barret, 2002).

These statistics suggest that many women, people of color, persons with disabilities, and gay/lesbian/bisexual/transgender individuals regularly experience discriminatory practices in hiring and promoting, insufficient financial resources, and a lack of role models and mentors. Thus, it may be that traditional approaches are not appropriate for assisting members of diverse groups in their career development (Sue, Arrendondo, & McDavis, 1992). If so, then career development interventions in the 21st century must be reconceptualized to more adequately meet the career development needs of the members of an increasingly diverse society (Arbona, 1990; Leong, 1986).

Tips from the Field

We are all alike and we are all different from each other. Work to understand both and to incorporate that understanding in your career interventions.

TRADITIONAL ASSUMPTIONS OF CAREER THEORIES IN THE UNITED STATES

Historically, career development theories and interventions, especially in North America, have emphasized a psychological perspective highlighting the role that intra-individual variables (e.g., motivation, internal locus of control, perseverance, ability) play in shaping one's career. Comparing career development theories in the United States with those in the United Kingdom, Watts, Super, and Kidd (1981) noted that career development theories in the United States have focused

> on the actions of individuals, while in Britain indigenous theoretical work has been more preoccupied with the constraints of social structures. . . . Thus, in the United States a dominant career-related belief is that the individual controls his or her own career destiny. Although individual control clearly plays a vital role, control is exerted within a context that varies relative to the degree to which it provides support for a person's career aspirations. Clearly, factors such as racism, sexism, socioeconomic status, ageism, and heterosexism constrain access to occupational opportunities for many people. Although theories in the United Kingdom may overemphasize social structures, theories in the United States have generally underemphasized the contextual influences shaping career development. (p. 3)

Gysbers, Heppner, and Johnston (2003) pointed out that career development interventions in the United States, having arisen out of a specific context, tend to favor five tenets reflecting a European-American perspective: (a) individualism and autonomy, (b) affluence, (c) structure of opportunity open to all, (d) the centrality of work in people's lives, and (e) the linearity, progressiveness, and rationality of the career development process. These tenets reflect specific assumptions that do not represent the contextual experiences many people encounter. Accordingly, Herr and Cramer (1996) remind us that "decision making, the development of self-identity, and life changes . . . occur within political, economic, and social conditions that influence the achievement images and belief systems on which individuals base their actions" (p. 203). Stead (2004) notes deficiencies in most extant career theories for their ethnocentrism and challenges the appropriateness of attempts at simply adapting existing theories to other cultures. He contends that from their beginnings culturally sensitive theories need to be grounded in specific cultural contexts to be relevant for those respective contexts. Young, Marshall, and Valach (2007) reinforce Stead's viewpoint by noting the variance in meaning attached to the word "career," even in English-speaking, Western industrialized countries.

Although many early theories of career development acknowledged the influence of such person-environment interactions in shaping careers, descriptions of these interactions were not developed fully. Despite these theoretical inadequacies, Leong and Brown (1995) suggest that it is premature to regard these theories as inapplicable to diverse populations, as some have concluded (e.g., Cheatham, 1990). Such a conclusion ignores the fact that "at least some concepts drawn from extant theories have found demonstrable empirical support when applied to some diverse populations" (Leong & Brown, p. 147). However, it is clear that a more diversified career counseling clientele and a heightened awareness of the important role that culture plays in career choice and career counseling highlights the need for theorists and practitioners to integrate multicultural perspectives into their theory descriptions and career interventions (Swanson, 1993).

UNIVERSAL VERSUS CULTURE-SPECIFIC MODELS

Many statements pertaining to multicultural career development interventions reflect the tension between *etic* (i.e., universal) and *emic* (i.e., culturally specific) approaches to counseling. Etic perspectives maintain that career development interventions for members of minority groups should be the same as the career development interventions used for those representing the majority. As such, proponents of etic perspectives contend that current career theories and techniques are robust enough to have universal applicability.

Emic perspectives, on the other hand, highlight the importance of designing career development interventions that are specific to the client's culture. Wohl (1995) suggests that "culturally specific approaches are psychotherapeutic methods designed to be congruent with the cultural characteristics of a particular ethnic clientele, or for problems believed to be especially prominent in a particular ethnic group" (p. 76). By extension, then, culture-specific career development theories are required to provide more comprehensive and accurate descriptions of the career development process for diverse groups.

Several authors resolve the tension between etic versus emic approaches by incorporating useful elements of both perspectives into multicultural career development theory and practice (Fischer, Jome, & Atkinson, 1998; Leong, 1993). For example, Leong focuses on similarities and differences in the career counseling process for majority and minority clients by adapting Kluckhorn and Murray's (1950) tripartite personality theory to the career counseling process. Kluckhorn and Murray contended that personality consists of universal (individuals are like all others in certain ways), group (individuals are like some others in certain ways), and individual (individuals are unique in certain ways) dimensions. Career counselors act in culturally encapsulated ways (Wrenn, 1962) when they attend to only the universal levels of their clients and ignore clients' important group, cultural, and individual dimensions. Leong & Brown (1995) argues that "effective cross-cultural counseling would consist of the appropriate shifting between dimensions as the counseling relationship develops" (p. 195).

Fischer et al. (1998) contend that researchers have focused a significant amount of attention on culturally specific (emic) counseling interventions, perhaps "at the expense of attention to common factors in multicultural counseling and research" (p. 528). Proposing a common factors perspective in multicultural counseling, Fischer and her associates suggest that "the curative properties of a given psychotherapy lie not in its theoretically unique components (e.g., insight for psychoanalytic approaches, modification of cognitions for cognitive approaches) but in components common to all psychotherapies" (pp. 529–530). Thus, Fischer and her associates identify four factors that appear to be "the universal elements of healing in all cultures" (p. 532). These factors are: (1) the therapeutic relationship, (2) shared worldview, (3) client expectations, and (4) ritual or intervention. A cornerstone of the therapeutic relationship is the establishment of trust and rapport between the counselor and client. Fischer et al. cite the strong research support indicating that the establishment of an effective therapeutic relationship is a significant predictor of therapeutic outcome.

A key aspect in establishing the therapeutic relationship is a shared worldview between the counselor and client. This common factor reflects Rogers' notion of empathic understanding, which he defined as "trying to experience the client's world as if it were your own without losing the 'as if' quality" (1957, p. 97). Fischer et al. (1998) suggest that understanding each other's worlds enables the client and counselor to establish the therapeutic relationship and sets the stage for positive expectations regarding counseling outcomes. Empathic understanding also minimizes the probability that counselors will operate on the myth of cultural uniformity, "which assumes that all individuals regardless of race, ethnicity, sex, age, and social class" have values and goals that are similar to the counselors' values and goals (Leong, 1993, p. 32). Thus, achieving this type of understanding is critical for providing effective multicultural career development interventions and requires the counselor to have adequate knowledge, skills, and awareness of the client's culture. Obviously, counselors must also be aware of their own cultural biases and assumptions within this process.

The third common factor identified by Fischer and her colleagues is client expectations. "Counselors and healers raise client expectations and gain credibility through the setting in which they conduct therapy, the training and degrees they possess, working within a shared worldview with the client, and developing a therapeutic relationship with the client" (Fischer et al., 1998, p. 538). When clients have positive expectations for their counseling experience, there is a greater likelihood that positive outcomes will occur (Torrey, 1986).

The first three common factors set the stage and are preconditions for the fourth common factor, which is ritual or intervention. Fischer et al. (1998) point out that "an intervention that is relevant and effective for one client may not be as relevant for another client, depending on the degree of relationship, shared worldview, and positive expectation" (p. 540). All of these factors are relevant to the career development intervention process, regardless of the career practitioner's theoretical orientation. Providing appropriate interventions requires career counselors to be aware of several important additional issues: ethnocentrism, acculturation, and identity development.

ETHNOCENTRISM

When counselors assume that one value system (their own) is superior and preferable to another, they engage in ethnocentric behavior that is insensitive to their clients' worldviews. Ethnocentrism can easily occur in career development interventions when counselors assume that individualistic and self-sufficient actions are preferable to collectivistic actions reflecting interdependence and group loyalty. Individualists use individual attitudes, private interests, and personal goals to guide their behavior, whereas collectivists rely on shared interests, group norms, and common goals to inform their decision making (Hartung, Speight, & Lewis, 1996). For many people the emphasis on individualism found within numerous theories of career development generated in the United States does not mesh with worldviews in which the family or group is the principal arbiter of appropriate occupational choices.

Clearly, Ju-Shin, the client presented at the beginning of the chapter, is in the process of making a career decision from a collectivistic perspective. Another illustration of this point is provided by the career counseling case of "Munier." Having recently relocated to the United States from Iraq, Munier came to the career services office during his first year in college with the concern of whether poor performance in his physics and math courses would prevent him from being able to major in chemical engineering. In the course of meeting with Munier it became obvious that, although his concerns were projected toward a college major in engineering, his interests and abilities pointed toward a program of study in a nonscience area. In fact, he had failed physics in high school and just barely passed a math course in his first semester of college. He thoroughly enjoyed literature and had performed well in classes related to this area in both high school and college. When asked to discuss his tentative decision to pursue a major in engineering, it quickly became apparent that this decision was based in a collectivistic worldview. His father had made his career plans for him.

When asked about the appropriateness of this goal, given his prior academic performance and his interests, it was clear that Munier was not going to enlarge the range of options under consideration. In this case, a counselor blindly adhering to the need for students to develop traditional, Western career development values of individual action and an internal locus of control may decide to use a counseling strategy that would challenge Munier's tendency to adhere to the wishes of others (his father in this case) rather than to make decisions based on his own sense of what was right for him. The projected treatment plan may even include assertiveness training with the goal of having Munier confront his father about his career development goals. Unfortunately, this type of counseling strategy is not sensitive to Munier's culture of origin, in which it is not uncommon for fathers to dominate the career decision making of their sons. In fact, it is a responsibility that the father takes seriously and a duty about which the child feels strongly. Any attempts at influencing the career direction of Munier would need to be sensitive to this very important cultural dynamic. Culturally diverse students such as Munier must be provided with opportunities to sort through the implications of these cultural differences for their own career development and to learn coping strategies for dealing with differences in cultural expectations. Often, as in the case of Munier, this sorting process must occur within the context of the family.

Such value conflicts illustrate the point that decision making, the development of self-identity, and life choices do not occur in a vacuum. They occur within political, economic, and social conditions that influence the achievement images and belief systems on which individuals base their actions. There are numerous instruments available that can be used to assess the worldview construct. For example, the "Scale to Assess World Views" (Ibrahim & Kahn, 1987; Ibrahim & Owens, 1992) and "The Person-in-Culture Interview" (Berg-Cross & Zoppetti, 1991) are examples of useful assessments for exploring the worldview construct.

ACCULTURATION

Although knowing that specific cultures are oriented toward individualism (e.g., European Americans) or collectivism (e.g., Asian Americans) is useful, it is also inappropriate to apply this knowledge to clients in a stereotypical fashion (e.g., "all European Americans are individualistic," "all Asian Americans are collectivistic"). Thus, another important variable to assess in understanding the client's worldview is that of acculturation. Acculturation can be defined as "the process of adopting the cultural traits or social patterns of another group" (Stein, 1975, p. 10). Results of acculturation research conducted in the United States have indicated that English-language proficiency is one of the best measures of acculturation (Fouad, 1993). However, acculturation is a complex and multifaceted process.

Early models of acculturation (e.g., Park & Burgess, 1921) were based on assumptions that reflected an "either/or" perspective toward acculturation (e.g., one either accepted the "new" culture and rejected the "old," or one rejected the "new" and maintained acceptance of the "old" culture). Inherent in such models is the notion of the *marginal person* (Park, 1928). The marginal person is someone who is psychologically "caught" between two cultures. Marginal persons hold negative views toward both their own culture and the host culture, such as when a Chinese American woman is unwilling to give unquestioned obedience to the traditional values of her Chinese parents, but also finds it difficult to accept many of the values inherent in a European American culture associated with racist attitudes and behaviors (Leong & Brown, 1995). Such instances often result in the experience of an identity crisis characterized by chronic restlessness, self-consciousness, and feelings of inferiority (Atkinson, Morten, & Sue, 1993).

More recent models of acculturation, however, reflect a bicultural perspective toward acculturation. Such models embrace the notion that individuals can be highly acculturated to multiple cultures—a sort of "both/and" approach versus the earlier "either/or" models. Atkinson et al. (1993) note that the bicultural person and the marginal person respond differently to their socialization in two cultures. The marginal person "feels caught between the conflicting values of two cultures and consequently feels little commitment to either" (Atkinson et al., p. 23). In contrast, the bicultural person "feels committed to both cultures and selectively embraces the positive aspects of each culture" (Atkinson et al., p. 23). Thus, the client's level of acculturation is an important within-group variable that must be addressed to provide appropriate career interventions.

It is important that counselors do not assume that the client's level of acculturation is at the same level as the client's family. Differences in this regard are important to address in the career development intervention process—especially for young people attempting to crystallize initial occupational preferences. Grieger and Ponterotto (1995) noted that it is not uncommon for first-generation, U.S. college students to experience cultural or bicultural strain, and consequently conflict when their families' level of acculturation is at variance with their own. This could have been the case with Munier had he been oriented to more Western notions concerning the career decision-making process rather than the values inherent in his culture of origin.

Numerous factors contribute to the degree to which individuals experience acculturative change. For example, Padilla (1980) noted that language familiarity and usage, cultural heritage, ethnicity, ethnic pride and identity, interethnic interactions, and interethnic distance influence acculturative change. Each of these factors clearly influences people differently, in both degree and kind. Sue and Sue (1990) pointed out that even small variations in the influence of these variables can have powerful effects on the career development intervention process. Such variability reinforces the important notion that general statements about cultural groups must not be applied uniformly (cultural uniformity myth). These general statements (e.g., White Americans tend to be individualistic, Asian Americans tend to be collectivistic) must be tempered by understanding how factors such as those identified by Padilla influence the individual's goals, career behavior, and career decision making.

IDENTITY DEVELOPMENT MODELS

The factors discussed by Padilla (1980) influence the client's level of identity development. Understanding the client's stage of identity development is essential for providing appropriate career development interventions.

Racial Identity Models

Models of racial identity help us understand that the status of racial identity (for both counselors and clients) can influence the career development intervention process at several levels. For example, Atkinson, Morten, and Sue (1989, 1993) describe five stages of racial identity development, each with corresponding counseling implications: (a) conformity, (b) dissonance, (c) resistance and immersion, (d) introspection, and (e) synergy.

Individuals in the *conformity* stage adhere to the dominant culture's value system, including its perception of racial/ethnic minorities. Their self-perceptions, as well as their perceptions of others, are viewed through the lens of the dominant culture. They tend to deny the existence of racism and discriminatory treatment on the part of the dominant culture and have a strong desire to "assimilate and acculturate" (Atkinson et al., 1993, p. 29). Moreover, their attitudes toward members of their own group may be very negative. In other words, individuals in the conformity stage may experience feelings of racial self-hatred as a result of cultural racism. Because of their strong identification with the dominant culture, individuals in the conformity stage may express a preference for a career counselor from the dominant culture. In the career development intervention process, they may display a high level of compliance and a need to please the counselor. Atkinson et al. (1993) suggest that these clients are likely to present career concerns that are most amenable to career development interventions focused on problem-solving approaches.

Individuals often move gradually into the *dissonance* stage, but the occurrence of significant events can serve as catalysts for propelling a person into the dissonance stage. In either scenario, the process of movement into the dissonance stage typically occurs when the individual in the conformist stage encounters a person or situation that runs counter to conformist-stage beliefs (for example, when an Asian American in the conformist stage, and thus adhering to negative stereotypes regarding the Asian culture, encounters a person who expresses pride in her Asian heritage, or when an African American in the conformist stage experiences racism on a personal level). In such instances, information is acquired that suggests alternative views toward the culture of origin (e.g., that there are positive aspects in cultural traditions, values, and customs) and the dominant culture (e.g., certain behaviors and practices in the dominant culture are discriminatory). Such information causes denial to break down and opens a window to further identity development. Specifically, individuals moving from conformity to dissonance may increasingly engage in self-exploration regarding self-concepts, identity, self-esteem, and group affiliation (Atkinson et al., 1989). Career development practitioners working with individuals in the dissonance stage need to have a thorough understanding of the individual's culture of origin.

Individuals adhering to beliefs and attitudes reflecting Atkinson et al.'s (1989) third stage of racial identity development, *resistance and immersion*, tend to reject the views and values of the dominant culture. They express a complete endorsement of the views and values of their culture of origin. Additionally, their resolution of the confusion experienced in the dissonance stage often leads to intense anger as they become more aware of racism and how it has impacted their lives. Sue and Sue (1990) note that as individuals begin to question their feelings of cultural shame, they often experience guilt and anger for having "sold out in the past and contributed to his/her own group's oppression, and anger at having been oppressed and 'brainwashed' by the forces in the dominant society" (cited in Atkinson et al., 1993, p. 31). Individuals in this stage often view oppression as the primary source of their career development concerns. Atkinson et al. suggest that individuals in this stage tend not to seek counseling, but if they do it is likely to be with an ethnically similar counselor and for more crisis-like concerns. Individuals in the resistance and immersion stage may also prefer group career counseling that is action-oriented and directed toward challenging racism. Sue and Sue point out that counselors, regardless of their degree of similarity to their clients, will be challenged concerning their own racism and role in society by clients in the resistance and immersion stage.

As individuals begin to experience discomfort with the rigidly held beliefs characterizing the resistance and immersion stage (e.g., "all Whites are bad") they begin to focus on greater individual autonomy. That is, as they move into the *introspection* stage, they begin to entertain the notion that perhaps not everything in the dominant culture is negative. Instead of holding on to blind adherence to positive or negative views toward cultural systems, there is a greater need to examine the merits of any particular cultural system on a more personal level. This notion emerges as a greater sense of security is experienced with one's own racial identity. As the individual becomes more autonomous, a more personal value system is developed. Atkinson et al. (1993) suggest that the emerging need for personal freedom in the face of a preponderant identification with their culture of origin often leads individuals to seek counseling to sort through the growing tension created by these conflicting dynamics. In such instances, career counselors who are similar to clients in race and ethnicity are often preferred; however, counselors from other cultures may be accepted if they share an appreciation for the client's cultural dilemma. Atkinson et al. suggest an approach that emphasizes self-exploration and decision making when working with clients in the introspection stage.

The final stage of the Atkinson et al. (1989) model is labeled as *synergistic articulation and awareness*. Individuals in this stage objectively examine the cultural values of their own group as well as those espoused by the dominant group. They accept or reject cultural values based on their experiences in earlier stages of identity development. They experience a genuine desire to eliminate all forms of oppression in society. Consequently, individuals in the synergistic stage tend to experience a sense of self-fulfillment regarding their cultural identity. Atkinson et al. suggest that because clients in this stage have developed "the internal skills and knowledge necessary to exercise a desired level of personal freedom . . . attitudinal similarity between the client and counselor becomes a more important determinant of counseling success than membership-group similarity" (1989, p. 36).

The model developed by Atkinson and his colleagues has similarities with Nigrescence theory of Black identity development first articulated by Cross (1971) in the early 1970s and then revised in 1995. Cross notes that Nigrescence theory essentially describes a resocializing experience that Cross (1995) describes as "the transformation of a preexisting identity (a non-Afrocentric identity) into one that is Afrocentric" (p. 97). The first stage in the Cross model is labeled as the *pre-encounter* stage. In this stage, persons often place values in things other than in their Blackness (e.g., religious beliefs, occupation). Some individuals, however, adhere to anti-Black attitudes reflected in hatred for other Blacks. Persons in the pre-encounter stage often favor Eurocentric cultural perspectives.

The *encounter* stage is the second stage in the Cross model. Cross (1995) notes that the encounter stage in the Nigrescence process "pinpoints circumstance and events that are likely to induce identity metamorphosis" (p. 104). Rather than a single event, the encounter stage more often involves a series of episodes that move the person toward Nigrescence over time. These episodes create dissonance as the person discovers that there is another level of "Blackness" to which he or she should aspire. This realization tends to be accompanied by powerful emotional experiences (e.g., guilt, intense anger toward Whites). These experiences often create the opportunity for a more Afrocentric person to emerge.

The third stage in the Cross model is a transition stage labeled as *immersion-emersion*. Immersion reflects the process of immersing oneself in the "world of Blackness" (Cross, 1995, p. 107). The strong emotions emerging during the encounter stage provide the driving force for this intense immersion experience. Eventually, the person emerges from the emotionality of the immersion period and experiences a leveling off and greater control of his or her emotions. The new identity begins to be internalized.

The fourth stage in the Cross model is *internalization*. In this stage, the person ascribes high salience to his or her Blackness. Cross suggests:

> The internalized identity seems to perform three dynamic functions in the everyday life of a person: (a) to defend and protect a person from psychological insults that stem from having to live in a racist society, (b) to provide a sense of belonging and social anchorage, and (c) to provide a foundation or point of departure for carrying out transactions with people, cultures, and human situations beyond the world of Blackness. (p. 113)

The final stage is labeled as *internalization-commitment*. The main difference between blacks in the internalization or internalization-commitment stages is that in the latter there is a commitment to Black affairs that is expressed over an extended period of time. Future research in the Cross model will focus on fostering a more differentiated understanding of the internalization-commitment stage.

Cross and Strauss (1998) identified three functions of Black identity that describe how cultural identity statuses can help African Americans adapt to their environment: bonding, buffering, and bridging. Career counselors and their African American clients can clarify how clients' identity statuses function to support their affiliation with Black people (bonding) and non-Black people (bridging), and protect them from discriminatory encounters (buffering).

Gender Identity Models

Gender relates to differences in masculinity and femininity. Individual and societal expectations for men and women may differ across cultures, but we are all influenced by gender and gender expectations. Having a clear understanding of the influence of gender in career development is critical to providing appropriate career development interventions. Sex-role socialization exerts a powerful influence on girls and boys early in life (Gottfredson, 1981, 2002; Hageman & Gladding, 1983).

Stereotypically, this influence reinforces competition and skill mastery in boys and relationships and connectedness in girls (Gilligan, 1982). As men and women enter the workforce, sex-role socialization continues as women are often confronted with discrimination in selection and promotion practices. Such practices not only limit the opportunity for women to advance in the workplace, but also limit opportunities to receive mentoring because women are excluded from the informal social networks often used by men to advance in their occupations. Greater than 90% of workers employed as secretaries, dental hygienists, preschool and elementary school teachers, and speech therapists are women (Bureau of Labor Statistics, 2010). Nearly the opposite is true with regard to women working in engineering and other science-related occupations.

The influence of socialization is not felt only by women, however. Men are expected to achieve and to be ambitious in their occupational pursuits. Many consider those men who are striving to achieve a balance in their life roles as lacking in ambition and the desire to work hard to achieve success. Moreover, men employed in occupations typically populated by women (e.g., men working as day care providers, nurses, or clerical workers) are often viewed as overly feminine. Many men who place a high value on family involvement and career achievement experience increased rates of depression as they struggle to fulfill roles in both of these life domains (Lease, 2003).

Differential socialization of the sexes has led to their unequal representation within occupations. As Herr, Cramer, and Niles (2004) have written, "The fact that many occupations are sex-traditional simply perpetuates sex-role stereotypes, sustaining the division of labor as a self-fulfilling prophecy" (p. 260). Such sex-role stereotyping occurs beyond the life role of the worker. In a review of recent research related to life-role salience, Niles and Goodnough (1996) noted the significant influence of societal expectations on life-role participation. For example, it is a consistent finding that women place greater importance on the home and family than do men. It is also evident that those women who place importance both on work and on home and family are at risk for experiencing role conflict. For male-female couples, this conflict is exacerbated by the fact that men consistently report lower participation in the home and family role when compared with women. In this regard, it is important that men identify ways in which they can participate in activities within the home and family role that will allow them to express important values in this life role. Given the centrality of work in male identity, the exploration of fears and resistance to committing more time to home and family must often be addressed within the career development intervention process. Cook (1994) noted that in terms of life-role participation, "behaving differently may seem to be a practical option but it may feel like a gender role violation, or alternatively, a personal affirmation that had not been considered because of its novelty" (p. 90). To be clear, we are not suggesting that increased participation in home and family on the part of men will eliminate work-home role conflict; rather, a more likely outcome may be that this burden will be more equally shared.

It is also apparent from the research reviewed by Niles and Goodnough (1996) that women tend to rely on work to provide them with an important network for social support. It is important, therefore, that career counselors examine the degree to which their female clients experience a lack of social support when their participation in work is reduced. When social support is lacking, strategies for maintaining a network of support can be identified. Thus, it is evident that the construct of gender must be thoroughly integrated into the career development intervention process.

To help achieve the goal of integrating gender in the career development intervention process, Gysbers et al. (2003) recommend using gender-related identity development models. For example, they cite a feminist identity development model proposed by Downing and Roush (1985). This model consists of five stages: (a) Stage 1: passive acceptance, (b) Stage 2: revelation, (c) Stage 3: embeddedness-emancipation, (d) Stage 4: synthesis, and (e) Stage 5: active commitment.

Stage 1 involves the passive acceptance of sexism and discrimination. There is an implicit, if not explicit, acceptance of sex-traditional gender roles. Stage 2 occurs when a life event exposes oppression of women in a way that is not able to be denied (e.g., a woman may directly experience discrimination in job hiring or promotion). Stage 3 is characterized by the perception that men possess only negative traits (e.g., men are not trustworthy, all men treat women unfairly) and women possess only positive traits. There is a strong desire to separate from men and bond only with other women. All men are viewed as oppressors and all women are viewed as victims. In Stage 4, women view men as individuals rather than automatically considering all men to be members of an oppressive group. Women are also evaluated on an individual basis. The influence of internal and external factors is recognized in the behavior of both sexes. Finally, individuals in Stage 5 become actively involved in managing their career development and in changing oppressive environmental influences.

Oppressive environmental influences restricting the career development of women occur in the home, school, community, and workplace. Stereotypes are perpetuated pervasively in books, movies, television shows, and magazines. These stereotypes often result in women encountering issues such as the "glass ceiling" (i.e., the barring of women from upper levels of administration and leadership), a lack of available mentors, discrimination in hiring, sexual harassment, inadequate and unaffordable child-care options, and a general lack of support for women aspiring to nontraditional occupations. Gysbers, Heppner, and Johnston (2003) contend that "understanding feminist identity development may help us learn a great deal more about our clients' reactions to the gendered environment. For example, a woman whose attitudes and beliefs are at Stage 1 may either be unaware of, or actually accepting of, sex bias, whereas a client in the middle stages may prefer a female counselor and may benefit from processing the anger she feels about sexism" (p. 95).

To address inadequacies in career theories as they relate to the career development of women, Cook, Heppner, and O'Brien (2002) propose using an ecological perspective to help illuminate the dynamic interaction between the person and the environment. Cook and her associates suggest that an ecological perspective is particularly useful in addressing the White, male, and Western experiences and worldviews implicit in career counseling models. They note that an ecological perspective encourages greater sensitivity to ways in which environmental factors do not support the career development of women. Specifically, Cook et al. note the need for career counselors to address the following assumptions that are implicit in career development models: (a) the separation of work and family roles in people's lives, (b) the emphasis on individualism and autonomy, (c) the view that work is the central activity in people's lives, (d) the notion that career development is a linear and rational process, and (e) the White, male bias existing in the occupational opportunity structure. Additionally, Cook and her colleagues emphasize the need for career counselors to address ways in which female clients experience the macrosystem imperatives concerning caring for others (i.e., how the client assigns importance to the needs of significant others and family members in her career development); how women might be able to influence their microsystems (e.g., the workplace) through learning or refining negotiation skills to enable them to ask for what they need (e.g., more flexible work hours, salary increases); how to identify and access quality child care; empowering women to handle sexual harassment in the workplace, and, therefore, lessen the likelihood of victimization; and helping women to access mentors. Of course, each of these issues provides opportunities for macrosystem (e.g., advocating for equitable workplace policies and treatment) and microsystem (e.g., within the career counseling relationship) interventions. Focusing on the career development experience of young women, Frome, Alfeld, Eccles, and Barber (2006) investigated why some young women who espouse occupational aspirations within male-dominated fields during adolescence relinquish these aspirations by the time they attain young adulthood. Their findings from a longitudinal data set indicate that the desire for a flexible job, the high time demands of an occupation, and the low intrinsic valuing of physical science predicted shifting occupational aspirations out of male-dominated fields. Concern for balancing family and career combined with a lower value for science-related domains (and perhaps a lack of societal and/or familial support) continue to influence women away from occupations in traditionally male-dominated fields, where, in fact, their abilities and goals may reside. Relatedly, Louis (2006) shared her personal experience as a scientist and mother. She contends that the confidence mothers have in their careers is correlated with the quality of their children's care and challenges employers to provide the necessary infrastructure that scientist-mothers need to succeed.

Integrating gender into the career development intervention process is important in working with men as well. Men are socialized to value power, competition, action, strength, logic, and achievement (O'Neil, 1982). They are taught to avoid emotional intimacy and to fear femininity (Skovholt, 1990). O'Neil contended that this type of socialization process results in men being restricted in self-disclosure and in experiencing various physical and emotional problems. The push toward achievement and success leads many men to overemphasize work activity and to minimize their activity in the home and family (Niles & Goodnough, 1996). Many men realize too late in life that they have frequently missed opportunities to connect more meaningfully with their partners and/or children. Providing men with opportunities (via individual and/or group career counseling) to explore how the socialization process influences their career behavior, to learn how to express their feelings, to learn how to manage and reduce stress, and to identify strategies for participating more fully in life roles beyond work are important components of career development interventions for this population.

Understanding the identity development status of men can help career development practitioners provide appropriate career development interventions. In this respect, it can be argued that a model of identity development similar to the one offered by Downing and Roush (1985) could also be applied to men. For example, a man whose attitudes and beliefs are at Stage 1 (i.e., passive acceptance) may be unaware of his acceptance of sex bias in his career behavior, whereas a client in the middle stages may prefer a male counselor and may benefit from processing the anger he feels about pressure to compete, achieve, and succeed at work. Men at Stage 5 (active commitment) may find male support groups helpful in maintaining behaviors that do not coincide with sex-role stereotyping (e.g., spending more time in nurturing activities related to the home and family role). Helping men to understand the importance of actively engaging in life roles beyond work and supporting them in these involvements (e.g., by offering support groups) may empower men to move toward a less constricted range of life-role involvements. This outcome benefits men, women, and children.

Lesbian/Gay/Bisexual/Transgender/Questioning Identity Models

There has been little research in the career development of lesbian, gay, bisexual, transgender, and questioning people (LGBTQ). Because each of these groups experiences oppression, Morgan and Brown (1991) suggested using minority career development theories to describe the career development of experiences of persons who are LGBTQ. Although there is undoubtedly significant overlap due to oppressive environmental conditions, this suggestion offers, at best, a temporary solution to the lack of theory and research pertaining to these populations. However, as with racial and gender identity, the assessment of identity development levels of LGBTQ clients represents a crucial element in the career counseling process (Chung, 2003; Datti, 2009; Morgan & Brown, 1991; Paul, 2008; Pepper & Lorah, 2008; Pope, 1995). When working with LGBTQ clients, Orzek (1992) noted that counselors must understand the meaning that their clients attach to their sexual identity to construct career development interventions that mesh with their clients' stages of identity development.

According to Cass (1979), LGBTQ persons encounter six stages of identity development: (a) confusion, (b) comparison, (c) tolerance, (d) acceptance, (e) pride, and (f) synthesis. The stages in the Cass model parallel those in racial identity models. The Cass model proposes that, as progression is made through the six stages, LGBTQ persons experience an enhanced sense of self-acceptance and self-esteem; they become increasingly empowered to form a stronger community with other gay, lesbian, and bisexual individuals; they feel more comfortable in disclosing their sexual orientation; and they experience more congruence between their feelings and behaviors. Sophie (1986) proposed a four-stage model of lesbian identity development. The four stages consisted of:

1. Self-awareness of LGBTQ feelings without disclosing those feelings to others
2. Testing and exploration of emerging LGBTQ identity with limited disclosure to straight persons
3. Identity acceptance and preference for gay social interactions
4. Identity integration with movement from a dichotomous worldview to a more integrated worldview

Chapman and Brannock (1987) developed a five-stage model of lesbian identity development. Fassinger (1995, p. 151) described this model as follows:

1. Same-sex orientation, characterized by feeling different about other girls and women, but lacking a name for those feelings
2. Incongruence, social isolation, and confusion about heterosexual dating

3. Self-questioning and exploration, involving strong bonds with or attraction to other girls and women, and possible exploration of homosexuality
4. Identification, characterized by thinking or feeling "I am a lesbian"
5. Choice of lifestyle, characterized by a decision to seek women as long-term mates, or maintaining a lesbian orientation without choosing women as long-term mates

Chung (2003) conducted a SWOT (strengths, weaknesses, opportunities, and threats) analysis of the literature related to career counseling with LGBTQ persons. He identified several strengths within the existing literature. For example, Chung noted that recently numerous researchers have engaged in studying the career behavior of LGBTQ persons through the application of existing career theories (e.g., Holland, Super, and social cognitive career theory [SCCT]). Chung also noted the important contributions of researchers, such as Fassinger (1995) and Prince (1995), who have applied lesbian identity development and gay male identity development models, respectively, to career behavior. A third recent and important development within the literature noted by Chung has been the more focused attention given to career issues experienced by LGBTQ persons (e.g., sexual identity disclosure and management, work discrimination, and discrimination coping strategies). Future research is needed that integrates the latter body of research into theoretical models. In addition to the need for more theory-based research in this area, Chung calls for researchers to engage in more programmatic research efforts to advance understanding of the career development of LGBTQ persons. Finally, Chung highlights the fact that research related to the career development of lesbian and bisexual persons lags behind research efforts focused on gay men; thus, there is the important need for additional research in these areas in particular.

More recently, Chung, Williams, and Dispenza (2009) investigated the validity of Chung's (2001) work discrimination and coping strategy models for sexual minorities. Chung's Work Discrimination model describes work discrimination using three dimensions: (a) formal versus informal, (b) perceived versus real, and (c) potential versus encountered. Formal discrimination refers to official policies that affect an employee's employment status (e.g., being fired, promoted). Informal discrimination refers to the existence of a hostile workplace. Perceived discrimination refers to one's perceptions that behaviors are discriminatory. Real discrimination is based on actual experiences. Potential discrimination refers to possible discrimination that would occur should a person's sexual identity become known. "Encountered discrimination involves discriminatory acts that the person experiences. Collectively, these three dimensions ($2 \times 2 \times 2$) describe eight types of work discrimination (e.g., perceived-potential-formal discrimination, real-encountered-informal discrimination)" (Chung, Williams, & Dispenza, p. 163).

The second dimension of Chung's model is the coping strategy framework. The first part of this framework involves the Vocational Choice model. Three vocational choice strategies are identified in this model. The first, self-employment, involves being one's own boss in order to avoid a discriminatory workplace. The second, job tracking, involves assessing whether an occupation and/or particular position is welcoming to sexual minorities. The third, risk taking, involves choosing a vocational option knowing that there is the risk for encountering discrimination. The second dimension of the coping strategy framework is the Identity Management model. This refers to "how a person decides to manage disclosure of information about his or her sexual identity for the purpose of dealing with potential discrimination" (Chung, Williams, & Dispenza, 2009, p. 163). Strategies for identity management range from acting (pretending to be straight) to being explicitly out as a sexual minority.

Chung's third coping strategy model is Discrimination Management, which involves how a person responds to discrimination when it is encountered. Strategies here include: quitting, remaining silent, drawing upon social support, and confronting the discrimination directly. The Vocational Choice and Identity Management models deal with formal and informal potential discrimination. Discrimination Management focuses on responding to formal and informal discrimination. Coping strategies are selected based on the discrimination encountered.

Chung, Williams, and Dispenza (2009, p. 168) offer three important recommendations for career counselors working with clients who are sexual minorities. Specifically, they note that it is important to help clients understand that discrimination can be formal and informal regardless of nondiscrimination policies. Chung and his associates also suggest that it is important to help clients achieve realistic and accurate perceptions regarding discrimination and that they develop the capacity to accurately assess potential and encountered discrimination. Career counselors can help clients explore various options for coping with workplace discrimination using the strategies that Chung (2001) identifies. While engaging in such exploration with a client, it is very important that career counselors remain sensitive to the client's pace of identity development and cultural context. That is, career counselors should not push clients toward more self-affirming and assertive coping strategies if they are not ready for such strategies (Chung, Williams, & Dispenza).

Datti (2009) provides an example of how social learning theory can be used in career counseling with lesbian, gay, bisexual, transgender, and questioning young adults. Datti stresses the importance of including in initial assessments topics that adequately address issues that are significant to the career development of LGBTQ clients. For example, career counselors can help LGBTQ clients consider topics such as their perceived importance of separating personal and professional roles, their comfort in working with a variety of individuals, their interest in working for organizations that have tolerance and discrimination policies, their comfort level with disclosure of their sexual orientation, and whether they have developed a social support network. Assessing these factors can provide information about client attitudes as well as whether clients have developed career-related task-approach skills that are important for LGBTQ clients in managing their careers effectively.

Pope and Barret (2002) also note the need for more research related to the career development experiences of persons who are gay, lesbian, bisexual, or transgender. Using the extant literature, Pope and Barret identify several intervention strategies for career counselors working with gay and lesbian clients. For example, as a first step for career counselors, Pope and Barret stress the importance of counselors taking a personal inventory of ways in which subtle or unconscious biases may influence career counseling (e.g., when a heterosexually oriented career counselor attempts to move a young man toward becoming more masculine in his behaviors). Pope and Barret also stress the importance of becoming more familiar with gay and lesbian culture (e.g., by attending workshops, reading relevant literature, participating in lesbian/gay culture). They note the ethical necessity for career counselors who cannot be gay/lesbian affirmative to refer clients to a career counselor who has experience with sexual minorities and can work with clients in a more affirming manner. With regard to "client-focused" career interventions, Pope and Barret highlight helping clients to cope effectively with issues such as "coming out," dealing with workplace discrimination, negotiating dual-career couples' concerns (e.g., benefits issues, relocation issues), and the selection/use of assessment instruments. In addition to client-focused interventions, Pope and Barret discuss program-focused interventions. Recommended interventions in this category include: sharing information on existing gay/lesbian community resources, offering special programming such as talks by gay/lesbian professionals, arranging career shadowing opportunities with gay/lesbian workers, maintaining a list of "out" gay/lesbian individuals who are available for information interviews, facilitating experiential opportunities (e.g., internships, externships) with gay/lesbian owned or operated businesses, and establishing mentoring programs with gay/lesbian mentors. Finally, Pope and Barret stress the importance of career counselors engaging in advocacy or social action interventions. For example, positive advocacy for gay and lesbian clients could include lobbying for the inclusion of sexual orientation in nondiscrimination policies of local employers.

Persons with Disabilities

Persons with disabilities represent another group that commonly experiences discrimination in career development. "Individuals with disabilities lag behind those without disabilities in virtually every indicator of economic activity" (Ettinger, 1996, p. 239). For example, only 31% of persons with disabilities who were also college graduates were employed in 2009 (compared with 81% of those who were not disabled and possessed only high school degrees) (Innovative Placements, 2010). The average annual income for a person with disabilities is about $33,000 compared to $44,269 for persons without disabilities. Despite these facts, career development researchers pay little attention to the career experiences of persons with disabilities. For example, an examination of the last ten reviews of the literature contained in the December issue of *The Career Development Quarterly,* considered by many career experts to be the most thorough annual review of the career development literature, revealed that more often than not, little attention is paid to the career literature pertaining to persons with disabilities. Even scholars who call on the profession to engage in more advocacy often fail to identify the near silence that exists on behalf of persons with disabilities. This is perplexing given that one in five Americans (54.4 million) has a disability (U.S. Censure Bureau, 2005). Clearly, this is an embarrassing, and inexcusable, gap in the career development literature.

Herr et al. (2004) define a person with disabilities as "one who is usually considered to be different from a normal person—physically, physiologically, neurologically, or psychologically—because of accident, disease, birth, or developmental problems" (p. 280). The Americans with Disabilities Act of 1990 (ADA) identifies a person with disabilities as:

> A person who has physical or mental impairment that substantially limits one or more "major life activities," or has a record of such an impairment, or is regarded as having such an impairment. Examples of physical or mental impairments are contagious and noncontagious diseases and conditions such as orthopedic, visual, speech, and hearing impairments, cerebral palsy, epilepsy, muscular dystrophy, multiple sclerosis, cancer, heart disease, diabetes, mental retardation, emotional illness, specific learning disabilities, HIV disease, tuberculosis, drug addiction, and alcoholism. "Major life activities" include functions such as caring for oneself, performing manual tasks, walking, seeing, hearing, speaking, breathing, learning, and working. (U.S. Department of Justice, 1991, pp. 3–4)

The ADA stipulates that employers can consider only essential job functions when hiring or promoting employees. Employers may require prospective employees to demonstrate how they will perform specific job-related functions. Although employers can make employment decisions based on job-related qualifications, they cannot make employment decisions based on reasons that are related to the person's disability.

Additionally, employers must provide reasonable accommodations to qualified individuals with disabilities to enable them to do the essential functions of a job, unless the change imposes undue hardship on the employers. Those desiring more information about the ADA can write to the Office of the Americans with Disabilities Act, Civil Rights Division, U.S. Department of Justice, Box 66118, Washington, D.C. 20035–6118. (See Figure 4.1.)

Zunker (2006) identifies several career development issues that typically confront persons with disabilities. Specifically, he notes that issues related to adjusting to disabilities (as when people experience physical trauma and then have difficulty adjusting to and accepting their disability) include confronting attitudinal barriers based on misinformation and discriminatory beliefs; overcoming generalizations formed as a result of being labeled disabled or handicapped; having a lack of role models and norm groups; coping with issues associated with the age of onset of disability; developing social/interpersonal skills; developing a positive self-concept; and developing skills for independent living. These issues each require specific career development interventions to facilitate the career development of persons with disabilities.

For those lacking role models, exposure to employed individuals with similar disabilities can serve as an important source of self-efficacy enhancement (Bandura, 1986). Cook (1981) noted that those having difficulty adjusting to their disability due to physical trauma might need assistance in coping with grief associated with losing their prior level of functioning. Zunker (2006) notes that those experiencing a disability at an early age may require assistance in developing assertiveness and independence and those experiencing the onset of a disability in adulthood may need to be reintroduced to the overall career development process. Supported employment (e.g., sheltered workshops) opportunities may help persons with disabilities gain exposure to role models, experience enhanced self-esteem through work-related accomplishments, and develop important interpersonal skills.

Zunker (2006) and Levinson (1994) provide thorough descriptions of the assessment process for people with disabilities. For example, Levinson describes

General

- *Public accommodations such as restaurants, hotels, theaters, doctors' offices, pharmacies, retail stores, museums, libraries, parks, private schools, and day-care centers may not discriminate on the basis of disability. Private clubs and religious organizations are exempt.*
- Reasonable changes in policies, practices, and procedures must be made to avoid discrimination.

Auxiliary aids

- Auxiliary aids and services must be provided to individuals with vision or hearing impairments or other individuals with disabilities, unless an undue burden would result.

Physical barriers

- Physical barriers in existing facilities must be removed, if removal is readily achievable. If not, alternative methods of providing the services must be offered, if they are readily achievable.
- All new construction in public accommodations, as well as in "commercial facilities" such as office buildings, must be accessible. Elevators are generally not required in buildings under three stories or with fewer than 3,000 square feet per floor, unless the building is a shopping center, mall, or a professional office of a health care provider.
- Alterations must be accessible. When alterations to primary function areas are made, an accessible path of travel to the altered area (and the bathrooms, telephones, and drinking fountains serving that area) must be provided to the extent that the added accessibility costs are not disproportionate to the overall cost of the alterations. Elevators are required as previously described.

Employment

- Employers may not discriminate against an individual with a disability in hiring or promotion if the person is otherwise qualified for the job.
- Employers can ask about one's ability to perform a job, but cannot inquire if someone has a disability or subject a person to tests that tend to screen out people with disabilities.
- Employers will need to provide "reasonable accommodation" to individuals with disabilities. This includes steps such as job restructuring and modification of equipment.
- Employers do not need to provide accommodations that impose an "undue hardship" on business operations.

Who needs to comply

- All employers with 25 or more employees must comply, effective July 26, 1992.
- All employers with 15–24 employees must comply, effective July 26, 1994.

Transportation

- New public transit buses ordered after August 26, 1990, must be accessible to individuals with disabilities.
- Transit authorities must provide comparable paratransit or other special transportation services to individuals with disabilities who cannot use fixed route bus services, unless an undue burden would result.
- Existing rail systems must have one accessible car per train by July 26, 1995.
- New rail cars ordered after August 26, 1990, must be accessible.
- New bus and train stations must be accessible.
- Key stations in rapid, light, and commuter rail systems must be made accessible by July 26, 1993, with extensions up to 20 years for commuter rail (30 years for rapid and light rail).
- All existing Amtrak stations must be accessible by July 26, 2010.

Figure 4.1

Americans with Disabilities Act requirements specified in the Public Accommodations Fact Sheet.
Source: From *Americans with Disabilities Act Handbook* (Coordination and Review Section), U.S. Department of Justice, Civil Rights Division, 1991, Washington, DC: U.S. Department of Justice.

a comprehensive vocational assessment for persons with disabilities as including psychological, social, educational-academic, physical-medical, and vocational functioning assessments. Zunker suggests that vocational evaluations for persons with disabilities could include (in ascending order): gathering biographical data; conducting an evaluation interview; conducting psychological testing; providing opportunities to acquire occupational information and to engage in career exploration; completing work samples; completing situational or workshop tasks; conducting informal conferences with other staff members; offering job tryouts; holding formal staff conferences; and providing vocational counseling for career decision making, implementation, and adjustment to the career choice implemented (p. 151).

Cummings, Maddux, and Casey (2000) note that much of the career literature related to persons with disabilities focuses on persons with physical disabilities and little attention is directed toward those with learning disabilities. Persons with learning disabilities often experience challenges that negatively influence their career development. Some common challenges include: a failure to understand how personal characteristics relate to career choice, low self-esteem, an inability to engage in self-advocacy, difficulties in establishing routines, difficulties in accurately observing and effectively imitating the work habits of role models, challenges related to information processing, and a tendency toward passive learning styles. Cummings and her associates identify several strategies that career practitioners can use to more effectively address the concerns of persons with learning disabilities. First, and foremost, they note the need for career practitioners to help secondary school students with learning disabilities engage in more systematic transition planning as they move from high school to postsecondary experiences. To achieve this goal, counselors must work to improve the coordination between high schools and postsecondary education and community agencies. Although IDEA requires that each student's transition plan include information regarding postsecondary services (e.g., vocational rehabilitation, independent living options), linkages to these services are often not identified for students with learning disabilities. Because college students with learning disabilities often experience lower career decision-making self-efficacy and a more pessimistic attributional style for career decision making than their peers without disabilities (Luzzo, Hitchings, Retish, & Shoemaker, 1999), the need also exists to provide more systematic and adequate transition planning to students with learning disabilities who are moving from high school to postsecondary education. Finally, Cummings and her colleagues advocate for taking a K–12 approach to transition planning. In this regard, Levinson (1998) argues for a three-level transition assessment program for students with learning disabilities. Specifically, Levinson suggests a Level 1 assessment during the elementary school years that focuses on identifying the student's needs, values, abilities, interests, interpersonal skills, and decision-making skills. Assessment outcomes at this level should be connected to transition goals/objectives that focus on career exploration and self-awareness. Level 2 assessments should occur during the middle school years and should involve formal and informal measures related to interests, aptitudes, work habits, and career maturity. Assessment outcomes should be linked to additional career exploration moving toward a narrowing of tentative career options and goals. Level 3 assessment should include work samples and situational assessments and additional emphasis on identifying the student's skills, interests, and career goals. Empowering persons with learning disabilities to engage in effective self-advocacy is also essential.

The challenges experienced by persons with disabilities require career practitioners to work on multiple fronts to provide effective career assistance (Levinson, 1998). For example, because empirically supported career theories for persons with disabilities are lacking, career practitioners must consider how extant theories can be applied to foster understanding of the intra-individual and contextual factors that influence the career development of persons with disabilities. Hypotheses generated in this regard should be subjected to empirical validation to advance general understanding of career development processes for persons with disabilities. To generate sound hypotheses, career practitioners will need to possess specific knowledge that extends beyond a general familiarity with career theories. Specifically, career practitioners will need to have knowledge pertaining to the following:

1. Federal and state legislation, guidelines, and policies applicable to persons with disabilities
2. Types of disability classifications, diagnostic tools or processes, and their limitations
3. Informal assessment procedures for assessing interests, values, goals
4. Characteristics of different types of disabilities, their causes, and their likely effects upon work behavior
5. Opportunities available in the local labor market for persons with different types of skills and different types of challenges
6. The meaning of functional limitation and its use in counseling
7. The effects of social stigma, labeling, and stereotyping on the self-concept of persons with disabilities
8. Essential employability skills, the availability of training programs, and occupational and educational opportunities
9. Ways to work effectively with other specialists to facilitate a comprehensive approach to career exploration, career preparation, and career placement of persons with disabilities
10. Examples of job redesign that employers use to accommodate the capabilities and/or functional limitations for persons with various types of disability
11. Methods of developing individual employment plans and individualized educational plans
12. Fears, concerns, and needs of parents or partners of persons with disabilities, and ways to work systemically to foster the career development of persons with disabilities
13. Models of developing daily living, mobility, job search, and work skills
14. Strategies for teaching self-advocacy skills related to accessing disability-related services

Persons with disabilities encounter specific obstacles in their career development that are often due to a lack of awareness and sensitivity on the part of employers, educational institutions, and the general public. Many employers adhere to the false (and stereotypical) beliefs that persons with disabilities will be absent more often, less productive, and less invested in their career development than their nondisabled peers. Evidence exists to suggest hiring discrimination is most often directed toward persons with physical or sensory impairments (McMahon, Roessler, Rumrill, Hurley, West, Chan, & Carlson, 2008). The provision of effective career development interventions requires practitioners to possess the requisite knowledge, skills, and awareness for adequately addressing the career concerns of persons with disabilities. Many times, this requires career development professionals to play an advocacy role with prospective employers and coworkers to dispel discriminatory myths.

ASSESSMENT

Our discussion of career development interventions for persons with disabilities leads into some important points to consider in conducting career assessments with diverse client populations. Walsh and Betz (1990) defined assessment as "a process of understanding and helping people cope with problems" (p. 12). Often, assessment involves using a test as a "method of acquiring a sample of behavior under controlled conditions" (p. 21). However, as we discussed previously, assessment can also involve activities such as observing client behaviors as they engage in specific work-related tasks, participating in job simulation activities, and engaging the client in a counseling interview to gather both important current information pertaining to the client's career concerns and relevant client biographical data.

Fouad (1993) notes that career counselors must be mindful of the fact that the client's culture plays a significant role throughout all phases of the assessment process. For example, analyzing the client's needs requires counselors to understand a client's worldview. Empathizing with the client from the client's perspective requires counselors to be aware of their own cultural backgrounds and how the client's culture may influence the assessment process. When encouraging clients to discuss their understanding of the assessment results, career counselors must be sure that the client's cultural context is factored into the review process. For example, because the history of Native American identity is typically maintained through oral tradition, a Native American client is likely to define words as powerful and value-laden. Thus, the tendency to use words casually may be avoided at all costs (Sage, 1991) and silence may predominate in sessions. Such silences should be allowed to occur naturally and should not necessarily be determined as client resistance. In this regard, many of the points raised by Fischer et al. (1998) concerning multicultural counseling also pertain to conducting culturally appropriate career assessments.

When selecting a test, career counselors must ensure that the instrument is valid, reliable, and appropriate for the client's cultural and linguistic context. Fouad (1993) identified several important issues that need to be considered in conducting career assessments across cultures. Specifically, Fouad noted that career counselors must determine whether a test is functionally and conceptually equivalent for the client's culture. Functional equivalence relates to "the role or function that behavior plays in different cultures" (Fouad, p. 8). Conceptual equivalence "refers to the similarity in meaning attached to behavior or concepts" (Fouad, p. 8). Fouad also identified metric equivalence (i.e., whether the scales of a test measure the same constructs across cultures) and linguistic equivalence (i.e., whether the translation of items results in equivalent language across cultures) as important areas to address in test selection.

Fouad also urges career counselors to consider whether systematic bias exists in any test being considered for use in career counseling. For example, content bias exists when test items are more familiar to members of one group than they are to another group. Lack of familiarity with item content obviously places a test taker at a significant disadvantage and leads to spurious test results. Internal structure bias exists when the relationships among items are not consistent across cultural contexts. Finally, selection bias occurs when a test has differential predictive validity across groups.

As with any career development intervention, selecting tests properly requires career counselors to be aware of their own worldviews, a client's worldview, and the psychometric concerns identified by Fouad. Too many times, counselors have disregarded these factors when using tests in career counseling. In such instances, they do a disservice to the client and the profession. When used properly, assessments can provide clients with vital information for resolving their career concerns.

To conduct culturally competent career assessment, career counselors need to possess general counseling skills, multicultural counseling competencies, and career counseling competencies. Flores, Spanierman, and Obasi, (2003) note important professional and ethical considerations for conducting career assessment with diverse client populations. Specifically, they remind career counselors that it is important to engage in information gathering, both formally and informally, that is culturally encompassing. Data that career counselors gather through assessment should help to not only identify the client's presenting career concerns but also help the career counselor understand the client as a cultural being. Gathering data regarding culturally specific variables such as racial/ethnic identity, acculturation, worldview, socioeconomic status, gender-role expectations, primary language, family expectations, and so on, will help set the cultural context for understanding the client's situation and concerns.

Ponterotto, Rivera, and Sueyoshi (2000) use a culturally sensitive semistructured protocol during career counseling intake sessions. Their "career-in-culture" (CiCl) interview incorporates recent theoretical advancements in multicultural counseling and social cognitive career theory (Lent, Brown, & Hackett, 2002). The CiCl interview focuses on understanding the client from five spheres of career development influence: culture, family, and religion; community and larger society self-view and self-efficacy; barriers and oppression; and narrative and relationship. Questions from each sphere foster a collaborative career counseling relationship and move from a focus on individual-based questions to those more broadly focused on family, religion, culture, and community. For example, the career counselor encourages the client to consider the following:

1. Is there anything you would like to know about me and my role as a career counselor?
2. Tell me about yourself.
3. Tell me about your career concerns and career goals.
4. What are some things that are important to you (and unimportant to you) in a career?
5. What types of occupations were you aware of growing up?
6. Name three things you are good at, and why.

7. Name three things you are not good at, and why you think you are not good at them.
8. Do you believe you can accomplish whatever goals you set for yourself? What might stop you from achieving your goals?
9. Tell me about your cultural background.
10. Tell me about your religious background.
11. How has your family influenced your career goals?
12. How do your career goals match with your family's expectations?
13. Draw a family genogram and tell me about the lives and work experiences of the family members identified.
14. What are some organizations in your community that have influenced you?
15. Who are some of the people in your community who have influenced you?
16. As a _____ (race/ethnicity, female/male, older/younger, gay/lesbian/ bisexual/transgender/straight, abled/disabled) person, what do you see as your greatest challenges to pursuing your career goals?

The CiCl draws upon SCCT and multicultural counseling to directly address essential spheres of influence in living and makes clear from the start that these topics are important in considering career concerns.

Scholl (1999) devised the "Career Path Tournament" as group intervention for middle school through university levels to help students consider the effects of sociological influences on career development. The tournament uses a round-by-round elimination format to achieve the following goals: (a) to stimulate awareness of sociological barriers to career advancement; (b) to increase participants' awareness of feelings (e.g., anger, anxiety, confusion); (c) to gain a better understanding of the career development process as it is reflected in education practices, professional training, and employment practices; and (d) to increase awareness of the need to intentionally cope with discriminatory practices. Herring (2002) provides excellent suggestions for additional group and classroom activities that engage students in the consideration of cultural and sociological influences in career development.

Leong, Hardin, and Gupta (2007) proposed A Cultural Formulation Approach to Career Assessment and Career Counseling (CF). Specifically, the CF encourages career practitioners to attend to the following five dimensions in the career counseling and assessment process: (a) cultural identity, (b) cultural conception of career problems, (c) cultural context and psychosocial environment, (d) cultural dynamics in therapeutic relationship, and (e) an overall cultural assessment. A special issue of the *Journal of Career Development* (2010) illustrates the application of the Cultural Formulation Approach using five career counseling case studies involving African American, Latina/ Latino American, American Indian, Asian American, and international student clients.

Degges-White and Shoffner (2002) describe how the Theory of Work Adjustment can be used effectively to provide career counseling with lesbian clients. Casella (2002) describes how Super's theory can also be used to help lesbian clients advance in their career development. Additional interventions such as those from postmodern theoretical perspectives (e.g., career laddering, "my life as a book," life-role salience questions that incorporate family and societal expectations) can also be used to acknowledge the central role of culture in shaping identity and career development.

Among the many different identities, values, and perspectives that career clients comprise, spiritual and religious dimensions should not be overlooked. First, it may be helpful to distinguish the differences as well as the areas of overlap between spirituality and religion. Spirituality can be viewed as a more encompassing term than religion in that it includes many different beliefs and practices that can be quite personal and individual. According to Cashwell and Young (2005), it includes "one's beliefs, awareness, values, subjective experience, sense of purpose and mission, and an attempt to reach toward something greater than oneself" (p. 13). Due to the highly individualized nature of the construct, spirituality and spiritual experiences can be difficult to define using strict categories and delineations.

Religion, conversely, is more concrete and comprehensible. It refers to a set of beliefs and practices that are part of a religious institution. It tends to be expressed in ways that are "denominational, external, cognitive, behavioral, ritualistic, and public" (Richards & Bergin, 1997, p. 13). It is a form of spirituality in that religious individuals may feel that they express their spirituality through practices and beliefs that are part of a religious institution (Cashwell & Young, 2005). Persons who identify themselves as spiritual and not religious tend to feel restricted by religious institutions and their dogmas, rituals, and practices, whereas religious persons may feel they identify closely with both terms.

In line with developments in career theory and practice such as constructionist perspectives and an emphasis on meaning making for clients, religious and spiritual issues are important client components for career counselors to consider. A client's spiritual and/or religious beliefs may impact the way in which the client approaches choosing a major, a career, switching careers, and how he/she perceives career counseling. Counselor self-awareness is especially imperative when working with clients from different spiritual and religious backgrounds. Career counselors will be most effective with a client if they deepen their own awareness of their beliefs regarding religion and spirituality as well as the prejudices that accompany those beliefs and how they may impact clients (Hayes, 2002).

MyCounselingLab™

Go to Topic 5: *Career Development and Counseling of Special Populations* in the MyCounselingLab™ site (www.MyCounselingLab.com) for *Career Development Interventions in the 21st Century,* Fourth Edition, where you can:

- Find learning outcomes for *Career Development and Counseling of Special Populations* along with the national standards that connect to these outcomes.

- Complete Assignments and Activities that can help you more deeply understand the chapter content.
- Apply and practice your understanding of the core skills identified in the chapter with the Building Counseling Skills unit.
- Prepare yourself for professional certification with a Practice for Certification quiz.
- Connect to videos through the Video and Resource Library.

Summary

The tremendous changes occurring in the population demographics within American society have given rise to many important developments related to career development interventions. Many existing career development theories have been expanded to be more inclusive. New theories with a greater sensitivity toward describing the career development process for diverse populations are emerging (Leong, 2010). Career development practitioners are becoming increasingly sensitive to the fact that treating all clients in the same way is, in fact, discriminatory treatment because such an approach ignores the contextual factors shaping the client's career behavior.

Despite these advances, much more needs to be done. For example, research is needed to more fully understand the career development process for members of diverse groups. Career development theories continue to require examination of the degree to which they apply to diverse groups. One area of concern in this regard, which has not received adequate attention, relates to the career development experiences of persons who are economically disadvantaged. Blustein (2006) is the leading researcher in this area and has proposed a useful framework that should spawn more research addressing the career development of those who are economically disadvantaged. Career development interventions still need to be expanded to address both intra-individual and extra-individual variables influencing career behavior. Greater understanding is needed regarding how differences between the career counselor and the client regarding language, social class, and, most importantly, culture, influence the career counseling process. In this regard, Trusty (2002, pp. 204–207) offers several cautions to those engaged in research to advance our understanding of multicultural influences in career development processes:

1. Comparison studies have limited usefulness.
2. Many studies are piecemeal.
3. Researchers often ignore the possibility of interactions or other curvilinear relationships.
4. Too little attention is paid to external validity, transferability of findings.
5. Research and theory from areas other than multicultural and career counseling are often ignored.
6. There is a double standard regarding cause in correlational studies.
7. We need more studies that focus on the effectiveness of interventions.
8. More research is needed on developmental processes.

In addition to these suggestions that emphasize quantitative research methods, Trusty also views recent advances in qualitative research as very useful for helping to broaden our understanding of factors that are influential in career development processes for diverse populations. For example, Hernandez and Morales (1999) conducted a qualitative study to increase understanding related to Latinas working in higher education. Hernandez and Morales revealed strong images of an inhospitable and nonsupportive work environment for Latinas. The qualitative data from this study supported important career development interventions for addressing individual and environmental factors influencing the career experiences of Latinas and other members of underrepresented groups.

Beyond increasing the rigor and amount of research (quantitative and qualitative) related to multicultural career development, counselor preparation programs need to infuse multiculturalism into the curriculum, especially as it pertains to career development intervention courses (Swanson, 1993; Swanson & O'Brien, 2002). Students should be encouraged to consider how career theories are not and/or are relevant for diverse groups and how to identify culturally appropriate career interventions, which should be the rule within counselor training.

In short, our pluralistic society has provided an excellent catalyst to making career development theories and interventions more inclusive. It has also provided opportunities for the profession to grow while more effectively serving the needs of greater numbers of people. Toward this end, we offer the following suggestions to career counselors:

1. Career counselors should, above all, possess essential counseling knowledge, skills, and understanding that reflect multicultural competencies. The possession of these attributes however, does not represent an end state. Rather, it represents a lifelong commitment to self-awareness, learning from others, and professional development.

2. Career counselors should be aware of their own attitudes and values generally, but they should also understand how their own attitudes and values may interact with their client's attitudes and values; career counselors should work to ensure that their internal frames of reference do not form roadblocks to successful counseling. To acquire such awareness, the first important realization is that we all have unconscious biases and the tendency to exaggerate between group differences and within group similarities (Fiske, 1998). Although there is a certain efficiency to combining different racial, ethnic, and cultural groups into categories with generalizations and stereotypes instead of looking at each individual as unique and different, such generalizations can hinder our ability to empathize with another's worldview, a critical component of all counseling relationships, including career counseling (Bohart, 2002).

A helpful tool to deepen understanding of one's own identities, clients' identities, and the ways in which the two may interact is by using the ADDRESSING framework (Hays, 2002). Briefly, the ADDRESSING framework stands for **A**ge and generational influences, **D**evelopmental or acquired **D**isabilities, **R**eligion and spiritual orientation, **E**thnicity, **S**ocioeconomic status, **S**exual orientation, **I**ndigenous heritage, **N**ational origin, and **G**ender. Hays highlights the importance of paying close attention to our own dominant group identities and the ways in which power imbalances based on these dominant group memberships may negatively impact a client. For instance, if a career counselor is a White, Christian male and his client is a Middle Eastern, Muslim female, there might be ways in which the power differential negatively impacts the client and the career counseling relationship. The client may be more submissive and compliant to her career counselor than if her counselor had similar identities to her. Because race and culture-related conflicts can have pernicious effects on counseling outcomes (Constantine, 1997), career counselor preparedness for cross-cultural interactions is of utmost importance. Pope-Davis et al. (2002) note the importance of directly addressing counselor-client cultural differences. They found that clients are more satisfied with counseling and perceive their counselors as more multiculturally competent when this occurs.

3. Career counselors should be aware of their client's cultural context, but they should also understand that we are each first and foremost individuals and only secondarily representatives of our specific immediate and distal cultural contexts. Chan (1992) found that the salience of clients' identities fluctuate with the environment. This means that a career counselor working with a client who has multiple identities has to be tentative and refrain from prematurely drawing conclusions about the client's most salient identities. For instance, if a White, straight, male career counselor is working with an Asian American, gay, male, Buddhist college student who is majoring in math, the counselor may arbitrarily view the client's most salient identities as being Asian American and gay, when in reality the client's most salient identities within the career counseling relationship are his being Buddhist and a math major.

Sun (1995) found that when individuals can categorize others into multiple group memberships, they experience less prejudice toward the other. For instance, if a career counselor knows her client as "Lori, the young Native American woman," she may neglect to acknowledge other important aspects of Lori's identity. Lori may be a mother, a food-service worker, and a woman with a learning disability. With this more holistic view of Lori, the career counselor will have less tendency to generalize Lori's experience into a "Native American woman" experience and will in turn experience less-prejudiced attitudes toward her and develop a more complete (and accurate) understanding of Lori.

4. Career counselors should empower clients who experience discrimination to "reject the rejection" within discriminatory attitudes and behavior. Discriminatory behavior always reveals much more about the perpetrator than it does about the person being discriminated against. The deficiencies do not reside in a person's skin color, sex, sexual orientation, or ethnicity but in the thinking and behavior of the person committing the discrimination.

5. Career counselors must be sure that they understand how experiences with racist, sexist, homophobic, classist, ageist, and discriminatory practices toward persons who are disabled influence their clients' career development. Certainly, reading can facilitate such understanding. Most times, however, career counselors will need to move to more active attempts at developing their understanding of discrimination. Regardless of one's demographic characteristics, most of us have areas in which we need to learn more regarding discriminatory experiences. The young, middle-class, gay male with a learning disability most likely has experienced various forms of discrimination; however, he may not have developed an awareness of the ways in

which a 45-year-old, Native American, single mother working in a factory experiences barriers in her career development. Participating in social action activities (e.g., volunteering at a homeless shelter if one has never been homeless) helps advance understanding in important ways. Expanding one's social network to include people that look, act, and believe differently can also advance understanding of differences.

6. Career counselors should engage in proactive programming to provide experiential opportunities, information resources, mentoring opportunities, and psychoeducational activities that are relevant to persons from diverse groups. They should provide services in nontraditional locations, enlist the support of leaders representing diverse groups, and implement strategies that make career services more accessible to more people.

7. Career counselors must engage in social action and advocacy to address systemic discrimination. Career counselors cannot simply talk about the importance of society becoming less discriminatory; they must also find ways to become actively engaged in addressing practices that result in artificial limitations being placed upon the career development of a person and/or group.

8. Career counselors should engage in programmatic research efforts to develop and advance theories of career development that apply to diverse groups. Often researchers rely upon samples of convenience, which, most often, are comprised of traditional college students. Moving beyond samples of convenience requires networking, using the Internet, contacting groups comprised of diverse persons to invite study participation, and using other more aggressive strategies for reaching out to potential study participants.

Case Study   *Pat—The Case of the Loner*

Pat is a 17-year-old high school senior who attends a career-technical school in a large city and has taken courses in culinary arts. Pat notes that this decision was based on parental advice: "Dad

says I needed to learn something practical." Pat also notes that there is parental pressure for Pat to be self-supporting after high school graduation. Pat's father (Frank) works as a truck driver and he is away more than half of every month. Pat's mother (Marie) works as a cashier at a local grocery store. Pat is an only child and feels responsible for providing health care assistance to Marie who is not in good health.

Pat has worked bagging groceries at the same grocery store as Marie ever since he turned 16 years old. Pat has always felt like a loner, and spends much time alone at school. During free time he can often be found at Miller's Pond where he daydreams about writing poetry and acting. However, Pat has low self-efficacy related to both activities and states that "people usually make fun of my poetry and laugh at my dreams related to acting." He does not want to be a chef; he would like to do something that is meaningful, but does not know what that would be. Pat states that "I probably am not smart enough to ever amount to much of anything." Frank (Pat's dad) has stated that he expects Pat to be independent when he turns 18 in six months. Pat has come to see you to get some help figuring out "what would be a good job" after high school.

How do you conceptualize Pat's situation? Would it make a difference if he were female or male? Would it make a difference if he were Caucasian or a member of a racial minority? What if Pat had a disability? What if he were gay or lesbian? Do any of these possible demographic variables influence how you conceptualize Pat's career needs? Do any of them influence how you might work with him? If not, then what is your responsibility in helping Pat prepare for any discrimination he is likely to experience? Is it possible for these factors not to make a difference in a discriminatory world? If they could make a difference in how you conceptualize Pat's situation and how you might work with him, then identify some of the demographic categories and discuss how they would influence your work.

Student Activities

1. Identify ways in which you think culture and related factors have influenced your career development. Consider the ways in which your career development has been influenced by your family, your gender, your race, your socioeconomic status, your sexual orientation, your religion, the community in which you were raised, or whether you experience any disabilities; and the area of the country in which you were raised, the country in which you lived, the time in history in which you grew up, and so on. Try to identify an influence from each of these factors. In what ways have these factors supported your career development? In what ways have they presented obstacles to you?

2. As you think about the factors you identified above, imagine what your career development experience might have been like had these factors been different (e.g., instead of being female you were male; instead of being raised in the United States, you were raised in China; instead of being straight, you were gay). What obstacles might have you encountered? In what ways might your support systems have been different?

3. Engage in a discussion with a person who is different from you in terms of race, sex, sexual orientation, disability status, and/or national origin. Ask this person to describe her/his career development experiences. In what ways are your career development experiences similar to this person's? In what ways are they different?

4. Now that you have read about career development theories, consider how these theories may need to be expanded or revised to provide more inclusive descriptions of the career development experiences of more people.

References

Arbona, C. (1990). Career counseling research and Hispanics: A review of the literature. *The Counseling Psychologist, 18,* 300–323.

Arons, J. (2008). *Lifetime Losses: The Career Wage Gap.* Washington, DC: Center for American Progress.

Atkinson, D. R., Morten, G., & Sue, D. W. (1989). A minority identity development model. In D. R. Atkinson, G. Morten, & D. W. Sue (Eds.), *Counseling American minorities* (pp. 35–52). Dubuque, IA: William C. Brown.

Atkinson, D. R., Morten, G., & Sue, D. W. (Eds.). (1993). *Counseling American minorities* (4th ed.). Madison, WI: Brown & Benchmark.

Axelson, J. A. (1985). *Counseling and development in a multicultural society.* Pacific Grove, CA: Brooks/Cole.

Bandura, A. (1986). *Social foundations of thought and action: A social cognitive theory.* Englewood Cliffs, NJ: Prentice Hall.

Berg-Cross, L., & Zoppetti, L. (1991). Person-In-Culture interview: Understanding culturally different students. *Journal of College Student Psychotherapy, 5*(4), 5–21.

Blustein, D. L. (2006). *The psychology of working: A new perspective for counseling, career development, and public policy.* Mahwah, NJ: Lawrence Erlbaum Associates.

Bohart, A. C. (2002). Focusing on the positive, focusing on the negative: Implications for psychotherapy. *Journal of Clinical Psychology, 58,* 1–7.

Bureau of Labor Statistics. (2010). Employment status of the civilian population by sex, age, and disability status. Retrieved from http://www.bls.gov/news.release/empsit.t06.htm.

Casella, C. (2002). Using Super's theory in career counseling with lesbian clients. *The Career Development Quarterly, 50,* 306–310.

Cashwell, C. S., & Young, J. S. (Eds.). (2005). *Integrating spirituality and religion into counseling: a guide to competent practice.* Alexandria, VA: American Counseling Association.

Cass, V. C. (1979). Homosexual identity formation: A theoretical model. *Journal of Homosexuality, 7,* 219–235.

Chan, C. (1992). Cultural considerations in counseling Asian American lesbians and gay men. In

S. Dworkin & F. Gutierrez (Eds.), *Counseling Gay Men and Lesbians.* (pp. 115–124). Alexandria, VA: American Association for Counseling and Development.

Chapman, B. E., & Brannock, J. C. (1987). Proposed model of lesbian identity development: An empirical examination. *Journal of Homosexuality, 14,* 69–80.

Cheatham, H. E. (1990). Africentricity and career development of African-Americans. *The Career Development Quarterly, 38,* 334–336.

Chung, Y. B. (2001). Work discrimination and coping strategies: Conceptual frameworks for counseling lesbian, gay, and bisexual clients. *The Career Development Quarterly, 50,* 33–44.

Chung, Y. B. (2003). Career counseling with lesbian, gay, bisexual, and transgender persons: The next decade. *The Career Development Quarterly, 52,* 78–86.

Chung, Y. B., Williams, B., & Dispenza, F. (2009). Validating work discrimination and coping strategy models for sexual minorities. *The Career Development Quarterly, 58,* 162–170.

Constantine, M.G. (1997). Facilitating multicultural competency in counseling supervision: Operationalizing a practical framework. In D. B. Pope-Davis & H. L. K. Coleman (Eds.), *Multicultural counseling competencies: Assessment, education and training, and supervision* (pp. 310–324). Thousand Oaks: Sage.

Cook, D. W. (1981). Impact of disability on the individual. In R. M. Parker & C. E. Hansen (Eds.), *Rehabilitation counseling* (pp. 169–197). Boston: Allyn & Bacon.

Cook, E. (1994). Role salience and multiple roles: A gender perspective. *The Career Development Quarterly, 43,* 85–95.

Cook, E., Heppner, M. J., & O'Brien, K. M. (2002). Feminism and women's career development: An ecological perspective. In S. Niles (Ed.), *Adult career development: Concepts, models, and practices* (3rd ed., pp. 169–190). Tulsa, OK: National Career Development Association.

Cross, W. E. (1971). The Negro-to-Black conversion experience: Toward a psychology of Black liberation. *Black World, 20,* 13–27.

Cross, W. E. (1995). The psychology of Nigrescence: Revising the Cross model. In J. G. Ponterotto, J. M. Casas, L. A. Suzuki, & C. M. Alexander

(Eds.), *Handbook of multicultural counseling* (pp. 93–122). Thousand Oaks, CA: Sage.

Cross, W., & Strauss, L. (1998). The everyday functions of African American identity. In J. Swim & C. Stangor (Eds.), *Prejudice: The target's perspective* (pp. 267–279). San Diego, CA: Academic Press.

Cummings, R., Maddux, C. D., & Casey, J. (2000). Individualized transition planning for students with learning disabilities. *The Career Development Quarterly, 49,* 60–72.

Daire, A. P., LaMothe, S., & Fuller, D. P. (2007). Differences between Black/African American and White college students regarding influences on high school completion, college attendance, and career choice. *The Career Development Quarterly, 55,* 275–279.

Datti, P. (2009). Applying the social learning theory of career decision making to gay, lesbian, bisexual, transgender, and questioning young adults. *The Career Development Quarterly, 58,* 54–64.

Degges-White, S., & Shoffner, M. (2002). Career counseling with lesbian clients: Using the theory of work adjustment as a framework. *The Career Development Quarterly, 51,* 87–96.

Downing, N. E., & Roush, K. L. (1985). From passive acceptance to active commitment: A model of feminist identity development for women. *The Counseling Psychologist, 13,* 195–209.

Ettinger, J. (1996). Meeting the career development needs of individuals with disabilities. In R. Feller & G. Walz (Eds.), *Career transitions in turbulent times: Exploring work, learning and careers* (pp. 239–244). Greensboro, NC: Educational Resources Information Center, Counseling and Student Services Clearinghouse.

Fabian, E. S., & Liesener, J. J. (2005). Promoting the career potential of youth with disabilities. In S. D. Brown & R. W. Lent (Eds.), *Career development and counseling: Putting them and research to work* (pp. 551–572). Hoboken, NJ: Wiley & Sons.

Farmer, H., Rotella, S., Anderson, C., & Wardrop, J. (1998). Gender differences in science, math and technology careers: Prestige level and Holland interest type. *Journal of Vocational Behavior, 53,* 73–96.

Fassinger, R. E. (1995). From invisibility to integration: Lesbian identity in the workplace. *The Career Development Quarterly, 44,* 148–167.

Fischer, A. R., Jome, L. M., & Atkinson, D. R. (1998). Reconceptualizing multicultural counseling: Universal healing conditions in a culturally specific context. *Counseling Psychologist, 26,* 525–588.

Fiske, S. T. (1998). Stereotyping, prejudice, and discrimination. In D. T. Gilbert, S. T. Fiske, & G. Lindzey (Eds.), *Handbook of social psychology* (4th ed., Vol. 2, pp. 357–411). New York: McGraw-Hill.

Flores, L. Y., Spanierman, L. B., & Obasi, E. M. (2003). Professional and ethical issues in career assessment with diverse racial and ethnic groups. *Journal of Career Assessment, 11,* 76–95.

Fouad, N. A. (1993). Cross-cultural vocational assessment. *The Career Development Quarterly, 42,* 4–13.

Frome, P. M., Alfeld, C. J., Eccles, J. S., & Barber, B. L. (2006). Young women who changed their occupational aspirations. *Educational Research and Evaluation, 12,* 359–372.

Gilligan, C. (1982). *In a different voice.* Cambridge, MA: Harvard University Press.

Goleman, D. (1990, July 10). Homophobia: Scientists find clues to its roots. *New York Times,* pp. C1, C11.

Gottfredson, L. S. (1981). Circumscription and compromise: A developmental theory of occupational aspirations. *Journal of Counseling Psychology, 28,* 545–579.

Gottfredson, L. S. (2002). Gottfredson's theory of circumscription, compromise, and self-creation. In D. Brown & Associates (Eds.), *Career choice and development* (4th ed., pp. 85–148). San Francisco: Jossey-Bass.

Grieger, I., & Ponterotto, J. G. (1995). A framework for assessment in multicultural counseling. In J. G. Ponterotto, J. M. Casas, L. A. Suzuki, & C. M. Alexander (Eds.), *Handbook of multicultural counseling* (pp. 357–374). Thousand Oaks, CA: Sage.

Gysbers, N. C., Heppner, M. J., & Johnston, J. A. (2003). *Career counseling: Process, issues, and techniques* (2nd ed.). Boston, MA: Allyn & Bacon.

Hageman, M. B., & Gladding, S. T. (1983). The art of career exploration: Occupational sex-role stereotyping among elementary school children. *Elementary School Guidance and Counseling, 17,* 280–287.

Hartung, P. J., Speight, J. D., & Lewis, D. M. (1996). Individualism-collectivism and the vocational behavior of majority culture college students. *The Career Development Quarterly, 45,* 87–96.

Hayes, J. A. (2002). Playing with fire: Countertransference and clinical epistemology. *Journal of Contemporary Psychotherapy, 32*, 93–100.

Hernandez, T. J., & Morales, N. E. (1999). Career, culture, and compromise: Career development experiences of Latinas working in higher education. *The Career Development Quarterly, 48*, 45–58.

Herr, E. L., & Cramer, S. H. (1996). *Career guidance and counseling through the lifespan* (5th ed.). New York: HarperCollins.

Herr, E. L., Cramer, S. H., & Niles, S. G. (2004). *Career guidance and counseling through the lifespan: Systemic approaches* (6th ed.). Boston, MA: Allyn & Bacon.

Herring, R. D. (2002). Multicultural counseling for career development. In J. Trusty, E. J. Looby, & D. S. Sandhu (Eds.), *Multicultural counseling: Context, theory and practice, and competence* (pp. 219–246). Huntington, NY: Nova Science.

Ibrahim, F. A., & Kahn, H. (1987). Assessment of worldviews. *Psychological Reports, 60*, 163–176.

Ibrahim, F. A., & Owens, S. V. (1992, August). *Factor analytic structure of the scale to assess worldview.* Paper presented at the annual meeting of the American Psychological Association, Washington, DC.

Innovative Placements. (2010). The facts about employing people with disabilities. Retrieved from http://innovativeplacementswny.com/facts.html.

Ivey, A. E., D'Andrea, M., Ivey, M. B., & Simek-Morgan, L. (2009). *Theories of counseling and psychotherapy: A multicultural perspective* (7th ed.). Pacific Grove, CA: Brooks/Cole.

Kluckhohn, C., & Murray, H. A. (1950). Personality formation: The determinants. In C. Kluckhorn & H. A. Murray (Eds.), *Personality in nature, society, and culture* (pp. 35–48). New York: Knopf.

Lease, S. H. (2003). Testing a model of men's nontraditional occupational choices. *The Career Development Quarterly, 51*, 244–258.

Lee, C. C., & Richardson, B. L. (Eds.). (1991). *Multicultural issues in counseling: New approaches to diversity.* Alexandria, VA: American Association for Counseling and Development.

Lent, R. W., Brown, S. D., & Hackett, G. (2002). Social cognitive career theory. In D. Brown & Associates (Eds.), *Career choice and development* (4th ed., pp. 255–311). San Francisco: Jossey-Bass.

Leong, F. T. L. (1986). Counseling and psychotherapy with Asian-Americans: Review of the literature. *Journal of Counseling Psychology, 33*, 196–206.

Leong, F. T. L. (1993). The career counseling process with racial-ethnic minorities: The case of Asian Americans. *The Career Development Quarterly, 42*, 26–40.

Leong, F. T. L. (2010). A Cultural Formulation Approach to Career Assessment and Career Counseling: Guest Editor's Introduction. *Journal of Career Development, 37*, 375–390.

Leong, F. T. L., & Brown, M. T. (1995). Theoretical issues in cross-cultural career development: Cultural validity and cultural specificity. In W. B. Walsh & S. H. Osipow (Eds.), *Handbook of vocational psychology: Theory, research, and practice* (2nd ed., pp. 143–180). Mahwah, NJ: Erlbaum.

Leong, F. T. L., Hardin, E., & Gupta, A. (2007). Culture and self in vocational psychology: A cultural formulations approach to career assessment and career counseling. An invited paper presented at the Society for Vocational Psychology Biennial Conference, University of Akron, May 29–June 1.

Levinson, E. M. (1998). *Transition: Facilitating the post-school adjustment of students with disabilities.* Boulder, CO: Westview Press.

Levinson, H. (1994). Why the behemoths fell: Psychological roots of corporate failure. *American Psychologist, 49*, 428–436.

Lewin, T. (2010). One a leader, U.S. lags in college degrees. *New York Times,* Retrieved October 31, 2001, from http://www.nytimes.com/2010/07/23/education/23college.html.

Louis, L. (2006). Life as a mother-scientist. *The Chronicle of Higher Education, 53*, C1.

Luzzo, D. A., Hitchings, W. E., Retish, P., & Shoemaker, A. (1999). Evaluating differences in college students' career decision making on the basis of disability status. *The Career Development Quarterly, 46*, 142–156.

McMahon. B. T., Roessler, R., Rumrill, P. D., Hurley, J. E., West, S. L., Chan, F., & Carlson, L. (2008). Hiring discrimination against people with disabilities under the ADA: Characteristics of charging parties. *Journal of Occupational Rehabilitation, 18*, 111–132.

Morgan, K. S., & Brown, L. S. (1991). Lesbian career development, work behavior, and vocational counseling. *Counseling Psychologist, 19*, 273–291.

National Council on Disability (2000). Transition and post-school outcomes for youth with disabilities: Closing the gaps to post-secondary education and employment. Washington, DC: National Council on Disability, Social Security Administration.

Niles, S. G., & Goodnough, G. (1996). Life-role salience and values: A review of recent research. *The Career Development Quarterly, 45*, 65–86.

O'Neil, W. M. (1982). Gender role conflict and strain in men's lives: Implications for psychiatrists, psychologists, and other human-service providers. In K. Solomon & N. B. Levy (Eds.), *Men in transition* (pp. 5–44). New York: Plenum.

Organization for Economic Co-operation and Development. (2010). Babies and bosses: Key outcomes of the United States compared to OECD average. Retrieved from http://www.oecd.org/document/60/0,3343,en_2649_34819_39699452_1_1_1_1,00.html.

Orzek, A. M. (1992). Career counseling for the gay and lesbian community. In S. H. Dworkin & F. J. Guitierrez (Eds.), *Counseling gay men and lesbians: Journey to the end of the rainbow* (pp. 23–24). Alexandria, VA: American Association for Counseling and Development.

Padilla, A. M. (1980). The role of cultural awareness and ethnic loyalty in acculturation. In A. M. Padilla (Ed.), *Acculturation: Theory, models, and some new findings* (pp. 47–84). Boulder, CO: Westview.

Park, R. E. (1928). Human migration and the marginal man. *American Journal of Sociology, 33*, 881–893.

Park, R. E., & Burgess, E. W. (1921). *Introduction to the science of sociology.* Chicago: University of Chicago Press.

Paul, P. (2008). Applying a constructivist-developmental approach to issues of sexual orientation and religion in career counseling. *The Career Development Quarterly, 56*, 344–352.

Pepper, S., & Lorah, P. (2008). Career issues and workplace considerations for the transsexual community: Bridging a gap of knowledge for career counselors and mental health care providers. *The Career Development Quarterly, 56*, 330–343.

Ponterotto, J. G., Rivera, L., & Sueyoshi, L. A. (2000). The career-in-culture interview: A semi-structured protocol for the cross-cultural intake interview. *The Career Development Quarterly, 49*, 85–95.

Pope, M. (1995). Gay and lesbian career development: Introduction to the special section. *The Career Development Quarterly, 44*, 146–147.

Pope, M., & Barret, B. (2002). *Providing career counseling to gay and lesbian clients. In S. G. Niles (Ed.), Adult career development* (3rd ed., pp.215–232). Tulsa, OK: National Career Development Association.

Pope-Davis, D. B., Toporek, R. L., Ligiero, D., Ortega, L., Bashshur, M. L., Brittan Powell, C. S., Liu, W. M., Codrington, J., & Liang, C. (2002). A qualitative study of clients' perspectives of multicultural counseling competence. *The Counseling Psychologist, 30*(3), 355–393.

Prince, J. P. (1995). Career assessment with lesbian, gay, and bisexual individuals. *Journal of Career Assessment, 5*, 168–177.

Richards, P. S., & Bergin, A. E. (1997). *A spiritual strategy for counseling and psychotherapy.* Washington, DC: American Psychological Association.

Rogers, C. R. (1957). The necessary and sufficient conditions of therapeutic personality change. *Journal of Consulting Psychology, 21*, 95–103.

Sage, G. P. (1991). Counseling American Indian adults. In C. C. Lee & B. L. Richardson (Eds.), *Multicultural issues in counseling: Approaches to diversity* (pp. 23–36). Alexandria, VA: American Association for Counseling and Development.

Scholl, M. B. (1999). The career path tournament: Developing awareness of sociological barriers to career advancement. *The Career Development Quarterly, 47*, 230–242.

Skovholt, T. M. (1990). Career themes in counseling and psychotherapy with men. In D. Moore & F. Leafgren (Eds.), *Problem solving strategies and interventions for men in conflict* (pp. 39–53). Alexandria, VA: American Association for Counseling and Development.

Sophie, J. (1986). A critical examination of stage theories of lesbian identity development. *Journal of Homosexuality, 12*(3), 39–51.

Stead, G. B. (2004). Culture and career psychology: A social constructionist perspective. *Journal of Vocational Behavior, 64*, 389–406.

Stein, J. (1975). *The Random House college dictionary* (rev. ed.). New York: Random House.

Sue, D. W., Arrendondo, P., & McDavis, R. J. (1992). Multicultural counseling competencies/standards: A call to the profession. *Journal of Counseling and Development, 70*, 477–486.

Sue, D. W., & Sue, D. (1990). *Counseling the culturally different: Theory and practice* (2nd ed.). New York: Wiley.

Sun, K. (1995). The definition of race. *American Psychologist, 50,* 43–44.

Swanson, J. L. (1993). Integrating a multicultural perspective into training for career counseling: Programmatic and individual interventions. *The Career Development Quarterly, 42,* 41–49.

Swanson, J. L., & O'Brien, K. M. (2002). Training career counselors: Meeting the challenges of clients in the 21st century. In S. Niles (Ed.), *Adult career development: Concepts, issues, and practices* (3rd ed., pp. 354–369). Tulsa, OK: National Career Development Association.

Torrey, E. F. (1986). *Witchdoctors and psychiatrists: The common root of psychotherapy and its future.* New York: Harper and Row.

Trusty, J. (2002). Counseling for career development with people of color. In S. Niles (Ed.), *Adult career development: Concepts, models, and practices* (3rd ed., pp. 191–214). Tulsa, OK: National Career Development Association.

U.S. Bureau of Census. (2010). Demographic profiles. Retrieved from http://2010.census.gov/news/press-kits/demographic-profiles.html.

U.S. Department of Justice. (1991). *Americans with disabilities handbook.* Washington, DC: U.S. Government Printing Office.

Walsh, W. B., & Betz, N. E. (1990). *Tests and assessment* (3rd ed.). Englewood Cliffs, NJ: Prentice Hall.

Watts, A. G., Super, D. E., & Kidd, J. M. (1981). *Career development in Britain.* Cambridge, England: Hobson's Press.

Wohl, J. (1995). Traditional individual psychotherapy and ethnic minorities. In J. F. Aponte, R. Y. Rivers, & R. Young (Eds.), *Psychological interventions and cultural diversity* (pp. 74–91). Boston: Allyn & Bacon.

Worthington, R. L., Flores, L. Y., & Navarro, R. L. (2005). Career development in context: Research with people of color. In S. D. Brown & R. W. Lent (Eds.), *Career development and counseling: Putting theory and research to work* (pp. 225–252). Hoboken, NJ: Wiley.

Wrenn, C. G. (1962). The culturally encapsulated Counselor. *Harvard Educational Review, 32,* 444–449.

Young, R. A., Marshall, S. K., & Valach, L. (2007). Making career theories more culturally sensitive: Implications for counseling. *The Career Development Quarterly, 56,* 4–18.

Zunker, V. G. (2006). *Using assessment results in career counseling* (7th ed.). Monterey, CA: Brooks/Cole.

5

Assessment and Career Planning

Assessment is a process by which you learn about your abilities, likes or interests, personality, and values or those qualities that give you personal satisfaction. I prefer using self-assessment procedures because they directly involve the person in a self-discovery process. I have found that most individuals like knowing more about themselves, creating self-motivation for the process. Another assessment process is the use of tests that some professionals believe are more scientific procedures than self-assessments. In this process professionals learn information about the person and then filter the data back to that person. Tests rely on creating knowledge about a person in comparison with others. Depending on the situation, the comparability of the validity of either approach is equivalent.

I have been professionally associated with using ability, interest, personality, and value information to identify career goals. I like to remind people that this same information, however, is equally important for several other purposes. Abilities and personalities are involved in the development of self-concepts— critical dimensions of a person and his or her functioning. Also, consider the value self-knowledge plays in relationships. Awareness of similarities and differences, identifying commonalities of interests and values, and being sensitive to personal preference styles all contribute to the dynamics of developing relationships.

In sum, self-knowledge is a critical human development requirement. Assessment is a valuable skill that facilitates this goal.

Thomas Harrington, Ph.D. Professor Emeritus
Northeastern University

MyCounselingLab™

Visit the **My**CounselingLab™ site for *Career Development Interventions in the 21st Century,* **Fourth Edition** to enhance your understanding of chapter concepts. You'll have the opportunity to practice your skills through video- and case-based Assignments and Activities as well as Building Counseling Skills units, and to prepare for your certification exam with Practice for Certification quizzes.

Melissa, a college sophomore, encouraged by her parents and her academic advisor to choose a major, sought help from the career planning and placement center in making a career choice and selecting a related major. The counselor began by administering an interest inventory that summarizes interests related to the six ACT-Holland clusters. Melissa's profile of interests was low and flat; that is, there was very little difference among the scores for the six occupational clusters, and all were below the 25th percentile related to those of a norm group of college students. The counselor appropriately concluded that Melissa was not ready to make a selection of possible occupations or majors so the counselor developed a plan for additional assessment and counseling sessions before moving on with the specific goal stated by Melissa.

The context for making career choices in the 21st century is decidedly different from that of the 20th century. The tasks of occupations are constantly changing. Some occupations are rapidly becoming obsolete while others are emerging. Some experts and agencies even predict that the concept of *occupation* will disappear altogether and that we will think of ourselves as possessing a set of skills that can be applied to work tasks in many different settings, which will produce a variety of products and services. Work is done in a different way in this century; we are now using a constantly expanding array of electronic equipment that has led to a variety of new settings, including working from home, working with team members electronically, and sending work to distant countries because it can be done less expensively there and can easily be sent electronically to a central source. The impact of global recessions and economic crises is that a larger percentage of people will be without a job for significant periods of time and that a larger percentage of people will have to work in jobs that do not coincide with their interests and values.

Not only are jobs different in the 21st century, but so are the people who perform the jobs. The United States is progressively moving from its tradition as a White, Christian nation to one of incredible diversity. In 2009, about one in every three U.S. residents was part of a group other than single-race non-Hispanic White—according to national estimates released by the U.S. Census Bureau. In 2009, the nation's minority population totaled 107.7 million, or 35%, of the country's total of 309 million. Blacks are the largest minority group at 38.1 million (12.4%). The second-largest minority group was Hispanics at 30.4 million (10.1%), followed by Asians at 13.8 million (4.5%), American Indians and Alaska natives at 2.5 million (.8%), and native Hawaiians and other Pacific Islanders at 450,000 (.15%). The population of non-Hispanic Whites who indicated no other race totaled 199.4 million in 2009. Persons of other racial backgrounds or of two or more races combined represent a total of 22.4 million (7.3%). The non-Hispanic, single-race White population, which represented 64.7% of the total population, accounted for less than a fifth of the nation's total population growth, and is projected to make up only 46.3% of the total population by 2050 (U.S. Census Bureau, 2010).

Further, people of the 21st century face many more transitions in their work than their 20th-century counterparts. They need a broader base of general skills, a higher level of knowledge of technology, and a commitment to lifelong learning to upgrade and update their skills. They need to have a better knowledge of the career choice and planning process because they need to use it more often. They have to assume personal responsibility for their careers and financial security because the 20th-century model of the paternalistic corporation has disappeared. They increasingly view career development as an ongoing, lifelong process, one that needs to integrate the various life roles related to work, family, leisure, and community.

These changes in the context and core of career choice and development require a change in the purpose and use of assessment. The first model of career guidance is attributed to Frank Parsons (Miller, 1961), who founded the Boston Vocation Bureau. Parsons (1909) advocated a three-step process that became the basis for what is called the *trait-and-factor* approach of the 20th century. The steps include gaining knowledge of self, gaining knowledge of the world-of-work, and applying decision-making skill to making an occupational choice.

The development of many different kinds of tests in the 20th century, partly encouraged by two world wars during which it was important to identify specific levels of intelligence and ability, provided an array of instruments that people could use to gain knowledge of self. Similarly, it was easy in the 20th century to gain knowledge about the world-of-work. The tasks involved in occupations changed more slowly, and many individuals could assume that they would remain in the same occupation, even with the same organization, for a lifetime, while moving through the stages described by Super (1957) in his early theory. Typically, at least until the 1980s, education for life was attained between the traditional ages of 14 and 22 because the tools and tasks of work remained stable. For these reasons, accomplishing the second step of Parsons' formula for career guidance—gaining knowledge of the world-of-work—was feasible.

So it was that the trait-and-factor approach dominated the 20th century in helping individuals with career choice. The movement was led by giants in the field such as Thorndike, Hagen, Binet, Terman, Kitson, Strong, Kuder, Paterson, Super, and Williamson. Test development was promoted through funding from government agencies, such as the U.S. Employment Service, and by a myriad of for-profit and not-for-profit organizations.

Assessment—defined here as the use of any formal or informal technique or instrument to collect data about a client—should still be valued in the 21st century as a tool used by counselors or by clients themselves to gather data useful in the career planning process. Its most important use is to assist individuals at a given point in time to identify their current interests and skills in order to identify the next educational or vocational choice in the sequence that makes up career development. In the use of assessment there is a danger of leading the client to believe that the process of career planning and choice is simplistic.

Given the changes noted in both the context in which career planning occurs and in the experience of individuals, it is clear that the characteristics of the use of assessment should be markedly different in the 21st century in the following ways:

- The results of assessment tools (such as tests and inventories) should be viewed as *one* piece of data that the client and the counselor use as the client considers career options. Many other sources of data should also be used, including the

client's self-knowledge and intentionality, past educational and vocational experience, and the best predictions possible about work demands of the future.
- Assessment should be used less for prediction of valid options, as the future will be different from the present, and more for identifying new concepts of self, needed areas for growth, and new possibilities for exploration.
- The client should be more involved in making a decision about whether to engage in assessment, and for what purposes, and should be viewed as an equal participant in the assessment process, rather than as the receiver of knowledge to which a counselor has some special access and ability to decode.

THE RELATIONSHIP OF ASSESSMENT TO THE CAREER PLANNING PROCESS

The process of career development is complex and continuous, comprising multiple cycles of decision making. Each time a person faces a new career choice in the process, that choice, if informed, is likely to include the steps illustrated in Figure 5.1.

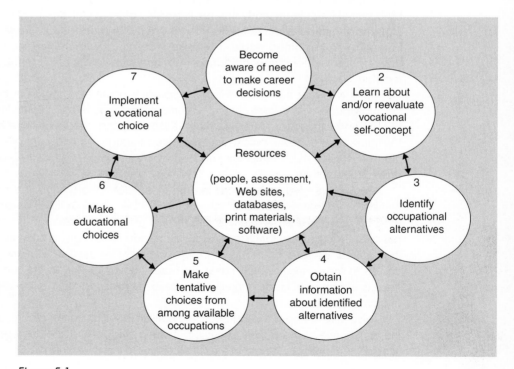

Figure 5.1

The career planning process.
Source: From *The Internet: A Tool for Career Planning,* 2nd Edition, by JoAnn Harris-Bowlsbey, Margaret Riley Dikel, and James Sampson, p. 2, published by the National Career Development Association (2002). Used by permission.

Step 1: Become Aware of the Need to Make Career Decisions

At first glance, this step may appear unnecessary. Psychologists tell us that we are not motivated to take new actions until and unless we are aware that we need to do so. Depending upon the work setting, clients may always come to counselors voluntarily as Melissa did. In that case, they do have some awareness of a need to make decisions, or they would not have initiated the contact. In other settings, such as in middle schools or high schools, students may be required to attend a career class or go to a counselor for help with career planning, but may, in fact, have no awareness that they need such help or how it may affect their futures. There are some assessment instruments, described later in this chapter, that counselors may administer at this step of the individual's career planning process to provide some information about the degree of awareness that clients have and also about their specific needs as they enter the process.

Step 2: Learn About or Reevaluate Vocational Self-Concept

We know from the theories of Parsons, Holland, and Super that work is satisfying when people are doing what they like to do (using their interests), when they have the needed skills to do their work (using their abilities), and when they believe their work is important to do (attaining their values). Thus, it is essential to focus on the client, who must focus on self during this step of the process.

In addition to what the counselor learns or helps the client to learn through interviewing, it may also be beneficial to use formal or informal assessment to expand this knowledge or confirm it. Either purpose is very valuable. With informal assessment, the client might be asked to use a checklist, a card sort, or a fantasy. These may be especially effective with clients who have difficulty talking freely in an interview. If formal assessment is used, the counselor might choose inventories or tests of interests, skills, abilities, values, and/or personality characteristics. In the case of Melissa, formal assessment of interests failed to reveal any pattern of defined interests and gave no indication of why this was true. The counselor might help Melissa identify some possible occupational goals by administering an assessment of skills, abilities, values, or personality characteristics.

Step 3: Identify Occupational Alternatives

At this stage, counselor and client are identifying occupations or jobs in which the client can implement his or her vocational self-concept (Super, Starishevsky, Matlin, & Jordaan, 1963). The profile that Melissa had on the interest inventory seemed to reveal that she had no defined picture of her vocational self-concept related to interests. When assessment is administered in print form, typically there are accompanying manuals that link the client's results to titles of occupations. When assessment is administered by a computer, a customized list of related occupations can be provided as part of the score report.

Step 4: Obtain Information About Identified Alternatives

At this step of the career planning process, clients are encouraged to gather extensive information about possible occupations through reading print materials, using computer databases and Web sites, job shadowing, and information interviewing. Assessment is not typically used at this step of the process.

Step 5: Make Tentative Choices from Among Available Occupations

At this step the client, with the counselor's assistance, is comparing alternatives and attempting to discard some while placing others in priority order. One type of assessment that may be helpful at this stage is formal or informal assessment related to work values. Though occupational alternatives may be identified on the basis of interests, abilities, and/or personality type, values serve as a filter to determine which of many options have highest priority. At this stage a counselor might use a values card sort, checklist, or inventory such as *Super's Work Values Inventory—revised* (Super & Zytowski, 2006). Follow-through would include the client's investigation to determine the potential of each occupation under consideration to satisfy the work values selected as most important.

Step 6: Make Educational Choices

Educational choices—high school courses, college major, and type and place of post-secondary education—should flow from selection of high-priority occupations. At this stage in the process, Web sites such as ACT's Map of College Majors (actstudent .org/majorsmap/plan.html) or the College Board's site (collegeboard.com/csearch/majors_ careers/profiles/) might be used to assist the client in identifying possible majors or training specialties. Further, instruments such as the *ACT Assessment Program* (ACT, 2011a) or the College Entrance Examination Board's *Scholastic Aptitude Test* (College Entrance Examination Board, 2011) are used for placement (in the case of the ACT) and/or for determining eligibility for entrance to specific schools. The *Armed Services Vocational Aptitude Battery* (see military.com/ASVAB; U.S. Department of Defense, 2005) is an instrument to provide guidance in selecting training programs in the branches of the military, using both interests and abilities as guidelines.

Step 7: Implement a Vocational Choice

At this step, clients enter the job market. Many organizations have their own instruments for screening applicants for jobs. Others use an instrument such as the *Position Classification Inventory* (Holland & Gottfredson, 1991), which determines a Holland code for a specific position or *WorkKeys* (ACT, 2010), which profiles a person's skills in 11 areas, comparing them to the level of skills needed in those same areas for specific jobs within an organization.

As indicated by the arrows between the steps of the model in Figure 5.1, the career planning process is cyclical and iterative. Note, for example, that a person may hold a job (Step 7) for a period of time and then move on to Step 1 again because of dissatisfaction with the job or a decision by the employer to reduce the number of employees. Also, note that career deciders may deal with the tasks of one step—such as identifying occupational alternatives (Step 3)—and then return to do more in-depth introspection (Step 2).

PURPOSES OF ASSESSMENT

Assessment should not be used unless there is a specific reason for doing so, a reason that both the client and counselor understand. Often, the findings identified through formal or informal assessment could be learned through an interview, a type of informal assessment. Choosing to substitute interviewing for more formal assessment depends on whether the counselor possesses knowledge comprehensive enough to sample the domains (such as areas of career maturity, interests, skills, and values) typically covered by assessment and has sufficient time to devote to comprehensive interviewing. Given the demands of time and knowledge in multiple domains, counselors typically rely on assessment for data gathering, both to alleviate these time and knowledge demands and to take advantage of the considerable benefits that scientific rigor adds to assessment.

What are the reasons that counselors ask their clients to spend time and perhaps money to engage in assessment? They can be summarized in three main categories: (1) learning more about the needs of an individual or group of individuals, (2) learning more about the characteristics of individuals and helping them learn more about themselves, and (3) determining the progress of a person or group of persons in areas related to career development. We will consider each of these in detail.

Learning More About the Needs of the Student or Client

School counselors are charged with helping all students with the career planning process through stages of career awareness (elementary school), exploration (middle school), and career preparation and decision making (high school and postsecondary). They typically accomplish this work through a systematic set of services offered to or required for all, though there is great variability in the needs of subgroups of the population.

In other settings in which more attention is given on a one-to-one basis, it is typical for counselors to ask clients to state the reasons for entering a counseling relationship. Many clients have sufficient awareness to be able to state their needs with considerable accuracy. Others are able to state the conditions they are experiencing without understanding the underlying reasons for these conditions (for example, "I can't seem to make up my mind about a major" or "My boss and I are very different, and I can't seem to learn how to get along with him"). Still others are completely unable to state the specific problems they need to deal with.

A counselor may administer certain assessments, to be described fully later in this chapter, in order to define the needs of the student or client more precisely. Melissa appears to be a case in which using assessment for further exploration of her needs is warranted. Here are two additional examples:

A high school counselor who was responsible for 500 students in all areas of school guidance wanted to devise a program of career planning services that would optimally meet the varying needs of all sophomores. He administered the Career Decision Scale (Osipow, Carney, Winer, Yanico, & Koschier, 1997). This 19-item inventory measures the degree of an individual's certainty or indecision related to career choice. In this case, the counselor was less interested in students' individual scores (and indeed did not reveal them to students) than in forming groups of students with similar needs so that these needs could be addressed in the most cost-effective ways. Using the results of the Career Decision Scale, he formed three groups of students according to their level of career decidedness and designed programs of services with different components for each of the three groups.

Iantha came to a career counselor stating that she needed help to identify some possible occupations so that she could declare a college major. Using a common interest inventory, the counselor helped her to identify some possible occupations. After spending considerable time researching most of these, Iantha was still as undecided as she was when she came in several sessions earlier. The counselor began to suspect that there were reasons for this continued undecidedness and administered the Career Thoughts Inventory (Sampson, Peterson, Lenz, Reardon, & Saunders, 1996). This 48-item inventory is designed to measure a person's dysfunctional thinking that may affect the career decision-making process. These items provide scores related to three scales: Decision-Making Confusion, Commitment Anxiety, and External Conflict. By looking at the scores on these scales and at the client's response to specific items, the counselor was able to identify and deal with some specific barriers in the client's thought processes before attempting to provide further assistance with selection of a college major.

Learning More About Clients and Helping Them Learn More About Themselves

Since the initial theory of Frank Parsons, supported by preeminent theorists in the field such as Donald Super (Super et al., 1963) and John Holland (1997), self-knowledge has been hailed as an absolute requirement for exploration and choice of occupations, majors, and jobs. The self-attributes most often proposed by theorists are interests, abilities, skills, values, and personality characteristics. An abundance of instruments exist to measure these characteristics. Sample instruments will be described later in this chapter.

Knowledge of all of these characteristics can be helpful to both the client and the counselor in synthesizing a self-image that can be matched to an environment (using Holland's terminology) or implemented in an occupation (using Super's terminology). Counselors may ask clients to take only one instrument, take an instrument that measures two or three of these characteristics, or take several instruments whose combined results provide a more comprehensive picture. Here are two examples:

Roberto, a high school junior, came to his counselor for assistance in identifying some possible occupations. He stated that he wanted to go to work immediately after high school. The counselor decided to ask him to take the Campbell Interest and Skill Survey (Campbell, 2000), which measures both interests and skills related to the six Holland-like clusters. The results showed high skill in the Technical cluster and high interest in both the Technical (called Producing) and Science (called Analyzing) clusters. From these results the counselor was able to help Roberto find occupations he could enter immediately after high school with some changes in his planned courses for the next three semesters. He was also able to help him learn about many additional occupations that he could consider if he would attend a two- or four-year college.

Mary Sue, a 35-year-old woman reentering the workforce after 10 years of child rearing, sought the assistance of a career counselor in determining possible jobs she could pursue. She stated that she did not have time to engage in further training or education but needed to find a job that could use her present skills. The counselor decided to administer WorkKeys (ACT, 2010), which measures an individual's current skills in 11 areas, including Reading for Information, Applied Mathematics, Listening, Writing, Locating Information, Applied Technology, Teamwork, Motivation, Learning, Observing, and Speaking. The counselor recommended that Mary Sue apply for jobs at three specific local companies that use the same instrument to profile the requirements of their positions. By talking with the human resource development personnel at these three companies, Mary Sue can identify jobs requiring her current level of skills and others that could be attainable in the future if she is willing to pursue additional training.

In both of these cases a counselor used the results of formal assessment to assist individuals to gain self-information that they had not been fully able to state or organize, as well as to gain information to guide their exploration.

Determining the Change or Progress of an Individual or Group

Some assessment instruments are designed to measure academic achievement, interests, or specific conditions, such as career maturity or career decidedness, over time, allowing the setting of benchmarks at specific points in a person's development. By comparing progress, change, or stability over time, it is possible to get a picture of a person's development. Following are two examples:

A middle school used the National Career Development Guidelines (association-database.com/aws/NCDA/asset_manager/get_file/3384), described in Chapter 10, as a framework for integrating career development concepts and activities into its curriculum. The superintendent required that the program include an evaluation component that would measure the degree to which the competencies stated in the guidelines had been reached. A customized version of the Iowa Career Learning Assessment (Kuder Inc., 1998) instrument was administered before delivery of the services and repeated afterward. There was a significant increase in scores in specific content areas after delivery of the program, providing objective data that the program was effective in building the desired competencies.

All of the students in a large, suburban school district took a series of tests called EXPLORE (eighth grade), PLAN (tenth grade), and the ACT Assessment Program (eleventh or twelfth grade), all developed and published by ACT, Inc. (ACT, 2007, 2011a, 2011b). Each of these three batteries of tests measures academic achievement in Language Usage, Mathematics, Social Studies, and Science as well as current interests by means of a 90-item interest inventory called UNIACT. By looking at the results of this group of tests at three different grade levels, a counselor in a university counseling center was able to show a student that each of three times he took the interest inventory he had made steady and good growth in the four academic areas, and that his most predominant area of interest was in the Social Service cluster. Based on these longitudinal results, the counselor felt secure in acquainting the student with the entire list of available university majors that relate to the Social Service cluster.

RESPONSIBILITIES AND COMPETENCIES OF THE COUNSELOR

Assessment and its interpretation can be harmful to clients if counselors are not adequately trained to deal with them. Counselors have responsibilities that are detailed specifically in the ethical guidelines that exist in the profession. Ethical guidelines, called the Code of Fair Testing Practices (Joint Committee on Testing Practices, 2004), have been developed by the American Education Research Association, the American Psychological Association, and the National Council on Measurement in Education. These are posted on the Web at theaaceonline.com/codefair.pdf and may be summarized into four areas: (1) developing and selecting tests, (2) interpreting scores, (3) striving for fairness, and (4) informing test takers. The Code of Professional Responsibilities in Educational Measurement (National Council on Measurement in Education, 1995), a document that covers the responsibilities of a wider audience—those who develop, market, select, administer, score, and interpret tests—is posted at natd.org/Code_of_Professional_Responsibilities.html.

Possess General Knowledge About Assessment

Agencies that govern the accreditation of counselor education programs and the licensing of individuals require counselors to take a course in tests and measurements. According to the standards included in *A Counselor's Guide to Career Assessment Instruments* (Whitfield, Feller, & Wood, 2009), published by the National Career Development Association (NCDA), counselors should possess the knowledge and competencies related to assessment shown in Figure 5.2. Students who have already taken the required course on assessment may want to use this form as a checklist for their own competencies.

Have Detailed Knowledge About the Instruments Used

Besides the general knowledge of testing just summarized, counselors need to have very detailed knowledge about the assessments they select for use. This knowledge can be gained in a variety of ways. It is likely that counselors will initially consider an instrument because they have identified it through a search on a Web site, from reading about it on the Web site of its publisher, from publications such as *A Counselor's Guide to Career Assessment Instruments* (Whitfield, Feller, & Wood, 2009), or because it was displayed at a conference. The first task, then, is to determine whether it has the characteristics—such as purpose, reading level, reliability, validity, and gender fairness—that it needs in order to qualify. These characteristics should be described in the technical manual that accompanies the instrument. The manual should report such important facts as the kind of research the instrument has undergone, what it is designed to measure, the norm groups that have been used in testing its properties, and its reading level. If there is no technical manual, the counselor must be wary about the amount of research that has been applied to the instrument.

It is also useful to read the critiques that others have written about the instrument. Such critiques are found in *A Counselor's Guide to Career Assessment Instruments* (Whitfield, Feller, & Wood, 2009), the Eighteenth *Mental Measurement Yearbook* (Spies, Carlson, & Geisinger, 2010), and on the Web site of the Buros Institute

Basic Concepts

Concepts important to the informal *use* of tests are listed below. Persons with final responsibility for *evaluating* and *selecting* assessment instruments will require knowledge beyond these basic concepts.

Use the following key in responding to the statements:

3 = I am able to apply the concept and explain it to others.

2 = I have some knowledge but little experience in applying the concept.

1 = I have little or no knowledge of this concept.

Enter the appropriate number in the blank at the left of each statement.

1. **Statistics used in testing and test manuals**
   - _____ a. Measures of central tendency (mean, median, mode)
   - _____ b. Measures of variability (range, variance, standard deviation)
   - _____ c. Distributions (frequency, normal)
   - _____ d. Scales of measurement (nominal, ordinal, interval, ratio)
   - _____ e. Correlation coefficients (Pearson product-moment, point biserial)

2. **Types of instruments**
   - _____ a. Measures of maximum performance
   - _____ b. Measures of typical performance
   - _____ c. Similarities and differences among measures of intelligence, aptitude, ability, and achievement
   - _____ d. Similarities and differences among self-reports, self-ratings, inventories, and tests

3. **Score reporting procedures**
   - _____ a. Percentile ranks
   - _____ b. Standard scores (including stanines)
   - _____ c. Grade placement (equivalent) scores
   - _____ d. Score profiles and profile analysis
   - _____ e. Group similarity indices
   - _____ f. Expectancy (experience) tables
   - _____ g. Estimates of probability of success and/or level of success; standard error of estimate

4. **Standardization and norms**
   - _____ a. Standardized administration and scoring
   - _____ b. Limitations of raw scores
   - _____ c. Types of norms (e.g., local, national, gender, grade); their applications and limitations
   - _____ d. Norm-based versus criterion-referenced interpretation

Continued on next page

5. Reliability

_____ a. Meaning of test reliability

_____ b. Sources of measurement error

_____ c. Types of test reliability (test-retest, parallel forms, internal consistency, including split-half, inter-rater)

_____ d. Standard error of measurement and error bands

6. Validity

_____ a. Meaning of test validity

_____ b. Implications of test use for validation procedures

_____ c. Types of test validity (content, criterion-related, construct)

_____ d. Factors affecting test validity

_____ e. Differential validity of test batteries for diverse criteria

_____ f. Potential sources of bias affecting validity

Figure 5.2

Assessment knowledge and competencies.
Source: From *A Counselor's Guide to Career Assessment Instruments* (pp. 42–43), by J.T. Kapes and E.A. Whitfield. Published by the National Career Development Association (2002). Used by permission.

(unl.edu/buros). Also, discussions with other counselors who have used the instrument can provide their views of its strengths and weaknesses.

Evaluate the Instrument for Usefulness with Diverse Populations

This particular step of the process is designed to assure that the instrument, in addition to having the purpose, reliability, and validity referred to in the above section, is suitable for use with the diverse populations that you may want to assess. There are many kinds of diversity. Those relating to age, reading and comprehension level, race, ethnicity, gender, and disability must be considered when assessment instruments are selected. Related to age, instruments are developed and normed for persons of a specific age range, and thus should be used to assess persons of that age range. Similarly, assessment instruments are written at a reading and comprehension level that can be determined. For example, there is a version of Holland's *Self-Directed Search, Form E* (1996) that is written at the fourth-grade reading level. This version of the instrument would, therefore, be the preferred version to administer to populations such as offenders or high school students with a reading deficit.

Further, race and ethnicity are important considerations when selecting instruments because cultural differences do affect the understanding and interpretation of inventory or test items. In a recent study with a sample of Mexican students, for example, Flores (Flores et al., 2006) found that the Holland typology did not fit Mexican American students well, especially males. Some instruments are accused of gender bias in the sense that their results encourage women toward certain occupational fields and men toward others. Learning style can also be a significant factor. Items on tests and inventories are typically presented as multiple-choice options working well for those who read well and think in a linear fashion. However, for persons of different learning styles, other methods of presentation might be far superior—such as analysis of vignettes provided as video clips, hands-on tasks or assignments, free-form essays, or oral presentations. Clearly, persons with specific kinds of disabilities need to be assessed in ways that accommodate their disabilities. When selecting instruments to respond appropriately to diversity, consider at least the nature of the items, the nature of the norm group, and the mode of administration and interpretation.

Items included on inventories measuring interests, skills, and values may be culture-bound. It is important to review the test or inventory items to determine if they represent activities or concepts that are compatible with the context of your students or clients. Providing norm-referenced results—that is, comparing the scores of one person against those of a representative sample—is a useful thing to do. In order to make this activity meaningful, however, that sample group needs to contain a representative sample of those like your population. When considering an instrument, read its technical manual and/or call its publisher to determine what percentage of the norm group has characteristics like the people to whom you plan to administer the instrument.

Finally, consider the method of administration of the instrument as it relates to your population. Some people love to use a computer and some don't. Some instruments are only available on the Web or delivered from a local computer, not in print form. Thus, a person who is uncomfortable with technology would be more comfortable and perhaps obtain more realistic results if administered an instrument that can be taken in print form. The Code of Fair Testing Practices (Joint Committee on Testing Practices, 2004) states the following two principles related to selection of instruments for persons of diversity:

- Make appropriately modified forms of tests or administration procedures available for test takers with disabilities who need special accommodations.
- Obtain and provide evidence on the performance of test takers of diverse subgroups, making significant efforts to obtain sample sizes that are adequate for subgroup analyses. Evaluate the evidence to ensure that differences in performance are related to the skills being assessed.

If the instrument passes this quality-control review, counselors may continue their exploration by taking the instrument themselves and getting a score report. This action will yield a firsthand knowledge of the kinds of items it has, the kind of score report it provides, and a sense of the accuracy of the instrument in measuring some characteristics about themselves. Next, the counselor may want to administer the instrument to a friend or to one or two individuals in order to become more familiar with it.

Prepare Students or Clients Adequately

Assuming that instruments have been selected, the counselor's next responsibility is to prepare those who will take the instrument for that experience. Such preparation consists of (1) explaining why they should take an assessment instrument, in other words, what they should expect to get from it; (2) getting agreement that they believe that its results will be helpful; (3) explaining what the items of the instrument are like and how long it will take to complete it; (4) telling them when the results will be available; (5) explaining what the score report will be like, perhaps by showing a mock score report; and (6) indicating what will happen to the results of the assessment—who will see them and where they will be stored.

Administer Instruments Properly

The manual provided with each formal assessment gives detailed instructions about the administration of the instrument. Some instruments, such as self-help interest inventories, can be given to an individual to take home. They are not timed, no supervision is needed, and there are no "right" or "wrong" answers. Other tests, such as college entrance examinations, are very high-stake tests and must be administered under the strictest conditions. These conditions include security of the test items prior to the testing session, identification of the examinee, room setup, lighting, silence, and exact timing. There are many other instruments that specify the conditions of administration somewhere between these two extremes. The point is to know, by reading the instructions provided with the instrument, what the appropriate conditions for administration are and then meet those conditions.

Interpret Instruments Properly

Correct interpretation of any instrument relates to three different considerations: (1) an overall understanding of the relevance of assessment to the process of career planning and choice, (2) the reason the individual has taken the instrument, and (3) the guidelines provided by the publisher for use of the instrument and/or the instrument's technical manual.

This chapter began with discussion of how the context of career planning and choice has changed in the 21st century. The discussion indicated that, concomitant with that changed context, the old model of the trait-and-factor approach (often called the "test-'em and tell-'em" approach) should be replaced with a view of assessment that has the following characteristics:

- Assessment is *one* of several tools that are used to assist the client with career choices; others may include interviewing, use of Web-based career planning systems and sites, group work, and completion of specific assignments (such as informational interviewing, job shadowing, internships, and coursework). Any plans that may emerge from use of these approaches should take into account the learning that occurs from all of these approaches.
- Assessment should be administered with the person's full understanding of its purpose and with agreement that the activity may provide some helpful information that can be used to guide exploration.
- The counselor has the responsibility to prepare the client well, administer the instrument correctly, treat the results in a confidential manner, and interpret the results in a knowledgeable way. The counselor also has the responsibility

to interpret the instrument flexibly; in other words, its results are not used as if they offer superior knowledge, but rather as data that may be used to stimulate further exploration of alternatives, growth or change, or confirmation of information already possessed. Clients have the responsibility to evaluate the results of the assessment and determine whether they are appropriate representations of the self-attributes the instrument is designed to measure, and how, if at all, to use the results as a part of the data that guide personal decision making.

The reason why the counselor has asked the client to take the assessment also guides the appropriate interpretation of the instrument. For example, a counselor may suggest that a client take the *Strong Interest Inventory* (Strong, 2004) in order to confirm a tentative occupational choice he or she has made, in accordance with a scale on the *Strong Interest Inventory*. The counselor will have also suggested that the client engage in other activities—such as taking related coursework, having informational interviews with people in the occupation, and participating in job shadowing or an internship—that will or will not contribute to this confirmation. In this case, however, the counselor would provide a general interpretation of the inventory, but would also focus on the client's scores as they relate to the profile of the norm group for the specific occupation of the client's choice.

A second example: if the purpose for suggesting that a client take the *Myers-Briggs Type Indicator* (Myers & Briggs, 1998) was to help the client understand why she is having difficulty in relating to a supervisor, the counselor would not only interpret the instrument in general, but would also ask the client how she would assess the supervisor on each of the four pairs of personality dimensions covered by the instrument. Where there were contrasts, the counselor would interpret the client's results in a way that would help her to get a clearer picture of why the supervisor's style and expectations are different from her own.

Finally, it is imperative that counselors interpret instruments within the confines of the research and the intentions of the authors and publishers of the instrument. Some publishers offer—even require—thorough training on their instruments by means of a nationwide series of workshops. These publishers are demonstrably concerned about having their instruments interpreted correctly. Other publishers require that those who want to purchase their instruments have training related to the instrument before allowing them to make purchases.

If, however, counselors are using assessments without these requirements, they have the ethical responsibility to train themselves to have competence: reading the manuals that the publisher provides with the instrument, attending workshops or sessions offered at professional conferences, and/or acquiring training through a graduate course that focuses on career planning instruments.

Follow Through with Clients

Assessment is a waste of time and money if its results are not used to inform decision making. Counselors have an ethical responsibility to move beyond interpretation in order to assist the client or student to use the results in the clarification of self-concept and/or the making of informed career choices. This is the most difficult step in the process because it involves making a leap from presentation of objective data to making inferences about the meaning of those data. Such inferences must be made within the context of all that a counselor knows about a student or client, not from test data alone. Thus, there are no prescriptive answers, but here are some suggestions:

- Think about the characteristics (such as liking to work with people face-to-face and using verbal skills) that are measured by the instrument and then assist the individual to think broadly about how that combination of characteristics may relate to a wide array of occupations, not only to the specific titles provided in the publisher's materials.
- Assist the individual to think about the implications for education, training, and/or certification of the occupational options provided by the assessment, and discuss these.
- Assist the individual to think about the lifestyle implications of the occupational options identified by an instrument, including work hours, time to be with family, requirement for travel, income, and capability to merge dual careers.
- Prescribe near-to-reality ways for individuals to explore occupational options once they are identified. Such ways include related coursework, videos, job shadowing, internships, part-time jobs, informational interviewing, and mentoring.
- After individuals pursue one or more of these ways to do reality testing, follow through with interviews to help them evaluate what they have learned and to make choices about keeping specific occupations on a short list of options or discarding them.

Tips from the Field

Before you administer any assessment, either informal or formal, give careful thought to the purpose of the assessment and how you will help your counselee or client use its results.

INFORMAL ASSESSMENTS

Assessment instruments and techniques are commonly divided into two broad categories: *informal* and *formal*. Checklists, games, fantasies, forced-choice activities, card sorts, and structured interviews are examples of informal assessments. Some recent studies (Miller, M. J., 2007) indicate that very comparable results can be gained from informal assessment and formal assessment related to specific tasks, such as determining one's Holland code.

A *checklist* is a series of items that may relate to an individual's preferred work setting, job characteristics, work tasks, work values, or skills. Such a checklist may be developed by the counselor, or the counselor can borrow—with permission—one that someone else has developed, or purchase one. As an illustration, assume that you are working with a group of women who are planning to return to the workforce after some years of child rearing. Such women often have the perception that they have few or no work skills that employers would value. As a means of helping them change this perception, the counselor may give them a checklist containing the following items and ask them to check those that they believe they possess to a moderate or high degree:

_____ Manage multiple tasks at the same time	_____ Teach or train others
_____ Decide which of competing tasks has priority	_____ Resolve conflicts between and among individuals
_____ Manage time	_____ Create and maintain an attractive environment
_____ Budget and manage money	_____ Manage people

A *game* may be used with small or large groups to make individuals aware of realities related to career choice and planning. As a part of such a game, an individual may be asked to play a specific role in a simulated environment or become subject to a variety of opportunities and setbacks represented on the game board. One good example of this kind of informal assessment is the *Real Game Series* (Real Game, 2008), available in six versions for different age populations, ranging from grade 3 through adults. Information about these games is available at realgame.com. Though many versions of the game are classroom- and print-based, a Web-based version is available for secondary school students.

A *career fantasy* is an activity in which a counselor asks one or more individuals to relax, close their eyes, and imagine an ideal day that includes time at a worksite. Individuals' fantasies can be stimulated by using instructions such as the following:

> I'd like you to relax, close your eyes if you wish, and put out of your mind any concerns that you may be dealing with. I want you to imagine that this is an ideal day of work. During this activity, you can have any job you want, and you have the skills and education to perform it.
>
> Imagine that you have completed breakfast and that you are now leaving your home to go to work. What kinds of clothes are you wearing—informal clothes, some kind of uniform, a business suit? How are you getting to work—on the metro, in your car, on a train, on an airplane, or are you working from home? How long does it take to get to work? What does your place of work look like? How many other people work directly with you? What is your relationship to these people?
>
> What are your work tasks today? Do you have any flexibility in how you perform them, or does someone supervise you closely? What kinds of tools or equipment do you work with? How much responsibility do you have for what you do? Is your pace frenetic, leisurely, or something in between?

This is a brief illustration. This fantasy can be embellished and expanded not only to include work activities but also to relate work to lifestyle, such as the kind of home, neighborhood, car, and leisure activities the person fantasizes. Discussion of this activity with individuals or small groups can help identify many characteristics that they desire in a job or lifestyle that the income from a job may impact. This technique might work with Melissa, because the counselor could identify key components in the ideal workday she describes that express interests and values.

A *forced-choice activity* is one in which an individual is asked to make a choice between two options that are quite different from each other or to rank-order three or more activities. This kind of assessment may be applied to work values, job characteristics, and work settings, for example. Following are three illustrations of the kind of items that may be used for these three purposes:

Work values: Through your life's work, would you rather

_____ make a lot of money   or   _____ make a contribution to society?

Job characteristics: In your ideal job, would you rather

_____ tell someone else what to do   or   _____ have someone tell you what to do?

Work setting: In your ideal job, would you rather

_____ work outside   or   _____ work inside?

This technique might be used with Melissa. Since it forces some choice, and therefore does not allow a series of responses such as "indifferent," it will reveal some interests.

A *card sort,* another informal assessment tool that might be helpful with Melissa, is an activity in which an individual or a group is given a deck of cards. Each card represents something related to career choice, such as a work value, a skill, a work task, or a characteristic of a work setting. Typically, the card would contain the name of the characteristic (such as Variety, Managing People, or Making or Repairing Things) and a definition of it.

If the number of cards in the deck is relatively few (up to 15), clients may be asked to rank-order the cards, placing the one that is most important in first position, followed by all of the others in priority order. If the number of cards in the deck is large, clients are typically asked to sort them into three different stacks: those that are very important or essential, those that are somewhat important, and those that are not important. Such a card sort may be made by the counselor or may be purchased from those who have specialized in the development of such instruments. If it's self-made, it is important to cover the full range of possible values, skills, work tasks, or characteristics that clients might choose—a process that will require review of the literature.

Finally, in a *structured interview* a counselor asks questions that are related to some theoretical base. For example, during an intake interview, a counselor might ask a student to provide information about coursework, past jobs, or extracurricular or volunteer activities and prompt or organize the responses around Holland's or ACT's six clusters of occupations. With sufficient knowledge about the characteristics of these six work environments, the counselor can formulate questions and analyze responses in skillful ways that yield an accurate assessment of a person's Holland code (see Chapter 2 for information about Holland's theory and codes) as well as acquire a great deal of information about the client. This approach would be a very helpful one with Melissa and others who have undifferentiated profiles of interest. Similarly, with sufficient knowledge of Jungian types (Jung, 1959), a skillful counselor might estimate a person's Jungian type without administering one of the instruments that measures personality type in these terms.

Informal assessment instruments have characteristics that are quite different from those of formal assessments, which we will examine next. Some of the characteristics of informal assessments are as follows:

- They have not been subjected to scientific rigor, nor do they have known *properties*, such as reliability and validity.
- They are not supported by any data that allow a person to compare his or her results with those of other people.
- Though inferences can be made by the client and the counselor, there are no documents that facilitate a connection between the choices made by the client and specific occupations.
- There is no standard way to interpret the results of these activities, which leaves such interpretation totally to the competence of the counselor.

The advantages of informal assessments include the following: (1) they are low-cost or free of charge, (2) they may not require the ordering of materials in advance, (3) they may not require as much time to administer as formal assessments, and (4) they may be less anxiety-producing for the client.

FORMAL ASSESSMENTS

Assessments labeled *formal* may be timed standardized tests or nontimed standardized inventories. It is common to call an instrument an *inventory* if it is assessing content areas in which there are no right or wrong answers, and to call it a *test* if the items do have right or wrong answers. Thus, an instrument measuring a person's interests is an inventory, whereas an instrument measuring a person's achievement in mathematics is a test.

The hallmark of formal assessments is that they have been subjected to scientific rigor; that is, authors and publishers have invested professional expertise, time, and money in order to develop a quality product. They have performed research on the instrument in an effort to assure quality and to be able to know the *properties* that the instrument possesses. Some of the most important properties that counselors need to know when selecting instruments include the following:

- *Validity.* There are several types of validity, and it is beyond the scope of this book to define them. An instrument is said to have *validity* if it measures what it is supposed to measure. For example, if the instrument purports to measure interests, does it do so (as opposed to measuring skills or work values)? An ethical counselor will need to read the technical manual provided by the publisher in order to learn what procedures have been taken to assure that it measures what its marketing literature says it does.
- *Reliability, often called test-retest reliability.* The construct of reliability deals with whether an instrument will measure what it is purported to measure reliably over time. In other words, if a client takes an interest inventory today and then takes it again three weeks from now, will the results be the same or

approximately the same? Intervals of time used for testing reliability typically range from two weeks to several months. Obviously, some factors related to career choice, such as interests, skills, and work values, can and do change over time. Thus, the challenge with measuring reliability is to have a sufficient period of time between the first administration and a subsequent one so that the client is unlikely to remember the items or previous responses to them. On the other hand, if the period of time is too long, change in the way the client responds may be at least partially the result of normal development.

Test-retest reliability is measured as a *correlation coefficient,* defined as the correlation between two measurements obtained in the same manner. A test-retest correlation coefficient of .8 is considered good and acceptable for selection of an instrument. Data about reliability should be provided in the technical manual as well as a description of how it was established, including the size and characteristics of the group used for this purpose.

- *Fairness related to diversity.* Increasingly in the 21st century counselors will deal with clients who represent a wide range of diversity—in gender, sexual orientation, ethnic background, race, age, and types of disability. It is important to know about the populations that are used to test and norm the instrument. The groups used for such testing need to be large enough to include a wide range of diversity, or the author and publisher need to state that the instrument has been tested only with selected populations. The former approach allows us to assume that the characteristics of clients are similar to those in the populations used for testing. This statement has profound implications for the use of instruments with members of diverse populations.

- *Comparison.* This property refers to whether or not the results that clients receive compare them to other people or rank-order characteristics related only to themselves. For example, some interest inventories are *norm-referenced;* an individual's scores are compared with those of one or more "norm" groups. For some inventories the score report will indicate that the examinee's responses place him or her, for example, at the 85th *percentile* compared with a norm group of persons of a similar age. This group of persons, or *norm group,* may be small or large, may be representative in various demographic ways of the population in general or only of a subset, may be national in scope or relatively local, or be comprised of both genders or one gender. In contrast, a different inventory may provide *raw scores;* that is, the total number of responses related to some category (right or wrong, or assigned to some scale) is reported. Such data do not provide a picture of how examinees compare with others but do allow them to rank-order their own interests, values, abilities, or whatever is being measured. Further, if norms are being used, the individual's standing related to them may be expressed in a variety of ways, including percentiles, stanines, and standard scores, to be explained later in this chapter.

Types of Formal Assessments

Earlier in this chapter three different purposes for assessment were described: to identify clients' needs, to help clients and the counselor know more about the self, and to measure progress or change. This section of the chapter describes more specifically the types of instruments, and provides a sample list of the most common ones that can be organized into each of these three categories.

IDENTIFYING THE NEEDS OF CLIENTS.   Instruments that fall into this category may be administered to a single client or may be administered to a target group of clients. In the first case, the counselor is attempting to identify the needs of a specific client and may, therefore, interpret the results to that client as a part of the career counseling process. For example, if a counselor finds that the usual technique of assessing interests, identifying some occupations, and learning about those occupations does not seem to be helping a client to deal with career concerns, he or she may want to determine if this client has barriers, such as irrational beliefs, that prevent moving forward. Under these circumstances the counselor might choose *The Career Beliefs Inventory* (Krumboltz, 1991) and suggest that the client take it. If that inventory reveals that the client is invested in a belief that he or she cannot enter a specific occupational field because the opportunities are too limited, the counselor may suggest that the basis for this belief be investigated through some occupational research before further work is done to consider other possible career choices.

On the other hand, a counselor may be seeking to identify different levels of need for career services in the target population. He or she might administer *My Vocational Situation* (Holland, Daiger, & Power, 1987) to the entire group and then make some informed assumptions about the needs of those whose scores placed them in the top 25% of the distribution, those in the middle 50%, and those in the lower 25%. In this case, it is unlikely that the counselor would interpret individual scores for members of the group because that was not the designated purpose for the assessment.

Some examples of this type of instrument, with a brief description and information about the publisher, are listed next. However, new instruments emerge with frequency, and some cease to be published. When selecting an instrument, counselors should consult the latest versions of reference books that summarize what is currently available and consult the Web sites of major publishers (provided at the end of this chapter).

Career Attitudes and Strategies Inventory (CASI), Holland and Gottfredson, 1994. A self-scored instrument designed to identify the attitudes, feelings, and obstacles that affect the careers of adults. The scales are Job Stability, Family Commitment, Risk-Taking Style, Geographical Barriers, Job Satisfaction, Work Involvement, Skill Development, Dominant Style Career Worries, and Interpersonal Abuse. Published by Psychological Assessment Resources, Odessa, FL.

Career Beliefs Inventory (CBI), Krumboltz, 1991. For persons over 13 years of age, designed to identify career beliefs that may be preventing them from reaching career goals. There are 25 scales organized under five categories: My Current Career Situation, What Seems Necessary for My Happiness, Factors That Influence My Decisions, Changes I Am Willing to Make, and Effort I Am Willing to Initiate. Published by Consulting Psychologists Press, Mountain View, CA.

Career Factors Inventory (CFI), Chartrand, Robbins, and Morrill, 1997. For persons over age 13, designed to identify persons' difficulties in the career planning and decision-making process. The scales are Need for Information, Need for Self-Knowledge, Career Choice Anxiety, and Generalized Indecisiveness.

Career Maturity Inventory (CMI), Crites and Savickas, 1995. Designed to measure how ready a student is to make a career decision. For students in grades 6–12. See vocopher.com.

Career Thoughts Inventory (CTI), Sampson et al., 1996. Designed to identify irrational thoughts that the client may have that could affect the career decision-making process. For use with students and clients from the high school level through adulthood. Published by Psychological Assessment Resources, Odessa, FL.

Career Development Inventory (CDI), Super, Thompson, Lindeman, Jordaan, and Myers, 1984. Designed to measure career development and career maturity. For use with high school and college students. See vocopher.com.

Career Decision Scale (CDS), Osipow et al., 1997. Designed to measure the reasons for career indecision and inability to make a vocational choice. For use with high school and college students. Published by Psychological Assessment Resources, Odessa, FL.

Career Decision Profile (CDP), Jones, 1986. Designed to measure level of decidedness about career choice, self-knowledge, and knowledge about occupations and training. Published by Lawrence K. Jones, Department of Counselor Education, North Carolina State University, Raleigh, NC.

My Vocational Situation (MVS), Holland et al., 1987. Designed to measure the degree to which lack of vocational identity, lack of information or training, and barriers may affect a person's ability to make a career choice. For use with students in grade 9 through adult years. Published by Consulting Psychologists Press, Mountain View, CA.

Most of the instruments just listed are designed for use with high school students and adults. This is the case because they measure constructs (such as career maturity, career beliefs, and decision-making skill) that are developmental in nature and should not be measured prior to the life stage in which their development is expected.

LEARNING MORE ABOUT CLIENTS.   In this category there is a rich array of inventories of interests, skills, abilities, work values, personality types, and combinations of these. In each case, the purpose is to allow the client and the counselor to explore characteristics that may help identify occupations or jobs for consideration. Following the theoretical work of Holland and Super, and of trait-and-factor theory in general, the purpose of these instruments is to identify personal characteristics that can be related to those of occupations or jobs in order to focus exploration of options. The lists and short summaries provided next divide the most common instruments into those measuring interests, abilities, skills, work values, personality types, and combinations of any of these.

Interest inventories. *Career Assessment Inventory (CAI)*, Johannson, 1986. Designed to measure interest in Holland's six personality types, 23 basic interest scales, and 111 occupations. Can be used with high school students, college students, and adults. Published by Pearson Assessments, Bloomington, MN.

Career Occupational Preference Survey (COPS), Knapp and Knapp, 1995. Designed to measure interest in eight career clusters, five of which are divided into professional and skilled levels. Can be used with students in grades 7–12, college students, and adults. Published by Edits, San Diego, CA.

Harrington-O'Shea Career Decision Making System (CDMS), Harrington and O'Shea, 2000. Designed to measure interest in Holland's six personality types, though names of scales have been changed. Different versions allow use from grade 7 to adulthood. Published by Pearson Assessments, Bloomington, MN.

Interest Determination, Exploration, and Assessment System (IDEAS), Johansson, 1996 and 2000. Two self-scored inventories—one for middle and high school students and one for adults—that measure interest in 16 areas. Published by Pearson Assessments, Bloomington, MN.

Interest Explorer, Riverside Publishing, 1998. For use with middle school students, high school students, and adults, the inventory measures interest in 14 career areas that are linked to the *Guide for Occupational Exploration, Occupational Outlook Handbook*, and *O*Net*. Published by Riverside Publishing, Rolling Meadow, IL.

Jackson Vocational Interest Survey (JVIS), Jackson, 1999. Designed to measure interests on 34 basic interest scales. For use with high school students, college students, and adults. Published by Sigma Assessment Systems, Port Huron, MI.

Kuder Career Search with Person Match™, Zytowski and Kuder, 2003. Designed to measure interest in six Holland-like occupational clusters or the states' 16 career clusters; also compares the profile of the inventory-taker with those of more than 2,000 real people and identifies and describes the specific jobs of the top matches. For use with high school students, college students, and adults. Available only on the Internet. Published by Kuder, Inc., Adel, IA.

O*Net Interest Profiler, United States Department of Labor, Employment and Training Administration, 2001a. Self-scored or Web-based instrument designed to measure interests by Holland's six personality types for persons in middle school through adult. May be printed out, copied, and distributed along with the score report and an interpretive booklet from onetcenter.org. Executable code may also be downloaded from this site onto a compact disc. An online version is also available at MyNextMove.org.

Self-Directed Search (SDS), Holland, 1996. Designed to measure personality type and interest in six different occupational groups. There are multiple forms for different age ranges, languages, and reading levels. Can be used with high school students, college students, and adults. The assessment is also available on the Web at self-directed-search.com. Published by Psychological Assessment Resources, Odessa, FL.

The Strong Interest Inventory, Strong, 2004. Measures interests in eight different areas—occupations, school subjects, activities, leisure activities, types of people preferred as coworkers, preference between two activities, personal characteristics, and preference in the world-of-work. Provides a Holland code, scores on 30 basic interest scales, five personal style themes, and similarity of examinee's profile to the profile of workers in 244 occupations. Available in English, French, and Italian. Appropriate for use with high school juniors and seniors, college students, and adults. The assessment offers many different score reports, including those for high school students, those for college students, and reports combined with the results of the *Myers Briggs Type Indicator* and the *Skills Confidence Inventory*. Published by Consulting Psychologists Press, Mountain View, CA.

Unisex Edition of the ACT Interest Inventory (UNIACT), Swaney, 1995. Measures interest in the six Holland types and uses the Holland code to suggest career areas on the World-of-Work Map for exploration. Due to different sets of items and norms, it is appropriate for use with high school students, college students, and adults. Included in DISCOVER (a Web-based system), the *Career Planning Survey* (ACT, Inc., 1997), and as a part of ACT's tests called *EXPLORE, PLAN,* and the *ACT Assessment.* Published by ACT, Inc., Iowa City, IA.

Skills inventories. *SkillScan*, Beckhusen, 2010. Provides opportunity for users to sort manually a large number of skills by areas of competence, preference, and need for development and to identify skills with a combination of high competence and preference. A Web-based version is now available at skillscan.com/products-services/individual-user-products. Appropriate for use with high school students, college students, and adults. Published by SkillScan Professional Pack, Martinez, CA.

WorkKeys, ACT, 2010. Measures skills in 11 areas: Reading for Information, Applied Mathematics, Listening, Writing, Locating Information, Applied Technology, Teamwork, Motivation, Learning, Observing, and Speaking. Specific jobs can be profiled on the same skills, allowing the relationship of an individual's skills with the level required by specific occupations and jobs. Can be used with high school students and adults. Published by ACT, Inc., Iowa City, IA.

Combination of interests and skills. *Campbell Interest and Skill Survey (CISS)*, Campbell, 2000. Measures interests and self-reported skills in seven areas that are roughly parallel to the Holland six types and contains 25 basic scales and 60 occupational scales. The basic scales are subscales under the six Holland-like types, expressed as Influencing, Organizing, Helping, Creating, Analyzing, Producing, and Adventuring. There are parallel skills scales for each of the interest scales. Can be used with high school students, college students, and adults. Published by Pearson Assessments, Bloomington, MN.

The Armed Services Vocational Aptitude Battery (ASVAB), U.S. Department of Defense, 2005. Measures abilities in 10 content areas and includes measurement of interests by Holland typology and personal preferences (values). Designed for high school seniors and adults. Used for admission to various specialties in the armed forces but is also provided to high school seniors in general. Published by the U.S. Department of Defense.

The Career Planning Survey (CPS), ACT, 1997. Measures abilities in three areas and interests in the six Holland personality types, linking these to the World-of-Work Map. Can be used with high school students, college students, and adults. Published by ACT, Inc., Iowa City, IA.

Abilities. *O*Net Ability Profiler*, United States Department of Labor Employment and Training Administration, 2001b. The O*Net Ability Profiler uses a paper and pencil format with optional apparatus parts and computerized scoring. Individuals can use O*Net Ability Profiler results to identify their strengths and areas for which they might want to receive more training and education, or to identify occupations that fit their strengths.

The O*Net Ability Profiler measures nine job-relevant abilities: Verbal Ability, Arithmetic Reasoning, Computation, Spatial Ability, Form Perception, Clerical Perception, Motor Coordination, Finger Dexterity, and Manual Dexterity. This instrument can be downloaded without charge from the O*Net Web site at onetcenter.org/AP.html.

Inventories of personality type. *The Personality Type Profiler*, Golden, J. (2004). The *Golden Personality Type Profiler* identifies both a Jungian four-letter type and a fifth element for stress, as well as provides scores for 18 traits (facets) that help describe the unique personality of each person. Score reports can be provided either for individuals or for teams. The assessment is administered online at talentlens.com/en/index.php. Published by Pearson Pubishing, San Antonio, TX.

The Myers-Briggs Type Indicator (MBTI), Myers & Briggs, 1998. Measures the psychological types described by Jung, yielding a four-letter code that can be related to typical profiles of groups of people who work in specific occupations or that can be used to develop teams or understand the interactions among members of a team. The results of the assessment are expressed as an individual's preference along a continuum on scales titled Extraversion-Introversion, Sensing-Intuition, Thinking-Feeling, and Judging-Perceiving. Combined score reports for the MBTI and the Strong Interest Inventory are available. MBTI is available in Spanish, German, French, Dutch, Canadian French, Italian, Korean, Portuguese, Danish, Norwegian, Chinese, Swedish, and Russian. Can be used with high school students, college students, and adults. Can be taken on the Web at mbticomplete.com/en/index.aspx?gclid=CJXax8Oqp6cCFaJl7AodTB5fEA. Published by Consulting Psychologists Press, Mountain View, CA.

Note that as with the previous group of assessment instruments, these are targeted primarily to individuals in the high school, college, and adult years. This is the case because interests are not crystallized until the adolescent years, and the development of abilities and skills to support them typically occurs in the high school and college years.

Inventories measuring work values. *O*Net Work Importance Profiler*, United States Department of Labor, Employment and Training Administration, 2001c. The *Work Importance Profiler* measures the importance of six work values—achievement, independence, recognition, relationships, support, and working conditions. Individuals who take the instrument begin by rank-ordering 21 work need statements by comparing them with one another. The results are linked to occupational titles. The instrument can be downloaded without charge either as a print document or as executable code from onetcenter.org.

Super's Work Values Inventory—revised, Super and Zytowski, 2006. Measures importance of 12 of Super's work values and provides percentile scores of level of importance. For use by high school students and adults. Available only in Web-based form as a part of the Kuder Career Planning System at kuder.com. Published by Kuder, Inc., Adel, IA.

MEASURING PROGRESS OR CHANGE. In the third category of reasons to use assessment, instruments are used to measure some kind of change that is considered desirable in an individual or a group of individuals. For example, it is common to use a pretest and a posttest to measure change that should occur because of some kind of treatment—such as a career guidance curriculum, a series of workshops, or use of a Web-based system. In this case, the purpose of the assessment is to note the difference in an individual's or group's scores before the treatment and after the treatment. The same instruments listed under category one (finding out the needs of clients) can be used to measure this progress or change.

WAYS IN WHICH ASSESSMENT INSTRUMENTS MAY BE ADMINISTERED

Traditionally, assessment instruments have been provided in print form. They are administered either by licensed or certified professional counselors or, more recently, by trained career development facilitators. In this mode, instructions are read by the administrator, and the examinee responds to the items of the instrument on a worksheet or optical scan form. The results may then be calculated by the examinee, by the test administrator, by computer software that has been acquired for that purpose, or by computer scoring at some central place. These different options for scoring also determine how soon the results will be available for interpretation to the client.

In recent years, the widespread availability of computers and access to the Internet have introduced additional ways in which administration and interpretation take place. Beginning in the late 1960s with the advent of computer-based career planning systems, some types of instruments—such as inventories of interests, skills, abilities, and values—became a part of such systems, described more fully in Chapter 7. In keeping with ethical standards, developers of computer-based systems engaged in research to assure that instruments delivered in this way yielded the same results as if they were administered in print form. In this mode, it became possible for an inventory or test to be scored immediately and for the computer to provide a very standard report, though customized for the individual examinee, that could be viewed on the screen and/or printed. The report was typically also made available electronically to a counselor who could follow through with the client for more in-depth interpretation and application of the results to the client's specific needs.

Subsequent to their inclusion in computer-based career planning systems, many assessment instruments became available from their publishers in software form. In this mode, a site can purchase a computer disk that contains the instrument and the computer code required to administer and interpret it. This software may be installed on machines at the user site and is typically limited according to how much has been paid for it or for how many individual uses the site has been authorized.

The advent of the Internet and its ever-increasing use has introduced yet another venue for administration and interpretation of assessment. It has also made it more difficult to determine the quality of available assessments, especially those offered by sites that do not charge a fee and cannot provide a manual that describes the research and development work invested in the instrument. As trends continue in these areas, three different observations can be made: (1) many instruments and their results are available to the general public without charge and without opportunity to learn about the quality of the instrument; (2) well-known and researched instruments are being offered via the Internet for a fee, and their results are available immediately to the examinee; and (3) well-known and researched instruments are being offered via the Internet, and their results are electronically sent to a counselor specified by the examinee; the results are interpreted either face-to-face or via electronic exchange with the counselor.

Numerous inventories are available on the Internet—some without fees and others on a fee basis. Examples of formal and informal no-fee assessment Web sites are as follows:

- University of Waterloo Career Services: cdm.uwaterloo.ca/step1.asp—A collection of career planning activities, including assessment tools that can be printed out and completed, covering personality and attitude, skills and achievements, knowledge and learning style, values, interests (based on Holland's types), and entrepreneurism.
- The Career Key: careerkey.org/cgi-bin/ck.pl?action=choices—An interest inventory for middle school students, high school students, or adults that yields a Holland code.
- iSeek Skills Assessment: iseek.org/careers/skillsAssessment—Based on data from O*Net, the iSeek Skills Assessment is a fairly simple tool that allows the user to rate him- or herself on 35 different skills and then see which occupations match those skills identified as the being most important to the user. The entire tool takes 5 to 10 minutes to complete and the results are presented immediately upon completion, offering the user information on each career, how his or her skills match this profile, and the level of education or training usually required to perform this particular job.
- Motivational Assessment of Personal Potential: assessment.com—Offers an interest inventory that measures one's interest in working with people or things and other job characteristics; suggests occupations linked to their O*Net descriptions.

Often there is little or no information about the developers of these instruments and sites. Counselors have the ethical responsibility to become knowledgeable about the quality of an instrument before recommending that students or clients take it.

Some of the inventories described earlier are available as part of a comprehensive Web-based career planning system. These for-fee sites include the following:

- ACT's *DISCOVER:* act.org—Offers ACT's UNIACT interest inventory, a self-rating of abilities inventory, and a values assessment. Results of the first two inventories suggest regions and career families on ACT's World-of-Work Map. Provides a complete career guidance system for students in grades 6–16.
- Kuder's *Navigator* and *Journey* career planning systems: kuder.com—Offer the *Kuder Career Search with Person Match* (an interest inventory), the *Kuder Skills Assessment*, and the revised *Super's Work Values Inventory*. The first two inventories provide a rank-ordered percentile score profile relating the user's interests to the States' 16 career clusters. *Navigator* provides a complete career guidance system for students in grades 6–16 while *Journey* addresses the career planning needs of postsecondary students and adults. The assessments provide an interactive score report with linkage to occupational information, information about postsecondary majors, and their related schools. Includes a lifetime electronic portfolio.

The availability of an expanding plethora of instruments and their interpretation via the Internet poses a significant professional challenge. Counselors who prescribe the use of such instruments have an ethical responsibility to find out about and be professionally satisfied with the quality of the instrument before prescribing it.

Another trend of the 21st century is to administer many kinds of tests—such as tests that govern entrance to colleges, graduate schools, or licensure or certification for a given occupation—through secure test sites in addition to (or instead of) through the traditional paper and pencil approach. Because tests of this nature are used to make decisions that appreciably affect people's lives, their items must be kept secure; and it must be assured that examinees do not use materials that will help them identify the correct responses. They must be administered in secure environments. That means that specific places are designated to which examinees must travel. These places have computer equipment that provides good service and response time. Monitors at these locations assure that the persons taking the tests are those who registered to take them and that the test items themselves are sent to work stations from central computers where security is guarded. This method of administration also has the capability to immediately score the tests, electronically send the results to persons or organizations authorized to receive them, and use adaptive tests. *Adaptive tests* are those that include a large number of items that measure a specific content field. These items are arranged in hierarchical order related to their level of difficulty. Using formulas developed with scientific rigor, the computer software begins by presenting a few items that are easy. If the examinee answers these correctly, the software displays items of greater difficulty. This pattern continues until the general level of the examinee's knowledge is determined. Then, a greater number of items is presented from this category of items. The characteristics of this type of testing are (1) shorter testing time in general, (2) variable testing time for each examinee, (3) immediate scoring and feedback to authorized persons, and (4) potential capability to do a more thorough testing at the specific competency level of the examinee.

TYPES OF REPORTS

Reports of the result of a test or inventory typically come to a client in print form. If the instrument has been taken on a computer or from a Web site, the report may also appear on the screen, but typically can also be sent to a printer. Counselors may receive reports in print form, on a computer disk from which they can be printed, or by electronic transfer via the Internet.

The results provided in the report may be idiosyncratic—that is, related only to the individual for whom the report was prepared—or may compare that person with one or more norm groups. If the report is idiosyncratic, the results are typically provided as raw scores and may also be represented in some graphic form. The examples on the following page illustrate both approaches.

Percentile scores, such as those reported on the Kudor Career Search report on the next page, indicate a point or range on a normal distribution where the examinee's score falls compared with the scores of those in the norm group. A percentile score indicates

Raw Scores on Sample Copy of *Self-Directed Search*™

	R	I	A	S	E	C
Activities	10	1	0	3	6	4
Competencies	3	0	2	2	1	3
Occupations	1	0	0	1	2	2
Self-Estimates	1	1	1	2	1	2
	2	1	1	3	2	5
Total Scores	17	3	4	11	12	16

Profile on the *Kuder Career Search*™

Scale	Score	Profile
Business Operations	91	xxxxxxxxxxxxxxxx
Sales & Management	88	xxxxxxxxxxxxxxx
Social & Personal Services	84	xxxxxxxxxxxxxx
Outdoor & Mechanical	51	xxxxxxxxxx
Arts & Communications	47	xxxxxxxxx
Science & Technical	28	xxxxxx

the percent of the norm group that scored lower than the examinee and, by subtraction of the score from 100, provides the percent of the norm group that scored higher. Norm groups can vary widely, and the score reports of some instruments will report the examinee's position related to more than one norm group. Depending on the specific instrument, a norm group may be a large national sample representative of those for whom the instrument is suggested, including both genders, a variety of ages, racial-ethnic diversity, and a variety of educational levels. Other norm groups may be one gender; specific grade level; local school district, state, or national representation; or with some interest and abilities measures, by occupational group membership.

Further, scores for some instruments will be reported as a single-point score on a continuum or as a range, typically called a *band of confidence*. Reporting a band of confidence is an indication by a publisher that the examinee's score falls somewhere within that range, though an exact point is uncertain. Instruments have a property called a *standard error of measurement*, and the band of confidence shows what the range of this error of measurement may be.

Percentile scores are always on a range of 1 to 99. Another way of expressing a similar concept, but with less precision, is to report a *stanine*. By definition, a stanine is a prescribed range of percentile points, and that range is the same for all instruments and all populations to which they are administered. The nine stanines have the following definitions:

Stanine 1 = the lowest 4% of a distribution
Stanine 2 = the next 7%, percentile values 5 to 11
Stanine 3 = the next 12%, percentile values 12 to 25
Stanine 4 = the next 17%, percentile values 26 to 40
Stanine 5 = the next 20%, percentile values 41 to 60
Stanine 6 = the next 17%, percentile values 61 to 77
Stanine 7 = the next 12%, percentile values 78 to 89
Stanine 8 = the next 7%, percentile values 90 to 96
Stanine 9 = the top 4%, percentile values 97 to 100

In summary, stanines 1 through 3 represent the lowest quarter (called a *quartile*) of any distribution; stanines 4 through 6, the middle 50%; and stanines 7 through 9, the top quarter (*quartile*).

A third way of describing how an individual's score relates to that of a norm group is the concept of a *standard score* (also called a *T-score*). This term is related to the term *standard deviation*, which is a way of measuring how far an individual's score is from the middle (that is, the 50th percentile) of the distribution. *Standard T-scores* range from 20 to 80, with 50 at the mean (50%), and each standard deviation is counted as 10 percentile points. Thus, an individual's score may be said to be two standard deviations above the mean (that is, at the 70th percentile), or 2.5 standard deviations below the mean (that is, at the 25th percentile).

SELECTION OF INSTRUMENTS

In summary, there is a wide variety of types and purposes for assessment, and the results emanating from assessment can take many forms. Instruments represent a wide variety of quality related to their psychometric properties and may be based on a wide range of theory or on none at all. Further, these instruments can be administered to individuals or groups and in multiple modes. Counselors may choose to administer only one assessment, a variety of different assessments, or a "package" of instruments placed together so that they can measure different but complementary attributes. These facts combined with the ethical standards that are cited in this chapter make the task of selecting instruments complex. When selecting an assessment instrument, counselors must be mindful of these guidelines:

- Determine the specific purpose(s) for assessment. Then, begin by identifying instruments that fit that purpose.
- Consider the characteristics of the person or group for whom the instrument is being selected. Determine if gender, racial or ethnic background, reading ability, intelligence level, or disability signal an alert to take special care in selection.

- Review the data about the groups used for testing and norming the instrument. Determine whether these groups are representative of those to whom the instrument will be administered or that they at least contain a reasonable number of persons similar to the population to be tested.
- For instruments that still qualify, search their technical manuals for data about reliability (.80 or above) and evidence of their validity.
- Read critical reviews of the instruments in reference books and/or Web sites. Talk with at least three other counselors who use the instrument.
- Purchase a sample copy of the instrument and take it. Study the score report, and consider whether its results seem appropriate. Read the manual to understand how the publisher suggests that the instrument be interpreted.
- Before adopting the instrument for wide use, administer it to a few individuals, and practice preparing them for taking it and providing an interpretation.
- If the instrument still qualifies, find out how much it costs, its various modes of administration and scoring, and adopt it.

MyCounselingLab™

Go to Topic 15: *Assessment in Career Guidance and Counseling* in the MyCounselingLab™ site (www.MyCounselingLab.com) for *Career Development Interventions in the 21st Century,* Fourth Edition, where you can:

- Find learning outcomes for *Assessment in Career Guidance and Counseling* along with the national standards that connect to these outcomes.

- Complete Assignments and Activities that can help you more deeply understand the chapter content.
- Apply and practice your understanding of the core skills identified in the chapter with the Building Counseling Skills unit.
- Prepare yourself for professional certification with a Practice for Certification quiz.
- Connect to videos through the Video and Resource Library.

Summary

Assessment, in its many and varied forms, has been presented as one tool among many that counselors can use with students and clients for three specific purposes: to identify their needs, help them learn more about themselves, and monitor their progress. The responsibilities of the counselor were listed. A plea was made for using assessment in combination with many other tools and techniques, in harmony with where a client is in the career development process. Cautions were stated related to not overinterpreting the meaning of scores, and counselors were admonished to use

the data from career planning instruments for exploration, guidance, and confirmation rather than for prediction. In this process the client is proposed as an active agent and is encouraged not to position the counselor in a role of superior knowledge.

The types, purposes, and characteristics of assessment instruments and their reports were reviewed. Some of the most common instruments were named and briefly described, and the counselor was encouraged to explore beyond this list. Finally, guidelines for selecting instruments for individuals or groups of clients were listed.

Case Study

Georgina is a 45-year-old single mother with two teenage children. For the past twenty years she has worked as an accountant for a small company. In that role she has focused entirely on budgets, expenditures, cost analyses, and report writing. Her company was recently acquired by a much larger one, and she and everyone else in her department have been replaced by staff from that company. She has been terminated with 3 months of severance pay. She has come to your office in a community–based counseling center to ask for help in deciding what to do next.

In the first interview Georgina asks you to give her "one of those tests that tell you what to do." You temporarily bypass this request and ask her to describe her work over the past twenty years, indicating what she liked about it and what she did not. You learn that her primary dissatisfaction in her past job was that there was very little opportunity to interact with people. You also ask about her interest in getting additional education or training for the purpose of being able to enter an entirely different occupation. You learn that Georgina feels strongly that she cannot pursue more or different training at this time due to family responsibilities.

You then return to the subject of her request to take one or more assessments. What do you decide to tell her? And if you decide to give her access to any kinds of assessments, which do you choose, and why?

Student Activities

1. At the beginning of this chapter you learned about Melissa. Write a one-page, double-spaced response to the following questions about her case.

   a. Given the results of Melissa's interest inventory (all six ACT/Holland groups below the 25th percentile), would you recommend additional assessment? Why or why not?

   b. If you answered "yes" to the above question, what would you select as assessment tools? Defend your selection of each of these.

   c. What other approaches, in addition to or instead of assessment, would you take with Melissa?

2. Refer to the MyCounselingLab™ Video and Resource Library and select the video entitled *21st Century Application of Holland's Theory with a College Student: Dr. Janet Lenz,* in which the client's results from having taken the *Self-Directed Search* are interpreted.

   Then, write a short paper that provides responses to the following items:

   a. List and describe at least three things that the counselor did well in the interpretation of the *Self-Directed Search*.

   b. What additional things might you have done or said in this interview?

   c. In Holland terminology, explain the discrepancy that the counselor uncovered between the client's current major (Kinesiology) and the results of her SDS profile.

3. Refer to the MyCounselingLab™ Video and Resource Library and select the video entitled *21st Century Career Assessment Interpretation with a College Student: Dr David Reile,* which shows a professional counselor interpreting the results of the *Campbell Interest and Skill Survey (CISS)* with a student who is unsure about his selection of major. Then,

   a. List and describe at least five positive things that the counselor did as he interpreted the Campbell Interest and Skill Survey.

b. List and describe at least two additional things that you would have done in this interview.

c. Using this interview as a model, list at least five basic guidelines for the interpretation of an inventory or test.

References

ACT, Inc. (1997). *Career Planning Survey.* Iowa City, IA: Author.

ACT, Inc. (2007). *EXPLORE.* Iowa City, IA: Author.

ACT, Inc. (2010). *WorkKeys.* Iowa City, IA: Author.

ACT, Inc. (2011a). *PLAN.* Iowa City, IA: Author.

ACT, Inc. (2011b). *ACT Assessment Program.* Iowa City, IA: Author.

Beckhusen, L. (2010). *SkillScan.* Orinda, CA: Skill-Scan Professional Pack.

Campbell, D. (2000). *Campbell Interest and Skill Survey.* Bloomington, MN: Pearson.

Chartrand, J. M., Robbins, S. B., & Morrill, W. H. (1997). *The Career Factors Inventory.* Palo Alto, CA: Consulting Psychologists Press.

College Entrance Examination Board. (2011). *Scholastic Aptitude Test (SAT).* New York: Author.

Crites, J., & Savickas, M. (1995). *Career Maturity Inventory.* Boulder, CO: Crites Career Consultants.

Flores, L. Y., Spanierman, L. B., Armstrong, P. I., & Velez, A. D. (2006). Validity of the strong interest inventory and skills confidence inventory with Mexican American high school students. *Journal of Career Assessment, 14*(2), 183–202. Retrieved October 23, 2009, from SAGE Journals Online.

Golden, J. (2004). *The Golden Personality Type Profiler.* San Antonio, TX: Pearson.

Harrington, T., & O'Shea, A. (2000). *Harrington-O'Shea Career Decision Making System.* Bloomington, MN: Pearson.

Holland, J. L. (1996). *Self-Directed Search™.* Odessa, FL: Psychological Assessment Resources.

Holland, J. L. (1997). *Making vocational choices: A theory of vocational personalities and work environments* (3rd ed.). Odessa, FL: Psychological Assessment Resources.

Holland, J. L., Daiger, D. C., & Power, P. G. (1987). *My Vocational Situation.* Palo Alto, CA: Consulting Psychologists Press.

Holland, J. L., & Gottfredson, G. D. (1991). *Position Classification Inventory.* Odessa, FL: Psychological Assessment Resources.

Holland, J. L., & Gottfredson, G. D. (1994). *Career Attitudes and Strategies Inventory.* Lutz, FL: Psychological Assessment Resources.

Jackson, D. N. (1999). *Jackson Vocational Interest Survey.* Port Huron, MI: Sigma Assessment Systems.

Johansson, C. B. (1986). *Career Assessment Inventory.* Bloomington, MN: Pearson.

Johansson, C. B. (1996, 2000). *Interest Determination, Exploration, and Assessment System (IDEAS).* Bloomington, MN: Pearson.

Joint Committee on Testing Practices. (2004). *Code of fair testing practices.* Washington, DC: Author.

Jones, L. K. (1986). *Career Decision Profile.* Raleigh, NC: Author.

Jung, C. G. (1959). The archetypes and the collective unconscious. In C. G. Jung, *Collected works* (vol. 9, part I). Princeton: Princeton University Press.

Knapp, R. R., & Knapp, L. (1995). *Career Occupational Preference Survey.* San Diego, CA: EDITS.

Krumboltz, J. D. (1991). *The Career Beliefs Inventory.* Palo Alto, CA: Consulting Psychologists Press.

Kuder, Inc. (1998). *Iowa Career Learning Assessment.* Adel, IA: Author.

Miller, C. H. (1961). *Foundations of guidance.* New York: Harper & Row.

Miller, M. J. (2007). Examining the degree of congruency between a traditional career instrument and an online self-assessment exercise. *Journal of Employment Counseling, 44*(1), 11–16. Retrieved October 6, 2009, from ABI/INFORM Global.

Myers, I., & Briggs, K. (1998). *The Myers-Briggs Type Indicator.®* Palo Alto, CA: Consulting Psychologists Press.

National Council on Measurement in Education. (1995). *The code of professional responsibilities in educational measurement.* Washington, DC: Author.

Osipow, S. H., Carney, C. G., Winer, J., Yanico, B., & Koschier, M. (1997). *Career Decision Scale.* Odessa, FL: Psychological Assessment Resources.

Parsons, F. (1909). *Choosing a vocation.* Boston: Houghton Mifflin.

Real Game. (2008). *The real game series.* Memramcook, NB: National Life Work Centre.

Riverside Publishing. (1998). *Interest Explorer.* Itasca, IL: Riverside Publishing.

Sampson, J. P., Peterson, G. W., Lenz, J. G., Reardon, R. C., & Saunders, D. E. (1996). *Career Thoughts Inventory*. Odessa, FL: Psychological Assessment Resources.

Spies, R. A., Carlson, J. F., & Geisinger, K. F. (Eds.). (2010). *The eighteenth mental measurements yearbook*. Lincoln, NE: Buros Institute.

Strong, E. K. (2004). *The Strong Interest Inventory*. Palo Alto, CA: Consulting Psychologists Press.

Super, D. E. (1957). *The psychology of careers*. New York: Harper.

Super, D. E., Starishevsky, R., Matlin, N., & Jordaan, J. P. (1963). *Career development: Self-concept theory* (Research Monograph No. 4). New York: College Entrance Examination Board.

Super, D. E., Thompson, A. S., Lindeman, R. H., Jordaan, J. P., & Myers, R. A. (1984). *Career Development Inventory*. Palo Alto, CA: Consulting Psychologists Press.

Super, D. E., & Zytowski, D. G. (2006). *Super's Work Values Inventory, revised*. Adel, IA: Kuder, Inc.

Swaney, K. B. (1995). *Technical manual: Revised unisex edition of the ACT Interest Inventory (UNIACT)*. Iowa City, IA: ACT, Inc.

U.S. Census Bureau. (2010). *Wikipedia*. Retrieved March 1, 2011.

U.S. Department of Defense. (2005). *Armed Services Vocational Aptitude Battery*. Monterey, CA: Author.

U.S. Department of Labor Employment and Training Administration. (2001a). *O*Net Interest Profiler*. Washington, DC: Author.

U.S. Department of Labor Employment and Training Administration. (2001b). *O*Net Ability Profiler*. Washington, DC: Author.

U.S. Department of Labor Employment and Training Administration. (2001c). *O*Net Work Importance Profiler*. Washington, DC: Author.

Whitfield, E. A., Feller, R.W., & Wood, C. (2009). *A counselor's guide to career assessment instruments*. Tulsa, OK: National Career Development Association.

Zytowski, D. G., & Kuder, F. (2003). *Kuder Career Search with Person Match*.™ Adel, IA: Kuder, Inc.

Publishers

ACT, Inc.
P.O. Box 168
Iowa City,
IA 52240
URL: act.org

American Guidance Service
4201 Woodland Road
Circle Pines,
MN 55014
URL: agsnet.com

Consulting Psychologists Press
P.O. Box 10096
Palo Alto,
CA 94303
URL: cpp-db.com

EDITS
P.O. Box 7234
San Diego,
CA 92167
URL: edits.net

Kuder, Inc.
302 Visions Parkway
Adel,
IA 50003
URL: kuder.com

Pearson Assessments
One Lake Street
Upper Saddle River,
NJ 07458
URL: pearsoned.com

Psychological Assessment Resources (PAR)
P.O. Box 998
Odessa,
FL 33556–9908
URL: parinc.com

chapter 6

Career Information
and Resources

*Career information can be a dry topic to learn and teach. Labor market
information (LMI) can appear cold and "unsexy" to counselors-in-training.
The daily accountability of counselor educators may create gaps between
understanding the changing school and workplace and providing current
career information resources. Though entering counselor training to enjoy
nurturing relationships, some counselors give little attention to the systems
clients face as they move through career transitions. Moving immediately
into "trait-factor" matching mode to provide just the right occupational or
education information to gain the client's respect is also a common trap.
Knowing how to integrate LMI into the career development intervention
process is an essential skill for helping others move forward in their career
development.*

Dr. Rich Feller
Professor, Colorado State University

Clarice is a 28-year-old single parent of three children who lives in a modest
apartment and receives support from public aid. She dropped out of high school
in her sophomore year after her first child was born. She has held part-time jobs
at various fast-food restaurants since that time. Clarice goes to a no-fee community
agency for assistance in determining if she can get any funding for additional training or education.

Chapter 5 addressed assessment as a tool that counselors can use to help an individual make informed choices in the career planning process. Similarly, what is commonly called *career information* needs to be placed within this same context. As with assessment, counselors often make the mistake of viewing career information as an end in and of itself. Actually, it is another tool that the counselor can use to assist clients to make informed choices.

As suggested by the title of this chapter and its introductory paragraph, the common term for what will be presented is career *information*. The authors of this text, however, prefer career *data*, meaning a collection of facts about occupational and educational opportunities. Borrowing from Tiedeman and O'Hara (1963), the authors endorse the perspective that students and clients, often with the assistance of counselors and technology, collect *data*. These data become *information* only when they are understood by clients and used to *inform* decision making—that is, to assist them to choose one alternative over another.

For the sake of making the linkage between data and an individual's career planning process, refer back to Figure 5.1. Notice the centrality of the oval labeled Resources. This is a pool of data that should be available to a person who is in the process of career planning. Notice that at each of Steps 2 through 7, the person making a career choice needs to access data. These data may be contained in the results of assessment instruments, in print materials, in curricula, or in computer databases resident on Web sites. At Step 2, data gained from instruments measuring interests, skills, abilities, personality type, and/or values may be very useful.

At each step of the career planning process, the type, quantity, and depth of data needed may be different. This difference relates to the age of the persons going through the process. Middle school students may learn about themselves through informal assessment techniques; they may learn only about clusters of occupations (rather than individual occupations) and about possible ways of getting training and the importance of getting and maintaining satisfying jobs. Adults, on the other hand, may take formal assessment inventories and tests, and may seek the assistance of professional counselors in gaining self-information, read highly specific occupational and educational information, and need detailed information about companies and specific jobs. In other words, the process is common whereas the level of specificity of the data required at each step changes with age and population.

At Step 3, search strategies that help students and clients find the titles of occupations that have or relate to the characteristics they have selected are most helpful. At Step 4, clients need to access databases or print materials that contain detailed descriptions of these identified occupations—including their work tasks, requirements for training, employment outlook, benefits and limitations, typical salary range, and sources for further information. At Step 5, which requires eliminating some of the identified occupations and keeping others, even more detailed data are needed about each. At this step, students and clients may seek data by talking with individuals who have experienced these occupations or by seeking some direct contact with the worksite as well as by reading and viewing slides and videos.

At Step 6, students and clients need data about different ways (that is, apprenticeship, two-year college, four-year college, vocational-technical school, etc.) to get training for occupations of their tentative choice and about options within the category they have chosen. At Step 7, students and clients need data about specific job openings and the companies or organizations that offer them.

THE COUNSELOR'S ROLE IN PROVIDING DATA

Counselors have three specific responsibilities related to career data. First, they have the responsibility to select high-quality print materials, computer-based systems, and Web sites—the most common sources of career data—that conform to the guidelines provided by professional associations. The most comprehensive set of guidelines is provided by the National Career Development Association (NCDA), and these are available in their entirety at ncda.org under the section titled "Guidelines." (These are also available in the NCDA's publication, *Guidelines for the Preparation and Evaluation of Career and Occupational Information Literature* [1991].) Counselors choosing resources should become familiar with this entire document.

Following are some of the salient points[1]:

- The source of the data should be clearly stated.
- Data should be updated on a regular schedule, and the date of last update should be displayed clearly.
- The material should be accurate and free from distortion caused by self-serving bias, sex stereotyping, or dated resources. Whenever possible, resources more than five years old should be avoided. Occupational descriptions should be written or at least reviewed by persons knowledgeable about each occupation.
- The data should be conveyed in a clear, concise, and interesting manner. A standard style and format for grammar should be adopted and used throughout the documents.
- The vocabulary and reading level should be appropriate for those who will be reading the material. Technical terminology or jargon should be fully explained or avoided, and use of nonsexist language is essential.
- Care should be taken to eliminate bias and stereotyping against persons with a disability or based on gender, race, social status, ethnicity, age, or religion.
- Any graphics or pictures should be current, should accurately depict the environment, and should represent without stereotype persons of both genders and of different races, ages, and physical abilities.
- If the data source deals with occupations, it should describe clearly the duties and nature of the work, work settings and conditions, preparation required for entry, special requirements or considerations, methods of entry, earnings and

[1]NCDA Policy Statements on Career Information. Copyrighted by the National Career Development Association. Reprinted with permission from NCDA.

other benefits, usual advancement possibilities, employment outlook, opportunities for experience and exploration, related occupations, and sources of additional information.

A second responsibility of counselors is to make the availability of these high-quality resources known to students and clients and to make them as user-friendly as possible. A later section of this chapter will describe a *career center*, the usual repository for these resources and methods of organizing it. Counselors have the responsibility to acquaint students and clients with the resources, to illustrate how they can be accessed, and, even more importantly, to refer them to the specific ones that may be most helpful at a given point in their decision-making process. This statement underscores the fact that counselors must know these resources in detail in order to refer clients to them and to be able to discuss their content. For example, students' and clients' use of a Web-based career planning system or of a Web site will be far less effective if counselors simply direct them to the system or site as opposed to providing a marked flowchart or site map accompanied with a statement such as "I'd like you to use *CareerInfoNet,* selecting the option titled Occupation Information on the opening screen."

A third and more difficult responsibility of the counselor is to assist the client to process, or make meaningful use of, the data acquired. The goal is to turn the *data* into *information*—in other words, for the client to absorb and understand the data so that they can place some alternatives in high priority while discarding others. This is the most important of the counselor's roles. The counselor should have the following concerns:

- Is this client ready to receive data and deal with it effectively?
- What barriers does the client potentially have to using data effectively?
- What kinds of data, and how much, will be most helpful?
- What methods of receiving data—print material, Web sites, personal contact—will be most effective?
- What kind of decision style does the client use, and how will that affect his or her ability to use data effectively?

Barriers and Decision Styles

Students and clients may experience a variety of barriers as they search and use data. Some of these barriers may be physical, such as sight or hearing disabilities. Others may be intellectual, such as poor reading skill, poor comprehension skill, or low intelligence. Others may be cognitive, such as possession of irrational beliefs (Krumboltz, 1991) or negative thoughts (Sampson, Reardon, Lenz, & Peterson, 2003). Another barrier may be the lack of a strong self-concept or vocational identity, what some call a sense of self-efficacy. Sampson and his colleagues describe a condition of cognitive inability to understand or follow a logical information-processing model. They also underscore the premise that clients cannot make maximum use of data if they do not have the cognitive and emotional readiness to receive it.

Dinklage (1968) studied the way in which different individuals face the decision-making process. Little is known about how people acquire a specific decision-making style, but it is clear from the definitions of the eight types of "deciders" identified by Dinklage that the role of data, and therefore the work of the counselor, is different for each style. The eight types of deciders are as follows:

- *Planful.* One who approaches decision making in a systematic, step-by-step manner. Steps include setting a goal, identifying alternatives that will help reach the goal, collecting information about those alternatives, identifying one that is most likely to reach the goal, and taking action steps to implement that alternative. Persons with this decision-making style are likely to be able to make effective use of data.
- *Agonizing.* One who attempts to engage in decision making in a systematic, step-by-step manner but becomes so engrossed in finding alternatives, collecting data about them, and trying to choose one over others that he or she is never able to reach a decision. For persons of this decision-making style, the more data that are available, the more difficult the decision becomes.
- *Impulsive.* One who does not know how to follow a systematic process or does not value it; rather, this type of decider selects an alternative quickly and does not spend the time to identify alternatives or collect data about them. Persons of this decision-making style do not recognize the need for or value of data.
- *Intuitive.* One who seems to be able to select one alternative over another (with good outcomes) without having to go through the steps of the planful process. This type of decider seems to be able to determine what his or her personal goals are quite quickly and then substitute experience and good judgment for extensive data collection. Persons of this decision-making style appear to need little data.
- *Compliant.* One who, either due to personal style or societal norms, allows others to make decisions for him or her. Persons of this decision-making style rely on the data that others may have collected.
- *Delaying.* One who recognizes that a decision needs to be made but continues to delay making it out of fear, lack of data, or lack of motivation. Persons of this decision-making style are not ready to collect or use data.
- *Fatalistic.* One who believes that he or she does not have control over the events of life, but that they are largely determined by external forces. Persons of this decision-making style are not ready to collect or use data.
- *Paralytic.* One who recognizes the need to make a decision but is not able to move forward in the process because the process or the possible outcomes are very frightening. As with the previous two types, these types of deciders are not ready to collect or use data. In fact, having a lot of data may cause them to be even more paralytic.

So students and clients present a variety of decision-making styles and levels of belief about their self-worth and self-efficacy. Many families in the White, non-Hispanic culture teach their children to follow a step-by-step, planful decision-making process in order to increase the probability of making informed decisions that yield *outcomes* or *consequences* that bring profit to the individual. On the other hand, putting the family or some other collaborative group's well-being first, ahead of personal interests and goals, is highly valued in many other cultures. Thus, the counselor should be aware that there is a cultural influence on how and why decisions are made, and these cultural differences need to be respected.

Career Information and Diversity

Some students or clients who seek career information will need help that may include one-on-one assistance, special software or hardware, and/or language translation. Students with severe reading disabilities may need to have assessment items or occupational descriptions read to them. This service may be provided in Web-based systems by an on-screen character (called an avatar), by complementary audio files, or by the assistance of a volunteer or paraprofessional.

Students or adults with visual disabilities will need the support of special equipment such as screen readers and related software. The sites they use will need to conform to the Bobby standards (mardiros.net/bobby-accessibility-tool.html) and those of the Association of Computer Systems for Career Information, now merged into an organization called Alliance for Career Resource Professionals (see acrna.net). Still others will have better understanding of the data available on the Internet if it can be displayed or described in their first language. Instructions or translation into another language can be done via an avatar or audio file. Because the software governing avatars can produce many different languages by reading a Word file of text in a given language, it is now relatively easy for developers to provide this opportunity. Further, the nongraphic content of any Web site can be translated from or to any of 36 different languages by accessing it through babelfish.yahoo.com, specifying the languages.

THE CLIENT'S ROLE IN RECEIVING DATA

Although the counselor has a significant role in the data-gathering process, students and clients also have responsibilities: (a) to complete the assignments or suggestions provided by the counselor; (b) to work with the counselor to process the data, that is, to use them in ways that inform personal decision making; and (c) to assume responsibility for their own decision making.

The first responsibility of students and clients is to complete the data-gathering assignments that counselors give them. Unfortunately, many students and clients want quick and easy answers to their questions about career choice or change. Some expect a Web-based career planning system, a Web site, or a test to provide those answers. Others want counselors to advise them what to do and would like to shift the responsibility for decision making to them. The fact is, though, that the process of career choice and development is difficult and time consuming. It requires that one commit the time and energy to develop skill at data processing. Students and clients should be informed early in the counseling relationship about the need to spend considerable time doing the data-gathering homework that is assigned.

A second primary responsibility of students and clients is to engage in activities with the counselor that will help with the processing—that is, analyzing and making personal application—of the data that have been gathered. A student or client may, for example, read and print out the descriptions of 20 occupations identified by an interest inventory. The time required to complete that work may be wasted if the counselor and the client do not move from there to answer the question, "So what?" Interests, abilities, and personality traits are very useful constructs to help students and clients identify possible occupations. Their use usually results in the identification of far more options than can be followed. The data-processing function occurs, then, when the counselor assists the client to identify and apply criteria that can be used to rank-order alternatives.

Criteria that guide decisions are typically called *values* or *characteristics*. Thus a counselor might use interviewing, a values inventory, or a card sort to help the client select several values and characteristics that can be used to eliminate and rank-order alternatives. Values are broader and deeper than characteristics. Examples of values are independence, altruism, high income, prestige, and authority. Examples of characteristics, applied to occupations, are working outside, being able to avoid overtime and night work, having longer-than-average vacations, and being able to enter the occupation without a college degree. Once preferred values and characteristics have been identified, it is possible to examine each identified alternative, using the data collected, for its potential to satisfy these. Doing so will provide a framework for eliminating some alternatives and rank-ordering the remainder, resulting in a short list of good alternatives.

A third responsibility of students and clients is to assume responsibility for their decisions. Some types of deciders—such as those described as compliant, paralytic, and agonizing—may attempt to relinquish to the counselor their right and responsibility to make decisions. It is wise to structure the expectations of the client early in the career planning process by reviewing the roles of the counselor and the client. There are times when counselors have to confront students and clients with the fact that they are not carrying out their responsibilities in the relationship.

TYPES OF DATA NEEDED BY CLIENTS

Career planning is defined as the sequential process of making educational and vocational choices based on knowledge of self and of the environment. Using this definition, it follows that, in addition to developing information about the self, students and clients need to learn about programs of study, occupations, schools and other types of training, financial aid opportunities, military service, and organizations offering jobs. Each of these databases will be considered separately.

Programs of Study

The term *programs of study* is used to describe sequences of high school courses; specialties in vocational-technical schools, apprenticeships, and the military; and majors in colleges and universities. Though it is highly desirable for individuals to have a broad base of knowledge in the liberal arts and a set of work skills like those described in the SCANS Report (U.S. Department of Labor, 1992), it is also highly desirable that individuals have coursework and training directed to the specific skills needed in the occupations of their choice. For that reason, it is very helpful to organize the courses in the high school curriculum, the specialties in on-the-job training opportunities, and the majors in college by the same organizational system used for occupations when these are presented to students. Further, the assessment used to identify interests, abilities, and/or values would also ideally be linked to the same organizational system.

Holland's typology has been applied to people through assessment instruments such as *The Self-Directed Search™* (Holland, 1994b), *The Career Assessment Inventory* (Johansson, 1984), *The Career Decision-Making System* (Harrington & O'Shea, 2000), the *UNIACT Interest Inventory* (ACT, 1989b), the *Inventory of Work-Relevant Abilities* (ACT, 1989a), and the *Campbell Interest and Skill Survey* (Campbell, 1992). The same system has been applied to occupations in *The Occupations Finder* (Holland, 1994a), *The Dictionary of Holland Occupational Codes* (Gottfredson & Holland, 1996), and the *O*Net* (U.S. Department of Labor, 2011) database. It has been applied to vocational-technical and college majors in *The Educational Opportunities Finder* (Rosen, Holmberg, & Holland, 1999), now out of print, and on Web sites such as hollandcodes.com/college-major-search.html and careersmarts.com.

The Holland codes have also been applied to leisure activities in *The Leisure Activities Finder* (Holmberg, Rosen, & Holland, 1999); they could be used to describe job openings and company positions as well. Given this fact, one way to help students and clients process data that they collect about themselves, occupations, and educational opportunities is to organize all of this information—as well as school course offerings, career days, and data in the career center—within the same structural framework. Thus, a listing of courses offered at the high school level or majors/specialties offered at the postsecondary level, organized by the Holland typology, would be very useful in decision making.

Another system, described later in this chapter, that can be used to organize all of these pieces is ACT's World-of-Work Map (Prediger, 1981), based on the Holland typology. In this organizational scheme, ACT's assessment instruments (such as *The Career Planning Survey* in print form and parts of *DISCOVER* in Web-based form) would be used, along with ACT's *Career Area Charts* or *DISCOVER* databases.

The most comprehensive source of general information about postsecondary majors and programs of study is the *Classification of Instructional Programs* (U.S. Department of Education, 2002). As suggested earlier, high schools and colleges could easily provide a listing and descriptions of their courses and majors by Holland or World-of-Work Map categories, thus creating a local, organized database of descriptions of majors. Data about programs of study and how they relate to occupations are most relevant at Step 6 of the career planning process.

Extensive data about military programs of study are offered on Web sites such as todaysmilitary.com/military-careers/ and armedforcescareers.com. In addition, each branch also has its own Web site:

- U.S. Army: goarmy.com
- U.S. Navy: navy.com
- U.S. Air Force: af.mil
- U.S. Marine Corps: usmc.mil
- U.S. Coast Guard: uscg.mil/top/careers.asp

Data about military training programs are particularly relevant at Step 6 of the decision-making model as it may be possible to get the training needed for a chosen civilian occupation in the military. If not, serving in the military may provide the educational benefits needed to take coursework while serving or to continue education after leaving.

Data about apprenticeship programs in general and about programs offered in a given state are available from the Federal Bureau of Apprenticeship and Training (doleta.gov/oa/eta_default.cfm) and from state apprenticeship offices. Such programs allow high school graduates to receive 144 hours of classroom instruction annually, typically provided without charge at the local community college, and the practical experience of learning a trade from an experienced worker while receiving a salary.

For college students, an internship program offers a valuable opportunity to learn about an occupation by experiencing it. These work-study programs allow students to work in a given occupation under supervision, receive pay for doing so, and typically earn college credit simultaneously. Data about apprenticeships and internships are relevant at Step 6 of the career planning process.

Print resources:

- *The Internship Bible, 10th Edition* (Princeton Review, 2005)
- *The Intern Files: How to Get, Keep, and Make the Most of Your Internship* (Fedorko & Allott, 2006)
- *The Back Door Guide to Short-Term Job Adventures: Internships, Extraordinary Experiences, Seasonal Jobs, Volunteering, Work Abroad* (Landes, 2005)
- *Internships2005: The Largest Source of Internships Available* (Peterson's Publishing, 2004)

Web site for apprenticeships:

- Bureau of Apprenticeship and Training: doleta.gov/oa/eta_default.cfm

Web sites for internships:

- **About.com:** internships.about.com
- **Internship Programs:** internships.wetfeet.com
- **MonsterTrak:** college.monster.com/education
- **MonsterCollege:** college.monster.com/content/internships?WT.srch=1&WT.mc_n=olmsrchtrk

Occupations

The guidelines for occupational information provided by the NCDA (1991) indicate that occupational descriptions should provide content in the following 11 areas: duties and nature of the work, work setting and conditions, preparation required, special requirements or considerations, methods of entry, earnings and other benefits, usual advancement possibilities, employment outlook, opportunities for experience and exploration, related occupations, and sources of additional information. The single most important source for data about occupations is the U.S. Department of Labor. In addition to providing descriptions of work tasks, work settings, entry methods and requirements, related occupations, and sources of additional information, the Department of Labor also conducts surveys about the *labor market* in general and its needs. The term *labor market* refers, on the one hand, to the supply of individuals who want and are able to work and, on the other hand, to the demand for workers from public and private employers. Surveys conducted at the state and federal level yield salaries for hundreds of occupations at the entry, median, and upper levels of experience. They also provide data about the expected growth or decline in the number of workers needed at both federal and state levels for hundreds of occupations. These figures are based upon estimates of the number of persons in an occupational group who will retire; number of students preparing for entry into the occupation, and number of openings expected due to growth. Labor market forecasts for different occupations are provided by the Department of Labor in the following standard categories:

Changing Employment between 2004 and 2014

If the Statement Reads:	Employment Is Projected to:
Grow much faster than average	Increase 27 percent or more
Grow faster than average	Increase 18 to 26 percent
Grow about as fast as average	Increase 9 to 17 percent
Grow more slowly than average	Increase 0 to 8 percent
Decline	Decrease any amount

Counselors need to remember that there is a great variance in the number of people in the hundreds of occupations about which the Department of Labor makes projections. Thus, the percentage of growth is meaningful only in combination with the number of people in the occupation. For example, growth of 14% in an occupation that has 130,000 incumbents represents more potential job openings than growth of 20% in an occupation that has 39,000 incumbents.

The most definitive source of occupational information is O*Net, a database developed and maintained by the U.S. Department of Labor. It is available in print form, within the prominent Web-based career information systems, and on a Web site at onetcenter.org. This database describes more than 1,100 occupations by hundreds of characteristics and is available in both English and Spanish (onetcenter.org/db_spanish.html). The organization of this database allows students and clients to relate information about themselves in many different ways, focusing on single characteristics or a combination of characteristics. It also provides a skills inventory; completion of this inventory identifies occupations in the database. Further, the site allows the download of three assessment instruments—the O*Net Interest Profiler, the O*Net Ability Profiler, and the O*Net Work Importance Profiler—either in print form or as executable code. Its latest development, added in 2011, is the addition of a companion site (mynextmove.dol.gov) called My Next Move. From this site users may take the O*Net Interest Profiler, whose results are provided in the form of a Holland code. Upon selection of a level of achieved or planned education, users receive a list of suggested occupations and can receive descriptions of these.

A second publication of the U.S. Department of Labor 2012 is The Occupational Outlook Handbook (OOH), available both in print form and on a Web site (bls.gov/oco). This book, updated every two years, provides extensive data about approximately 250 occupations, covering about 104 million jobs. Lengthy descriptions include all of the topics included in the NCDA's guidelines. The content of this book is updated and expanded on a quarterly basis in *The Occupational Outlook Quarterly (OOQ)*, a publication available by subscription and at bls.gov/opub/ooq/ooqhome.htm.

The U.S. Department of Labor Web site, *CareerInfoNet* (acinet.org), is a very rich source of occupational information. The site offers a keyword-search capability for more than a thousand occupations (same titles as the *O**Net database) as well as extensive descriptions of them, including detailed data about their employment outlook and salary range as a national average and by each state. There are also videos about the work tasks of most of the occupations. The site also provides a listing and data about the fastest-growing occupations, those with the largest employment, those that are declining, those that pay the highest salaries, and those related to the greening of America. The Resources section of the site offers linkages to a wide array of Web sites that provide assessment, occupational information, resume-writing instruction, job-seeking instruction, and general career planning support. The site also provides a military-to-civilian occupation translator.

In addition to the publications, Web sites, and databases developed by the federal government, many private publishers offer high-quality material. Examples of these are listed next. Searches for relevant occupational titles and detailed descriptions of them are most useful at Steps 3, 4, and 5 of the career planning process model.

Representative print resources include:

- *Encyclopedia of Careers and Vocational Guidance* (J.G. Ferguson Publishing, 2010)
- *The Occupational Outlook Handbook* (U.S. Department of Labor, 2012)
- *Young Person's Occupational Outlook Handbook* (Jist Publications, 2010)

Representative software:

- *CareerCruising* (Career Cruising, 2011)
- *Career Futures for Middle Schools* (Xap Corporation, 2011a)
- *Choices Explorer* (Xap Corporation, 2011b)
- *COIN* (Coin Educational Products, 2011)
- *DISCOVER* (ACT, 2011)
- *Galaxy* (Kuder, Inc., 2011a)
- *Journey* (Kuder, Inc., 2011b)
- *Navigator* (Kuder, Inc., 2011c)
- *Paws in Jobland* (Xap Corporation, 2011c)

Representative Web sites:

- U.S. Department of Labor sites: acinet.org (*CareerInfoNet*), onetcenter.org (*O**Net), bls.gov/oco (*Occupational Outlook Handbook*), and mynextmove.dol.gov (*MyNextMove*).
- State of Nebraska: nebraskacareerconnections.org
- State of Missouri: missouriconnections.org
- State of South Carolina: palmettopathways.org
- State of Kansas: kansascareerpipeline.org
- State of Michigan: michigan.gov/careers

Schools

Prior to seeking data about individual schools, students and clients need to understand the various types of schools, training, and degrees or certifications. These types include the following:

1. **Private (often called *proprietary*) vocational-technical schools.** These are for-profit schools that typically provide training for specific vocational fields within a three-month to two-year time frame. Though some offer associate degrees, most offer certificates that document the fact that students have successfully completed a program of study. There is a wide variation in the quality of these schools.

   Representative print data sources:

   - *Peterson's Vocational and Technical Schools* (Peterson's Publishing, 2006)

   Representative Web sites:

   - Guide to Career Education: guidetocareereducation.com
   - RWM Vocational Schools Database: rwm.org/rwm
   - Peterson's: petersons.com/college-search/career-college.aspx
   - College Surfing: collegesurfing.com
   - Search 4 Career Colleges: search4careercolleges.com

2. **Public community colleges.** These schools offer two categories of majors: transfer and career-related. Students who enter the transfer program plan to continue at a 4-year institution after 2 years at the community college where they typically receive an associate degree. Students in the career-related program expect to end formal education after completion of a career-technology program in fields such as electronics, information sciences, auto body repair, X-ray technology, and many more. These students receive either a certificate (in a program of less than two years' length) or an associate degree. Community colleges offer training in the same fields as private vocational-technical schools, often with much lower tuition fees and higher-quality teaching.

   Representative print resources:

   - *Peterson's Two-Year Colleges* (Peterson's Publishing, 2011)
   - *Two-Year College Databook* (Chronicle Guidance, 2009a)

   Representative Web-based systems:

   - *CareerCruising* (Career Cruising, 2011)
   - *Choices Explorer* (Xap Corporation, 2011b)
   - *DISCOVER* (ACT, 2011)
   - *Navigator* (Kuder, Inc., 2011c)
   - *Journey* (Kuder, Inc., 2011b)

3. **Four-year colleges and universities.** These come in many sizes and types. They may be funded by private or public funds, may be liberal arts colleges or universities, may be church-related or not, and may have a wide range of admission standards. They also have a wide variety of majors, and different schools have outstanding programs in specific areas.

Representative print resources:

- *Colleges That Change Lives: 40 Schools That Will Change the Way You Think About Colleges* (Pope, 2006)
- *Four-Year College Data Book* (Chronicle Guidance, 2009b)
- *Guide to the Most Competitive Colleges* (Barron's Educational Publications, 2011)
- *Peterson's Four-Year Colleges* (Peterson's Publishing, 2010b)
- *The Big Book of Colleges* (College Prowler, 2010)

Representative software:

- *CareerCruising* (Career Cruising, 2011)
- *Choices Explorer* (Xap Corporation, 2011b)
- *COIN* (Ebsco Publishing, 2011)
- *DISCOVER* (ACT, Inc., 2011)
- *Journey* (Kuder, Inc., 2011b)
- *Navigator* (Kuder, Inc., 2011c)

Representative Web sites:

- **CollegeNET:** collegenet.com
- **CommunityCollege.com:** communitycollege.com
- **COOL: College Opportunities Online:** nces.ed.gov/ipeds/cool
- **Go College:** gocollege.com
- **I'm Higher:** communitycolleges.imhigher.com
- **Peterson's Education Center:** petersons.com
- *U.S. News and World Report:* usnews.com
- **Yahoo, HigherEducation:** yahoo.com/education/highereducation

4. **Graduate schools.** These include universities offering master's degrees, certificates of advanced study, and doctorates, as well as schools of medicine, dentistry, veterinary science, and pharmacy.

Representative print resources:

- *ABA-LSAC Official Guide to ABA-Approved Law Schools: 2012 Edition* (Margolis, 2012)
- *Barron's Guide to Medical and Dental Schools, 12th Edition* (Wischnitzer & Wischnitzer, 2009)
- *Graduate Schools in the U.S. 2011* (Peterson's Publishing, 2010c)
- *Insider's Guide to Graduate Programs in Clinical and Counseling Psychology* (Mayne, Norcross, & Sayette, 2010)
- *The Best 168 Medical Schools, 2011 Edition* (Princeton Review, 2010a)
- *Peterson's Graduate Programs in Engineering and Applied Science* (Peterson's Publishing, 2010a)
- *Medical School Admission Requirements 2011–2012: The Most Authoritative Guide to U.S. and Canadian Medical Colleges* (Association of American Medical Colleges, 2011)

Representative software:

- *CareerCruising* (Career Cruising, 2011)
- *Choices Explorer* (Xap Corporation, 2011b)

- *DISCOVER* (ACT, Inc., 2011)
- *Journey* (Kuder, Inc., 2011b)

Representative Web sites:

- **Grad Schools:** gradschools.us.com/?kw=default&afid=101&seed=Grad+School#_firstStep
- **Peterson's Education Center:** petersons.com
- *U.S. News and World Report*: usnews.com

The United States Department of Labor is predicting that, in the early 21st century, approximately 20% of jobs will require a bachelor's or advanced degree; 65% will require some education or training after high school, up to two years; and the remaining 15% can be filled by high school graduates or dropouts. This information may help students and their parents make informed decisions about the levels of postsecondary education to pursue.

Financial Aid

Many students need financial aid in order to pursue the type of education they would like to have. Most schools use a federally established formula for determining whether a family or independent student needs financial assistance. This formula is embodied in the *Free Application for Federal Student Aid (FAFSA)*, a form that students and parents complete and submit for processing. It is available in print form from high school counselors or college financial aid officers and on the Internet at fafsa.ed.gov. Completing the form results in a number, called the *expected family contribution,* which reveals the dollar figure that a family (or an independent student not supported by family) is considered capable of contributing toward a year of college. The formula used in FAFSA can be summarized as follows:

Total cost of one year at college minus Expected Family Contribution for one year equals Unmet need.

Using this general formula, note these two examples:

$40,000 (expensive college)	$22,000 (less expensive college)
$14,600 (expected family contribution)	$14,600 (expected family contribution)
$25,400 (unmet need)	$ 7,400 (unmet need)

The college financial aid officer at the expensive college would try to provide financial assistance to the student who filed this application in the amount of the *unmet need,* that is, $25,400. This amount may be awarded from three kinds of resources: private, state, or federal grant funds; federal loan funds; and/or part-time work on campus. Money allocated from the first source would not have to be repaid. Loans, however, would have to be repaid. Typically, repayment starts after graduation and entry into a job, and the rate of interest is reasonable.

High school counselors and college financial aid officers know about many hidden sources of financial aid information. These may be grants from community organizations, professional associations, companies, and individuals who have set up trust funds for this purpose. Further, many types of financial aid are provided by the state and federal governments. In addition to learning about private sources on the job, counselors find the following resources to be valuable.

Representative print resources:

- *Chronicle Financial Aid Guide 2009–2010: Scholarships and Loans for High School Students, College Undergraduates, Graduates, and Adult Learners* (Chronicle Guidance Publications, 2009c)
- *College Board Scholarship Handbook 2011* (College Entrance Examination Board, 2010)
- *Paying for College Without Going Broke 2011* (Princeton Review, 2010b)
- *The Ultimate Scholarship Book 2011: Billions of Dollars in Scholarships, Grants, and Prizes* (Tanabe & Tanabe, 2010)

Representative software:

- *CareerCruising* (Career Cruising, 2011)
- *Choices Explorer* (Xap Corporation, 2011b)
- *DISCOVER* (ACT, Inc., 2011)
- *Navigator* (Kuder, Inc., 2011c)
- *Journey* (Kuder, Inc., 2011b)

Representative Web sites:

- CollegeBoard: apps.collegeboard.com/cbsearch
- FastWeb: fastweb.com
- Scholarships.com: scholarships.com/scholarship-search.aspx
- *U.S. News and World Report*: usnews.com
- United States Department of Education: studentaid.ed.gov/PORTALSWebApp/students/english/index.jsp
- National Association of Financial Aid Administrators: finaid.org

Information about financial aid is relevant at Step 6 of the career planning process.

Jobs

In many settings counselors assist students and clients in writing resumes, learning job interviewing skills, and identifying job openings, activities related to Step 7 of the career planning process. Adults can seek such services from their state Job Service offices (often called career centers or one-stop centers). The locations and services of these offices can be found at servicelocator.org. In addition, there are many good Web sites that assist with this step.

Especially in the present economic downturn, counselors need to be prepared to assist clients with grieving job loss, and with learning how to survive while unemployed and how to find a job. Many adults who find themselves out of work have not had to face the job market for many years. They do not know how to prepare or update their resumes, how to apply their skills to other occupations, or how to present themselves in a job interview. Young people and adults do not know how to use social networking wisely in the job search, and indeed, many are never invited to an interview because of the kinds of public posting they have done on sites like Facebook. Chapter 7 provides more information about the power of the Web for creating and sustaining a social network that can be positive for job searching.

There are multiple books on all of these topics, but the Web is an abundant and rapidly updated source of information about jobs and job-seeking. Two sites that offer a large amount of information on these topics as well as the capability to post resumes and see employer job listings are Riley's Guide (riley.com) and Job Hunters Bible (jobhuntersbible.com).

Representative Web sites:

- Most states have a Web-based job bank, listing open positions in their state. Go to or call the nearest Job Service office (servicelocator.org) to use this job bank or get its URL for your state.
- CareerBuilder: careerbuilder.com
- Indeed: indeed.com
- NationJob: nationjob.com
- MonsterBoard: monsterboard.com
- Richard Bolles's site: jobhuntersbible.com
- The Riley Guide: rileyguide.com

OTHER METHODS OF COLLECTING DATA

The previous section focused on collecting data to inform the decision-making process through reading books, Web sites, or computer databases. Reading the resources listed in this chapter will be very helpful to support Steps 3 (identify occupational alternatives), 4 (collect data), 5 (make tentative choices), 6 (make educational choices), and 7 (implement a vocational choice). However, it will be even more helpful at Step 5 (make tentative choices) to collect data from additional sources, including career days, job shadowing, part-time jobs, and internships.

Career days, commonly offered in high schools, expose students to a wide variety of occupations through direct contact with people who work in those occupations. Speakers may be brought in to the school, or students may be taken to workplaces. In either case the experience will have greater meaning if (a) the occupations are categorized in some meaningful way and (b) there has been some prior activity that suggests specific occupations for exploration. The occupations represented in the career fair may be organized by the six Holland or ACT clusters or by the 16 States' industry-based clusters (see careerclusters.org). Assessment may have been administered to identify the students' preferred clusters. Students can then be scheduled to hear speakers or visit sites that represent those clusters.

Common ways for students to learn about occupations are mentoring (which may be e-mentoring) and job shadowing. In job shadowing (see ja.org/programs/programs_job_shadow.shtml), arrangements are made for students to spend a day with a person in an occupation they are considering. This firsthand experience allows students to view day-to-day activities of the occupation, experience a typical worksite, and ask questions of a person in the occupation. Part-time jobs, carefully chosen, can offer the same kind of experience for a longer period of time. At the college level, students may apply for an internship in an occupation of their choice. An internship allows students to take coursework and work part-time simultaneously. Students receive pay for the work and may also receive college credit.

These methods of providing on-site exploration of occupations can be very valuable when well supported. First, they need to be well planned and organized so that students with specific interests are matched with people and sites that represent those interests. Second, students should be prepared for the experience in advance. Such preparation would include explaining the purpose of the experience and providing worksheets or guidelines for what the student should learn. It is as valuable to find out that interest in the occupation is not confirmed as it is to find out that there is interest in that occupation. Finally, as with all kinds of data collection, there should be a follow-through activity, either individual or group, that helps students analyze what they have learned and what the learning means for personal decision making or further exploration.

ORGANIZING OCCUPATIONS

In the former *Dictionary of Occupational Titles* (U.S. Department of Labor, 1991), nearly 13,000 occupations were described. and more than 1,100 groups of occupations are detailed in the *Dictionary's* replacement, called *O*Net*. This vast difference in number of occupations exists because *The Dictionary of Occupational Titles (DOT)* breaks occupations into finer divisions; for example, the DOT describes multiple types of cooks (fast-food cook, pastry cook, pizza cook, etc.), whereas *O*Net* provides a general description of cook.

Even with the smaller number of 1,100 occupations, it is necessary to present these to career planners in some organized way. It is impossible to learn about all occupations individually, and providing information about groups of occupations allows students and clients to narrow their search to specific groups prior to getting into great detail. There are four common organizational systems used in schools and agencies: Holland's system (Holland, 1997), ACT's classification system (Prediger, 1981), the Department of Labor *O*Net* system, and the States' career clusters. Each is briefly described.

The Holland System

Holland's theory (1997) proposes that work environments can be described as combinations of six different types: Realistic, Investigative, Artistic, Social, Enterprising, and Conventional. Definitions of these six types are provided in Chapter 2. Based on more than 30 years of research, Holland and his collaborators have provided three-letter Holland codes for most occupations. *The Occupations Finder* (wahyan.edu.hk/paulsir/occupation/occupations%20finder.pdf) provides codes for 1,224 occupations; the *Dictionary of Holland Occupational Codes* (Gottfredson & Holland, 1996) provides codes for 12,860 occupations. The *O*Net* database provides a two-letter Holland code for each of its occupations. As reviewed in Chapter 5, taking one of several inventories of interests and/or skills will provide a personal Holland code for a student or client. Use of such assessment will make it easy for counselors to recommend, or students to choose, speakers or sites that are most likely to be of interest to them.

The World-of-Work Map

Based on the research done by Holland while employed by ACT, the original hex-agonal model was expanded to a circle called the World-of-Work Map (Figure 6.1). In addition to changing the hexagon to a circle, the six Holland personality types describing characteristics of people were changed to titles for six groups of occupa-tions that provide work tasks and environments that the persons of a given Holland type would be likely to enjoy. Further, the concept of primary work tasks—that is, working with People, Data, Things, and/or Ideas—was added based on further re-search (Prediger, 1981). Thus, the Holland types have the following equivalents on the World-of-Work Map:

Holland type	ACT occupational cluster	Primary work tasks
Social	Social Service	Work with People
Enterprising	Administration/Sales	Work with People and Data
Conventional	Business Organization	Work with Data and Things
Realistic	Technical	Work with Things
Investigative	Science and Technology	Work with Things and Ideas
Artistic	Arts	Work with Ideas and People

Finally, ACT's research identified 26 families of occupations called *career areas,* groups of homogenous occupations, based on their work tasks. These 26 career areas were plotted on the Map based on the degree to which the occupations in the group require work with data, people, things, and/or ideas. On a horizontal continuum through the Map, those groups that require relatively more contact with people are placed to the left of center, and those requiring more work with things/equipment are plotted to the right of center. On a vertical continuum through the Map, those families that require relatively more work with data are plotted above the center line of the Map, and those requiring relatively more work with ideas are plotted below the center line of the Map.

Using *Career Area Charts* (ACT, 2007) or ACT's Web site (actstudent.org/career/aboutwwm.html), it is possible to find out where more than 500 common occupations and majors are plotted on the Map. Using ACT's career planning assessments or *DISCOVER,* it is possible to plot individuals on the Map based on their interests and/or self-estimated abilities. High schools, vocational-technical schools, and col-leges can assign their majors to the 26 career areas and thus to occupations. ACT's Web site at actstudent.org/career/majors.html also offers exploration of postsecondary majors by clusters and career areas on the Map.

O*Net Classification System

O*Net has become the foundational source for occupational information, avail-able at onet.center.org. As mentioned earlier, it offers a very detailed description of more than 1,100 occupational groups related to the content and context

Figure 6.1
World-of-work map.
Source: Copyright © 2001 by ACT, Inc. All rights reserved. Used by permission.

of work. Occupations are described by more than 300 characteristics, including worker requirements, knowledge areas needed, basic and cross-functional skills needed, associated work values, Holland code, work tasks, education requirements, experience, and training. A skills search allows individuals to assess their own skills and to relate them to occupations in the database.

The results of the *O*Net Interest Profiler*, *Ability Profiler*, and *Work Importance Locator* link individuals directly to occupations in this database. The My Next Move Web site (mynextmove.dol.gov) offers an online version of the *O*Net Interest Profiler* whose results suggest a list of occupations related to the user's interests and planned education level. Selecting any of the occupations on the list provides a short description of the occupation and offers a link to online *O*Net* for a more detailed description.

U.S. Department of Education (Now Called The States') Career Clusters

The U.S. Department of Education established 16 broad career clusters. Each cluster consists of entry-level through professional-level occupations in a broad industry area. The cluster also includes the academic and technical skills and knowledge needed for further education and work in the occupations contained in the cluster. Occupations assigned to a cluster are divided into sub-groups, or specialties called *career pathways*. Descriptions of these clusters are available at careerclusters.org. The *Kuder Career Search with Person Match* interest inventory (Kuder & Zytowski, 1999) and the *Kuder Skills Assessment* link individuals to the titles of occupations and postsecondary majors in these clusters through Kuder's career planning systems, *Navigator* and *Journey*.

THE CAREER CENTER

The resources cited in this chapter and many others—including videos, journals, books, assessment instruments, and a variety of software programs—need to be housed in some physical place, typically called a *career center*. This physical place should be of sufficient size to handle the collection, be an attractive place to read or use computers, be centrally located within the larger facility, and be well organized. Especially given the growing importance of Web sites as providers of career data, the center should contain computers both for the use of locally resident software and for linkage to the Internet. It also should contain equipment for viewing videos and taking assessment instruments.

There are various methods of organizing materials in a career center: (1) by type (print, video, software locally used, Internet access); (2) by content (self-information, occupational information, school information, financial aid information, etc.); (3) by step of the career planning process; or (4) by life role (student, worker, parent, leisurite, citizen, etc.).

Career centers should be staffed with one or more trained persons who have extensive content knowledge of all of their resources. In recognition of the need for trained personnel to work in career centers in support of counselors and clients, the National Occupational Information Coordinating Committee (NOICC) funded the development of a curriculum in the early 1990s for training paraprofessionals. This new occupation has been titled career development facilitator (CDF). The curriculum addresses 12 basic competencies that these paraprofessionals need, including basic helping skills, knowledge of labor market and occupational information, job-seeking skills, and ability to navigate computer-based systems and Web sites. Upon successful completion of this curriculum (for detailed information, see ncda.org) and application to the Center for Credentialing and Education (CCE), individuals can be certified. Trained CDFs can help students and clients acquire data to assist with career planning. Counselors need to assume responsibility for assisting students and clients in processing and making effective use of those data for personal decision making.

Virtual career centers are increasingly being developed on the Internet. Typically, these contain a combination of online assessments, locally developed databases (such as descriptions of majors available at a given institution), linkages to a selected and organized list of Web sites, and support from a counselor via the Internet. Such support may be by synchronous (both persons at the computer at the same time) or asynchronous (persons not at the machine at the same time) e-mail or video conferencing using a product such as Skype. With the rapidly expanding technology that allows images to be transmitted in real time, it has become feasible for counselors and clients to have real-time, face-to-face conversation via the Internet, removing the barrier of distance.

Tips from the Field

Despite a wealth and often an overload of data about occupations, majors, schools, and financial aid, counselors must assist their students/clients in processing these data through their own interests, skills, and values. In other words, the data only have meaning when they inform an individual's personal decision making.

HELPING CLIENTS TURN DATA INTO INFORMATION

The most difficult and also the most essential role of the counselor is to assist students and clients to make sense out of what can be an overload of data about occupations, schools and other training opportunities, financial aid, and so on. The goal is to use the data to make it clear which of the various alternatives (about occupational choice, type of training or school, scholarships available, and/or jobs to apply for) should be further explored and which should be removed from consideration. This section of the chapter illustrates how counselors can perform this essential work and offers two case studies.

Chris is a high school junior who feels pressured by both his counselor and his parents to state an occupational goal and an educational plan. As a part of some special career guidance activities the counselors are doing in English classes, he spent two hours in the school's career center. While there he took an interest inventory included in a computer-based career planning system, which provided a printout with the titles of 48 occupations. At the direction of the paraprofessional in the center, he found many facts about 12 of these occupations through reading reference books, using the system's database, and linking to some sites on the Internet. As a result, he has 34 pages of print-out and feels more confused about his possible choice of occupation than he did when he came into the center. Fortunately, he is going to have an interview with his counselor; he hopes that she can help him out of his confusion.

In this typical case, what can a counselor do to provide helpful assistance that will cut through this pile of paper and help the student move to some certainty about next career planning steps? Here are some suggestions:

- If the student has taken the interest inventory only in the Web-based system, the counselor should consider what other kind(s) of assessment, if any, might be helpful in this specific case. Since Chris is a high school junior, an assessment of values might be premature. A simple checklist of job characteristics, from which Chris is asked to select 5 to 10 items that are most important, would be one good approach.
- The counselor may ask Chris to tell about some of the most interesting courses, experiences, or leisure activities he has had and ask why he found these interesting, relating these reasons to characteristics of occupations.
- A review of Chris's high school record may help him identify some courses and abilities that surpass others. The counselor may also ask him about his plans or aspirations for education after high school.
- Chris may be asked to list occupations about which he has daydreamed in the past and tell what was attractive to him about these, even though he may not know the details of the work tasks or training. From this activity and previous ones, he can make a list of characteristics (such as having a lot of independence, making more than the average amount of money, not having to travel long distances as a requirement of work, or not working with numbers and mathematics) of importance to him.
- Chris could share the list of occupations identified by the interest inventory he took, relating which, if any, of these occupational titles were attractive to him, and why. He could state which, if any, of these he would not consider and why, and compare the characteristics of occupations on the list with the personal list he has just developed.
- Using the list from the Web-based system and any others that may have been added during interviews, Chris might be asked to place the titles in three columns: those he would definitely not pursue, those that hold some promise, and those that he is favoring most.
- Chris should be given assignments designed to help him learn more about the list of occupations he is favoring most. This may initially include further research in the career center, using books, software, or Internet sites, depending on whether Chris has already adequately researched the favored occupations in this way. Additional activities may be designed to put Chris directly in touch with people who work in this occupation. This may be a job-shadowing assignment or an information interview with one or more persons who work in each of these occupations. He should be given a worksheet as a part of the assignment to assure that he collects the data that he needs. This worksheet should include questions

that he suggests as well as the ordinary ones, such as benefits and limitations of the job, training required, opportunities for promotion, degree of independence, and what the person wishes he or she had known before entering the occupation.

- Following this assignment, Chris should be scheduled for another interview to discuss what he has learned from these assignments. He may analyze each of the occupations he has researched further by the list of important characteristics developed in the previous session and write down his current list of preferred occupations in priority order. He should be aware that he will make numerous career changes during his lifetime and that he should consider and be prepared for more than one occupation.

- With a short list of occupations in mind, Chris and his counselor should review the amount and type of education needed for these jobs and determine whether they all require the same level of education, such as community college or four-year college, or whether some could be entered through apprenticeship. Based on this review, Chris may be able to select a postsecondary educational goal. This might be an ideal time to include his parents in the discussion of his goals.

- Dependent upon the postsecondary plans, Chris may be directed to other resources (computer searches, Web sites, books) that will assist with the selection of schools in which the needed training can be acquired. The counselor can provide a worksheet that lists the characteristics (such as geographic location, size of school, level of admission selectivity, type of school, cost range, student activities, etc.) that he and his parents can consider. He also needs to determine how various selections (such as how large the school is or how far away from home it is) will affect him and his parents.

- The counselor may help Chris to select the most relevant courses for his senior year and to make a timetable for coming back to talk about school selection, taking entrance tests, and filing applications for entry and financial aid.

This suggested approach combines good use of technology for acquiring data with counselor support for processing the data in a way that helps Chris and his parents make informed decisions.

As indicated at the beginning of this chapter, Clarice is a 28-year-old single parent of three children who lives in a modest apartment and receives support from public aid. Recent legislation, however, has mandated that she go to work within a year and has provided access to funding for some training. She dropped out of high school in her sophomore year after her first child was born. She has held part-time jobs at various fast-food restaurants since that time. Clarice goes to a no-fee community agency for assistance in determining what she can do to meet the requirements of the legislation.

What can a counselor do? Here are some suggestions:

- An extensive intake interview is a needed first step. During this interview, the counselor can learn about high school courses taken, expressed interests, motivational level, skills, details of part-time jobs, family situation, support system (network of friends and family), barriers (such as physical handicaps, need for child care, and lack of transportation), and goals.

- The counselor might decide to administer some assessment, such as an interest inventory (to broaden the options that the client may have expressed). From the list of occupations suggested by this inventory and the intake interview, the counselor and client can develop a list of reasonable (in terms of the amount of training needed) options. Clarice and the counselor make a list of five characteristics that are most important for the occupation to be selected: (1) does not require more than two years of training beyond high school completion, (2) does not require work during the evening or on weekends, (3) offers an opportunity to work directly with people and with equipment, (4) offers an opportunity for career growth when additional education can be attained when children are older, and (5) offers a beginning salary of at least $30,000 per year.

- The counselor asks Clarice to go to the local library and access *The Occupational Outlook Handbook* and *CareerInfoNet* to learn details about the identified occupations. Clarice has not used the Internet before, so the counselor provides a worksheet with step-by-step instructions about how to access each of these sites and how to find the assigned information. Further, the counselor instructs the client to go to a specific person at the library to receive some general instruction about how to use the equipment and how to obtain assistance that may be needed in completing the assignment. The counselor asks Clarice to bring the printout to the next session or good, detailed notes if the library charges for printed pages and the cost of this is not feasible.

- Clarice completes the assignment and comes back the next week with printed descriptions of several occupations that require high school completion and training beyond that. The counselor helps Clarice evaluate each of the occupations in relation to the five criteria developed during the intake interview. Three occupations pass that review: radiation therapist, dental assistant, and dental hygienist. According to *CareerInfoNet,* there is a high demand for workers in all three of these occupations in Clarice's state of residence, and beginning salaries for all three are above $30,000.

- The counselor suggests that Clarice complete two homework assignments before the next session: (1) have an informational interview with a person in each of these three occupations, and (2) investigate sources of getting a high school diploma by taking the General Educational Development (GED) exam. The counselor explains what an information interview is and gives Clarice a list of suggested questions to which she can add others. The counselor makes some phone calls and sets up these three interviews at times when Clarice's mother will care for the youngest child. The counselor also gives Clarice the URL address of the Web site of the state labor department. One section of this site provides a list of opportunities for completing the GED exam.

- Clarice returns after completion of these assignments with enthusiasm about the opportunity to prepare for taking the GED exam through a course offered by the local community college. Her mother has agreed to stay with the children one night per week so that she can attend this course. Further, she indicates that, based on the visits she has made, she would like to pursue training to become an X-ray technician.

- The counselor works with Clarice, using a specific form, to develop an action plan and a time schedule designed to accomplish two primary goals: (1) getting a high school diploma by preparing to take the GED exam and (2) seeking entry into the X-ray technician program at the community college. The plan includes funding by the agency for the GED preparation course and coursework in the X-ray technician program at the community college. The plan also includes child care during class times and transportation to the community college. The counselor invites Clarice to call her at any time and indicates that she should call each month to make an appointment so that they can review progress in completion of the action plan.

MyCounselingLab™

Go to Topic 14: *Information in Career Guidance and Counseling* in the MyCounselingLab™ site (www.MyCounselingLab.com) for *Career Development Interventions in the 21st Century,* Fourth Edition, where you can:

- Find learning outcomes for *Information in Career Guidance and Counseling* along with the national standards that connect to these outcomes.

- Complete Assignments and Activities that can help you more deeply understand the chapter content.
- Apply and practice your understanding of the core skills identified in the chapter with the Building Counseling Skills unit.
- Prepare yourself for professional certification with a Practice for Certification quiz.
- Connect to videos through the Video and Resource Library.

Summary

This chapter has described various types of resources available in print and electronic form that are critical sources of data as individuals engage in the career planning process. The responsibilities of counselors in selecting and using these resources wisely are reviewed. Similarly, the responsibilities of students and clients to spend the time and effort needed to acquire data are reviewed. Great emphasis is placed upon the fact that providing good data to students and clients is not in and of itself sufficient to ensure that career decision making will be informed. The counselor's responsibility and role to help students and clients sort through a mass of data and transform elements of it into meaningful information is stressed. Finally, two cases have been presented with suggestions about how a counselor might deal with them.

Case Study

Roel is a college sophomore, and he is faced with the need to declare a major. He comes to you in his college counseling center to ask for your assistance. You ask him how he has reached other major decisions in his life, such as which part-time jobs to accept, which car to buy, or which college to attend.

As Roel recounts how he has made these decisions and others, you begin to see the pattern that he typically is an impulsive decider, selecting an alternative that sounds good at the moment without seeking other alternatives or in-depth information.

Given this past history, how would you go about helping Roel to select one of more than one hundred majors available at your college?

Student Activities

The suggestions provided for Clarice on pages 221–223 are quite traditional and reflect a cognitive decision-making approach. This approach serves many clients well, but is not helpful for others. Think about and write an answer to these two questions within one double-spaced page:

- For what kinds of clients might this approach **not** be helpful? Why?

- What alternate approaches might a counselor use to help Clarice reconstruct her life?

References

ACT, Inc. (1989a). *Inventory of Work-Relevant Abilities.* Iowa City, IA: Author.

ACT, Inc. (1989b). *UNIACT Interest Inventory.* Iowa City, IA: Author.

ACT, Inc. (2007). *Career area charts.* Iowa City, IA: Author.

ACT, Inc. (2011). *DISCOVER* [Computer software]. Iowa City, IA: Author.

Association of American Medical Colleges. (2011). *Medical school admission requirements 2011-2012: The most authoritative guide to U.S. and Canadian medical colleges.* Washington, DC: Author.

Barron's Educational Publications. (2011). *Guide to the most competitive colleges.* Hauppauge, NY: Author.

Campbell, D. (1992). *Campbell Interest and Skill Survey.* Minneapolis, MN: NCS Assessments.

CareerCruising. (2011). CareerCruising [Computer software]. Toronto, Canada: Author.

Chronicle Guidance Publications. (2009a). *Four-year data book.* Moravia, NY: Author.

Chronicle Guidance Publications. (2009b). *Two-year college data book.* Moravia, NY: Author.

Chronicle Guidance Publications. (2009c). *Financial aid guide.* Moravia, NY: Author.

Coin Educational Products (2011). *COIN.* Toledo, OH: Author.

College Entrance Examination Board. (2010). *College board scholarship handbook.* New York: Author.

College Prowler. (2010). *The big book of colleges 2011.* Pittsburgh, PA: Author.

Dinklage, L. B. (1968). *Decision strategies of adolescents.* Unpublished doctoral dissertation, Harvard University, Cambridge, MA.

Ebsco Publishers. (2011). *COIN* [Computer software]. Ipswich, MA: Author.

Fedorko, J., & Allott, D. (2006). *The internship files: How to get, keep, and make the most of your internship.* New York: Simon & Schuster.

Gottfredson, G. D., & Holland, J. L. (1996). *The dictionary of Holland occupational codes.* Odessa, FL: Psychological Assessment Resources.

Harrington, T., & O' Shea, A. J. (2000). *Career decision-making system.* Circle Pines, MN: American Guidance Service.

Holland, J. L. (1994a). *The occupations finder.* Odessa, FL: Psychological Assessment Resources.

Holland, J. L. (1994b). *The Self-Directed Search™.* Odessa, FL: Psychological Assessment Resources.

Holland, J. L. (1997). *Making vocational choices: A theory of vocational personalities and work environments* (3rd ed.). Odessa, FL: Psychological Assessment Resources.

Holmberg, K., Rosen, D., & Holland, J. L. (1999). *The leisure activities finder.* Odessa, FL: Psychological Assessment Resources.

J. G. Ferguson Publishing. (2010). *Encyclopedia of careers and vocational guidance.* Chicago, IL: Author.

Jist Publications. (2010). *Young person's occupational outlook handbook.* St. Paul, MN: Author.

Johansson, C. B. (1984). *Career Assessment Inventory.* Minneapolis, MN: NCS Assessments.

Krumboltz, J. D. (1991). *The Career Beliefs Inventory.* Palo Alto, CA: Consulting Psychologists Press.

Kuder, F., & Zytowski, D. (1999). *The Kuder career search with Person Match.* Adel, IA: Kuder, Inc.

Kuder, Inc. (2011a). *Galaxy* [Computer software]. Adel, IA: Author.

Kuder, Inc. (2011b). *Journey* [Computer software]. Adel, IA: Author.

Kuder, Inc. (2011c). *Navigator* [Computer software]. Adel, IA: Author.

Landes, M. (2005). *The back door guide to short-term job adventures: Internships, extraordinary experiences, seasonal jobs, volunteering, work abroad.* Berkeley, CA: Ten Speed Press.

Margolis, W. (Ed.). (2012). *ABA-LSAC official guide to ABA-approved law schools: 2012 Edition.* Lawrenceville, NJ: Arco.

Mayne, T. J., Norcross, J. G., & Sayette, M. A. (2010). *Insider's guide to graduate programs in clinical and counseling psychology.* New York: Guilford Press.

National Career Development Association. (1991). *Guidelines for the preparation and evaluation of career and occupational information literature.* Broken Arrow, OK: Author.

Peterson's Publishing. (2004). Internships 2005: The largest source of internships available. Lawrenceville, NJ: Author.

Peterson's Publishing. (2006). *Peterson's vocational and technical schools.* Lawrenceville, NJ: Author.

Peterson's Publishing. (2010a). *Graduate programs in engineering and applied science.* Lawrenceville, NJ: Author.

Peterson's Publishing. (2010b). *Peterson's four-year colleges 2010.* Lawrenceville, NJ: Author.

Peterson's Publishing. (2010c). *Graduate schools in the U.S. 2011.* Lawrenceville, NJ: Author.

Peterson's Publishing. (2011). *Peterson's two-year colleges 2011.* Lawrenceville, NJ: Author.

Pope, L. (2006). *Colleges that change lives: 40 colleges that will change the way you think about colleges.* New York: Penguin.

Prediger, D. P. (1981). Aid for mapping occupations and interests: A graphic for vocational guidance and research. *Vocational Guidance Quarterly, 30,* 21–36.

Princeton Review. (2005). *The internship bible: 10th edition.* New York: Author.

Princeton Review. (2010a). *The best 168 medical schools.* New York: Author.

Princeton Review. (2010b). *Paying for college without going broke.* New York: Author.

Rosen, D., Holmberg, K., & Holland, J. L. (1999). *The educational opportunities finder.* Odessa, FL: Psychological Assessment Resources.

Sampson, J. P., Reardon, R., Lenz, J., & Peterson G. (2003). *Career counseling and services: A cognitive information processing approach.* Florence, KY: Brooks/Cole.

Tanabe, G., & Tanabe, K. (2010). *The ultimate scholarship book 2011: Billions of dollars in scholarships, grants, and prizes.* Belmont, CA: SuperCollege.

Tiedeman, D., & O'Hara, R. (1963). *Career development: Choice and adjustment.* New York: College Entrance Examination Board.

U.S. Department of Education. (2002). *Classification of instructional programs.* Washington, DC: Author.

U.S. Department of Labor. (1991). *The dictionary of occupational titles.* Washington, DC: U.S. Government Printing Office.

U.S. Department of Labor. (1992). *What work requires of schools.* SCANS Report. Washington, DC: U.S. Government Printing Office.

U.S. Department of Labor. (2011). *O*Net occupational database.* Washington, DC: Author.

U.S. Department of Labor. (2012). *The occupational outlook handbook.* Washington, DC: U.S. Government Printing Office.

Wischnitzer, S., & Wischnitzer, E. (2009). *Barron's guide to medical and dental schools.* Hauppauge, NY: Barron's Educational Publishers.

Xap Corporation (2011a). *Career futures for middle schools.* [Computer software]. Culver City, CA: Author.

Xap Corporation (2011b). *CHOICES Explorer.* [Computer software]. Culver City, CA: Author.

Xap Corporation (2011c). *Paws in jobland.* [Computer software]. Culver City, CA: Author.

7

Using Technology to Support Career Counseling and Planning

Technology changes lives. For some, the changes are better; for others the changes are perceived as negative. In many ways career counselors have been at the forefront of changes in society and mental health. They have been among the first to use new tools and techniques in their work. Nowhere has this been truer than in the use of technology. The use of computers and, more recently, the Internet have changed the ways in which career counselors assist their clients. Though career counselors are, first and foremost, counselors, they are also providers of information. The provision of information when assisting clients with resumé writing, interview coaching, networking, and choosing education and training venues has been made better, faster, and more comprehensive through the Internet. Career counselors are now able to devote more time to counseling and coaching their clients while being able to quickly and easily locate information that supports their work. Popular Web sites have come and gone. But in the years since the Internet became mainstream, it has significantly changed the way career counselors do their work. Now there is no going back. We must learn to use technology to be effective and to provide our clients with the service they need and expect.

David M. Reile, Ph.D., NCCC
Career Development Alliance

MyCounselingLab™

Visit the **MyCounselingLab**™ site for *Career Development Interventions in the 21st Century,* Fourth Edition to enhance your understanding of chapter concepts. You'll have the opportunity to practice your skills through video- and case-based Assignments and Activities as well as Building Counseling Skills units, and to prepare for your certification exam with Practice for Certification quizzes.

In Chapter 2 you learned about Juanita, a 17-year-old Hispanic student in the eleventh grade, who appears to be struggling with poor self-concept, low motivation, low career maturity, lack of role models, and other factors related to making an informed vocational choice. Using one or more theoretical models presented earlier in the text, Juanita's counselor dealt with these factors through one-to-one and small-group interventions. After noting positive change in self-concept, motivation, and career maturity, the high school counselor decided to give Juanita some specific assignments related to the Web-based career planning system that the school has and use of several Web sites. You will note those assignments as you read this chapter.

The purposes of this chapter are to define and describe the primary technologies that have an impact on the delivery of career planning services in the 21st century and to propose how they can best be used to enhance the delivery of career planning services. There is an understandable tendency to confine our perception of technology to that provided by the computer or the Internet. Actually, the field of career planning has been impacted by technologies other than the computer—the test-scoring machine, the video camera, and the telephone, for example. Computers, however, have exerted the most powerful impact on the field because of their capabilities to administer, score, and interpret tests and inventories; teach skills and concepts; facilitate interactive dialogue; store, search, and interrelate huge databases; store a record of the user's interaction; and prompt and monitor a user's interaction with the system. These computer capabilities have been progressively developed and applied to the field of career counseling and support since the late 1960s. Progress of computer-based technology can be viewed in the light of two different contexts. The first context relates to the ever-growing capability of computers progressing from early, stand-alone mainframe computers to networked mini- and personal computers to the World Wide Web of computers, with each of these progressive steps offering the opportunity to serve an increased number of individuals.

The second context is the growing knowledge and body of research that informs counselors about the effectiveness of computer-delivered services for different populations and for different purposes. Many of these purposes have already been covered in Chapters 5 and 6 due to the fact that assessment, occupational information, educational information, and a host of other applications relevant to career planning are now almost exclusively accessed on the Web.

HISTORICAL PERSPECTIVE

Computer-assisted career guidance systems had their genesis in the late 1960s. The IBM Corporation released a computer monitor in the mid-1960s, moving computers from batch-processing work to the capability of simulating an interactive dialogue between the machine and a user at a terminal device, which, at that time, could be as far as 1,000 feet away. This invention prompted several early developers—JoAnn Harris, Joseph Impelleteri, Martin Katz, Donald Super, and David Tiedeman (Super, 1970)—to design systems that could simulate the kind of career counseling interview that a counselor might have with a student or client.

The theorists in the early development group—Katz, Super, and Tiedeman—viewed the computer as a tool that could be used to teach their theories directly to users and hoped that those users would be able to internalize the processes learned. Katz (1963) developed the *System for Interactive Guidance Information (SIGI)* and designed it to teach 10 specific work values (such as prestige, high income, early entry, leisure, leadership, helping others, variety, and security) that he had identified through extensive research; SIGI then assisted the user in assigning each value a level of importance. These weighted values were used to identify occupations from the computer's database that could help the user attain the selected values. Next, test scores measuring the user's abilities were used to estimate the latter's probability of being able to complete the education needed for each of the identified occupations. By multiplying the value of the occupation by the probability of successfully completing the required education, a numerical score could be assigned to each occupation under consideration, ranking them in order of desirability. This early system became the basis for later versions, including the current *Sigi 3* (Valpar International Corporation, 2011).

Working as a consultant to the IBM Corporation, Super developed the *Education and Career Exploration System (ECES)*. This system operationalized some parts of Super's theoretical work, specifically, the capability to use the results of assessment to identify occupations for exploration and the capability to engage in exploratory behavior by accessing microfilm files of occupational descriptions that included black-and-white pictures of work settings and tasks as well as text. Though this system was a significant one in its theoretical base, it was not taken to market by IBM; instead, it was given to Genessee County, Michigan, the site of its field trial.

David Tiedeman, who had a large grant at Harvard University from the U.S. Office of Education, developed the *Information System for Vocational Decisions (ISVD)*. His goal was to have the computer monitor the user's path through an extensive system and teach his seven-step decision-making paradigm (Tiedeman & O'Hara, 1963). In addition to engineering its elegant content design, Tiedeman included two features that were many years ahead of their time: multimedia and natural language capability. The multimedia consisted of the mainframe computer triggering the display of slides by a carousel projector that showed pictures of colleges and occupations. The natural language capability offered the user the opportunity to type in any question or request and have the computer "understand" the meaning sufficiently to provide a logical answer. Due to the great sophistication of this system before technology could support it, it never became operational outside of its developmental setting.

Other developers—practitioners in orientation—developed less-elegant systems. At Pennsylvania State University, Impelleteri (1970) developed the *Computer Occupational Information System (COIS),* which allowed students to explore a variety of vocational-technical programs of study and occupations and make a selection. His untimely death in the early 1970s resulted in the demise of this system. Harris (1970), director of guidance at Willowbrook High School in Illinois, developed the *Computerized Vocational Information System (CVIS)* with funding provided by the Illinois State Board of Vocational Education. This system gave students the opportunity to explore and get information about occupations, colleges, military programs, and apprenticeships. The occupational database was organized by Roe's (1956) classification system, which divides occupations into six educational levels and eight interest fields. Choice of interest field was guided by the results of the *Kuder Preference Record* (Science Research Associates, 1968) interest inventory, and selection of educational level was determined by the student. This system also included a variety of online capabilities for counselors, including the changing of student schedules and review of student records. CVIS was a precursor to *DISCOVER* (ACT, 2011), a more elegant system.

In summary, the earliest computer-based systems had several things in common, as follows:

- They were comprehensive career planning systems, offering a planned sequence of activities for the user.
- They were based, at least in part, on the career development theory available at the time—that of Super, Tiedeman, Katz, and Roe.
- They stored a user record so that a summary of a person's use was kept in order to be accessed by a counselor for follow-through work and to allow the user to continue sequentially from past use.
- They implicitly or explicitly taught a decision-making process considered by the developer to be the most appropriate for career planning.
- They were supported by external sources of public or private funding.
- They operated on large mainframe computers, and, each in its own way, pushed the limit of capabilities of the host machine.

Following these early systems came the era of less comprehensive information systems. These systems were not based on a theoretical model, did not intend to support the entire career planning process, and focused on databases and search strategies. Bruce McKinlay led the development in this arena with the *Career Information System (CIS)* (University of Oregon, 2011). Coming from the labor market information perspective rather than the career development perspective, CIS and other systems that followed it had the occupational database and strategies to search it as their hallmark. In these systems there was very high concern for the quality and currency of the occupational information. As development continued, these systems were expanded to include multiple databases, including searches for vocational-technical schools, two-year and four-year colleges, and financial aid opportunities.

In 1976, a federal organization called the National Occupational Information Coordinating Committee (NOICC) was formed. One of the many initiatives that this organization championed was the development of state *career information delivery systems* (CIDS), computer-based delivery systems that provide occupational and educational information, typically customized for students and adults in a specific state. CIS was used, and still is used, as a basis for these systems in many states. These systems were supported by a combination of federal funding, state funding, and user fees. These state systems collaborated through a professional association called the Association of Computer-Based Systems for Career Information (ACSCI), now encompassed in the Alliance of Career Resource Professionals (ACRP), which has set standards for its quality and promotes its continual expansion and improvement. Similarly, the National Career Development Association (NCDA) has developed standards (NCDA, 1991) for the quality of computer-assisted systems. These standards are available at these organizations' Web sites— acrpro.org and ncda.org.

Characteristics of systems that focus on information are as follows:

- They typically offer multiple databases (occupations, schools, financial aid, etc.), and great care is given to the quality and timeliness of the data.
- They typically provide labor market information (that is, employment outlook and salary) for specific states and regions within the state.
- They typically do not store a user record.
- They do not attempt to provide support to all components (i.e., assessment, instruction, etc.) of the career planning process.
- They are neither theory-based nor do they attempt to teach a planful decision-making process.

Systems of the 21st century are characterized by some new features, representing a synthesis of capabilities not possible in earlier versions. These include the following:

- Almost all systems and applications are Web-based rather than installed on individual computers or networks.
- There is ever-expanding use of dynamic graphics, audio, and streaming video to enhance the message of the systems.
- There are multiple linkages to other sites on the Web and then back to the system itself for the purpose of expanding exponentially the amount of information a user can gain while still being "shepherded" within the confines of an integrated system.
- With more comprehensive systems, it is very common to offer the user the capability to start an e-portfolio at first sign-on and then to maintain and update that portfolio over the lifespan.
- With more comprehensive systems, there is a trend to include content for multiple audiences (i.e., students in grades 5–6, grades 7–8, high school, post-secondary level; adult workers; parents; administrators and counselors) within one system, and to direct the user to appropriate material based on information gained at sign-on.
- There is an increased capability to store documents (such as scanned certificates, transcripts, resumes, cover letters, and work samples) in the user's e-portfolio and then to send these to schools or employers as needed.
- There is a trend for the development of an integrated Web site for no-fee use by all citizens in a given state (such as in Nebraska, Missouri, Kansas, South

Carolina, and Arkansas) through cooperative development and funding by the departments of education, labor, economic development, and/or commerce.

- There is a trend to develop systems in which the text and assessment instruments are available in either English or Spanish.

CURRENT STATUS OF WEB-BASED SYSTEMS

Moving from that rich historical perspective, we now look at the state of this art in the early 21st century. Although this description is confined to what is happening in the United States, it is important to note that the use of Web-based services via computers, iPads, and smart phones is in common practice worldwide. Developing countries appear to be jumping over the computer age to develop telephone-based applications, due to the fact that a larger proportion of their populations have Web access via a phone than by computer.

Integrated Career Planning Systems

Although both Chapters 5 and 6 list a multitude of Web sites that offer either assessment tools or databases, the application described here is a Web site that incorporates tools and databases that assist users through a sequential process that includes multiple steps in the career planning process. The process is typically devised for a specific population such as elementary school students, middle school students, secondary school students, postsecondary students, unemployed adults, veterans, older unskilled adults, or unskilled youth in need of job skills. In other words, for each of these populations a developer has gone through the process of identifying the needs of some specific population and of creating content designed to address those needs. For elementary students, for example, those needs could be gaining some self-awareness, awareness of the breadth of the world-of-work and of the fact that there is a relationship between the two. For older, low-income, unskilled adults, as another example, the needs might be to assess current interests and work skills, provide training to improve skills, assist with developing a resume, teach job interviewing skills, and provide a searchable database of jobs. In other words, integrated career planning systems offer a planned sequence of activities or resources specifically designed to meet the needs of a given target population. Typically, an electronic portfolio is developed for each user as a repository of choices made while using the system, resumes, cover letters, references, assessment results, and documents such as certificates of achievement or career readiness.

Integrated career planning systems are typically developed as a whole with many different content topics, each of which may be used independently, but all of which contribute to the interaction of the total system. In more specific terms, such systems may have an online interest assessment, a searchable occupational database, a searchable national postsecondary school database, a resume writer, and a database of job openings. Some users may take only the interest assessment, use the searchable occupational database, and get occupational descriptions. Other users may go directly to the resume writer and then to the searchable jobs database. Some systems are "intelligent" enough to identify the users' needs and to direct them to the specific parts of a large system that they need to use at a current decision point. An electronic portfolio that monitors and saves the results of use serves as the integrating piece of the system.

Most of the integrated career planning systems available in the United States have already been mentioned in Chapters 5 or 6, as they also offer assessment and provide educational and career information. Some companies that develop such systems offer only one version for all populations, while others offer different versions for persons of different age ranges. Some of these companies offer only a standard system while others offer a wide range of customization options, including developing totally customized systems for users in a specific state, agency, or country. As the developers of these systems often respond to competitive Requests for Proposals that require functionality beyond their usual offerings, there is also a growing tendency for them to partner with other companies that can offer additional services, such as electronic transfer of transcripts, online college applications, or preparation for taking college-entrance examinations. Below is a list of the most widely used systems in the United States and their contact information.

Career Information System (Oregon Career Information System, 1244 University of Oregon, Eugene, OR 97403-1244)

  Career Trek (elementary students)

  Career Information System (for high school, middle school, high school, college students, adults)

Choices (Xap Corporation, 3534 Hayden Avenue, Culver City, CA 90232-2413)

  Jobs in Pawland (elementary school)

  Career Futures (middle school)

  Choices Explorer (high school)

  Choices Planner (high school)

  Choices Planner CT (college students and adults)

DISCOVER (ACT, Inc., P.O. Box 168, Iowa City, IA 42243-0168)

FOCUS (Career Dimensions, Inc.; careerdimensions.com/contact.php)

  My Own Career Profile (middle and high school students)

  FOCUS-2 (college students and adults)

  My Golden Career (adults in transition)

Kuder Career Planning Systems (302 Visions Parkway, Adel, IA 50003)

  Kuder Galaxy (elementary school)

  Kuder Navigator (middle and high school)

  Kuder Journey (college students and adults)

Naviance (1850 K Street NW, Suite 1000, Washington, DC 20006)

SUCCEED

System for Integrated Guidance Information (Sigi3)

Virtual Career Centers

Another version of the integrated career planning system is a *virtual career center*. A virtual career center is a well-planned Web site that creates a master menu of existing no-fee sites that offer component pieces of an integrated career planning system. For example, one site may offer an interest inventory that yields a Holland code; a second site might allow a search for occupations and postsecondary majors by Holland code; a third site might offer a postsecondary school search; while a fourth site offers excellent instruction and tools for the job search. Thus, someone who understands the elements of an integrated career planning system may formulate a list of well-developed sites and put them all together under one menu that offers many or most of these components. In doing so, using a Google search to find such sites would be very helpful. Using the screened list maintained by Margaret Dikel and displayed on the Web site of the National Career Development Association (associationdatabase .com/aws/NCDA/pt/sp/resources) would be an even better way to identify sites for use in a virtual career center.

The advantages of a virtual career center over licensing an integrated career planning system are lower cost and the ability to place local resources (such as parts of a university's own Web site or the site of a local state agency) into the menu. Important weaknesses of this approach are (a) the lack of the capability to guide a user to move from one activity to the next and (b) the inability to store assessment, information, choices made, notes, and a collection of valuable documents in an electronic portfolio that can be accessed and edited through life. Further, it is impossible to collect data about users and their progress in this type of system, and thus there is no reporting capability about use of the system or longitudinal research about its outcomes. Unlike integrated career planning systems, it is also impossible for counselors to communicate with the users of a virtual career center through e-mail, cell phone communication, or notes posted in their portfolios. The following sites are representative of the topics and appearance of virtual career centers: the University of Maryland Career Center, careercenter.umd.edu/ page.cfm?page_ID=7&Section_ID=1); and the Department of Labor's Career One-Stop (careerinfonet.org).

Social Networking

The newest phenomenon related to the use of technology to support career planning is social networking. Networking, not of the electronic kind, has long been hailed as the most effective single approach to finding job openings. On Web-based social networking sites, users create a profile, and provide as much personal and professional information as they wish. They may also upload photos, videos, and links. Individuals can also easily create Web logs, also known as blogs, in which they can journal in a forum that can be joined by others. Members of online social networks invite individuals to join their network or to "friend" them. This process connects two individuals with the added benefit of allowing the newly linked members to see all the other "friends" in each others' network. This kind of social networking can be used to develop a job network as well.

Regrettably, many young people today are posting messages and videos on their "walls" that are creating poor images of themselves as potential employees. Two researchers (Kolek & Saunders, 2008) found, in looking at Facebook profiles of students from a large public university, that the majority of students had profiles, and many contained large amounts of public personal information, including pictures of alcohol consumption. It is a known fact that employers are doing a social network search on job applicants prior to deciding whether to invite them to a job interview. Thus, any person who may be looking for a job should be very careful about the messages and postings that are associated with his or her name.

Some social networking sites—such as Facebook and MySpace—are intended solely to be vehicles for social communication. Others such as LinkedIn are professional social networks, and their purpose is to connect professionals for both social and business purposes. LinkedIn (linkedin.com) boasts over 50 million users, with executives from all Fortune 500 companies, 170 industries, and 200 companies represented. The site screens acceptance of members and requires that contacts know each other or be introduced to each other from a common contact. LinkedIn offers the opportunity to build a professional profile. Members can write endorsements for other members that serve as letters of recommendation and can be seen by employers. Members can use an advanced search function to find contacts related to a specific company, or browse through company profiles. LinkedIn also allows companies to post jobs, and allows individuals to link their blogs to their profiles.

Given these two kinds of networks, clients need to learn how to use both, considering the increasing importance of such networks for job-seeking and finding. Individuals should be extremely careful about what they post on purely social sites such as Facebook and MySpace, remembering that if they use their real names, prospective employers may view what they post. Individuals can make good use of such social sites by posting statements such as "I'm looking for a job as a medical technologist. Do you know of any places in the Chicago area that are hiring medical technologists?"

A good plan is for job seekers to belong to both a carefully used social networking site and a professional networking site such as LinkedIn. On the professional site they should build a carefully worded and accurate professional profile, and they should systematically construct a network of those who might be helpful in finding or recommending a job of the kind they want.

Mobile Phone Applications

The latest technology tool for delivery of career planning information and support is the smart phone. This application is being applied in other countries more than in the United States at this time. In countries such as India or South Africa, there is a larger percentage of people with Web connection through their phones than through computers. Thus, in such places it is logical to use the telephone as the delivery mode.

Due to the screen size on phones and the mobility of the person owning the phone, career guidance services must be delivered in small packages—quite the opposite of the content provided by the integrated career planning systems described earlier. For example, individuals might be able to recall their electronic portfolios and download a resume to a wireless printer. A person on the way to a job interview might review a list of tips or likely interview questions. Another person might take a short interest assessment and receive a list of suggested occupations. Still another might retrieve the description of a college in preparation for a campus visit. One might consider these capabilities as a "just in time" approach to retrieving information needed in the career planning and job-seeking process. In some places, such as the United Kingdom, call centers have been established and staffed with people who are qualified to talk with individuals who contact them with questions that are prompted by the information provided in the mobile phone application.

In many other sites, including services offered to the Transportation Security Administration (TSA) employees in the United States, the telephone is the medium for delivering counseling interviews. The telephone can also be used in conjunction with the integrated career planning systems described earlier. In this application, activities completed at a computer can trigger text messages or e-mails sent to a telephone. For example, assessment results from a child's use of an integrated career planning system might be sent to a parent's mobile phone as a text message. Students might be encouraged to use the next logical piece of an integrated career planning system by a text message sent to their mobile phones.

COMPUTER CAPABILITIES THAT SUPPORT CAREER GUIDANCE

The sequence of development and use of computer-assisted systems from the late 1960s to the present—spanning the generations of the mainframe, minicomputer, microcomputer, and now the World Wide Web—has identified and confirmed the strengths of computer technology related to assisting people in the career planning process. Those strengths are as follows:

- *Test and inventory administration and interpretation.* Computers can consistently administer inventories of interests, abilities, skills, experiences, personality, values, and so on, and score them, providing a comprehensive printed report. In the multimedia age, they can also enhance items by displaying images or graphics that help to communicate the meaning of an item. Score reports are interactive, linking from a profile to descriptions of the clusters of occupations suggested by that profile and the specific occupations and postsecondary majors included in them. Further, the meaning of a profile may be explained in text and/ or in audio.
- *Database searches.* Computers can search large databases of occupations, majors, schools, financial aid opportunities, and military programs quickly by using many different search characteristics in combination. Further, they can display data and provide multimedia treatment (slides, audio, video, graphics) about the options identified in the search. These databases can be updated quickly at periodic intervals—even daily, if the system is connected to an Internet site that maintains them continually.
- *Crosswalking.* Computers are capable of crosswalking, that is, relating one database to another with ease. For example, when users are learning about a specific occupation, they might crosswalk to a database of majors to read the descriptions

of those related to that occupation. From the database of majors, the user might select one and crosswalk to the financial aid database to determine if there are scholarship programs for those who pursue this major. Similarly, the user might crosswalk from the database of majors to schools that offer a specific major.

- *Standard delivery.* Computers are uniquely capable of delivering the same service to users at any time from any location that has appropriate technology. The content is provided in a standard way, but if a record is kept in the computer for each user, this standard content can be customized for each individual based on the results of assessment, past use, identified need, and/or age range. For example, the computer may select different interest inventory items for persons of different age ranges, use different norms tables to score inventories, or display information at different reading levels.

- *Monitoring progress of the user through the career planning process.* By use of a computer-stored record that retains information about users, the computer can monitor a user's progress through the system and report it to those who need to know it, which provides an opportunity to link human support services with computer support services. Many systems now offer the capability for the user to build and maintain an electronic, Web-stored portfolio. Users may release parts of that portfolio for others to view (such as counselors or employers), and may continually update it.

- *Delivering instruction.* Computers provide a strong capability of interactive instruction. Examples of instructional topics related to career planning include how to make decisions, how occupations can be organized, how to write an effective resume, or how to conduct a job interview. The instruction may include the use of graphics, audio, video, interactive activities, and quizzes.

- *Linking resources.* It is possible to expand the user's resources by linking from the career planning software to Web sites or individuals that can provide further information. For example, an occupational description stored within the system may be expanded by a link to the description on the U.S. Department of Labor's site called *CareerInfoNet* (acinet.org). Similarly, a student who is interested in learning more about a particular occupation may be connected by e-mail to alumni or community members who work in that occupation.

THE INTERNET AS THE DELIVERER OF CAREER GUIDANCE

Most computer-based career planning systems are now delivered on the Internet. The Internet as a delivery tool—in contrast to a stand-alone or networked computer—has the following advantages:

- The system is available from home, the library, and many other places on a 24/7 basis. Further, it is available from a computer and potentially also from a smart phone.
- There is a potential to serve an incredibly larger audience.
- E-portfolios can be developed and maintained on a Web site to which users may have lifelong access and from which documents (such as resumes, evidence of certifications, transcripts, etc.) can be sent to employers or schools.

- Databases can be updated more frequently because they are developed and updated from one central source to which all end-user stations are connected.
- Linking to the resources of the Internet and to e-mail communication can be more seamlessly included in the system.
- Technology now makes it possible for a counselor to communicate with system users, also via the Internet, while they are online.

At this time there are also the following disadvantages to using the Internet for delivery of computer-assisted services:

- Access and operation can be slow, depending upon the user's hardware configuration and the traffic on the Web site providing the service.
- The Internet is not a secure environment; thus, user data may not be confidential.

Just as early developers struggled with similar problems in the early years with stand-alone computers, current Internet-delivered systems face these obstacles, which will be solved as the capabilities of the Internet expand.

CHOOSING A WEB-BASED CAREER GUIDANCE SYSTEM

Counselors are typically included as part of a team that decides which of the systems should be selected for use at their site or if the one presently being used should be replaced by another. In this event, it is necessary to gain in-depth knowledge of each system under consideration. Although presentations made by marketing representatives are helpful, the best ways to gain truly in-depth knowledge are to acquire and read the system's professional manual and then, or simultaneously, to use the entire system as a student or client would. Listed next are the critical topics to use as benchmarks while making an evaluation.

- *Theoretical base of the system.* Some systems, such as those that focus on file searches and data displays, are atheoretical; that is, they do not propose any process for career decision making, nor do they offer any content that is related to the work of any specific theorist. Other systems do both; they propose and offer a specific process for career decision making and use the theoretical work of one or more of the theorists included in this text as the basis for that process and/or other content. Clients need to follow an exploratory process. Counselors need to decide whether the computer will be the presenter and monitor of that process or whether the counselor will play a more active role, using the computer as a support system at points in the process.
- *Presence of online inventories and/or the capability to enter the results of assessment taken in print form.* For most clients and students, assessment of interests and skills/abilities—and perhaps also work values—is important. This being the case, counselors need to determine how such assessment will be administered. There are two possibilities, each of which can be used exclusively or combined with the other. First, assessment can be administered, scored, and interpreted online as a part of a Web-based career planning system, an Internet Web site, or by software licensed from a test publisher and resident on a local computer. Second, assessment may be administered in print form and either self-scored

(possible for some types of inventories) or sent elsewhere for scoring. In the latter case, the Web-based career guidance system may allow individual users to enter their own scores or clerical support persons may enter the results for multiple individuals into the system so that they can be used to assist with their search for occupations.

- *Quality and comprehensiveness of databases.* Databases are an essential part of Web-based career guidance systems and their quality is critical to the quality of the system. Such quality includes accuracy of descriptions of items in the databases (occupations, schools, financial aids, etc.), sources of data, and currency and frequency of update. Some systems contain only two databases—usually, occupations and schools. The school database may comprise four-year colleges only or may also include vocational-technical schools, two-year colleges, and graduate schools. These files could be only for the state of installation, for a geographic region, or for the entire nation. Some systems offer data about 200 to 300 occupations, whereas others include more than a thousand. Some have many databases in addition to occupations and schools, including financial aid, apprenticeships, internships, military occupations, and majors. Some vendors make maximum use of databases developed by reliable government sources, such as the departments of labor, education, and defense; others do not. Some vendors of systems update their files once annually; others send a quarterly or biannual update. Another factor to consider is the style of writing used for the databases. Some systems use a factual, documentary writing style, whereas others describe an occupation in an informal, "what I do on the job every day" kind of format. It is also important to note the reading level of these descriptions.
- *Ease of searches.* Being able to search databases by specific characteristics is a core function of Web-based systems. Searches can be intuitive and user-friendly, or they can be awkward. When you are reviewing a system, note how easy or difficult it is to remove an already selected search characteristic, or to add one or go back to the results of your last search and change only one or two variables.
- *Content of system.* The first item in this list addressed the matter of theoretical base, and the second dealt with assessment, both of which are elements of content. However, there can be other, vast differences in content. Some systems contain instructional material, such as how occupations can be organized, how to write a resume, how to participate in a job interview, and how to find possible job openings through networking. The content desired in a system obviously relates both to the needs of the people served and to the elements of content provided in other ways.
- *User-friendliness and appeal.* The appearance of a Web-based system is determined by its graphics and icons, its color scheme, the availability of multimedia (video, still images, audio), the simplicity and attractiveness of screen layout, and the readability and attractiveness of the fonts used for text. Items that relate to user-friendliness include having a consistent way of navigating throughout the system, moving from one part to another, and integrating all materials needed within the system rather than having to rely on two or more media.
- *Multimedia capabilities.* Users of Web-based systems find them more appealing and are more motivated to use them if they have multimedia assets such as

dynamic graphics, streaming video, and audio. The positive aspect of having multimedia is its motivational appeal and capability to give much more information to a user about occupations or schools, for example, than text alone. The challenging side of multimedia is the software and hardware requirements. These features may require specific software on users' machines as well as high-speed communication lines with significant bandwidth.

- *Quality and track record of vendor.* Some career planning systems and Web sites have been developed on a low budget by individuals who are not known in the career development field. Further, the support capabilities they offer related to training and technical support are sparse. Other systems are developed and maintained by large organizations that have a long history of high-quality support and product development. These organizations are able to invest a large portion of their revenue in enhancing systems, training, and keeping up with the next technological trend.

The NCDA has a document titled *Software Review Guidelines,* which is available on its Web site at ncda.org. It lists 67 items that should be reviewed, and the worksheet allows the system reviewer to rate each item on a scale of 1 to 5 with 1 being unsatisfactory and 5 being outstanding.

Tips from the Field

Research consistently indicates that the most effective method of assisting individuals with career planning is a combination of Web-delivered service and counselor face-to-face support—either individual or in a group.

ADDING HIGH TOUCH TO HIGH TECH

The list of capabilities of Web-based systems is impressive. At first glance, it might appear that such systems could provide career planning services without counselor support. There are at least three reasons why this is not the case. First, when students or clients say that they need help with career planning, their statement may mask a variety of other needs and concerns. As a counselor talks with a student or client, these other needs become apparent, if they exist. Obviously, a computer does not have this power of discernment. Second, not all individuals with a primary need for career planning can profit optimally from receiving these services by computer because everyone has a different learning style and personality type. Further, some clients are not ready to receive information because of a lack of readiness to process it effectively. Third, research (Taber & Luzzo, 1999; Whiston et al., 2003) designed to determine the best way to deliver career planning services has consistently indicated that the optimal treatment for students/clients is the combination of human support services and computer services. In a recent study (Herman, 2010) using Career HOPES (an Internet-delivered group counseling intervention designed to facilitate occupational exploration and career decision making), experimental subjects showed greater gains than control group participants in career decidedness as measured by the Occupational Alternatives Questionnaire, occupationally relevant self-knowledge, and emission of career exploration behaviors. In the experimental group, the online group discussions were moderated by a psychologist with career counseling experience; in the control group, the discussions were unmoderated. Professional moderation resulted in better outcomes on several variables and greater overall satisfaction with the intervention.

As indicated by this and other studies as well as experience, invaluable responsibilities of counselors include the following:

- Determining the readiness of the person to receive information from a computer and apply it effectively
- Expanding on the interpretation of tests and inventories so that they are more likely to inform the client's decision making appropriately
- Assisting the client to identify the personal values that will guide the reduction of options provided by the computer
- Providing motivation and emotional support for continued work related to career planning
- Suggesting creative alternatives that the computer doesn't "know"

Some recent studies provide evidence of the effectiveness of computer-based systems and Web sites. In a longitudinal study in Israel, Gati et al. (2006) tested the predictive validity of Making Better Career Decisions (MBCD), a computer-assisted career decision-making system. Seventy clients who had used the system six years earlier were interviewed by telephone about their present field of study or occupation and the degree of their satisfaction with their occupational choice. The participants were divided into two groups: one consisted of clients whose chosen occupation was on the list of occupations recommended by MBCD, whereas the other consisted of clients whose chosen occupation was not on the recommended list. In the first group, 84% were highly satisfied with their occupational choice and 16% were satisfied to a moderate extent. Among those whose chosen occupation was not on the recommended list, only 38% were highly satisfied with their chosen occupation, 44% were satisfied to a moderate extent, and 18% were dissatisfied with their choice.

A study done by researchers at ACT (Gore et al., 2006) describes the career exploratory behaviors of high school and college students and offers a typology of users of *DISCOVER*, a Web-delivered career planning system. Access to the records of 87,293 high school and college students allowed for the identification and replication of three emergent types of users: a general browser, a focused user, and an in-depth user. Exit surveys of subsequent career exploratory behavior outside of the Web application for a subset of users (n = 1655) helped to clarify differences in exploration by user type, with in-depth and focused users more likely to seek additional information and to talk with others about their career decisions.

THE COUNSELOR AND THE COMPUTER

As indicated earlier in this chapter, a sequence of studies (Taber & Luzzo, 1999; Whiston et al., 2003) provides data indicating that the most effective means of providing career planning assistance to students or clients is by a combination of computer and counselor. The same studies indicate that receiving assistance from a computer-delivered system provides better outcomes than no assistance at all, but significantly greater gains are achieved when counselors can lend specific competencies to the picture. Pyle (2001) has identified the following list of needed counselor competencies:

- *Knowledge of computer-assisted software and Web sites.* Good content knowledge of valid and reliable Web-based guidance systems and Internet sites.
- *Capability to diagnose.* Ability to diagnose a client's needs effectively in order to determine whether use of a technology-assisted intervention is appropriate.
- *Capability to motivate.* Ability to explain the value of Web-based systems or sites in a way that will motivate the client to invest time in using them.
- *Capability to help the client process data.* Ability to assist a client to turn data into personally meaningful information.
- *Capability to move the client to an action plan.* Ability to assist a client to develop an action plan and then move forward on it.

These competencies may be applied in combination with different models of service delivery combining technology and counselor support, of which there are at least four: one-to-one counseling plus use of technology, group guidance plus use of technology, group counseling plus use of technology, and counselor support via the Internet plus use of Web sites.

In one-to-one counseling plus use of technology, the counselor gives the student or client specific assignments to use a Web-based system or sites between sessions. It is important that the assignments be specific instead of referring individuals to an integrated career guidance system or Web site without direction about which specific part(s) to use. For example, Juanita's counselor determined that she would profit from taking *The Self-Directed Search* (Holland, 1994). The counselor asked Juanita to take the instrument from its Web site, print out and read the extensive report, and return the next week. At the second session, the counselor expanded on the interpretation of the instrument and helped Juanita develop some guidelines for determining which of the many occupations suggested by the instrument to explore. Together, they developed a short list. The counselor asked Juanita to gather information about this list of occupations by using the *Occupational Outlook Handbook* (bls.gov/oco) and *CareerInfoNet* (acinet.org) online. At the third session, the counselor and Juanita discussed the information collected, and Juanita decided to learn more about training opportunities for Web designers. The counselor suggested that she search for such opportunities by using the National Center for Educational Statistics site (nces.ed.gov/ipeds/cool) and to bring a printed list of information about each of the identified schools to the next session. This example illustrates how counselors can use either an integrated career planning system or a Web site as a valuable resource to help clients identify options and gain information about them.

The group guidance or classroom-plus-technology model is highly similar, though it may serve a group of 15 to 30 simultaneously. For example, a community college may offer a two-credit course in career planning, and its enrollment may be as many as 30 students. During class sessions, the instructor teaches basic concepts of career planning, using a curriculum such as *Take Hold of Your Future* (Harris-Bowlsbey, 2009) and leads the group in activities designed to apply those concepts to personal decision making. Further, the instructor may give specific assignments to use parts of *Journey* (Kuder, Inc., 2011), for example, between class sessions to take inventories online, to identify occupations, to get occupational descriptions, to select a major, to identify schools, and to learn job-seeking skills. This approach not only makes wise use of technology, but gives the instructor class time to offer additional activities.

The group-counseling-plus-technology model is similar, but it serves students in groups not larger than eight and features counseling as opposed to guidance. Pyle (2001) has developed a model that requires three 1 and 1/2-hour group sessions and use of a Web-based system or site between the first and second and the second and third sessions.

The age of cybercounseling is upon us. *Cybercounseling* is the provision of counseling support to a client by a qualified professional via the Internet. Hardware and software exist to make such service possible, and indeed there are a few Web sites offering it; however, experience and ethical guidelines are insufficient at this time to allow an evaluation of its effectiveness. In such service delivery, a cybercounselor and a cyberclient may be physically located anywhere there is an Internet connection, and they can communicate with each other synchronously (that is, at the same time) via interactive e-mail or video conferencing (being able to see each other because both have digital cameras and appropriate software on their machines). Although it is probably less effective, the interaction could take place asynchronously (that is, the two are not at the machine at the same time). In such a relationship, the counselor and client may discuss any topics for which the Internet is a secure-enough platform, and the counselor may or may not assign the use of Web sites appropriate to those topics. Ethical guidelines for cybercounseling have been developed by the NCDA 1997 (ncda.org), the National Board for Certified Counselors (NBCC) 2007 (nbcc.org), and the American Counseling Association (ACA) 1999 (counseling.org), and posted on their respective Web sites. These guidelines re summarized in Table 7.1.

Table 7.1

Comparison of Three Sets of Ethical Guidelines for Use of the Internet

	ACA	NBCC	NCDA
Responsibilities of Counselors	Develop procedures to maintain client communication as securely as possible	In situations where it is difficult to verify the identity of the Internet client, steps are taken to address impostor concerns, such as by using code words or numbers	Develop Web sites with content input from professional counselors
	Provide background information about all counselors related to site	Explain to clients the procedures for contacting the Internet counselor when he or she is off-line and, in the case of asynchronous counseling, how often e-mail messages will be checked	State, on site, the credentials of those who developed both content and site design

Table 7.1
(*continued*)

	ACA	NBCC	NCDA
	Indicate who will see client data, if it will be saved, and how it may be transferred	Explain to clients how to cope with potential misunderstandings when visual cues do not exist	Determine if content is appropriate for Internet and state appropriate topics on site
		Make clients aware of free public access points to the Internet within the community for accessing Internet counseling or Web-based assessment, information, and instructional resources	Must be aware of free public access points so that service can be available for all who desire it in this mode
			Assessment must meet same criteria online as in print format (or client must be informed)
Selection of Clients	Counselor cannot provide service in states in which professional counselors are not licensed	Determine if a client is a minor and therefore in need of parental/guardian consent	
	Clients must be above minority age and able to enter counseling relationship with informed consent (or have signed permission of authorized representative)	Within the limits of readily available technology, to make their Web site a barrier-free environment to clients with disabilities	Counselors must do appropriate screening by phone to determine if client can profit
	Counselor must verify client identity and have alternate ways of contacting client in case of emergency		Counselor must monitor the client's progress to assure that he or she is profiting from service in this mode
Client Responsibilities	Sign waiver statement acknowledging limitations and potential lack of security of Internet		
Content		Internet counselors are aware that some clients may communicate in different languages, live in different time zones, and have unique cultural perspectives	Databases must be of high quality and updated often (date listed on site)
Security of Information	Counselor can only transfer information to third parties if both sites are secure	Informs clients of encryption methods being used to help ensure the security of client/counselor/supervisor communications	

(*continued*)

Table 7.1
(continued)

	ACA	NBCC	NCDA
	Site must be secure through various methods (including encryption, firewalls, etc.) if one-on-one counseling is provided	Informs clients if, how, and how long session data are being preserved	
	Clients must be informed about levels of security and limitations of confidentiality	Follow appropriate procedures regarding the release of information to others by other electronic sources	
Links to Other Sites	Counselor is responsible for doing a quality check of Web sites to which his or her site is linked	Counselors should provide links to all appropriate certification bodies and licensure boards for the purpose of consumer protection	Web sites to which site is linked must also meet NCDA guidelines
Online Relationship	Counselor must have specified intake procedures to assure that client can profit from online counseling		Counselor should have a specific contract with client that includes counselor's credentials, client goals, cost of service, how client can report unethical behavior, security of the Internet, and what data will be stored and how long
	Counselor must develop with client individual counseling plans related to client needs and Internet limitations		
	Counselor must cease to provide services if it is evident that client cannot profit from cybercounseling. Must suggest alternate means of help, including other counselors and/or contact by phone, fax, and so on	Counselor must explain how to cope with potential misunderstandings arising from lack of visual cues	Counselor must identify appropriate counselor in client's geographic area if face-to-face is needed and make the referral

Source: American Counseling Association (1999); National Board for Certified Counselors (2007); and the National Career Development Association (1997).

ISSUES RELATED TO CYBERCOUNSELING

Although the prospect of providing good counseling service at a reasonable rate to a much larger audience through the Internet is bright, there are also issues and concerns that the profession must wrestle with and research. The most critical of these are counseling environment, content topics, client characteristics, security and confidentiality, counselor qualities and qualifications, and supporting services. Each of these will be addressed briefly.

Counselors have been traditionally trained to create a nonpressured, accepting environment and to use specific relationship-building skills, including eye contact, attending behavior, immediate feedback through reflection, and intuitive questioning. Despite the use of digital cameras on workstations and software like Skype, achieving a psychologically warm environment and good facilitative skills in the medium of the Internet is challenging and currently at a primitive stage. Responsiveness may be seriously impacted by the limitation of band width or simply by the lack of synchronicity in the communication.

A second concern relates to the selection of presenting problems for attention via the Internet. Clients typically begin a counseling relationship by discussing topics that they believe will be acceptable ones, such as making a career choice or dealing with stress. However, it is typical that other concerns surface as the counseling relationship builds. The current guidelines indicate that counselors should state on their Web sites the topics that they believe to be appropriate for cybercounseling. This raises a concern as to whether the Internet should be used for counseling or only for the provision of guidance and information. It also raises the question of whether it is possible to stack presenting problems in hierarchical order and to divide them into the categories of "appropriate" and "inappropriate" for cybercounseling.

A third concern relates to determining which clients can profit from service via cybercounseling. The guidelines indicate that it is the responsibility of a counselor to determine whether a given client has the capability to maintain a relationship via the Internet and to profit from it. Yet, as a profession we have neither researched nor defined what the client characteristics are that would enhance their capability to profit from service in this mode or how a counselor may identify them, especially without a face-to-face interview.

A fourth concern relates to the fact that the Internet is an insecure environment. The counseling profession has always placed very high priority on the necessity to keep client communication and records secure and confidential. Encryption and other methods are being used to minimize the risk of having counselor case notes, client communication, and client records accessed by unauthorized persons; yet, these methods are not ironclad. The current guidelines indicate that counselors have the responsibility to inform their clients that the Internet is an insecure environment, but this may not be an adequate way to absolve counselors of this responsibility.

A fifth concern is how to identify and train counselors to work in this new mode. It is likely that counselors who are effective in delivering service via the Internet have characteristics that are different from those of their colleagues who work in a direct, face-to-face service mode. It is also very likely that counselors need to be trained differently for effective cybercounseling than for traditional counseling. Research is needed to understand what those counselor personality and skill differences are so that appropriate people can be selected and be taught appropriate skills.

Finally, it would be very helpful to understand what kinds of supportive services cyberclients need and how to determine when they need them. The current guidelines suggest that online services might be supplemented by support by phone, fax, links to other Web sites, and referral to qualified face-to-face counselors. The issue here is how to know when service in other modes would be critical or beneficial and how best to provide those additional services.

MyCounselingLab™

Go to Topic 14: *Information in Career Guidance and Counseling* in the MyCounselingLab™ site (www.MyCounselingLab.com) for *Career Development Interventions in the 21st Century,* Fourth Edition, where you can:

- Find learning outcomes for *Information in Career Guidance and Counseling* along with the national standards that connect to these outcomes.

- Complete Assignments and Activities that can help you more deeply understand the chapter content.
- Apply and practice your understanding of the core skills identified in the chapter with the Building Counseling Skills unit.
- Prepare yourself for professional certification with a Practice for Certification quiz.
- Connect to videos through the Video and Resource Library.

Summary

The computer has been used as a powerful tool in the delivery of career planning information and service since the late 1960s when such systems had their genesis. Delivered initially by stand-alone mainframe computers, these services have migrated to networked computers of all sizes and, more recently, to the Internet. Although far more effective than no service at all, their function is optimally enhanced by the support of counselors in one-on-one counseling, group guidance, group counseling, or cybercounseling. The latter is in a primitive stage at this writing but will likely become an important delivery mode as technology, ethical standards, and cybercounseling training progress. In this chapter, three sets of ethical guidelines are summarized and compared, and six specific issues related to cybercounseling are defined.

Case Study

Casio is a 32-year-old Hispanic male who has recently lost a job due to a reduction in state government employees. In his initial visit with you in a one-stop center, he indicates that he is very comfortable with using the Internet as one way to help in his job search.

Which sites would you recommend to Casio, and for what purposes?

Student Activities

1. In order to have firsthand experience with a Web-based integrated career planning system that was developed for middle school and high school students, sign on (without charge) to the Kuder career planning system called *Navigator* and use parts of it by following these steps:

   a. Access careerinterventions.kuder.com.

   b. Complete the brief form provided at that site, including your name, your instructor's name, and the name of the university where you are taking this course.

   c. Upon completion of the form, Kuder, Inc., will send by e-mail an activation code—a number which you can use when you register to use *Navigator*. This number will allow you to use the system and build an electronic portfolio without charge.

   d. Upon receipt of the activation code, access Kuder *Navigator* at kuder.com.

   e. On the right side of the screen, choose *Navigator* (the system for middle school and high school students).

   f. Under the Login box, select *New Users Register Here*. Complete the registration form, indicating that you are in Grade 9. During that process you will be asked to enter the activation code you have received. You will also create a unique user name and password. Record the user name and password because you will enter the same ones each time you return to the system.

   g. Use the following parts of the system. You may sign off at any time and return to the system by entering the user name and password that you created at first use.

      i. Under the tab titled *Learn About Myself,* choose *Take an Assessment,* and then the Kuder *Career Search* (an interest inventory). If you have time, come back to this menu later and take Donald Super's *Work Values Inventory.*

      ii. Under the tab titled *Explore Occupations,* select the option to *Explore Occupations by Assessment Results.* This option will give you a list of occupations suggested by the results of your interest inventory and values inventory. Look at the descriptions of at least three occupations, and save them to your portfolio. From your portfolio, compare the descriptions of the three occupations side by side. While you are in that section, notice the other ways in which students can explore and identify occupations.

      iii. Under the tab titled *Plan for Education,* search for a college, using at least four different characteristics. Look at the descriptions of at least three colleges, save them to your portfolio, and compare them. While in that section, note the other content that is available to students.

      iv. Choose the tab *Plan for Work* and look at the menu options to get an idea of the content of this module.

      v. Choose the tab *Find a Job* and look at the menu options to get an idea of the content of this module.

   h. After this review, write a brief report related to these three items:

      i. At the freshman level, your high school is looking for ways to meet a career guidance objective which reads: "Provide activities that are designed to expose students to a large number of career options and motivate them to explore these." Assuming that you had approval to assign students to a laboratory setting which offers the use of a Web-connected computer for each student, which specific part of Kuder *Navigator* would best meet this objective, and why?

ii. You are a high school counselor with a responsibility for freshman students. A parent calls you and asks you to work with her son in regard to a career choice and development of a high school plan of study that would support that choice. As a part of your assistance to this student, which parts of *Navigator* might you assign, and why?

iii. Another counselor on your high school guidance staff works with college-bound juniors. Which parts of *Navigator* would you suggest that this counselor use with students, and why?

2. You are a high school counselor, and you have been asked to serve on a committee that will review three integrated Web-based career planning systems in order to choose one for your school. You have been asked to review the Kuder Career Planning System called *Navigator*. Your assignment is to sign on to *Navigator* (following the directions provided in Activity 1 above) and then to write a one- to two-page summary for the committee based on the criteria specified in this chapter, namely

- Theoretical base
- Presence of online inventories and/or capability to enter assessment scores
- Quality and comprehensiveness of databases
- Ease of searches
- Content of system
- User-friendliness and appeal
- Multimedia capabilities
- Quality and track record of vendor.

References

ACT, Inc. (2011). *DISCOVER* [Computer software]. Iowa City, IA: Author.

American Counseling Association. (1999). *Ethical standards for Internet on-line counseling.* Alexandria, VA: Author.

Gati, I. G., Reuma, D., & Shemesh, N. (2006). The predictive validity of a computer-assisted career decision-making system: A six-year follow-up. *Journal of Vocational Behavior, 68*(2), 205–219.

Gore, P. A., Jr., Bobek, B. L., Robbins, S. B., & Shayne, L. (2006). Computer-based career exploration: Usage patterns and a typology of users. *Journal of Career Assessment, 14*(4), 421–436.

Harris, J. (1970). The computerization of vocational information. In D. E. Super (Ed.), *Computer-assisted counseling* (pp. 46–59). New York: Teachers College, Columbia University Press.

Harris-Bowlsbey, J. (2009). *Take hold of your future.* Adel, IA: Kuder, Inc.

Herman, S. (2010). Career HOPES: An Internet-delivered career development intervention. *Computers in Human Behavior, 26*(3) (May), 339–344.

Holland, J. L. (1994). *The Self-Directed Search™.* Odessa, FL: Psychological Assessment Resources.

Impelleteri, J. (1970). A computerized occupational information system. In D. E. Super (Ed.), *Computer-assisted counseling* (pp. 60–63). New York: Teachers College, Columbia University Press.

Katz, M. (1963). *Decisions and values.* New York: College Entrance Examination Board.

Kolek, E. A., & Saunders, D. (2008). Online disclosure: An empirical examination of undergraduate Facebook profiles. *NASPA Journal, 45,* 2–35.

Kuder, Inc. (2011). *Journey.* Adel, IA: Author.

National Board for Certified Counselors. (2007). *The practice of Internet counseling.* Greensboro, NC: Author.

National Career Development Association. (1991). *Software review criteria*. Broken Arrow, OK: Author.

National Career Development Association. (1997). *NCDA guidelines for the use of the Internet for provision of career information and planning services*. Broken Arrow, OK: Author.

Pyle, K. R. (2001). Career counseling in an information age. *The Career Planning and Adult Development Journal* (vol. 16, no. 3). San Jose, CA: Career Research and Testing.

Roe, A. (1956). *The psychology of occupations*. New York: Wiley.

Science Research Associates. (1968). *Kuder Preference Record*. Chicago, IL: Author.

Super, D. E. (Ed.). (1970). *Computer-assisted counseling*. New York: Teachers College, Columbia University Press.

Taber, B. J., & Luzzo, D. A. (1999). *ACT Research Report 99–3: A comprehensive review of research evaluating the effectiveness of DISCOVER in promoting career development*. Iowa City, IA: ACT, Inc.

Tiedeman, D. V., & O'Hara, R. (1963). *Career development: Choice and adjustment*. New York: College Entrance Examination Board.

University of Oregon. (2011). *Career Information System* [Computer software]. Portland, OR: Author.

Valpar International Corporation. (2011). *SIGI 3*. Tucson, AZ: Author.

Whiston, S. C., Brecheisen, B. K., & Stephens, J. (2003). Does treatment modality affect career counseling effectiveness? *Journal of Vocational Behavior, 62*(3), 390–410.

8

Career Counseling Strategies and Techniques for the 21st Century

Because we're human beings, career counselors can fall into the understandable trap of hearing and interpreting clients' stories from our own frame of reference. Developing the discipline to thoughtfully apply a range of theories in our work with clients enables us to push beyond our own perspectives in conceptualizing salient issues and interventions. By challenging ourselves to consider clients' career and life choices from different theoretical frameworks, we can view their worlds through a variety of lenses, each bringing a distinct focus to the work. Sometimes, when mulling over a first session with a client and reasoning through the presenting information, I push myself a bit by asking, "How would Super—or Holland or Krumboltz or Schlossberg—view this client's situation; and what would each of them focus on in helping this client?" For me, the application of theory is a powerful tool that improves with frequent sharpening. It's a means for considering a series of possibilities and thus, for keeping the work fresh and honoring the uniqueness of each client.

Barbara Hilton Suddarth, Ph.D., NCCC
Kensington Consulting

MyCounselingLab™

Visit the **MyCounselingLab**™ site for *Career Development Interventions in the 21st Century,* Fourth Edition to enhance your understanding of chapter concepts. You'll have the opportunity to practice your skills through video- and case-based Assignments and Activities as well as Building Counseling Skills units, and to prepare for your certification exam with Practice for Certification quizzes.

Maggie, a 28-year-old, single, European American woman presented for career counseling. Maggie desperately wanted out of her current work situation because her retail sales position was simply not working out for her. However, Maggie had no clear sense of her career options. She also possessed very limited information about the career development process. At the first session, she was clearly distressed and anxious. She wondered whether there was any hope for her future and she wanted to move on to something else as soon as possible. This was her first experience in career counseling.

Career development interventions provide the historical foundation for the counseling profession (Dorn, 1992). Herr, Cramer, and Niles (2004) point out that the counseling field emerged from three distinct movements: (1) vocational/career guidance, (2) psychological measurement, and (3) personality development. Despite the substantial influence of career development interventions on the counseling field and recent advances in career development theory, we know relatively little about the career counseling process (Anderson & Niles, 2000; Swanson, 1995; Whiston, 2003). Career counselors rarely study how career counseling actually "works" (Swanson). Rather, many career development researchers focus their efforts on career counseling outcomes (e.g., studying whether a career counseling intervention leads to less career indecision). Although career outcome research is obviously important, we also need to learn more about what happens within the career counseling process.

The results of a small group of empirical studies account for much of what we know about the career counseling process. It is noteworthy that as we take a closer look at what happens in career counseling, we realize that career counseling and general counseling have much in common (Multon et al., 2001). For example, Holland, Magoon, and Spokane (1981) reported that positive career counseling outcomes were related to techniques and strategies that included cognitive rehearsals of clients' career aspirations, providing clients with occupational information and social support, and cognitive structuring of clients' dysfunctional career beliefs. Heppner et al. (1998) reported a positive relationship between career counselor confidence in establishing therapeutic relationships and client confidence in coping with career transitions. Heppner and Hendricks (1995) reported that both a career-indecisive client and a career-undecided client attached substantial importance to the development of a therapeutic relationship with their career counselor. Anderson and Niles (1995) reported that clients devoted considerable attention to noncareer concerns in career counseling sessions and often discussed family of origin and relationship concerns with their career counselors. Anderson and Niles (2000) reported that career counseling participants (i.e., counselors and clients) most frequently identified aspects of self-exploration, support, and educating as the most important and helpful career counseling interventions. One result from this small group of studies is the support for a close relationship between the processes of psychotherapy and career counseling. It is particularly evident that an effective working alliance is critical to positive outcomes in career counseling. Thus, many of the counseling skills used to establish rapport with clients (e.g., reflective listening, paraphrasing, demonstrating positive regard) also apply to effective career counseling.

Tips from the Field

Collaborate with your students and clients to co-construct career interventions that fit their life contexts.

Career counseling outcome research indicates that career counseling is moderately to highly effective in helping clients resolve their career concerns (Oliver & Spokane, 1988). Whiston (2002) also notes that there is convincing evidence that career interventions that do not include counseling are not as effective as career interventions that include a counseling component. Brown, Ryan, and Krane (2000) note that career counseling is most effective when it contains individualized interpretation and feedback, occupational information, modeling opportunities, attention to building support for the client's choices within the client's social network, and written exercises. Despite more general evidence that career counseling is effective, we know less about the effectiveness of specific career counseling models (Whiston, 2003). This lack of information becomes more glaring when considering the question of which career counseling models work with which clients under what conditions. These issues expose the rather substantial gap that exists between career counseling research and practice. We agree with Whiston's (2003) call for a "surge in research that focuses on the process and outcome of career counseling" (p. 40).

EXPANDING THE LIMITED VIEW OF CAREER COUNSELING

Despite the need for more career counseling process and outcome research, it is possible to offer some summary statements regarding needed changes within career counseling practice. For example, over the past 20 years researchers have noted the close relationship that exists between the processes of psychotherapy and career counseling (Subich, 1993). Despite this relationship, many people still conceptualize the career counseling process as limited to measuring individual characteristics to identify congruent matches between people and prospective occupational environments. It is not surprising that this perception persists given the close connection between the development of interest inventories and aptitude tests during the early part of the last century and the use of these measures to help young people and veterans of the armed forces identify occupational preferences. Generations of people were exposed to this approach, and, thus, the predominant perception that this is the only approach to career counseling is pervasive and long-standing. Although this emphasis on finding the "best occupational fit" was crucial to the evolution of career development interventions and is an essential aspect of many current career counseling strategies, it does not describe the totality of career counseling interventions.

Clearly, there is a substantial body of evidence providing empirical support for career counseling strategies focused on person-environment fit; however, this limited view of career counseling is often accompanied by some less than desirable outcomes. For example, the widespread use of standardized tests in career counseling has led many clients to make the following request when presenting for career counseling: "I want to take a test that will tell me what I should do." Although no such test exists, many practitioners have been eager to comply with these requests, usually for a fairly steep financial fee.

The notion that career counseling is a process limited to test administration and interpretation also contributes to less than enthusiastic attitudes toward career counseling on the part of students in counselor training programs (Heppner, O'Brien, Hinkelman, & Flores, 1996). Students often conclude that career counseling is a rather mechanical process with a sequence of interventions that resembles the following:

Step 1 The client presents for career counseling.
Step 2 The counselor gathers client information and administers a test battery.
Step 3 The counselor interprets the tests and identifies a few appropriate occupational options for the client.

In this approach the counselor is in charge of the process. The counselor is directive and authoritative. Clients are passive recipients of a predetermined test battery. In this scenario the career counseling "process" is described as "test 'em and tell 'em" and "three interviews and a cloud of dust." Because some counselors use the same test battery over and over, regardless of the client's background and context, career counseling in these instances becomes something that is done to clients rather than something the counselor and client participate in collaboratively.

Many mental health practitioners also lack enthusiasm for the practice of career counseling (Spokane, 1991). Perhaps this is because practitioners also conceptualize career counseling as a process of administering tests and providing occupational information. Such views freeze career counseling at the middle of the last century and do not acknowledge the increased use of a variety of creative counseling strategies within career counseling (Amundson, Harris-Bowlsbey, & Niles, 2005).

Increasingly, career counselors infuse career counseling with general counseling strategies (Fouad et al., 2007; Multon et al., 2001). There is a growing recognition on the part of practitioners that the perceived dichotomy between career and personal counseling is false and does not reflect life as most people live it. There is growing recognition that work and mental health are interwoven (Herr, 1989). Niles and Pate (1989) observe that:

> Given the relationship between work and mental health, it is perplexing that there has been an artificial distinction between career counseling and mental health counseling on the part of many clients and counselors. Career counseling and personal counseling are often referred to as if they were completely separate entities. In fact, there are few things more personal than a career choice. (p. 64)

Moreover, clients present with career concerns in virtually every setting in which counselors work. Accordingly, Niles and Pate (1989) argue for counselors to be systematically trained in both the career and noncareer intervention domains. Blustein and Spengler (1995) agree that a systematic and comprehensive integration of training experiences across career and noncareer domains is necessary to prepare competent counselors in the 21st century.

Although Brown and Brooks (1985) acknowledge that not all counselors can be skilled career counselors, they also encourage all counselors to at least become competent at recognizing situations in which career counseling is an appropriate intervention that warrants referral. To address the goals identified by career development scholars such as Brown and Brooks, we will now identify strategies for effective career counseling in the 21st century and offer a framework for conceptualizing the career counseling process.

CAREER COUNSELING IN THE 21ST CENTURY

Career counseling has evolved as both a counseling specialty and a core element of the general practice of counseling. The 2009 Standards for the Council for the Accreditation of Counseling and Related Educational Programs continue to identify career development as a core area of counseling competence (see Appendix D). Thus, career counselors are professional counselors or psychologists with specialized training in the delivery of career development interventions. Career counselors possess the competencies required to provide multiculturally competent general individual and group counseling interventions to their clients while also possessing knowledge, skills, and awareness particular to the career domain (e.g., career development theories; career counseling theories and techniques; occupational information resources; career concerns of diverse populations; career assessment, consultation, program management; and ethical issues related to career service delivery).

Career counseling can be classified within the general category of counseling because of the overlap in skills required to conduct general and career counseling (Sampson, Vacc, & Loesch, 1998). In this regard, Crites (1981) suggests that "career counseling often embraces personal counseling but it goes beyond this to explore and replicate the client's role in the main area of life—the world of work" (p. 11). Crites further contends that:

1. The need for career counseling is greater than the need for psychotherapy.
2. Career counseling can be therapeutic.
3. Career counseling should follow psychotherapy.
4. Career counseling is more effective than psychotherapy.
5. Career counseling is more difficult than psychotherapy. (pp. 14–15)

Brown and Brooks (1991) take a similar view and define career counseling as "an interpersonal process designed to assist individuals with career development problems" (p. 5). Career indecision, work performance, stress and adjustment, unsatisfactory integration of life roles, and person-environment fit concerns are some of the issues Brown and Brooks include within the career counseling domain.

Brown and Brooks (1991) also suggest that career counseling clients must possess *cognitive clarity* to be able to benefit from career counseling. They define cognitive clarity loosely by referring to it as "the ability to objectively assess one's own strengths and weaknesses and relate the assessment to environmental situations" (p. 5). Brown and Brooks suggest that when counselors determine that their clients do not possess cognitive clarity, they should postpone addressing the client's career concerns until cognitive clarity is attained. Although on the surface this notion seems reasonable, and probably is applicable for clients with more severe psychological disorders, there is little empirical evidence to support this view for clients with normal developmental concerns. In fact, it is typical that career and general counseling concerns are so intertwined within career counseling that compartmentalizing them is not realistic for most clients (Kirschner, Hoffman, & Hill, 1994; Subich, 1993). For example, Niles and Anderson (1995) examined the content of more than 250 career counseling sessions and investigated when clients discussed career and noncareer concerns within career counseling. They found no pattern for the presentation of career and noncareer concerns in the career counseling process. Thus, it may be more appropriate to view career counseling as a type of psychological intervention that, at times throughout the course of career counseling, may require the counselor and client to focus on noncareer concerns.

Rounds and Tinsley (1984) support this view, stating, "we believe that a conceptual shift in which career interventions are understood as psychological interventions (and career counseling as psychotherapy) would foster advances in the understanding of vocational behavior change and processes" (p. 139). In some instances, students and clients may simply need minimal self and/or occupational information to be able to cope with their career concerns. In other instances, more therapeutic interventions may be required to help students and clients move forward in their career development.

DESIGNING CAREER COUNSELING STRATEGIES FOR THE 21ST CENTURY

Such notions pertaining to career counseling reflect the widely recognized belief that career issues are contextual and that the context of the 21st century is not the same as the context of the early 20th century. Savickas (1993) argued for career counselors to respond to societal changes occurring in the new millennium by stating that "counseling for career development must keep pace with our society's movement to a postmodern era. Thus, counselors must innovate their career interventions to fit the new *zeitgeist*" (p. 205).

It should also be evident that the career counseling interventions used by professional counselors and psychologists must be guided by an understanding of how the current *zeitgeist* shapes the career tasks presented to students and workers. For instance, as we noted in Chapter 1, career counselors must be cognizant of the fact that the hierarchical organizational pyramids, which once fostered the notion that career success is represented by climbing up the corporate career ladder, have been flattened. Career patterns now resemble roller coasters rather than gradual inclines, thereby requiring workers to redefine notions of what it means to be a "success" in one's career. Many adults present for career counseling with concerns that reflect unsuccessful attempts at coping with such changes. Adolescents worry about what they will experience in their careers as they watch their parents struggle to manage their career development. Brown, Ryan, and Krane (2000) conclude from their meta-analysis of career counseling outcome studies that positive career counseling outcomes are likely to occur when career counselors have their clients compose written career goals, talk with the counselor about their future goals, become exposed to models of effective career decision making, assist in the search for and integration of occupational information, and establish a supportive network relative to achieving their future goals.

To respond to these issues effectively, we contend that professional counselors and psychologists must provide counseling-based career assistance and support to their students and clients (although these may at first glance appear to be obvious recommendations, we have too often observed career counselors who seem to blatantly disregard them in their work with clients). We view these recommendations as essential to providing career counseling that is sensitive to the career concerns young people and adults experience in the 21st century.

Providing Counseling-Based Career Assistance

Career counselors offering counseling-based career assistance do not view their clients as the problem and the counselor as the solution. Rather, they seek to empower clients to articulate their experiences, clarify their self-concepts, and construct their own lives. Accordingly, career counselors function as collaborators in this process and pay special attention to the therapeutic relationship. As we have noted, providing counseling-based career assistance requires counselors to possess multicultural competencies. These skills are essential in the career counseling process and every counseling relationship is cross-cultural (Leong, 1993). It is essential, therefore, that counselors understand how contextual factors such as gender, socioeconomic status, racial/ethnic identity, sexual orientation, and disability status influence each client's worldview, identity, and career goals.

To help counselors consider these factors in the career counseling process, Ward and Bingham (1993) devised a multicultural career counseling checklist that can be used to help counselors identify issues of race/ethnicity that may need to be addressed in career counseling. When necessary, counselors help their clients develop strategies for overcoming prejudice and discrimination in employment and training practices. Interventions such as cognitive-behavioral counseling techniques, mentoring, and advocacy are especially useful in this regard (Herr & Niles, 1998). Additional strategies for culturally appropriate career counseling (e.g., the Career-in-Culture Interview) were discussed in Chapter 4 and serve as foundational skills for effective career counseling.

Providing counseling-based career assistance to clients also requires the use of basic skills such as summarizing client statements, reflecting clients' feelings, paraphrasing, using indirect and/or open questions, expressing positive regard for the client, and empathic responding. These skills are essential for creating an effective working alliance with clients regardless of the theoretical perspective used by the counselor (Brammer, 1993).

Establishing an effective working alliance with clients is fairly straightforward when clients are eager career counseling participants who are motivated to make changes. However, not all career counseling clients are eager and motivated. Some secondary school students, for example, present for career counseling because their parents have pressured them to make career choices and these students do not yet see the importance of career planning in their lives. School systems expect all students to make curricular choices, which are essentially prevocational choices, at specific points in the educational process. Some students do not possess the readiness for making these choices and are not motivated to develop readiness, while others may be reluctant to identify career goals that run counter to their parents' plans for them. Adults who are victims of outplacement may experience resentment and bitterness toward their former employers. They may feel that what happens in their careers is out of their control and that it is useless to engage in career counseling. Other clients may be more comfortable dreaming about options than implementing them. Fears that they may fail or that the new options will not live up to the expectations they have for them may keep some clients "stuck." Expressing the need to make a career change is much easier for most people than taking actions to implement a career change. Clients in each of these situations can be described as *resistant clients*. Although they recognize at some level that their career concerns need to be addressed, they are fearful of making changes in their lives.

Resistance represents a particularly interesting paradox in general counseling, and career counseling is no exception. People present for career counseling out of a desire to make changes in their career situations, yet, due to fear of changing, they resist making career changes. Because resistance exists, at some level, within all clients, career counselors must be competent at recognizing and dealing with resistance when it occurs. A starting point for working effectively with resistance involves understanding the different forms in which clients can express their resistance. To this end, Otani (1989) offers a taxonomy for classifying various forms of client resistance. Her taxonomy includes four categories: (a) response-quantity resistance (e.g., silence, minimum talk, verbosity); (b) response-content resistance (e.g., intellectualizing, symptom preoccupation, small talk, future/past preoccupation); (c) response-style resistance (e.g., discounting, thought censoring, second-guessing, last-minute disclosing, externalizing, forgetting, false promising); and (d) logistic management resistance (e.g., poor appointment keeping, personal favor asking). Otani notes that for client behaviors to be appropriately labeled as resistant, they need to occur repeatedly over several sessions. Thus, occasional silence, for example, may simply reflect the fact that the client is pondering a particular point rather than being resistant to change. Being alert to resistant behaviors can help counselors identify client concerns that may be important to explore within career counseling. Understanding the various ways in which clients can express their fear of changing, or resistance, also helps counselors to manage their countertransference when they encounter client expressions of resistance. Clearly, understanding the client's motivation for resistance (i.e., the affective experience the client hopes to avoid encountering) is critical to working effectively with resistant clients.

Spokane (1991) suggests guidelines that career counselors can use to cope with client resistance. (Spokane adapted these guidelines to career counseling from suggestions Meichenbaum and Turk [1987] offered to encourage compliance in therapy.)

1. Anticipate resistance.
2. Consider the career counseling process from the client's perspective.
3. Foster a collaborative relationship with the client.
4. Be client oriented.
5. Customize interventions to meet the client's needs.
6. Enlist family support.
7. Provide interventions that are continuous and accessible (e.g., as in job-search groups).

8. Use other career personnel and community resources to increase the range of social support to which the client has access.
9. Manage your countertransference and don't give up. (pp. 45–47)

These strategies obviously require career counselors to use general counseling techniques in the career counseling process. Providing counseling-based career assistance helps clients to engage in career exploration and cope effectively with the career-change process.

Providing Support in Career Counseling

Given the career development challenges confronting people today, professional counselors recognize that offering support to clients is essential to effective career counseling (Brehm, 1987; Holland et al., 1981; Kirschner, 1988). Counselor-initiated supportive acts engender feelings of hope, confidence, and purpose within clients (Highlen & Hill, 1984; Kalton, 2001). As Brammer (1993) notes, support "helps to counter feelings of 'falling apart,' 'being at loose ends,' or 'pulled in many directions at once'" (pp. 105–106). When clients acknowledge that they are unsure about their current and/or future career goals, it is common for them to experience feelings such as hopelessness, anxiety, confusion, and/or depression. Career counselors offering supportive acts help their clients to begin the process of coping more effectively with their career dilemmas.

Career counselors offer support to clients in a variety of ways. As noted, establishing an effective relationship between the counselor and the client is an essential first step in the career counseling process. However, the type of support clients need depends on the stage of career counseling and the specific career concerns being addressed. For example, Amundson (1995) discussed the importance of support in helping clients cope with unemployment. Specifically, he advocated connecting cognitive reframing interventions with the client's time perspective by focusing on the client's past (e.g., normalizing reactions to unemployment, recalling accomplishments, and identifying transferable skills), present (e.g., affirming the client's capacity to cope, externalizing the problem, limiting negative thinking), and future (e.g., identifying new cycles of activity, creating focused goal statements).

Support is also useful for highly self-conscious clients who are having difficulty making career decisions (Leong & Chervinko, 1996). Adolescents who have little work experience and limited self-knowledge to draw upon in their career planning may be tentative and insecure decision makers. Leong and Chervinko found that individuals who fear making a commitment and who internalize high standards from parents and significant others (i.e., socially prescribed perfectionism) also tend to have career decision-making difficulties. Counselors can help these clients by encouraging them to examine the beliefs that stop them from making commitments and moving forward with their career decision making. In this regard, it may be useful to have clients first identify barriers to their career development and then focus on what clients have done in the past to overcome similar barriers (Luzzo, 1996). Counselors may need to take a more educative role in helping clients who have limited experience in coping with the barriers they are encountering (Krumboltz, 1996).

By offering support, career counselors help clients cope with the challenges they encounter as they attempt to manage their career development more effectively. Supportive acts in career counseling include all counselor-initiated interactions that involve one or more of the following key elements: affect, affirmation, and aid (Kahn & Antonucci, 1980). Supportive acts can be used to extend emotional support, informational support, and assessment support to clients (House, 1981).

Emotional support involves providing caring, trust, and empathy to clients. Informational support involves providing clients with information they can use in resolving their career concerns. Assessment support involves providing clients with information that is useful in making accurate self-evaluations (e.g., interest inventories, card sorts, measures related to career thoughts and beliefs). Although it is possible to make distinctions among the types of support that counselors provide to clients, the three types of support we have identified are not mutually exclusive (e.g., providing clients with assessment support can be an emotionally supportive act as well). Informational and assessment support, however, focus on the transmission of information rather than the affect involved in emotional support (House, 1981).

EMOTIONAL SUPPORT IN CAREER COUNSELING.   The need to provide emotional support to clients is a basic presupposition of most forms of career counseling (Amundson, 1995; Crites, 1976; Salomone, 1982; Super, 1957). Caring and empathy are the essential supportive acts involved in extending emotional support to clients. These acts of emotional support are important throughout career counseling, but they are especially critical in the early phase of career counseling when an effective working alliance is being established (Amundson, 1995; Kirschner, 1988).

Offering emotional support requires that career counselors understand their clients' multiple perspectives and subjective experiences. Emotionally supportive acts, therefore, are grounded in multicultural counseling competencies (Pope-Davis & Dings, 1995; Sue et al., 1982). Although this seems to be a statement of the obvious, career counselors often act otherwise. That is, some career counselors demonstrate insufficient understanding of clients' multiple perspectives, as evidenced by the inappropriate use of assessment instruments (Fouad, 1993), the application of culturally inappropriate career counseling processes (Leong, 1993), and the lack of attention given to career concerns beyond the exploration stage of career development (Niles & Anderson, 1995).

To provide culturally appropriate career counseling assistance, Savickas (1993) recommends that career counselors move from acting as experts to acting as "cultural workers," from focusing on occupational choice to focusing on life design, and from focusing on test scores to focusing on clients' stories (pp. 210–214). Ignoring clients' perspectives and subjective experiences (at best) minimizes opportunities for providing effective emotional support to career counseling clients. The absence of an emotionally supportive relationship in career counseling increases the risk of poor goal clarification and the use of inappropriate career interventions (Leong, 1993).

Providing emotional support to clients in career counseling essentially helps clients feel as though they "matter" (Schlossberg, 1984). Schlossberg refers to this as *mattering*, which she defines as the "beliefs people have, whether right or wrong, that they matter to someone else, that they are the object of someone else's attention, and that others care about them and appreciate them." Amundson et al. (2005, p. 45) note that helping clients feel as though they matter requires skilled actions as well as good intentions on the part of career counselors. Amundson and his associates recommend that career counselors use the acronym PLEASE as an aid for expressing mattering to their clients.

P—protecting. Providing a secure and safe haven for exploratory efforts. Ensuring that clients receive all of the benefits to which they are entitled.

L—listening. Taking the time to hear all aspects of a person's story. Paying attention to underlying feelings in the telling of the story.

E—enquiring. Expressing interest in the story through questions and requests for clarification. Being naturally curious and asking about events in the person's life.

A—acknowledging. Noticing the other person and expressing greetings both verbally and nonverbally.

S—supporting. Expressing encouragement and praise. Identifying positive attitudes and behaviors and providing specific feedback.

E—exchanging. Sharing information about oneself. This self-disclosure should be genuine and appropriate to the situation. (p. 40)

Helping clients feel that they matter is clearly an effective way to extend emotional support and to establish a firm foundation for career counseling interventions. Although emotional support is a necessary condition for effective career counseling, it is usually not sufficient for supporting clients as they develop their careers.

INFORMATIONAL SUPPORT IN CAREER COUNSELING. Informational support is an additional form of support that aids clients in their career development. Essentially, informational support empowers clients to help themselves. There are numerous examples of supportive acts that career counselors can use to extend informational support to their clients. Among these are teaching clients job search strategies, providing clients with access to lists of job openings, teaching decision-making strategies, examining clients' dysfunctional career beliefs, and providing clients with lists of reading materials that are relevant to their career concerns.

Informational support can also be provided to clients in the early phase of career counseling. Specifically, supportive acts can be used to provide information about the structure of career counseling. Because so many clients enter career counseling expecting counselors to use tests, it is important that career counselors discuss the career development process as well as the career counseling process with their clients. For instance, clients can be informed that career counseling is a collaborative process in which counselors offer feedback, affirmation, and support as clients interpret their needs and shape their lives. This information helps counteract clients' expectations to be tested by an expert who will then identify appropriate career options. Clarifying roles and responsibilities for career counseling helps clients understand that career counseling is a shared experience in which they are active participants. Informing a client that most people make career changes multiple times during their lives and that career change is often a very adaptive response to personal changes and/or changes in work helps normalize the client's career concerns.

Thus, extending informational support in the early phase of career counseling allows clients to take full advantage of the career counseling experience. Providing clients with emotional support and informational support in the early phase of career counseling helps to establish an effective working alliance and sets the stage for the incorporation of assessment support in the career counseling process.

ASSESSMENT SUPPORT IN CAREER COUNSELING. Assessment support provides clients with opportunities to acquire information that is useful in making accurate self-evaluations (see Chapter 5). Assessment information can be used in the early phase of career counseling to support clients as they clarify their career concerns and identify their career counseling goals. Here again, exploring clients' multiple perspectives is an important step in providing culturally sensitive assessment support (Ibrahim, Ohnishi, & Wilson, 1994), because clients' patterns of career concerns are influenced by various personal and situational determinants that shape their life-role self-concepts (Super, 1980). Some individuals view work as the central role in life, whereas others see it as being on the periphery. Some view a career choice as the expression of personal fulfillment and others view it as the fulfillment of familial expectations. Thus, understanding the client's worldview, cultural identity, gender identity, sexual orientation, and disability status is a prerequisite for engaging in effective assessment activities.

Given the uncertainty related to career paths today, it should be clear that providing clients with information about themselves and the world-of-work through objective, standardized assessments is necessary, but often not sufficient, for empowering people to manage their careers effectively. To be sure, having information about how one's interests compare with others is helpful in the process of identifying viable career options. But, an overreliance on objective assessment ignores that "what exists for individuals is purpose, not positions on a normal curve" (Savickas, 1993, p. 213). Thus, two people with similar aptitude test and interest inventory results may select different occupations due to other factors influencing their decision making and sense of self. Our unique life experiences provide the clay out of which we sculpt our career decisions. To help people make meaning out of life experiences, career counselors pay attention to each client's subjective career (Carlsen, 1988). Most likely, the experiences that capture the most attention are those that have been the most painful (Adlerians call it "actively mastering what we at one time passively suffered" [Watkins & Savickas, 1990, p. 104]). Counselors can help clients sift through these experiences by augmenting traditional standardized assessment strategies with interventions that help clients translate their subjective experiences into purposeful career activities.

Savickas (1989) offers the career-style assessment model as a strategy for helping clients to identify subjective themes that guide their career developments. In this approach, Savickas queries clients as to their early role models; early life recollections; their favorite books, movies, and magazines; and their life mottoes. The answers to these questions contain themes that clients use to guide their decisions as they work to turn their problems into opportunities. For example, one of our career counseling clients (Verneda) noted that her role model in early life was her high school principal because she "helped others overcome obstacles in their lives." Verneda, an African American woman, had experienced early life tragedies, serious chronic illness, and numerous instances of discriminatory treatment. Through the use of the career-style assessment, Verneda became aware of her life theme—"overcoming obstacles"—and decided to become a counselor to "help others overcome obstacles." She actively mastered what she had passively suffered early in her life and turned her preoccupation (overcoming obstacles) into an occupation (helping others overcome obstacles) through her work as a counselor. Savickas' approach focuses on working collaboratively with clients to translate their life themes into career goals. The use of projective techniques, autobiographies, laddering techniques, and card sorts are also useful, subjectively oriented strategies for incorporating life experiences into the career counseling process (Neimeyer, 1992; Peavy, 1994).

More recently, Savickas (in press) offered a new paradigm for career intervention that acknowledges the impact that the digital revolution and the global economy have had on work and workers. Savickas' life-design structures interventions to (a) *construct* career through small stories, (b) *deconstruct* these stories and reconstruct them into an identity narrative or life portrait, and (c) *co-construct* intentions that lead to the next *action* episode in the real world.

Life-design intervention draws heavily upon narrative and begins by having career counseling clients describe both (a) the incident that dislocates them from the current episode in their career story and (b) their goals for a new scenario that they want to co-construct with their counselor. Life-design intervention focuses on narrative stories because stories help clients build their identities and careers out of complex social interactions. As Savickas (in press) notes, "storytelling makes the self and crystallizes what clients think of themselves. The more stories they tell, the more they develop their identities and careers." Stories help people organize their life events into a sequence that describes their career development.

Desconstruction helps identify self-limiting thoughts and ideas that clients may adhere to, the cultural barriers they may experience, and the confining life roles in which they participate. Deconstruction seeks to make these factors more obvious so that they can be introduced into career counseling with the goal of considering strategies for rethinking limiting thoughts, addressing cultural barriers, and redefining unnecessarily limiting life-role participation—all with the intent of helping clients identify ways to move forward in their career development—to advance their career story.

As such, deconstruction of clients' career stories fosters the reconstruction process. Reconstruction involves the career counselor actively gathering "the story threads and weaving them together into one tapestry to craft a unified sense of individuality" (Savickas, in press) so that a larger career story is constructed. This larger career story reflects the client's identity narrative. The larger career story contains the personal meaning and reveals life themes that the client uses to understand his/her past and present. This understanding then facilitates and guides future movement as the career counselor and the client co-construct a life portrait that portrays the client's story as accurately as possible relative to life themes, patterns, and personal meaning. "With new language, fresh perspectives, and expanded vistas clients may reorganize their meaning system and clarify what is at stake in the next episode of their career story" (Savickas). Essentially, the process fosters greater self-clarity relative to the client's career story and past, present, and future goals so that the client can take intentional actions to link a personal story with career possibilities.

Watkins and Savickas (1990) note that four types of clients tend to benefit the most from incorporating subjective assessment strategies into career counseling: (a) indecisive clients, (b) "difficult cases" or clients who have received career counseling but have yet to resolve their career concerns, (c) mid-career changers, and (d) culturally diverse clients who may not be served adequately by objective-only interventions. To be of most use to clients, Savickas (1993) contends that counselors should augment, rather than replace, objective and standardized assessments focusing on congruence, developmental tasks, vocational identity, and career adaptability with subjective-oriented assessment strategies. Thus, career counselors must understand the purposes, strengths, and limitations of subjective and objective assessments. Specifically, subjective assessment strategies can be used to help clients address the following questions:

1. How do my life experiences connect to my career development?
2. What gives me meaning?
3. What sort of life do I want to construct?
4. What do I want to be able to express through my work?
5. Which work options will allow me to come the closest to expressing who I am?

Objective assessment strategies help clients address questions such as:

1. How do my interests compare with others?
2. How much aptitude do I possess in specific areas?
3. How strong are my values in specific areas (e.g., economic rewards, aesthetics, ability utilization)?
4. What is my readiness for career decision making?

Of course, each approach has its own strengths and limitations that guide career counselors in decisions about which might be more useful to a client. The strengths of subjective assessments include:

1. They help clients understand themselves on a deep level.
2. They help clients consider the relevance of their life experiences to their career development.
3. They help clients attach a sense of purpose to their activities.
4. They are often inexpensive to use.
5. They actively engage clients in the career counseling process.
6. The assessment results are clearly connected to client responses to assessment questions.

The limitations of the subjective approach to assessment include:

1. They lack psychometric evidence related to the assessment activities.
2. They require substantial career counselor time within the career counseling process.

3. They typically have no clear interpretation guidelines for career counselors to follow.
4. They typically require more work on the part of the client than do objective assessments.

The strengths of objective assessments include:

1. They allow the client to make comparisons with others.
2. They are outcome oriented.
3. They do not require as much in-session career counselor time as subjective assessments.
4. They often provide a useful starting point for subsequent consideration of career options.

The limitations of objective assessments include:

1. The results are not easily connected to specific responses.
2. They are counselor controlled.
3. They can be expensive.
4. Clients often have inappropriate expectations for what can be accomplished through the use of an objective assessment.
5. Measures do not always fit the client's context.

Career counselors need to adapt their assessment strategies to their clients' career concerns. Being skilled in incorporating objective and subjective assessments in career counseling helps counselors to more effectively serve their clients.

A FRAMEWORK FOR CAREER COUNSELING

Numerous frameworks exist for conducting career counseling. For example, Isaacson (1985) suggests that over the course of career counseling, counselors typically address six issues: (1) getting started, (2) helping clients deal with change, (3) helping clients engage in self-assessment activities, (4) helping clients learn about the world-of-work, (5) helping clients expand or narrow choices, and (6) helping clients make plans.

Gysbers, Heppner, and Johnston (2003) view the career counseling process as typically progressing through several phases: (a) an opening phase in which the working alliance is established, (b) a gathering information phase in which the counselor and client gather data about the client's career situation, (c) a working phase in which the counselor and client use the information gathered to develop career goals and action plans, and (d) a final phase in which the counselor and client bring closure to career counseling.

Spokane (1991) proposes that career counseling consists of three overlapping and sequential phases labeled as a beginning phase, an activation phase, and a completion phase. During the beginning phase, career counselors provide clients with (a) structure concerning the career counseling process, (b) opportunities to rehearse their career aspirations either to themselves or to others, and (c) opportunities to uncover or identify conflicts engendered by their aspirations. During the activation phase, counselors provide support to clients as they process self-assessment data, test hypotheses about their career aspirations based on the new data they acquire, and begin formulating a commitment to a particular career option. During the completion phase, the career counselor helps the client implement and sustain a commitment to a career choice while also focusing on termination of the career counseling process.

Crites (1981) integrates multiple career counseling theories in his comprehensive model of career counseling and offers a generic framework for considering the career counseling process. In his model, Crites suggests that career counseling typically proceeds from an initial focus on diagnosis, in which the client and counselor work collaboratively to understand the client's career concerns, to a focus on process, which encompasses the implementation of career counseling interventions to address the client's career concerns. It then proceeds to an examination of the outcomes in which the career counselor and client reexamine the status of the client's concerns and determine whether additional career counseling is needed or if termination is appropriate.

Regardless of the framework used to conceptualize the career counseling process, most experts agree that career counseling typically involves a beginning or initial phase, a middle or working phase, and an ending or termination phase.

The Beginning or Initial Phase of Career Counseling

During the initial phase of career counseling, an effective career counseling relationship is developed, the counselor begins the process of gathering information about the client, and preliminary goals for career counseling are identified. Many career counselors begin sessions with their clients by asking them how they can be useful to the client. To clarify concerns, counselors encourage clients to identify individual and contextual factors contributing to their career dilemmas. Career counselors invite clients to discuss the strategies they have tried thus far to resolve their career dilemmas. Career counselors also seek to gather preliminary data concerning the clients' values, interests, and skills. Perhaps most importantly, career counselors work to establish rapport with their clients (Anderson & Niles, 2000; Fouad et al., 2007).

The initial phase of career counseling involves counselors providing clients with structure concerning the career counseling process. Career counselors work to clarify their clients' preferences and expectations for career counseling. Because clients seem clearer about what they prefer in career counseling than what they anticipate occurring, it is essential that counselors discuss with clients what they can expect to experience during the course of career counseling (Galassi et al., 1992; Swanson, 1995). For example, Spokane (1991) recommends that counselors distribute to clients a brief handout describing the career counseling process and what is likely to occur in career counseling sessions. Informing clients about what they can anticipate within the process helps them to clarify the types of concerns that are appropriate to discuss in sessions. Additional structuring topics include the payment of fees, the length of sessions, confidentiality, counselor–client roles and responsibilities, and the career counselor's theoretical framework.

Theoretical frameworks help to organize the data that counselors collect from clients. For example, using Holland's theory, a career counselor could focus on collecting data to organize the counselor's understanding of the client's Holland types. This information helps counselors make initial assessments concerning the client's degree of congruence (What is the goodness of fit between the person's characteristics and the expectations of the person's current and/or most recent occupational environments?), consistency (How diverse or focused are the client's interests and competencies?), and aspirations (To which environments does the client aspire?).

A counselor relying on Super's (1990) life-span, life-space theory would be concerned with understanding the constellation of career development tasks confronting the client (e.g., Is the client an adolescent engaged in exploration stage tasks for the first time or an adult recycling through exploration stage tasks while also coping with tasks of other career stages?) and the client's life-role salience (e.g., What does the client hope to accomplish in each salient life role? To what degree is the client able to express important values in salient life roles?). Collecting this information in the initial phase of career counseling helps the counselor understand the client's life-role self-concepts (Super, 1990).

A career counselor operating from Krumboltz's (1996) learning theory of career counseling might organize the information collected from the client to understand the client's self-observation generalizations (How does the client describe himself or herself?), career beliefs (What does the client believe about the career development process? Are the client's beliefs functional or dysfunctional?), and which learning experiences have been most influential in the client's career development.

In these ways, career counseling theories provide the organizing structures used by career counselors to understand the information presented by their clients. Theories help shape the content of career counseling and provide a structure for conceptualizing clients' career concerns. Theories also provide a vocabulary the counselor and client can use to discuss the client's experiences.

Regardless of the theoretical perspectives used by career counselors, the following topics are addressed in the initial phase of career counseling:

1. The client's view of self; self-characteristics, worldview, racial/ethnic identity, view of the future; the client's health and physical status; the client's previous experiences in counseling (if any); and the client's presenting concerns and goals.
2. The client's family (e.g., Who are they? What has been their influence? What type of relationship does the client have with family members? What goals and aspirations do the family members have for the client? What is the client's attitude toward the family members?); the client's educational background (What type and level of education does the client have? Is the client open to considering additional education? What is the likelihood that the client could pursue additional education if desired?); and cultural influences (e.g., What cultural factors influence the client's attitudes, behavior, goals?).
3. The client's significant work and life experiences (e.g., How have these experiences influenced the client's attitudes, behavior, and goals? How has the client coped with difficulties in the past?); and significant individuals in the client's life (e.g., What role models does the client have? In what ways have the client's role models influenced the client's attitudes, behavior, and goals? What sources of support does the client have?).

Isaacson (1985) recommends using a checklist to estimate clients' attributes for career counseling. At the onset of any career counseling relationship, career counselors should conduct a needs assessment to ascertain the client's concerns, expectations, and goals for career counseling.

Goals for career counseling must achieve several criteria. Goals should be specific, observable, time-specific, and achievable. Sometimes, goal identification can be facilitated by helping clients clarify the questions they are asking when they present for career counseling. For example, Maggie (the client introduced at the beginning of the chapter) presented for career counseling and declared in the first 10 minutes of her first session that her goal was "to get out of my miserable work situation" (she worked as a sales associate in a department store at the local mall). The counselor responded supportively to Maggie by reflecting her feelings of frustration and anger. This encouraged Maggie to tell more details about her work situation. When asked what occupations she had in mind, Maggie expressed in frustration that she didn't know, but that "anything has to be better than what I am doing now." These statements provided the career counselor with a clear sense that Maggie wanted things to change and that she was not happy in her current job; however, it did little to provide the counselor and client with an indication as to what Maggie wanted to move toward in her career. Thus, the counselor clarified with Maggie that she already knew that she wanted to stop doing what she was currently doing but that she did not know what she wanted to do next. The counselor provided Maggie with informational support by explaining the career development and career counseling process to her. The counselor was careful to emphasize the necessity of clarifying important self-information before attempting and acquiring relevant occupational information prior to making career decisions. To help Maggie clarify important self-information, the counselor asked Maggie for more information:

Counselor: Maggie, can you tell me some more about what you don't like about your current job?

Maggie: I work for a sexist creep who takes credit for my work and never has anything positive to say about what I do. I have no opportunities for advancement and the pay stinks.

After discussing with Maggie what specifically was wrong in her current situation and what she would like more of in her next situation, Maggie began to crystallize more specific, observable, time-specific, and achievable goals for career counseling. By clarifying the questions she was asking about her career situation, Maggie was able to state that her initial goal for career counseling was to identify occupational options that would allow her to engage in activities she enjoyed, use the skills she prized most, and express her important values. Maggie also felt that she was currently underemployed and hoped to get a job that would allow her to use her bachelor's degree in business administration. Thus, Maggie quickly acknowledged that her statement that "anything would be better than what she was doing now" was not exactly accurate and did not reflect the questions she was asking about her career. There were certain things she wanted in a job and certain things she did not want to be part of her work.

To help Maggie answer the question as to what job she would like to pursue next, Maggie felt that focusing on clarifying her interests and values would be especially useful. After additional discussion of Maggie's interests, values, and skills, Maggie stated that "In the next few career counseling sessions, I would like to learn more about my interests and values. After we do that, I would like to identify some jobs that make sense for me." Articulating and clarifying goals provides the opportunity for the counselor and client to identify an initial plan of action for career counseling.

The initial phase of career counseling culminates in the establishment of an effective counselor–client relationship, a mutual understanding of the structure of the career counseling experience (e.g., roles, responsibilities, limits), and a shared understanding of the client's presenting issues and initial goals for career counseling. Providing emotional and informational support to clients also helps establish an effective working alliance in career counseling.

The Middle or Working Phase of Career Counseling

The middle or working phase of career counseling is the time when a client's concerns and goals are explored in depth and a specific plan of action for career counseling is more fully developed and implemented. Career counseling goals are often revised and/or refined in the middle phase of career counseling. For example, to help Maggie clarify her interests and values, she and her career counselor decided to use an interest inventory and values card sort exercise. Thus, assessment support became an important component of the middle phase of career counseling with Maggie. As Maggie proceeded to clarify important self-information, she was able to clarify a plan of action by stating that "In 6 months I would like to have a job that allows me to have more opportunities to use my verbal and computer skills. I want to work more independently and have more control over my success. I also want a job with more income potential and that offers opportunities for advancement into higher levels of management."

Maggie and her counselor then began the process of identifying prospective occupational options related to her interests, values, and skills. Based on this exploration, Maggie came to the tentative conclusion that a career in computer sales offered her the opportunity to express her most important characteristics. To gather more information about computer sales positions, Maggie and her counselor decided that information interviewing would be useful. Maggie had never engaged in information interviewing, so she and her counselor decided that learning how to conduct an information interview would be a good first step in gathering additional occupational information. As they reviewed the steps involved in information interviewing, it became evident to the counselor that Maggie lacked assertiveness skills. Thus, the counselor and Maggie decided that it would be helpful to focus on developing assertiveness skills because these skills are essential for effective interviewing for occupational information (and interviewing for jobs). Maggie and her counselor engaged in assertiveness training.

Soon, Maggie was ready to begin information interviewing. A family friend actually worked in computer sales and Maggie thought that this person would provide a good starting point for her information interviewing. They met for a 30-minute interview during which Maggie received answers to many of her questions pertaining to work as a computer salesperson. At the end of the interview, Maggie asked for names of other computer salespeople with whom she could meet. Before she could schedule her second information interview, however, her interviewee learned of a vacancy in his company. He recommended Maggie for the position and she was offered an interview that resulted in her being hired as a computer salesperson.

Career counseling theories provide guideposts to direct the career counseling process. For example, interventions with Maggie focused on her information and skill deficits. Such interventions reflect a behavioral or social learning theory approach to career counseling. A developmental counselor working with Maggie might have encouraged her to clarify her life-role salience by constructing current and ideal life-career rainbows (Super, Savickas, & Super, 1996). This information would be useful in helping Maggie sort through occupational options (e.g., she could evaluate each option in light of the opportunity each option provided for participating in life roles that were important to her).

A counselor oriented toward using Holland's theory might have decided to teach Maggie Holland's typology. Learning the Holland types would provide a structure and vocabulary that Maggie could use to increase her self-understanding and sort through prospective occupational options. A counselor oriented toward Krumboltz's (1996) learning theory of career counseling might have encouraged Maggie to identify her career beliefs. The counselor may have administered the Career Beliefs Inventory (Krumboltz, 1988). Results from the Career Beliefs Inventory might have been used to highlight the specific beliefs causing Maggie difficulty and could have provided a starting point for forming more functional beliefs about the career development process.

Of course, how career counselors intervene depends not only on the counselor's theoretical framework but also on the type of decisional difficulty clients are experiencing. Decision-making difficulties occurring at the *beginning* of the decision-making process may be due to a lack of self- and/or occupational information, dysfunctional career beliefs, a lack of motivation, or more general indecisiveness within the client (Gati, Krausz, & Osipow, 1996). Decisional difficulties occurring *during* the career decision-making process could be due to insufficient information, conflicts related to personal characteristics and occupational options (e.g., skill levels insufficient for the occupation desired), and conflicts due to the influence of significant others (Gati et al.). Difficulties arising after decisions have been implemented may be the result of a poor choice of occupation, problems within the occupational environment, or the inability of the client to adjust to a particular work or educational situation.

When clients have made a poor occupational choice, they will need to recycle through Super's (1990) exploration-stage tasks. Maggie recycled through exploration-stage tasks as a more informed career explorer. She used information from her first sales position to help crystallize more appropriate occupational options.

Clients experiencing problems within the occupational environment may need to consider other jobs within the same occupation or may focus on strategies they can use to change their current work environment (e.g., clarifying with a supervisor one's roles and responsibilities, confronting a coworker). Maggie's situation was very limited in this regard. Her boss was not likely to change his attitudes and behaviors.

Clients having difficulty adjusting to their work environments may need to focus on developing important effective work competencies, such as developing interpersonal skills, assertiveness, and reliability. For example, an unassertive client experiencing ambiguity regarding work responsibilities may need assertiveness training to approach a supervisor to ask for more clarity concerning work tasks. Maggie decided that approaching her boss concerning his sexist attitudes was not as important to her as developing assertiveness skills to engage in information interviewing. These skills were essential to her in learning more about her new occupation and in succeeding in her job search.

It is interesting to note that career counseling research typically focuses on issues related to helping clients make and implement career choices. However, as implied by the previous discussion, career concerns continue after choices have been implemented (Carson, Carson, Phillips, & Roe, 1996). Indeed, many individuals have difficulty adjusting to the work they have chosen. Hershenson (1996) offers a systems model for career counselors to use in addressing work adjustment issues. Hershenson's system for work adjustment highlights the relationships among the subsystems of the person (work personality, work competencies, and work goals), the elements of the work setting (behavioral expectations, skill requirements, and rewards/opportunities), and the components of work adjustment (work-role behavior, task performance, and worker satisfaction). The formative influences of culture, family, school, and peer/reference group are also addressed in Hershenson's model of work adjustment. Thus, career counseling for work adjustment focuses on the relationship between the worker and the work environment.

Career counseling for work adjustment begins by assessing whether the problem is related to work-role behavior, task performance, worker satisfaction, or some combination of these three factors. If it is the former, then interventions focus on work personality. For issues of task performance, work competencies are addressed. Issues related to worker satisfaction require addressing work goals. Contextual factors (e.g., family, culture, and economics) are considered in all cases.

Thus, career counseling interventions are theory based and emerge from information gathered during the initial and middle phases of career counseling. When selecting interventions, the counselor provides the client with an explanation as to how the proposed intervention relates to the client's career concern and how the intervention might be useful to the client. The counselor and client discuss collaboratively whether the intervention seems appropriate. When it does, then there is a clear sense as to how career counseling will proceed. When the intervention does not make sense to the client, then there may be the need for thecounselor to clarify his or her understanding of the client's concerns. Perhaps the counselor has missed important elements of the client's situation. For example, a client who is dissatisfied in his current job may be reluctant to engage in broad career exploration with the goal of entering a new and potentially more satisfying occupation when he has significant financial obligations that restrict his ability to sustain substantial periods of time without a paycheck. Although finding a more satisfying occupation may be an ideal goal from the counselor's perspective, in this instance it may not be realistic from the client's perspective.

When counselors discuss their understanding of clients' career concerns and propose interventions for addressing the those concerns, they have the opportunity to receive important formative feedback from clients. Establishing an effective working alliance allows clients to feel comfortable discussing their perceptions of the career counseling process thus far. Working collaboratively in this fashion provides the opportunity for the client to take ownership of the career counseling process and outcome because the client has been actively involved in the entire career counseling experience.

Moreover, during the middle phase of career counseling, clients may become aware of important aspects of their career concerns that they were not aware of in the initial phase of career counseling. This new information may influence the client's goals for career counseling and result in the identification of alternative interventions that may be more appropriate for addressing the client's revised goals and concerns. In fact, Niles, Anderson, and Cover (2000) suggest that clients typically revise their concerns and goals during the course of career counseling, and counselors need to be alert to this phenomenon. Therefore, counselors should maintain flexibility in responding to clients' concerns as they emerge during the course of career counseling and, when necessary, invite clients to consider revising their goals for career counseling.

Maggie and her counselor began by focusing on helping her to clarify the questions she was asking about her career. Maggie was also encouraged to learn more about her important self-characteristics. As she learned more about herself, especially her interests and values, she began to crystallize a career preference. As career counseling progressed, it became clear that Maggie would need to learn new skills to move forward in her career development. Thus, the counselor and Maggie revised their goals for career counseling to include training in information interviewing and assertiveness.

The Ending or Termination Phase of Career Counseling

In the ending or termination phase, career counselors connect the work done in the beginning and middle phases of career counseling by assessing the client's current status and relating that status to the client's goals for career counseling. If the client's goals have been achieved, then termination becomes the focus. Steps are taken to prepare for ending the career counseling relationship. The counselor and client review the progress the client has made; discuss what the client has learned as a result of career counseling; consider how the learning the client has experienced can be generalized into future scenarios; and review what the client can do if difficulties are encountered in the future.

In reflecting on where the client was initially and where the client is now in his or her career development, differences in cognitions, affect, and behavior can be highlighted. For example, when Maggie presented for career counseling she was confused, angry, and ready to quit her job for any job that she could get. As career counseling progressed, she became more focused on the specific questions she was asking. She became more focused on what she needed to do to move forward in her career. She systematically acquired new information and skills she needed to cope more effectively with her career concerns. As Maggie did this, she began to crystallize new options that connected more closely with important self-characteristics. Additionally, Maggie became an active participant in her career planning. As she became more active (e.g., participating in information interviews), Maggie developed important skills for helping her acquire a job she wanted. The ultimate reward was that she eventually acquired a more satisfying job. This process would be important for Maggie and her counselor to review. By reviewing her progress, Maggie's counselor can take opportunities to reinforce important learning experiences in Maggie's career counseling:

Maggie: When I think about how I felt when I first came to see you, I remember feeling anxious, frustrated, and even somewhat hopeless.

Counselor: How does that compare to how you feel now?

Maggie: I've come 180 degrees. I now feel more in control, confident, and satisfied.

Counselor: What do you think has helped you to feel so good?

Maggie: Obviously, having my new job helps! But, I think that I learned to approach my career more systematically. I never really thought that much about my interests and values. Career counseling helped me organize that information and connect it with career options. I think I am much more in control of my career now. I also know how good career decisions are made. I don't think I really understood that before.

Maggie and her counselor continued to discuss what Maggie learned in her career counseling. The counselor was careful to point out the many strengths that Maggie exhibited in her career counseling (e.g., she took control of her situation, she was willing to learn new skills, she was able to put her new skills to use in effective ways, she was able to communicate clearly to the counselor and others, she followed through on assignments the counselor gave to her). They also considered how Maggie could put her new learning to use in the future. However, the counselor invited Maggie to return for career counseling in the future if she felt the need. Finally, Maggie and her counselor discussed what was most useful to Maggie in her career counseling as well as what Maggie thought was not as useful to her. Acquiring this information from the client's perspective provides important evaluative data that the counselor can use to improve his or her career counseling skills. To help structure the feedback Maggie provided, she was given an evaluation form (see Figure 8.1) to complete. Finally, Maggie was encouraged to consider whether there were any things that she would like to say to the counselor before terminating. As a result of her career counseling, not only did Maggie feel more satisfied with her new job; she also felt more confident about her ability to manage the career concerns she would encounter in the future.

Not all termination experiences are as positive as Maggie's, however. Termination can also occur when the client decides that now is not the time to take action. This decision can occur for a variety of reasons. For example, it may be that the client has decided to attend college but cannot do so at this time due to financial constraints. Or the client may decide that the current situation is simply preferable to a change and, therefore, may lack motivation for changing. In these instances, the counselor can discuss the steps the client can take if, in the future, making a change seems more reasonable.

There are also instances of "premature closure" that occur when clients end counseling before the counselor thinks the client is ready. Brown and Brooks (1991) suggest four possibilities as to why premature closure occurs: (1) clients believe that

CAREER COUNSELING EVALUATION

This evaluation of the Counseling Center's career counseling services will help us improve the quality of assistance to the students.

Use the rating scale below to indicate your response to each statement. Write the number that corresponds to your response in the blank.

0	1	2	3	4
Not Applicable	Strongly Disagree	Disagree	Agree	Strongly Agree

_____ 1. The counselor understood what my noncareer concerns were.

_____ 2. The counselor understood what my career concerns were.

_____ 3. The counselor has helped me to identify effective ways to cope with my noncareer concerns.

_____ 4. The counselor has helped me to identify effective ways to cope with my career concerns.

_____ 5. The time and activities spent learning about my interests, skills, and values were helpful.

_____ 6. The time and activities spent in learning about my different occupational and/or educational choices were helpful.

_____ 7. The time and activities spent in learning about the career planning and decision making process were helpful.

_____ 8. Career counseling is helping me to achieve personal and career goals.

_____ 9. Career counseling is helping me to function more effectively as a student, worker, and as a human being.

_____ 10. Overall, my career counseling experience has been helpful to me.

Please describe below the most helpful activities and moments in career counseling.

Please describe below the least helpful activities and moments in career counseling.

Your social security number will allow us to connect your responses to demographic data to help understand our effectiveness with various populations. It will also identify you to your counselor and help them better understand your evaluation so your counselor can improve his/her effectiveness. Your reply, as well as all other information you provide to the Center, will be kept confidential. If you would prefer to respond anonymously, leave the social security number blank.

Social Security Number: _____   Date: _____

Counselor name: _____

Approximate number of counseling sessions: _____

Thank you for your assistance.

Figure 8.1
Sample career counseling evaluation.

they have achieved their goals, (2) the career counseling experience does not meet clients' expectations, (3) clients fear what may be uncovered in career counseling, and (4) clients lack commitment to career counseling. When premature closure happens, it is essential that the career counselor try to understand the reasons for it occurring. In such instances supervision or consulting with a colleague can be very useful. For example, if the client terminated because the career counseling experience did not meet the client's expectations, the counselor and supervisor can explore what factors might have contributed to the client drawing this conclusion. Was the counselor sensitive to the client's concerns? Did the counselor establish an effective working relationship with the client? Were there factors associated with the client's background or concerns that were difficult for the counselor and therefore limited the counselor's effectiveness with this particular client?

Gysbers et al. (2003) note that when a client terminates prematurely by unexpectedly dropping out of career counseling, then the counselor must make a decision as to how this will be handled. What the counselor decides to do in these instances is based on the counselor's beliefs about how much responsibility he or she should take in encouraging a client to return to career counseling. Gysbers and his colleagues suggest that placing a phone call to the client has several advantages:[1]

1. It allows for the expression of caring and concern for the client.
2. It gives the counselor a chance to collect information about the client's reasons for terminating.
3. It provides the counselor with the opportunity to make a referral that is appropriate.
4. It provides the counselor with the opportunity to "leave the door open" for counseling in the future. (p. 363)

Although it is not a pleasant experience, premature closure provides opportunities for counselors to learn about themselves and the career counseling process. Career counselors should take full advantage of these opportunities by consulting with other professionals and, when possible, communicating with clients.

Clearly, termination is an important phase of career counseling. It provides an opportunity for the career counselor and client to review the important work they have done together. It provides important feedback to the counselor and helps the client to consider what he or she can do to cope with future career concerns. Given the importance of termination, it clearly should be a career counseling phase for which the counselor and client prepare ahead of time. The counselor must alert the client to the fact that termination is approaching. The counselor can help the client prepare for termination by encouraging the client to consider what has been learned in the time they have spent together and how the client feels about termination. The counselor also needs to be in touch with his or her feelings about termination. Because career counseling is an interactive experience, counselors often learn a great deal about themselves as a result of any career counseling relationship. It is important that the counselor reflect on what has been learned as a result of working with each client.

[1]From Gysbers, N., Heppner, M., & Johnston, J. *Career counseling: Process, issues, and techniques* (2nd ed.). Boston: Allyn & Bacon . Copyright © 2003 by Pearson Education. Reprinted/adapted by permission of the publisher.

To assess whether termination has been handled thoroughly, Gysbers et al. (2003) offer a seven-point checklist and recommend that the counselor ask:[2]

1. Did I review the content of what happened in counseling?
2. Did I review the process of what happened in counseling?
3. Did I reemphasize the client's strengths that were evident in counseling?
4. Did I evaluate what went well and what went poorly?
5. Did I explore things unsaid in counseling?
6. Did I discuss feelings related to the ending of the counseling relationship?
7. Did I provide clear and direct structure for the client's next steps? (p. 363)

Taking a planful approach to termination contributes to a positive career counseling experience and helps the client, and counselor, take full advantage of the career counseling process.

CAREER COUNSELING GROUPS

Group counseling offers a mode of service delivery that can be used instead of, or in addition to, individual career counseling. Hansen and Cramer (1971) describe group counseling as an intervention for 5 to 15 members, with 5 to 8 members optimal. Structured career counseling groups address a specific issue that is a common concern to the group members (e.g., job search, outplacement, choosing a college major, career decision making, career planning). Activities in structured career counseling groups tend to resemble group career-guidance activities. Because structured groups focus on specific career development topics, there is often a teaching component provided by the group leader. Thus, structured groups tend to be more information oriented and didactic than less-structured groups. Structured career counseling groups typically meet for three to seven sessions.

Teaching students and clients about job-search strategies represents an excellent topic for a structured group experience. For example, in session one, the career counselor can provide an overview of job-search strategies. Active and passive job-search techniques could be described, resume styles reviewed, job interview techniques highlighted, and strategies for managing a job search could be discussed.

Session two could address active versus passive job-search strategies in depth. Specifically, the career counselor could teach group participants about the importance of engaging in an active job-search campaign, noting that many people rely solely on a passive approach to job searching—they compose a general resume and send it to employers who have placed advertisements for a specific job opening. This approach has a low probability of succeeding for a variety of reasons. First, because it is a common approach it is likely to result in a large number of applications being submitted for the same position. Second, employers favor hiring "known commodities." That is, they are more comfortable employing a person with whom they have had previous contact or who has been highly recommended by a trusted associate. When employers have multiple applicants for a position,

[2]From Gysbers, N., Heppner, M., & Johnston, J. *Career counseling: Process, issues, and techniques* (2nd ed.). Boston: Allyn & Bacon. Copyright © 2003 by Pearson Education. Reprinted/adapted by permission of the publisher.

persons having had positive previous contacts with the employer have a decided edge over those without such contacts. Finally, when all a job searcher knows about a vacancy is what is listed in the job vacancy announcement, it is rather difficult to compose a cover letter and resume that connects closely with the specific opening. Resumes composed in a general way are almost always poor ones. When employers read resumes they look for connections with the skills required for being successful in the position for which they are hiring. A general, or "shotgun," approach to composing a resume is likely to miss its target. Those candidates using a focused (rather than general) resume that clearly connects with the responsibilities related to the job for which one is applying are the candidates most likely to be invited for an interview. Thus, describing relevant accomplishments in action-oriented terms (e.g., *managed, led, organized, developed, coordinated*) is key to an effective resume.

Active job searchers do not rely on employers to announce job vacancies. Rather, they actively engage in meeting with those who may be most likely to employ people to do what it is that the job searcher wants to do. Active job searchers work diligently to activate and develop a *network* of persons who fit this description. They attend professional meetings and explore employment possibilities with friends, acquaintances, and relatives. They query others as to whether they know people who work in a job in which they are interested and/or whether they know people who hire people to work in a job in which they are interested. They rely upon information interviewing to gather data about specific jobs and work environments as well as to expand their network of personal contacts within their field of interest. They activate a system of contacts that eventually helps them to connect with prospective employers in a personal way. After discussing the importance of networking, the career counselor could conclude session two by demonstrating effective information-interviewing skills and then having the group members engage in a role play using these skills (e.g., by asking questions related to what the person likes about his/her job, what sort of training is required, what the challenges of the job are, what a typical day is like, and whether the interviewee would be willing to provide a name of another person likely to be an information interview candidate).

Session three could address the different styles of resumes job searchers use and the pros and cons of each. For example, most people use (and employers tend to prefer) a chronological resume. Chronological resumes contain important information related to the job searcher's educational and work experiences, listed in reverse chronological order. A useful strategy for composing a chronological resume is to first itemize the essential skills required to succeed in the job in which the person is interested. Then, the job searcher should consider ways in which his or her experience can be described to match the requisite skills. As much as possible these skills should be described as achievements within each listing on the chronological resume. The determination of whether particular information should be included on the resume is based upon whether the information is relevant to the job for which the person is applying. Although employers prefer a one-page resume, workers with extensive experience may opt for two pages. In all cases, the resume should be neat, professional in appearance, and error-free. Many job searchers find it helpful to review many sample resumes as they seek to identify a format that they will use.

When job searchers do not have experiences that connect directly with the skills required for success in the job they are seeking, they often resort to using functional resumes, which rely on the use of functional skill categories (e.g., managerial skills, organizational skills, communication skills, computer skills) that are relevant to the job. The job searcher first identifies the essential skills for the job being pursued and then lists accomplishments/experiences within each of the functional skills categories. The most relevant and highest-priority skills areas should be listed first on the resume. Functional resumes become useful when a job searcher has developed relevant skill sets via activities such as volunteering and independent learning. A final option for job searchers is a hybrid or chronological/functional resume. Hybrid resumes can be used when a job searcher has some relevant employment experiences but also has developed relevant skills in nontraditional ways. In all cases a resume should convince prospective employers that the job searcher could do the job. If the resume does not connect to the job the searcher is pursuing, then it will be viewed as weak and will not accomplish the goal of gaining an interview. At the conclusion of session three the career counselor could assign participants the task of developing a resume. The career counselor could meet with the participants individually to provide ongoing feedback pertaining to the resume being developed. The following resources provide resume samples and useful information for this dimension of the job search process:

e-Resumes Part I
Describes the purpose of converting resumes to a plain text format; provides tips; contactpoint.ca/index.php?option5com_content&view5article&id5349:faqs-about-e-resumes-part-1&catid558:spring-2003&Itemid575

e-Resumes Part II
Discusses privacy and confidentiality concerns; contactpoint.ca/index.php?option5com_content&view5article&id5336:faqs-about-e-resumes-part-2&catid557:summer-2003&Itemid575

HR Professional Resume Preferences
Presents survey results from 213 government and corporate HR managers and recruiters from the greater Washington, DC, area on what they prefer and dislike in resumes; rcjobs.com/issues/1_1/seeker_resources/17-1.html

References and Letters of Recommendation
Tips for requesting references and recommendations; sample letters provided; jobsearch.about.com/od/referencesrecommendations/a/recommendation.htm

Resume Styles
Examples of chronological, functional, and combination resumes; distinctiveweb.com/choose.htm

Targeted Resume
Sample of a resume targeted to a specific job ad; jobsearch.about.com/od/resumes/a/target.htm

After reviewing resumes with group participants, the career counselor could explore the essentials of job interview skills in session four. For example, the counselor could explain that all job interviews involve getting responses to three questions: Can you do the job? Will you do the job? Will you fit in? These are the essential questions employers have in mind when meeting with job candidates. A goal of the interviewee should be to address these three questions (whether the interviewer asks them or not). If the job searcher has engaged in a thorough process of self-assessment to decide which job(s) she or he wants to pursue, then the answers to these three questions should be apparent. That is, the job searcher should be clear about the relevant interests, skills, values, and other self-characteristics that predict a high probability for success in the job. Moreover, by identifying the requisite skills for success in the job when composing a resume, the job searcher has already taken an important step in preparing for the job interview.

During the interview, the job searcher offers specific examples of relevant accomplishments that provide important data to the employer (the best predictor of success in the future is having been successful at a similar task in the past). For example, group participants can be told that rather than simply stating that you are confident in your organizational skills, you can also provide specific examples in which you successfully demonstrated organizational ability.

The question pertaining to whether the job searcher will "fit in" represents a key concern in the interview process. Perhaps more than anything else, employers want to know if a job candidate will demonstrate the sort of behaviors that contribute positively to the work climate. Skills such as getting along well with others, having effective communication skills, being reliable, being dependable, being stable in one's behavior, and staying on task represent the sort of self-management skills that employers strongly desire in their employees. Job interviewees must communicate that they possess these skills. This can be demonstrated in multiple ways (e.g., being on time for the interview, demonstrating effective interpersonal skills in the interview, dressing appropriately for the interview, discussing the fact that the job searcher possesses these skills—"I tend to be the sort of person who gets along well with others and works hard to contribute positively to my work environment, for example, . . ."). Finally, the career counselor can demonstrate effective (and not-so-effective interview skills) in the group session and then have group members discuss the demonstration before practicing effective job interview role plays.

The final group session can address the activities required for managing a job search effectively (e.g., keeping records of all contacts, setting goals to make a particular number of contacts each week, the importance of engaging in good self-care and positive self-talk, connecting with others who can be supportive, joining a job search group). Last, but not least, the final session should involve collecting evaluative data to inform the career counselor about ways in which the experience can be improved in the future.

Typically, structured groups like the one we have just described blend didactic information with experiential information as career counselors seek to help their clients acquire pertinent knowledge, awareness, and skills connected to the purpose of the group. The career counselor should identify specific goals, objectives, and outcomes for each group session.

Career counseling groups can also be more process oriented and less structured. Less-structured groups tend to focus on the intrapersonal and interpersonal concerns clients experience in their career development. They also tend to be more affective oriented than structured group experiences. Spokane (1991) contends that less-structured career counseling groups will increase in popularity as career development interventions and general counseling interventions become more interwoven. Less-structured career counseling groups tend to meet over a longer period of time than structured groups. Pyle (2000) contends that less-structured groups are often useful for clients struggling with career choice or direction. Job searchers who are fully engaged in the job search process (i.e., they have already learned the skills described in the structured group) can also benefit from a process-oriented group experience. Riordan and Kahnweiler (1996) provide an excellent description of ways in which job search support groups can be beneficial to job seekers.

The skills required for group career counseling are the same as those required in any group counseling experience; however, the counselor also needs to possess the requisite career knowledge pertaining to career development theory and practice. Pyle (2000, pp. 122–127) identifies four stages in group career counseling:

1. **Opening Stage:** The group members meet, the counselor provides an overview of the content of the group program, and goals are established. The counselor uses basic counseling skills, such as attending, concreteness, and genuineness.
2. **Investigation Stage:** Members focus on discussing the issues and topics pertinent to the group's purpose. For example, they may explore self-information (e.g., values, skills, interests), barriers to career development, or understanding the world-of-work. The counselor uses skills such as facilitative responses, self-disclosure, and personalizing to encourage group discussion.
3. **Working Stage:** Members process, synthesize, and identify actions they can take to advance their career development. The counselor uses skills such as accurate empathy, confrontation, providing feedback, and information processing to help clients during this stage.
4. **Decision/Operational Stage:** Members take action and provide support to each other regarding their action steps. The counselor uses skills such as drawing conclusions, helping members articulate their action plans, and bringing closure to the group experience.

There is mixed research evidence related to the effectiveness of career counseling groups. However, most of this evidence focuses on the effectiveness of structured group experiences. Most experts agree that there are several advantages to group career counseling experiences. For example, group career counseling is an efficient mode of service delivery. It maximizes the use of the counselor's time. This is especially important in school settings in which counselors often have very high caseloads and cannot offer individual counseling to every student for which they are responsible.

Kivlighan (1990) notes that career groups also provide opportunities for group members to (a) learn new information about themselves and others, (b) receive social and emotional support from other group members, and (c) learn from peers who are in similar situations. Group interventions also offer the opportunity for group members to share resources and ideas with each other, thereby maximizing opportunities for learning new strategies for coping with their career concerns. For example, Sullivan and Mahalik (2000) found that encouraging group members to focus on performance accomplishments, emotional arousal, vicarious experiences, and verbal persuasion was effective in helping group members increase career self-efficacy. Mawson and Kahn (1993) found that information-sharing aspects of the group process were helpful to group members in identifying stable career goals.

Group career counseling experiences are enhanced when the counselor is able to create a cooperative and inclusive group environment in which the members focus on commonly accepted goals. Hansen and Cramer (1971) note six additional criteria that contribute to successful groups:

1. Members of the group are in interaction with one another (i.e., there is open communication among group members).
2. Members of the group share a common goal.
3. The group members set norms that direct and guide their activities.
4. The group members develop a set of roles to play within the group.
5. The group members develop a network of interpersonal attraction (i.e., they develop likes and dislikes for each other).
6. The group works toward the satisfaction of individual needs of the group members.

CAREER COUNSELING PROFESSIONAL DESIGNATIONS AND RELATED SERVICE PROVIDERS

Regardless of whether a career counselor provides individual and/or group career assistance, we encourage counselors to develop a professional disclosure statement describing their training, experience, services offered, and approach to service delivery. This is important for a variety of reasons. As we have noted, many clients have clear expectations for career counseling (i.e., that they will be tested and informed as to which occupations are appropriate for them), and these expectations often do not mesh with current approaches to career counseling. Moreover, career services providers differ substantially in their training and areas of expertise, thus making the process of selecting a service provider an overwhelming one for consumers. For example, a popular movement today is the emergence of career coaching (Chung & Gfroerer, 2003). Career coaches can range from persons with professional counseling degrees and expertise in career development interventions to persons who are essentially paraprofessionals attempting to practice career counseling without the proper training and credentials. Generally, career coaches aspire to help people identify their skills, make better career choices, and become more productive and satisfied workers. Career coaches seek to help their clients identify strategies for accomplishing their goals in their work lives. We take the view that (because few things are more personal than a career choice) it is difficult to engage in career coaching without delving into issues/concerns that require professional training as a counselor or psychologist. We agree with the NCDA's view that career coaching is an essential role for career counselors as exemplified by the fact that it is one of the core career counseling competencies identified by the NCDA (NCDA, 1997).

Unfortunately, when career coaches lack proper training and credentials, they can easily engage in what professional counselors and psychologists label as *unethical practice.* Chung and Gfroerer (2003) recently highlighted the professional and ethical issues existing within the practice of career coaching. Chung and Gfroerer point out the lack of training, the absence of enforceable ethical standards, weak professional credentials, and the paucity of research investigating the efficacy of career coaching practices as areas that pose substantial difficulties for those engaging in career coaching without professional counselor training. When career counselors provide a clear description of their training and credentials to prospective clients, they help consumers understand the difference between professionals who provide career coaching as part of their career counseling practice and others who lack appropriate credentials and expertise.

One important designation for career counselors is the Master Career Counselor (MCC) designation currently offered by the NCDA. An MCC requires at least three years of post-master's experience in career counseling; an MCC is also nationally certified as a licensed professional counselor, and/or licensed psychologist. MCCs must have successfully completed at least three credits of coursework in each of the six NCDA career counseling competency areas and must have completed a supervised career counseling practicum or two years of supervised career counseling work experience under a certified supervisor or licensed counseling professional. MCCs are skilled in administering and interpreting career assessments and provide the highest quality of career counseling services. What should be evident throughout the process of career counseling, whether it is done individually or in groups, is the importance of counselor sensitivity to the client's context. When interventions are designed collaboratively with the client, the chances of this occurring are increased. As noted, a strength in subjective assessments is that they, almost by definition, engage clients in the process of designing their career counseling experience. Understanding the client's values, worldviews, familial orientations, religious/spiritual perspectives, and so on, is a core task in providing culturally appropriate career counseling. Clearly, this requires career counselors to achieve the same understanding and awareness of their own values, worldviews, and so on. These learning processes regarding self and others' cultural contexts are lifelong.

MyCounselingLab™

Go to Topic 16: *Research and Social Issues in Career Guidance and Counseling* in the MyCounselingLab™ site (www.MyCounseling-Lab.com) for *Career Development Interventions in the 21st Century,* Fourth Edition, where you can:

- Find learning outcomes for *Research and Social Issues in Career Guidance and Counseling* along with the national standards that connect to these outcomes.

- Complete Assignments and Activities that can help you more deeply understand the chapter content.
- Apply and practice your understanding of the core skills identified in the chapter with the Building Counseling Skills unit.
- Prepare yourself for professional certification with a Practice for Certification quiz.
- Connect to videos through the Video and Resource Library.

Summary

Career development interventions are the cornerstones of the counseling profession (Dorn, 1992). However, we know relatively little about the career counseling process. Many view career counseling from a perspective that is frozen in the past. Rounds and Tinsley (1984) suggest that conceptualizing career counseling as psychotherapy "would foster advances in the understanding of vocational behavior change and processes" (p. 139). Such notions pertaining to career counseling reflect the widely recognized belief that career issues are contextual and that the context of the 21st century is not the same as the context of the early 20th century. Savickas (1993) encourages career counselors to respond to the societal changes occurring in the new millennium by stating that "counselors must innovate their career interventions to fit the new *zeitgeist*" (p. 205).

It should also be evident that the career counseling interventions used by professional counselors and psychologists must be guided by an understanding of how the current *zeitgeist* shapes the career tasks presented to students and workers. To help clients address career tasks in contemporary society, career practitioners should provide counseling-based career assistance and support to their students and clients. By expanding their career interventions in these ways, career counselors provide assistance that is sensitive to the career concerns students and clients experience in the 21st century.

Case Study

Hyung Joon is a 40-year-old, Korean male who appears for his first session presenting as clean and neatly dressed in casual business wear. He is paraplegic resulting from an automobile accident when he was 27. He lives in a large city in California. He has been a househusband for approximately the past 13 years, but he has had a number of part-time jobs, primarily as a travel agent. He earned an associate's degree in business management 10 years ago.

Hyung Joon declared that he wanted help in deciding how to obtain work in which he can use the skills he learned in his business management degree program. He expressed very strongly that he does not want to be working as a travel agent for the rest of his life. He also expressed interest in obtaining additional education in the same area that he has begun in business management. He was fairly happy being a househusband but now feels a need to find employment, expand his work experience, and have more intellectual interaction in his life and work.

Hyung Joon has not expressed any unhappiness concerning his home life other than his desire for more intellectual stimulation in a job. He stated that his wife and family were supportive of his interests in pursuing a career at this time. Hyung Joon seemed happy with himself for achieving his associate's degree, yet he felt it was just "not enough."

Hyung Joon seems self-motivated to obtain information, support, and resources about what he wants to accomplish. He is not very knowledgeable about the range of opportunities and occupations that are available to him. He expressed his desire to expand his experiences and develop his skills. Hyung Joon stated that he liked a lot of variety in his work environment, and he disliked jobs that required him to do routine, monotonous tasks.

Which theories would guide you in your work with Hyung Joon? How do you conceptualize his career situation? In what ways might his disability impact his

career development process? In what ways might his cultural background influence his career development at this point in his life? What career interventions are you likely to use in your work with him?

Student Activities

1. If you have never been a career counseling client, try to find someone who has (perhaps your course instructor can facilitate this). Ask if they would be willing to talk with you about what was helpful to them in this experience and what was not so helpful. If you have been a career counseling client, make a list of what was helpful to you in career counseling and what was not. Reflect upon the ways in which what was helpful and what was not have implications for career counseling practice.

2. Consider what you think is helpful about the "test 'em and tell 'em" approach to career counseling. Make a list of the ways in which you think this approach can be helpful to clients. Now, consider the limitations of this approach. Make a list of these.

3. Consider what you think is helpful about the more expansive view of career counseling described in this chapter. Make a list of the ways in which you think this approach can be helpful to clients. Now, consider the limitations of this approach. Make a list of these.

4. What are the advantages of conducting career counseling groups? What are the disadvantages? Which career development concerns do you think might be most appropriate for a group career counseling experience? What career development concerns do you think might be inappropriate for a group career counseling experience?

5. How could you evaluate the effectiveness of career counseling?

References

Amundson, N. E. (1995). An interactive model of career decision making. *Journal of Employment Counseling, 32,* 11–21.

Amundson, N. E., Harris-Bowlsbey, J., & Niles, S. G. (2005). *Essential elements of career counseling.* Upper Saddle River, NJ: Merrill/Prentice Hall.

Anderson, W. P., & Niles, S. G. (1995). Career and personal concerns expressed by career counseling clients. *The Career Development Quarterly, 43,* 240–245.

Anderson, W. P., & Niles, S. G. (2000). Important events in career counseling: Client and counselor descriptions. *The Career Development Quarterly, 48,* 251–263.

Blustein, D. L., & Spengler, P. M. (1995). Personal adjustment: Career counseling and psychotherapy. In W. B. Walsh & S. H. Osipow (Eds.), *Handbook of vocational psychology* (2nd ed., pp. 295–329). Hillsdale, NJ: Erlbaum.

Brammer, L. M. (1993). *The helping relationship: Process and skills* (5th ed.). Boston: Allyn & Bacon.

Brehm, S. S. (1987). Social support and clinical practice. In J. Maddux, C. Stoltenberg, & R. Rosenwein (Eds.), *Social processes in clinical and counseling psychology* (pp. 26–38). New York: Springer-Verlag.

Brown, D., & Brooks, L. (1985). Career counseling as a mental health intervention. *Professional Psychology: Research and Practice, 16,* 860–867.

Brown, D., & Brooks, L. (1991). *Career counseling techniques.* Needham Heights, MA: Allyn & Bacon.

Brown, S. D., Ryan, J. M., & Krane, N. E. (2000). Four (or five) sessions and a cloud of dust: Old assumptions and new observations about career counseling. In S. D. Brown & R. W. Lent (Eds.), *Handbook of counseling psychology* (3rd. ed., pp. 740–766). New York: Wiley.

Carlsen, M. B. (1988). *Making meaning: Therapeutic processes in adult development.* New York: W. W. Norton.

Carson, K. D., Carson, P. P., Phillips, J. S., & Roe, C. W. (1996). A career retrenchment model: Theoretical development and empirical outcomes. *Journal of Career Development, 22,* 273–286.

Chung, Y. B., & Gfroerer, M. C. A. (2003). Career coaching: Practice, training, professional, and ethical issues. *The Career Development Quarterly, 52,* 141–152.

Crites, J. O. (1976). A comprehensive model of career development in early adulthood. *Journal of Vocational Behavior, 9,* 105–118.

Crites, J. O. (1981). *Career counseling: Models, methods, and materials.* New York: McGraw-Hill.

Dorn, F. J. (1992). Occupational wellness: The integration of career identity and personal identity. *Journal of Counseling & Development, 71,* 176–178.

Fouad, N. A. (1993). Cross-cultural vocational assessment. *The Career Development Quarterly, 42,* 4–13.

Fouad, N. A., Chen, Y. L., Guillen, A., Henry, C., Kantamneni, N., Novakovic, A., Priester, P. & Terry, S. (2007). Role induction in career counseling. *Career Development Quarterly, 56,* 19–33.

Galassi, J. P., Crace, R. K., Martin, G. A., James, R. M., & Wallace, R. L. (1992). Client preferences and anticipations in career counseling: A preliminary investigation. *Journal of Counseling Psychology, 39,* 46–55.

Gati, I., Krausz, M., & Osipow, S. H. (1996). A taxonomy of difficulties in career decision making. *Journal of Counseling Psychology, 43,* 510–526.

Gysbers, N. C., Heppner, M. J., & Johnston, J. A. (2003). *Career counseling: Process, issues, and techniques.* Boston: Allyn & Bacon.

Hansen, J. C., & Cramer, S. H. (Eds.). (1971). *Group guidance and counseling in the schools.* New York: Appleton-Century-Crofts.

Heppner, M. J., & Hendricks, F. (1995). A process and outcome study examining career indecision and indecisiveness. *Journal of Counseling & Development, 73,* 426–437.

Heppner, M. J., Multon, K. D., Gysbers, N. C., Ellis, C. A., & Zook, C. E. (1998). The relationship of trainee self-efficacy to the process and outcome of career counseling. *Journal of Counseling Psychology, 45,* 393–402.

Heppner, M. J., O'Brien, K. M., Hinkelman, J. M., & Flores, L. Y. (1996). Training counseling psychologists in career development: Are we our own worst enemies? *The Counseling Psychologist, 24,* 105–125.

Herr, E. L. (1989). Career development and mental health. *Journal of Career Development, 16,* 5–18.

Herr, E. L., Cramer, S. H., & Niles, S. G. (2004). *Career guidance and counseling through the lifespan: Systemic approaches* (6th ed.). Boston: Allyn & Bacon.

Herr, E. L., & Niles, S. G. (1998). Career: Social action in behalf of purpose, productivity, and hope. In C. Lee & G. Walz (Eds.), *Social action: A mandate for counselors* (pp. 117–136). Alexandria, VA: American Counseling Association.

Hershenson, D. B. (1996). Work adjustment: A neglected area in career counseling. *Journal of Counseling & Development, 74,* 442–446.

Highlen, P. S., & Hill, C. E. (1984). Factors affecting client change in individual counseling: Current status and theoretical speculations. In S. Brown & R. Lent (Eds.), *Handbook of counseling psychology* (pp. 334–396). New York: Wiley.

Holland, J. L., Magoon, T. M., & Spokane, A. R. (1981). Counseling psychology: Career interventions, research, and theory. *Annual Review of Psychology, 32,* 279–300.

House, J. S. (1981). *Work stress and social support.* Reading, MA: Addison-Wesley.

Ibrahim, F. A., Ohnishi, H., & Wilson, R. P. (1994). Career assessment in a culturally diverse society. *Journal of Career Assessment, 2,* 276–288.

Isaacson, L. E. (1985). *Basics of career counseling.* Boston: Allyn & Bacon.

Kahn, R. L., & Antonucci, T. (1980). Convoys over the life course: Attachment, roles, and social support. In P. B. Baltes & O. Brim (Eds.), *Lifespan development and behavior* (vol. 3). Boston: Lexington Press.

Kalton, C. A. (2001). Client psychological distress: An important factor in career counseling. *The Career Development Quarterly, 49,* 324–335.

Kirschner, T. (1988). *Process and outcome of career counseling.* Unpublished doctoral dissertation, University of Maryland, College Park.

Kirschner, T., Hoffman, M. A., & Hill, C. E. (1994). Case study of the process and outcome of career counseling. *Journal of Counseling Psychology, 35,* 216–226.

Kivlighan, D. M. (1990). Career group therapy. *The Counseling Psychologist, 18,* 64–80.

Krumboltz, J. D. (1988). *Career Beliefs Inventory.* Palo Alto, CA: Consulting Psychologists Press.

Krumboltz, J. D. (1996). *A social learning theory of career counseling.* Stanford, CA: Stanford University.

Leong, F. T. L. (1993). The career counseling process with racial-ethnic minorities: The case of Asian Americans. *The Career Development Quarterly, 42,* 26–40.

Leong, F. T. L., & Chervinko, S. (1996). Construct validity of career indecision: Negative personality traits as predictors of career indecision. *Journal of Career Assessment, 4,* 315–329.

Luzzo, D. A. (1996). Exploring the relationship between the perception of occupational barriers and career development. *Journal of Career Development, 22,* 239–248.

Mawson D. L., & Kahn, S. E. (1993). Group process in a women's career intervention. *The Career Development Quarterly, 41,* 238–245.

Meichenbaum, D., & Turk, D. C. (1987). *Facilitating treatment adherence: A practitioner's guidebook.* New York: Plenum Press.

Multon, K. D., Heppner, M. J., Gysbers, N. C., Zook, C., & Ellis-Kalton, C. A. (2001). Client psychological distress: An important factor in career counseling. *The Career Development Quarterly, 49,* 324–325.

National Career Development Association. (1997). Career counseling competencies. Tulsa, OK: Author.

Neimeyer, G. J. (1992). Personal constructs in career counseling and development. *Journal of Career Development, 18,* 163–174.

Niles, S. G., & Anderson, W. P. (1995). A content analysis of career and personal concerns expressed by career counseling clients. *Educational and Vocational Guidance Bulletin, 57,* 59–62.

Niles, S. G., Anderson, W. P., Jr., & Cover, S. (2000). Comparing intake concerns and goals with career counseling concerns. *The Career Development Quarterly, 49,* 135–145.

Niles, S. G., & Pate, R. H. (1989). Competency and training issues related to the integration of career counseling and mental health counseling. *Journal of Career Development, 16,* 63–71.

Oliver, L. W., & Spokane, A. R. (1988). Career-intervention outcome: What contributes to client gain? *Journal of Counseling Psychology, 35,* 447–462.

Otani, A. (1989). Client resistance in counseling: Its theoretical rationale and taxonomic classification. *Journal of Counseling and Development, 67,* 458–461.

Peavy, R. V. (1994). A constructivist perspective for counseling. *Educational and Vocational Guidance Bulletin, 55,* 31.

Pope-Davis, D. B., & Dings, J. G. (1995). The assessment of multicultural counseling competencies. In J. G. Ponterotto, J. M. Casas, L. A. Suzuki, & C. M. Alexander (Eds.), *Handbook of multicultural counseling* (pp. 287–311). Thousand Oaks, CA: Sage.

Pyle, K. R. (2000). A group approach to career decision-making. In N. Peterson & R. C. Gonzalez (Eds.), *Career counseling models for diverse populations: Hands-on applications for practitioners* (pp. 121–136). Belmont, CA: Wadsworth/ Thompson Learning.

Riordan, R. J., & Kahnweiler, W. (1996). Job support groups: Three configurations. *Journal of Counseling & Development, 74,* 517–520.

Rounds, J. B., & Tinsley, H. E. A. (1984). Diagnosis and treatment of vocational problems. In S. Brown & R. Lent (Eds.), *Handbook of counseling psychology* (pp. 137–177). New York: Wiley.

Salomone, P. R. (1982). Difficult cases in career counseling: II. The indecisive client. *The Personnel and Guidance Journal, 60,* 496–500.

Sampson, J. P., Vacc, N. A., & Loesch, L. C. (1998). The practice of career counseling by specialists and counselors in general practice. *The Career Development Quarterly, 46,* 404–415.

Savickas, M. L. (1989). Annual review: Practice and research in career counseling and development, 1988. *The Career Development Quarterly, 38,* 100–134.

Savickas, M. L. (1993). Career counseling in the postmodern era. *Journal of Cognitive Psychotherapy: An International Quarterly, 7,* 205–215.

Savickas, M. L. (in press). Life design: A paradigm for career intervention in the 21st century. *Journal of Counseling & Development.*

Schlossberg, N. K. (1984). *Counseling adults in transition, linking practice with theory.* New York: Springer.

Spokane, A. R. (1991). *Evaluating career interventions.* Upper Saddle River, NJ: Prentice Hall.

Subich, L. M. (1993). How personal is career counseling? *The Career Development Quarterly, 42,* 129–131.

Sue, D. W., Bernier, J. E., Durran, A., Feinberg, L., Peterson, P., Smith, E. J., & Vasquez-Nutall, E. (1982). Position paper: Cross-cultural counseling competencies. *The Counseling Psychologist, 10*(2), 45–52.

Sullivan, K. R., & Mahalik, J. R. (2000). Increasing career self-efficacy for women: Evaluating a group intervention. *Journal of Counseling & Development, 78,* 54–62.

Super, D. E. (1957). *The psychology of careers.* New York: Harper & Row.

Super, D. E. (1980). A life-span, life-space approach to career development. *Journal of Vocational Behavior, 16,* 282–298.

Super, D. E. (1990). A life-span, life-space approach to career development. In D. Brown, L. Brooks, & Associates (Eds.), *Career choice and development: Applying contemporary theories to practice* (2nd ed., pp. 197–261). San Francisco: Jossey-Bass.

Super, D. E., Savickas, M. L., & Super, C. (1996). A life-span, life-space approach to career development. In D. Brown, L. Brooks, & Associates (Eds.), *Career choice and development* (3rd ed.). San Francisco: Jossey-Bass.

Swanson, J. L. (1995). The process and outcome of career counseling. In W. B. Walsh & S. H. Osipow (Eds.), *Handbook of vocational psychology: Theory, research, and practice* (pp. 217–259). Hillsdale, NJ: Erlbaum.

Ward, C. M., & Bingham, R. P. (1993). Career assessment of ethnic minority women. *Journal of Career Assessment, 1,* 246–257.

Watkins, C. E., Jr., & Savickas, M. L. (1990). Psychodynamic career counseling. In W. B. Walsh & S. H. Osipow (Eds.), *Career counseling: Contemporary topics in vocational psychology* (pp. 79–116). Hillsdale, NJ: Erlbaum.

Whiston, S. C. (2002). Applications of the principles: Career counseling and interventions. *The Counseling Psychologist, 30,* 218–237.

Whiston, S. C. (2003). Career counseling: 90 years old yet still healthy and vital. *The Career Development Quarterly, 52,* 35–42.

Designing, Implementing, and Evaluating Career Development Programs and Services

MyCounselingLab™

Visit the **MyCounselingLab™** site for *Career Development Interventions in the 21st Century*, Fourth Edition to enhance your understanding of chapter concepts. You'll have the opportunity to practice your skills through video- and case-based Assignments and Activities as well as Building Counseling Skills units, and to prepare for your certification exam with Practice for Certification quizzes.

It is evident that career counseling embraces career/life-planning concerns. What is not as obvious is that providing career services demands structures that encompass business principles.

Those principles address such issues as strategic planning, program design, financial and marketing concerns, evaluation and review processes. Being exposed to the development of successful programs that deliver effective services strengthens the foundation of all we learn in our graduate programs.

Martha Russell, M. S. NCC
Career Services Board of Directors NCDA

It has been reported that the majority of Americans who purchase a new car now consult one of several services that evaluate the quality of different cars being offered. The popularity of these services is attributable to the often-stated view of car purchasers that a new car purchase is too important a decision to base on the unevaluated claims of the manufacturers.

If the choice of a new car is important enough for people to want a source that provides reliable evaluations of the cars offered, it only seems reasonable that career planning services that deal with potentially life-enhancing or life-damaging career advice and information should also be the object of responsible evaluation.

Careful reading of this chapter will enable you to design and plan your own evaluations. Additionally, you will be able to assess if the evaluations undertaken by other services are adequate, a handy thing to know if you wish to refer people to quality programs and services. Specifically, you should be able to determine if the evaluation is formative (useful for improving an ongoing program) or summative (judging the overall worth of the program) or some of both. A useful skill to have, wouldn't you say?

Garry R. Walz, Ph.D., NCC
Counseling Outfitters, CEO
University of Michigan, Professor Emeritus (Past President of the American
Counseling Association and the National Career Development Association)

Previous chapters, especially Chapters 4 through 8, have provided a great deal of information about the content of career planning services. This chapter focuses on the process of designing these programs and then delivering them to the students or clients for whom they are developed. The step-by-step process of design, development, delivery, and evaluation is described, and five sample programs are presented as examples.

There are important reasons for engaging in program design. The first is that it is impossible for counselors in any setting other than private practice to provide all of the assistance needed by the students or clients they serve on a one-to-one basis. Schools typically have counselor-student ratios ranging from 1:300 to 1:1000, and among the mix of services provided by school counselors, attention to career concerns is low. Thus, without having a systematic program of career planning services that can be offered to groups of students, only a very small percentage of students would receive assistance.

Even if these services could be provided on a one-to-one basis, this would be a cost-ineffective way to provide them to all. The goal of career guidance services should be to provide the maximum benefit to students and clients at the lowest per-person cost. Clearly, given the workload and time restraints of counselors in schools and other settings, the goal should be to save one-on-one time for persons that need such specialized service while providing service to most students through a variety of methods, including classroom instruction, group guidance, group counseling, and Web-based career planning systems and sites.

A second rationale for careful program planning is to require that career services be carefully thought out before their delivery. Such thought, following a process detailed later in this chapter, results in much higher program quality. It also provides the basis for determining program content, methods of delivery, evaluation, and a clear description of the program for administrators, parents, and recipients of the program.

Counselors may play a variety of roles related to the design and implementation of career development programs and services in their work settings. These roles may include advocacy, coordination, participation, design, management, and evaluation. Let's look at each of those roles separately.

In the role of advocacy, counselors use their skills and influence to work with the various stakeholders, which may include faculty, administrators and managers, and, in some settings, parents, to achieve improved career planning services. This role may include serving on advisory boards or committees, making presentations, or exerting influence in a variety of other ways.

In the role of coordination, counselors collaborate with internal staff (such as other counselors, teachers, and managers) and external entities (such as employers, advisory board members, agencies, community organizations, and parents) to deliver parts of the program of services. They may work with teachers to develop a curriculum that includes career planning concepts, with managers to develop workshops, with community organizations to serve as mentors for students, with parents to raise money for some parts of the program, or with employers to offer job-shadowing experiences or internships.

In the role of participation, counselors personally deliver all or part of the program of service. They may do this through a combination of group work, one-to-one counseling, instruction, assessment, and support of use of Web-based systems and sites.

Counselors may be the only people in schools or other organizations who are trained in career development theory and practice. Thus they are likely to be the people who are called upon as designers, developers, and managers of services for students or clients. They may also be called upon to provide evidence of the effectiveness of these services, and be instrumental in planning and carrying out their evaluation. For example, a counselor may be employed by a middle school, high school, or university that wishes to provide career development services for all of its students. Or, a counselor may work in a corporation as a personnel worker and be called upon to develop services that meet immediate needs caused by corporate restructuring, downsizing, or other kinds of changes. A company undergoing such changes would likely ask a counselor to develop ways to help employees make these upsetting transitions with less stress and with a better image of the company.

If the school, university, or company has hundreds or thousands of students or employees who need to benefit from career planning services, it is impossible to meet this need by dealing with everyone on a face-to-face, interview basis. It is essential to design a program and then to deliver it in ways that will reach the largest number of people and will do so cost-effectively. A process for accomplishing this is presented in 10 steps, each explained in detail.

STEPS FOR DESIGNING AND IMPLEMENTING A CAREER DEVELOPMENT PROGRAM

Step 1: Define the Target Population and Its Characteristics

The purpose of this step of the program design process is to get a clear picture of the people whom the program will serve. It is necessary to describe the population with some clarity as indicated in the following illustrations. This description might contain demographic data such as racial-ethnic background, mean and range of scores on achievement or aptitude tests, gender, age range, and types of diversity.

HIGH SCHOOL. Midtown High School has 673 students who are fairly evenly divided over the four years (freshman, sophomore, junior, senior). They come from families in a small city and areas as far as 10 miles from the city. Sixty-one percent of the students are male and 39% are female. Seventy percent are Caucasian, 14% African American, and 16% Hispanic. Most students come from middle-income families in which wage-earners work in the area's tourist industry, or are retail merchants, or work as assembly workers in the local factories. In the past, no attention has been given to teaching students about planning for future jobs.

COLLEGE/UNIVERSITY. Upstate University, located in a rural area of the state, has approximately 14,000 full-time undergraduate students, 900 full-time graduate students, 1,700 part-time undergraduate students, and 2,500 part-time graduate students. It draws students from all over the state as well as 12% from other states and 5% from other countries. The mean age of undergraduate students is 19.4 years, and graduate students, 29.4 years. Twenty percent of undergraduate students continue on to graduate school; the rest seek jobs immediately after graduation, most of them within the state. Job placement for those who complete the university's undergraduate and graduate programs has traditionally been very high, approaching 95% within three months after completion. Within the past three years, however, this figure has declined to approximately 90%, likely because major corporations in the state are reducing the number of new employees in order to be able to retain as many of their current employees as possible. In the past, no services have been provided to students to help them to seek employment or plan their careers.

CORPORATION. The Royal Corporation, located about 40 miles south of a large urban area, has almost 12,000 employees, ranging in age from 18 to 65. The corporation makes audio and video boards for computers. It offers positions in management, sales, advertising, and light factory-assembly work, in which manual dexterity and accuracy are critical to the quality of its products. The turnover rate of employees is 26% each year. In this company no assistance has ever been provided with topics such as how to make transitions, how to conduct a successful job search, or how to analyze one's skills so that they can be transferred to another position.

JOB SERVICE OFFICE. This office serves the northeast area of the city. Typical clients include adults in the age range of 35 to 65 who have been laid off, or are displaced homemakers, veterans, ex-offenders from the local state prison, or persons on public aid. Most clients have very low skill levels in reading, mathematics, and language use and have no or little past work experience. Further, they have a mean educational level of sixth grade and have not acquired marketable job skills.

There are at least two ways to gather the information that will provide a description of a target population in some detail. One way that may yield sufficient details is to review the records that already exist in a school, agency, or company. The second way is to develop a questionnaire to administer to all potential students or clients, or at least to a group that has been selected as a random sample. A random sample is a small group taken from the whole group by using a computer program or by drawing specific numbers (which may be student- or employee-identification numbers) from a book of random numbers. Before using this approach, one should consult someone who knows research and sampling techniques or read a chapter on this topic in a relevant book.

It is important to understand the nature of a target population before beginning to design a program of services. This information provides insight about the topics, reading level, methods, tools, time available, and level of sophistication for the material to be presented in the career planning program.

Step 2: Determine the Needs of the Target Population

Obviously, it is impossible for counselors to develop a program of services to meet student, client, or employee needs if they do not know in considerable detail what those needs are. If the target population consists of high school students, it is possible to infer from their age and stage in career planning that they have certain needs, such as deciding whether to attend a vocational-technical school, attend a university, or go directly to work. It is also safe to assume that they need assistance in selecting the occupation(s) they plan to enter. But, there may be other needs that cannot be identified by age or life stage alone—such as a need to have more information about the community colleges in the area—if needs are not assessed in a more formal way.

If the target population is in a college or university, it can be assumed, because of the age of these students and their stage in career planning, that they need to (1) understand the relationship between majors and specific occupations, (2) select one or more occupations, and (3) learn how to find job openings and get a job effectively. It cannot be known, however, without a needs assessment, if a large percentage of the students do not know how changes in the job market may affect their career planning significantly.

If the target population consists of employees in a corporation, then less is known from theory about their needs. One may surmise that those who will be laid off need to learn how to write a resume and engage in job interviews, but program designers might not assume that a significant percentage would like to leave the corporation voluntarily because of job dissatisfaction without administering a questionnaire or working with focus groups.

There are at least four ways to identify the needs of any group. First, there may be some information already available from past questionnaires that can be used to identify some needs. Second, a short questionnaire can be made and administered in written form to everyone in the target group, potentially via the organization's intranet or in several small, focus groups. A focus group is a group of 10 to 15 people who are selected for a specific purpose (in this case, to help identify needs) and are believed to be representative of the total population. Use of a focus group allows not only the completion of a questionnaire, but also the opportunity to discuss the answers given by people in the group, thus gaining more in-depth information. Third, consultants may be hired to make recommendations based upon their knowledge of normal developmental needs or of the needs of others in similar settings.

Finally, there are often needs in schools (such as a high percentage of drop-outs) or corporations (such as unmotivated employees) that are related to poor or inadequate career planning. Thus in some settings it would be wise and helpful to ask administrators and managers to identify problems that need solutions. Then, services can be devised that address those particular problems. If solutions are found, it is likely that there will be support from management for the delivery of the career planning service. Following are examples of the kinds of needs that might be identified for different settings.

MIDDLE SCHOOL.   According to theory, these are the years for broad-based exploration of occupations and gaining awareness of the work world through becoming acquainted with clusters of occupations. It is also the time to motivate awareness on the part of the students that career choices need to be made in the future and that there is a relationship between current schoolwork and future plans.

HIGH SCHOOL.   Almost no students realize that there have been many changes in the past few years that will make their approach to career planning quite different from that of their parents. Students have no knowledge of how occupations are organized or how their work tasks vary. Few students can describe their interests or their best abilities, and those who can do not know how these may relate to their future work. Many students do not understand that different jobs require different amounts of education, and they cannot define the different paths of education (i.e., vocational-technical school, two-year college, university, apprenticeship, military service, etc.) that lead to work.

COLLEGE/UNIVERSITY.   As with the high school students, few realize that there have been many changes in the past few years that should make their approach to career planning different from that of their parents. Further, they do not realize that they are likely to change occupations several times during their lifetime and that this will become the accepted pattern. Students on the whole do not understand how the world-of-work is organized, nor how specific subject-matter specialties relate to this organization and to jobs that they will be seeking. Many cannot state their personal interests, their best skills or abilities, nor the values that they would hope to attain through work. Many have had no instruction about how to decide what kinds of jobs they might like, how to find openings in these jobs, how to have successful job interviews, how to make effective use of social networking, or how to evaluate one job over another in accordance with personal preferences.

CORPORATION.   Some workers still believe that the corporation should be responsible for their career planning or progression. Many have no knowledge about how to plan for a career change, leaving one company and going to another or to self-employment. Still others cannot identify their transferable skills or identify other jobs that will make use of those skills. Those who have been in one job for many years do not know how to write a resume that can be transmitted electronically, to use face-to-face and social networking to identify job openings, or to feel comfortable in either a face-to-face or virtual job interview.

Step 3: Write Measurable Objectives to Meet Needs

A measurable objective is the clear statement of a goal, including how to determine whether or not the goal has been reached. There are at least two reasons for writing objectives for the career planning services. First, having to follow the discipline of writing objectives will require a counselor to think carefully about what he or she is trying to achieve and how to know if it has been achieved. Second, the objectives will become the basis for the content and evaluation of the services. It is almost universally true that management will not support a program, either psychologically or financially, that is not explained adequately and does not show evidence of being effective. So, in order to get and retain support for career planning services, it is necessary to define them clearly (via the objectives) and also to measure the outcomes of providing them (via evaluation).

The identified needs of the target population become the basis for writing measurable objectives. If, for some reason, the time and money required to do a needs analysis is not available, it may be necessary to use broad statements of goals at the various age levels provided by such documents as the National Career Development Guidelines, funded by the U.S. Department of Education, Office of Vocational and Adult Education (see associationdatabase.com/aws/NCDA/asset_manager/get_file/3384), presented in Chapters 10 and 11, or similar documents developed by state or local entities. Measurable objectives should always begin with the statement, "At the end of this (workshop, program of services, school year, course), students (employees, clients) will be able to. . . ". The statement of the objective, described in some way that makes it possible to measure its accomplishment, should follow this general statement. Some sample measurable objectives are listed next.

HIGH SCHOOL.   By the end of the second year of high school, students will be able to:

1. Describe changes in the American workplace that will affect their own career planning;
2. State at least two areas of interest, using either Holland (1997) clusters or job families on the World-of-Work Map (ACT, 2000) for future work;
3. Describe the courses or curricula available in their high schools to help prepare them for these areas of work;
4. Describe different paths of education or training that they might pursue after high school related to these areas of work.

By the end of the third year of high school, students will be able to:

1. State one or more tentative occupational choices;
2. List specific schools or ways in which they can get the postsecondary training needed for these occupations;
3. Complete an action plan that lists the steps needed to move from these choices through the education needed to enter the occupation;

4. Demonstrate job-seeking skills such as completing a job application and engaging effectively in mock job interviews (for those not planning to seek further education).

COLLEGE/UNIVERSITY.   By the end of the first year, students will be able to:

1. State at least two areas of their highest interest, using either Holland (1997) clusters or job families on the World-of-Work Map (ACT, 2000);
2. Describe in detail at least three occupations in each of these two areas, based on research through use of Web sites, Web-based career planning systems, and informational interviews;
3. Tentatively select an occupation or group of occupations;
4. Select a major that is related to the occupational choices.

By the end of the third year, students will be able to:

1. List at least three companies in the geographic area where they offer positions like those desired;
2. Describe each of these companies in terms of its products, number of employees, recent history related to reducing its workforce and/or restructuring, and potential for employees' further growth or training;
3. Write a high-quality resume in at least two formats;
4. Exhibit skill, through participation in mock interviews, in the job-interviewing process;
5. State five personal criteria for identifying jobs or for selecting one job offer over another.

CORPORATION.   At the end of this series of workshops, employees will be able to:

1. State how recent changes in the American workplace are affecting their personal careers;
2. Describe the career planning process that they may need to use either because they choose to make career changes or because the company needs to make adjustments;
3. List their top-10 transferable skills should they need to make a career change;
4. Write a high-quality resume that describes their education, work skills, and employment history;
5. State the type and length of training that would expand or update some of their job skills, making them more productive for the company or more marketable should they decide to leave the company.

AGENCY SERVING LOW-INCOME ADULTS.   At the end of these three sessions, participants will be able to:

1. Identify skills learned in home management and state how to describe them in a resume;
2. Identify jobs in which these identified skills can be used;
3. Write an attractive resume that capitalizes on these skills.

As indicated, these objectives become the basis for the content of career planning services as well as the methods of evaluating them.

Step 4: Determine How to Deliver the Career Planning Services

In this step, the goal is to provide as rich an array of services to as many people as possible in the most cost-effective way. Providing service via one-to-one interviews is the most expensive and the most time-consuming way to deliver service. For this reason, it is desirable to do as much as possible through other methods that are effective but demand less time. Methods other than one-to-one interviewing include the following (of course, any of these could be combined with one-to-one interviewing):

- Offering special courses or units within existing courses about career planning topics (middle school, high school, and perhaps college/university) in face-to-face and/or Web-based delivery
- Offering workshops that serve 8 to 15 people (university and corporation)
- Creating a virtual career center that organizes high-quality Web sites that provide career planning content
- Assigning use of one of the comprehensive Web-based career planning systems described in Chapter 7
- Providing self-help materials that may include assessment inventories and a companion workbook

The methods chosen to provide the career planning services will relate to available time, staff, budget, and resources (such as assessment inventories or self-help books) that fit the population's needs and objectives; the amount of time people have to spend on career planning needs at the school or worksite; and available technical resources (for use of Web-based career planning systems or Web sites).

MIDDLE SCHOOL AND HIGH SCHOOL. Much of the content could be provided in the classroom by training teachers to include some of the topics in their curriculum or through a well-planned and staffed career center. Alternatively, a career planning course may be offered to students during designated class periods or through homeroom or advisement periods. This curriculum may be developed locally, or the site might use a curricular package such as *Direct Your Future* (Harris-Bowlsbey, 2010b). Individual interviews with counselors could be offered to students who need individualized help.

COLLEGE/UNIVERSITY. The content could be provided through a series of workshops, offered by a career counselor or certified career development facilitator, as a part of the services of a well-equipped physical career center, through a virtual career center (i.e., a Web site), and/or through individual interviews with students who need them. Another viable method is offering a for-credit, one-semester career planning course. This course may be developed at the local level or may utilize an already developed course such as Take Hold of Your Future (Harris-Bowlsbey, 2010a).

CORPORATION.   The content could be provided through a series of workshops provided by a career counselor or a certified career development facilitator, through workshops and individual interviews provided by a trained manager, or via the corporation's intranet or Web site. Many corporations have a career management center that provides a wealth of printed information, access to Web sites, and one-to-one counseling provided by a certified, professional counselor.

COMMUNITY AGENCIES.   The content may be provided through a series of workshops or through one-to-one interviews. Web sites may also be used for assessment, career information, and job searching. Individual counseling may also be available.

Step 5: Determine the Content of the Program

The content of the program is determined by its objectives, so it is necessary to look at each objective and imagine different ways it could be addressed. Here is one example for each of the populations.

HIGH SCHOOL.   Objective: Describe changes in the American workplace that affect personal career planning.

Methods of meeting objective: Ask representatives from companies or government organizations to describe these changes in a scheduled meeting; ask students to read a book, use Web sites, or read several articles on this topic. Hold a group discussion after use of any of these methods of providing the basic information.

COLLEGE/UNIVERSITY.   Objective: State at least two areas of their highest interest, using either career areas on the World-of-Work Map or Holland clusters.

Methods of meeting objective: Administer one or a combination of instruments that measure interests and skills by Holland typology. Provide score reports to students, and interpret the results for them.

CORPORATION.   Objective: Describe the career planning process that they may need to use either because they choose to make career changes or because the company needs to make adjustments.

Methods of meeting objective: Provide a workshop in which the career planning process is described; prepare a brochure for all employees; train managers in this process, and ask them, in turn, to provide this information and instruction in meetings that they have with employees; place this information on the corporate intranet or Web site.

Step 6: Determine the Cost of the Program

It is rare indeed that any project will be approved without knowledge of its cost. In order to calculate cost accurately, it is necessary that the objectives be defined, that the method(s) of meeting each objective be detailed, and that the content proposed for each objective be solidified. At that point, it should be possible to calculate a budget that includes all of the following components:

- Staff time for designing, developing, and evaluating the products and services
- Staff time needed either to deliver or to train others to deliver the program
- A Web-based career planning system that may be needed
- Equipment and materials needed such as computers, reference books, or copies of assessment inventories
- Printing costs, if any
- Technical costs (if a virtual career center is being developed, for example)
- Cost for using facilities, if any
- Cost of refreshments for participants, if any

A manager would want to know how much of the total cost requires spending additional money and how much represents the use of staff, equipment, and materials that already exist. In some settings, it may also be necessary to project expected gains from having delivered the program of services. For example, if it is offered in a university setting and the expectation is that the services will reduce the loss of enrolled students, the strategy of comparing the cost of delivering the service to one current student with that of recruiting and orienting one new student may be effective. If it is a corporate setting the goal of a program of services is to improve the satisfaction of employees, resulting in higher productivity, cost may be justified by comparing the cost of delivering the service to one employee to the value of the increased productivity of that employee.

Because managers are always very busy, the budget should be presented in a very succinct way that summarizes the services, the benefits that are expected from the services, and the total or per-client cost of delivering them.

Step 7: Begin to Promote and Explain Your Services

In any environment there are always some who are willing to support career planning services and others who are ready to criticize them. It is important to build an understanding and supportive environment for the introduction of any new program. There are several ways to accomplish this:

- Early in the design process, invite or appoint a committee of people to help design the program, or at least to provide feedback about preliminary plans. It is important to choose people who are respected by others and who are influential. When others see that the proposed program is being supported by these people, they will be more likely to do so as well.
- As soon as preliminary ideas are formed, begin to explain them to managers and ask for their input, either in individual meetings or through the circulation of a document to which they are invited to add their comments.
- Start with a small pilot test. Try to get some respected and visible students or employees to participate in the pilot test. Not only will a pilot test help to expand and refine ideas and procedures, but it will also begin to provide publicity

by word of mouth. Capitalize on that by having short articles in the school or corporate newsletter in which someone talks about the new program and how it has benefited him or her.

- If the school or company is facing challenges or problems that might be alleviated by some part of the proposed career planning program, begin with that part. Ideally, the career planning assistance will help solve those problems and will thus be viewed positively when it is time for expansion.

> **Tips from the Field**
>
> The quality of the program of services, when it is delivered, will correspond directly to the time and energy put into the first seven steps of planning.

Step 8: Start Promoting and Delivering the Full-Blown Program of Services

It is important to notice that seven time-consuming planning steps have occurred before starting to deliver the services that have been designed and planned. Although this seems tedious, the time and energy spent in the long planning cycle will result in a higher-quality end product.

No matter how good a product or service is, it will not meet its objectives if people do not avail themselves of it. It is very important, at the same time the content is being designed, to plan how the program will be promoted. Therefore, plans for promotion should be ready to implement prior to the time the service itself is implemented.

Just as the first impression in a job interview is extremely critical, so is the impression that is created the first time new services are offered. Make sure that everything is ready for launching the program before beginning and that its first round of delivery is of very high quality, thereby ensuring that the program will gain an image of quality and usefulness from the outset.

Step 9: Evaluate the Program

Because evaluation is a time-consuming and expensive process, let us consider four reasons why evaluation is important. The predominant reason is to determine whether the program is helping people to achieve the objectives for which it was defined. Those objectives were written in order to meet the needs identified in the target population. If the program does not help people to achieve those objectives, it is not meeting needs.

Second, it is necessary to evaluate the services so that they can be improved. No matter how well the design and development stages have been accomplished, implementation of a new program will always identify additional needs, different possible approaches, and good ideas for enhancement. Program development and delivery is a cyclical process; new ideas should be included in the program at next delivery.

Third, evaluation provides ongoing information to supervisors and other stakeholders about the results of the program, meeting the requirement of accountability.

Administrators typically want to know how many people are availing themselves of the program and about the effectiveness of the program in meeting identified needs.

Fourth, evaluation is sometimes done in order to determine whether the outcomes of delivering services are worth the money and other resources being invested. The focus of such evaluation is to make a decision to retain, expand, or discontinue services.

Evaluation is typically categorized as being *formative, summative,* or both. According to the Joint Committee on Standards for Educational Evaluation (2011), formative evaluation is done for the purpose of improving an ongoing program, whereas summative evaluation has the goal of drawing conclusions about the overall worth of a program in order to determine whether to retain it. Thus, the first three reasons just given for evaluation fall into the category of formative, whereas the fourth reason fits the category of summative. Evaluation can, of course, be designed to meet all four purposes.

Planning Evaluation

In planning evaluation it is necessary to follow several standard steps that will provide the structure for the implementation of the evaluation plan. The first step is to determine whether the evaluation is formative, summative, or both. The kinds of data collected depend on the answer to this question. For example, in formative evaluation, there will be questions about how the content of the program can be improved and about how the participants valued it. For summative evaluation, it is likely that there will be measurement of outcomes and cost, begging the question of whether or not the outcomes were worth the expenditures to accomplish them. This planning step may also include decision making about who will receive the data.

A second step is to determine what specific knowledge, skills, attitudes, or behaviors are to be evaluated. These may include global constructs, such as change in career maturity, decision-making skill, or self-concept; skills, such as job interviewing; or knowledge, such as how to research occupations. Longer-term behaviors, such as consistently getting to work on time or maintaining a job for a long period of time, may be measured. What is measured should relate directly to the statement of objectives for the program.

A third step is to determine what the source(s) of the evaluation data will be. In formative evaluation it is likely that the data will be sought from clients, program participants, or trained observers. In summative evaluation the data may be collected from records, budgets, and follow-up studies. For example, if a correctional system is doing a summative evaluation of a new program of vocational training and counseling services to offenders, the offenders themselves may never evaluate the program. Rather, data collection will focus on calculating the per-offender cost of providing the service and comparing it to the change in job placement rate and, in turn, the effect on recidivism.

A fourth step is to determine how the data will be collected. There is a wide range of formal and informal methods from which to choose. Formal methods include the administration of standardized instruments, structured observation, and follow-up studies. Informal methods include group feedback, questionnaires, and interviews. This planning step will include review and selection of instruments (if these are to be used), development of questionnaires or observer checklists, and/or the design of follow-up studies. This step should also include decisions about who will administer these data-collection instruments and how the data will be collected, tallied or entered, and prepared for analysis.

Related to this step is the question of when the data will be collected. For formative evaluation, administering a questionnaire or holding exit interviews may be sufficient to provide the feedback needed for program improvement. A higher level of evaluation may involve assessing—through instruments, observation, or changed behaviors—whether a specific knowledge or skill has been acquired. Such evaluation is likely to be done immediately after delivery of the program or treatment. If the focus of evaluation is to determine how skills, attitudes, or knowledge has changed as a result of the program, data may be collected both before and after the treatment.

A fifth step is to determine how the data will be analyzed. This step includes decisions about whether data will simply be tallied, providing the number of respondents and a breakdown of their responses, or whether specific statistical tests will be applied to it. Such tests would likely be selected to compare differences between experimental and control group results, or pretreatment and posttreatment results, and to determine their significance.

Stakeholders

Depending upon the evaluation purpose, data may be sought from sources in addition to the persons who received the services. For example, when evaluating services provided to elementary students, a counselor would likely seek input from parents and school administrators, as well as from the students themselves. At the middle school level, evaluation might be sought from students, parents, teachers, and administrators. At the high school level, these same audiences could be supplemented by colleges and employers who receive graduates. At the college level, evaluative input might be sought from students, administrators, and employers. At the community agency level, clients, employers, and organizations that fund the services could evaluate services.

Before designing evaluation, then, it is necessary to consider who the stakeholders are—that is, who is receiving the services and who cares about them, who profits from them, who needs to be informed, and who provides the approval and funding for their continuation. Ideally, representatives of all of these stakeholders would serve on a committee that drafts the evaluation plan.

Types of Data Collected

The term *evaluation* implies the collection of data. These data may either be *quantitative* or *qualitative*. Quantitative data reports numbers and these numbers would answer questions, such as the following, that are often posed by administrators:

- How many elementary school children received help with career awareness through the classroom units taught by the counselor?
- How many sixth graders participated in the career fair?
- Of the seventh graders who participated in the fair, what percentage made a tentative selection of a career cluster?

- How many eighth graders brought their parents for an interview to develop a four-year plan related to a selected career cluster?
- How many tenth graders were served by the special series of homeroom programs about career planning?
- What percentage of seniors who went to full-time employment after graduation entered an occupation listed in their career portfolios or a highly related one?
- What percentage of college-bound seniors entered one of the majors selected in their career plans?
- What percentage of these was still pursuing that major in the sophomore year?
- How many students at each high school grade level were interviewed by counselors specifically for career planning?
- What percentage of students who attended the job-seeking workshops found a job that was desirable to them within 60 days of graduation?
- How much does it cost each time a counselor spends an hour with a student?
- How many clients have been served this calendar year in the one-stop center?
- What is the breakdown of clients by problem presented?
- Of those seeking jobs, what percentage found them within 60 days after receiving service?

Qualitative data provide information about the perceived value of the services and the extent to which predefined program outcomes were achieved. The indicators to measure quality may be different for different stakeholders. Let us imagine that a full-blown career guidance program was approved and funded for a large, urban high school. Different stakeholders may be interested in different outcomes of the intervention. Their different hoped-for outcomes might be as follows:

- Students—that they can decide upon a major (those going on to postsecondary education) and an occupation
- Counselor delivering the program—that the students will experience growth in career maturity, including decision making
- Principal—that the school dropout rate will be reduced because students become aware of the relationship between school and work
- Parents—that students will be directed to occupations and postsecondary education that are "good" for them so that money will not be wasted on further education
- Employers—that students will learn job-seeking skills, especially job-retention skills
- Teachers—that the program is worth the class time that they and the students give up

This list illustrates why individuals representing a range of stakeholders need to be involved in evaluation design.

Benchmarks for Evaluation

The word *evaluation* implies that outcomes will be compared with a desired standard. Thus, evaluation is impossible unless a standard has been set for desirable outcomes. Because there are different types of career planning services, each with different expected outcomes and stakeholders, the standard used for evaluation may be different for each.

One primary mode of delivering career services is through one-on-one, face-to-face interviewing. It is customary in such a relationship for clients, assisted by counselors, to set goals for the relationship. Examples of such goals are as follows:

- To identify and discard the irrational beliefs that the client holds that are preventing him or her from being able to formulate career goals and move ahead with them
- To develop a clearer and more positive self-concept
- To identify skills learned from past work experience and to determine how to transfer them to at least three occupations that are different from the ones already pursued
- To learn how to market oneself in a job interview

In the case of individual counseling, then, the standard for evaluation for the counselor and the client is whether or *to what extent the relationship results in accomplishment of the client's goal(s)*. It is likely that such accomplishment can be measured only by two people—the client and the counselor. Qualitative evaluation of accomplishment with this mode of service delivery may be as simple as these three steps:

- Early in the counseling relationship, specific goals are set by the client and the counselor, and these are placed in writing.
- At the end of the counseling relationship, the client and the counselor separately rate, on a scale of 1 to 5, the degree to which each goal has been accomplished.
- These ratings are shared and discussed.

An administrator in this setting is likely to want to know the number of individual clients served in a year by counselors, the mean number of sessions per client, and the hourly cost of counseling service. Data to answer these questions may be collected by requiring that counselors keep log sheets on paper or electronically or by setting up a system by which a clerical support person logs these data for everyone in the counseling or career planning center.

In group counseling, group guidance, or a career planning class, the goals are typically set for the participants by the facilitator or instructor. As described earlier in this chapter, these goals are stated in the form of *measurable objectives* that begin with the phrase "At the end of this series of____, participants will be able to . . . ," a second kind of benchmark for program evaluation. Accomplishment of these types of objectives can typically be measured by a questionnaire developed by the counselor or program administrator. Such a questionnaire could provide both quantitative and qualitative data. The following illustrate statements that include both qualitative and quantitative data: After completion of the program,

- 87% of elementary students who participated in it were able to match appropriate work tasks with the four dimensions of the World-of-Work Map—People, Data, Things, and Ideas;

- 92% of middle school students were able to sort a list of 30 occupations into the correct Holland clusters;
- 96% of high school students were able to list two or three job families by name in which they have interest, including the titles of specific occupations in those families.

Administrators may value additional data, including:

- The number of students, clients, or employees served by the program (quantitative)
- The per-person cost of providing the service (quantitative)
- Participant satisfaction with the program measured by a questionnaire in which participants are asked to rate the quality or value of the program (qualitative)
- Feedback from parents about the program (qualitative)

Parent evaluation could be assessed by a questionnaire sent to homes, including questions similar to the following:

- Did your child talk about the career exploration program at home? If so, what kinds of things did he or she say?
- Did this program trigger any conversations at home about your child's career planning? If so, what were the topics of those conversations?
- To what extent, if any, do you think that this program helped your son or daughter to determine either what he or she wants to do in work or does not want to do?

A third benchmark for evaluation of individuals' progress related to career planning is *national* or *local guidelines* that have been adopted. The latest version of the National Career Development Guidelines was developed by the U.S. Department of

Indicator	One Way to Assess
Identify your interests, likes, and dislikes.	After appropriate interventions, ask students to list three fields/clusters of their primary interest.
Identify your abilities, strengths, skills, and talents.	After completion of a skills bombardment activity, during which all members of a group are asked to tell each person what his or her primary strengths are, ask students to indicate what they have learned from the activity and how their view of self has been modified.
Identify your positive personal characteristics (e.g., honesty, dependability, responsibility, integrity, and loyalty).	Ask students to write a short essay about the positive personal characteristics that they believe they have, how they acquired these characteristics, and how they believe that they exhibit them.
Identify your work values/needs.	Using the results of a recent work values inventory, ask students to share the most important ones with others in a small group and indicate how they think they can attain these values in work.
Describe aspects of your self-concept.	Ask students to bring three pictures of themselves to class, each of which demonstrates some part of their self-concept. In a small group, have them show each other the pictures and describe what they say about themselves.

Super's Developmental Tasks	Possible Methods of Evaluation
Crystallization: shortening a list of occupations to a small number that have the highest potential to implement the self-concept.	After having offered interventions that assist students to develop a list of preferred occupations, ask them to circle three to five that they are considering most seriously. Ask students to write or talk about why they have kept these on the list while discarding others.
Specification: one occupation is selected from the short list of occupations.	Ask students to indicate the occupation that they will plan to enter, what training they will need to complete in high school and thereafter, what the typical duties of this occupation are, what the future employment outlook is, what the beginning salary range will be, which other occupations are closely related (using the same or a similar set of skills), and how they will learn more about this occupation and test it out in reality before further commitment.
Implementation: engaging in the coursework that is desirable or required for the occupation.	Ask students to make a four-year plan, listing courses available at their high school that will best prepare them for the occupation. Also ask them to describe the post-high school training needed, where it is available, and how they plan to take advantage of it.

Education, Office of Vocational and Adult Education in collaboration with several professional organizations. They address desired competencies and behaviors in three domains, eleven goals, and multiple indicators (see associationdatabase.com/aws/NCDA/asset_manager/get_file/3384). These have been adopted by many school districts across the nation. Above are a few sample behavioral indicators from the high school version of these guidelines, accompanied by an example of how the existence of the indicator might be assessed.

Local school districts or state educational systems often develop their own guidelines for career interventions, modeled after career development theories or this national set of guidelines. When schools adopt or develop guidelines, these should become the basis for both program content and evaluation.

A fourth kind of standard for evaluation is *theory*. Think, for example, about the first three of Super's (1957) five developmental tasks, listed above. These could be used as the basis for both program content development and evaluation at the secondary level.

Methods of Evaluation

As indicated at the beginning of this chapter, the primary purposes of evaluation are to determine whether specified outcomes are being achieved, to improve services, to provide data to supervisors and other stakeholders, and to make decisions about continuation of services related to cost-effectiveness. Evaluation is possible only through collection and organization of data. The data collected must be directly relevant to answering the evaluation questions, and evaluation questions are possible only when clear objectives for services have been identified. Thus, the evaluation cycle is as follows:

- Determine the specific measurable objectives (desired outcomes) of the program or service.

- Determine the *indicators* or *behaviors* that will be tell-tale signs of having reached the stated objectives.
- Identify the best way(s) to observe or measure these indicators or behaviors.
- Collect data using these methods.
- Organize the data in ways that will answer the specific evaluative questions posed by different stakeholders.
- Deliver the data to these stakeholders.
- Use relevant data for the various purposes of evaluation: to determine whether the program achieved its objectives, to improve the services for future delivery, to serve public relations purposes, and/or to make decisions about program retention.

There are several common ways of collecting the data needed for evaluation. One is through a carefully planned *questionnaire* or *interview*. In either case the same standard questions would be asked, either in written form or in a face-to-face interview process. Examples of such questionnaire items have been provided throughout this chapter. Following are general guidelines for writing items (which may either be questions or statements, such as "List the three best sources of information about job openings"):

- Make sure that the items relate directly to the indicators, behaviors, or outcomes you are trying to evaluate.
- Avoid questions that can be answered with *yes* or *no*.
- Make sure that the items are written clearly, without ambiguity.
- Make sure that the items are at an appropriate reading level for their audience.
- Make sure that the items cover all of the indicators or topics you need to cover in the evaluation.
- Modify the items as needed for different stakeholders.
- Make the questionnaire or interview as short and succinct as possible while still getting the core data that you need.

In most cases, questionnaires are administered to all persons who received a service (the subjects) immediately or in a relatively short time (one week to one month) after its completion. Sometimes, for the sake of documenting change, the same questionnaire is administered prior to receiving the service (called the *treatment*) and again after receiving the service. This type of evaluation allows a comparison of data before and after, leading to evaluative statements such as "Before the career planning unit was taught to all sophomores, 85% of them indicated that they had no idea about their future vocational choice. After the completion of the unit, only 24% indicated that they had no idea."

A second method of evaluation is the *administration of more formal instruments* developed by test publishers, some of which are described in Chapter 5. Such instruments measure global constructs (career maturity, decision-making skill, career decidedness, career concerns, and career beliefs) rather than the accomplishment of specific objectives. If the goal of offering a specific service was to increase or modify one or more of these global constructs, use of such instruments could be helpful. These are listed and described in detail in *A Counselor's Guide to Career*

Assessments, 5th edition (Whitfield et al., 2009), published by the NCDA and updated periodically.

As with questionnaires, these instruments may be administered to the same group or individual, both before and after the career planning service has been provided, or only after. Typically, the before-after administration is used when the study is nonscientific; that is, when there is no *control group* considered equivalent to the *experimental group* that was denied the service at the time of the evaluation. The use of randomly selected groups is typically required in *research studies*. However, in *evaluation studies* this design is not typically used because it is very difficult to achieve in day-to-day operational settings.

Another common method of collecting data is the *follow-up study*. In such a study, those who have participated in some form of treatment are contacted by phone, e-mail, regular mail, or in person at one or more intervals of time after completion of the program. The purpose of this contact, of course, is to determine whether specific predefined outcomes have been or are being experienced as a result of the treatment. As an example, suppose that an instructional unit was provided to high school seniors who are not planning to enter any kind of postsecondary education. The unit provides extensive instruction about job-seeking skills. A primary objective was stated as follows: "Upon completion of this unit and graduation from high school, at least 85% of students will get a job within a month after graduation." In this case, a counselor might conduct a follow-up study by either sending a questionnaire to graduates, sending an e-mail, or placing a phone call, any of which would be designed to find out if the graduate had found a job and begun work. Thus, it would be easy to determine whether the objective set for the instructional unit had been met.

Using the Results of Evaluation

The reason for which evaluation is done determines how the results will be used. Imagine that evaluative results—both qualitative and quantitative—have been collected for the delivery of a unit of career planning instruction to middle school students. Briefly stated, the results are as follows:

From *administrators* (based on receipt of a content outline of the program): This program looks exceptionally good, and its content is needed by all students. Be careful not to take too much class time for the program, however, especially from the core subjects.

From *parents* (based on a short questionnaire included with report cards for students who participated in the program):

- 99% indicated that their students need this instruction;
- 76% indicated that their child talked about the program at home;
- 32% indicated that their child formed a tentative career goal as a result of the instruction;
- 45% indicated that their child would use what was learned in the instructional unit to help with the development of a four-year plan;
- 90% indicated that they thought the school should continue the program.

From the *students* (based on an end-of-unit questionnaire):

- 88% of students, when given a list of 30 occupational titles with short descriptions, could place each title in the correct Holland cluster;
- 95% of students selected one of the six Holland clusters as a "first-choice" cluster;
- The same 95% of students drafted a mock four-year plan for selection of high school courses related to the cluster of their first choice.

When asked what they learned during the unit,

- 81% indicated that they learned how occupations can be organized;
- 92% indicated that they learned more about their own interests;
- 73% indicated that they learned about the relationship between school subjects and work.

When asked what they liked best about the unit (listing the five top choices),

- 97% selected the field trips;
- 94% selected the use of a Web site which explains the six clusters and gives titles and descriptions of occupations;
- 85% selected the guest speakers;
- 76% selected the videos about the six clusters;
- 74% selected the use of a Web-based system that provides titles and occupational descriptions by cluster.

When asked what they liked least about the instructional unit,

- 94% selected the requirement to write a short paper about the cluster of occupations they liked best;
- 90% selected the requirement to interview someone who works in the cluster selected as favorite;
- 85% selected having to complete a four-year high school plan for the cluster selected;
- 61% selected having to memorize a definition of each of the six clusters;
- 25% selected having to miss English class for three days.

From *classroom teachers who gave their classrooms and class time to make the unit possible* (based on a short interview with each):

- The counselor should have made arrangements for this unit no later than September 15 so that lessons and assignments for the English class could have been modified earlier.
- Students seemed to have more freedom while the counselor was teaching this unit. As a result, the room was more disorderly than usual.
- The bus that took students on the field trip returned to school late, resulting in a need for the teacher to write a late pass for every student before he or she went to the next class period.
- In casual conversation, students showed a lot of enthusiasm for the unit.
- Students need to know this content, but it would be better if it could take less time away from the English class.

Assuming this evaluative feedback, how will the counselor use it to improve the unit the next time it is delivered? These conclusions could be drawn from the data:

- The basic methods of presenting the content (field trip, speakers, videos, Web sites) are well received by the students.
- Specific assignments, though disliked by the students, should be kept because of their value.
- Based on administrator, teacher, and student feedback, the length of the program should be cut without losing its valuable outcomes.
- Great care should be taken to work with English teachers very early in the semester, or even at the end of the previous semester, so that their lesson plans can be modified both to reflect the content being taught in this special guidance unit and to accommodate for the time loss it causes.
- The schedule for field trips must be very carefully monitored so that students never return to the school building late.

How could a counselor use the same results to determine whether program objectives have been met? Although not stated here, let us imagine that the counselor had several clearly written and measurable objectives for this program and that data listed at the beginning of the previous list indicated that the objectives had been met at an even higher level than indicated in the objectives. Such data would confirm that program objectives had been met.

How would a counselor use these results to promote and explain the program as well as to ensure that it continues? Here are some ideas in that regard:

- A short executive summary of the results could be sent to the administrator, along with a memo that thanks him or her for continued support for the program and indicates that its length, now 6 hours, has been reduced to 4 hours for the next year in order to ensure that the amount of time taken away from English classes is not excessive. The report might contain not only the basic data, but also several positive quotes from parents, teachers, and/or students. The cover memo might also include a summary of the plans for the next semester or year.
- A short summary of the results could be included in the school newsletter to parents, along with some student quotes. Further details might be presented at a PTA meeting.
- An article about the program could be written and sent to the local newspaper. A cover letter might state when the program will be offered again and invite a reporter to cover one or more of the main events (such as the field trip to show the different kinds of work tasks included in the six clusters of occupations) next time.
- A report about the success of the program could be sent, along with a thank you letter, to the English teachers who gave up class time for the program and to their department chair. The letter might include a paragraph that indicates that some time has been cut from the program in order to use as little English-class time as possible and that greater care will be taken in the future about the condition of classrooms and the prompt arrival of buses from field trips.

How might an administrator use the data to determine whether to retain the program of services or to discontinue it? An analysis of the number of hours spent by the counselor and the number of students served reveals that the cost of delivery was $2.45 per student. Based on the strong parent and student feedback, the principal decides to retain the program in spite of some faculty resistance about the fact that class time is taken for its delivery.

Roadblocks to Evaluation

It is not easy to find the time or the motivation to do evaluation of career counseling and career planning services. Most counselors work in settings in which there are many conflicting demands on their time and priorities. The crisis situations—such as dealing with violence, drugs, excessive absence, and a variety of behavioral problems—receive first priority. In high school settings, planning and changing course schedules often demands second priority; making or finding time to provide career planning services receives, at best, third priority; and designing or evaluating any of these services falls near the bottom of the priority list. Patrick and Niles (1988) identified three additional roadblocks, as follows:

- Because evaluation is designed to reveal the quality of services as perceived by those who receive them, the potential for negative results is threatening. If evaluation did result in negative findings, funding, staff, and program approval could be in jeopardy.
- Unless the services of a guidance or student affairs office have been designed in the way described in this chapter, its offerings may be so nonsystematic—that is, without defined objectives—that it is difficult or impossible to evaluate them.
- Many counselors believe that the kind of work they do cannot be objectively evaluated because it is not quantifiable or definable. Thus, they resist any method of evaluation.

In addition to these roadblocks, counselors may not have the financial resources to purchase instruments that would be helpful in evaluation or conduct a follow-up study. Further, they may not have the time or expertise to develop questionnaires, observer checklists, or exit interviews to be used. In cases in which better data would be acquired if there could be an experimental-control group design, the realities of the work setting may not support such a design.

Step 10: Revise the Program as Needed

In this step of the process, developers use the results of evaluation of the previous delivery of the program, feedback from managers, and additional creative ideas in order to revise the program and prepare for its next delivery. Revisions are a very normal part of the process because it is never possible to anticipate how students or clients will react to interventions until they have been tested with members of the target population. Revisions may include changes to content, time allocated to different activities, facilities, personnel, and methods of evaluation. The number of changes will decrease as the number of times the program is delivered is increased.

SOME SAMPLE PROGRAMS

A wealth of information about career development theory and practice has been covered in this book. The purpose of this content, of course, is to enable counselors to create programs to serve different kinds of clients in a variety of settings by using curricular, group, and one-to-one approaches, all enhanced by the use of Web-based career planning systems and sites. This section of the chapter provides examples of the program design process in five different settings. These are merely illustrations provided for the purpose of offering further clarity about the development process.

Example 1: A Middle School

You have been a teacher in a middle school (grades 6 to 8) of approximately 400 students. You recently completed a master's degree in counseling, and your principal has asked you to work with a task force of teachers to figure out how to incorporate career guidance objectives and content into the curriculum. Your team used the National Career Development guidelines for the middle school years (see Chapter 11) as the basis for this work. Although individual teachers have provided some content and activities related to occupational choice, there has been no integrated plan for providing career exploration for the students. For that reason, under your leadership, the task force begins by writing a document for the principal, briefly describing your proposal.

EXECUTIVE SUMMARY.   Career development is a lifelong process. Within the context of this process, students at the middle school level should be encouraged to engage in career exploration; that is, to become aware of their personal characteristics (self-awareness), occupations and their similarities and differences (occupational exploration), and career preparation (curricular choices). The U.S. Department of Education (2003), Office of Vocational and Adult Education, in collaboration with appropriate professional organizations, has developed detailed guidelines. The committee has used the middle school guidelines as the basis for its own development of specific objectives for our school.

NEEDS.   The needs of middle school students are well defined by the National Career Development Guidelines. The specific objectives included are drawn both from theory (especially that of Donald E. Super) and from the demands of their transition to high school. Thus, the needs are to develop a strong base of self- and occupational knowledge during these years and to accomplish the objectives provided below.

SPECIFIC OBJECTIVES.   By the time students transition to high school, they will be able to:

1. Describe the world-of-work as six clusters of occupations and differentiate the work tasks, work settings, skills, and educational levels unique to each cluster;
2. Select one or two clusters of highest interest;

3. Develop a tentative four-year high school plan that would prepare them for work in or further educational preparation for work in the selected cluster(s);

4. Describe work as one significant role among others that make up one's personal career.

PROPOSED PLAN. In order to accomplish the objectives listed above, the following steps are suggested:

1. It is proposed that the World-of-Work Map (ACT, 2000) be taught in social studies classes at the sixth-grade level as a way to help students understand how occupations are organized and the different roles that workers play in our society in order to make it function economically with sufficient production of goods and services. Also, Super's (1980) definition of career as a combination of life roles being played at any point in life will be used and explained.

2. At the seventh-grade level, a concerted effort would be made to provide information to students about the work tasks, work setting, and academic preparation needed for work in each of these six clusters. In order to facilitate this, school subjects would be assigned to each of the six clusters, and teachers of those subjects would be provided with a list of occupations (at various educational entry levels) that belong to the cluster to which their subject matter is related. Teachers would be asked to make linkages as often as possible between subject matter being taught and tasks of occupations in the cluster. They would also be encouraged to invite speakers into the class to talk about occupations in the cluster and how the subject matter being taught relates to their work. Further, the school counselor will coordinate a career day that is organized by the six clusters, inviting representatives of many occupations to the school so that students can talk with them. The counselor will also increase the resources of the career center and organize all occupational information by the same six clusters.

3. The counselor will work with the high school to organize the high school curriculum by the same six clusters. During the eighth grade the counselor will work with students and their parents in groups to draft a four-year high school plan related to each student's selected cluster(s) and future educational plans.

RESOURCES NEEDED. In order to implement the proposed program, the following resources will be needed:

1. Purchase of posters from ACT that provide a graphic representation of the World-of-Work Map and copies of the Career Area Charts that list occupations. (Note: These materials can be found online at act.org/wwm/index.html and used by students in that mode if access to the computer lab is possible.)

2. One to two hours of time in department or faculty meetings during which the counselor can explain these materials to teachers and suggest ways in which they may be used as a part of their course.

3. A budget of $500 to be used for expenses related to planning for, advertising, and sponsoring the career day.

4. Time allocated to the counselor to organize and be in charge of the career day.

5. Time allocated to the counselor to meet with members of the high school guidance department to plan and complete the work related to organizing the high school courses by the World-of-Work Map organizational system.

EXPECTED OUTCOMES.   The following outcomes are expected as a result of program delivery:

1. Students will be able to make meaningful relationships between schoolwork and later work.
2. Students will gain broad awareness of the meaning of career and of how the world-of-work is organized.
3. Students will make informed occupational choices and take high school courses that will validate and/or prepare them for those choices.

METHODS OF EVALUATION.   The following methods are suggested for the purpose of evaluation:

1. Students will have a quiz after instruction on the World-of-Work Map. They will be asked to place occupational titles (which include short descriptions) into the six clusters.
2. Students will be asked to select one or two clusters of their preference and to list at least five occupations in each of these clusters in which they might have interest.
3. Students will develop a four-year high school plan related to the cluster(s) they have selected.

Example 2: A High School

Suppose that you have just been hired as a counselor in a local high school that has approximately 1,500 students. The first thing you did was to request space and funds for a career center equipped with computers and Web access so that students could access the resources described in Chapter 6. This request was granted, and the equipment been ordered.

In the past there has been no service of any kind for helping students plan for future occupational choices. Some time can be made available during the school day for sophomores, so you decide to begin your program at this level. Further, you decide to develop a program that provides service to all sophomores in a cost-effective manner, though you are willing to see those with special needs individually. The school principal asks you to provide a short document that describes what you have in mind and what your needs are. Your document might look like the one that follows.

EXECUTIVE SUMMARY.   This brief document describes the needs, objectives, content, expected outcomes, and requested resources for a career guidance program proposed for all sophomores. The needs listed can be assumed from our knowledge of career development theory and of the context in which the young people of the United States find themselves. Based on these needs, several specific objectives for the program are listed, and content and activities are proposed. Finally, the document summarizes expected outcomes, resources needed, and methods of evaluation.

NEEDS.   Given the age of these students and the contextual changes occurring in the United States, sophomore students have the following needs:

1. To understand the changes in the workplace and how these changes will affect their personal career planning;
2. To learn the process of career planning that they can apply now and will need to apply again and again throughout their lives;
3. To identify their personal interests and abilities;
4. To relate these interests and abilities to possible occupations;
5. To learn about these occupations;
6. To select courses in high school that will lay the academic basis for further education and entry into one or more of these occupations.

SPECIFIC OBJECTIVES.   At the end of the proposed program, at least 80% of the students who complete the program will be able to:

1. Describe in detail three significant trends in the United States that are changing employers and jobs, and include the implications of these for personal career planning;
2. Describe the steps of a planful process for making career decisions;
3. State three to five groups (families) of occupations that relate to their personal interests and abilities;
4. Make a list of occupational titles from those groups;
5. Describe in detail at least five occupations from that list;
6. Select at least three occupations of highest interest;
7. State the educational implications of preparing for those three occupations.

SUMMARY OF PLAN.   It is proposed that the following sessions be held with sophomores:

Session 1: Learn about changes that are occurring in the workplace.

Three speakers will be invited from three different companies. Each will talk about changes that have occurred in the past five years and what the projected changes are for the future, including what these may mean for young people entering the job market.

All sophomores will be assembled in the auditorium. A one-page worksheet will be given to each student on which he or she can record the main points of each speaker as well as a summary that includes at least three implications of what speakers said for personal career planning.

Projected time: 1½ hours

Session 2: Learn a process for making personal career decisions.

The career planning process (copy of a graphic enclosed for your information) will be described by the counselor to sophomores in groups of 40 using a PowerPoint presentation. Students will receive a short handout that provides a graphic of the career decision-making process and an explanation of each of its steps.

An interest inventory (copy enclosed for your information) will be administered to each group of 40 students. Answer sheets will be scored and results printed, using the computer program licensed with the instrument.

Proposed time: 2 hours—1 hour for presentation of the career planning model (including answering student questions) and 1 hour for describing the purpose and administering the interest inventory. Because there are 400 students in the sophomore class, this will require 20 hours of counselor time plus another 3 hours for preparation of visual materials and handout.

Session 3: Interpret the results of the interest inventory to students in groups of 40.

Give each student his or her score report. Describe the score report by use of a sample (for some fictitious student) score report projected on the screen, and explain each section of the report. Then ask the students to look at their own reports. Answer as many questions as possible in the group sessions. If students have additional questions, invite them to make an appointment for an interview. Ask students to circle the names of three clusters that interest them on the material provided with the score report.

Projected time: 1 hour for each of 10 groups of students, requiring 10 hours of counselor time for presentations, an additional 2 hours for preparation, and an estimated 10 hours for individual interviews requested by students or invited by the counselor because of the pattern of results.

Session 4: Assist students to identify occupations that belong in the three career clusters they have selected and to get information about those occupations.

Schedule students in groups of 20 to come to the career center. Provide brief instruction about the materials in the center that contain occupational descriptions, including two specific Web sites. Also, explain what an information interview is and how students can find people who are willing to talk with them. Provide students with a worksheet that will guide their use of materials so that they can record the titles of occupations and information gained about each. Assign an information interview for each of three occupations, and provide a worksheet for students' use in summarizing their learning.

Projected time: 2 hours each for 20 groups of students—a total of 40 hours of counselor time.

Session 5: Offer opportunities for students to discuss their learning from the research in the career center and from informational interviews, and give students time to complete a personal Career Action Plan.

Students will come to the center in groups of 20. Students will be asked to share with the group some of the things they learned by doing the research and by interviewing individuals who work in occupations that interest them. Ask students to complete a one-page career action plan which lists three occupations of highest interest at this time, indicates the level and kind of education needed for entering each occupation, and lists next steps. These steps may include taking courses that are needed in high school, researching the occupation further, or requesting an interview with the counselor.

Projected time: 40 hours of counselor time for the group sessions plus an estimated 10 additional hours for individual interviews.

RESOURCES NEEDED.   It is anticipated that the following resources will be needed in order to deliver this program:

1. Use of the auditorium and audiovisual equipment for Session 1
2. 400 copies of the interest inventory
3. Permission to duplicate handouts for students that will total about 20 pages per student

EXPECTED OUTCOMES.   As a result of the delivery of this program, the following outcomes are expected:

1. High student motivation because of school's concern for their future planning
2. Improved student choice of curriculum while in high school
3. Learning of decision-making and research skills that will be needed many times later in life
4. Support and involvement of parents

METHODS OF EVALUATION.   The following are suggested as methods of evaluation:

1. Review work forms completed by students to assure that they have been able to complete assigned tasks.
2. Provide questionnaire that each student completes at the end of the five sessions.
3. Interview 20 randomly selected students to ask them how they rate the effectiveness of the program and to capture ideas they have for improvement.

Another idea related to this program is to have an evening meeting with parents prior to beginning the program. If this is not feasible, then it may be possible to send a letter from the principal to each home. Either of these approaches would explain the purpose of these meetings with students, describe the general content, and offer parents a chance to talk with a counselor if they have questions.

Example 3: A University

Imagine that you have just been hired as a career counselor at a major university. Other than the assistance that faculty mentors may give to students, there has previously been no staff or program to assist students with the selection of majors, occupations, or jobs. One of the conditions you stated when you considered the job was that the university would invest in the facilities and resources needed to establish a career center for students and alumni. This request was granted, and you are in the process of drawing a layout for the center and of ordering the furnishings and resource material. You are anxious to get permission for a program of services for students, but because this is a new idea, your dean asks you to provide a short proposal, which you do, as follows.

EXECUTIVE SUMMARY.   This document describes a voluntary program of services for seniors at the university that will assist them to prepare the documents needed for searching for jobs and will provide them with skills to identify job openings, secure job interviews, conduct themselves effectively in job interviews, and select a good place of employment.

NEEDS.   The needs stated here have been identified both by a review of the career development literature and by a random survey of alumni who graduated from the university last year. Based on these sources, graduates of this university have the following needs:

1. To understand how the workplace they are about to enter has changed;
2. To learn a process for career decision making that they can use now and in the future;
3. To develop an effective resume for today's job market;
4. To know how to find or create job openings;
5. To know how to identify personal skills and relate them to job openings;
6. To know how to participate in an effective interview.

OBJECTIVES.   Based on these identified needs, students who participate in the program of services described next will be able to:

1. Describe at least three trends in the United States today that affect their personal careers and what they should expect of their future employers;
2. Describe a process for making career choices;
3. Show a personal resume, in at least two formats (e.g., chronological and functional), that can be used for a job search;
4. In mock interviews, demonstrate an ability to participate effectively in job interviews, including relating personal skills to a job opening.

CONTENT.   The content described next will be presented in a series of three workshops to be presented four times throughout the academic year.

Session 1 (1 hour): A presentation by the counselor, using audiovisual aids, about the systemic changes in the workplace, how these will affect personal careers, and how individuals will need to take responsibility for their own career choices; presentation (with handout) of a career decision-making model.

Session 2 (1 hour): Presentation about the purpose of a resume and of two different formats for preparing one. Via a handout, show good examples of sample resumes, and provide worksheets that each student can use to write his or her own resume in both formats. Ask students to prepare these sample resumes by the next session. Invite students who wish to come for an individual interview to do so. Offer to review and make suggestions about their resumes. Show good examples of Web-based e-portfolios and how a resume is used as a central part of that portfolio.

Session 3 (2 hours): Presentation about the characteristics and stages of an effective interview, with handout. Following that, do a mock interview with one student. Then hand out descriptions of a job opening and an applicant; ask students to form triads, with one playing the role of an employer; one the role of an applicant, and the third the role of an observer who is noting whether the characteristics of a successful interview are present. Videotape the job interviews, and use these videos as a basis for discussion of effective and ineffective interview behaviors.

EXPECTED OUTCOMES. As a result of delivery of this program, the following outcomes are anticipated:

1. Students will learn about changes in the U.S. job market that affect their careers and what their expectations of employers should be in the future.
2. Students will learn a decision-making model that they can use to assume personal responsibility for their own career decisions again and again.
3. Students will be able to prepare an effective resume and post it for review by employers.
4. Students will be more comfortable and more effective in job interviews.

RESOURCES NEEDED. The following resources will be needed:

1. Capability to advertise these workshops in all university media
2. Permission to duplicate handouts to support these workshops
3. Use of a larger facility if the number of students who wish to attend exceeds the capacity of the career center
4. Postage and time for follow-up study

METHODS OF EVALUATION. The program will be evaluated in the following ways:

1. Ask students who attended all three workshops to complete a questionnaire at the end of the sequence.
2. Tally the number of students who attend each workshop and the number who attend all three.
3. Do a follow-up survey by mail of 100 students one year after the workshop series to determine what percentage have jobs, their degree of satisfaction with these jobs, and how they believe the workshops helped them to find and acquire employment.

Example 4: A Corporation

Imagine that you have just been hired as a career counselor by a large corporation that needs to reduce the size of its workforce. It is doing this by offering older employees an early retirement financial package and terminating 456 middle managers. When you were hired, you were told that your services were desperately needed to help these two specific target populations. You asked for the physical space and the funds to set up a career management center, and these requests were granted. You are asked to provide a proposal for serving one of these two target populations as soon as possible. You decide to initiate a program for the 456 mid-level managers first because their needs are more immediate than those of the early retirees who have six more months of employment left. You submit the following proposal.

EXECUTIVE SUMMARY. This document describes a program of services that will be initiated with 456 middle managers who are to be terminated in two weeks. The program focuses on assisting them to learn and practice job-search skills so that they can find another job quickly.

NEEDS. These employees are understandably in a state of shock, anger, and denial. They need an opportunity to talk about the present situation, with the hope that they will be able to get through the anger and denial stages and move quickly to being able to formulate an action plan for reemployment. Also, because these employees are in the age range of 42 to 50 and most have worked for this company for many years, it is assumed that they need to review the latest job-search techniques and to practice these until they are comfortable.

OBJECTIVES.   At the end of this series of workshops, employees who are going to be terminated will be able to:

1. Recognize that the situation they are facing is a result of economic conditions and resultant corporate decisions and that it has no relationship to their work performance;
2. Accept that, though the situation is unfortunate and stressful, it is not catastrophic and that they can find a way to make a successful transition;
3. Write an effective resume in multiple formats that adequately expresses their skills and experience;
4. Participate effectively in mock job interviews;
5. Describe three effective ways of finding job openings;
6. Using Schlossberg's model, develop a plan for coping successfully with this transition.

CONTENT. Employees will be allowed to use normal working hours to attend a series of workshops, have individual interviews with the counselor, and use the Career Management Center. There will be a series of four two-hour workshops, which these employees will be encouraged to attend. Because 30 people would be a maximum number for each workshop, multiple sequences of these workshops will be scheduled.

Workshop 1 (2 hours): This workshop will be less structured than the remaining three. Because employees are unlikely to be able to focus on action planning until they have been able to express their anger and grief about job loss, this session will allow individuals to talk about their feelings. Several people from top management will be invited to attend, and, when appropriate, they may answer questions or provide information about the events that led the corporation to make the decision about termination of these employees.

Workshop 2 (2 hours): This session will focus on the preparation of a good resume, in at least two formats, that expresses the skills and experience of each employee. A presentation will be made about how to develop such a resume, and good examples will be provided as handouts. Individuals will spend the remaining time preparing a first draft of their own resumes. They will be invited to make individual interviews with the counselor, if they wish, and/or to leave their resumes in the counselor's office for review and feedback.

Workshop 3 (2 hours): This session will focus on a review of good interviewing skills. The various stages of the job interview will be described. Particular emphasis will be placed on teaching individuals how to research companies via the Internet and other means so that when they have interviews, they are able to relate their skills and experience to the particular job for which they are applying. Two good interviews will be role-played for the group. A checklist will be provided that outlines the characteristics of a good interview. Then, members of the group will be asked to divide into triads. One will play the role of interviewer; one the role of job seeker; and the third the role of observer, evaluating the interview using the checklist of characteristics.

Workshop 4 (2 hours): This session will focus on how to find job openings (including use of placement agencies, Web-searching, social networking, and direct application to companies) and on learning how to network with others to identify job openings that are never publicly listed. Schlossberg's model for coping with transition will be described, and a worksheet will be provided on which individuals in the group can list ways they will cope with the transition by planning specific action steps. Members of the group will share these plans with others in the group.

EXPECTED OUTCOMES. As a result of delivery of the program, the following outcomes are anticipated:

1. Terminated employees will be able to get rid of some of their anger and frustration and may leave the company with a more positive attitude.
2. Terminated employees will have improved chances of finding another job within a reasonable time because of instruction on job-seeking documents and skills.

RESOURCES NEEDED. In order to deliver the program effectively, the following resources will be needed:

1. Permission to invite people to come to the workshops on company time
2. Cooperation from division heads to help publicize and promote the workshops through newsletters and other communications
3. A budget for refreshments
4. Use of audiovisual equipment and printing facilities
5. Permission to use Survey Monkey to conduct a follow-up study

METHODS OF EVALUATION. The following methods of evaluation are planned:

1. Provide a questionnaire that participants will complete at the end of the four sessions.
2. Follow up with a random sample of participants 90 days after completion of the workshop to determine if they have found a job and if the content of the workshop helped them to do so.

Example 5: A Community Agency

Imagine that you have accepted a position as a counselor in a one-stop center. Your manager asks you to develop a service to assist community adults who, for whatever reason, want to pursue a different occupation from the one in which they are currently engaged.

EXECUTIVE SUMMARY. This document describes a proposed program of service for adult men and women who come to the agency seeking assistance with making a new career choice. Given the restraints of time, these individuals will be offered three group sessions with the requirement of an intake interview prior to the first session and an opportunity for a counseling interview following the three group sessions. The content of these sessions has been determined by the counselors' past experience with similar clients as well as through work with a randomly selected focus group of members of the target population. The intake interview, workshop sessions, and potential content of the counseling interview are described. Further, a summary of needed resources and the plan for evaluation are provided.

NEEDS. The needs identified for this population are as follows:

1. To understand the implications of career change
2. To assess the resources and barriers related to making the change
3. To consider possible choices and to define one
4. To draft a realistic action plan for making the change

OBJECTIVES. By the end of the sequence of activities, clients will be able to:

1. Describe realistically the transition they have chosen to make;
2. Identify forces for and forces against accomplishing the change;
3. State a definite career goal and how they plan to reach it.

CONTENT. Each client who expresses a desire to make a career change (that is, select and pursue a different occupation) will be asked to participate in an intake interview. The format of intake interviews will be the same for all clients. Questions asked by the interviewer will address the following topics:

*   Past work history
*   Client's view of his or her best skills and greatest work-related accomplishments
*   Client's reasons for desiring to make an occupational change
*   Ideas the client has about what this change might be
*   How much the client knows about the occupation or field he or she now wants to enter
*   Resources that support the client's ability to make a change (such as financial situation, persons who will be supportive, children grown and independent, etc.)
*   Barriers the client will need to surmount (such as lack of support from some important persons, need for retraining, etc.)
*   Willingness to make a commitment to the three group sessions and the follow-up counseling session

The three group sessions will be scheduled for two hours on the same night in three consecutive weeks. Their content will be as follows:

Session 1: Sharing within the group in regard to the kinds of changes they are seeking to make and the supports and barriers they confront for the transition. Following this, individuals will take three assessment inventories contained in a Web-based career planning system: an interest inventory, a skills inventory, and a values inventory. They will receive their results from these inventories immediately and can print them out.

Session 2: The counselor will provide a group interpretation of the three assessments, using a fictitious composite score report and a PowerPoint presentation. Group members will have an opportunity to ask questions in general or about their own reports. Members of the group will then share their specific occupational goals or dreams and indicate whether or not the results of the assessment support those ideas. The counselor will facilitate discussion. If individuals in the group need individual assistance in identifying possible occupational alternatives, they may make an appointment with the counselor for an individual interview before Session 3.

Session 3: Using worksheets based on the Schlossberg model for transition, clients will draft a plan to pursue a goal they have set for themselves. In this process they will identify specific steps they need to take (such as getting some training or having an information interview), assign a feasible timeline for completion of each step, and identify barriers and methods of dealing with these.

Following the three sessions, each participant will have an individual interview with the counselor. The purpose is to review the action plan together so that the counselor may be able to provide further information or suggest strategies for following the plan.

EXPECTED OUTCOMES.   As a result of this sequence of activities, it is expected that clients will:

1. Have a specific plan for making a career change.
2. Have a realistic career goal in keeping with self-information that has been gained.
3. Experience the support of the counselor and the group for moving forward with this plan.

RESOURCES NEEDED.   Delivery of the program as designed will require the following resources:

1. For the first session, a meeting room equipped with computers and Web access that will hold 15 people. Meeting room space, but without computers, will also be needed for an additional two consecutive weeks;
2. Equipment to display a PowerPoint presentation at each session;
3. Fifteen copies of the Schlossberg model worksheet;
4. Use of the center's career development facilitator to conduct the intake interviews;
5. Counselor time for preparing PowerPoint presentations, facilitating the three workshop sessions, and conducting individual counseling sessions.

METHODS OF EVALUATION.   The following methods of evaluation will be used:

1. Ask each client to complete a questionnaire, either in print form, or via Survey Monkey on the Web, at the end of the entire sequence.
2. Contact participants by phone or e-mail three months after the sequence of activities to assess the degree to which they have followed, or are following, the action plan they developed.

MyCounselingLab™

Go to Topic 15: *Assessment in Career Guidance and Counseling* in the MyCounselingLab™ site (www.MyCounselingLab.com) for *Career Development Interventions in the 21st Century*, Fourth Edition, where you can:

- Find learning outcomes for *Assessment in Career Guidance and Counseling* along with the national standards that connect to these outcomes.

- Complete Assignments and Activities that can help you more deeply understand the chapter content.
- Apply and practice your understanding of the core skills identified in the chapter with the Building Counseling Skills unit.
- Prepare yourself for professional certification with a Practice for Certification quiz.
- Connect to videos through the Video and Resource Library.

Summary

After building a rationale for program development and defining the roles counselors may play in it, this chapter has described a 10-step process for developing a program of career planning services for a specific target population. This process begins with understanding the characteristics of the target population, assessing its needs, and writing clear, measurable objectives focused on meeting those needs. It then includes developing program content, determining a combination of ways in which the program will be delivered, and determining how to promote and evaluate the program. Significant attention is given to the purposes and methods of evaluation and to ways in which its results can be used.

In order to make this process more practical, five sample programs for different target populations are described in some detail. They are proposed only as examples of the many different approaches to providing career planning service.

Case Study

Your high school has a dropout rate of 19%, far higher than desired by the faculty and members of the school board. As director of guidance, you are asked by your principal to develop an initiative that would (a) identify students who are at risk of drop out, (b) provide special services that may reduce that risk, and (c) evaluate the success of one year of delivery of these services.

How would you go about meeting the request of your principal?

Student Activities

1. Refer to the MyCounselingLab™ Video and Resource Library and select the video entitled *21st Century Career Development* *Interventions in the Schools: Dr. Carol Dahir*, which is an interview between Dr. Spencer Niles, the lead author of this

text, and Dr. Dahir, who was the lead author of the American School Counselor Association (ASCA) national model, which includes career development. Then, write a short paper that provides responses to these questions:

a. List and describe at least two trends in the career development field that these two professionals talked about.

b. From the many ideas that Dr. Dahir shared, did you get any ideas for a program of services that you would like to develop in a setting where you expect to work?

c. Based on what you learned in this video, what are some of the barriers that school counselors have as they attempt to provide career planning services to students?

2. By this time in the course, you may have watched videos of several clients who participated in one-on-one counseling with professional counselors in a community counseling center. Suppose that you are the director of this center and you are told that it must serve more clients than can be dealt with in one-on-one mode with the allocated budget. Write a one- or two-page, double-spaced paper that addresses the following questions:

- What kinds of programs of service could you develop within the same budget to serve the needs of more clients who need career counseling?

- What are some of the first steps you would take in developing these programs, and why?

3. Choose a setting where you hope to work as a counselor after you complete your training. Then, write a short paragraph about each of the following:

- Some basic facts about the students or clients (target population) you hope to work with

- What you believe their career (vocational and educational) development needs may be

- The kinds of interventions you would provide to meet these needs

References

ACT, Inc. (2000). *World-of-Work Map, 2000 revision*. Iowa City, IA: Author.

Harris-Bowlsbey, J. (2010a). *Take hold of your future*. Adel, IA: Kuder, Inc.

Harris-Bowlsbey, J. (2010b). *Direct your future*. Adel, IA: Kuder, Inc.

Holland, J. L. (1997). *Making vocational choices: A theory of vocational personalities and work environments* (3rd ed.). Odessa, FL: Psychological Assessment Resources.

Joint Committee on Standards for Educational Evaluation. (2011). *The program evaluation* (3rd ed.). Thousand Oaks, CA: Sage.

Patrick, J., & Niles, S. G. (1988). Establishing accountability and evaluation procedures in student affairs offices. *NASPA Journal, 25*(4), 291–296.

Super, D. E. (1957). *The psychology of careers*. New York: Harper.

Super, D. E. (1980). A life-span, life-space approach to career development. *Journal of Vocational Behavior, 16*, 282–298.

U.S. Department of Education. (2003). *The National Career Development Guidelines*.

Whitfield, E. A., Feller, R. W., & Wood, C. (2009). *A counselor's guide to career assessment instruments*. Broken Arrow, OK: National Career Development Association.

10

Career Development Interventions in the Elementary Schools

Providing career development interventions in my work as an elementary school counselor is important because it allows children to gain an awareness of careers in their community. It helps children to identify their own skills, abilities, and interests related to the world-of-work. Students gain an understanding of what makes them special and unique. Most importantly, career development activities allow students to connect school to their hopes and dreams about what they want to be when they grow up.

Colleen Yeager
Professional School Counselor North Graham Elementary School Graham, NC

MyCounselingLab™

Visit the **MyCounselingLab**™ site for *Career Development Interventions in the 21st Century,* Fourth Edition to enhance your understanding of chapter concepts. You'll have the opportunity to practice your skills through video- and case-based Assignments and Activities as well as Building Counseling Skills units, and to prepare for your certification exam with Practice for Certification quizzes.

Rosita was only five years old, but she had already experienced many difficult situations in her life. Her father, Enrique, left home before she was born. Her mother, Rosa, struggled with substance abuse problems. Rosa's lack of education (she never completed high school) severely limited her employment opportunities. She was able to find occasional employment as a waitress; however, she had a pattern of absenteeism and tardiness. These behaviors typically resulted in her termination from work.

During her periods of unemployment, Rosa often turned to drugs to numb the pain. Rosa loved Rosita, but did not know how to extricate herself from this self-defeating behavioral pattern. Fortunately, Rosa's mother lived nearby and provided much-needed emotional support to her daughter and granddaughter. Despite this support, Rosita struggled with her father's absence and her mother's frequent bouts with substance abuse and unemployment. Today, however, Rosita had other thoughts. It was her first day of school. She felt scared and anxious as she wondered what school would be like. She took comfort in the fact that her best friend, Melissa, was also starting kindergarten today.

OVERVIEW OF CAREER DEVELOPMENT INTERVENTIONS IN THE SCHOOLS

Throughout their history, professional school counselors have been engaged in helping students, such as Rosita, advance in their career and educational planning. The National Standards for School Counseling Programs (Campbell & Dahir, 1997) and the American School Counselor Association (ASCA) National Model for School Counseling (ASCA, 2003) reinforce this fact by identifying career development as an essential element in effective school counseling programs (Dimmitt & Carey, 2007). The National Standards, which were developed to address the growing need for standardization and accountability in school counseling programs, consist of four components (the foundation, the delivery system, the management system, and the accountability system). The foundation consists of program philosophy statements; it connects with the mission of the school and contains information regarding expected student competencies in the three domains (academic, career, and personal/social development). There are also nine standards (three per domain) that, in turn, are each connected to student competencies linked to specific knowledge and skills that students will develop as outcomes of their exposure to school counseling programs. Specifically, the career development domain in the National Standards contains the following standards, competencies, and indicators:

Standard A: Students will acquire the skills to investigate the world-of-work in relation to knowledge of self and to make informed career decisions.

C:A1 Develop Career Awareness

C:A1.1	Develop skills to locate, evaluate, and interpret career information
C:A1.2	Learn about the variety of traditional and nontraditional occupations
C:A1.3	Develop an awareness of personal abilities, skills, interests, and motivations
C:A1.4	Learn how to interact and work cooperatively in teams
C:A1.5	Learn to make decisions
C:A1.6	Learn how to set goals
C:A1.7	Understand the importance of planning
C:A1.8	Pursue and develop competency in areas of interest
C:A1.9	Develop hobbies and vocational interests
C:A1.10	Balance between work and leisure time

C:A2 Develop Employment Readiness

C:A2.1	Acquire employability skills such as working on a team, problem solving, and organizational skills
C:A2.2	Apply job readiness skills to seek employment opportunities
C:A2.3	Demonstrate knowledge about the changing workplace
C:A2.4	Learn about the rights and responsibilities of employers and employees
C:A2.5	Learn to respect individual uniqueness in the workplace
C:A2.6	Learn how to write a resume
C:A2.7	Develop a positive attitude toward work and learning
C:A2.8	Understand the importance of responsibility, dependability, punctuality, integrity, and effort in the workplace
C:A2.9	Utilize time- and task-management skills

Standard B: Students will employ strategies to achieve future career goals with success and satisfaction.

C:B1 Acquire Career Information

C:B1.1	Apply decision-making skills to career planning, course selection, and career transition
C:B1.2	Identify personal skills, interests, and abilities and relate them to current career choice
C:B1.3	Demonstrate knowledge of the career planning process
C:B1.4	Know the various ways in which occupations can be classified
C:B1.5	Use research and information resources to obtain career information
C:B1.6	Learn to use the Internet to access career planning information
C:B1.7	Describe traditional and nontraditional career choices and how they relate to career choice
C:B1.8	Understand how changing economic and societal needs influence employment trends and future training

C:B2 Identify Career Goals

C:B2.1	Demonstrate awareness of the education and training needed to achieve career goals
C:B2.2	Assess and modify their educational plan to support career goals
C:B2.3	Use employability and job-readiness skills in internship, mentoring, shadowing, and/or other work experience
C:B2.4	Select coursework that is related to career interests
C:B2.5	Maintain a career planning portfolio

Standard C: Students will understand the relationship between personal qualities, education, training, and the world-of-work.

C:C1 Acquire Knowledge to Achieve Career Goals

C:C1.1	Understand the relationship between educational achievement and career success
C:C1.2	Explain how work can help to achieve personal success and satisfaction
C:C1.3	Identify personal preferences and interests influencing career choice and success
C:C1.4	Understand that the changing workplace requires lifelong learning and acquiring of new skills
C:C1.5	Describe the effect of work on lifestyle

C:C1.6   Understand the importance of equity and access in career choice
C:C1.7   Understand that work is an important and satisfying means of personal expression

C:C2 Apply Skills to Achieve Career Goals
C:C2.1   Demonstrate how interests, abilities, and achievement relate to achieving personal, social, educational, and career goals
C:C2.2   Learn how to use conflict management skills with peers and adults
C:C2.3   Learn to work cooperatively with others as a team member
C:C2.4   Apply academic and employment readiness skills in work-based learning situations such as internships, shadowing, and/or mentoring experiences (ASCA, 2003, pp. 79–80)

Clearly, the National Standards represent a comprehensive and holistic view of career development. By themselves, however, the standards could seem overwhelming to the novice professional school counselor seeking to use the standards as a developmental framework from which specific career development programs can be designed and implemented. Fortunately, the ASCA National Model for School Counseling Programs links with other national standards such as the National Career Development Guidelines. Essentially, the current guidelines update those developed in 1989. More specifically, in 2003, the U.S. Department of Education's Office of Vocational and Adult Education (OVAE) embarked upon an effort to revise the National Career Development Guidelines (NCDG). The specific goals of the revision project were to: update and revise the framework of competencies and indicators to align with the goals of *No Child Left Behind*; expand the target audiences to include K–12 students and their parents, teachers, counselors and administrators, postsecondary students, and other adults and the business community; provide the target audiences with accessible career development information, learning activities, and strategies that lead to informed career decision making; and create a career development Web site to deliver career development information, learning activities, and strategies. (Extensive links to multiple resources professional school counselors will find helpful are available at cte.ed.gov/nationalinitiatives/gandctools.cfm?&pass_dis=1.)

The revision resulted in a new framework that is organized into three domains. In addition, there are goals for each domain and mastery indicators for each goal. The indicators are further grouped by learning stage. The domains for the Guidelines are: Personal Social Development (PS), Educational Achievement and Lifelong Learning (ED), and Career Management (CM). Interestingly, the three domains provide a parallel to the National School Counseling Model. Each domain contains goals that define broad areas of career development competency. Under each goal in the framework are mastery indicators that highlight the knowledge and skills needed to achieve that goal. Each indicator is presented in three learning stages based upon *Bloom's Taxonomy*: knowledge acquisition, application, and reflection. Unlike·the previous Guidelines, the current ones are not tied to an individual's age or level of education. This change acknowledges both the heterogeneity in career development and the fact that people recycle through career development tasks.

Persons engaged with knowledge acquisition-stage tasks focus on expanding their knowledge awareness and building comprehension. They have the capacity to recall, recognize, describe, identify, clarify, discuss, explain, summarize, query, investigate, and compile new information about the knowledge they have acquired. Persons at the application stage are able to apply acquired knowledge to situations and to self. They seek out ways to use the knowledge. They have the capacity to demonstrate, employ, perform, illustrate, and solve problems related to the knowledge they have acquired. Persons engaged with reflection-stage tasks have the capacity to analyze, synthesize, judge, assess, and evaluate knowledge in light of their own goals, values, and beliefs. They decide whether to integrate the acquired knowledge into their ongoing response to situations and whether to adjust their behavior accordingly.

The NCDG framework uses a coding system (PS–Personal Social Development; ED–Educational Achievement and Lifelong Learning; CM– Career Management) to identify domains, goals, indicators, and learning stages (see associationdatabase.com/aws/NCDA/asset_manager/get_file/3384). The coding system is intended to makes it easy to use the NCDG for program development and to track activities by goal, learning stage, and indicator. Thus, goals are coded as PS, ED, or CM and then listed numerically under the respective domains. For example, under the Personal Social Development domain:

Goal PS1: Develop understanding of yourself to build and maintain a positive self-concept.

Goal PS2: Develop positive interpersonal skills including respect for diversity.

Indicators and Learning Stages (K–Knowledge Acquisition; A–Application; R–Reflection) are coded numerically by domain, goal, and learning stage. For example, the second indicator under the first goal of the Personal Social Development domain:

PS1.K2: Identify your abilities, strengths, skills, and talents.

PS1.A2: Demonstrate use of your abilities, strengths, skills, and talents.

PS1.R2: Assess the impact of your abilities, strengths, skills, and talents on your career development.

The NCDG framework can be used in various ways to inform the creation, implementation, and evaluation of career intervention programs. For example:

Youth and adults can use the goals and indicators as an informal checklist to determine areas of competency and gaps that need attention.

Parents, guardians, spouses, or family members can use the framework to better understand how to help someone with career development questions.

Teachers can use the framework to review their curriculum and existing lessons for career development connections.

Teachers can use the framework to write new lessons that enhance academic rigor by infusing career development concepts.

Counselors, career practitioners, and administrators can use the framework to review an existing career development program for students or adults to see what competencies are covered and where the gaps are.

Counselors, career practitioners, and administrators can use the framework to craft needs assessments for youth and adults.

Counselors, career practitioners, and administrators can use the framework to craft a new competency-based career development program for youth or adults.

Counselors, career practitioners, and administrators can use the framework to develop a program evaluation and accountability plan.

Counselors, career practitioners, and media specialists can use the framework to review materials and resources on hand or those being considered for purchase.

The framework can serve as the basis for staff development workshops offered locally, statewide, or regionally (e.g., American School Counselor Association workshops).

The framework can inform the development of professional standards, accreditation, certification, and legislation and policy at both the national and state levels.

Product developers can use the framework to target their materials to meet specific career development needs of potential customers (acrnetwork.org/ncdg/ncdg_what.htm).

We contend that these two national models present an outstanding structure that professional school counselors can use to construct career development interventions. For example, in the Personal Social Development domain (PS1–Develop understanding of yourself to build and maintain a positive self-concept), the following activities can be used:

About Me—Introduces students to tools and concepts that will help them explore their interests, skills, and abilities (high school).

Being Positive Has Payoffs!—Explores how attitude can affect life outcomes by taking students through a series of scenarios and asking them to make choices (high school).

You've Already Got a Lot to Offer—Shows students how everyday activities help develop valuable skills (high school).

ME, Inc.—Uses the analogy of a corporation to illustrate important components of one's life and asks student "CEOs" to consider how values influence decisions (high school).

When constructing career development interventions, we think it is especially important for professional school counselors to be cognizant of the ways in which environmental constraints (e.g., sexism, racism, heterosexism, discrimination experienced by students with disabilities) negatively affect students' career development. Clearly, career development interventions must be designed to address these experiences (Holcomb-McCoy, 2007; Jackson & Grant, 2004).

Tips from the Field

Career development is alive and often not doing so well in childhood. Media and stereotypes influence what children think is possible . . . challenge this process!

Several authors (e.g., Gysbers & Henderson, 2001; Lapan, 2004; Schmidt, 2003) advocate for making career development programs an integral part of the school curriculum rather than an ancillary service. Niles, Trusty, and Mitchell (2004) take a systems perspective to designing career development interventions and emphasize that professional school counselors must communicate effectively with important subsystems (students, teachers, administrators, parents and families) regarding the goals and objectives of the career development program. Effective communication with students includes conducting a needs assessment to guide professional school counselors in the construction of career development programs and to serve as a basis for evaluation of program effectiveness. Effective communication with parents and families includes helping parents understand how they can positively influence their children's career development.

Teachers need assistance connecting academic content to career and educational planning. Providing and/or delivering classroom career guidance activities assists teachers in making such connections. Professional school counselors can also help teachers become aware of research data that indicate the positive correlation between career planning and school success (Herr, Cramer, & Niles, 2004). Educating administrators regarding these data also helps increase the probability that the career development program will be an integral part of the school curriculum. The critical point here is that, in a very real sense, professional school counselors operate within a political context that does not always understand and support the need for career services. Therefore, professional school counselors must work as advocates for career development as they deliver systematic and coordinated career services to students (Perusse & Goodnough, 2004).

Those questioning the usefulness of career development interventions assume that career-related activities take students away from time spent focusing on core academic subjects. Additionally, career education critics assume that career education programs pressure students to pursue work immediately after high school rather than pursuing a college education. Many people who are unfamiliar with how careers develop do not understand why career development interventions are important at the elementary and secondary school levels. The fact that career education initiatives were funded with monies external to school districts and that, in many instances, career education proponents had not generated local support for career education were also factors contributing to negative attitudes toward the career education movement (Herr, Cramer, & Niles, 2004). Thus, career education initiatives often become entangled in the political issues common to education today (e.g., the "back-to-basics" movement, the push to eliminate teaching of values in education, and the misconception that career education is the same as vocational education).

Those questioning the usefulness of career interventions in the schools are often even more adamant about their opinion that career interventions are not necessary for elementary school students. Those arguing against career interventions for elementary school students often view career decision making as events that occur at particular points during the course of secondary school education (e.g., when students must select a curriculum of study, when they leave high school). Such perspectives lack an appreciation of the precursors to effective career decision making.

Another issue related to the implementation of career education programs relates to the fact that many school districts do not provide career development programs in a systematic and coordinated fashion (Herr et al., 2004; Walz & Benjamin, 1984). The piecemeal implementation of career development interventions obviously limits the degree to which such interventions can positively influence students. Moreover, such an approach often creates confusion as to the meaning and purpose of career development programs by those not directly involved in their creation and implementation. Thus, it is essential that school counselors at the elementary and secondary school levels engage in systematic and coordinated planning prior to implementing career development programs (Gysbers & Henderson, 1998; Myrick, 1993).

SYSTEMATIC AND COORDINATED PLANNING FOR CAREER DEVELOPMENT PROGRAMS IN THE SCHOOLS

Herr et al. (2004) recommend using a five-stage planning model for facilitating the implementation of systematic career development intervention programs. The stages are:

Stage 1: Develop a program rationale and philosophy
Stage 2: State program goals and behavioral objectives
Stage 3: Select program processes
Stage 4: Develop an evaluation design
Stage 5: Identify program milestones

An important component of Stage 1 involves conducting a needs assessment to determine appropriate program rationales, goals, and interventions (Niles et al., 2004). As we have noted, the needs assessment provides benchmarks against which program outcomes can be assessed. Herr et al. (2004) emphasize the importance of incorporating teachers, students, parents, and community participants in the needs assessment to increase understanding of, and involvement in, career development programs. Clearly, a properly conducted needs assessment provides a firm foundation upon which effective career development intervention programs can be constructed.

Walz and Benjamin (1984) also provide important recommendations for developing systematic career development intervention programs. Their recommendations include the following:

1. Involve a team of knowledgeable professionals, parents, and representatives from the community in all phases of program planning.
2. Use developmentally appropriate interventions.
3. Be sure that the program goals and objectives are clearly communicated to all involved in the program.
4. Make sure the program is based on student needs.
5. Have an evaluation component to determine the degree to which the program goals and objectives have been achieved.
6. Make sure that those involved in program delivery are highly competent.

Once again, the implicit theme in both sets of recommendations just mentioned is that professional school counselors need to be sensitive to the political climate in which they operate. For example, in some locations, not clearly connecting career development interventions to student academic achievement will significantly decrease the chances of program success. Also, not adequately communicating successful program outcomes will result in the program resources being vulnerable to funding cuts. If school personnel view the program as an additional burden to their already heavy workloads, then there is little chance that the program will succeed. Thus, the "marketing" of the program to all stakeholders becomes an important aspect of program development and implementation. Having clearly defined behavioral objectives that address the specific needs of program participants will be useful in marketing the program and providing outcome data demonstrating program benefits.

Similar to the systems approach advocated by Niles et al. (2004), these recommendations highlight the importance of taking a team approach to service delivery. Although there is no one prescription for how the roles and responsibilities for delivering career development interventions should be distributed, it is logical that counselors take the lead (not the sole) role in developing and implementing career development programs. Counselors are often the only professionals in the school system with specific training in career development. Therefore, counselors possess the knowledge of career development theory and practice necessary for formulating appropriate career development program interventions. Moreover, the processes typically used in program delivery relate to counselors' primary areas of expertise. These processes are counseling, assessment, career information services, placement services, consultation procedures, and referrals. Professional school counselors can use their knowledge and skills related to career development to empower teachers and parents/guardians to function as collaborators in career services delivery.

The development of a systematic and coordinated career development program across grades K–12 requires an understanding of the developmental tasks confronting students as they progress through school. Having an awareness of the tasks students deal with at all levels of schooling prepares school personnel to work collaboratively in program development and implementation. A comprehensive understanding of the career development process also sets the stage for developing program interventions that are sequential and cohesive. Thus, the following sections of this chapter (and the primary topics of the following chapter) focus on career development tasks, program goals, and recommended interventions for elementary, middle/junior high school, and high school students, respectively.

CAREER DEVELOPMENT IN THE ELEMENTARY SCHOOLS

Careers unfold and develop throughout the life course. Ignoring the process of career development occurring in childhood is similar to a gardener disregarding the quality of the soil in which a garden will be planted. For children and adolescents, school and leisure activities represent their work. These activities provide essential learning experiences that shape self-perceptions and understandings of the world-of-work. They form the seedbed from which children begin to identify their preferences and connect themselves to their futures as workers.

Prior to entering elementary school, children have moved through the first two of Erikson's (1963) eight stages of development. Those who have coped successfully with these stages have developed a sense of trust and autonomy. Thus, children ideally enter school believing they can trust the adults in their world and that they will be able to cope successfully with challenges they will encounter. Children operating from a perspective of trust and self-sufficiency are likely to approach school tasks with a positive and enthusiastic attitude. Children who have not been as successful in developing trust and autonomy will operate from a different attitudinal stance. These children will be more likely to question whether they can trust others. They may also lack confidence concerning their ability to master the tasks they confront. Erikson notes that when trust and autonomy are not achieved, children experience the emotional consequences of mistrust, doubt, and shame. To overcome these negative consequences, it is critical that children experience success and support.

Havighurst (1972) notes that during infancy and early childhood (ages 0 to 5), children encounter a series of critical developmental tasks. For example, during this developmental stage children:

1. Learn to walk
2. Learn to eat solid foods
3. Learn to talk
4. Learn to control elimination of bodily wastes
5. Learn sex differences and modesty
6. Learn to relate emotionally to family members
7. Prepare to read
8. Learn to identify the difference between right and wrong

Havighurst notes that to progress to subsequent stages of development, children must be successful in coping with these tasks. Failure to cope with these tasks successfully "leads to unhappiness in the individual, disapproval of society, and difficulty with later tasks" (p. 2).

Rosita, introduced earlier in the chapter, had experienced events in her life that did not foster the acquisition of many of the skills identified by Havighurst (1972). Her father's absence and her mother's drug-induced emotional absences also made it difficult for Rosita to believe that she could count on adults being there for her. She also wondered about her own self-worth and capabilities. She hoped that she would do okay at school, but deep down she was convinced that she would not do well. What she needed most as she entered school was to encounter adults who consistently supported her. She would also need remedial assistance to enhance her interpersonal and academic skills, especially in the area of reading.

During the elementary school years, children begin formulating a sense of identity through greater interaction with the world beyond their immediate families. Interactions with peers, teachers, parents, and community members shape the child's self-perceptions. Through exposure to adult life patterns via observations in schools, community activities, home, and the media, children draw conclusions about their lives. The conclusions children draw include assumptions about their current and future place in the world.

Porfeli, Hartung, and Vondracek (2008, p. 28) summarize their review of the literature pertaining to career development in childhood, and note that: (a) children know much more about the world-of-work than many people believe; (b) career aspirations of children are influenced by gender-based stereotypes and these aspirations tend to be stable across the elementary school years; (c) career aspirations are influenced by occupational stereotypes that move girls away from science, technology, engineering and math-related occupations and boys away from female-dominated occupations; (d) children from economically challenged situations, Hispanic, and African American children tend to identify less-prestigious career aspirations than do their more affluent and Caucasian peers; and (e) children tend to relinquish more glamorous aspirations for more realistic ones that are in line with their skills and interests as they progress through elementary school.

Erikson (1963) proposes that during elementary school, children encounter developmental stages related to developing initiative (ages 4 to 6) and industry (ages 6 to 12). These qualities are essential to the career development process. If they are not developed, then children experience guilt and inferiority. These negative consequences do not foster the sort of active and broad-based exploration that is necessary for children to advance in their career development. When a sense of initiative and industry are achieved, then children use their curiosity as a stimulus for exploring and gathering information about themselves and their worlds. Moreover, children experience feelings of personal effectiveness when they begin to do things on their own and experience positive outcomes associated with their self-initiated activities.

Havighurst (1972) suggests that during middle childhood (ages 6 to 11), children encounter an array of developmental tasks related to motor coordination, emotional development, and attitudinal perspectives related to self and others. Specifically, he notes that children during this stage must:

1. Develop physical skills for participating in games
2. Build positive attitudes toward themselves
3. Develop interpersonal skills
4. Become more tolerant
5. Learn appropriate gender social roles
6. Develop academic skills in reading, writing, and mathematics
7. Achieve a greater sense of independence
8. Develop attitudes toward groups and institutions

Applying these tasks to Rosita, it is clear that to advance in her career development Rosita would need continued support and assistance. Positive reinforcement for her accomplishments, encouragement to engage in new activities that interest her, and guidance in helping her identify tasks and chores that would foster a sense of industry are all important developmental interventions for Rosita. Although some interventions would require Rosita to work independently, it would also be important for her to engage in some group-oriented activities. Group activities would provide Rosita with opportunities to develop her interpersonal skills while also increasing her circle of friends. Thus, Rosita provides an excellent example of how general statements of developmental tasks must be contextualized for the individual student.

GOALS OF CAREER DEVELOPMENT INTERVENTIONS AT THE ELEMENTARY SCHOOL LEVEL

Obviously, there is tremendous variability in the quality of the life patterns to which children are exposed. Television, for example, often provides children with examples of men and women in gender-stereotyped roles and occupations (e.g., only women working as nurses, only men working as auto mechanics, women taking the primary or sole responsibility for homemaking and parenting). Children use this information to draw conclusions about the life patterns that are appropriate for them. As children are increasingly exposed to stereotypical behaviors and expectations, they begin to eliminate nontraditional life patterns and occupations from further consideration. Gottfredson (2002) contends that this gender-based elimination process begins as early as age 6. Gottfredson also suggests that between the ages of 9 and 13, children begin to eliminate those occupations from further consideration that they perceive to be less prestigious for their social class. Such variables as sex-typing and prestige rankings interact with self-perceptions of abilities and interests, as well as with family and community expectations, to shape the decisions young people make about potential occupational options. Geography also factors into this equation because children in rural areas tend to be exposed to different (and often fewer) occupational options than children in more urban locations (Lee, 1984). Because elementary school children have not yet had the opportunity to fully explore their options and potentialities, an important goal of career development interventions in elementary school is to counteract environmental factors that pressure students to prematurely commit to educational and occupational options (Marcia, 1966). The use of nontraditional role models (e.g., male nurses, male secretaries, female physicians, female engineers) and exposure to a broad range of occupational environments in career development interventions is encouraged during the elementary school years.

Rosita could benefit from being exposed to women working in a wide variety of occupational environments. Because the women in her immediate and extended families have worked in traditional occupations, it would be useful for Rosita to learn about women working in nontraditional occupations. Having the opportunity to be mentored by a woman in an occupation of interest to her might also help Rosita develop a sense of trust, autonomy, initiative, and industry.

Another goal of career development interventions with elementary school children is to provide an environment in which each student's natural sense of curiosity can flourish (Super, 1990). Curiosity provides the foundation for exploring. Children naturally express curiosity through fantasy and play. For example, children often engage intensely in fantasy-based play related to occupations such as physician, firefighter, teacher, professional athlete, and nurse. Curiosity can be guided to help students learn accurate information about themselves and their environments. For example, field trips to occupational environments related to a child's fantasy-based occupational interests reinforce the child's sense of curiosity and stimulate further exploring and the gradual crystallization of interests (Super, 1957).

It obviously would be useful for Rosita if her counselor would encourage her to identify and explore activities of high interest and then work with Rosita to help her process what she learns about herself as a result of participating in exploratory activities. Fostering a sense of curiosity related to herself and the world-of-work will help to increase Rosita's sense of what might be possible and to counteract environmental limitations she may be experiencing. In other words, it is a way to begin empowering Rosita.

Encouraging students to participate in activities relating to their interests nurtures a sense of autonomy, the anticipation of future opportunities for exploring, and the beginning of planful behaviors (Watts, Super, & Kidd, 1981). When interests connect with skills and capacities, a positive self-concept emerges which, in turn, provides the foundation for coping with the career development tasks of adolescence (Super, 1994). As children move toward adolescence, they must accomplish four major career development tasks. Specifically, they must (a) become concerned about the future, (b) increase personal control over their lives, (c) convince themselves to achieve in school and at work, and (d) develop competent work habits and attitudes (Super, Savickas, & Super, 1996, p. 131).

Unfortunately, when these four tasks are compared with data from the National Assessment of Educational Progress's Career and Occupational Development Project (a survey of approximately 28,000 9-year-old children), one might conclude that elementary school students have been only marginally successful in accomplishing these tasks. Results from this survey indicate that children have limited self-knowledge and limited occupational information and take limited responsibility for their behavior and future career decision making (Miller, 1977). Clearly, these results provide cause for concern because children who are not able to accomplish the career development tasks they encounter in the elementary school are at risk for even more difficulty when they encounter the career development tasks presented to them during their secondary school experience. Thus, there is the need to consider how career development interventions might be provided to elementary school students in a more systematic and effective fashion.

Based on the counseling and developmental literature, career development goals for elementary school children should be directed toward helping children develop basic skills and awareness in the following areas:

Self-knowledge

Skills to interact with others

Basic skills in educational and occupational exploration

Awareness of the benefits of educational achievement

Awareness of the relationship between work and learning

Basic skills to understand and use career information

Awareness of the importance of personal responsibility and good work habits

Awareness of how work relates to the needs and functions of society

An understanding of how to make decisions

Awareness of the interrelationship of life roles

Awareness of different occupations and changing male/female roles

Awareness of the career planning process

CAREER DEVELOPMENT INTERVENTIONS IN THE ELEMENTARY SCHOOLS

When combined with the ASCA National Model and the National Career Development Guidelines (see Appendix E), these goals provide a framework for establishing career development goals and interventions. Because self-awareness provides the foundation for processing career information, career development interventions in the primary grades can focus first on helping students develop more sophisticated self-knowledge. For example, in grades K and 1, students can increase their self-knowledge by describing themselves through drawings, writing sentences describing the things they like and the things that are important to them, and bringing some of their favorite things to school to show to their classmates. Sharing their self-descriptions with others helps students to clarify their self-concepts. Each of these activities can also emphasize the importance of appreciating the similarities and differences that exist among students in the classroom. Differences among students can be described as valuable contributions to the learning process because we often learn more from students who are different from us than those who are like us in our interests, skills, or backgrounds. Activities that encourage students to focus on clarifying their global self-concepts can be emphasized and can be easily infused into the curriculum during the first years of school. Differences in cultural traditions among students can be highlighted and celebrated.

In clarifying her self-concept, it is likely that Rosita would benefit from understanding that her family situation is not something that she caused. Emphasizing her positive relationship with her grandmother may be useful as well. In processing the contextual differences among students, it would be important for Rosita's teacher to discuss the different ways to define "family." This may help Rosita focus on what she has rather than what she has lost regarding her family structure.

Activities that help students learn more about themselves can be supplemented with activities that focus on educational and occupational exploration as children progress through the primary and intermediate grades. For example, in the primary grades students can identify the occupations of their family members (e.g., parents, grandparents, aunts, and uncles) as well as the level and type of education each family member attained. As students share this information, the relationship between education and work can be stressed (e.g., some jobs require a college education and others may require a different type of training such as trade school or an apprenticeship). Differences in family members' occupations can be discussed as strengths (e.g., it takes people working in a wide variety of occupations to make our society function effectively). To counteract occupational sex-typing, men and women working in nontraditional occupations can be invited to school to discuss their work. (To expand Rosita's awareness of occupational options, it would be useful for Rosita to be exposed to Latinas working in professional occupations.)

Beale and Williams (2000) discuss the "anatomy of a school-wide career day" in an elementary school setting. Specifically, they point out that much planning goes into making the career day successful. They note that successful career days provide opportunities to break down occupational stereotypes, to involve parents/guardians as well as community and business representatives in the school counseling curriculum, and to help students begin making positive connections between themselves and their futures.

To prepare for the career day, Beale and Williams (2000) suggest that a planning committee (involving the counselor, teachers, administrators, community representatives, and parents) be established. The first step of the planning committee is to establish goals and objectives (e.g., expand students' awareness of the school-work connection, increase students' understanding of workers in the community, increase students' understanding of the interrelatedness of workers, increase students' awareness of traditional and nontraditional careers) for the career day.

Next, the planning committee should identify a timeline for completing specific tasks (writing and mailing letters informing parents and teachers of the date, time, place, goals, and objectives of the career day). Concerning the timing of the career day, counselors may want to connect the career day to the NCDA's Career Development Month (usually in November). The NCDA sponsors a poetry and picture contest during National Career Development Month and offers resources that counselors can use to prepare for activities such as a school-wide career day. Clearly, the planning committee must systematically select speakers for career day. Using Holland's occupational categories (i.e., Realistic, Investigative, Artistic, Social, Enterprising, and Conventional) as a guide for identifying representative occupations may be useful. Surveying teachers and parents, contacting the local chamber of commerce, and soliciting suggestions from the planning committee members are ways to identify potential career-day speakers. When inviting potential speakers to participate, it helps to identify the time and place of the event, the purpose of the career day, the specific topics to be discussed, and the format (e.g., "show and tell" versus lecture) for discussing the work-related topics. Once workers agree to participate, Beale and Williams (2000) recommend sending speakers a confirmation letter containing the vital information for their participation. As the day approaches, school announcements reminding students and school personnel of the event should be made.

Additional issues to be addressed by the planning committee include deciding on the format to be used during the career day (e.g., whether a central location will be used, whether students will rotate from classroom to classroom to meet with speakers, or whether speakers will rotate from classroom to classroom). Once the plans for the career day are finalized, counselors should construct a detailed schedule to distribute to all participants.

Student preparation for the career day can include creating a mural of all workers in the school, having students interview their parents/guardians to gain information about their work, having students create poster presentations of workers using pictures in magazines and newspapers, and having students generate a list of possible interview questions to be used during the career day.

On career day, volunteers should be assigned to meet speakers when they arrive and help them get oriented. Speakers should also be asked to complete an evaluation of their experience that can be turned in at the end of the day. Evaluating the effectiveness of the day is important for improving future career days. Thank you notes should be sent to all involved. After the career day, counselors can engage in classroom guidance activities to help students assimilate the information they learned, discuss their perceptions of the jobs they learned about, and identify next steps to take to learn more about the world-of-work.

Students in grades K and 1 can begin the process of learning about work by focusing on occupations with which they have the most immediate relationship (e.g., occupations of family members, occupations in the school setting, occupations in their neighborhoods). Then, elementary school students can gradually learn about occupations that are more remote (e.g., occupations in the community, occupations in the state, occupations in the nation, and occupations throughout the world) as they progress from grades 2 to 5. Using a proximity-distance scheme to guide students in the acquisition of occupational information helps students understand the relevance of work in their lives and the ways in which various workers contribute to society. At each level of proximity, the relationship between work and the educational requirements for performing specific occupations can be highlighted. Students can also discuss what is required to perform occupations successfully. Job-content skills (the specific skill requirements for each occupation), functional skills (the skills that are transferable across occupations), and self-management skills (e.g., being reliable, getting along with coworkers, being trustworthy, completing assignments on time) can be integrated into these discussions as well.

Beale (2000) provides an excellent example as to how a well-conceived field trip can enhance career awareness in elementary school students. Using a field trip to a hospital as an illustrative example, Beale notes that for this sort of activity to be useful it must be carefully planned and implemented. For example, in planning for a career awareness field trip, counselors need to involve teachers, students, workplace personnel, and parents. In addition to identifying specific objectives of the trip; securing consent from administrators, parents, and teachers; counselors should also engage in a "dry run" through the worksite prior to the trip. During the preliminary worksite visit, the counselor should meet with worksite representatives (e.g., administrators and workers with whom the students will interact) to clarify the purpose and duration of the visit and what opportunities will be made available to the students. Copies of any interview questions the students will be asking should be provided to all relevant employees. Eliminating surprises during the visit and helping employees to be prepared will help to maximize the effectiveness of the trip.

It is important to note, however, that students also need to be well prepared for the field trip. Strengthening the pre-visit interest and motivation of students will increase the chances of the trip being successful. Ways to accomplish this involve engaging students in pre-trip classroom career activities. For example, in preparing bulletin boards related to the field trip, students can bring in pictures of workers and services provided in the worksite. Students can engage in classroom discussions on what to look for during the field trip. Preparing sample questions (e.g., How long have you been doing this kind of work? What do you like best/least about your job? How long did you have to go to school to do what you do?) that students can ask of workers helps to guide student learning for the field trip. (It is also important to let students know that questions such as "How much money do you make?" are inappropriate.) Having workers come to the classroom (in their work clothes) can also raise student interest and motivation for the field trip. Here, counselors should keep in mind the importance of providing examples of non-stereotypical workers (e.g., a female physician, a male nurse, an African American female CEO). Additional preparatory activities can include drawing pictures of the worksite, looking in the Yellow Pages or surfing the Web to identify the number of related worksites in the area, and talking about whether they have ever visited a similar worksite.

Beale (2000) also recommends that counselors use the time en route to the worksite as an opportunity for preparing students. For example, giving each student a list of specific occupations to look for in the worksite, and providing them with scrambled work sheets, hidden word puzzles, or crossword puzzles using words related to the different occupations, work materials, and equipment that they will see on the tour, are ways to focus student thinking en route to the worksite.

After the visit, Beale (2000) recommends activities that reinforce student learning and career awareness. For example, class discussions related to student reactions to the visit that focus on listing the occupations observed, identifying school subjects related to the occupations the students observed, and discussing the interrelationship of various occupations (e.g., "What would happen if there were no nurses, custodians, receptionists, orderlies, etc.?") represent useful follow-up activities. Having students prepare a scrapbook containing information related to the field trip, and/or developing a slide presentation of the visit (in which students compose and narrate the script) also represent important activities that can be connected to the curriculum. Conducting an evaluation of the activity (e.g., asking students to identify whether they learned more about work in the worksite visited and whether they enjoyed the activities before, during, and after the visit) is an important final step in the process.

Educational and occupational exploration activities can be infused into the curriculum in a variety of additional ways. For example, assignments highlighting the various types of work required in different geographical locations can be integrated into the social studies curriculum. Language arts assignments (e.g., short-story writing) can also be constructed to help students learn more about what workers do in different occupations and to express their important self-characteristics (e.g., writing an autobiography). The art curriculum can include drawing, painting, and photographing workers in various occupations.

Activities to help students learn about the career planning and decision-making process could include having students read biographies and then discussing the important career decisions people made in the biographies they read. Students can be encouraged to consider what constitutes a "good" rather than "bad" career decision as they discuss the biographies they read. Additionally, students can use a timeline to chart the important events that influenced the decisions that the people they read about made in their lives.

Encouraging students to read stories about people working in nontraditional occupations can contribute to counteracting the effects of occupational sex-typing. Discussions can include the ways in which culture, gender, and social class may have influenced the career development of the person in the biography.

Another key focus in providing career development interventions at the elementary school level is that of increasing students' awareness. Interventions that increase students' self-awareness, occupational awareness, awareness of the relationship between work and education, and awareness of how career decisions are made are all important topics to address with elementary school students. Students should be encouraged to engage in activities that foster broad self- and career exploration to arouse interest in the future. A sense of internal control (e.g., "I can influence my direction"); the belief that it is important to be concerned about the future (e.g., "what happens to me is important to me"); and an attitude of personal competence or self-efficacy (e.g., "I am able to do what I am expected to do") should also be outcomes of career development interventions at the elementary school level (Super et al., 1996). Armed with these beliefs, students are prepared to cope with the career development tasks they will confront at the middle/junior high school level.

Magnuson and Starr (2000) offer the following thoughts to guide the planning of career development interventions:

1. Become a constant observer of children:

   Notice how children approach tasks.

   Notice the activities in which children choose to participate.

   Observe and encourage the child's initiative taking.

   Notice the thematic patterns emerging in each child's activities.

2. Consider the processing of an activity as important as the activity itself.

   To help children develop a sense of industry rather than inferiority, focus feedback on the specifics of children's efforts.

   Accompany career awareness and career exploration activities with opportunities for students to express their beliefs about themselves in relation to various occupations. (p. 100)

PARENTAL INVOLVEMENT

Parents have substantial influence over the career development of their children. Basow and Howe (1979) examined the career development of 300 college students and found that parents had the greatest influence in the career development of the students participating in their study. This finding is not surprising. Parents provide the greatest amount of indirect and direct exposure to work for their children. Most adults can recount numerous instances in which they recall their parents conveying positive and negative expressions of their work experiences. These expressions influence children vicariously as they formulate their understanding of an area of life they have yet to encounter directly. Thus, children rely upon adults and peers for information. As has been noted, children use the information they receive to make preliminary decisions about the appropriateness of the occupational options of which they are aware.

Young (1994) suggests that the influence parents exert on the career development process is most effective when it is planned, intentional, and goal-oriented. However, many parents possess minimal knowledge regarding career development theory and how environmental factors influence the career development process of children. Thus, it is important that counselors help parents to learn ways to contribute positively to the career development of their children. Counselors can begin by providing parents with information about the career development process (e.g., during elementary school, children are encouraged to expand their awareness related to self and the world-of-work). Counselors can also explain to parents how the environment affects options children are willing to consider. For example, the influence of occupational stereotyping within the media and gender-role stereotyping can be discussed with parents. Finally, counselors can help parents identify specific strategies they can use to facilitate career development in their children. Engaging in conversations in which parents provide accurate occupational information and challenge occupational stereotyping represents an obvious, yet important, way that parents can foster positive career development in their children. Parent-child career conversations regarding career development should foster a sense of curiosity, openness to possibilities, awareness of options, and a positive attitude toward the world-of-work.

Herr, Cramer, and Niles (2004) identify eight ways parents can help children advance in their careers. These strategies include:

1. Parents can encourage children to analyze important self-characteristics (e.g., interests, capacities, and values).
2. When parents are familiar with specific work requirements for jobs, they can communicate these to their children.
3. Parents can discuss the importance of work values in work behavior.
4. Parents can explain the relationship between work, pay, and the economic condition of the family.
5. Parents can connect children with informational resources (e.g., other workers, books, films) for acquiring accurate career information.
6. Parents can be careful to avoid stereotyping occupational alternatives and workers.
7. Parents can provide children with opportunities for work in the home and community.
8. Parents can provide children with opportunities to learn and practice decision-making skills. (p. 364)

Helping parents become aware of their own attitudes toward work and occupations, exposing children to work opportunities in the home and community, and providing support to children as they engage in career decision-making tasks are all ways to help children cope effectively with the career development process. By empowering parents with knowledge and information that can be used to help their children cope effectively with career development tasks, counselors make an important contribution to the career development of the students with whom they work.

Both Rosita and her mother could benefit from learning more about the career development process. Helping Rosa understand how careers develop would give her information that she could use to manage her own career development more effectively. Coaching Rosa as to the ways she could help Rosita with her career development would not only help Rosita but would also help Rosa feel more effective as a parent. Strengthening the bond between Rosa and Rosita would help Rosita develop the trust and autonomy she needs to move forward in her development.

MyCounselingLab™

Go to Topic 7: *Elementary School* in the MyCounselingLab™ site (www.MyCounselingLab.com) for *Career Development Interventions in the 21st Century*, Fourth Edition, where you can:

- Find learning outcomes for *Elementary School* along with the national standards that connect to these outcomes.
- Complete Assignments and Activities that can help you more deeply understand the chapter content.

- Apply and practice your understanding of the core skills identified in the chapter with the Building Counseling Skills unit.
- Prepare yourself for professional certification with a Practice for Certification quiz.
- Connect to videos through the Video and Resource Library.

Summary

New parents often wonder which occupations their children will select later in life. What many parents do not realize is that children begin charting courses toward specific occupations early in life. Occupational selection represents the confluence of genetic and environmental influences that shape the career course. Like any developmental task, the career development process can be approached systematically and intentionally, or it can be approached haphazardly and passively. Most parents would prefer that their children receive systematic career development assistance oriented toward providing children with the competencies required for managing their careers effectively. For elementary school children, the task is to learn more about themselves and the educational/occupational options that are available. By providing support and helping children acquire accurate information about themselves and the world-of-work, counselors provide children with the foundation for effective career planning and decision-making.

Case Study

Robert is a 9-year-old African American male in the fifth grade at a local urban elementary school. Robert is a below-average student. Although he is at the top of his class in science, his reading and writing skills are below grade level. His teacher describes Robert as a likable, outgoing child who causes too many disruptions in the classroom. Although Robert responds well to the adults in the school, he has been referred to the principal several times for bullying other students.

Robert's life outside of school is challenging. His biological father left home after a divorce when Robert was six and is now incarcerated for dealing drugs. His mother remarried and moved to another state when he was seven, and he has lived with his legal guardians, his paternal grandparents, since his mother left. Although he visits his father in prison, he has seen his mother infrequently since she left. Robert's grandfather is a retired police officer who is not involved much with Robert (he says he already raised his kids). Robert's grandmother is the primary caregiver and has met with school administrators and you (school counselor) expressing her concerns about Robert (low achievement, referrals, and lack of friends).

When prompted, Robert identifies sports as his main interest. He cannot identify anything in school that he really likes besides gym class. In casual conversation, Robert talks about being a professional athlete when he gets older. In three meetings with you at school, Robert has talked excitedly about rejoining his father when he is released from prison, but resists any discussion about his mother. He seems ambivalent about his grandparents and struggles to identify any friends in school. Robert explains that he spends most of his time outside of school at the park with boys from the middle school.

If you were Robert's school counselor, how would you address Robert's career development needs? Who would you involve in your career work with him? Which theories do you think would be helpful to you in understanding his situation? How might you foster a stronger sense of self-esteem and motivation in him?

Student Activities

1. What career development tasks do you think are most important to help elementary school–aged children address?

2. What factors do you think could negatively influence the career development of children?

3. What are three strategies you could use to foster positive career development in children?

4. Why do you think there is resistance to providing career interventions with elementary school children?

5. How could you help parents/guardians to help their children experience positive career development?

6. Interview an elementary school student about his or her career development. Ask this student what occupations s/he thinks are possible for him/her. Ask whether the student thinks there are any occupations that are not possible. Ask your interviewee to discuss why s/he thinks certain occupations may not be possible. Ask what occupation s/he would choose if s/he could choose anything. Then, explore with your interviewee what s/he thinks is attractive about that occupation.

7. Refer to the **MyCounselingLab** Video and Resource Library and select the video entitled, "21st Century Career Development Interventions in the School: An Interview with Dr. Carol Dahir." How would you use Dr. Dahir's comments to convince your principal and school board of the importance of career development interventions in elementary schools?

References

American School Counselor Association (ASCA). (2003). *The ASCA National Model: A framework for school counseling programs.* Alexandria, VA: American School Counselor Association.

Basow, S. A., & Howe, K. G. (1979). Model influences on career choices of college students. *Vocational Guidance Quarterly, 27,* 239–243.

Beale, A. V. (2000). Elementary school career awareness: A visit to a hospital. *Journal of Career Development, 26,* 65–72.

Beale, A. V., & Williams, C. J. (2000). The anatomy of an elementary school career day. *Journal of Career Development, 26,* 205–213.

Campbell, C. A., & Dahir, C. A. (1997). *The national standards for school counseling programs.* Alexandria, VA: American School Counselor Association.

Dimmitt, C., & Carey, J. (2007). Using the ASCA National Model to facilitate school transitions. *Professional School Counseling, 10,* 227–232.

Erikson, E. H. (1963). *Childhood and society.* New York: W. W. Norton.

Gottfredson, L. S. (2002). Gottfredson's theory of circumscription, compromise, and self-creation. In D. Brown & Associates (Eds.), *Career choice and development* (4th ed., pp. 85–148). San Francisco: Jossey-Bass.

Gysbers, N. C., & Henderson, P. (1998). *Developing and managing your school guidance program.* Alexandria, VA: American Counselors Association.

Gysbers, N. C., & Henderson, P. (2001). Comprehensive guidance and counseling programs: A rich history and a bright future. *Professional School Counseling, 4,* 246–256.

Havighurst, R. J. (1972). *Developmental tasks and education* (3rd ed.). New York: D. McKay.

Herr, E. L., Cramer, S. H., & Niles, S. G. (2004). *Career guidance and counseling through the lifespan: Systematic approaches* (6th ed.). Boston: Allyn & Bacon.

Holcomb-McCoy, C. (2007). Transitioning to high school: Issues and challenges for African American students. *Professional School Counseling, 10,* 253–260.

Jackson, M., & Grant, D. (2004). Fostering positive career development in children and adolescents. In R. Perusse & G. Goodnough (Eds.), *Leadership, advocacy, and direct service strategies for professional school counselors* (pp. 125–154). Belmont, CA: Brooks/Cole.

Lapan, R. T. (2004). *Career development across the K–16 years.* Alexandria, VA: American Counseling Association.

Lee, C. C. (1984). Predicting the career choice attitudes of rural Black, White, and Native American high school students. *Vocational Guidance Quarterly, 32,* 177–184.

Magnuson, C. S., & Starr, M. F. (2000). How early is too early to begin life career planning? The importance of the elementary school years. *Journal of Career Development, 27,* 89–101.

Marcia, J. E. (1966). Development and validation of ego-identity status. *Journal of Personality and Social Psychology, 3,* 551–558.

Miller, J. (1977). *Career development needs of nine-year-olds: How to improve career development programs.* Washington, DC: National Advisory Council for Career Education.

Myrick, R. (1993). *Developmental guidance and counseling: A practical approach* (2nd ed.). Minneapolis, MN: Educational Media.

National Occupational Information Coordinating Committee (NOICC). (1992). *The National Career Development Guidelines Project.* Washington, DC: U.S. Government Printing Office.

Niles, S. G., Trusty, J., & Mitchell, N. (2004). Fostering positive career development in children and adolescents. In R. Perusse & G. Goodnough (Eds.), *Leadership, advocacy, and direct service strategies for professional school counselors* (pp. 102–124). Belmont, CA: Brooks/Cole.

Perusse, R., & Goodnough, G. (2004). *Leadership, advocacy, and direct service strategies for professional school counselors.* Belmont, CA: Brooks/Cole.

Porfeli, E. J., Hartung, P. J., & Vondracek, F. W. (2008). Children's vocational development: A research rationale. *The Career Development Quarterly 57,* 25–37.

Schmidt, J. J. (2003). *Counseling in schools: Essential services and comprehensive programs* (4th ed.). Boston: Allyn & Bacon.

Super, D. E. (1957). *A psychology of careers.* New York: Harper & Row.

Super, D. E. (1990). Career and life development. In D. Brown & L. Brooks (Eds.), *Career choice and development: Applying contemporary theories to practice* (2nd ed., pp. 197–261). San Francisco: Jossey-Bass.

Super, D. E. (1994). A life-span, life-space perspective on convergence. In M. L. Savickas & R. W. Lent (Eds.), *Convergence in career development theories: Implications for science and practice* (pp. 63–74). Palo Alto, CA: CPP Books.

Super, D. E., Savickas, M. L., & Super, C. M. (1996). The life-span, life-space approach to careers. In D. Brown & L. Brooks (Eds.), *Career choice*

---

and development: Applying contemporary theories to practice (3rd ed., pp. 121–178). San Francisco: Jossey-Bass.

Walz, G. R., & Benjamin, L. (1984). A systems approach to career guidance. *Vocational Guidance Quarterly, 33*, 26–34.

Watts, A. G., Super, D. E., & Kidd, J. M. (1981). *Career development in Britain*. Cambridge, England: Hobson's Press.

Young, R. A. (1994). Helping adolescents with career development: The active role of parents. *The Career Development Quarterly, 42*, 195–203.

Sample Career Development Activities for Elementary School Students

Interesting Activities

NOICC CAREER DEVELOPMENT GUIDELINES: Self-Knowledge

ASCA STANDARDS: Standard A—Students will acquire the skills to investigate the world-of-work in relation to knowledge of self and to make informed career decisions.

PURPOSE: To discuss interests related to various activities.

OBJECTIVE: Students will learn to connect interests to activities.

MATERIALS: Magazines and scissors

INTRODUCTION: Discuss the importance of participating in activities that we find enjoyable. All activities, including work, can be fun when we participate in activities that we enjoy. The opposite is also true, however. When we participate in activities, including work, that we do not enjoy, we experience different reactions. Ask students to discuss how they feel when they participate in activities they like versus activities they do not like.

ACTIVITIES: Have each student cut out pictures from magazines demonstrating people engaged in activities that the student enjoys. Students will share the pictures with the class and tell what the activity is and what they like about it using the following phrase: "What I find interesting about this activity is . . . .".

DISCUSSION: Discuss the different activities and interests revealed. Ask students if any of them liked the activities that were shared by any of the other students. Have the students identify which activities they like and say what they find interesting about that activity. Ask students if they disliked any of the activities shared. Have the students identify which activities they do not like and what they do not like about that activity.

CLOSURE: Emphasize that there is no "right or wrong" associated with the likes and dislikes expressed by students. What really matters is that the students are clear about what they find interesting. Discuss how students' interests can be linked to vocational and avocational activities. Emphasize the importance of both types of activities for providing outlets for expressing interests.

TIME: 45 minutes

EVALUATION/ASSIGNMENT: Have students construct a list of the activities they find interesting and the activities that they do not find interesting.

Skills I Have

NOICC CAREER DEVELOPMENT GUIDELINES: Self-Knowledge

ASCA STANDARDS: Standard A—Students will acquire the skills to investigate the world-of-work in relation to knowledge of self and to make informed career decisions.

PURPOSE: To discuss the skills students have developed.

OBJECTIVE: Students will be able to identify the skills they possess.

MATERIALS: Skills list handout, paper, and pencils

INTRODUCTION: Discuss the fact that all people have many skills. Some skills are learned in school, some are learned at home or in play, and others seem to be "natural" skills. Distribute a list of skills to the students. Review the list to be sure that the students understand the skills listed.

ACTIVITIES: Have students list three activities they participate in that they enjoy. Divide students into groups of four. Assign each student one of the following roles: interviewer (2 students), interviewee, and recorder. The interviewee must identify one activity that he or she enjoys. The interviewers must try to identify as many skills as possible that the interviewee uses when participating in the activity. The interviewee must say either "yes" or "no" to the skills the interviewers identify. The recorder lists the skills that the interviewee uses in the activity. After 10 minutes, the leader should stop the activity and ask students to rotate their roles. At the conclusion of each interview, the recorder's list is given to the interviewee.

DISCUSSION: Discuss the importance of recognizing the skills we possess. Indicate the reasons why it is useful to identify the skills we use when we participate in activities that we enjoy. Review how identifying these skills can be useful in career planning.

CLOSURE: Repeat the activity until the students have a skills list for all three activities (it is recommended that this activity take place over multiple sessions, e.g., three 30-minute sessions). Have students review their skills lists. Ask them to circle the skills that appear on more than one list. Discuss the importance of focusing on these skills in career exploration.

TIME: 60–90 minutes

EVALUATION/ASSIGNMENT: Ask students to identify occupations relating to the skills appearing on more than one list.

Feelings

NOICC CAREER DEVELOPMENT GUIDELINES: Self-Knowledge

ASCA STANDARDS: Standard A—Students will acquire the skills to investigate the world-of-work in relation to knowledge of self and to make informed career decisions.

PURPOSE: To discuss the importance of understanding the feelings of others.

OBJECTIVE: Students will identify feelings from nonverbal cues and identify ways to respond to the feelings of others.

MATERIALS: Pictures of persons expressing various emotions, chalkboard, and chalk

INTRODUCTION: Explain the importance of being sensitive to the feelings of others. Talk with students about how they feel when others are insensitive to their feelings. Contrast these situations with those in which others are sensitive to students' feelings. Begin by brainstorming feelings. List the feelings students identify on the board.

ACTIVITIES: Brainstorm feelings and list them on the board. Then show students pictures of persons expressing various emotions. Have students guess the feelings being expressed. List the feelings on the board.

DISCUSSION: Discuss with students how they could respond to each of the feelings listed. Role play various responses (noneffective responses and effective responses). Have students react to each response by identifying how they might feel if someone responded to them in that way.

CLOSURE: Emphasize that being able to recognize and respond to the feelings of others is very important in effective interpersonal communication.

TIME: 45 minutes

EVALUATION/ASSIGNMENT: Give students three statements, each of which expresses different feelings (e.g., happiness, sadness, anger). For example, "It hurt my feelings when the teacher yelled at me for something I did not do." Instruct the students to write how they would respond to each statement if it were expressed by one of their friends (e.g., "You sound sad that the teacher yelled at you.").

What Is a Friend?

NOICC CAREER DEVELOPMENT GUIDELINES: Self-Knowledge

ASCA STANDARDS: Standard A—Students will acquire the skills to investigate the world-of-work in relation to knowledge of self and to make informed career decisions.

PURPOSE: To identify what is valued in friendships with others.

OBJECTIVE: To enhance self-awareness and the awareness of others; to determine valued attributes in a friend.

MATERIALS: Paper, pencils, poster board or chalkboard

INTRODUCTION: Ask students the question, "What is a friend?"

ACTIVITIES: Students will answer individually or divide into groups to answer the question, "What is a friend?" The leader will write on the chalkboard or poster board words that describe a friend. Students may then draw an illustration of "what a friend is."

DISCUSSION: Discuss students' definitions of what a friend is; prioritize these definitions (e.g., number them from 1 to 10); ask students if they have followed their own guidelines of "friendship" and why or why not; ask: Is it important and why? Focus on how friends can provide a source of support that helps one achieve goals or on how they can influence a person in ways that are counterproductive to goal achievement.

CLOSURE: Discuss how true friends help each other to achieve their goals.

TIME: 30–45 minutes

EVALUATION/ASSIGNMENT: Have students list five characteristics they want in a friend.

The "Problem Bucket"

NOICC CAREER DEVELOPMENT GUIDELINES: Self-Knowledge

ASCA STANDARDS: Standard A—Students will acquire the skills to investigate the world-of-work in relation to knowledge of self and to make informed career decisions.

PURPOSE: To discuss a range of problems that individuals are experiencing and possible solutions.

OBJECTIVE: Students will assist one another in thinking about problems that each is experiencing and possible solutions.

MATERIALS: Pencils, container ("bucket"), and note cards

INTRODUCTION: Explain to students the purpose of the "problem bucket": Individuals anonymously contribute, into the bucket, problems facing them. The problems will then be discussed and solutions explored.

ACTIVITIES: Ask students to write down on note cards the problems they are experiencing. Put these note cards into the bucket. Move students into small groups to discuss the problems and possible solutions. Ask students to handle information seriously and confidentially and to respect the anonymity of contributors.

DISCUSSION: Allow small groups to present problems they were discussing, as well as any solutions they developed, to the larger group. Encourage other groups to offer solutions as well.

CLOSURE: Discuss how many students share similar problems. Focus additional discussion on how it feels to talk with others about problems and on how almost all problems have solutions.

TIME: 30–45 minutes

EVALUATION/ASSIGNMENT: Ask students to write a response to the following question: As a result of this activity, what did you learn about "problems" and how to solve them? Answers should focus on the topics discussed in the activity, especially on the closure segment of the activity.

Comic Strips

NOICC CAREER DEVELOPMENT GUIDELINES: Self-Knowledge; Educational and Occupational Exploration

ASCA STANDARDS: Standard A—Students will acquire the skills to investigate the world-of-work in relation to knowledge of self and to make informed career decisions; Standard C—Students will understand the relationship between personal qualities, education, training, and the world-of-work.

PURPOSE: To explore the ways in which comic strips reflect human behavior, personality, lifestyle, and so on.

OBJECTIVE: Students will be able to identify and discuss the ways in which comic strips reflect real people and society.

MATERIALS: A newspaper comic strip, comic books, books with collections of comic strips, etc.; pencil, paper, chalk, and a blackboard

INTRODUCTION: Students will be asked to look through the newspaper comic section or comic books to find the ways in which comics reflect truth about life.

ACTIVITIES: Ask students to list the ways in which characters in the comics reflect human behavior and personality. Ask students to find examples in the comics of a family crisis, a conflict, a human value, a social problem, a prejudice, stereotypes (particularly about work-related issues, if desired), and a problem at work. Then ask students to draw their own comic strips about a particular aspect of their own lives, such as school, a sport they play, or their choice of occupations.

DISCUSSION: Ask students how these comics reflect or fail to reflect real life in our culture. Discuss how the comics are humorous and why students think others laugh at the situations in comics. Ask students to choose a comic character whom they would like to be and why. Ask students if they feel comics are purposeful, or if the influence of comics is somehow negative (e.g., violence in a comic might be seen as a negative influence on children).

CLOSURE: Comics tell us about both common experiences in our culture and culture-specific problems people encounter. They often reveal how culture influences our responses to the problems we encounter. Finally, the main theme of comics is the importance of keeping perspective in dealing with problems and of maintaining a sense of humor. By developing effective coping strategies, one can manage all problem situations more effectively and the situations are less stressful.

TIME: 1 hour, but this activity can also be used over multiple meetings, especially if students are assigned to draw their own comic strip

EVALUATION/ASSIGNMENT: Students can respond to the following question: "How does humor help you handle the problems you encounter?"

Workers I Know

NOICC CAREER DEVELOPMENT GUIDELINES: Educational and Occupational Exploration

ASCA STANDARDS: Standard A—Students will acquire the skills to investigate the world-of-work in relation to knowledge of self and to make informed career decisions; Standard B—Students will employ strategies to investigate the world-of-work in relation to knowledge of self and to make informed career decisions.

PURPOSE: To introduce students to occupations that they encounter each day.

OBJECTIVE: Students will identify the workers that they see every day in their lives.

MATERIALS: Chalkboard, chalk

INTRODUCTION: Discuss the fact that there are many types of workers that students encounter each day. Emphasize the point that each of these workers plays an important role in keeping our society functioning.

ACTIVITIES: List the workers that students see each day. Identify the role that each worker plays in helping the community function.

DISCUSSION: Discuss the importance of each occupation listed, the training required for each occupation, and the benefits associated with each occupation. Be sure to address gender stereotyping with each occupational selection (i.e., challenge students who assume that only members of one gender can perform a particular occupation).

CLOSURE: Reinforce the importance of learning more about occupations. Encourage students to continue listing occupations that they observe for the next 2 days.

TIME: 30–45 minutes

EVALUATION/ASSIGNMENT: Ask students to list the workers and their occupations that they observe in their school and community for the next two days.

Women and Men at Work

NOICC CAREER DEVELOPMENT GUIDELINES: Self-Knowledge; Educational and Occupational Exploration

ASCA STANDARDS: Standard A—Students will acquire the skills to investigate the world-of-work in relation to knowledge of self and to make informed career decisions; Standard C—Students will understand the relationship between personal qualities, education, training, and the world-of-work.

PURPOSE: To discuss gender-role stereotyping in work.

OBJECTIVE: Students will recognize that occupational selection does not have to be gender based.

MATERIALS: Two flip charts, markers

INTRODUCTION: Ask students to think about the workers that they see each day.

ACTIVITIES: Ask students to list on a sheet of paper at their desks the workers they see each day and whether they are male or female (e.g., principal—female; custodian—male; bus driver—female). Then, using two flip charts, label one "women" and the other one "men." Have students call out occupations that they have noticed. List the occupation under either

"women" or "men," depending on the gender of the worker in the occupation the student noticed.

DISCUSSION: Discuss the overlap of occupations on the "women" and the "men" charts. Ask students what conclusions they draw from the overlap. For occupations listed only on one chart, ask students to discuss whether they think a person of the opposite sex could perform those jobs. Challenge gender-based assumptions expressed by students.

CLOSURE: Emphasize the importance of not assuming that an occupation is for "women only" or for "men only" just because a particular occupation may be more populated by members of one gender than another.

TIME: 30–45 minutes

EVALUATION/ASSIGNMENT: Ask students to identify two people who are opposite in gender from the workers they listed originally. For example, if on the original list students noted a principal who was female, instruct them to identify a male who is a principal. If they cannot identify someone in their immediate environment, they can ask their family members if they know anyone who works in a particular occupation and is opposite in gender from the person on the original list.

Future Skills

NOICC CAREER DEVELOPMENT GUIDELINES: Self-Knowledge; Educational and Occupational Exploration; Career Planning

ASCA STANDARDS: Standard A—Students will acquire the skills to investigate the world-of-work in relation to knowledge of self and to make informed career decisions; Standard B—Students will employ strategies to achieve future career goals with success and satisfaction; Standard C—Students will understand the relationship between

personal qualities, education, training, and the world-of-work.

PURPOSE: To discuss the future and the impact of technology on our daily lives.

OBJECTIVE: Students will become aware of the impact of technology on their future lives.

MATERIALS: Chalkboard and chalk

INTRODUCTION: Discuss how many of the things we do today are influenced by technology. For example, communication via e-mail, satellite television, microwave ovens, computers in cars, facsimile machines, and car phones all allow us to do things in ways that are very different than when our parents were growing up. Discuss the jobs that exist now because of technology. Compare how things are accomplished today with how things were done 100 years ago.

ACTIVITIES: Divide students into groups. Have each group work collaboratively on creating posters in which they make drawings of "life in the future."

DISCUSSION: Have students share their drawings and discuss the pictures they drew. Discuss what the pictures

suggest regarding jobs in the future. Discuss what jobs might not exist in the future due to technology.

CLOSURE: Emphasize the implications of life in the future for career planning. For example, students can discuss the skills that will be needed to work in the future.

TIME: 45 minutes

EVALUATION/ASSIGNMENT: Have students write a short report identifying what they think will be fun about work in the future and what they think will be scary about work in the future.

Picture This!

NOICC CAREER DEVELOPMENT GUIDELINES: Self-Knowledge; Educational and Occupational Exploration; Career Planning

ASCA STANDARDS: Standard B—Students will employ strategies to achieve future career goals with success and satisfaction; Standard C—Students will understand the relationship between personal qualities, education, training, and the world-of-work.

PURPOSE: To discuss assumptions students make about workers based on race/ethnicity and gender.

OBJECTIVE: Students will recognize that race/ethnicity and gender are not occupational requirements.

MATERIALS: Magazines and scissors

INTRODUCTION: Explain to students that many people draw conclusions about occupational requirements based on false assumptions and factors that have nothing to do with the tasks of the job.

ACTIVITIES: Show students pictures of persons employed in different occupations (be sure to use a diverse sample of persons at work). Ask students to guess each person's occupation.

DISCUSSION: Discuss the assumptions students made in guessing each person's occupation. Discuss why it is not appropriate to relate demographic information to occupations. Discuss ways in which students' assumptions may be counterproductive in their own career development (e.g., because it can lead to eliminating occupations that might be very appropriate for the student).

CLOSURE: Encourage students to identify reasons that they might eliminate nontraditional occupations from consideration in their own career planning. Discuss whether these reasons are a good basis for career decision making.

TIME: 45 minutes

EVALUATION/ASSIGNMENT: Have students interview one person employed in a nontraditional occupation and ask the person to respond to questions such as:

1. What do you like about your occupation?
2. Was it difficult to choose a nontraditional occupation?
3. What are the challenges you face working in a nontraditional occupation?
4. Would you encourage others to consider working in a nontraditional occupation?

ABC List of Occupations

NOICC CAREER DEVELOPMENT GUIDELINES: Educational and Occupational Exploration

ASCA STANDARDS: Standard B—Students will employ strategies to achieve future career

goals with success and satisfaction; Standard C—Students will understand the relationship between personal qualities, education, training, and the world-of-work.

PURPOSE: To have students list as many occupations as they can think of alphabetically and determine which require the most work from the worker.

OBJECTIVE: To identify occupations and consider which students think would require the most energy to perform.

MATERIALS: Chalkboard, pencils, and paper

INTRODUCTION: Ask students to construct an ABC list of occupations so that you have one job listed for each letter of the alphabet. Ask students which three jobs they think require the most work from the worker and why (be sure to have them discuss the criteria they used for defining the "most work"—manual labor, hours worked per day, etc.).

A variation of this activity is to divide the group into two and have each group compete against each other in constructing an alphabetical list of occupations within a pre-specified amount of time (e.g., 2 minutes). The leader can time the activity.

ACTIVITIES: Students will list occupations on the board or on paper.

DISCUSSION: Discuss how the students perceive the definition of work and the energy required in performing specific occupations. Discuss whether the jobs with the least or the most energy requirements are the least or most desirable to the students and why. Ask students which jobs they feel earn the most money. Do they feel energy expended always leads to higher pay?

CLOSURE: Discuss the importance of knowing about jobs and job requirements. Emphasizing how our personal preferences influence our opinions about jobs is also an important part of this activity. The latter point also reinforces the notion that there is no one way to list preferred jobs. Each person will have his or her own list and reasons for preferring certain jobs and particular types of jobs.

TIME: 30–45 minutes

EVALUATION/ASSIGNMENT: Ask each student to write responses to the following questions: What type of "work" do I prefer? After this activity, I think I know (choose 1): (a) a lot about jobs, (b) an average amount about jobs, or (c) a little about jobs. Then ask students to identify three jobs they would like to learn more about based on this activity.

School and Work

NOICC CAREER DEVELOPMENT GUIDELINES: Career Planning; Self-Knowledge; Educational and Occupational Exploration

ASCA STANDARDS: Standard B—Students will employ strategies to achieve future career goals with success and satisfaction; Standard C—Students will understand the relationship between personal qualities, education, training, and the world-of-work.

PURPOSE: To discuss the relationship between school and work.

OBJECTIVE: Students will identify occupations that relate to specific school subjects.

MATERIALS: Chalkboard, chalk, pencils, and paper

INTRODUCTION: Begin by discussing the relationship between school and work.

ACTIVITIES: List school subjects (e.g., math, science, language arts, music, and physical education) on the chalkboard. Divide students into small groups. Ask students to list occupations under each school subject that require the use of that subject (e.g., math—accounting, bank teller, cashier). Have each group write its list on the board.

DISCUSSION: Review the list from each group. Have students identify how they think the subject matter is used in each occupation. Discuss what would happen if a person in each occupation didn't have a background in a relevant subject matter.

CLOSURE: Reinforce the connection between school subjects and work.

TIME: 30–45 minutes

EVALUATION/ASSIGNMENT: Have students interview their family members to identify the subject areas that are important for performing their jobs.

Leaders and Followers

NOICC CAREER DEVELOPMENT GUIDELINES: Self-Knowledge; Educational and Occupational Exploration

ASCA STANDARDS: Standard A—Students will acquire the skills to investigate the world-of-work in relation to knowledge of self and to make informed career decisions; Standard B—Students will employ strategies to achieve future career goals with success and satisfaction; Standard C—Students will understand the relationship between personal qualities, education, training, and the world-of-work.

PURPOSE: To discuss the attributes of individuals considered to be "leaders."

OBJECTIVE: Students will be able to identify characteristics of a "leader" and compare them with the characteristics of a "hero."

MATERIALS: Chalkboard, pencils, and paper

INTRODUCTION: Begin by brainstorming the words that come to their minds when students think of the words leader and follower. List the words on the chalkboard under each term.

ACTIVITIES: Students should make a list of persons they consider to be great leaders including artists, athletes, politicians, scientists, writers, pioneers, businesspersons, and entertainers. Write down the major achievements of these leaders and five common traits these individuals share (e.g., hard worker, natural talent, etc.). Ask students to name someone they know that has these leadership qualities (from home, school, etc.). Discuss the difference between a leader and a follower. What are the positive traits of both?

DISCUSSION: Review the characteristics of a leader. Ask if being a leader is always a good thing, and why or why not. Ask students to discuss if they prefer being a leader or a follower and to identify reasons for their preferences. Note that they may have preferences for leading in certain situations. When this latter situation occurs, ask students to discuss why they may prefer leading in certain situations but not in others. They should focus on the activities they are engaged in, how they feel about their abilities to complete these particular activities, and so on. Finally, discuss how people become leaders (e.g., Are they "born leaders" or can these skills be developed?). The same discussion can take place for "followers."

CLOSURE: Discussion should focus on the importance of leaders and followers in the workplace. Emphasize the importance of both. What would happen if everyone wanted to be a leader? What would happen if everyone wanted to be a follower?

TIME: 30–45 minutes

EVALUATION/ASSIGNMENT: Have students write down what skills they need to develop to become better leaders and better followers.

School: The Good and the Bad

NOICC CAREER DEVELOPMENT GUIDELINES: Self-Knowledge; Educational and Occupational Exploration

ASCA STANDARDS: Standard A—Students will acquire the skills to investigate the world-of-work in relation to knowledge of self and to make informed career decisions; Standard C—Students will understand the relationship between personal qualities, education, training, and the world-of-work.

PURPOSE: To have students explore their feelings about school in general.

OBJECTIVE: Students will think about what they like about school as well as their complaints about school.

MATERIALS: Chalkboard, chalk

INTRODUCTION: Make two lists on the board with headings "good" and "bad."

ACTIVITIES: Ask students to take turns writing something under a list of good or bad things about school. If the first student writes under the "bad" list, the next student must write under the "good" list, and vice versa. Examples might be, "I get to see my friends" or "I hate the school lunches."

DISCUSSION: Have students discuss the items on the lists. Encourage them to think of the ways school enhances their lives. Students will then brainstorm ideas for turning "bad" items into "good" items. For example, if a bad item is "homework," then participants can discuss what might be useful about homework. Students could also share strategies they use for making homework better or more enjoyable. Students can also talk about how and when they do their homework. Different strategies can be discussed. The same approach can be used for other "bad" items. Note that it is likely that all "bad" items may not be converted into "good" items. The leader will need to select which items to focus on in this exercise.

CLOSURE: Center the discussion on whether anything in life is all good. Emphasize the importance of turning "bad" into "good."

TIME: 30–45 minutes

EVALUATION/ASSIGNMENT: Students can list three items in their "bad" category that they could change into "good." Strategies for converting these items from bad to good should be identified.

Changes

NOICC CAREER DEVELOPMENT GUIDELINES: Self-Knowledge; Educational and Occupational Exploration; Career Planning

ASCA STANDARDS: Standard A—Students will acquire the skills to investigate the world-of-work in relation to knowledge of self and to make informed career decisions; Standard C—Students will understand the relationship between personal qualities, education, training, and the world-of-work.

PURPOSE: To explore the ways people change.

OBJECTIVE: Students will be able to discuss ways in which they have experienced change as individuals and changes that may likely occur in the future.

MATERIALS: Pencils, paper

INTRODUCTION: Ask students to list or name something about themselves that has changed.

ACTIVITIES: The activity leader will ask students to name something about themselves that has changed: in the past 24 hours (such as clothes); in the past week (something new learned in school); in the past year (joined a sports team, changed grades); since birth. Students will then be asked to predict changes that are likely to occur in the future (next year, in 5 years, in 10 years, etc.).

DISCUSSION: Discuss the changes that each student has experienced and whether he or she considers these changes positive or negative. Discuss which changes students feel have had the greatest impact on who they are today. Discuss fears about changes likely to occur in the future and how individuals successfully deal with change in their lives. Ask what students might like to change about themselves or their environment and what impedes these changes from occurring.

CLOSURE: Review the discussion and ask students to write down things they notice about themselves that are changing in the next week or month. Request that each student choose something they would like to work on changing in the next few weeks, and ask that they keep a journal of their progress regarding this change (e.g., get homework done on time, get up 10 minutes earlier, help with household chores, change looks somehow, etc.).

TIME: 45 minutes to 1 hour

EVALUATION/ASSIGNMENT: Share the journal with the leader.

Career Investigators

NATIONAL CAREER DEVELOPMENT GUIDELINES: Educational and Occupational Exploration.

ASCA STANDARDS: Standard C—Students will understand the relationship between personal qualities, education, training, and the world-of-work.

PURPOSE: Knowing where and how to obtain information about the world-of-work and postsecondary training/education.

OBJECTIVES: Students will be able to identify roles and responsibilities of individuals in the world-of-work.

MATERIALS: A big magnifying glass (paper or real); "tool box": a collection of tools that workers use

INTRODUCTION: Have or make an oversized magnifying glass (you can easily make one by duct-taping a roll of masking tape to a magic marker). Tell the students that you are investigating the work people do. Ask the students to help you in the investigation.

ACTIVITY:

1. Walk around classroom using BIG magnifying glass to get a closer look at various people and things in the room—act like a detective . . . without talking directly to students.
   - Make comments like "hmmmm," "this is interesting," "I can use this as evidence."
   - As you're walking around, gather "evidence" of a teacher's work role and responsibilities.
2. Explain to students that they will help you investigate what people do while they are working. Ask 3-4 students to tell the class their definition of "investigate," "work," and "workers."
3. Reveal the "Tool Box." Pull out one or two tools; ask individual students to help you by holding the tools.
   Use questions to prompt student discussion/participation such as:
   - "Hmmm . . . I wonder who would use this tool at work?"
   - "Who will demonstrate how a worker uses this tool?"
   - "What skills does someone need to use this tool at work?"
   - "Does anyone have a family member who uses this tool at work?"

Follow the same procedure with 3 or 4 more tools (depending upon students' attention span).

DISCUSSION: As you close the lesson for this day, ask students to tell one thing they have discovered about workers.

CLOSURE: Ask students to help you learn more about what people do at work by observing workers at home or wherever they go.

- "When you go home, look at your parents or grandparents or older sister or brother, or whoever else might live in your house with you. Try and notice the things that they do for work. Maybe you'll even want to ask them what they do at their work or what tools they get to use!"
- "During our next lesson together, we will talk about your observations and you will get to see more of the tools in the Tool Box."

TIME: 30 minutes

EVALUATION/ASSIGNMENT: Students will demonstrate their engagement by following with their eyes, and will contribute to the discussion by helping the investigators to identify occupations. Students may also volunteer definitions of "investigate" and "work" and workers.

VOCABULARY:

- tool
- job title
- role
- responsibility
- investigate
- worker
- work

Possible "Tools" and Corresponding Occupations

Tool	Job Title	Role	Responsibility
Hammer	Carpenter	Builds/repair houses	Follow plans/directions from homeowner.
Wrench	Mechanic	Repair vehicles	Repair what the owner asks.
Paintbrush	Painter (Could also be an artist)	Paint rooms/houses	Change color to satisfy the owner.
Pencil	Writer	Write books	Meet deadlines.
Hair Dryer	Beautician	Fix people's hair	Talk with people about what they want done with their hair.
Bowl and Spoon	Chef	Cook meals	Follow recipe.
Stethoscope	Doctor	Help people who are sick	Listen to patient.
Ruler	Architect	Design buildings	Make sure the building is safe.
Books	Librarian	Provide information and resources	Help people find books.
Telephone	Receptionist	Answer questions	Provide accurate information.
Calculator	Banker/Teller	Manage accounts	Accurately count money.
Needle and Thread	Seamstress	Construct/repair garments	Create or repair clothing to meet the interests of people.
Tractor	Farmer	Plant/grow crops	Take care of the crops/soil.

A modified version of the original, retrieved from: http://missouricareereducation.org/curr/cmd/guidanceplacementG/lessons/kind.php.

A Few of My Favorite—And Not So Favorite!—Things

NATIONAL CAREER DEVELOPMENT GUIDELINES: Self-Knowledge.

ASCA STANDARDS: Standard C—Students will understand the relationship between personal qualities, education, training, and the world-of-work.

PURPOSE: To develop awareness of self, work, and workers.

OBJECTIVE: Students will be able to identify likes and dislikes at home and at school.

MATERIALS: Puppet and activity sheet

INTRODUCTION: Puppet and counselor will facilitate a discussion with students including the following questions:

- "Is it important to have things you like to do? Why?"
- "What if I don't like everything I do? Is that okay?"
- "What are some favorite things you like to do at home? At school?"
- "What are some things you don't like to do at home? At school?"

ACTIVITY:

1. As both yourself the counselor, and as the puppet, use the previous questions to conduct a discussion of students' favorite and least favorite things to do at school and at home. Feel free to be silly and energetic as the puppet! Because students will be excited to share their ideas with the puppet, it will be extra necessary to encourage students to raise a quiet hand, take turns, and help them to focus their responses.

2. As the puppet, ask three or four students what their favorite subjects are at school. The puppet can share his/her favorite subject as well.

3. The puppet will continue the discussion by asking what activities the students like and dislike when they are at home. As the puppet, ask three or four more students to share their least favorite things at home. Be sure to include all students by using questions like "Who else feels this way?" or "Who else likes/dislikes to do that too?" Encourage quiet hands instead of calling out.

4. Counselor and puppet will hand out *My Favorite/Least Favorite Things Activity Sheet*. In the first column, students will draw one thing they like to do at school, and one thing they like to do at home. In the second column, students will draw something they dislike doing at school and one for at home.

5. Once students have completed their drawings on the activity sheet, encourage them to share their drawings. (If there is space, students may come to the carpet. If not, they can stay at their desks/tables and share. If you decide to move to the carpet be sure to allot a few minutes for students to collect on the carpet and get themselves ready to share and listen). As each student shares, the puppet should give undivided attention to the student who is speaking, while the counselor can help make sure that everyone is using his or her listening ears. In large classes, you may want to divide the class in half—one side sharing what they like best, and the other side sharing what they like least.

6. As the counselor, ask, "How do you know what you don't like?" "How do you know what you do like?" Students' responses will indicate an early awareness of influences in their lives, that is, "I don't like getting dirty," or "My brother likes drawing, but I like playing outside."

DISCUSSION: Puppet and counselor will conduct a summarizing discussion. Include:

a. Everyone had great ideas!
b. There were so many different ideas.
c. Everyone has different and similar ideas of what are his or her favorite and not-so-favorite things to do—and that is okay because that's what makes you YOU!
d. Some of our favorite and not-so-favorite things will stay the same as we grow up, and some of them will change as we grow up and change too.
e. We make choices based on what we like and what we don't like.

Students will respond to and discuss these topics to show that they understand the concepts, especially that each person has favorite and not-so-favorite things he or she does, such as, "Jayden likes math, and I like music!"

CLOSURE: Counselor tells the puppet it's time to go and the puppet is at first sad to leave, but then remembers how much fun he/she and the students had together and praises the students for their hard work. The puppet then thanks the students for letting him/her come to their classroom and promises to come back again soon.

EVALUATION/ASSIGNMENT: Students' drawings pertain to their likes and dislikes. Students are able to differentiate between the feelings they have when they are doing something they like, and the feelings they have when they are doing something they dislike. Students will contribute to the discussion and listen to their peers.

TIME: 30 minutes

VOCABULARY:
- Favorite
- Least favorite/Not-so-favorite

WORKSHEET:

My Favorite Things . . .	My Least Favorite Things . . .
Draw a picture of one or more of your favorite things.	Draw a picture of one or more of your least favorite things.
at school . . .	at school . . .
at home . . .	at home . . .

Let's Play Dress-Up!

NATIONAL CAREER DEVELOPMENT GUIDELINES:
Educational and Occupational Exploration

ASCA STANDARDS: Standard A—Students will acquire skills to investigate the world-of- work in relation to knowledge of self and to make informed career decisions.

PURPOSE: Learning about the variety that exists in the world-of-work. Exploring specific occupations and their tasks and responsibilities.

OBJECTIVES: Students will identify a worker that they see or interact with regularly in their daily lives. Students will then dress like that specific worker, and role play with the class. Students will provide a brief summary about the responsibilities and tasks of a worker in that profession.

MATERIALS: For this activity, students will mainly be bringing their own materials from home. In case students have limited materials available to them at home, be sure to have extra hats, jackets, and props for each student's occupation.

INTRODUCTION: Tell students to think about workers they see every day. Help remind them about all the different people they interact with throughout their day. This can include their parents/guardians, siblings, neighbors, bus drivers, crossing guards, teachers, administrators, and so on. Have students brainstorm a list and write down what they come up with.

ACTIVITY:
1. In the initial guidance lesson with students after brainstorming a list of workers, explain to students that for next time they will need to come prepared to class dressed like one of the people they see working on a daily basis. This can include teacher, homemaker, businessman/-woman, artist, bus driver, and so on . . . the possibilities are endless! Each student will then sign up for a specific occupation. It is okay if 2-3 (but no more than 3) students choose the same occupation, as there may be some variation within that occupation (for example, one might choose a Kindergarten teacher, while another might choose a fifth-grade teacher; business employees might also have similar but different tasks and responsibilities).

2. Interview the worker or use the Internet to research tasks and responsibilities of a worker in that profession.
3. Students will present to class what they learned about the worker. You may invite parents to hear their child's presentation!
4. After presentations, students can have a "party" in which they mingle with one another and role play as their worker. Snacks are optional based on budget or how much time is available. Most importantly, students should be able to tell other students about their "job" and what they have learned through their research.

DISCUSSION: To close the session, ask students how it felt to be someone else for a day. Encourage students to tell you what they liked or disliked about the job that they chose.

CLOSURE: In your next visit to the class, spend one guidance lesson conducting a follow-up discussion with students. Ask them what it was like to interview the worker they imitated or to research their occupation.

- "What things surprised you about the worker and their job?"
- "What do you like about the kind of work you explored? Dislike?"
- "Do you think you want to do the work you chose when you grow up?"
- "Tell me some new things that you learned from your classmates." (Make a brainstorm list together.)

After discussing as a class, provide children with paper and crayons, markers, or colored pencils. Have students draw a picture of themselves as the workers they presented. Post them on the wall or bulletin board under a career-themed title. This will be a fun way to conclude the project and for kids to proudly demonstrate what they presented and learned!

TIME: 30–45 minutes

EVALUATION/ASSIGNMENT: Students will research their chosen occupation (help from grown-ups is permitted). Type of research (interview, Internet searches, or library) is up to grade level, ability, and availability. After researching, students will be able to "teach" what they have learned about their chosen occupations to their peers with the use of role play.

VOCABULARY:
- explore
- interview
- worker
- occupation
- role play

Career Collage Comic Strip

NATIONAL CAREER DEVELOPMENT GUIDELINES: Career Planning.

ASCA STANDARDS: Standard B—Students will employ strategies to achieve future career goals with success and satisfaction.

PURPOSE: Being able to picture a future career goal and then be able to identify steps to achieving that goal. Students will demonstrate goals and steps through pictures and collage.

OBJECTIVE: Students will identify a career that they would like to strive toward or one that they can see themselves participating in. Using this image as a goal, students will then identify specific steps in order to move from where they are today toward their goals. Each step and goal will be demonstrated in comic strip form using drawing, painting, written dialogue, or collage.

MATERIALS: Newspapers and magazines, poster boards, watercolor paints, crayons, markers, colored pencils, glue sticks, and scissors. Before the lesson, cut poster boards in half; students will not need entire poster boards for this activity; a half of a poster board is the perfect size for each student to map out his or her goal and steps.

INTRODUCTION: Ask students to share some of the things they might like to be when they grow up. Go around the room and let a few students tell the class their ideas. You can even share some of the things that you wanted to be when you were a kid. Ask students, "What does it take for someone to get to do their dream job?" On the board, make a list of what the students tell you (answers can include: education, working hard, doing a lot of jobs, going to college, meeting people, etc.). Emphasize that we do not wake up one day and magically get to be what we dreamed of, but rather that it takes a lot of hard work, planning, and time. To get there, it takes many small and big steps.

ACTIVITY:
1. After sharing, tell the students to close their eyes and imagine themselves in their dream career (if some students have more than one dream career, tell them to pick one for today. It's okay if it changes later on). Prompts include:
   a. "Imagine what you would be doing at your job."
   b. "Think about who you would be working with? How old are the people you would be working with?"
   c. "How much money would you get paid at your job?"
   d. "What do you wear to your job?"
   If it helps, students can write down the ideas that come to mind as they are imagining themselves in their dream job.
2. After the students have solidified an idea of their dream job, tell them that this will be their goal. Then, talk with them about some of the steps that might help them get to their dream job. Students can share their goals for examples. As the steps become clearer, students can write these down on a sheet of paper as well. Have students number their steps. Students should have about five to six steps each (no more than ten).
3. Once students have identified their goals and steps, hand out the poster boards to each student. Tell students to divide their poster into enough boxes or spaces so that each of their steps and their goal can have one space each (you may want to demonstrate this on the board or your own sheet of poster board). Then, students should number their boxes per number of steps and write "My Goal" in the box where their goal will be. It should look something like this:

Step 1:	Step 2:	Step 3:	Step 4:	MyGoal!:

4. If there is time, students may title their steps (i.e., Step 1: Practice a lot. Step 2: Do all my homework, etc.). After mapping out their posters, pass around the materials. Tell students that now they can look for pictures that demonstrate what their steps or goals look like. If they can't find a picture, they can draw things instead. Students may use words, but encourage them to demonstrate their goals through pictures as much as possible. Students can take time drawing, flipping through magazines, cutting out pictures, and gluing pictures to their comic strip collage. Note: this may take more than one guidance lesson to complete.
5. After day one, collect what the students have started and encourage them to continue thinking about their posters. On day two, students can pick up where they left off and complete their posters. After finishing, close day two with a discussion about goals and steps.

DISCUSSION: Have students explain the difference between long- and short-term goals. Talk about what it takes to reach a long-term goal. Ask students what kinds of things came up for them when they were planning for their long-term goal. Ask students, "Do you like every single one of your steps? Is it okay if we like some of our steps but not others?"

CLOSURE: Remind students that things that they are doing now will impact them in the future and that is why it is so important for them to work hard now. Encourage students to recognize when one of their steps is successful and that each day they are getting closer and closer to their goals. Students can then take home their comic strip collages, or if there is space hang the collages on a bulletin board, in the hallway, or around the room.

TIME: Two 45 minutes lessons (Total of 90 minutes)

EVALUATION/ASSIGNMENT: Students will visualize their goals and steps through pictures. Students will show the counselor and the class that they can see and explain their goals and what goes in to planning and reaching their goals. Students' pictures will demonstrate an understanding of career planning and short- and long-term goals.

His Job or Her Job?

NATIONAL CAREER DEVELOPMENT GUIDELINES: Career Planning: Awareness of different occupations and changing male/female roles.

ASCA STANDARDS: Standard B—Students will employ strategies to achieve future career goals with success and satisfaction.

PURPOSE: To describe traditional and nontraditional careers and how they relate to career choice.

OBJECTIVE: Students will learn about the challenges and benefits of pursuing a non-traditional career.

MATERIALS: White board, paper, and coloring materials for each student

INTRODUCTION: Tell students that they'll be doing some drawing that relates to careers.

ACTIVITY:
1. Help students fold paper into three sections (like a brochure). Tell students these are three separate sections. If it helps them to visualize the sections, they can draw a line down each fold.
2. Explain that in each section they'll draw an image of a person in a particular career. No talking or looking at other students' papers. Give 3–5 minutes for each drawing.
3. Tell students to draw the following three occupations. Give students time between each occupation.
   a. First, tell students to draw what a NURSE looks like.
   b. Second, an AIRPLANE PILOT.
   c. Third, a MUSICAL PERFORMER.
4. Circulate the room to make sure students are drawing independently and have enough time to complete three detailed drawings. Instruct them to put their drawing utensils down after the third drawing.
5. Make a chart on the board to document the gender of the people drawn for each job. Ask

how many students drew a male nurse and then how many drew a female. Next ask how many drew a female pilot and then how many drew a male. The order is not important for the musical performer—it should be rather even.

DISCUSSION: Discuss why their images of nurses are primarily female and pilots primarily male. Offer statistics (dol.gov/wb) about how many men are nurses (5.7%) and how many females are pilots (3.4%). Challenge students to think of a career that can only be performed by one gender. (Be prepared

to prove them wrong!) Then lead students through a brainstorm about the benefits and challenges of pursuing a nontraditional career.

CLOSURE: Remind students to think about careers in terms of their interests instead of gender traditions.

EVALUATION/ASSIGNMENT: Students will challenge gender traditions in careers. In discussion, students will identify reasons to pursue nontraditional careers. If time allows, have students write a five-minute reflection.

What Subjects Do Workers Like?

NATIONAL CAREER DEVELOPMENT GUIDELINES: Educational and Occupational Exploration: Awareness of the relationship between work and learning.

ASCA STANDARDS: Standard C—Students will understand the relationship between personal qualities, training, education, and the world-of-work.

PURPOSE: To discuss the relationship between subjects at school and the world-of-work.

OBJECTIVE: Students will identify occupations related to specific school subjects. Subjects will include core subjects as well as specials such as music, art, physical education, and so on.

MATERIALS: Paper, pencils, chalkboard or butcher paper and markers

INTRODUCTION: Talk with students about the connection between school and work. Ask students to share some examples of similarities between school and work, as well as some of the differences. "What are some things that you do at school that you will need for working?" (Answers can include reading, writing, knowing how to do math, reading music, knowing about science, etc.)

ACTIVITY: List school subjects along the top of the chalkboard or on butcher paper. Ask a few students to give examples of jobs that use things from the

school subjects; for example, a banker uses math and a journalist uses language arts. You can ask students to share and record their answers, or allow students to come up one at a time and write their ideas. After a few ideas have been written on the board, divide students into small groups to brainstorm their own ideas. Circulate throughout the room to make sure students understand. After 10–15 minutes, have each group write the jobs it came up with on the board under each subject.

DISCUSSION: Go over each group's list. Have the students give examples of how the school subject might be used in each occupation. Be sure to point out some ways that a job might use a subject that students might not guess at first (Musicians use counting and numbers—that's math!). Talk with students about why it is important that each worker in a certain occupation has a background in his or her specific subject.

CLOSURE: Remind students how we decided school and work are similar and are closely related.

TIME: 45 minutes

EVALUATION/ASSIGNMENT: Students will talk to other workers they see on a daily basis to learn more about which subjects are important for doing their jobs.

Guess Who: Careers

NATIONAL CAREER DEVELOPMENT GUIDELINES: Educational and Occupational Exploration

ASCA STANDARDS: Standard A—Students will acquire the skills to investigate the world-of-work in relation to knowledge of self and to make informed career decisions.

PURPOSE: To be able to describe elements, responsibilities, and tasks of specific careers. To expand students' vocabulary related to occupations.

OBJECTIVE: Students will be able to use clues to describe occupations to their classmates. Students will also be able to guess specific occupations based on the clues they are given.

MATERIALS: Note cards (one for each student and yourself), a marker, masking tape

INTRODUCTION:
a. Before visiting the class, create a list of occupations including a variety of occupational types. The list should include occupations that students will be familiar with, but also some that are more challenging. After the list is finalized, use a marker to write one occupation on each note card. Students should be able to read the note card from across the room.
b. Take occupation note cards and masking tape to the classroom. Before starting, have the students make a circle with their desks or sit in a circle on the floor.
c. Explain to the students, "I want to see how much each of you know about different occupations. In this activity, show me what you know by giving your classmates clues about specific occupations. If you're not sure you know what clues to give about an occupation, ask me or someone else and we can help each other out."

ACTIVITY:
1. With the teacher or a helper, go around the room and tape one note card to each student's forehead. The student should not look at or be able to see what is written on his or her note card. "Do not look at your note card. You are going to have to guess what is written on it based on the clues your classmates give you!"
2. Once each student has a note card, tape the remaining note card to your forehead in order to participate with the students. You can start the activity or take a volunteer to be the first guesser. Ask three or four students to raise their hands and each give one clue about what is written on the guesser's forehead note card. Help students to stay relevant with their clues. Clues can include:
   a. "You work in a school."
   b. "You use your hands to work."
   c. "You use tools to fix things."
   d. "You like people/animals."
   Students may not use a part of the word on the note card in their clue (i.e., if the word is Teacher, students cannot say "You teach kids"). Encourage students to use clues relating to context, environment, tasks, tools implemented, and so on.
3. Go around the room until each student has guessed his or her occupation note card. Encourage all students to give clues.

DISCUSSION: Ask students, "What was it like to give your classmates clues? To receive clues?" Talk with students about any words that came up that they were unfamiliar with. Help students to understand that there are many different titles of occupations and that usually there are many different parts to an occupation. For example, a school counselor has to know how to give classroom guidance, but also needs to know how to talk with people one-on-one.

CLOSURE: Encourage students by telling them the positive things you noticed about the clues they gave each other. Reiterate that there are many different job titles and many different things that workers do.

TIME: 30 minutes

EVALUATION/ASSIGNMENT: Students will participate in the activity and give appropriate and relevant clues. Students will then go home and ask parents/guardians, siblings, or other workers they see about the many different aspects of their work.

How Do I Get There from Here?

NATIONAL CAREER DEVELOPMENT GUIDELINES: Career Planning

ASCA STANDARDS: Standard C—Students will understand the relationship between personal qualities, education, training, and the world-of-work.

PURPOSE: To acquire knowledge to achieve career goals.

OBJECTIVE: Students will understand the relationship between educational achievement and career success.

MATERIALS: Computer with Internet access for each student or pair of students. Worksheets—one for each student, large poster board or butcher paper for the class

INTRODUCTION: Discuss how school subjects are related to careers and career choices. Introduce the activity and go through the directions, explaining that only a small number of careers will be listed for each subject area on the Web site ("Your fantasy job may not be listed. If it's not, try and find a different one to learn about.") Encourage students to look for a job that they don't already know a great deal about.

ACTIVITY: Assist each student in accessing the Bureau of Labor Statistics Web site for kids - bls.gov/k12/ and monitor their browsing. When each student has completed the chart on the worksheet, record the data from the whole class on a large chart for students to compare findings. Note which careers require

the most/least training, are growing/shrinking in demand, and earn the highest/lowest salaries.

CLOSURE: Emphasize that students' performance in school has a significant influence on their readiness to enter a training program, educational program, or career. Help students understand that they do NOT need to know right now what they want to do when they grow up, but instead that by trying out different classes and putting in their best effort can help them to learn more about what they like or dislike. Stress the importance of working hard and encourage students to keep an eye out for and to celebrate the results and successes.

TIME: 30 minutes

EVALUATION/ASSIGNMENT: Students will turn in the worksheet with data completed. Evaluate for participation and completion. Students will then be able to share their findings with the class on a chart (each student will be able to share at least one finding and put it on the chart).

WORKSHEET

Directions: Choose one of the areas that interests you, select it, and then choose one career from those listed and select it. For that job, read "What is this job like?" and "How do you get ready?" Then complete the chart below by finding the information you need from "How much does this job pay?" "How many jobs are there?" and "What about the future?"

Job Title _____

Number of jobs	Available	Preparation	The future	$$ Pay $$

11

Career Development Interventions in Middle and High Schools

Providing career development interventions in my work as a middle school counselor is important because students need to learn how to explore their interests and strengths. By offering career guidance at this level, counselors can help middle school students build the foundation necessary to understand possibilities and expectations in the world-of-work.

Many of the work habits that students develop at this level are carried over to high school and beyond. It is crucial that educators provide the assistance students need to form healthy habits and make informed decisions. The earlier students learn about careers and occupations, the better prepared they are to explore the pathways leading toward their own future goals.

Through interest inventories, career fairs, mock job interviews, visits from community business members, and numerous other middle school activities, students are introduced to career development. Teachers from all disciplines combine to provide a full-circle approach to educating students on the importance of career exploration.

Self-awareness is critical at the middle school level. These activities provide a realistic view of potential career paths and opportunities for students to match them with their likes and abilities. Our middle school also offers numerous clubs and activities so students can try out new ideas and experiences to further define their future aspirations.

Overall, the more we encourage our students to pursue interests and new experiences, the more we help them to form good work habits and positive life skills. These skills highlight the importance of using sound judgment when exploring careers and planning for the future.

Michael J. Brannigan
Professional School Counselor
Queensbury Middle School
Queensbury, NY

Career development interventions in my work as a high school counselor are important because high school counselors are preparing students to go into the working world. At the high school level, career development involves teaching students how to plan and prepare for the workforce. Many teenagers have no idea what direction they want to head into and need help sorting through their interests and abilities. This can dictate everything from how they choose their postsecondary education to what jobs they search for while in school. As such, they need to know how to create résumés, fill out applications, and prepare for interviews. Counselors must also teach students life management skills and how career choice can affect your ability to support yourself and others. An additional aspect of career development for counselors can be job placement, more unique to the high school level. Students of all levels are looking for various types of employment. Some students need help finding part-time positions to help pay for expenses or save for college. Other students need training and basic skills for full-time employment that will begin as soon as they graduate. High school counselors must be in contact with community resources and businesses to find out what positions are available to students and sometimes to monitor a student's on-the-job performance. These contacts not only may employ students, but also provide opportunities for apprenticeships, internships, job shadowing experiences, and coming into the schools for presentations or recruitment. Career development for counselors in high schools serves to bring students and the workforce together to find the best fit.

Megan Martin, M.Ed.
Professional School Counselor
Orange County High School
Hillsboro, NC

MyCounselingLab™

Visit the MyCounselingLab™ site for *Career Development Interventions in the 21st Century,* Fourth Edition to enhance your understanding of chapter concepts. You'll have the opportunity to practice your skills through video- and case-based Assignments and Activities as well as Building Counseling Skills units, and to prepare for your certification exam with Practice for Certification quizzes.

Antonio was new to the school. He and his parents had recently moved from Los Angeles to rural Pennsylvania. As a seventh grader in L.A., Antonio had lots of friends, knew most of his teachers, and was one of the star players on the soccer team. In Belltoona, Pennsylvania, Antonio was new, disoriented, and unsure of himself. He was angry about moving; he felt alone, and he was depressed. Antonio's parents noticed that he had become apathetic and uninvolved in many of the activities that once gave him a sense of satisfaction and pride.

Tips from the Field

Adolescents need to engage in broad exploration to know which educational and career paths make the most sense for them. Help them to view their experiences through the lens of accurate self-understanding.

MIDDLE/JUNIOR HIGH SCHOOL

Antonio's situation represents what many middle school students experience. Students at the middle/junior high school level are confronted with a more sophisticated set of developmental tasks than they experienced during their elementary school years. Erikson (1963) notes that between the ages of 12 and 18 adolescents must clarify their identities. If identity clarification is not achieved, then adolescents will experience confusion as they attempt to negotiate the tasks presented to them. Specifically, Havighurst (1972) suggests that adolescents must accomplish the following developmental tasks:

1. Achieve new and more sophisticated relations with peers;
2. Achieve emotional independence from parents and other adults;
3. Set vocational goals;
4. Prepare for marriage and family life;
5. Develop skills for civic competence;
6. Acquire a set of values and an ethical system as a guide to behavior;
7. Set realistic goals and make plans for achieving these goals.

These tasks present a daunting challenge to young people as they move from childhood to adolescence and early adulthood. The often stormy experience of transitioning from childhood to adolescence not only presents a challenge to the young person experiencing this transition but also to those who are part of the young person's social network. Physiological and social development encourage the preadolescent to take strides toward independence. Strides toward independence, however, are often accompanied by feelings of insecurity, conflict, fear, and anxiety; as Vernon (1993) states, "Dramatic changes in cognition and the intensification of affect contribute to a fluctuating sense of self" (p. 10). Bireley and Genshaft (1991) describe early adolescence as the process of "struggling toward maturity" (p. 1). As a result of their advancing development, middle/junior high school students are preoccupied with belonging and are influenced significantly by their same-sex peers. Thus, counselors providing career interventions for middle school students need to challenge students to become active agents in the career development process while at the same time offering supportive assistance as students acquire additional self- and career information.

Antonio's parents asked his school counselor to meet with Antonio. They wanted Antonio to become more connected with the school and to begin working harder at making new friends. During their meeting, Antonio's counselor convinced him to join a school activity. Together, they explored the wide range of activities available at Antonio's school. The school counselor also encouraged

Antonio to explore the various options with his parents. After these discussions, Antonio reluctantly agreed to join a community service group at the school. The counselor also asked the captain of the middle school's soccer team to "mentor" Antonio and help him to become more familiar with the school and other students. Antonio met with his counselor on a regular basis for the first half of the school year and was clearly becoming more connected with the school and making new friends. Antonio and his counselor discussed a variety of topics, including Antonio's experience in the community service group. These discussions also focused on other areas of interest for Antonio. A seemingly natural leader, Antonio's counselor encouraged him to assume a leadership role within the community service group. Antonio liked "being in charge" and at the next election of group officers, he was voted in as the president. Because Antonio had not thought much about life after high school, his counselor suggested that they spend some time discussing his career plans. Soon, Antonio and his counselor began to explore how his interests related to various occupational options.

Understanding the career development status of middle school students is crucial for developing goals for career development interventions. As is true at the elementary school level, counselors in secondary school settings view providing career assistance to students as central to their work (American School Counselor Association, 2003; Campbell & Dahir, 1997). Career assistance provided to middle school students must be sensitive to the contextual, physical, and emotional transitions that students experience. Akos (2004) highlights the shifts occurring from elementary to middle school, noting that rising middle school students encounter "multiple teachers, larger school buildings, block scheduling, lockers, and new and different peers" (p. 881). These contextual changes occur concurrently with significant physical and emotional development changes during puberty. Researchers have found that students making the transition to middle school often experience decreases in self-esteem, increases in psychological distress, and decreases in academic achievement (Akos).

Akos, Konold, and Niles (2004) found that middle school students exhibit distinct patterns of needs regarding developing their readiness for career decision making. Some students reflect developmentally appropriate career indecision or moratorium status, some indicate the need for more focused and intense personal and career counseling interventions, whereas others may highlight premature career identity foreclosure and are disengaged from the career decision-making process. Understanding a student's career decision-making needs helps counselors to identify specific career development interventions that may be most useful in fostering a student's career development. Here again, data from the National Assessment of Educational Progress's Project on Career and Occupational Development provide useful information for understanding the career development status of middle/ junior high school students. For example, survey results from a national sample of 38,000 13-year-olds indicate that young people at this age have made progress in crystallizing their self-concepts, as exemplified by the fact that they tend to be able to identify their strengths and weaknesses. Students at this age also evidence a growing understanding of the world-of-work. Often this progress is the result of students participating in school activities, hobbies, and/or part-time work. Boys and girls at age 13 tend to be equally knowledgeable about highly visible occupations and can link at least one school subject to a job. Most students at this age indicate that they have at least started the process of thinking about a future job. Interestingly, their choices for future jobs tend to be occupations requiring college degrees or lengthy training periods beyond high school, rather than jobs now held by the majority of the workforce (i.e., those not requiring a college degree). Of most concern in the data provided by the National Assessment of Educational Progress's Project on Career and Occupational Development is the fact that racial minority students and students living in economic poverty tend to lag behind other students in their career development. Thus, the effectiveness of current career development interventions provided to middle/junior high school students is variable.

This variability points to the importance of being clear about the societal expectations placed on students in middle/junior high school. As these students transition between Super's growth and exploration stages, they encounter the task of crystallizing occupational preferences. They are expected by teachers, counselors, and designers of the school curriculum to develop a realistic self-concept and to acquire additional information about more opportunities (Super, 1984). Specifically, middle/junior high school students are required to learn about themselves and the world-of-work and then translate this learning into an educational plan for the remainder of their secondary school education. Super, Savickas, and Super (1996) refer to the crystallization process by noting that "when habits of industriousness, achievement, and foresight coalesce, individuals turn to daydreaming about possible selves they may construct. Eventually, these occupational daydreams crystallize into a publicly recognized vocational identity with corresponding preferences for a group of occupations at a particular ability level" (p. 132). Thus, to establish an appropriate course of action for high school and beyond, career development interventions during middle/junior high school must be directed toward helping students cope successfully with the tasks of crystallizing and specifying occupational preferences (Super et al., 1996).

The ASCA National Standards (2003) also provide direction for professional school counselors as they construct career development interventions for middle school students. Specifically, the standards indicate that middle school students should: "(a) acquire the skills to investigate the world-of-work in relation to knowledge of self and to make informal career decisions, (b) employ strategies to achieve future success and satisfaction, and (c) understand the relationship between personal qualities, education and training, and the world-of-work" (p. 17).

During his meetings with his counselor, Antonio discussed how working in the community service group helped him feel less lonely and better about himself in general. Antonio enjoyed planning and organizing the group's service activities. He had quickly become a leader in this group and enjoyed this role as well. Antonio confided to his counselor that he had often dreamed about being a CEO for a company that does something to help others. He stated that "being in charge" and "helping others" were two things that were fun and important to him. Antonio's counselor carefully listened to Antonio's important self-referent statements. The counselor helped underscore for Antonio how this self-knowledge could be used to direct Antonio's further exploration of career options. Specifically, Antonio's counselor suggested that he use the computer information delivery system available at the school to find out which occupations would provide him with opportunities to "be in charge" and "help others." After generating a list from the computer, Antonio met with his counselor to discuss the options on the list and determine where he could get more information about the options that interested him the most.

Career Development Goals for Middle/ Junior High School Students

Based on the career development literature and the National Career Development Guidelines, the following career development goals can be identified for middle/junior high school students:

1. Enhance self-understanding
   a. Increase awareness related to the influence of a positive self-concept on career-related behavior
   b. Develop more advanced interpersonal skills
2. Learn how to engage effectively in educational and occupational exploration
   a. Understand the transition from educational achievement to career opportunities
   b. Understand the relationship between work and learning
   c. Develop the skills to locate, understand, and use career information
   d. Develop job search skills
   e. Understand how work relates to the needs and functions of the economy and society
3. Career Planning
   a. Develop the skills to make effective decisions
   b. Understand the interrelationship of life roles
   c. Develop knowledge of different occupations and changing male/female roles
   d. Understand the process of career planning

A variety of career development interventions can be constructed systematically by using the ASCA Standards and National Career Development Guidelines. Prior to discussing possible interventions, however, it is useful to examine the career planning considerations offered by Herr, Cramer, and Niles (2004):

1. Because middle school is a transitional experience from the structured and general education of the elementary school to the less structured but more specialized education of the secondary school, students must be provided with a broad opportunity to explore their personal characteristics as well as those of the educational options from which they must choose. Opportunities to relate curricular options to the possible and subsequent educational and occupational outcomes seem highly desirable.

2. Because wide ranges in career maturity, interests, values, and abilities characterize middle school students, a variety of methods are needed to accommodate the range of individual differences. Students whose parents have not completed high school frequently have not had the developmental experience or occupational knowledge enjoyed by students from homes in which the parents are well educated.

3. Although students in middle school are capable of verbal and abstract behavior, exploration will be enhanced if they are given concrete, hands-on, direct experiences as well.

4. Fundamental to the rapid changes that students experience in middle school is a search for personal identity. Therefore, career guidance programs must encourage students to explore feelings, needs, and uncertainties as a base for evaluating educational and vocational options. Values clarification and other similar processes are helpful in this regard (p. 392).

In addition to these important considerations, professional school counselors need to remain cognizant of the ways in which gender and racial stereotyping related to occupational options can artificially constrict the range of options students are considering. Clearly, counselors must deliver career development interventions that aggressively attack these discriminatory influences.

Career Development Interventions in Middle/ Junior High Schools

Thematic consideration of middle/junior high school–level career development competencies reveals the importance of students acquiring the necessary knowledge, skills, and understanding to advance in their career development. Interventions that combine psychoeducational activities and experiential tasks are useful in helping students cope with the career development tasks confronting them. Examples of the former include teaching students about the relationship between education and work (e.g., by interviewing workers of their choice and asking the workers how academic subjects connect their work tasks); the importance and interaction of life roles (e.g., by asking students to identify how they spend their time in the course of a typical week and then to identify the values they express in how they spend their time). It is also important to help students understand issues related to equity and access in career choice (e.g., by sponsoring a career fair comprised of nontraditional workers representing a wide range of occupations, such as female carpenters, African American female engineers, etc.). Finally, helping students develop awareness regarding the career development tasks they will confront now and in the future (e.g., by having students construct their ideal future life and then discuss how prepared they feel for taking on those future tasks, what they can do between now and then to become better prepared for them, etc.); and the ways in which they can access and evaluate occupational information (e.g., by educating students about ways to identify bias in occupational information) are central to effective educational and career planning in secondary school. These interventions can easily occur in group and/ or classroom guidance activities. The ASCA National Model (ASCA, 2003) provides an excellent guide for identifying topics to incorporate in psychoeducational activities with students. Examples of experiential tasks include job shadowing; attending career fairs; conducting occupational information interviews; and engaging in activities to clarify interests, values, and skills. Both psychoeducational and experiential activities help students acquire the knowledge, skills, and understanding needed to develop the attitudes and skills of readiness for educational and career decision making (Super, 1990).

With the help of his counselor, Antonio decided that it would be helpful to him to speak with a local hospital administrator, the executive director of a local social service agency, and the minister of his church. The purpose of the meetings was to learn more about each of these occupations (e.g., what each person liked and did not like about his or her occupation, training required for each of the occupations, and the academic subjects that were more important for doing the work well). After conducting these occupational information interviews, Antonio expressed an interest in job shadowing with the hospital administrator. He also stated that after he finished high school, it would be important for him to attend college.

It is also important at this developmental level that career interventions continue to stimulate curiosity in students. Students who are curious about their emerging self-concepts (e.g., their avocational and vocational interests, skills, and values) are more likely to engage in exploratory behavior to acquire the information they need for self-concept clarification (Super, 1981). Helping students identify and connect with role models can also facilitate a sense of internal control and future time perspective, which can, in turn, lead to planful behaviors and the development of effective problem-solving skills (Super, 1990). Stott and Jackson (2005) found that a service learning approach with middle school students was very useful in helping them make stronger connections between academics and career possibilities.

To help guide students in their exploration, counselors can administer career assessments. In selecting career assessments, it is important that the reading level, language, and normative samples are appropriate for the school population with which the assessments will be used. Interest inventory results can foster more systematic thinking about the activities in which students enjoy participating. Aptitude tests can also help students acquire accurate estimates of their abilities. Interest and aptitude assessments are often administered to students during the middle/junior high school grades. The combination of interest inventory results and aptitude test results provides a useful foundation for the exploration process. Students will find it useful to explore occupational areas for which they have high interest and high aptitude. When the results of an interest inventory suggest that a student has no area of above-average or high interest, it may be that he or she needs exposure to activities across several interest areas to determine what will interest the student. Thus, a key to making assessments (especially interest inventories) useful is that students must have the experiential base to draw upon to respond to assessment items. Students with limited exposure to a variety of activities will be forced to guess at appropriate responses to questions requiring them to identify their likes and dislikes. (One counselor related that he attempted to administer an interest inventory to his daughter when she was in sixth grade. Her reading level at that time far exceeded the reading level of the inventory, but her experiential base was such that she did not understand many of the items presented to her on the inventory. It very quickly became evident that the inventory results would not serve to foster her career development!) When school systems have a systematic career development intervention program in place for all grades, it is safer to assume that middle/junior high school students have been exposed to activities that have fostered their self- and career exploration. When no such programs exist, counselors must be especially cognizant of the possibility that many students will need more remedial career development interventions prior to being administered career assessments.

Providing middle school students with exposure to work facilitates the acquisition of knowledge, skills, and awareness related to the career development domains within the National Career Development Guidelines. These activities also connect to Standards C:A1 (Develop Career Awareness) and C:B1 (Acquire Career Information) of the ASCA's National Standards. Teaching students how families of occupations can be clustered according to factors such as skill requirements, interests, and/or training helps students organize the world-of-work and connect their characteristics to occupational options (ASCA's Develop Career Awareness and Identify Career Goals standards). For example, Holland's classification system uses the six personality types, described in Chapter 2, to group occupations. *Realistic* occupations include skilled trades and technical occupations. *Investigative* occupations include scientific and technical occupations. *Artistic* occupations include creative occupations in the expressive arts. *Social* occupations include the helping professions. *Enterprising* occupations involve managerial and sales occupations. Last, *conventional* occupations include office and clerical occupations. Occupations are classified according to the degree to which the activities of the occupation draw upon the Holland types. The three most dominant types reflected in the occupation are used to classify each occupation.

Antonio was administered The Self-Directed Search and obtained the Holland code of enterprising, social, and artistic. He met with other students and the counselor to discuss the inventory results. They talked about their Holland codes and whether they thought the codes were accurate. With the counselor's assistance, they also brainstormed a list of occupations for each Holland type. Antonio decided that it made sense for him to continue to explore the occupations of hospital administrator and social service director.

The U.S. Office of Education (USOE) clusters occupations according to whether they involve producing goods or providing services. The two broad categories are then subdivided into 16 occupational clusters as follows:

1. Agriculture, Food, and Natural Resources
2. Architecture and Construction
3. Arts, A/V Technology, and Communications
4. Business Management and Administration
5. Education and Training
6. Finance
7. Government and Public Administration
8. Health Science
9. Hospitality and Tourism
10. Human Services
11. Information Technology
12. Law, Public Safety, Corrections, and Security
13. Manufacturing
14. Marketing
15. Science, Technology, Engineering, and Mathematics
16. Transportation, Distribution, and Logistics

The National Career Clusters Framework groups occupations based on similar skill sets, interests, abilities, and activities. The clusters contain subgroupings called Career Pathways. The pathways identify the knowledge and skills required for a particular career field. The pathways link academics with career fields. Career pathways can help students understand the vital connection between the courses they take in high school and particular career fields that interest them. Students can explore career clusters based on their interests and then examine a variety of postsecondary options—higher education, training, or apprenticeship—that will help them succeed in those career fields.

Clustering systems such as the career clusters and Holland's system can be used to guide career exploration by using the types to organize career information resources, career fairs, curricula experiences (e.g., students can be assigned the task of writing an essay about occupations that fall within their dominant Holland type), job-shadowing experiences, participation in extracurricular activities, avocational pursuits, college exploration, and part-time employment experiences. Specific educational plans can be developed for specific career pathways (e.g., careerclusters.org/resources/pos_ks/POS/AG-1-POS.pdf).

To develop effective interpersonal skills related to the work environment (ASCA's Develop Employment Readiness competency, C:A2), students can be provided with difficult interpersonal interactions (e.g., a coworker who interacts angrily for no apparent reason, an angry boss who places unreasonable demands on workers); and students can brainstorm ways of coping with the situation. Students can then role play solutions to handling difficult interpersonal interactions at work.

To increase students' thinking about the interrelationship of life roles (ASCA's Acquire Knowledge to Achieve Career Goals competency, C:C1, and NCDG's Personal Social Development domain), counselors can use a group guidance format to help middle/junior high school students examine their current life-role salience by responding to such questions as: How do you spend your time during a typical week? How important are the different roles of life to you? What do you like about participating in each of the life roles? What life roles do you think will be important to you in the future? What do you hope to accomplish in each of the life roles that will be important to you in the future? What life roles do members of your family play? What do your family members expect you to accomplish in each of the life roles?

Obviously, patterns of life-role salience are significantly influenced by immediate (e.g., family, cultural heritage, level of acculturation) and distal (e.g., economics, environmental opportunities for life-role participation) contextual factors (Blustein, 1994). Contextual factors, therefore, contribute to patterns of life-role salience. However, many middle/junior high school students lack an awareness of the ways in which contextual factors (such as the dominant culture and the student's culture of origin) interact with identity development to shape life-role salience (Blustein). Group discussions pertaining to these topics can help middle/junior high school students develop their sense of which life roles are important to them now, which life roles will be important to them in the future, and how life roles interact to influence life satisfaction.

An effective tool for helping middle/junior high school students engage in purposeful planning, exploring, information gathering, decision making, and reality testing related to two prominent life roles (i.e., student and worker) is an educational and career planning portfolio. Educational and career planning portfolios are typically used to help students chart their academic and career decision making. This charting process can begin in middle/junior high school and continue until the student leaves high school. By making at least annual entries into the portfolio, the student and counselor can track the student's career development progress. They can also make systematic educational and career plans that build upon the growing base of self- and occupational knowledge the student is developing. In essence, the portfolio provides a vehicle for the student and counselor to discuss what the student has done and what the student will do next to advance his or her career development. There are several very useful portfolios available (e.g., "Get a Life" developed by the American School Counselor Association), and portfolios are fairly easy to develop locally (see the portfolio developed by Niles for the Virginia Department of Education in Appendix B).

By completing the educational and career planning portfolio on a regular basis, students, their parents, and school counselors can trace students' academic, cocurricular, extracurricular, and career exploration activities. When portfolios are completed at least annually, they provide the focus for goal identification and further intentional educational and career planning. We encourage you to examine the portfolio in Appendix B as well as the portfolio available through your access to Kuder's Navigator career planning system for middle and high school students. Using the most recently completed portfolio, the student, his/her counselor, and his/her parents can review past career goals and determine whether they continue to make sense, and whether there are ways they may need to be revised based on new experiences the student has had. The latter, in particular, can be used to set goals for the forthcoming year. Using a career and educational planning portfolio in this way helps the student learn how to make career decisions systematically.

To help students focus on the interrelationship of life roles and to engage in planning related to their salient life roles, the educational and career planning portfolio can be expanded to a *life-role portfolio* by addressing students' readiness for life roles beyond those of student and worker. Students can be encouraged to plan, explore, and gather information for each of the major roles of life. For example, students who anticipate being parents in the future can plan for this role by considering how parenting interacts with other roles. Students can explore different styles of parenting by interviewing parents about their parenting practices and philosophies. Students can also gather information about the skills required for effective parenting (perhaps by taking a class). Through these activities they can learn the things that are important to consider in making decisions about parenting. Finally, students can reality-test their interest through participating in child-care activities. Thus, the life-role portfolio serves as a stimulus for counselor and student meetings focused on planning, exploring, information gathering, decision making, and reality testing vis-à-vis the major life roles. When the portfolio is used over successive years, it also provides developmental documentation of activities and decisions related to major life roles.

This expanded use of the planning portfolio is an example of a counseling activity that is intended to help students cope with the developmental task of identity formation within the context of developing life-role readiness. It also provides additional opportunities for discussing contextual influences on life-role salience. Regardless of the life role, it is important that counselors are sensitive to cultural diversity in life-role salience and life-role behaviors among their students.

HIGH SCHOOL

Although the developmental shifts and contextual changes between middle and high school are not as dramatic as those between elementary and middle school, the educational stakes rise relative to their long-term implications for each student's future academic and career success. As students rise through middle school and into high school, so too, does the intensity of the academic expectations they encounter. Likewise, the need for high school students to engage systematically in educational and career planning also increases during this educational period. "Students often choose academic tracks that impact not only the next four years of high school, but also their future post-secondary and work options" (Akos, 2004, p. 883). As with all developmental transitions, the transition to high school offers opportunities for actively engaging students in career development interventions that can strengthen their academic motivation, bolster their self-esteem, and help them to make connections between their school experiences and their future academic and career opportunities.

More specifically, as students transition to high school, they focus more directly on the tasks of identifying occupational preferences and clarifying career/lifestyle choices (these tasks build upon all of the ASCA competencies within the Career Development domain as well as all of the tasks within the National Career Development Guidelines). According to Super (1957), the tasks of crystallizing, specifying, and implementing tentative career choices occur during early (ages 12 to 15), middle (ages 16 to 18), and late (ages 18 to 24) adolescence. Super et al. (1996) described the process of coping with these career development tasks of crystallizing and specifying as follows:

> When habits of industriousness, achievement, and foresight coalesce, individuals turn to daydreaming about possible selves they may construct. Eventually, these occupational daydreams crystallize into a publicly recognized vocational identity with corresponding preferences for a group of occupations at a particular ability level. Through broad exploration of the occupations in this group, individuals eventually complete the task of specifying an occupational choice by translating the privately experienced occupational self-concept into educational/vocational choices. (p. 132)

Antonio acquired other experiences through volunteering in the local hospital and a local social service agency. These experiences helped him to learn more about himself and the world-of-work. The more he learned, the more he liked the idea of becoming a hospital administrator. He decided that this would be his tentative career goal. He used this information to guide his exploration of postsecondary educational opportunities.

When adolescents complete the relevant training/preparatory experiences, they then implement their occupational choices by acquiring positions in their specified occupations. Implementation is followed by a period of adjustment to the occupational requirements and workplace expectations of the implemented choice

(Tiedeman, 1961). Thus, the key elements to a successful school-to-work and school-to-school transition involve being able to implement and adjust to career choice.

In this regard, it is important to note that a substantial portion of secondary school students in the United States enter work immediately upon leaving high school or prior to completing a college degree (Marshall & Tucker, 1992). Although 84% of high school seniors plan to get a two- or four-year college degree, only 41% of high school graduates age 30 to 34 actually have college degrees (Rosenbaum & Person, 2003). Feller (2003) reports that over 70% of high school seniors expect to hold professional jobs (i.e., those requiring a college degree). Many school counselors, Feller notes, hesitate to confront this "silent dream" of obtaining a college degree.

This trend toward "college for all" aspirations emerged from three revolutionary changes (Rosenbaum & Person, 2003, p. 252). First, the labor market dramatically increased its skill demands and augmented the earnings advantages for college graduates. Second, college enrollment became dramatically more accessible in recent decades. Third, community colleges instituted an open admissions policy. Although there has been a popular concern about school counselors being too restrictive by encouraging some students not to attend college, now the opposite situation may be true. The point here is that school counselors need to do a better job of informing students, parents, and school personnel that jobs leading to rewarding careers exist in a wide variety of fields, including technical specialties, financial services, construction, and trades. Unfortunately, too little is known about jobs in these areas. Moreover, because 31% of college entrants (52% of whom are students with high school grades of C or lower) actually earn no college credits (Rosenbaum, 2001), these students are in reality work-bound and they do not benefit from the "college for all" approach. Thus, we believe that professional school counselors should help students make choices from a full range of options, including those occupations not requiring a college degree. Rosenbaum and Person recommend that professional school counselors also help others become aware of the following new rules regarding the labor market and college:

- All students can attend college, but low-achieving students should be cautioned about the need to take remedial courses once they enter college.
- Even if high school students have college plans, they must prepare for work.
- College plans require substantial effort and good academic planning in middle/high school.
- Many good jobs do not require a college degree.
- High school students improve their chances for obtaining good jobs by having better academic achievement, taking vocational courses, getting job-placement assistance from teachers, and developing "soft skills" such as interpersonal competence and good work habits.

These points highlight the importance of developing workforce readiness to cope successfully with the school-to-work transition. The definition of *workforce readiness* changes with the times. Until recently this term may have focused solely on helping adolescents acquire training for a specific job, but now employers are more concerned with "finding youth who can read and write, have a good attitude, are motivated, are dependable, follow directions, and can be good team members"

(Krumboltz & Worthington, 1999, p. 316). Academic skills, interpersonal skills, and engaging in lifelong learning have emerged as important skills for youth to acquire if they are to be successful workers. In this regard, Hansen (1999) argues for expanding school-to-work career development interventions to include student development in addition to the more traditional emphasis on workforce development. Hansen points to curricula such as the Missouri Life Career Development System, the Minnesota Career Development Curriculum, and a model development by the Florida Department of Education titled "A Framework for Developing Comprehensive Guidance and Counseling Programs for a School-to-Work System" as excellent examples of comprehensive career development interventions to help youth prepare for the transition from secondary school to work.

Baker and Gerler (2008) emphasizes the importance of school counselors providing "transition enhancement" assistance to secondary school students as they progress toward further education, training, or employment. Because such transitions are a regular part of high school students' development, Baker recommends that counselors view transitions as a process rather than as events or a sequence of events. The basic needs of students coping with the transition process can be classified into the categories of support, awareness, and skills.

Students need emotional support to lessen the anticipatory anxiety they may experience as they consider the transitions they will encounter. Moving from the familiar to the unknown creates anxiety in all people. However, it is reasonable to expect this anxiety to be fairly high among adolescents who have lived their lives primarily in the arenas of home and school. Postsecondary work, training, and education present new challenges and experiences. Although some of these challenges may seem somewhat intimidating, counselors can remind students that the competencies they have developed thus far in their lives will also be helpful to them as they negotiate the postsecondary transition experience. Reassuring students that it is "normal" to feel a bit anxious during a transition also provides emotional support to students as they move forward in their career development plans. In many respects, school counselors are the human development specialists in the schools. Educating stakeholders about the developmental process students will experience as they move through school helps students, teachers, administrators, and parents develop the awareness to think proactively about the tasks students will encounter. Thus, infusing the academic and school counseling curricula with developmental concepts helps students acquire the awareness that fosters a planful approach to coping with career development tasks.

When conceptualized as a process, the skills required for coping with the school-to-work and school-to-school transition are linked to the elementary and middle school career development competencies discussed previously. That is, transition skills build upon the self-awareness, occupational awareness, and decision-making skills students have developed throughout their educational experience. Transition skills also build upon the basic educational competencies related to reading, writing, and arithmetic (Baker, 2000). For example, composing a resume and cover letter requires writing skills. Performing effectively in a job or college interview requires skills in oral communication and interpersonal communication. Acquiring information about jobs, colleges, and training programs requires research, technology, and reading skills. Transition skills can also be expanded to include those related to stress and anxiety management. The ASCA (1985) takes the position that counselors in the schools must assume the primary (but not the sole) responsibility for fostering these skills in students: "The school counselor's role covers many areas within the school setting and career guidance is one of the most important contributions to a student's lifelong development" (p. 165). Thus, proactively bolstering students' readiness to cope with the career development tasks they are likely to encounter is a primary component of the school counselor's role. Likewise, counselors must be competent in strategies to help students who encounter difficulty in coping with career development tasks.

Much of Super's research focused on understanding how adolescents can develop their readiness to cope effectively with the various career development tasks confronting them. The term initially used by Super (1955) to describe career readiness in adolescence was *career maturity*. Because the career development tasks confronting adolescents emerge from expectations inherent in academic curricula and society (e.g., family, teachers), the career development process during this life stage is more homogeneous than in adulthood. The school system expects students to make career decisions at specific points in the curriculum (e.g., eighth graders choosing an academic program that they will study in high school). Because the timing of these career development tasks can be predicted, career development practitioners can provide a systematic set of interventions to foster adolescent career development. Super et al. (1996) reinforced this point in stating that adolescent career development can be guided "partly by facilitating the maturing of abilities, interests, and coping resources and partly by aiding in reality testing and in the development of self-concepts" (p. 125).

Other researchers such as Marcia (1966) have also identified important variables for adolescent career development. Specifically, Marcia focuses on two variables—crisis/exploration and commitment—as central to the career development process during adolescence. Crisis/exploration refers to the process of sorting through identity issues; questioning parentally defined goals, values, and beliefs; and identifying personally appropriate alternatives regarding career options, goals, values, and beliefs. Commitment refers to the extent that the individual is personally involved in, and expresses allegiance to, self-chosen aspirations, goals, values, beliefs, and career options (Muuss, 1998). The degree to which adolescents resolve the tasks associated with crisis/exploration and commitment provides the conceptual structure for Marcia's taxonomy of adolescent identity (Marcia, 1980). This taxonomy comprises four identity statuses: identity diffused (or identity confused), foreclosed, moratorium, and identity achieved.

1. The *identity-diffused* person has yet to experience an identity crisis or exploration and has not made any personal commitment to an occupation, much less to a set of goals, values, and beliefs.
2. The *foreclosed* person has yet to experience an identity crisis or exploration but has committed to an occupation and to a set of goals, values, and beliefs (usually due to indoctrination or social pressure by parents and/or significant others). This type of foreclosure is premature because it has occurred without exploring

and struggling with the basic existential questions related to identifying one's values, beliefs, goals, and so on.

3. The *moratorium* person is engaged in an active struggle to clarify personally meaningful values, goals, and beliefs. Committing to a particular set of values, goals, and beliefs has been placed "on hold" until the process of identity clarification is more complete.

4. The *identity-achieved* person has sorted through the process of identity clarification and resolved these issues in a personally meaningful way. Moreover, as a result of exploring and resolving identity issues, the identity-achieved person commits to an occupation and a personal value system.

Rather than being a singular process of exploring and committing to a set of values, goals, and beliefs, identity formation occurs across several domains, such as occupation, religion, politics, and sexuality. In many respects, these domains parallel Super's (1980) notion of life-role self-concepts (e.g., worker, leisurite, student, and homemaker) and reinforce Hansen's (1999) call for holistic career development interventions in the schools. Additionally, the individual's identity status within each domain is not static but rather an ongoing process involving back-and-forth movement across stages (Muuss, 1996). Marcia (1980) notes that although any of the identity statuses can become terminal, the foreclosed person experiences the greatest risk of closed development. Thus, career development interventions for preadolescents and adolescents (who by definition enter into these life stages with a relatively diffused identity) should be carefully designed to foster exploration and identity development related to the career domain. For example, Kolodinsky et al. (2006) described the ways in which a career fair designed to expose students to nontraditional workers resulted in both greater exploration and a broader understanding of potential occupational options for student participants. Specifically, these researchers designed a one-day fair with 11 females employed in nontraditional occupations such as border patrol officer, emergency medical technician, computer repair technician, cable technician, firefighter, military officer, and water treatment technician, and 4 males employed as hair stylist, nurse, respiratory therapist, and receptionist, respectively. Each discussed and demonstrated his or her experiences with nontraditional careers. After listening to and interacting with the presenters, students demonstrated increased occupational self-efficacy and relinquished stereotypical beliefs about what is "women's work" and what is "men's work." They also demonstrated increased interest in specific occupations represented by the workers. Given survey results such as those obtained by Gibbons et al. (2006) indicating that ninth graders expressed a desire for additional career information as it relates to developing their career and educational plans, the provision of interventions such as a career fair comprised of nontraditional workers can be an important intervention that offers students accurate information about potential career options.

Career Development Goals for High School Students

The extensive body of literature related to adolescent career development helps counselors identify appropriate career development goals and interventions for high school students. The specific career development competencies identified as being appropriate for high school students are:

1. Develop more advanced self-knowledge
   a. Develop skills to interact positively with others
   b. Understanding the implications of continued growth and development for career planning
2. Develop skills for engaging in educational and occupational exploration
   a. Understand the relationship between educational achievement and career planning
   b. Understand the need for positive attitudes toward work and learning
   c. Develop the skills to locate, evaluate, and interpret career information
   d. Develop more sophisticated job-search skills
   e. Understand how societal needs and functions influence the nature and structure of work
3. Strengthen the skills to make decisions
   a. Understand the interrelationship of life roles
   b. Understand the continuous changes in male/female roles
   c. Develop skills in career planning

In constructing interventions to foster the development of these competencies, Herr, Cramer, and Niles (2004) recommend attending to several potential issues confronting high school students. For example, it is essential that students construct and know how to implement a career plan. School counselors must also address the fact that students differ in their readiness to address career and educational planning tasks. Thus, career interventions need to be flexible enough to account for these student differences in readiness for career decision-making. Finally, students must develop awareness related to post-secondary options, specifically the pro's and con's of each option under consideration (e.g., joining the military, enrolling in community college, attending a four-year university).

Career Development Interventions in High Schools

The emphasis on knowledge, skills, and understanding that emerged in the middle/junior high school level competencies is continued in the high school competencies. The high school competencies, however, challenge students to become more focused on making career plans by translating their self- and career information into career goals. Savickas (1999) proposed career development interventions that foster the sort of self-knowledge, educational and occupational exploration, and career planning described in the high school competencies. Specifically, these interventions focus on (a) orienting students' comprehension of careers, (b) developing students' competence at planning and exploring, (c) coaching students to develop effective career management techniques, and (d) guiding students in behavioral rehearsals to become prepared for coping with job problems (pp. 331–333). Interventions that focus on these areas address the ASCA standards in the Career Development domain.

To orient ninth-grade students to the planning tasks they will encounter as they move through high school, Savickas (1999) recommends using a group guidance format to discuss items on career development inventories, such as the Career Maturity Inventory (Crites, 1978) or the Adult Career Concerns Inventory (Super et al., 1988). Using inventory items to orient students to the tasks they need to address to manage their career development effectively helps provide a stimulus for planning and exploring behaviors (Savickas, 1990). For example, the Adult Career Concerns Inventory (ACCI) (Super et al., 1988) measures developmental task concern for the career stages of Exploration, Establishment, Maintenance, and Disengagement. Reviewing the career stages and tasks within the ACCI teaches high school students about the general process of career development. Using ACCI items, adolescents can identify those career development tasks they are likely to encounter in the near future. Strategies for coping with current and near-future career development tasks can be identified. In this way, high school students' understanding of time perspective or "planfulness" can be enhanced (Savickas, Stilling, & Schwartz, 1984). These activities connect with Standards A, B, and C in the Career Development domain of the National Standards for School Counseling.

Antonio's counselor used a group guidance format to discuss students' scores on Holland's Self-Directed Search. They brainstormed occupational options for each type and then discussed what sort of education would be required to enter each occupation. The group members also discussed which school subjects they thought would be most important for each occupation.

Sharing this information with parents and guardians helps foster parental awareness of the career development tasks confronting their children. Keller and Whiston (2008) found a significant relationship between parental behaviors and middle school students' career decision-making self-efficacy. To foster parental awareness of, and involvement in, the career development process, evening informational sessions and newsletters provide opportunities to orient parents and guardians to the career development tasks they can expect their children to encounter. These activities also provide opportunities to advise parents as to how they can help their children manage these career development tasks more effectively (Turner & Lapan, 2002).

Antonio's counselor sent materials home that described the Holland types and the Self-Directed Search. The counselor invited parents to an evening meeting in which they were given an informal assessment of their Holland types. In a fashion similar to what the counselor had done with the students, parents were then encouraged to brainstorm occupations for each type, identify educational requirements for each occupation, and then list the academic subjects they thought were most important for each occupation. After this activity, the counselor identified ways in which the parents could help their children use the information they had acquired in their career planning.

To help increase self-knowledge and to encourage educational and occupational exploration (ASCA Standards A and C in the Career Development domain), counselors can facilitate student participation in informational interviews. To prepare for these experiences, counselors and teachers guide students in composing interview questions that relate to the high school–level career development competencies. For example, questions pertaining to the importance of interpersonal communication, positive work attitudes, and the relationship between educational achievement and career planning can be identified.

Results from interest and abilities measures administered at the end of middle school or at the beginning of high school provide direction as to which occupational environments offer the best potential for fruitful exploration. As noted previously, the range of career assessment possibilities that can be used systematically with youth is substantial. To measure interests, counselors can use instruments that provide information related to students' Holland types, such as the Self-Directed Search (Holland, 1985) and the Career Assessment Inventory (Johansson, 1986). Ability measures include the Differential Aptitude Test (Bennett, Seashore, & Wesman, 1992), the Ability Explorer (Harrington, 1996), and assessments of functional skills from school transcripts or educational and career planning portfolios. Areas of high interest and ability can be matched to occupational clusters and students can identify specific occupations for in-depth exploration (C:B2 in the National Standards).

Although interest and ability assessment results provide important data pertaining to career choice content (i.e., relating students' abilities and interests to occupational options), these data fail to address whether students have developed readiness for career decision making (Super, 1983). Approaches to career assessment must attend to both content and process variables in order to adequately address the needs of youth (Savickas, 1993). Specifically, interests and abilities can be considered as career choice content data that must be viewed in light of career choice process data such as readiness for career decision making, life-role salience, and values—which can be labeled as moderator variables (Super et al., 1992). To be ready to effectively choose, and adapt to, an occupation, it is important for high school students to "see themselves as coping with certain developmental tasks, at a stage in life at which they are expected, and may expect themselves to make certain decisions and acquire certain competencies" (Super, 1983, p. 559). Students who have not successfully accomplished the career development tasks presented to them at previous educational levels will need remedial interventions (e.g., additional opportunities for self-concept clarification, training in acquiring occupational information) prior to focusing on career decision making.

From this perspective, addressing career choice readiness (Super, 1990) becomes a necessary precursor to the effective use of ability- and interest-assessment data. According to Super, career choice readiness involves five dimensions: (a) having a planful attitude toward coping with career stages and tasks, (b) gathering information about educational and occupational opportunities, (c) exploring the world-of-work, (d) knowing how to make good career decisions, and (e) being able to make realistic judgments about potential occupations (p. 231). These dimensions (which relate to Standards A–C in the National Standards) are important because, if an adolescent knows little about the world-of-work, his or her interest inventories that use occupational titles or activities may produce misleading scores and the student may make poor choices (Super et al., 1996). Likewise, when adolescents do not engage in appropriate career planning, they often encounter career tasks for which they are not prepared (Herr, Cramer, & Niles, 2004). Thus, assessing high school students' resources for choosing, and adapting to, an occupation requires conducting appraisals of career choice content (e.g., abilities, interests, values) and process (e.g., life-role salience, career choice readiness) variables. When a student is lacking in any of the five dimensions that make up career choice readiness, then the counselor should focus on interventions to help the student progress in that particular domain prior to focusing on career choice content.

It is important to note that traditional assessment approaches focusing only on career choice content variables assume that all individuals place a high value on work, and that all individuals view work as the prime means of values realization. It can be argued that this is a Western, middle class, male view of career development and, thus, is a culturally encapsulated view of life-role salience. Different patterns of life-role salience exist and they must be considered in helping high school students clarify and articulate their career goals (Niles & Goodnough, 1996). For example, when salience for the work role is high, youths view work as providing meaningful opportunities for self-expression. In such cases, high school students are often motivated to develop the career maturity necessary (e.g., to be planful, to explore opportunities, to gather information) for making good career decisions. When work-role salience is low, however, adolescents often lack motivation and career maturity. In the latter instances, counselors need to begin the career development intervention process by arousing the individual's sense of importance for the worker role (Super, 1990). Disputing irrational beliefs, exposing young people to effective role models, and providing mentors are examples of activities that foster career arousal (Krumboltz & Worthington, 1999).

To help young people further clarify their life-role self-concepts, counselors can encourage high school students to revisit life-role salience questions posed during the middle/junior high school years (e.g., How do I spend my time during the course of a typical week? What changes would I like to make in how I spend my time? How important is each life role to me? How important is each life role to my family? What do I like about participating in each life role? What do I hope to accomplish in each life role? What does my family expect me to accomplish in each life role? What life roles do I think will be important to me in the future? What must I do to become more prepared for the life roles that will be important to me in the future?). Discussing these questions helps high school students clarify and articulate their life-role self-concepts. Specifically, by discussing these questions during the first years of high school, adolescents can become clearer as to the values they seek to express in each life role. This information is vital not only for guiding high school students in the selection and pursuit of appropriate educational and occupational options, but also in developing appropriate expectations for values satisfaction within the respective life roles.

These discussion questions also provide opportunities for exploring the individual's level of acculturation, cultural identity, and worldview. For example, high school students can discuss family expectations and other cultural factors influencing their life-role participation. Finally, discussing these questions helps counselors become aware of potential barriers, as well as potential sources of support, for students as they move closer to negotiating the school-to-work or school-to-school transition. These discussions also foster the acquisition of the high school–level career development competencies related to understanding the interrelationship of life roles and understanding the changing nature of male/female roles. This information also helps high school students identify those roles in which they spend most of their time, those to which they are emotionally committed, and those that they expect to be important to them in the future. By clarifying information concerning life-role salience (and the cultural factors influencing role salience), high school students establish the foundation for making accurate self-evaluations and for developing career choice readiness.

An important task in acquiring adequate self-knowledge for effective educational and occupational exploration is clarifying values. Clarifying values is important because values are indications of the qualities people desire and seek in "the activities in which they engage, in the situations in which they live, and in the objects which they make or acquire" (Super, 1970, p. 4). Because values reflect the individual's goals, they provide a sense of purpose and direction in the career planning process. However, though many agree that values clarification is critical to choosing an occupation, relatively few put forth the effort to examine their values in a systematic way (Harrington, 1996). Values card sorts (e.g., Career Values Card Sort Kit, Nonsexist Vocational Card Sort) and instruments such as the Career Orientation Placement and Evaluation Survey (COPES) are instruments that are useful in values clarification. Interest inventory results can also be used to identify work-related activities that provide opportunities for values expression.

Regarding parental involvement in the career intervention process, Amundson and Penner (1998) recommend that professional school counselors consider involving parents/guardians directly in the career counseling experience. To this end, Amundson and Penner devised an innovative, parent-involved career exploration process (PICE) that includes five steps. In step one (Introduction), two students and at least one parent, or guardian, for each student are invited to participate in an innovative career exploration activity. The participants' roles are explained (it is the student's career counseling session and parents are invited as observers) and the participants are introduced. The next step is labeled as the Pattern Identification Exercise (PIE) activity and requires the students to each identify a leisure activity and specify an instance when their participation in the activity went very well and an instance when it was less than positive. The counselor works with each student to elaborate regarding the people involved in both instances and the student's feelings, thoughts, challenges, successes, and motivation. The purpose of this discussion is to elucidate each student's strengths and weaknesses. Once a full description is outlined, each student is asked to consider the types of patterns suggested in the information presented. Specifically, students are asked to consider the various goals, values, aptitudes, personality traits, and interests revealed in the information. The final step in the PIE activity links the identified patterns to the career choices the student is facing. Then, the counselor invites input from the students' parents. Parents can confirm what has been discussed and add their perspectives. The next step in PICE is to examine the academic experience. Specifically, students discuss what courses they are taking, how they are performing in each of their courses, and what their feelings are about each of the courses. As before, parents are then asked to provide their perspective of the information the student has shared. Next, students discuss the options under consideration in light of the current labor market situation (e.g., current labor market trends, the need for flexibility, information interviewing, anxiety about the future, admissions to postsecondary opportunities, etc.). Parents are also asked to contribute to this discussion and offer their perspectives about labor market trends and strategies for coping with the current nature of work. The final step in

PICE involves action planning. Students and parents are provided with information about school and community career resources. Students are asked to identify what step(s) they will take next in their career planning.

Collectively, these interventions represent examples of ways in which secondary school counselors can help students prepare for a successful school-to-work or school-to-school transition. When counselors at all grade levels work collaboratively to develop systematic career development interventions, then there is the likelihood that high school students will be prepared for the career development tasks they will encounter as they move through secondary school. Two more recent publications provide additional examples of effective strategies for fostering career development in students. Specifically, Perusse and Goodnough (2004) and Erford (2003) are excellent resources for professional school counselors. Both publications contain chapters that address career development with recommended activities, which, in the case of Perusse and Goodnough, are connected to the National Standards.

Although we realize that group and classroom career interventions represent the most reasonable way for school counselors (who, on average nationally experience student-counselor ratios of 476:1) to provide career assistance to students, overreliance on group approaches can foster a "one size fits all" mentality. Clearly, such a mentality does not lend itself to addressing individual and group differences in career development processes. As we have noted in previous chapters, students from collectivistic cultures approach the career development process differently from those who adhere to more of an individualistic worldview. Due to prejudice, students who are ethnic/racial minorities, disabled, sexual minorities, members of economically challenged groups, and so on, must cope with the career development challenges they experience as a result of discrimination. School counselors must empower students to address these challenges constructively. Thus, effective school counselors understand the processes and the potential effects of discrimination and contribute to helping students develop the knowledge, skills, and awareness necessary for managing their careers in a world in which some people try to limit the opportunities available to others. Surely, individual career assistance and targeted group interventions addressing topics such as the importance of offering and receiving emotional and informational support, challenging occupational stereotypes, and empowering students to acquire the skills/attitudes essential for confronting discrimination are necessary but addressing such issues also requires school counselors to be actively engaged in advocating with employers, school personnel, and community members in efforts to eradicate discrimination in workplace, school, community, and family settings.

Career Development Interventions for At-Risk Students

Successfully completing high school is critical for each student's future success. A male high school graduate who works until age 65 will earn, on average, nearly $333,000 more than a student who leaves school without graduating and a worker with some college will earn $538,000 more (National High School Center, 2008). In 1964, a high school dropout earned 64 cents for every dollar earned by an individual with at least a high school diploma. In 2004, students who dropped out of high school earned only 37 cents for each dollar earned by an individual with more education (Wise, 2007). Yet, every school day 7,000 U.S. students leave high school, never to return. In 2004, approximately 3.8 million 16- through 24-year-olds were not enrolled in high school and had not earned a high school diploma or alternative credential, such as a GED. Based on calculations per school day (180 days of school, seven hours each day), one high school student drops out every nine seconds. Male students are consistently 8% less likely to graduate than female students, and the gap is as large as 14% between male and female African American students (National High School Center).

The benefits of earning a secondary degree are clear, but our educational system performs poorly relative to preparing minority students and students with disabilities to enter and succeed in higher education. For instance, while 65% of White high school graduates entered college immediately upon graduation in 2001, only 56% and 53% of African American and Latino graduates did the same, respectively (Haycock, 2004). Forty percent of White students graduating from high school in 2002 were considered "college-ready," compared to 23% of African American students, and 20% of Latino students (Greene & Winters, 2005). Nine percent of students with disabilities have attended a four-year college after leaving high school, with 6% doing so in 2003, and although this figure is up from previous years, it is still significantly lower than the general population (Wagner et al., 2005).

Jerald (2006) notes that the three secondary school requirements for postsecondary school success are: (a) high expectations and rigorous instruction for all students, (b) equal access to rigorous coursework, and (c) adequate support for student success. As such, it is reasonable to expect in a democratic society that all students will have access to these requirements. However, while 65% of high-income and nearly half of middle-income students are participating in a college preparatory curriculum, only 28% of low-income students are enrolled in a similar program (Pathways to College Network, 2004). African American students are half as likely to be enrolled in "gifted" programs and three times more likely to be enrolled in special education than their White classmates (Pathways to College Network). African American students make up 17% of the public high school population, yet represent 4% of AP Exam test takers. The statistics are similar for Latino students (Barton, 2003).

Such disparities reflect serious deficiencies in the educational system within the United States. In addition, ensuring equal access to the three requirements identified by Jerald, helping students make connections between their academic experiences and future educational and career opportunities fosters academic motivation and achievement. For example, McLaughlin, Sum, and Fogg (2006) report that exposure to work experiences in high school is linked to both greater success in the workforce and in postsecondary education. Given the current lack of job opportunities for young people, however, school counselors need to be actively engaged in advocating on behalf of their students in order to help them gain access to work experiences during high school. Creating volunteer opportunities, job-shadowing experiences, internship experiences, and so on, represent ways in which school counselors can help their students bridge the school-to-work connection. Here again, disparities exist as more White teens—sometimes twice as many—held summer jobs in 2006 than non-White teens; further, teens with higher family annual incomes engage more in summer employment opportunities than students from lower-income families (Sum, McLaughlin, & Khatiwada, 2006). When school counselors help create workplace opportunities for students from lower-income families, they help address the fact that high school students from low-income families (the lowest 20%) are six times more likely to drop out than students from higher-income families. The Alliance for Excellent Education (2006) has estimated that the more than 12 million students who will drop out over the next decade will cost the nation $3 trillion dollars. Thus, when school counselors develop and deliver effective career guidance programs to address school retention, they provide important data for policy makers regarding the essential nature of career development services in education.

Froeschle (2009) provides an excellent example of a career development program that was created to influence dropout rates for at-risk students. The program consists of four distinct components: mentorship, small-group solution-focused counseling sessions, psychoeducational career lessons led by counselors and mentors, and implementation of solution-focused skills within the classroom.

Mentors should be individuals who are committed to participating in training sessions, who are willing to meet students on a weekly basis, and who should pass a background check (per local or state district policy). Mentors listen to student concerns and offer empathy, support, and advocacy while modeling good behaviors and decision making (Froeschle, 2009). Being consistently engaged with the student is crucial for the program's success. Mentors are also encouraged to consult with the school counselor after each student meeting to provide updates and solicit advice regarding the mentor's work with the student. The school counselor should also offer students an opportunity to discuss mentoring sessions before, during, or after small-group counseling sessions.

The small-group component of the program uses solution-focused counseling strategies to encourage students to share positive accomplishments, and to refocus thoughts on positive personal traits that led to past successes, exceptions to problems, and leadership skills (Froeschle, 2009). Using solution-focused techniques such as the miracle question, exception questions, complimenting, and scaling questions connected to school performance and career development, small-group meetings seek to empower at-risk students to develop skills to address barriers to achieving career adaptability and school success.

To provide solution-focused strategies in the classroom, school counselors train teachers to focus on students' positive attributes to create an encouraging classroom atmosphere. For example, teachers are trained to notice and record times when students are performing well or have shown improvement. These success lists are provided to the school counselor to share with students in small-group counseling sessions and/or teachers can share the list privately with students (Froeschle, 2009).

Psychoeducational sessions focus on teaching social skills, providing career information to facilitate goal setting, and creating social support for the students (Froeschle, 2009). Social skills training is linked with positive classroom behavior; developing a career goal is a protective factor connected to positive youth development; and social support provides a coping resource for persevering through challenging times. These groups meet monthly and alternate between being resource focused (e.g., having a guest speaker who provides career information relevant to the participants' interests) and fun activities (field trips to educational and workplace settings; attending events such as sporting activities, plays, movies, which provide the basis for group discussions related to important topics such as teamwork, discipline, overcoming challenges, etc.).

Froeschle (2009) concludes that programs such as this one, which are strengths-based and solution focused "form a school based career counseling program with the potential to reduce dropout rates among minority students. Advocacy for policy changes along with the implementation of this program will result in a better educated class of minority students with greater academic and career potential, maturity, and choices" (p. 18).

MyCounselingLab™

Go to Topic 8: *Junior High/Middle School* and Topic 9: *Senior High School* in the MyCounselingLab™ site (www.MyCounseling-Lab.com) for *Career Development Interventions in the 21st Century,* Fourth Edition, where you can:

- Find learning outcomes for *Junior High/Middle School* and *Senior High School* along with the national standards that connect to these outcomes.

- Complete Assignments and Activities that can help you more deeply understand the chapter content.
- Apply and practice your understanding of the core skills identified in the chapter with the Building Counseling Skills unit.
- Prepare yourself for professional certification with a Practice for Certification quiz.
- Connect to videos through the Video and Resource Library.

Summary

Today, perhaps more than ever, systematic career development interventions are needed to help young people advance in their career development. The nature of work is changing dramatically, requiring new skills sets (e.g., transition skills, stress management, the ability to engage in lifelong learning, personal flexibility, computer skills) that suggest that change, rather than constancy, will be the norm. Workers in the 21st century will experience multiple career changes that will bring associated levels of stress that must be managed effectively. It is naive to expect parents, many of whom are struggling to manage their own careers effectively, to provide children and adolescents with the competencies they need to advance in their careers. Career development interventions help students prepare for the tasks they will encounter as adults. Moreover, career development interventions help students connect current school activities with their futures. This connection is key to increasing school involvement and school success. Clearly, "when professional school counselors provide career and educational guidance to their students, they influence the future by helping clarify developmental decisions that often last a lifetime" (Erford, 2003, p. 153).

Case Study

James is a 13-year-old Caucasian boy in the eighth grade. His parents were divorced when he was in the first grade. Since then, James has had sporadic contact with his father (although his father seems to genuinely care about him). After the divorce, James's mother relocated to an upper-class suburban town in New Jersey. James lives with his mother and older sister (age 18). James's father lives in the town where James was born, which is two hours away. James's other sister (age 16) lives with her father and his second family. Although his parents' divorce was very difficult, no one in the family has received any counseling relative to this event.

James's parents are college graduates. James's father has a master's degree in educational leadership and has worked as a middle school teacher. However, he is currently employed as the head of the personnel department for the National Guard. He changed occupations to increase his salary ("You can't pay the bills on what they pay you as a teacher"). James's mother is employed as a high school Spanish teacher. James's older sister is an airline ticket agent. His younger sister is a successful athlete and good student in the eleventh grade.

Until now, James has given very little attention to his career. His major interests revolve around sports. He plays baseball, basketball, and football. He follows the local sports teams as well as the professional sports teams in his area. His heroes are all professional athletes and James dreams of being a professional athlete one day. He has no other hobbies.

Interpersonally, James is a friendly, but shy, boy. Lately, he has started to associate with a group of boys in his neighborhood who tend to get into trouble at school. A few have even gotten into minor problems (e.g., vandalism) with the law. James has not been a disciplinary problem.

In school, James has been an average to above-average student. He finds history and English to be interesting but struggles with mathematics. Not surprisingly, his favorite class is physical education. James has a general lack of confidence when it comes to his academic ability. He likes school because it is where he gets to play sports with his friends. His mother would like you to help him identify some career goals. Ideally, James's mother thinks he should be a lawyer because they "earn a good living and it is a prestigious occupation." But, James thinks it would be "fun" to be a coach. James's mother dismisses this as an appropriate occupation, telling James that he will "never make any money as a coach" and that one day he will be "too old" to be involved in sports. James and his father have never discussed what James might do "when he grows up." His mother has spoken with the school principal about having the school counselor give James some sort of test that will identify appropriate career options for him. The principal has asked you (the school counselor) to help out.

What are James's career development needs? What other issues does James present? What career tasks must he complete to begin to engage in effective educational and career planning? How will you work with James to help him move forward?

Student Activities

1. What career development tasks do you think are most important to help middle school students address?

2. What factors do you think could negatively influence the career development of middle school students?

3. What are three strategies you could use to foster positive career development in middle school students?

4. What do you think is the most common type of career assistance provided to middle school students? Do you think this type of assistance is helpful? If so, why? If not, why not?

5. How could you help parents/guardians to help their middle school students experience positive career development?

6. Interview a middle school student about his or her career development. Ask this person what occupations s/he thinks are possible for him/her. Ask your interviewee whether there are any occupations that are not possible for him/her. Ask the person to discuss why certain occupations may not be possible. Ask what occupation your interviewee would choose if s/he could choose anything. Then, explore with your interviewee what s/he thinks is attractive about that occupation.

7. What career development tasks do you think are most important to help high school students address?

8. What factors do you think could negatively influence the career development of high school students?

9. What are three strategies you could use to foster positive career development in high school students?

10. What do you think is the most common type of career assistance provided to high school students? Do you think this type of assistance is helpful? If so, why? If not, why not?

11. How could you help parents/guardians to help their high school students experience positive career development?

12. Interview someone who is a high school student about his or her career development. Ask what occupations s/he thinks are possible for him/her. Ask your interviewee whether there are any occupations that are not possible for him/her. Ask the person to discuss why certain occupations may not be possible. Ask what occupation s/he would choose if s/he could choose anything. Then, explore with your interviewee what s/he thinks is attractive about that occupation.

13. Ask a group of middle school students (or one student if a group is not available) what life roles they hope to play when they are adults (you will need to provide examples of life roles). Then, ask if they think they will be able to perform well in each of those life roles. Ask how they think they will learn the skills required for successful performance in each of those life roles. Now, ask the same questions of high school students.

14. Refer to the MyCounselingLab™ Video and Resource Library and select the video entitled, "21st Century Career Development Interventions in School: An Interview with Dr. Carol Dahir." How would you draw upon Dr. Dahir's comments to convince your principal and school board of the importance of career development interventions in middle and high school settings?

References

Akos, P. (2004). Transition programming for school counselors. In B. Erford (Ed.), *Professional school counseling: A handbook of theories, programs, and practices* (pp. 881–888). Austin, TX: Caps Press - PRO-ED.

Akos, P., Konold, T., & Niles, S. G. (2004). A career readiness typology and typal membership in middle school. *The Career Development Quarterly, 53*, 53–66.

Alliance for Excellent Education. (2006). *Paying double: Inadequate high schools and community college remediation*. Washington, DC: Author. Available online at http://www.all4ed.org/publications/remediation.pdf.

American School Counselor Association (ASCA). (2003). *The ASCA National Model: A framework for school counseling programs*. Alexandria, VA: American School Counselor Association.

American School Counselor Association (ASCA). (2004). The role of the school counselor in career guidance: Expectations and responsibilities. *The School Counselor, 29*, 164–168.

Amundson, N. E., & Penner, K. (1998). Parent involved career exploration. *The Career Development Quarterly, 47*, 135–144.

Baker, S. (2000). *School counseling for the 21st century* (3rd ed.). Upper Saddle River, NJ: Merrill/Prentice Hall.

Baker, S. B., & Gerler, E. R. (2008). *School counseling for the twenty-first century* (5th ed.). Upper Saddle River, NJ: Merrill/Prentice Hall.

Barton, P. (2003). *Parsing the achievement gap: Baselines for tracking progress*. Princeton, NJ: Educational Testing Service.

Bennett, G. K., Seashore, H. G., & Wesman, A. G. (1992). *Technical manual: Differential Aptitude Tests* (5th ed.). San Antonio, TX: The Psychological Corporation.

Bireley, M., & Genshaft, J. (1991). Adolescence and giftedness: A look at the issues. In M. Bireley & J. Genshaft (Eds.), *Understanding the gifted adolescent: Educational, developmental, and multicultural issues. Education and psychology of the gifted series* (pp. 1–17). New York: Teachers College Press.

Blustein, D. (1994). "Who am I?" The question of self and identity in career development. In M. L. Savickas & R. W. Lent (Eds.), *Convergence in career development theories* (pp. 139–154). Palo Alto, CA: Consulting Psychologists Press.

Campbell, C. A., & Dahir, C. A. (1997). *The national standards for school counseling programs*. Alexandria, VA: American School Counselor Association.

Crites, J. O. (1978). *Theory and research handbook for the Career Maturity Inventory*. Monterey, CA: CTB, McGraw-Hill.

Erford, B. T. (2003). *Transforming the school counseling profession*. Upper Saddle River, NJ: Merrill/Prentice Hall.

Erikson, E. H. (1963). *Childhood and society*. New York: W. W. Norton.

Feller, R. W. (2003). Aligning school counseling, the changing workplace, and career development assumptions. *Professional School Counseling, 6*, 262–271.

Froeschle, J. G. (2009). Using career counseling to influence minority dropout rates. In G. R. Walz, J. C. Bleuer, & R. K. Yep (Eds.), *Compelling counseling interventions: VISTAS* (pp. 11–20). Alexandria, VA: American Counseling Association.

Gibbons, M. M., Borders, L. D., Wiles, M. E., Stephan, J. B., & Davis P. E. (2006). Career and college planning: Needs of ninth graders—as reported by ninth graders. *Professional School Counseling, 10*, 168–178.

Greene, J. P., & Winters, M. A. (2005). *Public high school graduation and college readiness rates: 1991–2002* (Working Paper No. 8). New York: Manhattan Institute for Policy Research [Online]. Retrieved June 17, 2011, from www.manhattan-institute.org/html/ewp_08.htm.

Hansen, L. S. (1999). Beyond school-to-work: Continuing contributions of theory and practice to career development of youth. *The Career Development Quarterly, 47*, 353–358.

Harrington, T. (1996). *Ability Explorer*. Itasca, IL: Riverside Publishing.

Havighurst, R. J. (1972). *Developmental tasks and education* (3rd ed.). New York: D. McKay.

Haycock, K. (2004, May 10). Written testimony of Kati Haycock, president of the Education Trust, before the national commission on accountability in higher education. Retrieved June 17, 2011, from http://www2.edtrust.org/EdTrust/Federal+and+State+Policy/kati+NCA.htm.

Herr, E. L., Cramer, S. H., & Niles, S. G. (2004). *Career guidance and counseling through the lifespan* (6th edition). Boston, MA: Allyn & Bacon.

Holland, J. L. (1985). *Making vocational choices: A theory of vocational personalities and work environments* (2nd ed.). Upper Saddle River, NJ: Prentice Hall.

Jerald, C. D. (2006). *Measured progress: A report on the high school reform movement* (Educator Sector Reports). Washington, DC: Educator Sector.

Johansson, C. B. (1986). *Career Assessment Inventory*. Minneapolis, MN: NCS Assessments.

Keller, B. K., & Whiston, S. C. (2008). The role of parental influences on young adolescents' career development. *Journal of Career Development, 16,* 198–217.

Kolodinsky, P., Schroder, V., Montopoli, G., McLean, S., Managan, P. A., & Pedersen, W. (2006). The career fair as a vehicle for enhancing occupational self-efficacy. *Professional School Counseling, 10,* 161–167.

Krumboltz, J. D., & Worthington, R. (1999). The school-to-work transition from a learning theory perspective. *The Career Development Quarterly, 47,* 312–325.

Marcia, J. E. (1966). Development and validation of ego-identity status. *Journal of Personality and Social Psychology, 3,* 551–558.

Marcia, J. E. (1980). Identity in adolescence. In J. Adelson (Ed.), *Handbook of adolescent psychology* (pp. 159–187). New York: Wiley.

Marshall, R., & Tucker, M. (1992, November 9–15). The best imports from Japan and Germany. *Washington Post National Weekly Edition,* p. 24.

McLaughlin, J., Sum, A., & Fogg, N. (with Khatiwada, I., & Palma, S.). (2006, April). The summer teen job market in 2005 and the predicted outlook for 2006: Implications of summer employment for jobs for America's graduates' programs (prepared for Jobs for America's Graduates, Alexandria, VA). Boston: Center for Labor Market Studies, Northeastern University.

Muuss, R. L. (1996). Marcia's expansion of Erikson's theory of identity formation. In R. Muuss, H. Porton, & Associates (Eds.), *Adolescent behavior and society: A book of readings* (5th ed., pp. 260–270). New York: McGraw-Hill.

National High School Center. (2008). *Linking research and resources for better high schools.* Retrieved June 17, 2011, from http://www.betterhighschools.org/.

Niles, S. G., & Goodnough, G. E. (1996). Life-role salience and values: A review of recent research. *The Career Development Quarterly, 45,* 65–86.

Pathways to College Network. (2004). *A shared agenda: A leadership challenge to improve college access and success.* Boston: Author.

Perusse, R., & Goodnough, G. (2004). *Leadership, advocacy, and direct service strategies for professional school counselors.* Belmont, CA: Brooks/Cole.

Rosenbaum, J. E. (2001). *Beyond college for all.* New York: Russell Sage.

Rosenbaum, J. E., & Person, A. E. (2003). Beyond college for all: Policies and practices to improve transitions into college and jobs. *Professional School Counseling, 6,* 252–261.

Savickas, M. L. (1990). The career decision-making course: Description and field test. *The Career Development Quarterly, 38,* 275–284.

Savickas, M. L. (1993). Predictive validity criteria for career development measures. *Journal of Career Assessment, 1,* 93–104.

Savickas, M. L. (1999). The transition from school to work: A developmental perspective. *The Career Development Quarterly, 47,* 326–336.

Savickas, M. L., Stilling, S. M., & Schwartz, S. (1984). Time perspective in vocational maturity and career decision making. *Journal of Vocational Behavior, 25,* 258–269.

Stott, K. A., & Jackson, A. P. (2005). Using service learning to achieve middle school comprehensive guidance program goals. *Professional School Counseling, 9,* 156–159.

Sum, A., McLaughlin, J., & Khatiwada, I. (2006, September). *The 2006 summer job market for the nation's teens: Who got the jobs and who didn't and why we should care* (prepared for Jobs for America's Graduates, Alexandria, VA). Boston: Center for Labor Market Studies, Northeastern University.

Super, D. E. (1955). Transition: From vocational guidance to counseling psychology. *Journal of Counseling Psychology, 2,* 3–9.

Super, D. E. (1957). *A psychology of careers.* New York: Harper & Row.

Super, D. E. (1970). *The Work Values Inventory.* Boston: Houghton Mifflin.

Super, D. E. (1980). A life-span, life-space approach to career development. *Journal of Vocational Behavior, 16,* 282–298.

Super, D. E. (1981). Approaches to occupational choice and career development. In A. G. Watts, D. E. Super, & J. M. Kidd (Eds.), *Career development in Britain.* Cambridge, England: Hobson's Press.

Super, D. E. (1983). Assessment in career guidance: Toward truly developmental counseling. *Personnel and Guidance Journal, 61,* 555–562.

Super, D. E. (1984). Leisure: What it is and might be. *Journal of Career Development, 11,* 71–80.

Super, D. E. (1990). Career and life development. In D. Brown & L. Brooks (Eds.), *Career choice and development: Applying contemporary theories to practice* (2nd ed., pp. 197–261). San Francisco: Jossey-Bass.

Super, D. E., Osborne, W. L., Walsh, D. J., Brown, S. D., & Niles, S. G. (1992). Developmental assessment and counseling: The C-DAC model. *Journal of Counseling and Development, 71,* 74–80.

Super, D. E., Savickas, M. L., & Super, C. M. (1996). The life-span, life-space approach to careers. In D. Brown & L. Brooks (Eds.), *Career choice and development: Applying contemporary theories to practice* (3rd ed., pp. 121–178). San Francisco: Jossey-Bass.

Super, D. E., Thompson, A. S., Lindeman, R. H., Jordaan, J. P., & Myers, R. M. (1988). *Adult Career Concerns Inventory: Manual for research and exploratory use in counseling.* Palo Alto, CA: Consulting Psychologists Press.

Tiedeman, D. V. (1961). Decision and vocational development: A paradigm and its implications. *Personnel and Guidance Journal, 40,* 15–20.

Turner, S., & Lapan, R. T. (2002). Career self-efficacy and perceptions of parent support in career development. *The Career Development Quarterly, 51,* 44–55.

Vernon, A. (1993). *Developmental assessment and intervention with children and adolescents.* Alexandria, VA: American Counseling Association.

Wagner, M., Newman, L., Cameto, R., Garza, N., & Levine, P. (2005, April). Postsecondary education: Participation of youth with disabilities. In *After high school: A first look at the postschool experiences of youth with disabilities. A report from the National Longitudinal Transition Study-2 (NLTS2)* (Chap. 4). Menlo Park, CA: SRI International. Available online at www.nlts2.org/reports/2005_04/nlts2_report_2005_04_complete.pdf.

Wise, R. (2007, June). Systems of support for high school improvement. Presented at the National High School Center Summer Institute, June 11–13, 2007, Washington, DC. Retrieved June, 16, 2011, from http://www.betterhighschools.org/summerinst/SI2007SystemsofSupport.asp.

Sample Career Development Activities for Middle/Junior and High School Students

An Interesting Journal

NATIONAL CAREER DEVELOPMENT GUIDELINES: Personal Social Domain: PS1.K1; PS1.A1; PS1.R1

ASCA STANDARDS: Standard A—Students will acquire the skills to investigate the world-of-work in relation to knowledge of self and to make informed career decisions; Standard C—students will understand the relationship between personal qualities, education, training, and the world-of-work.

PURPOSE: This activity encourages students to identify their interests and to consider how their interests can inform their career decisions.

OBJECTIVE: To help students identify their interests and connect their interests to career possibilities.

MATERIALS: Notebook or journal

INTRODUCTION: Discuss how our interests should guide career plans: "Do what you enjoy and you will never work a day in your life." By focusing on the things that we find most enjoyable, we can begin to clarify those activities that we should incorporate into our career plans.

ACTIVITIES: Instruct students to keep a log of how they spend their out-of-school time over the course of 1 week. As they enter the activity in their journals, they should give the activity a rating from 1 ("hated it") to 5 ("loved it"). The time frame can be lengthened to get a better sense of the activities students liked and disliked.

DISCUSSION: Students can discuss the activities they liked and did not like. They can also identify reasons for their reactions to their activities.

CLOSURE: The leader can help students understand how they can use their interests to guide their career exploration. For example, if a student enjoys working with animals, then the group can brainstorm additional activities that can provide that student with the opportunity to work with animals. The group can also brainstorm career opportunities that provide people with the opportunity to work with animals. As each student discusses his or her likes, the group can brainstorm in a similar fashion.

Values Sorting

NATIONAL CAREER DEVELOPMENT GUIDELINES: Personal Social Domain: PS1.K4; PS1.A4; PS1.R4; Career Management Domain: CM2.K5; CM2.A5; CM2.R5

ASCA STANDARDS: Standard A—Students will acquire the skills to investigate the world-of-work in relation to knowledge of self and to make informed career decisions.

PURPOSE: Good career decisions are values-based. However, few career options provide individuals with the opportunity to express all of their important values. Thus, we must prioritize values and identify those that are most important to us. We must be clear as to which values we are willing to part with, if necessary. Each decision we make requires us to sort our values and make choices accordingly. Being able to select career options that provide us with maximal opportunities for values expression requires us to subjectively define our important values. For example, although many people value "financial rewards," this value is defined somewhat definitely across individuals. Understanding how we define the most important values in our lives helps us to determine which options fit best. Finally, it is important to understand how values are connected to our participation in the life roles we play.

OBJECTIVES: As a result of participating in this activity, participants will (a) learn the importance of values clarification, (b) become aware of their most important values, and (c) understand the importance of considering values in career decision making and career planning.

MATERIALS: Handouts of the values list and five slips of paper per participant

INTRODUCTION: Introduce this activity as an exercise that helps participants identify and define important values in their lives.

TIME: 45–60 minutes

EVALUATION/ASSIGNMENT: At the end of the activity, students should identify two activities in which they are interested and two things they can do to gain additional exposure to their interests.

ACTIVITY: To start this activity, give participants a list of values such as this one:

VALUES LIST

_____ Financial security

_____ Job security

_____ Good family relationships

_____ A world that is free of discrimination

_____ Creativity

_____ Having a set routine

_____ Time by myself

_____ Community activities

_____ Physical activities

_____ An attractive physical appearance

_____ Variety

_____ Power

_____ Recognition

_____ Prestige

_____ Freedom from stress

_____ Associating with people I like

_____ Success

_____ Freedom to live where I choose

_____ Leisure time

_____ Fame

_____ Strong religious faith

_____ Adventure

_____ World peace

_____ Helping others

_____ Having children

_____ Good health

_____ A beautiful home

_____ Autonomy

_____ Other

_____ Other

Instruct students to identify their top-10 values from this list by putting an X next to the values that are most important to them (the values chosen are not ranked at this point). Then, after discussing their experience of conducting this initial values sort, provide participants with five slips of paper. Ask them to identify their top-5 values from the list of their top-10 and to write one value on each slip of paper (again these values are not ranked). Participants are then informed that the activity leader will be taking a value from them, one at a time. Thus, participants must now decide which of their top-5 values they are willing to part with first. At this point, the activity leader actually goes around the room taking a value from each participant.

Immediately after students give a value to the leader, instruct the participants to record and define what that value means to them (e.g., "financial rewards: having an income of more than $45,000/year with good health and retirement benefits"). Continue this process for each of the remaining values. At the conclusion of the exercise, participants have a list of their top-5 values, with definitions, in descending order. For example, here are five value definitions:

5. Financial rewards: having an income of more than $45,000/year with good health and retirement benefits

4. Autonomy: being able to make my own decisions as to how to best accomplish my job duties, but having a colleague who can give me advice when I need it

3. Associating with people I like: being friends with my coworkers and doing things together outside of work

2. Good health: eating right and exercising three times per week

1. Strong religious faith: going to church on a regular basis and volunteering at a soup kitchen

DISCUSSION: After completing the exercise, explain how the activity relates to career decision making. Explain that in every decision there is the promise of gain and the threat of loss (otherwise, one could simply choose the "perfect" option in every instance). The risk involved in decision making is lessened when options are selected based on the individual's key values.

CLOSURE: Encourage participants to consider how they spend their time in the course of a typical week and if they spend time in activities reflecting their top values. If the answer is no, then encourage participants to identify strategies for increasing their participation in activities reflecting their values (e.g., agreeing to a moderate exercise program, identifying opportunities for volunteering).

TIME: Approximately 30 minutes

EVALUATION/ASSIGNMENT: Students will list their five most important values and identify three jobs in which they could express these values.

The Pie of Life

NATIONAL CAREER DEVELOPMENT GUIDELINES: PS1.K4; PS1.A4; PS1.R4; Career Management Domain: CM2.K5; CM2.A5; CM2.R5

ASCA STANDARDS: Standard A—Students will acquire the skills to investigate the world-of-work in relation to knowledge of self and to make informed career decisions; Standard B—Students will employ strategies to achieve future career goals with success and satisfaction; Standard C—Students will understand the relationship between personal qualities, education, training, and the world-of-work.

PURPOSE: To focus on how students spend their time now and how they hope to spend their time in the future.

OBJECTIVE: To enhance self-awareness regarding values and life-role participation.

MATERIALS: Paper, pencils

INTRODUCTION: Encourage students to consider a typical week in their lives and ask them how they spend their time. Emphasize with students the importance of spending time in activities that reflect their interests and values.

ACTIVITIES: Ask each student to draw a circle on a piece of paper. Encourage students to consider the circle as if it were a "pie of life." Instruct them to consider how they spend their time over the course of a typical week (24 hours a day, 7 days a week). Tell them to divide the circle or pie into "slices" according to how much of their time is spent in each activity over the course of a week. Once they have divided their pies into slices, ask students to write answers to the following question: "What conclusions could someone draw from your 'pie of life' about what you like to do and what you value?"

DISCUSSION: Divide students into small groups. Encourage them to share their "pies of life" with each other. Then encourage students to share with the entire class any reactions they had to dividing their "pies of life" into slices as well as any reactions they had to hearing how their peers divided their pies.

CLOSURE: Emphasize the importance of having a "pie of life" that reflects your interests and values as much

as possible. If students do not have a pie that reflects their interests and values, then encourage them to consider what changes they can make to increase the degree to which their "pies of life" reflect their values and interests.

TIME: 45 minutes

EVALUATION/ASSIGNMENT: Have students draw a second circle that reflects their lives as an adult (choose a specific age, such as 35 years old). Instruct them to divide their "pies of life" into slices according to how they hope to spend their time in the future. Ask them to identify how their slices relate to their interests and values. Ask them to identify the life roles reflected in their future slices of life. Finally, ask students to identify five things they can do between now and when they turn age 35 to increase the chances that their future "pies of life" will come true.

Time Capsule

NATIONAL CAREER DEVELOPMENT GUIDELINES: National Career Development Guidelines: PS1.K4; PS1.A4; PS1.R4; Career Management Domain: CM2.K5; CM2.A5; CM2.R5

ASCA STANDARDS: Standard A—Students will acquire the skills to investigate the world-of-work in relation to knowledge of self and to make informed career decisions; Standard B—Students will employ strategies to achieve future career goals with success and satisfaction; Standard C—Students will understand the relationship between personal qualities, education, training, and the world-of-work.

PURPOSE: To explore what possessions are valuable to students and why.

OBJECTIVE: Students will learn about themselves and others by examining a valued possession; students will explore what they would like future generations of people to know about them. Students will also discuss how the possessions they value are influenced by the culture in which they live.

MATERIALS: Ask students to bring a valued object from home, something that tells something about them that

they might leave behind in an imaginary time capsule for future generations of middle school students.

INTRODUCTION: Ask students to bring an item from home to show other participants; students should be prepared to explain what the item is and why it is important to them.

ACTIVITIES: Each student will describe the possession, explain why it is important to him or her, how it reflects something about the student, and what he or she would like to communicate to future middle school students by placing this item in an imaginary time capsule.

DISCUSSION: Students may discuss the items, any common concerns/messages for future generations, what they would like others to know about them, what is valued and why, and so on. Students will also discuss the group similarities and differences in the items they chose as valuable. Students can discuss how these items might be different if they lived in another country.

CLOSURE: Students can discuss the fact that the things we value are reflected in the things that are valuable to us. They are, in essence, symbolic representations of things that are important to us due to a variety of reasons (e.g., what the objects represent, because a person who is important to us gave us the object). The uniqueness of the objects selected tells us something important about ourselves.

TIME: 45 minutes to 1 hour

EVALUATION/ASSIGNMENT: Students will complete the following sentences: "Three things that are important to me are _____." and "These objects are important to me because _____."

Becoming a Member of Another Culture: A Fantasy

NATIONAL CAREER DEVELOPMENT GUIDELINES: Career Management Domain: CM2.A5; Personal Social Domain: PS2.K9; PS2.A9; PS2.R9

ASCA STANDARDS: Standard A—Students will acquire the skills to investigate the world-of-work in relation to knowledge of self and to make informed career decisions; Standard B—Students will employ strategies to achieve future career goals with success and satisfaction; Standard C—Students will understand the relationship between personal qualities, education, training, and the world-of-work.

PURPOSE: For students to learn what it would be like to suddenly find themselves as members of another culture.

OBJECTIVES:

1. For students to think about what privileges go along with certain cultures.
2. For students to recognize how they perceive their culture and others' cultures.

MATERIALS: None

INTRODUCTION: Say to students, "I am going to need everyone to relax and close his or her eyes. We are going to use our imaginations in this exercise to think about what it would be like to be a member of another culture."

ACTIVITY: (Read aloud) "You're feeling relaxed now; you're very calm; it's the middle of the week, just prior to bedtime. You find yourself sitting in your comfortable

chair, very relaxed. Your eyes are closed. . . . You are tired, very tired, and decide to go to bed. You enter a very restful sleep, very restful sleep. (Pause 10 seconds.) Now, visualize yourself awakening the next morning. You see yourself entering your bathroom. Take a careful look in the mirror; you see there's been a rather startling transformation during the night. . . . You woke up as a member of another culture with physical characteristics typical of those from that culture. . . . You went to bed a member of one culture and you woke up a member of another! (Pause.) How does it feel? (Pause.) Now you find yourself walking outside and meeting your best friend. How does your friend react? (Pause.) Now, visualize yourself walking across the campus. How do people react to you? You meet your favorite teacher—what happens? How do you feel? What is the overall reaction toward you? (Pause.) Okay. Open your eyes now."

DISCUSSION: Place students in small groups to take turns sharing their fantasies. Ask members to ask each other open-ended questions about what they share (what, how, when, or where). Request that they do not "interpret" another's fantasy.

CLOSURE: Discuss some of the themes in the students' fantasies and their specific reactions to suddenly being a member of a different culture.

TIME: 20–30 minutes

EVALUATION/ASSIGNMENT: Ask students to write two paragraphs describing how it felt to be a member of a culture different from their own.

Who Am I?

NATIONAL CAREER DEVELOPMENT GUIDELINES: Career Management Domain: CM2.A5; Personal Social Domain: PS2.K9; PS2.A9; PS2.R9

ASCA STANDARDS: Standard A—Students will acquire the skills to investigate the world-of-work in relation to knowledge of self and to make informed career decisions; Standard B—Students will employ strategies to achieve future career goals with success and satisfaction; Standard C—Students will understand the relationship between personal qualities, education, training, and the world-of-work.

PURPOSE: To help members learn more about themselves and each other in the group.

OBJECTIVE: Students will have an increased level of understanding among students about what makes each of them uniquely different and also what are some of their similarities.

MATERIALS: Pins, 4 × 6 cards for each student

INTRODUCTION: Tell students: "We will be learning a lot about who we are. It is important to understand yourself and what has influenced who you are today. The activity we will be starting with is a great way to remind us about what things are unique to each of us and help us to recognize the differences in others."

ACTIVITIES: Give each student a 4 × 6 card and read aloud the following instructions.

A. Print your first name in the center of the index card. Write large enough so other people can read it.
B. In the upper left-hand corner, write or put a symbol for:
1. Where you were born
2. A favorite place you would like to visit on a vacation
C. In the upper right-hand corner, put a symbol or write words that depict something you like to do to have fun.

D. In the lower left-hand corner, write three words your best friend might use to describe you if you were not present.
E. In the lower right-hand corner, describe one characteristic about the specific culture to which you belong (Anglo, African American, etc.) that you value and appreciate.
F. Finally, somewhere on your card put another symbol that tells something you are really looking forward to doing in the future.

After they have completed their "Who Am I" card, have students fasten the cards to the fronts of their shirts or blouses. Then ask them to find an individual they do not know very well, preferably of a different culture or gender, someone with whom they can pair up. Each pair should interview one another concerning the data on the cards for 10 minutes.

DISCUSSION: Next, form a large circle with pairs standing together. Each pair should in turn step forward and introduce one another to the group. Afterward, have students share something they have learned regarding a student and what they would like to know more about.

CLOSURE: Ask the participants to wear their name tags to subsequent sessions until everyone knows everyone else.

TIME: 1 hour

EVALUATION/ASSIGNMENT: Have students follow through on the activity by instructing them to learn more about one person in the group.

Responding to Labels

NATIONAL CAREER DEVELOPMENT GUIDELINES: Career Management Domain: CM1.K1; CM1.R1; Personal Social Domain: PS2.K9; PS2.A9; PS2.R9

ASCA STANDARDS: Standard A—Students will acquire the skills to investigate the world-of-work in relation to knowledge of self and to make informed career decisions; Standard B—Students will employ strategies to achieve future career goals with success and satisfaction; Standard C—Students will understand the relationship between personal qualities, education, training, and the world-of-work.

PURPOSE: For students to think about some of the ways society labels people and how one can sometimes use some of the conflict resolution techniques when they feel like they are possibly being labeled.

OBJECTIVE:

1. Let the students experience what it is like when society labels certain individuals.
2. Help students to decide how to handle labeling, such as peer-group labels.

MATERIALS: Sheets of paper, tape, and a marker

INTRODUCTION: Place labels on certain individuals' backs. People in the room will respond to these individuals according to the labels they have on their backs. The individuals with labels will not know what they are and should pay close attention to how others in the room are treating them. While doing this activity, think about other labels that society gives people. For example, there are probably labels that your peers give to people in school.

ACTIVITIES: Write one of the following labels on separate sheets of paper and tape them on a few of the students' backs. Have the students without the labels walk around and react to the students as if they actually were what they are labeled.

- Famous movie star
- Person with HIV
- Mental patient
- Deaf person
- Criminal
- Drug addict
- Famous athlete

DISCUSSION:

1. Have the students who had labels talk about what it felt like to wear the labels. Have each guess what they think his or her label might be.

2. Next, have the students who did not have labels talk about how it felt to treat people according to their labels.

Ask the students if they think this happens in our society. What are some of the labels people attach to others? Have students consider how damaging these labels can be to the individuals assigned the labels by society. Ask the students what they can do to deal with labeling. Have them refer back to some of the skills they learned in the conflict resolution activities. List their answers on the board.

CLOSURE: Ask students to think about how knowledge gained from this activity can make us more aware of labeling in our society and ways of handling situations in which someone is being labeled.

TIME: 30 minutes

EVALUATION/ASSIGNMENT: Ask students to list ways in which they encounter labeling each day (e.g., television, music, newspapers, family, and friends).

Educational and Occupational Exploration Informational Interviewing

NATIONAL CAREER DEVELOPMENT GUIDELINES: Personal Social Domain: PS2.K9; PS2.A9; PS2.R9; Career Management Domain CM2; CM3.K2; CM3.A2; CM3.R2; CM3.K4; CM3.A4; CM3.R4; CM3.K5; CM3.A5; CM3.R5; CM3.K6; CM3.A6; CM4.A5; CM4.R5; CM4.A6; CM4.R6

ASCA STANDARDS: Standard A—Students will acquire the skills to investigate the world-of-work in relation to knowledge of self and to make informed career decisions; Standard B—Students will employ strategies to achieve future career goals with success and satisfaction; Standard C—Students will understand the relationship between personal qualities, education, training, and the world-of-work.

PURPOSE: To provide students with information concerning their possible career goals.

OBJECTIVE: Students will learn about specific occupations. Students will gather information pertaining to occupational requirements, training requirements, occupational conditions, and so on, for occupations that interest them.

MATERIALS: Writing materials and interview guide

INTRODUCTION: Tell students: "To get real-life information about jobs, it is useful to interview people working in a job in which you are interested. Workers can provide important information concerning what they like about their work and what they do not like. They can also tell you about the training requirements involved in preparing for the job."

ACTIVITIES: Students will interview workers who enjoy doing their jobs and are good at them. In other words, the interviewees will need to be screened to ensure that they meet these two requirements (the first requirement being more important than the second). Students will conduct a structured interview asking the following questions:

1. What do you like most about your job?
2. How did you decide that this job was a good choice for you?
3. What type of training is required for this job?
4. What types of benefits are provided in a job like this?
5. How many hours do you usually work each week?
6. How much vacation time do you have each year?
7. What are the most important things for doing this job well?
8. What things do you not like about your job?
9. What is the most important piece of advice you would give to someone interested in doing this job?
10. Is there anything else you think I should know?

DISCUSSION: Have students review the responses to these questions and share them with the group. Have them respond (in writing and/or verbally) to the following question: "This job would or would not (select one) be a good match for me because _____."

CLOSURE: Encourage students to compare the information they learned about the job with the information they have learned about themselves (e.g., their interests, values, skills, etc.). Students can eliminate jobs that do not seem like a good fit from further consideration. Students can identify next steps for additional exploration of jobs that seem like a good fit, such as participating in job shadowing and engaging in additional research to learn more about the job.

TIME: Varies depending on the number of interviews; each interview should take 20–30 minutes

EVALUATION/ASSIGNMENT: Students will complete the question listed in the Discussion section.

Work Lessons

NATIONAL CAREER DEVELOPMENT GUIDELINES: CAREER MANAGEMENT DOMAIN: CM2.R4; CM3.K2; CM3.A2; CM3.R2; CM3.K4; CM3.A4; CM3.R4; CM3.K5; CM3.A5; CM3.R5; CM3.K6; CM3.A6; CM4.A5; CM4.R5; CM4.A6; CM4.R6

ASCA STANDARDS: Standard A—Students will acquire the skills to investigate the world-of-work in relation to knowledge of self and to make informed career decisions; Standard B—Students will employ strategies to achieve future career goals with success and satisfaction; Standard C—Students will understand the relationship between personal qualities, education, training, and the world-of-work.

PURPOSE: To provide students with information concerning the jobs their family members have held.

OBJECTIVE: Students will link their family's history with the world-of-work.

MATERIALS: Interview guide

INTRODUCTION: Remind students that we learn a lot about work from our family members. Often, family members pass on to their children and grandchildren

the lessons they have learned from their work experiences.

ACTIVITIES: Students will interview immediate and extended family members concerning their work experiences. Students will conduct a structured interview asking the following questions:

1. What jobs have you held in your life?
2. How did you choose each of these jobs?
3. Which job did you like the most and why?
4. What type of training is required to do the job you liked most?
5. What are the most important skills and interests for doing this job well?
6. What did you learn about working as a result of doing this job?
7. Would you recommend this job to me? Why or why not?
8. What job did you like least and why?
9. What did you learn about working as a result of doing this job?
10. What is the most important piece of advice you could give to me about making a career choice?

DISCUSSION: Students can review the responses to these questions and share them with the group. They can also respond (in writing and/or verbally) to the following question: "The job that one of my family members has held that is most interesting to me is _____. This job is interesting to me because _____."

CLOSURE: Encourage students to discuss what they learned about work as a result of interviewing their family members. Encourage students to talk about what they like or dislike about what they learned. Finally,

encourage students to discuss how they can use what they learned in their own career planning.

TIME: Varies depending on the number of interviews; each interview should take 20–30 minutes

EVALUATION/ASSIGNMENT:

1. Students will complete the questions listed in the Discussion section.
2. Students can gather information about the job that they liked most.

Family Meeting Role Play

NATIONAL CAREER DEVELOPMENT GUIDELINES: Career Management Domain: CM2.R4; CM3.K2; CM3.A2; CM3.R2; CM3.K4; CM3.A4; CM3.R4; CM3.K5, CM3.A5; CM3.R5; CM3.K6; CM3.A6; CM4.A5; CM4.R5; CM4.A6; CM4.R6

ASCA STANDARDS: Standard A—Students will acquire the skills to investigate the world-of-work in relation to knowledge of self and to make informed career decisions; Standard B—Students will employ strategies to achieve future career goals with success and satisfaction; Standard C—Students will understand the relationship between personal qualities, education, training, and the world-of-work.

PURPOSE: To explore the pros and cons of, and concerns about, college attendance, from the points of view of a range of family members.

OBJECTIVE: To clarify values in and identify obstacles to going to college (real, imagined, attitudes, etc.).

MATERIALS: Students may role play family members and/or bring in family members for this activity; use hats or costumes if desired.

INTRODUCTION: Explain to students the role-play task: Each student must role play a family member other than himself or herself. Then students switch roles

to see different points of view or concerns of all family members. Encourage real family members to participate when possible. Identify questions to ponder, such as, "Where will the money for college come from?" "Will a parent/sibling be okay when the college student leaves home?" "Why do you want to go to college when there are jobs here at home you can do?"

ACTIVITIES: Conduct the role plays and follow-up questions. Monitor group discussions and identify a note-taker that lists barriers, concerns, and general attitudes.

DISCUSSION: Review concerns and barriers, discuss solutions, and identify feelings that arise and the impact of those feelings upon college decisions.

CLOSURE: Focus on sorting out which concerns are real and which are imagined. Identify solutions (via brainstorming) to the real concerns. Encourage students to "let go" of the imagined concerns.

TIME: 30 minutes to 1 hour

EVALUATION/ASSIGNMENT: Have students complete a table with two columns in which they list the real concerns about attending college in one column and the imagined concerns about attending college in the other column.

What Can I Buy? Comparing Incomes: College or No College

NATIONAL CAREER DEVELOPMENT GUIDELINES: Educational Achievement and Lifelong Learning Domain: ED1.R2; ED1.R3; ED1.K5; ED1.A5; ED1.R5; Career Management Domain: CM1.A1; CM1.A2; CM1.K5; CM1.A5; CM1.R5

ASCA STANDARDS: Standard A—Students will acquire the skills to investigate the world-of-work in relation to knowledge of self and to make informed career decisions; Standard B—Students will employ strategies to achieve future career goals with success and satisfaction; Standard C—Students will understand the relationship between personal qualities, education, training, and the world-of-work.

PURPOSE: To compare an average college graduate's income with the income of a high school graduate, and give examples of what extra income might be used for in a given period of time.

OBJECTIVE: Students will be able to visually compare the purchasing power a college degree income has over that of a high school degree.

MATERIALS: Store catalogs with pictures, car brochures, newspaper photos (e.g., houses for sale), and so on

INTRODUCTION: Ask students if they would rather earn more money or less money in their lives. Then tell students that there is a way to increase significantly the probability that they will be able to achieve their goals of earning more money. Use the chart that follows to explain to students that a man or woman with a college degree may earn from 82% to 96% more than a person with a high school diploma. Show examples of annual differences in income, five-year differences, and ten-year differences on the blackboard.

ACTIVITIES: Have students draw, cut out pictures, or describe verbally what the differences in incomes could purchase for an individual with a college degree (e.g., first year—number of pairs of sneakers, basketballs, a small car; fifth year—two medium-sized cars; tenth year—a home). Ask students to construct a weekly budget based on a high school degree versus a college degree.

DISCUSSION: Review income differences and examples of the purchasing power of college versus no college incomes. Ask students, "Is this important?" "Why?"

CLOSURE: Discuss how extra effort (e.g., staying in school four years longer) can make a significant difference in one's life. Emphasize that the decisions we make, especially about education, have real and long-term effects in our lives.

TIME: 30–40 minutes

EVALUATION/ASSIGNMENT: Have students respond to the following question: "What is meant by the phrase 'the more you learn, the more you earn'?"

The Value of Work

NATIONAL CAREER DEVELOPMENT GUIDELINES: Educational Achievement and Lifelong Learning Domain: ED1.R2; ED1.R3; ED1.K5; ED1.A5; ED1.R5; Career Management Domain: CM1.A1; CM1.A2; CM1.K5; CM1.A5; CM1.R5; CM3.K1; CM3.A1; CM3.R1; CM3.R3; CM3.K4; CM5.K1

ASCA STANDARDS: Standard A—Students will acquire the skills to investigate the world-of-work in relation to knowledge of self and to make informed career decisions; Standard B—Students will employ strategies to achieve future career goals with success and satisfaction; Standard C—Students will understand the relationship between personal qualities, education, training, and the world-of-work.

PURPOSE: To learn that the compensation for work is not always equal to the value of a particular service provided by workers.

OBJECTIVE: Students will be able to state which occupations they feel are the most valuable and/or which they feel should be compensated at a higher rate for the work performed.

	H.S. Grad.	College Grad.	Difference
In 1 year	$10,000	$19,000 (90% more)	$9,000
In 5 years	$50,000	$95,000	$45,000
In 10 years	$100,000	$190,000	$90,000

MATERIALS: Pencils, paper, and a blackboard and chalk

INTRODUCTION: Give students a list of jobs and services, including teacher, police officer, garbage collector, professional athlete, firefighter, secretary, computer programmer, doctor, writer, bus or cab driver, rock musician.

ACTIVITIES: Have students rank the jobs according to the amount they feel they should be paid, from lowest to highest salary.

DISCUSSION: Have students compare their lists and discuss the reasons for ranking each as they did.

CLOSURE: Discuss with the students the difference between the economic value of a job (i.e., the salary of a job determined by the economic principles of supply and demand) and the social value of a job (i.e., the degree to which the job contributes to society and others).

TIME: 30 minutes

EVALUATION/ASSIGNMENT: Each participant will be able to list three jobs with high economic value (i.e., those that pay well but do not necessarily contribute to society, such as athlete and performer). Each participant will be able to list three jobs with high social value (i.e., those that contribute to the betterment of society).

People and Things

NATIONAL CAREER DEVELOPMENT GUIDELINES: Educational Achievement and Lifelong Learning Domain: ED1.R2; ED1.R3; ED1.K5; ED1.A5; ED1.R5; Career Management Domain: CM1.A1; CM1.A2; CM1.K5; CM1.A5

ASCA STANDARDS: Standard A—Students will acquire the skills to investigate the world-of-work in relation to knowledge of self and to make informed career decisions; Standard B—Students will employ strategies to achieve future career goals with success and satisfaction; Standard C—Students will understand the relationship between personal qualities, education, training, and the world-of-work.

PURPOSE: To explore tasks that require interpersonal skills and those that do not.

OBJECTIVE: Students will be able to identify activities that require interpersonal skills and differentiate between tasks that do or do not require interpersonal skills.

MATERIALS: Paper; pencils; lists of activities, such as hobbies, pet care, sports, clubs, going to school, and so on.

INTRODUCTION: Ask students to list activities that they or others might do in any given day.

ACTIVITIES: Ask students to differentiate between the activities requiring interpersonal skills and those that do not. Write these lists on the blackboard.

DISCUSSION: Review and compare the lists of activities. Ask students to determine which of these activities are their favorites, which they'd like to avoid, which are particularly difficult due to the need for compromise with others, and so on.

CLOSURE: Emphasize the importance of focusing on the category of activities (those relying on a high level of interpersonal skills vs. those that do not) to which students seem most drawn in their career planning. Encourage students to identify occupations within each category.

TIME: 30–45 minutes

EVALUATION/ASSIGNMENT: Ask students to list occupations that fall within two categories: (a) those that rely heavily on interpersonal skills and (b) those that do not rely heavily on interpersonal skills.

Career Planning: Map of My Life

NATIONAL CAREER DEVELOPMENT GUIDELINES: Personal Social Domain: PS1.K4; PS1.A4; PS1.R4; Career Management Domain: CM1.A1, CM1.A2, CM1.K5, CM1.A5, CM1.R5, CM3.K1, CM3.A1, CM3.R1, CM3.R3, CM3.K4, CM5.K1

ASCA STANDARDS: Standard A—Students will acquire the skills to investigate the world-of-work in relation to knowledge of self and to make informed career decisions; Standard C—Students will understand the relationship between personal qualities, education, training, and the world-of-work.

PURPOSE: Students will recognize how different events and people have changed their lives.

OBJECTIVE: Each student will construct a personal road map with dates, his or her birthplace, family, schools, friends, significant influences, accomplishments, setbacks, interests, and short- and long-term goals.

MATERIALS: Large piece of art paper and colored markers

INTRODUCTION: Tell students: "You will be making a map of your life on a large piece of art paper.

To learn more about ourselves and events and people who have influenced who we are today, we are going to make a personal road map."

ACTIVITIES: Have students complete their maps using words and illustrations and then pair off to discuss their maps.

DISCUSSION: Ask the class to discuss these questions: "Did anyone learn something new about themselves?" "Was it difficult to think of future goals?" and "Were some people surprised by how much they had on their maps?"

CLOSURE: Tell students: "I hope this activity helped you understand some of the things that have influenced you. It is important to have self-understanding before making decisions. We will be looking at our goals in some later activities."

TIME: 35 minutes

EVALUATION/ASSIGNMENT: Have students identify one long-term goal and three things they can do to achieve that goal.

My Roles in Life

NATIONAL CAREER DEVELOPMENT GUIDELINES: Personal Social Domain: PS4.K1; PS4.A1; PS4.R1; PS4.K2; PS4.A2; PS4.R2; PS4.K3; PS4.A3; PS4.R3; PS4.K4; PS4.A4; PS4.R4

ASCA STANDARDS: Standard A—Students will acquire the skills to investigate the world-of-work in relation to knowledge of self and to make informed career decisions; Standard B—Students will employ strategies to achieve future career goals with success and satisfaction; Standard C—Students will understand the relationship between personal qualities, education, training, and the world-of-work.

PURPOSE: To provide students with the opportunity to consider life roles that are and will be important to them.

OBJECTIVE: Students will engage in life-role planning.

MATERIALS: Writing materials, chalk, and a chalkboard

INTRODUCTION: Tell students: "While busy making livings, people are busy living their lives. All the things we do can contribute to our life satisfaction. We can describe our activities in life in terms of 'life roles.' For example, one life role most adults play is the role of 'worker.' Many adults are also parents. All young people play the life role of 'student.'" Discuss additional life-role possibilities for young people and adults. Write them on the chalkboard under either the heading of "young people" and/or "adults" according to which category or categories are most appropriate. Emphasize that participating effectively in the life roles we play (e.g., being a good worker, being a good parent, being a good student) has much to do with our life satisfaction, and we need to give

serious consideration to what life roles we want to play and how we want to play them.

ACTIVITIES: Have students respond to the following questions:

1. What life roles are important to me now?
2. What life roles will be important to me when I am an adult?
3. What can I do to prepare for the life roles that will be important to me in the future?

DISCUSSION: Divide students into small groups. Encourage students to share their responses to the first two questions listed in the Activities section. Then have the students brainstorm responses to the third question for each student.

CLOSURE: Discuss the importance of planning for future life-role participation. Ask each student to list the life roles they plan to participate in when they are adults. Have them list two things they can do between now and then to prepare for participating in that life role.

TIME: 45–60 minutes

EVALUATION/ASSIGNMENT: Have students discuss with their parents/guardians the following questions:

1. What life roles do you play?
2. What do you like about each life role you play?
3. What life roles do you expect me to play when I am an adult?
4. What do you expect me to accomplish in the life roles I will play as an adult?

Have students discuss in small groups the results of the interviews with their parents/guardians. Encourage them to consider how the results of their interviews may influence their career planning.

My Life as a Book

NATIONAL CAREER DEVELOPMENT GUIDELINES: Educational Achievement and Lifelong Learning Domain: ED1.R2; ED1.R3; ED1.K5; ED1.A5; ED1.R5; Career Management Domain: CM1.A1; CM1.A2; CM1.K5; CM1.A5; CM1.R5; CM3.K1; CM3.A1; CM3.R1; CM3.R3; CM3.K4; CM5.K1

ASCA STANDARDS: Standard A—Students will acquire the skills to investigate the world-of-work in relation to knowledge of self and to make informed career decisions; Standard B—Students will employ strategies to achieve future career goals with success and satisfaction; Standard C—Students will understand the relationship between personal qualities, education, training, and the world-of-work.

PURPOSE: To help students see the themes or patterns in their lives and to encourage students to consider their future "stories."

OBJECTIVE: Students will identify activities that they find meaningful and discuss ways to gain additional exposure to these activities. Students will identify goals toward which they would like to strive.

MATERIALS: Writing materials

INTRODUCTION: Explain to the student that a person's career is like a story. Each story has a beginning, middle, and end. Each person can take an active role in writing his or her own story or autobiography. Students should consider their lives as if they were books. Just as there are happy stories and sad stories, we can work hard to write the types of stories about our lives that we would like. By understanding our story or life as we have lived it thus far, each of us can decide if we want to continue in the same direction or make changes. By considering the direction we would like our lives to take, we can establish goals for our futures.

ACTIVITIES: Ask students to consider their lives as if they were books. They should give titles to their books or lives as they have lived them thus far (e.g., "The Baseball Player," "The Dancer," "The Next Bill Gates"). Then ask students to divide the lives they have lived thus far into chapters. Their chapters may reflect developmental stages (e.g., infancy, preschool, primary grades, intermediate grades) and/or they may reflect important life events (moving from home, parents divorcing, having a new sibling). Encourage the students to give titles to their life chapters. Next, have the students consider their futures. What do they want these chapters to be like? What goals can they identify in their future chapters?

DISCUSSION: Students can discuss their lives thus far and share the titles of their books. They can also discuss what future chapters they would like to live. In discussing future chapters, students can identify goals they would like to achieve and the group can help each student brainstorm strategies for achieving their goals.

CLOSURE: Tell students that each of them can take an active role in writing his or her own destiny. Our pasts can help us to make decisions about what we would like to achieve in the future. By identifying what we would like our futures to look like, we can identify goals toward which to strive. We can also then begin to develop a plan for achieving our goals.

TIME: 60–90 minutes

EVALUATION/ASSIGNMENT: At the conclusion of the activity, students should be able to identify two or three goals they would like to achieve in their lives and strategies that they can use to help them achieve their goals.

The Rocket Kid's Story

NATIONAL CAREER DEVELOPMENT GUIDELINES: CAREER MANAGEMENT DOMAIN: CM2.R4; CM3.K2; CM3.A2; CM3.R2; CM3.K4; CM3.A4; CM3.R4; CM3.K5; CM3.A5; CM3.R5; CM3.K6; CM3.A6; CM4.A5; CM4.R5; CM4.A6; CM4.R6

ASCA STANDARDS: Standard A—Students will acquire the skills to investigate the world-of-work in relation to knowledge of self and to make informed career decisions; Standard C—Students will understand the relationship between personal qualities, education, training, and the world-of-work.

PURPOSE: To learn about the life of a real scientist and explore the manner in which a boy achieved his career goal despite numerous obstacles.

OBJECTIVE: Students will be able to identify the goals of the movie characters in the film they are about to watch. They will also be able to identify the risks taken to achieve those goals and the role of teamwork in achieving goals.

MATERIALS: The movie *October Sky*, paper, pencils, a blackboard and chalk, rocket-making kit (if desired)

INTRODUCTION: Develop a list of questions for students to respond to such as, "Do you know anyone like the movie characters?" "How did teamwork play a role in the success of the 'rocket boys'?" "What was the father's attitude toward college and the son's career interests?" "What was the family's attitude toward sports, and what role did sports play in the lives of the young people?" "What was Homer's original destiny, and how and why did that change?" "What risks did Homer take to implement his career goal?"

ACTIVITIES:

1. Ask students to watch the video *October Sky* or, if preferred, to read the book *Rocket Boys* by Homer Hickam. (Note: Parents may need to give permission to see this movie, as its rating is PG-13, and there is some language that may be offensive to some individuals.) After watching the movie, students will respond to the questions in the Introduction section or others you develop. Follow this by actually building and/or setting off a rocket (kits to simplify the building can be purchased at toy and crafts stores), if circumstances allow.

2. Students can then list their "dream" jobs or "occupational fantasies."

3. To provide examples of people who have overcome obstacles and achieved their goals, invite past program participants to the session. The past participants could share their stories and discuss what obstacles they overcame to achieve their goals. If it is not possible to have past participants, consider videotaping interviews from past participants. In the interviews the past participants could share their stories and identify the obstacles they overcame to achieve their goals.

DISCUSSION: Review the questions in the Introduction section and others that arise as students watch the movie. Ask students to take notes or write down a list of questions that arise as they watch this video. Emphasize the risks taken by the characters in the story and the role of teamwork in creating success in one's career. Students should list the obstacles the movie characters overcame to achieve their goals. Feelings may also be discussed, such as, "Do you feel as if success similar to that of the movie characters is within your reach?" Share stories of past students who have achieved their goals (e.g., being admitted to college, graduating from college, attaining a job with a college degree).

CLOSURE: Discuss the fact that people must overcome obstacles to achieve their goals in life. Obstacles can be viewed as opportunities rather than reasons not to pursue a goal.

TIME: 2–3 hours

EVALUATION: Students can list the obstacles they have already overcome in their lives.

Resources for Information on Colleges

NATIONAL CAREER DEVELOPMENT GUIDELINES: Personal Social Domain: PS1.K4; PS1.A4; PS1.R4; Career Management Domain: CM1.A1; CM1.A2; CM1.K5; CM1.A5; CM1.R5; CM3.K1; CM3.A1; CM3.R1; CM3.R3; CM3.K4; CM5.K1

ASCA STANDARDS: Standard A—Students will acquire the skills to investigate the world-of-work in relation to knowledge of self and to make informed career decisions; Standard B—Students will employ strategies to achieve future career goals with success and satisfaction; Standard C—Students will understand the relationship between personal qualities, education, training, and the world-of-work.

PURPOSE: To provide students with information about colleges.

INTRODUCTION: Say to students: "There are many college resources available to you. Here are some ideas to get you started. Your school counselor should be your most valuable resource in your college search. Your counselor can provide you with help on testing, college requirements, choosing colleges to apply to, academic programs, the application process, and financial aid. You should visit your counselor as soon as possible to discuss your plans for after high school."

THE INTERNET

General College Sites
College Board Online: collegeboard.org

Connects to a tremendous range of college materials. Use the Fundfinder to search for scholarships, grants, internships, and loans. Use ExPan to get in-depth information about colleges, careers, and financial aid from 3,000 colleges. To custom-fit your search, create a program of your ideal college. ExPan will list colleges that match only your interests.

Minority Information: web.fie.com/web/mol Molis

(Minority On-Line Information Service) offers data on historically Black colleges and universities, Hispanic- and Tribal-serving institutions, and on financial aid for minorities.

Adventures in Education: tgslc.org

Includes a wide array of college and career information to help students and parents.

CollegeNET: collegenet.com CollegeNET

Lets students search for institutions by geography, tuition, enrollment, and college major. Provides separate databases for four-year colleges and community, technical, and junior colleges; lists colleges by category; and links to sources of financial aid information.

Internet College Exchange: usmall.com

Provides assistance in identifying potential colleges, finding financial aid, and completing college applications.

Peterson's Education Center: petersons.com

Peterson's Education Center includes information about educational programs at all levels and provides searchable databases of colleges and academic programs. All college/university sites provide basic information and many provide extensive descriptive material, online viewbooks, and applications.

Financial Aid Sites
FastWEB: fastweb.com

Includes a database of 375,000 scholarships; plug in your name for a free scholarship search.

FinAid: finaid.org

The Internet's most complete financial aid site, with links to other key college sites. It also includes a "Scholarship Scam Alert" with information about scams and how to avoid them.

The Federal Government's Sites
studentaid.ed.gov/

Offers information about the U.S. Department of Education's federal student financial aid programs.

fafsa.ed.gov/

Provides an on-line form you must complete in order to receive federal student aid. You can submit it by regular mail or at this site over the Internet.

College Loan Sites
Mapping Your Future: mapping-your-future.org

Sponsored by agencies that take part in the Federal Family Education Loan Program (FFELP).

Sallie Mae: salliemae.com

A financial services corporation that funds education.

College and University Home Pages
At individual college Web sites, you can read catalogs and admission requirements, check activities, and learn more about the school.

University Pages: isi-garnet.uah.edu/

Universities Courtesy of the University of Alabama at Huntsville, this site provides easy access (by state) to college and university home pages.

Yahoo: Yahoo.com/

Regional/Countries/United States/Educational/ Colleges and Universities.
This site contains brief descriptions of U.S. colleges and universities.

12

Career Development Interventions in Higher Education

It is now fairly universally acknowledged that career development is a complex, lifelong process—a process that many college students are ill prepared to negotiate effectively and that many find supremely challenging. It is further acknowledged that the career development needs of our increasingly heterogeneous, multicultural society do not lend themselves to one-size-fits-all, recipe-driven career interventions or service delivery models. In response to these acknowledged conditions and the recent societal trend away from institutional/corporate responsibility for career development and toward greater individual responsibility, institutions of higher education are struggling to implement career services, programs, and interventions that meet the ever-changing needs of today's college student. In an era of unprecedented accountability, college and university career services professionals must choose from a complex array of career interventions and career service–delivery models. This chapter provides the reader with exposure to the career development needs of higher education students; a discussion of the evolution of career development interventions in higher education; and some models, services, and standards for career development interventions in higher education. It is a "must read" for those charged with setting the future course for the delivery of career services in our nation's institutions of higher learning.

Jack Rayman, Ph.D.
Former Director of Career Services and Affiliate Professor, Counseling Psychology
Pennsylvania State University

Presently, almost all colleges and universities provide a variety of career interventions. Career guidance services have roots in counseling and testing centers established in the early 20th century to assist college students in clarifying career goals. Also, colleges routinely established placement offices to assist graduates in securing employment. During the later portion of the 20th century, many higher education institutions merged the missions for career guidance and employment and established career development and placement offices. These offices evolved to 21st-century career centers that hold the university-wide mission for career guidance, experiential education, and employer relations. Typically, comprehensive career centers today offer a variety of services ranging from career counseling, assessment, and programming through employment recruitment.

Technological innovations to career services have exploded during recent years to include many Web-based applications. Today's career centers continue to offer personal and group-based career interventions in addition to technologically driven services. Career services have gained considerable respect by higher education administrators and are viewed as important offices that support recruitment, retention, and fundraising efforts in facilitating the career preparation of graduates. As a result, career centers are often located in centralized, highly visible campus locations. Career development interventions are at the heart of the counseling profession. Today's comprehensive career centers boast services assisting thousands of clients annually, including college recruits, freshmen, seniors, graduate students, as well as alumni representing all career fields ranging from the liberal arts to business and engineering. This chapter reflects the dynamic and exciting nature as well as the significance of higher education career development interventions in the 21st century.

Jeff W. Garis, Ph.D.
Senior Executive Director
Career Services
Pennsylvania State University

MyCounselingLab™

Visit the **MyCounselingLab**™ site for *Career Development Interventions in the 21st Century,* Fourth Edition to enhance your understanding of chapter concepts. You'll have the opportunity to practice your skills through video- and case-based Assignments and Activities as well as Building Counseling Skills units, and to prepare for your certification exam with Practice for Certification quizzes.

Robert had experienced substantial success in his career since graduating with an associate's degree in business from the local community college. Over the past 15 years, he had worked his way up to a middle-management position with a medium-sized manufacturing firm. His success has come at a price, however. He has consistently worked long hours and weekends. He was increasingly uneasy with the time he was spending on the job. His two children were both in middle school and he realized that he had already missed important moments in their lives due to his involvement at work. Moreover, he had come to feel that his work was "not contributing anything positive to the world." A series of layoffs within his company heightened his sense that it was time to make a change. His precarious employment situation, combined with his desire to spend more time with his family and engage in work that he felt was meaningful, led him to decide to explore his career and educational options. After several sessions with a career counselor in the community, Robert decided he would like to return to college to earn a four-year degree. However, he was anxious about returning to school. Among other things, he wondered if he would be "smart enough" to finish his degree, if he would be able to cover the tuition costs, if his family would support his decision, and if, at age 35, he would be the "old man" in his classes. Because his desire to make a change was stronger than his anxieties about changing, he decided to meet with a career counselor at the local college. He hoped this person would help him sort through his educational and career options in a way that would turn his desire for change into a concrete plan.

Like Robert, a substantial portion of people in the United States view postsecondary education (i.e., four-year colleges, community colleges, career and technical education) as essential to their career development. According to the Bureau of Labor Statistics, in October 2011, 68.1% (2.2 million) of 2010 high school graduates were enrolled in colleges and universities. The college enrollment rate in 2010 for young women was 74% compared to 62.8% for young men. The college enrollment rate of Asians (84.0%) was higher than for recent White (68.6%), Black (61.4%), and Hispanic (59.6%) graduates. About 6 in 10 recent high school graduates who were enrolled in college attended four-year institutions. Of these students, 32.0% participated in the labor force, compared with 52.4% of recent graduates enrolled in two-year colleges (BLS).

Fry reported that in October 2009, some 3.1 million young adults, or 10.9% of all 18- to 24-year-olds, were enrolled in a community college. A year later, that figure had risen to 3.4 million students, or 11.8% of all 18- to 24-year-olds. Community college enrollments have long been considered somewhat countercyclical; that is, they tend to rise as the economy worsens. One reason is that community colleges are less expensive than four-year institutions—they average $6,750 per year (including tuition, fees, and room and board) in the net price for full-time students, compared with $9,800 for four-year public colleges and $21,240 for four-year private colleges. Community colleges offer university transfer programs, technical programs, job training programs, basic skills programs, and special interest programs of study and, therefore, appeal to an ever-increasing broad spectrum of students.

Approximately 14 million students participated in secondary and postsecondary career and technical education (CTE) programs during the 2007–2008 school year (Association of Career and Technical Education, 2011). One-third of college students are involved in CTE programs, and as many as 40 million adults engage in short-term, postsecondary occupational training. Career and Technical Education in the United States evolved from a relatively small number of vocationally oriented programs at the beginning of the 20th century into a much more comprehensive postsecondary system. Today's CTE educational options include a broad array of diverse subject areas that reflect the constantly changing global economy (ACTE, 2011).

The number of young students has been growing more steadily than the number of older students. Between 1995 and 2006, the enrollment of students under age 25 increased by 33%. Enrollment of people 25 and over rose by 13% during the same period. From 2006 to 2017, the National Center for Educational Statistics projects a rise of 10% in enrollments of people under 25, and a rise of 19% in enrollments of people 25 and over.

In 2007, slightly more than 18 million students were enrolled in 3,885 higher education institutions in the United States (Statistical Abstract of the United States, 2008). This number has increased by approximately 3 million since 2001. Many of these students emerge from high school experiences in which they received minimal career development assistance. For those students, who may also have diffuse vocational identities, negotiating the tasks of selecting a college major and identifying potential occupations is daunting at best. Statistics support this contention since only 50% of students who enter colleges and universities graduate in six years (Gray & Herr, 2000) and, according to Marklein (2011) only 63% of students who enroll in a four-year university will earn a degree. Clearly, many students are not prepared for what they encounter when they step onto a college or university campus. So, why do so many people choose to enroll in postsecondary education?

Survey results from the American Council on Education (1999) indicate that most first-year college students (77%) indicate that they chose to attend college to "get a better job" and 75% report that they chose to attend college "to make more money." Obviously, many students view higher education as a means for advancing their careers. Helping students crystallize and implement their career identities is a critical role of career services professionals in higher education.

It is important to note, however, that students enrolled in higher education today represent a vast array of cultural and ethnic backgrounds. Many students are, like Robert, returning adult students. Other students have disabilities that require accommodations. Still others represent the first generation in their families to attend higher education. Finally, a growing trend for students graduating from postsecondary education in the United States is that they are graduating having incurred substantial debt to pay for their education. For example, the Project on Student Debt (2010) reports that for the academic year 2007–2008, 67% of students graduating from four-year colleges and universities had student-loan debt. That represents 1.4 million students graduating with debt, up 27% from 1.1 million students in 2004. In 2008, 62% of graduates from public universities had student loans; 72% of graduates from private nonprofit universities had student loans; 96% of graduates from private for-profit universities had student loans (a major increase from 2004, when 85% of these graduates had student loans). Average debt levels for graduating seniors with student loans rose to $23,200 in 2008—a 24% increase from $18,650 in 2004. In 2008, 36% of enrolled students graduated from college in four years. Fifty-seven percent completed their undergraduate requirements in six years, at the same college in which they first enrolled (Singletary, 2009). Not surprisingly, there is a concomitant increase in pressure from parents, politicians, and students themselves to decrease the amount of time spent in postsecondary education, in order to reduce loan indebtedness. Career professionals in higher education can play a vital role in helping students achieve this goal. Thus, in this chapter we discuss the career needs of those enrolled in higher education today; the evolution of career services in higher education; the competencies students in higher education must develop to cope effectively with career development in adulthood; models, services, and standards for career services; and issues that must be considered in managing career services.

Tips from the Field

Students in higher education often think that career decision making occurs in the following manner: You must first know what you want to do before you can take action. Actually, just the opposite is true: In order to know what you want to do, you must first take action. Doing leads to knowing. Therefore, students in higher education need help in engaging in experiential career activities so they can make effective career decisions.

THE CAREER NEEDS OF HIGHER EDUCATION STUDENTS

Although a large number of students enroll in higher education immediately following their high school graduation, increasingly, these students do not fit the traditional stereotype of the American college student (i.e., age 18 to 22, enrolled full-time, and living on campus). In fact, fewer than one in six students in higher education fit this traditional stereotype (Colozzi, 2000). More than ever in the history of higher education, today's students represent a diverse mix in terms of their backgrounds, characteristics, developmental levels, and career development needs.

For example, Herr et al. (2004) note that there are approximately 6 million adults (i.e., those over the age of 25) attending college each year. The majority of adults returning to higher education do so primarily to enhance their career opportunities (Luzzo, 2000). However, many adult students must balance their pursuit of higher education with child rearing and other life-role responsibilities. Moreover, many adult students experience insecurity over their decision to return to school; they are uncertain about their ability to succeed academically and are anxious about whether they will be able to convert their academic experience into new career opportunities (Marron & Rayman, 2002). Women made up 56% (about 8 million) of the undergraduate student population and 59% (about 2 million) of the graduate students in 2005, according to the latest data released today by the U.S. Census Bureau on school enrollment in the United States. The majority of undergraduate students were enrolled in four-year colleges (69%). Of those enrolled in four-year colleges, 81% attended full-time (U.S. Census Bureau, 2007).

International students also represent a substantial percentage of those enrolled in higher education within the United States. For instance, Herr et al. (2004) report that approximately 500,000 international students were enrolled in higher education in 2001. Historically, international students have not received sufficient assistance with their career development. Specifically, international students tend to receive inadequate information concerning employment opportunities in their home countries; they often receive inadequate academic advice from advisors who are not sensitive to concerns of international students, and they frequently experience difficulty in self-expression in an unfamiliar culture. Since September 11, 2001, many international students from the Middle East have experienced undeserved hostility. These experiences do not foster career development and they reflect special needs that career practitioners must address to provide comprehensive career services to international students.

Within the past two decades, higher education institutions have also experienced a surge in enrollment of people with disabilities (Conyers & Szymanski, 1998). For example, more than 130,000 students with learning disabilities currently attend college in the United States (Ohler, Levinson, & Barker, 1996). The types of disabilities reported by these students include:

Learning disabilities	45.7%
Mobility or orthopedic impairments	13.9%
Health impairments	11.6%
Mental illness or emotional disturbance	7.8%
Hearing impairments	5.6%
Blindness and visual impairments	4.4%
Speech or language impairments	0.9%
Other impairments	9.1%

Source: *An Institutional Perspective on Students with Disabilities in Postsecondary Education,* National Center for Educational Statistics, Postsecondary Education Quick Information System, August 1999.

Two federal laws have opened the doors to higher education for many Americans with disabilities. Specifically, section 504 of the Rehabilitation Act of 1973 and the Americans with Disabilities Act of 1990 (and the ADA Amendments Act of 2008 (P.L. 110-325) created an environment of increased access to higher education for persons with disabilities. Despite increased access to higher education, people with disabilities have not fared well in the labor market (Hitchings & Retish, 2000). Thus, students with disabilities need assistance during their higher education experience to increase their chances of being successful in their careers following graduation. For example, Ohler and her colleagues report that students with learning disabilities who require many accommodations demonstrate lower levels of career maturity when compared with students with learning disabilities. Despite the need for career assistance, Friehe, Aune, and Leuenberger (1996) report that college students with disabilities use career services at a significantly lower rate than nondisabled students. Clearly, career practitioners in higher education must do a better job of meeting the career development needs of students with disabilities.

Although students in the early centuries of higher education were predominantly European American men, women now constitute the majority (57.5%) of students enrolled in higher education. Fassinger and O'Brien (2000) contend that the career development needs of female students are considerably different from those of college males. Specifically, Fassinger and O'Brien note that two themes character- ize the differences between female and male college students' career development: (a) women experience a pervasive and persistent underutilization of their abilities and talents resulting in occupationally segregating women into jobs that are typically lower in pay and status than jobs held by the majority of men, and (b) women experi- ence a higher level of participation in family roles than men. This results in a higher frequency of role overload issues that women experience as their career aspirations are juxtaposed with family responsibilities. Career practitioners must address these themes to foster the career development of women enrolled in higher education.

The percentage of students enrolled in higher education who are members of racial/ethnic minority groups has also increased in recent years. Herr et al. (2004) point out that the total enrollment for racial/ethnic minorities represented 22.5% of all stu- dents in higher education in 1999 and rose to 32% in 2007, according to the National Center for Education Statistics. Much of the change from 1976 to 2007 can be attrib- uted to rising numbers of Hispanic and Asian or Pacific Islander students. During that time period, the percentage of Asian or Pacific Islander students rose from 2% to 7% and the Hispanic percentage rose from 4% to 11%. The percentage of Black students was 9% at the beginning of the time period and it fluctuated during the early part of the period before rising to 13% in 2007. Nonresident aliens for whom race/ethnicity is not reported made up 3% of the total enrollment in 2007, according to NCES. Despite this level of enrollment within higher education, and despite these increases, ethnic minorities are still less likely than European Americans to attend college, complete college degrees, and enter professional training programs. Historically, occupational stereotyping by high school counselors, lack of role models, and few perceived oppor- tunities have led to restricted career choice patterns among ethnic minority students. The discriminatory treatment experienced by students of color presents a wide range of issues that must be addressed in the career development process.

Lesbian, gay, bisexual, transgendered, and questioning students also encounter numerous contextual barriers in their career development. Unfortunately, the career development needs of lesbian and gay students have long been ignored by career services in higher education. Pope, Prince, and Mitchell (2000) urge career professionals to work to change this by providing a safe and welcoming environment on college campuses for gay and lesbian students. One way to contribute to creating an environment that is more responsive to the needs of lesbian and gay students is to offer career services that more thoroughly address their career development needs. Pope and his colleagues note that lesbian and gay students are likely to have encountered biased career information, may be reluctant to consider certain career options because of concerns about discrimi- nation or negative stereotyping, and may need help in considering the advantages and disadvantages of coming out in the workplace. Career services can be provided to help lesbian and gay students cope with these and other career concerns related to their sexual orientation. For example, providing students with information on employment antidiscrimination laws and policies and with lists of gay and lesbian resources and com- munity agencies; encouraging gay and lesbian students to attend workshops addressing complex career/relationship issues; providing names of gay and lesbian alumni who are willing to provide mentoring and networking opportunities; and making sure that career development interventions are appropriate/relevant to lesbian and gay students are some of the ways in which career services can be made more responsive to this substantial population of students in higher education (Pope et al., 2000).

This sampling of the career concerns of students enrolled in higher education clearly paints a landscape that is very different than that of previous centuries. What was once an environment populated by European American men of privileged socioeconomic status is now characterized by heterogeneity at all levels. This increased diversity suggests that career development interventions in higher education must be comprehensive and planned systematically to meet the myriad career development needs of students today. The current scenario is very different from the one out of which career services in higher education emerged early in the last century.

THE EVOLUTION OF CAREER DEVELOPMENT INTERVENTIONS IN HIGHER EDUCATION

Career development interventions have a long history in higher education. Comprehensive career services ranging from helping students select a major to helping students find a job are relatively recent in higher education. Current approaches to career services were preceded by a "system" of service delivery that primarily depended upon the efforts of professors who provided mentoring and placement assistance to selected students. Herr, Rayman, and Garis (1993) note that:

> "career services" were essentially confined to how a professor or a don advocated for or mentored a student prodigy as part of his induction into a profession. This was a male-dominated activity, an "old boy's network" by which a faculty member would speak in behalf of a student to persons of importance who might employ him as a favor to, or out of respect for, the professor. (p. 1)

Job placement was the focus of this sort of career assistance. The rate of success for this placement activity depended on the professor's contacts and stature within the field as well as the professor's degree of regard for a particular student. In other words, this system probably worked well for some students, but not as well for other students.

In the early 1800s, commercial employment agencies offered placement services to graduates from teacher training programs. By the late 1800s there were nearly 200 employment agencies in the United States (Herr et al., 1993). As enrollments in higher education increased and student services emerged in university settings, placement offices were created to provide all students with placement assistance. For example, Yale University established a placement office in 1919 to provide vocational guidance to students and to match them with employment positions during the academic year, the summer months, and after graduation (Herr et al., 1993).

From prototypical efforts such as those initiated at Yale, the influence of the emerging vocational guidance movement being pioneered by the concepts of Frank Parsons in the early 1900s, and the growing interest of students and employers in placement assistance, employment offices or placement bureaus were instituted on campuses throughout the United States. Often these offices were combined with efforts of faculty, other college and university student personnel officials, and alumni who sought to identify employment opportunities and match students to them.

The focus on placement services resulted in the separation of placement offices from other student affairs functions that were more focused on student development. Rather than training in areas such as counseling and psychology, career placement "officers" tended to have a variety of backgrounds, but were often linked to business. Placement was a process by which the students were matched to the requirements of commerce, industry, and the professions based on the careers they had developed through their college experiences (Herr et al., 1993). Services provided by placement officials emphasized job-search skills (e.g., interviewing and resume writing). Typically, these services tended to be in more demand as students approached graduation. In contrast, counseling centers were more likely to be concerned with student development (e.g., the remediation of emotional or academic distress) and services were provided at any time during the student's collegiate experience.

A shift occurred in career services in higher education beginning in the late 1950s and early 1960s. Career planning activities that had been a part of many counseling centers were relocated to placement offices and combined with placement services: "In essence, in many colleges and universities, an organizational entity frequently known as the career planning and placement office or the career development and placement center or service was formed" (Herr et al., 1993, p. 4). This shift reflected an expanded perspective of career services that moved beyond a singular focus on placement to a developmental perspective of career planning. The developmental perspective included the use of interventions to help students engage in systematic career planning. Placement was now viewed as the culminating activity, rather than the only activity, in the career development of students enrolled in higher education.

Herr et al. (1993) note that currently "there is no single type of counseling center or career development and placement center. Each of these evolves from different institutional histories. In some cases, college and university counseling centers embrace the full range of career services; in others, they have essentially none" (p. 3). Survey results from 963 institutions participating in a study conducted by Whiteley, Mahaffey, and Geer (1987) provide evidence of the variety of approaches used for delivering career services in higher education today. Specifically, these researchers identified five major approaches used in higher education for delivering career services:

1. **Macrocenter:** broad range of services, including career and personal counseling, testing, and special functions such as training and consultation with some advising services offered
2. **Counseling orientation:** similar to macrocenters except with fewer career services
3. **General-level service:** broader functions, including some "dean of students"–type functions; more services to more students than a conventional counseling center
4. **Career planning and placement:** career-oriented services with minimal counseling and other functions
5. **Minimal service:** characterized by providing minimal services in all areas

It is unfortunate that some institutions of higher education are unwilling or unable to provide a full range of career services to students. For example, had Robert (the returning student mentioned at the beginning of this chapter) presented for assistance at a career services office focused exclusively on placement, he would have received limited assistance. The career placement officer may have provided him with placement statistics and information on job openings and job search strategies. But Robert was clearly at a place in his career development where he needed other assistance. He needed help clarifying his vocational identity and learning about the options available to him. He also needed information about financial aid. Finally, it would have been very useful for him to speak with someone who is knowledgeable about the concerns confronting returning students. In many ways, Robert's career situation reflects the variety of contextual and intrapersonal challenges students confront in their career development. Given this complexity, it is not surprising that most major surveys examining the needs of students enrolled in higher education reveal the fact that students express a strong desire for help with a variety of career-related concerns (Healy & Reilly, 1989; Weissberg et al., 1982). For example, Healy and Reilly report that the students in their study of 1,540 women and 1,386 men enrolled in 10 community colleges in California desired assistance in:

1. Knowing more about themselves
2. Identifying career goals
3. Becoming more certain of their career plans
4. Exploring career options
5. Educational planning
6. Learning job-search skills

Such survey results provide evidence that students enrolled in higher education, regardless of their backgrounds and characteristics, are very concerned about their ability to make and implement career choices. It seems reasonable to expect institutions of higher education to provide assistance to students as they attempt to translate their life and academic experiences into career choices. The Office of Post-secondary Education within the United State Department of Education offers a program guide that identifies excellent resources to helping postsecondary students manage their educational experience (2.ed.gov/about/offices/list/ope/opeprogramguide.html, retrieved June 18, 2011). In addition to being aware of useful resources, providing career assistance effectively requires understanding the career development tasks that students confront while they are enrolled in higher education and as they move forward in their career development beyond higher education.

CAREER DEVELOPMENT COMPETENCIES IN ADULTHOOD

Although they have since been revised and updated (see Chapters 10 and 11), the National Career Development Guidelines developed by the National Occupation Information Coordinating Committee (NOICC, 1992) are useful for identifying the competencies that postsecondary school students need to manage their careers effectively. These guidelines provide the target skills toward which comprehensive and systematic career services in higher education must be directed. Like the NOICC competencies identified for students in grades K–12, the adult-level competencies are categorized within three domains: (a) self-knowledge, (b) educational and occupational exploration, and (c) career planning.

Self-Knowledge

Self-knowledge competencies involve:

1. The skills to maintain a positive self-concept;
2. The skills to maintain effective behaviors;
3. Understanding developmental changes and transitions.

Adults need to develop a positive self-concept that encompasses an accurate understanding of their strengths, interests, abilities, and values. Moreover, adults need to understand how these important self-characteristics influence their career decisions. A holistic understanding of one's self-concepts across life roles provides the foundation for educational and career exploration. Skills related to interpersonal communication, stress management (e.g., engaging in positive self-care activities, identifying resources for social support, and overcoming self-defeating behaviors), and an understanding of life-span development are essential for helping adults manage their career development (NOICC, 1992).

Most often, career services providers help students in higher education to develop an accurate understanding of their self-characteristics through the use of self-assessment activities. Assessment results can be reviewed in individual career counseling or small-group counseling sessions. Career counselors provide a variety of standardized assessments, such as interest inventories, personality measures, and career maturity measures. Career counselors in higher education also expose students to computer-assisted career guidance systems that provide opportunities for engaging in self-exploration. To develop an understanding of life-span development and to enhance skills in areas such as stress management, practitioners encourage students to enroll in career planning courses. In these courses students receive career development assistance in large- and small-group interactions. Thus, skills in interpersonal communication are also enhanced. Students also learn about various approaches to career decision making (Niles et al., 1997). Reed et al. (2001) describe a career planning course based on the cognitive information-processing theory. Reed and her colleagues divide their course into three units. Unit I covers career concepts and applications focusing on self-knowledge, knowledge of options, and decision making. Unit II addresses social conditions affecting career development, focusing on current social, economic, family, and organizational changes affecting the career planning process. Finally, Unit III focuses on employability skills and strategies for implementing academic and career plans. To gain a fuller understanding of the range of material typically covered in career planning courses, we refer readers to the career planning course syllabus presented at the end of this chapter.

Education and Occupational Exploration

Competencies within the educational and occupational exploration domain involve:

1. The skills to enter and participate in education and training;
2. The skills to participate in work and lifelong learning;
3. The skills to locate, evaluate, and interpret career information;

4. The skills to prepare to seek, obtain, maintain, and change jobs;
5. An understanding of how the needs and functions of society influence the nature and structure of work.

Self-concepts evolve over time, making career choice and adjustment a continuous process (Super, 1984). Thus, adults must know how to access and use the information they gather in their educational and occupational exploration. Using self-knowledge and career information effectively requires the ability to identify short- and long-range career goals. Goals emerge from connecting self-knowledge with accurate career information. Making this connection requires the ability to locate relevant career information, identify job opportunities, understand training requirements related to jobs, and demonstrate a general understanding of the nature of work in a global economy (NOICC, 1992).

Inevitably, adults will need to develop strategies for overcoming obstacles in their career paths (e.g., finding adequate child care, obtaining financial resources to cover educational costs). Because engaging in lifelong learning is a common requirement for most career options, adults need to possess the requisite skills for experiencing academic success (e.g., skills related to taking tests, studying, and taking lecture notes). Successful career management also involves being able to seek, obtain, maintain, and change jobs (e.g., using effective job-search skills and demonstrating effective work attitudes and behaviors).

Career practitioners in higher education use a variety of interventions to help students develop knowledge, skills, and awareness in educational and occupational exploration. Career planning courses contain units to help students learn goal-setting skills. Instructors encourage students to identify short- and long-range career plans based on the occupational and self-information they have acquired. Career services centers in higher education contain resources related to educational and occupational information. Career information libraries provide students with printed materials describing educational programs, occupational options, and prospective employers. Career information delivery systems offer students state-specific information describing various educational and occupational opportunities. To access information online, career services centers provide students with listings of Web sites that provide useful occupational information. Career planning courses, workshops, and small groups give students opportunities to learn about the process of locating, evaluating, and interpreting career information. Externships provide students with opportunities to acquire hands-on exposure to specific occupational environments. Students are assigned to job shadow a person employed in an occupation that is of interest to the student. Typically, these assignments last from three to five days and provide students with important information they can use in their educational and career planning.

Career Planning

Career planning competencies include:

1. The skills to make decisions;
2. Understanding the impact of work on individual and family life;

3. Understanding the continuing changes in male/female roles;
4. The skills required to make career transitions.

Like the competencies involved in the two previous domains, effective career planning in adulthood involves a variety of skill sets. For example, adults need to possess sufficient self-understanding for making decisions about training, education, and work. Such understanding encompasses intra-individual characteristics (e.g., skills, values, interests, personality traits) and extra-individual factors (e.g., demands from nonwork life roles, accessibility of training opportunities, financial resources, family support). Because choosing and adjusting to choices are continual processes in career development, skills to manage transitions from one circumstance to another are also essential to effective career planning (NOICC, 1992). Skills in stress management and interpersonal communication and engaging in positive self-talk all contribute to coping with transitions. Because work activity occurs amidst demands from other nonwork life roles, being able to balance demands from multiple life roles is imperative for reducing the stress associated with making transitions. Thus, career planning involves not only planning for work but also planning for the sort of life one hopes to live. Because we live within a social system, planning is often a collective activity encompassing the needs and hopes of the individual and other prominent people in the individual's social network (e.g., partner, children, and parents).

Career practitioners help students in higher education develop career planning skills via individual and/or small-group counseling, workshops, and career planning courses. To develop decision-making skills, researchers suggest that it is important for students to understand multiple approaches that can be used for making decisions. For example, Johnson (1978) identified systematic, spontaneous, internal, and external decision-making styles. Individuals using the systematic decision-making style approach decisions in a rational and logical fashion. They actively seek all relevant information and accept personal responsibility for their decision making. Spontaneous decision makers make decisions holistically and quickly. Internal decision makers process information privately and quietly. External deciders think out loud and talk to others about decisions. Niles et al. (1997) found that students who rely upon a systematic/internal decision-making style tend to be less advanced in their career development and less confident in their ability to complete career development tasks than students who rely upon a systematic/external style. Moreover, the students in the Niles et al. study who had the highest career decision-making self-efficacy and the lowest career indecision were those who preferred a systematic/external decision-making style, had clarified their values, and had acquired occupational information. The students with the lowest career decision-making self-efficacy preferred a systematic/internal style of decision-making and were not clear about how to make career decisions. Thus, it seems important to provide career assistance that is sensitive to students' preferences for gathering and analyzing data in the decision-making process. For example, students who prefer to analyze data internally may benefit from maintaining career decision-making journals and writing career autobiographies. Additionally, to analyze data effectively, internalizers need accurate information about how career decisions are made. Students who prefer to analyze data externally are likely to find participating in career counseling groups and career planning classes to be useful forms of career assistance.

The goals of interventions directed toward helping students develop career planning skills include:

1. Helping students learn to identify and transfer career interests to a plan of action;
2. Helping students to relate interests and goals to opportunities;
3. Helping students to relate their career plans to life goals and opportunities;
4. Helping students learn how to evaluate their progress toward career goals through academic preparation.

Career planning courses contain content to help students understand life-structure issues and to help students formulate plans that provide opportunities for participating in their most salient life roles (Halasz & Kempton, 2000). Computer-assisted career guidance systems, such as *DISCOVER* (ACT, 1995), provide students with opportunities to clarify their salient life roles and consider which roles they think will be important to them in their futures. Standardized and nonstandardized assessment opportunities can be provided to help students consider the impact of work on individual and family life. Group discussions in career planning courses can focus on the continuing changes in male/female roles. By incorporating activities directed toward enhancing stress-management skills, counselors help students acquire skills that are essential to managing career transitions effectively.

Clearly, this list of competencies required for successful career management in adulthood is daunting. Moreover, one could analyze the competencies identified by NOICC at microlevel and expand the list of knowledge, skills, and behaviors exponentially. It is unrealistic to expect students to develop all of these skills while they are enrolled in higher education. However, career services practitioners in higher education can strive to help sensitize students to the challenges they are likely to encounter as their careers develop. Career practitioners in higher education can also foster students' career development by providing comprehensive and systematic interventions directed toward developing basic competencies in the three domains of self-knowledge, educational/career exploration, and career planning. Although our returning student, Robert, probably needs assistance across all three domains, he first needs help enhancing his self-knowledge and his understanding of the transition process, and in bolstering his self-esteem.

MODELS, SERVICES, AND STANDARDS FOR CAREER DEVELOPMENT INTERVENTIONS IN HIGHER EDUCATION

Models

To deliver career services systematically and comprehensively, practitioners are required to operate from models of service delivery that are also systematic and comprehensive. There are a variety of models for career services that can be used to develop the competencies that are essential for effectively managing one's career in adulthood (e.g., Colozzi, 2000; Crites, 1981; Reardon et al., 2000; Sampson, 2008). For example, Crites suggests that as students progress through higher education, they need assistance in narrowing the range of occupational options under consideration.

Typically, students begin the career development process in higher education by: (a) exploring a variety of options, (b) then crystallizing a narrow range of specific options, (c) at which point the student makes a commitment to a particular choice and specifies a college major, (d) which leads to implementing the option selected. Crites recommends that career development professionals help students progress through this process by first assessing each student's career development needs and then offering group and individual career development interventions based on the needs identified for each student. (Interventions with Robert need to begin with a comprehensive assessment of his needs; however, it seems clear he will need to begin at the beginning of the Crites model, i.e., exploring.) To further assess students' development, Crites recommends readministering the needs assessment to students at the end of their first year of study. Data from the second assessment can be used to identify further interventions needed to foster each student's career development.

Powell and Kirts (1980) propose a systems approach to career services in higher education. Their approach focuses on providing awareness programming to new students. Awareness programming involves giving all new students an overview of career services. In large-group meetings, career services staff members and upper-level students describe the career development process and the services available to help students advance in their careers. Voluntary small-group meetings of fewer than 30 students then follow these large-group meetings. In the small-group meetings career counselors and student peer counselors describe in greater detail the career services available and respond to students' specific questions and concerns. Students needing additional assistance are then referred to the appropriate career service (e.g., individual career counseling, career planning courses).

The second component in the Powell and Kirts (1980) model involves self-assessment activities. Powell and Kirts recommend offering small groups in which students first view a videotape of upper-class students who discuss the ways in which various career services have been useful to them. Students use information provided via the videotape to identify resources that they think might help them learn more about themselves (e.g., workshops, individual counseling, and groups).

The next phase in the Powell and Kirts model focuses on exposure as students engage actively in career exploration. Career exploration activities are offered to help students integrate self-assessment information and occupational information. Powell and Kirts note that, in this phase of their model, career counseling and traditional placement functions merge. They recommend using career courses in which alumni and local business leaders link educational and career information (i.e., they identify how academic subjects are relevant for various occupations). Alumni and local business leaders can also serve as resources for creating externship and internship opportunities to expose students to career opportunities.

The final phase of the Powell and Kirts model (1980) is training, which involves providing students who are approaching graduation with training in job-search skills. This phase of the model involves an approach similar to the one used in the awareness phase. Specifically, career services staff members provide students in their last year of study with a large-group (convocation-like) overview of placement services. Students are then invited to participate in small-group sessions according to their academic majors. These sessions focus on the specifics of job searching using videotapes of recent graduates discussing the requisite skills and attitudes for effective job searching. Subsequent group meetings focus on resume writing, mock interviewing, accessing information about job opportunities, and so on.

Awareness programming would be especially useful to Robert. As a returning student, Robert needs to learn about the range of services available to him. The inclusion of returning students in the videotapes focused on how students have found career services useful would be very important to Robert. Because Robert is experiencing many of the fears typically experienced by returning students, it would be beneficial for him to hear other returning students express similar concerns and discuss how they coped with them. As he moves through career exploration and placement activities, career counselors will need to be sensitive to Robert's life situation as a returning student with family responsibilities and, most likely, limited geographical mobility.

Reardon (1996) also describes a comprehensive career services model in use at Florida State University. The Florida State model is a curricular career information service (CCIS) model with five modules. In the CCIS model, career services focus on providing students with an introduction to the service, orienting students to the career decision-making process, helping students engage in self-assessment, helping students locate career information, and helping students match majors and jobs. A unique aspect of the CCIS model is that it is self-help oriented and uses paraprofessionals, instructional models, and multimedia resources in service delivery. The CCIS model is a comprehensive and efficient approach to career services. It also allows students to direct their learning about career planning and manage their own career development.

Recently, Sampson (2008) recommended that career programs in higher education use an eight-step model, which begins with evaluating and assessing current career resources and services and then, based upon the initial assessment, revising and adapting career resources and services. Then the revised and improved resources and services are integrated into the existing career services with appropriate staff training. Sampson notes the importance of conducting a pilot study to evaluate the new program. Data from the pilot test are used to further revise and develop the program prior to final implementation with ongoing training and evaluation.

Models for service delivery such as the ones discussed reflect not only the expanded and developmental perspective within career services but also expanded modes of service delivery. They clearly demonstrate the variety of ways in which career services in higher education have gone beyond their initial focus on placement to help students develop the knowledge, skills, and awareness required to manage their career development effectively.

For example, results from a survey by the National Association of Colleges and Employers (NACE) indicate that roughly four out of every five career centers provided group-oriented career counseling interventions and workshops (Collins, 1998). Fifty-two percent of the institutions participating in the NACE survey offered career planning courses. Hardesty (1991) conducted a meta-analysis focusing on the effectiveness of career planning courses and found that students completing career courses were "40% more capable of making career decisions than students who did not complete these courses" (p. 185). For students completing career planning courses, Hardesty found that they were 48% more certain about their career choices at completion of the course than they were at the beginning. A recent meta-analysis conducted by Whiston, Sexton, and Lasoff (1998) compared the effectiveness of workshops, career planning courses, computer programs, and individual counseling and found that individual career counseling was the most effective. However, when one considers the range of needs that must be addressed by career centers and the number of career counselors available, it becomes readily apparent that providing individual career counseling to all students is not possible. Moreover, some students may benefit from the peer support that is often experienced in group-oriented career interventions. Rayman (1996) contends that though individual career counseling is at the core of the profession, comprehensive career centers should use a wide range of approaches in delivering career services to students.

Services

The models discussed also reflect the fact that career services are delivered to students by a variety of people in a variety of venues. Herr, Cramer, and Niles (2004) identify four major approaches used for delivering career services to students in higher education: (1) courses, workshops, and seminars that offer structured group experiences in topics such as career decision making, career planning, and job-search skills; (2) group counseling activities directed toward students experiencing such issues as career indecision, career indecisiveness, and job-search anxiety; (3) individual career counseling; and (4) placement programs such as on-campus and/or online job interviewing. Obviously, the use of computer-assisted career guidance and computer information delivery systems offer vehicles for service delivery that range from career decision making to placement. Computer-assisted career guidance systems have existed for some time; more recent placement-oriented computer services include virtual job fairs, online resumes, and chat rooms for job seekers (Miller & McDaniels, 2001). Social networking Web sites such as Facebook, and software applications such as Skype provide opportunities for online career services delivery that many college and university students find appealing.

Davidson (2001) stresses that as career services professionals increase their reliance on technology in career services delivery, they also need to address the wide range of ethical issues associated with increased use of technology. For example, researchers suggest that it is important to balance "high-tech" with "high-touch." Students need access to humans as well as computer-based services. One does not replace the other. Computer-based services are not yet effective at providing empathy, addressing individual student needs, and responding to subtle, nonverbal expressions in client statements. Moreover, many online services have not been constructed according to the ethical and professional standards to which career services professionals adhere.

These multiple approaches for services delivery provide the means by which students receive a wide array of career-related services. For example, Reardon, Zunker, and Dyal (1979) identify 31 categories of career services delivered by 302 institutions of higher education. These services include, but are not limited to, providing occupational information via computerized and printed resources, job-search skills training, educational information, standardized and nonstandardized assessment opportunities, referrals to campus and community resources, self-help materials, training in decision making, assertiveness training, communications skills training, career planning courses, externships, internships, on-campus and off-campus job interview opportunities, and job interview training via videotaped role-play practice.

Herr (1989) observes that, in addition to individual career counseling of students, there are at least nine categories of career services in higher education. These categories affirm the comprehensiveness of career services and include approaches such as:

1. Infusing academic subject matter systematically with information pertinent to career development;
2. Providing courses for academic credit that focus on career development;
3. Using external resources (e.g., speakers, externships, and internships) to provide direct communication of career-related information;
4. Integrating placement and transfer processes in support of career planning;
5. Offering opportunities for work-study/cooperative education;
6. Providing decentralized counseling using academic departments as the location for counselors who, among other responsibilities, coordinate the career and academic advisement of students;
7. Providing seminars in residence halls, student unions, and so on, that focus on college life and educational and career planning;
8. Providing group counseling focused on self-awareness and career planning;
9. Providing interactive, computer-based career guidance and information systems.

From the perspective of the broad goals to be met in career services in higher education, Herr et al. (2004) contend that services such as these are offered to achieve the following goals:

1. Provide students with assistance in the selection of a major field of study;
2. Provide students with assistance in self-assessment and self-analysis;
3. Provide students with assistance in understanding the world-of-work;
4. Provide students with assistance in decision making;
5. Provide assistance that addresses the unique needs of various subpopulations of students;
6. Provide students with assistance with access to the world-of-work.

As Robert progressed through career counseling, he increased his career and self-awareness through self-assessment exercises. He also participated in a career planning group consisting of returning students focused on crystallizing their career choices after being employed in the labor force for substantial periods of time. These activities helped Robert decide to pursue a career in education. Specifically, he decided to become a social studies teacher at the secondary school level. He thought this career option would provide him with opportunities to help others in meaningful ways while also spending more time with his family than he had in his previous jobs.

Standards

Because various models and approaches to career development interventions in higher education exist, there is the need for the professional community to identify the essential components of career services programs. Standards provide useful guides for delivering career development interventions in higher education. The comprehensive career models and services discussed thus far are similar to the perspectives advocated by the Council for the Advancement of Standards for Student Services/Development Programs (CAS) (Council for the Advancement of Standards, 2010). The Council is a consortium of professional associations in higher education that collectively devised and published *Standards and Guidelines*, a document that recommends criteria for student services in colleges and universities. One of these student services is career planning and placement. In the CAS Standards, the mission for career services centers is described "assisting students and other designated clients in developing, evaluating, and implementing career, education, and employment plans" (CAS, 2010, p. 6). The CAS Standards and Guidelines also stipulate that career services programs in higher education should be institutional resources regarding career issues and employment data. Career services professionals in higher education should also develop positive connections with academic units and external constituents. Career services should be directed toward helping students to develop self-understanding and knowledge of occupational information and trends; to identify academic programs of study that match the student's interests and abilities; to increase each student's sense of ownership and responsibility related to coping effectively with career development tasks; to gain relevant career-related experiences (co-curricular, extracurricular, and experiential); to develop job-search skills and networking skills with alumni, prospective employers, and potential future academic programs; and to learn how to use technology to manage their career development.

To accomplish its goals, career services in higher education must provide the following services: career advising, counseling, and education, information and resources on careers and further study, opportunities for career exploration through experiential education, job-search services, graduate and professional school or further education planning, employer relations and recruitment services, consultation services to faculty and administrators.

The CAS Standards (CAS, 2010) also address topics that are essential for the day-to-day operation of career services in higher education. These topics include:

- *Leadership* (e.g., leaders of career services programs must have appropriate training; be able to articulate a clear vision for career services; set goals and objectives; prescribe and practice ethical behavior; and manage, plan, budget, and evaluate services/personnel)
- *Organization and Management* (e.g., policies and procedures must be current and accessible, there must be written performance expectations for all staff members, and processes for resolving grievances must be clearly stated)
- *Human Resources* (e.g., there must be adequate staffing, selection training and staffing procedures must be established, support staff must be adequate, affirmative action policies must be followed, and professional development opportunities must be encouraged and supported)
- *Financial Resources* (e.g., career services must have adequate funding)
- *Technology* (e.g., Internet-based resources providing current information regarding the mission, location, staffing, programs, and services available, computer-assisted career guidance systems, online recruiting and employment systems)

- *Facilities and Equipment* (e.g., facilities and equipment must be adequate and suitably located; facilities, technology, and equipment must comply with federal, state, and local requirements for access and safety)
- *Legal Responsibilities* (e.g., staff members must be knowledgeable about laws and regulations pertaining to service delivery)
- *Equity and Access* (e.g., staff members and services must not discriminate on the basis of age, color, disability, gender, national origin, race, religious creed, sexual orientation, and/or veteran status)
- *Campus and External Relations* (e.g., career services programs establish, maintain, and promote effective relations with relevant campus offices and external agencies)
- *Diversity* (e.g., career services staff members and programs must nurture environments in which similarities and differences among people are recognized and honored)
- *Ethics* (e.g., relevant ethical standards must be adhered to in all career services practices)
- *Assessment and Evaluation* (e.g., regular and systematic quantitative and qualitative evaluations must occur to determine program quality)

The CAS Standards (2010) reflect the fact that career services in higher education extend throughout the campus and beyond. Comprehensive career services interact with other student services units (e.g., counseling, residential life), academic units, and community resources. The Standards also provide career practitioners with a useful list of topics and issues that must be addressed in the overall operation of career services in higher education. In these ways, the Standards can be used as benchmarks against which quality and effectiveness of career services can be assessed.

The Professional Standards for College and University Career Services developed by the National Association of Colleges and Employers (NACE, 2010) overlap with the CAS (2010) Standards and Guidelines. According to the NACE Standards, key program components for career services in higher education must be defined clearly, designed in alignment with the student needs, and based upon contemporary career services practices. There is also the expectation that career services providers will work collaboratively with academic units, faculty members, and prospective employers. Drawing upon resources such as college newspapers, Web sites, and other electronic media helps to increase the reach of the career services provided. Specific program components include: (a) career advising/counseling, (b) career information, (c) employment services, (d) graduate school planning, and (e) experiential education.

Career advising and career counseling can occur through individual career counseling appointments, group programs, career planning courses, outreach programs, and via information technology. The primary intent of each of these services is to empower students to make informed educational and career choices based in accurate self-, educational, and occupational information. Career advising and career counseling services are sensitive to a student's cultural contexts as well as the developmental and personal contexts each student must address when constructing career and educational plans. Integrating experiential activities (e.g., job shadowing, volunteering, externships, externships, part-time employment) into career advising and career counseling helps students develop short and long-term career plans.

Career information includes helping students acquire accurate self-assessment activities, current occupational and labor market information, effective job-search strategies, and accurate employer information (NACE, 2010).

Employment services include helping students engage in exploration related to career possibilities that match their career goals, developing job-search competencies, obtaining employer information, making connections with prospective employers, and developing relevant job search networks (NACE, 2010).

Graduate school planning activities include helping students to identify graduate school opportunities that match their interests, skills, and goals; acquire information regarding prospective programs; learn how to apply to graduate school programs; and develop the skills to connect effectively with potential graduate school programs (NACE, 2010).

Experiential education activities include working with employers and academic units to help students experience career-related learning via job shadowing, volunteering, internships, externships, cooperative education, and apprenticeships. When necessary, career services should also include helping students identify potential funding sources for engaging in experiential education opportunities (NACE, 2010).

The comprehensive NACE 2010 Professional Standards for College and University Career Services also address other important topics for developing and delivering career services in colleges and universities. Specifically, the Standards address the following topics: program management, office organization, job descriptions for career services professionals, job responsibilities for career services directors, professional positions, pre-professional positions, professional student employee and volunteer positions, support staff and technical positions, financial resources, facilities and equipment, technology considerations, campus and external relations, employer relations and recruitment services, legal responsibilities, equal opportunity, access, affirmative action, diversity, ethics, program evaluation, assessment, and research.

MANAGING CAREER SERVICES IN HIGHER EDUCATION

The NACE (2010) and CAS (2010) Standards highlight important topics for the management of career services in higher education. Although a full discussion of topics pertaining to managing career services in higher education is beyond the scope of this chapter, there are a few topics that are important to review. For example, it is important to consider the organizational structure of the career services operation because it substantially influences the planning and delivery of career services.

A prominent issue influencing the delivery of career services in higher education is whether career services should be centralized or decentralized. A centralized structure is the most common one for organizing career services in higher education (Powell & Kirts, 1980). Centralized services have clear advantages. Because services are located primarily in one place, it is clear to faculty, students, and employers where career services are provided on campus. Herr et al. (1993) note additional advantages of a centralized, rather than decentralized, career services structure:

1. Centralized services are more likely to achieve a critical mass in terms of professional staff.
2. There are substantial efficiencies and economies of scale that occur in terms of interview room use, career information resources, and support staff.
3. Because a centralized career services structure draws a very heterogeneous student population, it creates a more vibrant, challenging, and interesting environment for students and staff. (p. 57)

Herr et al. (1993) are quick to point out, however, that there are also advantages to decentralized career services (e.g., the service may be viewed as more personalized and the services are likely to be more accessible because they are located closer to where students spend a substantial portion of their time). Some institutions provide a combination of centralized and decentralized career services. For example, career counseling services can be decentralized and placement services can be centralized. There is some logic to this approach due to the fact that in decentralized structures, career counselors often have more direct contact with students and, thereby, find it easier to establish relationships with the students with whom they work. Providing centralized placement services is likely to be less confusing to employers as it is clear to everyone where this activity occurs on campus.

Another issue pertaining to managing career services in higher education relates to the place of career services within the institutional structure. Career service units in higher education typically report to the chief administrator responsible for student services or the chief academic administrator. The results of a survey conducted by the College Placement Council (1991) indicate that nearly three-fourths of career services offices report to the vice president of student services. Reporting to the vice president of student services has several advantages. For example, in this administrative structure career services are likely to be viewed as an integral aspect of student services. Because in this structure career services personnel meet regularly with professionals representing other student services units, communication among career services staff members and other student services providers (e.g., counselors, residence life directors) will probably be enhanced. This facilitates service delivery in various ways (e.g., referrals, programming, collaboration among student services professionals). There is a strong possibility that the vice president of student services will have a good understanding of, and appreciation for, the complete range of career services provided by the unit. When career services offices report to the chief academic administrator, they are better aligned with the primary enterprise of the institution. This also provides benefits to career services, such as facilitating relationships with faculty.

The ways in which these administrative issues are resolved in specific institutions will most likely depend on the structure of the overall student services operation and the university itself. Although Herr et al. (1993) view this issue as important for career services delivery, they are careful not to overstate the case, noting that "clearly, the structure of career services must be compatible with the institution in which it operates. Our experience has been that excellent career services often exist despite, rather than because of, a particular organizational structure" (pp. 106–107).

Rayman (1999) identified 10 imperatives for career services in higher education for the next millennium. These imperatives provide college and university career practitioners with useful guidelines as they plan and evaluate the career assistance they provide to students.

- *Imperative 1:* We must acknowledge the lifelong nature of career development and initiate programs and services that enable and encourage students to take responsibility for their own career destinies.
- *Imperative 2:* We must accept and embrace technology as our ally and shape its use to free staff time for those tasks that require human sensitivity.
- *Imperative 3:* We must continue to refine and strengthen our professional identity and that of career services within the academy.
- *Imperative 4:* We must acknowledge and accept that individual career counseling is at the core of our profession and endeavor to maintain and enhance the centrality of individual career counseling in the career development process.
- *Imperative 5:* We must forge cooperative relationships with faculty, advising professionals, other student affairs professionals, administrators, parents, and student groups to take advantage of the "multiplier effect" that such collaborative relationships can have in furthering our goal of enhanced student career development.
- *Imperative 6:* We must redouble our efforts to meet the changing career development needs of an increasingly diverse student body.
- *Imperative 7:* We must accept our position as the most obvious and continuing link between corporate America and the academy, but we also must maintain our focus on career development and not allow ourselves to be seduced into institutional fundraising at the expense of quality career services.
- *Imperative 8:* We must acknowledge and accept that on-campus recruiting as we have known it is a thing of the past and develop alternative means of facilitating the transition from college to work.
- *Imperative 9:* We must resolve the ambiguities that exist about our role in delivering alumni career services and solicit from our alumni associations the resource support necessary to provide these services.
- *Imperative 10:* We must advocate more effectively for resources to maintain and increase our role in facilitating student career development within the academy, and we must become more efficient and innovative in our use of existing resources.

Rayman's imperatives reveal both the challenges and opportunities for career practitioners in higher education in the 21st century. Clearly, the challenges focus on dwindling resources within the context of a growing need to help students in higher education move forward in their career development. The growing need for career services represents a tremendous opportunity to equip students with the knowledge, awareness, and skills to manage their careers effectively in the emerging workplace.

MyCounselingLab™

Summary

Career services in higher education have a long and venerable history. In many ways, the evolution of these services reflects the evolution of the field in general as services evolved from an orientation toward job placement to a full range of career planning services being offered to meet the needs of diverse student populations. Increasingly, career services providers in higher education enlist a broad range of resources to deliver comprehensive career assistance to students. Alumni, faculty, peers, and community and business representatives are among those participating in the delivery of career services in higher education. Coordinating and providing comprehensive services requires careful and systematic planning, a familiarity with the career development competencies toward which services must be directed, knowledge of current standards for service delivery, awareness of the current literature identifying efficacious career development interventions, and skills in conducting formative and summative evaluations of career services. It is our hope that comprehensive career services, staffed by an adequate cadre of career professionals committed to meeting the career development needs of diverse student populations, will become the norm in higher education. Given survey results in which students identify career planning as their greatest concern, it would seem difficult, at best, for higher education institutions to justify anything less.

Case Study

Chandra is a 21-year-old junior at a large midwestern university. She was the youngest of four children and was raised by her mother and father who lived in New Orleans until hurricane Katrina destroyed their home and they were forced to move in with her father's parents in Alabama. Chandra lost all of her possessions in the devastation caused by Katrina (which occurred when Chandra was in her first year of college). During high school, she attended an urban parochial high school in New Orleans.

She has come to the university's career center to get some help in making a career decision. During her first session with the career counselor, Chandra talks about a number of occupations she has considered. She likes to write and has thought about working as a journalist or a researcher. She is also very concerned about the environment, but she is not aware of any occupations that would allow her to be involved in environmental issues. She also likes working with children and elderly people and wants to know how she can tie these interests into her career. She has considered the possibility of going to law school because it seems like a "smart thing to do." She is clear that her experience with Katrina has changed her and she wants to make a difference in the lives of others, especially those who are in "difficult situations" like she was.

Her struggle to make a career decision is also reflected in the difficulty she has experienced in selecting an academic major. After "trying out" several possibilities, Chandra decided to major in history and French. These majors seem a bit meaningless to her now. She is not involved in any extracurricular or community activities.

Chandra presents herself in a confident way. She is very talkative and animated and seems at ease throughout the session. Her primary concern is identifying what career would be best for her "given all that has happened" in her life. Toward the end of the first session, she asks you about how you got into counseling because it is another occupation that interests her.

What are Chandra's career development needs? Which career theories help you understand her situation? Are there any challenges you would experience in trying to understand her situation? What steps would you take to help her?

Student Activities

1. What career development tasks do you think are most important for students enrolled in higher education to address?

2. What factors do you think could negatively influence the career development of these students?

3. What are three strategies you could use to foster positive career development in these students?

4. What do you think is the most common type of career assistance provided to students enrolled in higher education? Do you think this type of assistance is helpful? If so, why? If not, why not?

5. What career development challenges did you experience in higher education? What would have helped you address these challenges effectively?

6. Why do you think so few students enrolled in higher education seek career planning assistance from their career services office? What are some strategies that you think could be effective in helping more students get more actively engaged in their career planning?

7. Refer to the MyCounselingLab Video and Resource Library and select the video entitled, *21st Century Application of Career Construction Theory with a College Student: Dr. Mark Savickas*. What are the benefits of using this model in a postsecondary school career center? What are the limitations of using this model in a career center?

8. Refer to the MyCounselingLab Video and Resource Library and select the video entitled, *21st Century Application of Holland's Theory with a College Student: Dr. Janet Lenz*. What are the benefits of using this model in a postsecondary school career center? What are the limitations of using this model in a career center?

References

ACT, Inc. (1995). DISCOVER for colleges and adults [Computer software]. Iowa City, IA: Author.

American Council on Education. (1999). *The American freshman national norms for fall 1998.* Washington, DC: Author.

Association for Career and Technical Education (ACTE). (2011). *CTE information.* Washington, DC: Author. Retrieved June 18, 2011, from http://www.acteonline.org/cte_info.aspx.

College Placement Council. (1991, July). *Career Planning and Placement Survey. Special report. Spotlight.* Bethlehem, PA: Author.

Collins, M. (1998). Snapshot of the profession. *Journal of Career Planning and Employment, 41,* 51–55.

Colozzi, E. A. (2000). Toward the development of systemic career guidance. In D. A. Luzzo (Ed.), *Career counseling of college students* (pp. 285–310). Washington, DC: American Psychological Association.

Conyers, L. M., & Szymanski, E. M. (1998). The effectiveness of an integrated career intervention for college students with and without disabilities. *Journal of Postsecondary Education and Disability, 13,* 23–34.

Council for the Advancement of Standards in Higher Education. (2010). *Career services: CAS standards and guidelines.* Washington, DC: Author.

Crites, J. O. (1981). *Career counseling: Models, methods, and materials.* New York: McGraw-Hill.

Davidson, M. M. (2001). The computerization of career services: Critical issues to consider. *Journal of Career Development, 27,* 217–228.

Fassinger, R. E., & O'Brien, K. M. (2000). Career counseling with college women: A scientist-practitioner-advocate model of intervention. In D. A. Luzzo (Ed.), *Career counseling of college students* (pp. 253–265). Washington, DC: American Psychological Association.

Friehe, M., Aune, B., & Leuenberger, J. (1996). Career service needs of college students with disabilities. *The Career Development Quarterly, 44,* 289–300.

Gray, K. C., & Herr, E. L. (2000). *Other ways to win: Creating alternatives for high school graduates* (2nd ed.). Thousand Oaks, CA: Corwin Press.

Halasz, T., & Kempton, C. B. (2000). Career planning workshops and courses. In D. A. Luzzo (Ed.), *Career counseling of college students* (pp. 157–169).

Washington, DC: American Psychological Association.

Hardesty, P. H. (1991). Undergraduate career courses for credit: A review and meta-analysis. *Journal of College Student Development, 32,* 184–185.

Healy, C. C., & Reilly, K. C. (1989). Career needs of community college students: Implications for services and theory. *Journal of College Student Personnel, 30,* 541–545.

Herr, E. L., Cramer, S. H., & Niles, S. G. (2004). *Career guidance and counseling through the lifespan: Systematic approaches* (6th ed.). Boston: Allyn & Bacon.

Herr, E. L., Rayman, J., & Garis, J. W. (1993). *Handbook for the college and university career center.* Westport, CT: Greenwood Press.

Hitchings, W. E., & Retish, P. (2000). The career development needs of students with learning disabilities. In D. A. Luzzo (Ed.), *Career counseling of college students* (pp. 253–265). Washington, DC: American Psychological Association.

Johnson, R. H. (1978). Individual styles of decision-making: A theoretical model for counseling. *Personnel and Guidance Journal, 56,* 531–536.

Luzzo, D. A. (2000). Career development of returning-adult and graduate students. In D. A. Luzzo (Ed.), *Career counseling of college students* (pp. 191–200). Washington, DC: American Psychological Association.

Marklein, M. (2011). *4-Year Colleges Graduate 53 percent of students in 6 Years.* Retrieved February 19, 2011, from usatoday.com.

Marron, D., & Rayman, J. R. (2002). Addressing the career development needs of adult students in research university settings. In S. Niles (Ed.), *Adult career development: Concepts, models, and practices* (3rd ed., pp. 319–334). Tulsa: OK: National Career Development Association.

Miller, K. L., & McDaniels, R. M. (2001). Cyberspace, the new frontier. *Journal of Career Development, 27,* 199–206.

National Association of Colleges and Employers (2010). Professional Standards for College and University Career Services–2009. Bethlehem, PA: Author.

National Occupational Information Coordinating Committee (NOICC), U.S. Department of Labor. (1992).

The National Career Development Guidelines Project. Washington, DC: U.S. Department of Labor.

Niles, S. G., Erford, B. T., Hunt, B., & Watts, R. H. (1997). Decision-making styles and career development of college students. *Journal of College Student Development, 38,* 479–488.

Ohler, D. L., Levinson, E. M., & Barker, W. F. (1996). Career maturity in college students with learning disabilities. *The Career Development Quarterly, 44,* 278–288.

Pope, M. S., Prince, J. P., & Mitchell, K. (2000). Responsible career counseling with lesbian and gay students. In D. A. Luzzo (Ed.), *Career counseling of college students* (pp. 267–281). Washington, DC: American Psychological Association.

Powell, R., & Kirts, D. K. (1980). *Career services today: A dynamic college profession.* Bethlehem, PA: The College Placement Council.

Project on Student Debt. (2010). *Quick Facts about student debt.* Washington, DC: Institute for College Access & Success. Retrieved on June 17, 2011, from http://projectonstudentdebt.org/files/File/Debt_Facts_and_Sources.pdf.

Rayman, J. R. (1996). Apples and oranges in the career center: Reaction to R. Reardon. *Journal of Counseling and Development, 74,* 286–287.

Rayman, J. R. (1999). Career services imperative for the next millennium. *The Career Development Quarterly, 48,* 175–184.

Reardon, R. C. (1996). A program and cost analysis of a self-directed career decision-making program in a university career center. *Journal of Counseling and Development, 74,* 280–285.

Reardon, R. C., Lenz, J. G., Sampson, J. P., Jr., & Peterson, G. W. (2000). *Career development and planning: A comprehensive approach.* Pacific Grove, CA: Brooks/Cole.

Reardon, R. C., Zunker, V., & Dyal, M. A. (1979). The status of career planning programs and career centers in colleges and universities. *Vocational Guidance Quarterly, 28,* 154–159.

Reed, C. A., Reardon, R. C., Lenz, J. G., & Leirer, S. J. (2001). A cognitive career course: From theory to practice. *The Career Development Quarterly, 50,* 158–167.

Sampson, J. P., Jr. (2008). *Designing and implementing career programs: A handbook for effective practice.* Broken Arrow, OK: National Career Development Association.

Singletary, M. (2009). The color of money: Getting through college these days. *The Washington Post.* Retrieved June 18, 2011, from http://www.washingtonpost.com/wp-dyn/content/article/2009/10/21/AR2009102103664.html? sub=AR.

Statistical Abstract of the United States. (2008). Washington, DC: U.S. Census Bureau.

Super, D. E. (1984). Leisure: What it is and might be. *Journal of Career Development, 11,* 71–80.

U.S. Census Bureau. (2007). http://www.census.gov/Press-Release/www/releases/archives/education/007909.html, retrieved December, 1, 2007.

Weissberg, M., Berenstein, M., Cote, A., Cravey, B., & Heath, K. (1982). An assessment of the personal, career, and academic needs of undergraduate students. *Journal of College Student Personnel, 23,* 415–422.

Whiston, S. C., Sexton, T. L., & Lasoff, D. L. (1998). Career-intervention outcome: A replication and extension of Oliver and Spokane (1998). *Journal of Counseling Psychology, 45,* 150–165.

Whiteley, S. M., Mahaffey, P. J., & Geer, C. A. (1987). The campus counseling center: A profile of staffing patterns and services. *Journal of College Student Personnel, 28,* 71–81.

Course Syllabus for a Career Planning Class

Effective Career Decision Making
Fall 2011
Tuesday and Thursday 11:15 AM–12:30 PM
202 Rackley

Office: Career Services
Office Hours: 2:00–3:00 p.m. Tuesday and Wednesday, and by appointment

Text: *The Career Fitness Program:*
Exercising Your Options (9th ed.)

Handout packet provided by the instructor

Purpose

This course is designed for students who are undecided about their major and career selection. This course is not appropriate for students who have already chosen a major and developed career goals. It does not cover topics such as job-search strategies, resume writing, cover letters, and interviewing skills. One of the other career courses offered by Career Services would be more appropriate for these students than this course.

Course Objectives

1. Engage in a variety of activities and experiences that are useful in building knowledge about yourself, careers, academic majors, and the world-of-work.
2. Know the core concepts and applications of basic career theories.
3. Identification and integration of personal history, interests, values, skills, and abilities.
4. Understand how career assessments (e.g., the Self-Directed Search and the Myers-Briggs Type Indicator) are used to facilitate career decision making.
5. Gain information and support through the use of the university's academic advising and career resources.
6. Learn how to use workplace trends to enhance current and future career decisions.

Students with disabilities who require accommodations should consult with the instructor within the first two weeks of class to address modifications that are needed to complete course requirements. Consistent with university policy, any student requesting an accommodation must provide documentation from the Office for Disability Services.

GRADING SCALE

A = 279–300	C+ = 231–239	Miscellaneous 15%
A– = 270–278	C = 210–230	Lifeline and Brief Paper 5%
B+ = 261–269	D = 180–209	Occupation Information
B = 249–260	F = Below 180	Interview Paper 20%
B– = 240–248		Career Autobiography Paper 20%
		Exams 20%
		Group Presentation 10%
		Attendance and Participation 10%

LATE ASSIGNMENT POLICY

Assignments: Lose one point per late class period. Career Autobiography Paper and Occupation Interview Paper: lose five points per late class period.

If you will be absent on a day the assignment is due, you are expected to turn the assignment in prior to your absence if possible.

Course Schedule

Date	Class Topic	Reading	Assignment Due
Tues., August 22	Introduction. Review of course syllabus and requirements. Discussion of student and instructor expectations. (Introduce Introductory Assessments.)		
Thurs., August 24	Effective career decision making. Career planning issues. Orientation to career services.		Introductory Assessments
Tues., August 29	Career development theories. (Introduce Lifeline assignment.)		
Thurs., August 31	Career development theories continued. (Hand out semester packets.)	Chapter 1 "Taking Stock"	
Tues., September 5	Career assessment strategies. The career counseling process. Orientation to academic majors. (Assign DISCOVER.) (Receive group assignments.) (Sign up for tour of Career Information Center.)		
Thurs., September 7	Small Group Workshop 1— Sharing and discussion of Lifelines		
Tues., September 12	Personal and career decision-making strategies. (Administer the Myers-Briggs Type Indicator.)	Chapter 8 "Making Decisions"	Exercises 8.1 and 8.15

Date	Class Topic	Reading	Assignment Due
Thurs., September 14	Values decisions in career and life planning. Values and work satisfaction. Lifeline Brief "Values Paper."	Chapter 3 "Values Clarification"	Lifeline Brief Paper Exercises 3.1 and 3.2
Tues., September 19	Interests. Holland's typology of personality and career interests. (Assign Self-Directed Search.)	"Focusing on You: Personality and Interests"	Interest Checklist for Worker Trait Groups pages 65–69
Thurs., September 21	Interpretation of the Self-Directed Search.		Self-Directed Search
Tues., September 26	Personality characteristics and workplace preferences. Interpretation of the Myers-Briggs Type Indicator.		
Thurs., September 28	Abilities and their role in academic and career planning. Synthesis–integration of internal information. (Introduce Career Autobiography.)	Chapter 5 "Skills Assessment"	Assessing Your Skills, pages 85–86 and Exercise 5.8
Tues., October 3	Exam 1		
Thurs., October 5	Small-Group Workshop 2—Review of assessment results. Bring results from Self-Directed Search, Myers-Briggs Type Indicator, Values and Skills exercises, Majors Checklist, DISCOVER, and Self-Assessment Summary.		Majors Checklist and Self-Assessment Summary
Tues., October 10	FALL BREAK		
Thurs., October 12	World-of-work work sectors; relationship between basic work tasks, academic majors, and career choice. (Assign Advising Interviews.)	Chapter 7 "Information Integration." Review pages 72–73.	Discover Reaction Paper
Tues., October 17 or Wed., October 18	Career information resources at Career Services. Class meets in room 410 Boucke at 5:00 p.m.		
Thurs., October 19	Small-Group Workshop 3—Planning for group presentation. Decision-making style and personal issues effect on major/career decision making.		Career Autobiography Paper
Tues., October 24	Interviewing for occupational information. (Introduce Occupation Informational Interview paper.)		
Thurs., October 26	Experiential Learning: Internships, externships, summer jobs, education abroad, activities, and volunteer work. Collegiate and community involvement and its role in career development.		Exercise 7.6
Tues., October 31	Guest speakers.		

Date	Class Topic	Reading	Assignment Due
Thurs., November 2	Discuss academic advising interviews.		Summaries of Advising Interview Experiences
Tues., November 7	Cultural Diversity: personal and career issues related to gender, race/ethnicity, and disability status.	Chapter 6 "The World and You"	
Thurs., November 9	Small-Group Workshop 4—Cultural Diversity. Discuss the impact of the culturally diverse workplace on career decisions.		Multicultural Me
Tues., November 14	Group Presentations.		
Thurs., November 16	Group Presentations.		
Tues., November 21	Workplace trends and issues.		Article from popular literature about a current workplace trend or issue for group discussion
Thurs., November 23	Thanksgiving		
Tues., November 28	Discuss Informational Interviews.		Occupation Informational Interview Paper
Thurs., November 30	Exam 2. Continue discussion of Informational Interviews.		
Tues., December 5	Course wrap-up and evaluations.		
Thurs., December 7	Small-Group Workshop 5—Putting it all together. Discussion of course learning as it applies to personal career situations. Next steps for career planning.		Putting It All Together

ASSIGNMENT DESCRIPTIONS

Assessments

You will be required to take three formal assessments: the Self-Directed Search, the Myers-Briggs Type Indicator, and DISCOVER.

Myers-Briggs Type Indicator (to be completed in class on September 12)

Self-Directed Search   Due: September 21

The Myers-Briggs and the Self-Directed Search are popular assessment tools that measure personality and interests, respectively. As we will discuss in class, personality preferences and tendencies and personal interests are important contributors to the career development process. The instruments will be administered in class. It is your responsibility to attend class and complete the assessments as instructed.

DISCOVER   Reaction Paper Due: October 12

DISCOVER is a computer-assisted career guidance system (CACGS) housed in Career Services, 410 Boucke, which can assist you with making career decisions. You will need to schedule a 1-hour appointment between September 6 and October 11. Appointments can be scheduled by going to 412 Boucke between the hours of 8:00 AM and 5:00 PM. More details on this assignment will be provided in class on September 5.

Lifeline and Paper   Lifeline Due: September 7
                                              Paper Due: September 14

The lifeline is a collection of important events in your personal development. There are two parts to this assignment. First, you will create the lifeline in any format you choose and present your project to your small-group members. Second, you will prepare a two-page written statement about your lifeline.

1. The lifeline can be presented in any format you choose. Previous lifelines have included:
   - Drawn, painted, or cartooned pictures of scenes throughout a lifetime
   - A poem describing feelings and/or major events (If you choose this format, make sure the content is substantial.)
   - A physical object representing a person's life, attitude, or an event (Include a written explanation.)
   - A recording of various relevant songs
   - Clip art, sculptures, collages, or creative writing

Although there are no formal requirements for length or content, grades will be determined by the amount of work, thought, or creativity evident through the presentation and the ability to express important events in a person's life.

You will present your lifeline at the first small-group session on September 7. Please be aware that you will have about 10 minutes to share your lifeline, so plan accordingly! If you have more to say, you can write about it in your summary.

Your project is to be turned in to your group leader.

2. A two-page summary of your lifeline should include your reactions to the presentations, thoughts that were triggered, the benefits of the assignment, and so on. Consider the following questions for group discussion and your paper:

Who are/were some of the significant people in your life?

Who has influenced you the most in terms of your educational and/or career planning?

What were some of the highs and lows or significant events in your life?

What accomplishments are you proudest of?

How did you decide to attend college and why did you choose Penn State?

What major(s)/career(s) were you considering when you first decided to attend Penn State?

Are you completely unsure of what you want to major in or what occupation you might enjoy?

How does it feel to be uncertain?

First Paper: Career Autobiography   Due: October 19

The Career Autobiography is meant to help you synthesize and process the information you have gained about yourself from class through various assessments, exercises, and discussions. The paper must be typed, approximately 5 to 7 pages long, and should include the following:

- A discussion of your background and significant life events. Include family background, careers you thought about as a child, how and why you decided to attend Penn State, and so on.
- Consideration of how your experiences to date, including work experience and extracurricular activities, have influenced your past or present educational and career plans.
- A review of the relationship between your life/career plans and information from the course. Discuss how well your assessment results from the SDS and Myers-Briggs "fit" you. Do you agree with your results? Why or why not? What did you learn about yourself from the values and abilities exercises? What is your decision-making style and how does it affect your choice of major? Which career theories apply to you? How? Be sure to cite some content from lectures, class discussion, assignments, and/or the text.
- A brief review of your present situation concerning your academic and career plans. Also, review possible future directions, including possible majors.

Please include a cover page. (Your cover page should include your name, course title, title of your paper, and the date.)

The following criteria will be used in grading your paper:

1. Integration of course concepts   20 pts.
2. Effect of your life experience on
   educational and career decisions   15 pts.
3. Present and future career issues   10 pts.
4. Overall presentation organization,
   grammar, and spelling   15 pts.

Total 60 pts.

Second Paper: Occupation Informational Interview   Due: November 28

Researching a career is essential to the career decision-making process.

The paper must be typed, double-spaced, approximately 5 to 7 pages in length, and should include the following:

- A review and discussion of an informational interview conducted with someone employed in a career area that may be of interest to you. Preferably, the person will not be a relative and will be employed outside of Penn State. (The instructor before the interview must approve relatives and Penn State employees.) Include the reason you chose to interview somebody in this particular field. Consider:

- The nature of the work (duties, responsibilities)
- Qualifications necessary (education and/or experience)
- Typical lines of advancement in this field
- Typical hiring organizations for this kind of job
- A summary of the nature of the organization in which the professional is employed. Consider:
  - The organization's structure
  - Profits or funding sources
  - Services or products
  - Work environment
  - Types of entry-level positions for college graduates
- If available, any handout information such as an annual report or organizational brochure. This would be included in an appendix.
- A review of your reaction to your interview with the professional.
- How similar or different was the information you obtained compared with your previous knowledge of the career field?
- What effect has this information had on your interest in the field and your decision to pursue it?
- What information do you still need about this career?
- What are your next steps or plans of action?
- A cover sheet with the name of the person you interviewed, name of the organization, date of the interview, and the interviewee's full mailing address and telephone number.

You will also be required to make a brief presentation about your informational interview on the day that it is due. You will not be graded on your presentation. The purpose is to share information about occupations to your fellow classmates.

Refer to the handout on "Occupational Information Interviewing" in your packet for ideas on questions to ask.

The following criteria will be used in grading your paper:

1. Information about the interviewee	15 pts.
2. Information about the organization	10 pts.
3. Your reaction and thoughts	20 pts.
4. Overall presentation organization, grammar, and spelling	15 pts.
Total	60 pts.

Group Report and Presentation

Due: November 14 and 16

Each discussion group will select a major and related occupation (or occupations) to research. It may not be possible to find a major and career that all group members would personally consider pursuing, so try to choose one that most members are curious to learn about. The group should review the following information for the selected major:

1. General nature of the program
2. Course and program requirements
3. Entrance requirements
4. Type and ranges of occupations associated with the major as well as opportunities for graduate/professional school
5. Sources of information and relevant student organizations

Information regarding the selected occupation(s) related to the major should include:

1. Nature of the work and typical responsibilities
2. Appropriate academic preparation and training; identify a range of undergraduate majors that could lead to the occupation(s)
3. Types and range of organizations/settings in which the occupation is performed
4. Job outlook and earnings
5. Sources of information and relevant student organizations

This presentation should be fun and informative for you and your classmates! Small skits, television shows, take-offs on movies, game-show-style presentations, and other creative ideas are encouraged! Your group will have a time range of 15 to 20 minutes.

The purpose of this assignment is to become familiar with the kinds of information necessary to make informed career choices and ways to research this information.

A few suggested resources: Academic Advising Centers, Student Organization Directory, Career Information Center, Pattee Library, and the Internet.

Each group will turn in a one-page, typed summary or outline of their presentation on or before the day of the presentation.

ASSIGNMENT DUE DATES AND COURSE GRADING CRITERIA

Date	Assignment	Points
August 24	Introductory Assessments	3 pts.
September 7	Lifeline	15 pts.
September 12	Myers-Briggs Type Indicator	2 pts.
September 12	Decision-Making Exercises 8.1 & 8.15	2 pts.
September 14	Values Exercises 3.1 & 3.2	2 pts.
September 14	Brief Paper	
September 19	Interest Exercise, pages 65–69	2 pts.
September 21	Self-Directed Search	3 pts.
September 28	Skills Exercise, pages 85–86 and Exercise 5.8	2 pts.
October 3	Exam 1	30 pts.
October 5	Majors Checklist	3 pts.
	Self-Assessment Summary	3 pts.
October 12	Discover Reaction Paper	5 pts.
October 19	Career Autobiography Paper	60 pts.

October 26	Gathering the Facts, Exercise 7.6	6 pts.
November 2	Academic Advising Summaries	6 pts.
November 9	Multicultural Me	2 pts.
November 14 & 16	Group Presentation	30 pts.
November 21	Work Trend Article	2 pts.
November 28	Occupation Info. Interview Paper	60 pts.
November 30	Exam 2	30 pts.
December 7	Putting It All Together	2 pts.
	Class Attendance & Participation	30 pts.
		Total 300 pts.

13

Career Development Interventions in Community Settings

So much

"To continue its good work in the next decade, the career counseling profession must intensify efforts to serve a diverse clientele in new settings, . . . construct new tools that exploit the potential of informational technology, . . . and assist counselors worldwide who seek to internationalize the profession of career counseling" ("Special Issue: Career Counseling in the Next Decade", 2004). These lofty aspirations for 2000–2010 suggest that never before has a profession expected so much of itself.

So many

A recent Gallup Organization survey conducted for the NCDA reported that a significant number of adult workers seek assistance from professionals in the careers field. The broadening list of presenting issues includes career dissatisfaction, work-life imbalance, job-loss grief, as well as the traditional job-search training. Will the dawn of the next decade witness increased public demand for professional career services? If so, then it may well be true that never before has so much been owed by so many individuals and their families.

So few

Some employers and professional organizations bemoan that there are so few highly trained professionals providing preventative (i.e., primary, secondary, and tertiary) career services. Small but growing is the demand for evidence-based career interventions that are deliverable in multiple formats (i.e., individual, couple/family, and group services), with returns on investment (ROI) that are measurable, sustainable, and replicable.

    A retrospective at decade's-end may prove whether the words of Prime Minister Winston Churchill during WWII's Battle of Britain characterize the

21st-century workforce: "*Never in the field of human conflict was so much owed by so many to so few*" (bartlyeby.com/59/10/Churchill.win.html).

Michael E. Hall, Ph.D., LPC, C.M.F.
Principal of a solo career-, marital-,
and leadership-development practice in Charlotte, North Carolina

MyCounselingLab™

Visit the **My**CounselingLab™ site for *Career Development Interventions in the 21st Century,* Fourth Edition to enhance your understanding of chapter concepts. You'll have the opportunity to practice your skills through video- and case-based Assignments and Activities as well as Building Counseling Skills units, and to prepare for your certification exam with Practice for Certification quizzes.

Alexa is a 30-year-old woman with a bachelor's degree in accounting. She has been working as an accountant for seven years and is greatly dissatisfied with her choice of occupation, one strongly suggested by her father. Not knowing how to get assistance in developing other occupational alternatives, she went to the local Job Service office. The counselor there was very helpful in teaching her how to use the state's electronic job bank to identify jobs that were available in her state and how to use other Web sites that would help her with labor market information and job seeking. She was, however, confused by the amount of information on these Web sites and realized that she needed extensive assistance in determining what her interests and values are in relation to work before being immersed in information and job possibilities. She called her former high school counselor, who was able to refer her to a local certified career counselor in private practice.

Although the profession of counseling had its genesis in 1908 in Frank Parsons' Vocation Bureau in Boston, which was a community-based setting, this specialty of career counseling has experienced a long struggle for recognition. Counseling was first recognized as a necessary function in public high schools; and the National Defense Education Act of 1958, which provided government funds for the training of counselors for placement in high schools, had a tremendous impact on institutionalizing high school counselors. Chapters 10 and 11 of this textbook describe the role and function of counselors in school settings, including elementary, middle, and high schools. Counseling in postsecondary educational settings, as described in Chapter 12, has become a recognized and essential component of the student services provided by two- and four-year colleges.

In addition, the need to provide career counseling to adult populations has been recognized. Responding to a need to have a professional organization for all counseling specialties, the American Personnel and Guidance Association (APGA), now the American Counseling Association (ACA), was formed in 1952 by the four professional associations—for career counselors, school counselors, college student personnel, and counselor educators and supervisors—then in existence. Since its founding, ACA has recognized the following specialties in counseling, which have become divisions within the main body of ACA:

- Association for Assessment in Counseling (AAC)
- Association for Adult Development and Aging (AADA)
- American College Counseling Association (ACCA)
- Association for Counselors and Educators in Government (ACEG)
- Association for Counselor Education and Supervision (ACES)
- Association for Gay, Lesbian, and Bisexual Issues in Counseling (AGLBIC)
- Association for Multicultural Counseling and Development (AMCD)
- American Mental Health Counselors Association (AMHCA)
- American Rehabilitation Counseling Association (ARCA)
- American School Counselor Association (ASCA)
- Association for Spiritual, Ethical, and Religious Values in Counseling (ASERVIC)
- Association for Specialists in Group Work (ASGW)
- Counseling Association for Humanistic Education and Development (C-AHEAD)
- International Association of Addictions and Offender Counselors (IAAOC)
- International Association of Marriage and Family Counselors (IAMFC)
- National Career Development Association (NCDA)
- National Employment Counseling Association (NECA)

Note that the names of these divisions vary in that some focus on the setting in which the counseling takes place (such as the American School Counselor Association); some, the population (Adult Development and Aging); and some, the primary concern of the counseling (such as the National Career Development Association). However, none of these specifically recognize the community as a setting for providing counseling and career development services. Further, though the members of the NCDA might have the highest degree of interest in providing career counseling and development services, the fact is that counselors who work in all of the specialties and settings represented by other divisions also inevitably work with clients who have major concerns with career choice and development. In addition to membership in these divisions of ACA, counselors specializing in career planning services in any setting might belong to a division of the American Psychological Association (APA), namely Division 17, comprised of members who specialize in vocational psychology.

TRAINING, CERTIFICATION, AND LICENSURE

The basic training for counselors in all specialties is a master's degree in a counseling curriculum that includes training in eight core areas and a supervised practicum. This training may be acquired in a graduate institution that is approved by the Council for Accreditation of Counseling and Related Educational Programs (CACREP) or one that is not CACREP-approved. CACREP-approved programs now require 48 semester hours for most counseling specialties but 60 hours for mental health and marital counseling) of graduate work in the field and 100 clock hours of supervised practicum followed by 600 hours of supervised internship. CACREP standards recognize specialties in both community and career counseling. There are nine graduate institutions with a specialty in career counseling and 181 that meet the requirements for training as a community counselor or clinical mental health counselor (now combined as one category).

The standards referred to in the previous paragraph are standards for graduate school programs; doubtless, these standards result in better preparation of those who attend schools that meet these standards. Other standards, notably those of the National Board for the Certification of Counselors (NBCC) and of state licensure boards, apply directly to the qualifications of individual counselors. NBCC offers certification to counselors who meet its requirements (48 semester hours of coursework, two academic terms of supervised field experience, and two years of postmaster's counseling experience); persons who qualify for certification may use the title National Certified Counselor (NCC). In addition to voluntarily applying for and maintaining certification, counselors must meet the requirements for licensure as defined in their own state's law. In addition to all of this, many career counselors (especially those who want to practice in higher education or in private practice) earn a Certificate of Advanced Study (CAS) or doctoral degree (Ed.D. or Ph.D.) with a specialty in career development theory and practice.

COMPETENCIES

It is easy to view community-based counseling as that which occurs in any setting other than education. This definition appears to be insufficient. A common definition (Hershenson et al., 1996) of community-based counseling is: "the application of counseling principles and practices in agency, organizational, or individual practice settings that are located in and interact with their surrounding community" (p. 26). This difference in approach implies that community career counselors need and use additional competencies beyond those needed in educational settings. These competencies include coordination, consultation, advocacy, and case management.

Coordination

Coordinating is the process whereby a counselor brings together the needs of a client and the resources of the community. A first step in being able to coordinate is to assess thoroughly the client's strengths and barriers and to investigate and become knowledgeable of the resources that the community has. A client's strengths and barriers are typically identified through informal and formal assessment techniques. The most common informal assessment technique is the interview. The first of such interviews is called an intake interview. It is a structured interview in which the counselor uses some predetermined questions to collect the information needed to understand the client's strengths and barriers. One model used for this process is based on Schlossberg's transition theory.

Schlossberg (1989) defines a transition as an event or nonevent that results in change that is significant enough to cause disruption in one's usual roles, relationships, and/or routines. Many of the concerns that send clients to community-based career counselors fit this definition.

Schlossberg proposes that the severity of such transitions can be controlled by use of a four-step process:

- Define the *situation* clearly. This step includes finding out how the client perceives the situation or problem, what its timing is, how long the client has had to absorb it, and how much control the client believes he or she can exert to resolve or manage the situation.
- Learn about the *self* or inner resources the client has. This step includes learning about how the client has dealt with past transitions; what his or her dominant goals, interests, and skills are; and what emotional and spiritual strengths lie in the personal reservoir.
- Learn about the *support system* that does or does not surround the client in this transition. This system includes the support of family, friends, agencies, and material goods that can assist with the transition.
- From the knowledge gained in these three areas, the counselor and the client can develop a *strategy* for coping with the present need or transition.

If a counselor were, for example, using this kind of theoretical base as a guide for asking open-ended questions (those that cannot be answered with a single word), this could be a valuable informal assessment technique for the identification of the client's strengths, barriers, and coping mechanisms.

In this technological age, Web-based integrated career guidance systems, such as Kuder's *Journey* (Kuder, Inc., 2011) may also ask users to identify needs or barriers that they have as they face the job market. In this system, users may identify any of the following as significant needs or barriers:

Needs	Barriers
Housing	Insufficient past work experience
Child care	Lack of enough education or training
Knowledge of job-seeking skills	Mental or physical health problems
Clothing	Addiction
Better reading skills	Inability to speak English well
Better math skills	
Completion of high school	

The system then provides a state-specific list of Web sites that identify community-based sources of assistance in each of the areas identified by the user. Further, the system provides individual reports for users that community-based counselors can access in order to develop a support plan for a given client.

As indicated with the example above, the other side of the equation is the identification of resources in the community that can meet the identified needs of the client or assist in removing barriers. In this process the career counselor spends significant time finding and cataloging community resources related to specific categories of need—such as job placement, shelter, vocational training, clothing, legal assistance, and other areas mentioned above. Because resources of this kind come and go, there is a need for an ongoing scan of the environment to identify new resources and resources that may no longer be available.

Identification of services is only the first step. The second step is to become knowledgeable about them: visiting the organization that provides the service; establishing and maintaining a personal contact; and getting detailed information about services provided, criteria for those who can access the services, length and cost of services provided, and the best way to access the services.

The third step is to make an informed linkage between the client and available services. One method is to organize client needs by the same descriptors as services provided by organizations. Given that client profiles and resource profiles are entered into a database, a counselor could easily relate the two by a simple computer search. Lacking this capability, counselors may maintain up-to-date print files or notebooks that describe community referral resources.

So, the process of coordination involves the steps of (1) identifying client needs, (2) matching client needs with community resources, (3) introducing the client to these resources through personal contact, (4) referring the client to the resource, and (5) following through with both the client and the resource to determine the effectiveness of the referral and what the next steps should be.

As an example of the task of coordinating, suppose that a counselor working in a prison setting identified vocational training as one of the primary needs of a client. The client is particularly interested in learning to cook, and The Salvation Army has a training program for cooks. The counselor follows all of the steps previously listed, including making a personal contact with The Salvation Army and setting an appointment for the client. The client presents himself effectively in the interview and is accepted in the culinary training program. The counselor is not yet finished; he or she needs to monitor the client's continuation and success in the program, especially during the first three to six months.

Consultation

Consultation is a second important competency for community-based career counselors (Dougherty, 1990). Consultation should not be confused with supervision, which implies that one person has the responsibility for directing the activities of another and for corrective action if performance does not meet expectations. Consultation, on the other hand, is the work of one professional with another in an attempt to find ways to identify interventions that will address the needs of a third party (the client).

As an example, suppose that a 45-year-old, single mother who comes to a community mental health center for career counseling has a heart condition that is potentially significant enough to affect the kind of work that she can do. As the counselor discusses the possible ways that she could afford additional training, he learns that she has always had a goal to attend college but does not believe it is possible considering her age and financial condition. The counselor describes the services of the Division of Vocational Rehabilitation and explains that there may be an opportunity for her to receive funds through this agency to attend the local community college or a state-supported university.

With the client's enthusiastic permission, the counselor makes an appointment with a staff member at the local office of the Division of Vocational Rehabilitation (DVR). During that meeting, the counselor describes his client and her needs. The DVR staff member and counselor compare the client's characteristics with the current policies of DVR and jointly conclude that the client is eligible for a service that would pay for tuition at a publicly supported institution of higher education. The counselor formally refers the client to the contact person at DVR, who proceeds to work with her to develop a formal application for services.

Many clients who receive services from community-based counselors lack the skills that are needed to overcome the barriers they face and reach the goals they seek. These skills may be social, academic, or psychological. In other words, there may be deficits in ability to communicate effectively with others, in specific skills needed to perform in a job, or in personal coping skills such as decision making or goal setting. As the counselor identifies these needs, he or she may seek ways to meet these deficits through consultation with persons in community agencies.

Advocacy

A third competency that Hershenson et al. (1996) attribute to community-based counselors is advocacy. This term describes a role that counselors may play to exert pressure on some aspect of the community in order to improve the resources available for clients. Advocacy may be exercised through representation on boards of referral agencies, pressing for specific legislation, writing newspaper columns, joining protests of various kinds, writing to legislators, exerting individual influence, or making presentations to groups that can have influence.

Suppose that you worked as a career counselor in a rehabilitation agency. A local community college offers an excellent program in desktop publishing, and five of your disabled clients are enrolled in it. However, it is very difficult for your clients to get a job, no matter how well they do in this program, because of the prejudice against persons with disabilities. You identify four major employers of persons trained in desktop publishing and make an appointment with the director of human resources in each of the four sites. When you visit, you take a copy of the performance-based curriculum that the community college offers. You also take some work samples and letters written by employers of past graduates of the program. Finally, you show pictures of your five clients and ask the director of human resources to grant an interview to these clients for the next desktop publishing job available. You commit to careful follow-through with your clients who become employees to increase the probability that they will be productive employees. Advocacy includes performance of all of the kinds of activities included in this example.

More than those in any other counseling specialty, community counselors must orchestrate a variety of people, resources, and services in order to meet the needs of their clients. This process of orchestration is called *case management*. In large agencies, the persons involved in case management may be different from those who provide counseling. More typically, however, the community counselor plays a multifaceted role that includes both counselor and case manager. This dual role demands diverse skills, ranging from the facilitative skills of a good counselor to the coordinating, consulting, and advocacy skills just described.

Case Management

The goal of case management is to assure that clients receive the sequence of services they need in a timely and coordinated fashion. Thus, one of the most critical roles of a community-based counselor is to develop a comprehensive case plan, which might be called an action plan, and then to monitor it continually. For some clients, services may be provided by the counselor and the agency that he or she represents with only one external service provider. For other clients, whose needs are complex and include needs outside the scope of the agency such as physical problems, housing needs, financial needs, and job needs, there may be several service providers external to the counselor's home site.

Tips from the Field

The services of coordination, consultation, and advocacy are delivered through the development and implementation of an effective case management plan.

The role of case manager demands skill in assessment (to determine needs), coordination with referral resources, evaluation of services provided, advocacy for the client, and continual follow-through with the client and the external service providers. Case management requires the development of a sound plan at the outset, establishment and maintenance of excellent relationships with specific persons within referral agencies, tact in communication and evaluation, ongoing instructional and emotional support to the client and perhaps the client's family, and wisdom about when to make a change in service provider or to terminate service to the client. The types of resources that may be included in a case plan are as varied as the needs of clients for whom plans are developed.

It is common for community-based centers to have differentiated staffing. A counselor addressing career concerns may be on a team with psychologists, social workers, nurses, medical doctors, and perhaps career development facilitators (CDFs). A career development facilitator is a paraprofessional trained to work under the supervision of a professional counselor to assist with a number of duties most directly related to career planning and job placement.

SIMILARITIES AND DIFFERENCES IN COMMUNITY-BASED SETTINGS

Career counseling provided to individuals or groups in community-based settings is both similar to and different from career counseling provided in other settings. It is similar to work in educational settings in that it draws upon the same counseling and career development theories for many of its tools and techniques and requires the same facilitative skills when working with clients. In addition, its clients may be dealing with career choice and development problems that in many ways parallel those of students.

Conversely, providing career development services in community-based settings differs from doing so in educational settings in the following ways:

- Clients who seek career counseling in community-based settings are typically adults who have major responsibilities in several life roles, such as spouse, parent, and citizen in addition to worker. They are typically facing one of the following areas of concern: (1) reentry into the workforce after child rearing or loss of job; (2) dealing with being plateaued and wanting to find greater job satisfaction through job change, upward mobility, or job enrichment; or (3) dissatisfaction with an occupation or job or a change in an occupation's requirements that necessitates significant retraining.

- The options they have for career choice or change are intimately tied to availability of resources and/or dilution of barriers in the community. *Community* is defined as all of that which surrounds the individual: that is, community may be the family, the neighborhood, and/or the organization in which one is imbedded.

- Based on this assumption, the counselor may spend as much time and effort in working with the community to make resources available as with the individual client.

- Work with the community may take the forms of finding training opportunities to augment the individual's current skills, advocating for additional or modified resources, removing barriers to those resources, consulting with appropriate persons or agencies, and/or coordinating between and among the client and community resources.

- The skills of coordination, consultation, advocacy, and case management—though also necessary in educational settings—may be needed and used more often in community-based settings than in school settings.

- These counselors work in the community in settings such as private practice, government agencies, mental health centers, drug and abuse centers, and corporations. They may also work in the global community by delivering services via the Internet.

SETTINGS FOR COMMUNITY-BASED CAREER COUNSELORS

There is an increasingly wide variety of settings in which community-based counselors work—some devoting full time to career-related concerns and others dealing with such concerns in the context of a much broader array. The most common of these community-based settings and the typical tasks of counselors who work in them are summarized next.

Private Practice

The term *private practice* implies that a trained counselor, who may have taken additional coursework related to career development, has chosen to form a company, market career development services, and identify clients who can and are willing to pay for services. Such a person would likely rent facilities or work from home and acquire clients through such approaches as newspaper ads, a Web site, listing in the

Yellow Pages, referrals, and word of mouth. Such a counselor might join a private practice made up of a group of counselors, and within that group, be the specialist in working with clients for whom career issues appear to be the leading ones.

Because this professional focuses his or her services on career concerns, clients are likely to state a career problem as the reason for seeking assistance. It may be stated as a need to find a different job (because of recent loss of a job or dissatisfaction with a current one), as a desire to get additional training in order to have new skills to use in a different kind of job, or as a desire to analyze the reasons why a recent potential for promotion has not been realized. It is rare, however, that the presenting problem is the only problem that needs to be addressed in the counseling sessions, because a career choice or change issue is likely to affect other life roles, such as spouse and parent. Further, the career problem presented may be affected by other problems, such as drug abuse, alcoholism, inability to sustain relationships, or poor self-concept. Thus, it is impossible to speak of "career counseling" with adults in community settings as purely related to career choices; presenting problems are almost inevitably entwined with a host of others.

At Alexa's first visit to a career counselor in private practice, she indicated that she was bored with her work as an accountant and was seeking assistance in identifying a different occupation, one in which she could work with people instead of numbers. As her story unfolded, however, she revealed that her father was a prominent figure in her life and that he had continually encouraged her to become an accountant, despite her lack of interest in detail. He thought that it was a high-paying occupation for a woman, one without significant emotional or physical stress. Through interviewing and assessment, the counselor helped Alexa to become aware of her interests and values related to working with people in some way. She also helped Alexa to delve deeply into her relationship with her father and the reasons she was still letting his influence affect major decisions in her life.

Alexa decided that she did not want to spend significant time in retraining because she had purchased a home and established a lifestyle that required continuation of her present level of income. Further, she realized that it would be very difficult for her to go against her father's wishes and advice about her occupational choice. Thus, the counselor suggested that Alexa explore other occupations related to accounting that would give her more opportunity to work with people on a face-to-face basis. After using print resources and Web sites to gather information about such specialties, Alexa had several information interviews with accountants who worked in entirely different settings—helping people with financial planning, providing service to professionals about retirement plans and options, and teaching accounting in a community college. This experience gave her perspectives on how she could use her accounting background in ways she had never thought of before, and she terminated her relationship with the counselor with a one-year action plan.

Career counselors in private practice typically work with their clients on a one-to-one basis through a sequence of interviews. As in other one-to-one settings, the counselor is likely to begin the sequence by assessing the client's needs and barriers, establishing goals with the client for the counseling relationship, working with the client to reach those goals, and ultimately terminating when the two agree that goals have been reached or that further work together will not be beneficial.

As in other settings, private practitioners, in addition to skilled interviewing, use the tools of assessment, technology (Web-based systems and Web sites), career information, referral, and advocacy to assist their clients to meet established goals. Their services may be short term, as would be the case if the goals are to write an effective resume, practice job interviewing, identify desirable job openings, and get a job. Conversely, the services may be long term, as would be the case if there are underlying problems of dysfunctional career beliefs, poor self-concept, drug abuse, or role conflict.

Counselors who work as private practitioners should have at least a master's degree in counseling with additional coursework in career development theory and practice. Many have doctorates and, through this additional study, have been able to acquire more background in career development theory than a master's degree counselor would have. They may and should be National Certified Counselors (NCCs) and preferably National Certified Career Counselors (NCCC). Unfortunately, the latter certification has been discontinued. However, the NCDA has established categories of membership that can be helpful to the consumer; those who qualify by educational background and experience to hold NCDA membership as a Master Career Counselor are likely to have the theoretical underpinnings and experience to work as private practitioners. In addition to these academic and experiential qualifications, counselors in private practice need business skills in order to market their services and to do the financial accounting required of small businesses. Further, as suggested in an earlier section, they may need additional skills in coordination, consultation, advocacy, and case management.

The World Wide Web: Cybercounseling

The year 2000 signaled the beginning of counseling services via the Internet. To date, these services are being offered by certified counselors who are working from their homes or offices. Their clients are self-selected on the Internet, and provision of service is brokered through a Web site that has the appropriate infrastructure to handle synchronous (both the client and the counselor are at a computer at the same time) text-based or video-based communication, appointment scheduling, and billing. Although initial sets of ethical guidelines have been developed by professional associations (described in Chapter 7), there are many unknowns about this form of counseling at this time. These relate to lack of knowledge about the types of clients and issues that may be addressed in this way, how to know when to refer clients for face-to-face counseling, and what counselor characteristics may predict counselor satisfaction and effectiveness in this mode of intervention. It appears, however, that cybercounseling may become a specialized version of private practice in the 21st century.

Mental Health Centers

Funded by both public and private organizations, community mental health centers assist citizens, regardless of their ability to pay, with concerns that may affect the quality of their lives and the community. These concerns include career-related problems. A major goal of mental health centers is early intervention, in an attempt to alleviate problems before they have greater impact on the individual and the community. Services for clients include individual counseling, assessment, referral, career information, skill-building, and perhaps job placement. Counselors use the techniques of group and individual counseling, instruction, consultation, referral, and advocacy.

The problems encountered and approaches used do not vary significantly from those encountered and used by a career counselor in private practice. A counselor in this setting may have a larger caseload than one in private practice; may spend less time per client; may have the advantages of a wider network for consultation and referral; and may have reduced responsibility related to promotion, marketing, and management.

Substance Abuse Centers

Counselors in substance abuse centers work with clients who have come voluntarily or have been referred by other organizations, including the courts. The centers may be located in hospitals, in a community mental health center, or in a separate organization. Typical services include individual and group counseling, support groups, educational programs about substance abuse, career counseling and assessment, referral for acquisition of job skills, and perhaps job placement. There may also be follow-through with employers for a period of time for the purpose of assisting substance-abuse offenders to develop job-keeping skills.

Rehabilitation Settings

Rehabilitation counselors deal with a variety of client concerns, including career counseling and job placement. They have more specialized training and certification than do counselors in more general settings, because of the additional knowledge and competency that are required.

The Division of Vocational Rehabilitation (DVR) is a government agency whose mission is to remove the barriers to satisfying and productive work that exist for persons with disabilities. Any person with a physical or mental disability that could affect employability may be eligible for the services of DVR. These services include counseling, vocational assessment, vocational training, on-the-job training, work adjustment training, funding for postsecondary education, job site modification, and purchase of equipment or technological devices that will assist the disabled person to perform work duties and maintain employment. Many rehabilitation counselors are employed in the nationwide network of offices of the DVR. Others are employed by private rehabilitation facilities.

Counselors who work with persons with disabilities use the same techniques and tools as other career counselors—including interviewing, assessment, career information, and technology—in assisting their clients. Because of their disabilities, clients are likely to have a restricted number of career options; they are likely to need a high level of support in accomplishing action plans and need counseling in areas such as self-concept and self-efficacy as well as career counseling. Further, counselors working with this population will use coordinating, consulting, advocacy, and case-management skills at a high level in helping their clients with job readiness and placement.

Corrections and Probation

The pendulum swings from time to time with regard to public opinion about the services that offenders and ex-offenders should receive. Currently, given the known relationship between getting and keeping a job upon release and recidivism, there is emphasis from the federal level on providing career planning and job placement services to offenders. These services are designed to contribute to offenders' capability to select, be trained for, and enter jobs in keeping with their interests and/or skills and to know how to retain those jobs.

The range of services available to offenders and the resources available to deliver them are limited. Work tasks in this setting include one-to-one interviewing, group instruction about career-related concerns, assessment, provision of career information, and job placement. This is a particularly difficult setting in which to work because the nature of the helping relationship, as traditionally defined by counselors, has to be substantially modified and, further, counselors can feel a continual pull between the client's needs and the needs of the prison and the larger society. Goals for career services in correctional facilities are also limited. They focus on acquiring some type of job training, getting a job, and being able to keep the job.

In the past few years there has been a national focus on training corrections staff as career development facilitators, called Offender Workforce Development Specialists (OWDS), in their environment. Teams from many states have been trained to develop programs of service for offenders prior to release or to ex-offenders after release. The goal is to assist ex-offenders to gain some work skills, learn how to behave in the work environment, get a job, and especially to keep a job. Research underscores the fact that there is a high relationship between getting and keeping a job and reduced recidivism.

Military Settings

Civilian counselors are common on military bases, and they work both with military personnel and members of their families. Counselors may engage in assessment, educational advisement, individual counseling related to career and personal issues, and referrals. In recent years, because of the significant downsizing of the military, counselors in this setting have focused on assisting military personnel with the transition from military to civilian occupations for which they have transferable skills and on the use of funding available to them to acquire additional education.

In times like the present, when large numbers of military personnel are coming home from long and stressful combat, there is an increase in services offered to veterans designed to assist with the transition to civilian life. Some of these services are offered virtually on sites such as Military.com (military.com/Careers/Home), which offer searches through job banks, assistance with resumes, information about job fairs, and the opportunity to network with other veterans. Another site, called TurboTAP.org, is the official site of the U.S. Department of Defense, and was developed to support the Transition Assistance Program. The site offers a wealth of information about services available to veterans and outlines a seven-step process for making a successful transition. Professional counselors are available at Transition Assistance offices to assist those separating from the military to plan for education or training funded by the GI Bill of Rights, to identify career options, to prepare for the job search, and to get a job. Mental health services are also provided by means of referral to appropriate professional personnel.

Job Service Offices and One-Stop Centers

By far, the largest proportion of community-based career guidance and support is provided by One-Stop Centers, of which there are more than 3,000 in the United States. Funded under the 1998 Workforce Investment Act (WIA), these centers represent a government initiative to place under one roof a variety of services needed by job seekers: unemployment compensation, access to the services of the Division of Vocational Rehabilitation, and access to a wide variety of services offered by One-Stop Centers. Individuals can find the center closest to their homes by accessing servicelocator.org.

These services include all of the following:

- Job-search and job-placement assistance
- Free access to computers, Internet, fax machines, and printers for job-search purposes
- Access to millions of job listings
- Labor market information for clients' state and regions within the state
- Assistance preparing resumes
- Comprehensive assessment of job skills, abilities, aptitudes, and needs
- Career counseling
- Workshops on topics such as interviewing skills
- Case management
- Prevocational support services (such as learning English, improving basic skills)
- Information on unemployment insurance
- Development of individual employment plans
- Training in literacy skills
- Rehabilitative services
- Referrals to training, education, and related supportive services (such as transportation and child care)
- Outreach and recruitment for business (job development)

Many of the job-search and labor market information services that One-Stop Centers offer are also available on the Internet at careeronestop.org. In addition, there is a tool, called the CareerOneStopCoach, which is available at careeronestopcoach .org. Typically, persons who staff One-Stop Centers are not trained as professional career counselors. Many have considerable experience in dealing with the challenges that One-Stop Centers tackle; and increasingly, centers are employing people who have become certified as Career Development Facilitators (CDFs), a paraprofessional level in the field.

One-Stop Centers serve a wide variety of clients, from Ph.D.s who have been laid off by NASA to the unskilled homeless. Other categories of clients include ex-offenders, high-risk youth, unemployed adults, displaced homemakers, veterans, older Americans, and persons with disabilities. In times like the 2009–2012 recession, when unemployment rates approach 10% (or more in some states), both the number and the diversity of clients who seek these free services increase significantly. As stated by the *New York Times* (February 20, 2010), "Call them the new poor: people long accustomed to the comforts of middle-class life who are now relying on public assistance for the first time in their lives—potentially for years to come."

The principles that guide the One-Stop Centers include the following:

- Streamline services through an integration of multiple programs, including Wagner-Peyser and Workforce Investment Act, at the service level;
- Empower individuals with information and resources they need to manage their own careers;
- Provide employer services that recognize business as a customer as well as a source for jobs leading to meaningful employment;
- Provide universal access for all job seekers to a core set of career decision-making and job-search tools;
- Increase accountability of the delivery system to achieve improved results regarding skill gains, credentials earned, job placement rates, earnings and retention in employment;
- Offer state and local flexibility to ensure that delivery systems are responsive to the needs of individual communities; and
- Offer the opportunity for local boards and the private sector to impact the design and operation of delivery systems.

In difficult economic times, One-Stop centers may receive increased funding as was the case with the American Recovery and Reinvestment Act (ARRA) which provided $1.25 billion for dislocated adult workers, such as those laid off or who have received advanced notice of a factory closing; $1.2 billion for dislocated youth workers; $500 million in state grants to provide assistance to low-income adults; and $500 million to fund training for sustainable energy jobs.

Besides the array of services listed earlier, One-Stop Centers are also the pipeline for providing assistance that may be required for diminishing barriers that low-skilled and low-income adults may have. This assistance may include food stamps, financial support for child care and/or transportation, the opportunity to learn English and other basic skills, and grants to underwrite a learning plan designed to provide education or training that develops marketable skills.

There have been strong accountability measures for One-Stop Centers. The 2009 data aggregated for all One-Stop Centers across the nation by the U.S. Department of Labor provided these numbers:

Percentage of clients who entered employment after One-Stop service:	54.0
Percentage of these who kept their jobs	77.7
Average annual earnings in these jobs	$ 13,712

One-Stop Centers also provide employers with a variety of services to meet workforce needs. Electronic job banks provide the needed link between employers and qualified job seekers. These offices also provide employers with reemployment services for dislocated workers, labor market information for planning business expansion, and focused recruitment for specialized workers needed due to new business ventures.

Faith-Based Organizations

Legislation enacted under the George W. Bush administration provided funding to faith-based organizations and other non-profit organizations that would devise programs to support the unskilled or low skilled, ex-offenders, and/or homeless. Typical support services offered by faith-based organizations include housing and food for the homeless, vocational training, mentorship, clothing, and sponsorship for job fairs. In fact, more than half of the job fairs offered across the nation are organized by faith-based organizations who make a tremendous contribution both in dollars and in volunteer support.

An outstanding example of the work of a non-profit organization is that of Goodwill Industries. Their mission is stated as "Goodwill Industries International enhances the dignity and quality of life of individuals, families and communities by eliminating barriers to opportunity and helping people in need reach their fullest potential through the power of work." (Retrieved from goodwill.org/about-us/our-mission, on March 10, 2011). In 2009 alone, Goodwill International provided training to 1.9 million individuals, workforce development services to 20.1 million, entry-level jobs to 155,000, and personal and family support services to 7.5 million.

The Association of Retired Persons (AARP) is a second outstanding example of a non-profit organization that is providing a wide range of career support services, using federal funding made available for older workers in need of employment. AARP offers no-fee services through hundreds of offices throughout the United States. These services include assessment (measurement of interests and skills), funding of training, and placement of low-income older adults who, especially in this depressed economy, need to continue to work in order to survive. Training is provided online for over 80 different certifications through the WorkSearch system, jointly developed by AARP and the National Business Services Alliance (NBSA). The certifications were created by NBSA in collaboration with a consortium of accredited universities. At the completion of the NBSA Certification Program, clients earn a certificate from a nationally known accredited state university. Participating universities not only validate NBSA's system of self assessments; they create and deliver course content to ensure that holders of an NBSA Skills Certificate are well prepared to do the job. All users of the WorkSearch system are offered free access to 17 essential skill courses. NBSA Certification Programs are geared toward jobs that are in high demand in the U.S. economy. This Certification Program also includes one-on-one assistance from a personal training advisor who helps to customize the learning experience for individuals.

There are some obvious differences in the services provided by U.S. Department of Labor One-Stop Centers and non-profit organizations from those provided in schools, universities, and private practice. First, the range of education, needs, and past experience possessed by clients is far wider than in other settings. Second, the treatment provided to these clients has to be all encompassing, ranging much farther than simply helping them get a job. Third, to be successful, the support provided needs to start with the initial interview and continue through at least the first six months after getting a job. Fourth, the array of services—which may include child care, transportation, training, resume preparation, and more—is offered through the collaboration of agencies and the merging of public and private funding.

Corporations and Other Organizations

Many organizations—such as the World Bank and the Federal Deposit Insurance Corporation—as well as private corporations, hire career counselors. They are typically housed in a facility that includes a well-furnished career center. Typical centers provide individual career counseling, assessment, use of the Internet or software, and group instruction.

Career counselors working in such settings deal with client concerns about career mobility within the organization or, in the case of downsizing, with client plans to move out of the organization. They may offer workshops on topics such as keeping one's resume updated, how to facilitate one's promotion, or how to profit from mentoring. They may also deal with plans for upgrading skills or acquiring new skills and with issues related to conflicts between supervisors and employees or between employees. Their job descriptions may also include the provision of counseling services that are unrelated to career progression.

In these diverse settings, fees for service may be nonexistent to clients, may be shared by clients in proportion to their ability to pay, or may be at full rate per session. For some clients in some settings (such as mental health agencies and private practice), the counselor may receive third-party payment, the counselor's services having been approved for coverage under an insurance plan.

MyCounselingLab™

Go to Topic 12: *Special Adult Career Concerns* in the MyCounselingLab™ site (www .MyCounselingLab.com) for *Career Development Interventions in the 21st Century*, Fourth Edition, where you can:

- Find learning outcomes for *Special Adult Career Concerns* along with the national standards that connect to these outcomes.
- Complete Assignments and Activities that can help you more deeply understand the chapter content.

- Apply and practice your understanding of the core skills identified in the chapter with the Building Counseling Skills unit.
- Prepare yourself for professional certification with a Practice for Certification quiz.
- Connect to videos through the Video and Resource Library.

Summary

This chapter has addressed the specialty of community-based career counseling that is practiced in a variety of noneducational settings. Not only is the setting for this career counseling specialty different from that of others, but the client characteristics, reasons for intervention, and the roles and functions of the counselor may also be different. Clients are typically adults who face career choice problems as a part of a much larger complex of issues and thus do not have as many options available to them as students do.

Intervention may be the free choice of individuals or may be forced due to layoffs, legislation, separation from the military or from prison, or some life event. Counselor functions extend beyond counseling to coordination, consultation, advocacy, and case management. Further, the counselor providing career assistance may work as part of a team that includes psychologists, social workers, medical specialists, and career development facilitators.

Case Study

Frank is a 25-year-old veteran who has served two tours of duty in Iraq. While there, he lost his right arm in trying to remove wounded soldiers from the combat zone. He is suffering from post-traumatic stress disorder. His military specialty is artillery maintenance specialist. Now he faces the need to get housing and a civilian job that provides enough income to support himself. What kinds of next steps would you investigate with him as you work on an action plan?

Student Activities

1. Refer to the **MyCounselingLab** Video and Resource Library and select the video entitled *21st Century Counseling with an Unemployed Adult: Dr. Barbara Suddarth.* Then write a short paper that responds to the following items:

   a. What practical suggestions was the counselor able to give this client?

   b. In what ways did the counselor provide emotional support to this client?

   c. What barriers to a successful job search does this client have?

   d. What are this client's strengths as he faces the job search?

2. Refer to the **MyCounselingLab** Video and Resource Library and select the video entitled *21st Century Job-Seeking Intervention with an Unemployed Adult: Dr. Michael Hall.* This counselor used a large number of techniques with this client. List and describe at least six of them.

References

Dougherty, A. M. (1990). *Consultation: Practice and perspectives.* Pacific Grove, CA: Brooks/Cole.

Goodman, P. S. (2010, February 20). Despite Signs of Recovery, Chronic Joblessness Rises. *New York Times,* p. A1.

Hershenson, D. B., Power, P. W., & Waldo, M. (1996). *Community counseling: Contemporary theory and practice.* Boston: Allyn & Bacon.

Kuder, Inc. (2011). *Journey.* Adel, IA: Author.

Schlossberg, N. K. (1989). *Overwhelmed: Coping with life's ups and downs.* Lexington, KY: Lexington Press.

Special Issue: Career Counseling in the Next Decade. *The Career Development Quarterly, 52*(1), 89. Retrieved May 11, 2004, from bartlyeby .com/59/10/churchill.win.html.

14

Ethical Issues in Career Development Interventions

Though not always evident and at the ready point of recognition, ethics is a constant of our daily lives. Frequently unconscious or professionally intuitive, some aspects of ethical decision making are readily evident and require careful attention and deliberation by all people. Vigilant adherence and commitment to ethics, ethical standards, and ethical principles are hallmarks of all professions, and all professionals are ethically accountable and liable. It may surprise many counselors and counselor educators to see the universality of many ethical principles manifest in ethical standards for professions as varied as computer associations, multinational corporations, and the U.S. military. Ethical principles common to the ethical standards of many professions center on respect for human beings; respect for privacy, accountability, responsibility, and truth; and crediting one's sources, among other principles.

Typically in counselor preparation and practice, ethics and ethical standards and principles are considered along with legal principles and practices, yet ethics is different from law in terms of the origins of ethics in philosophy and in terms of legality being far more explicitly definitive than ethics. In law, there is close attention to legal precedent and nuance refining principles of justice in guiding legal behavior and adjudication of perceived illegalities. In ethics, there is attention to more general ethical standards and principles guiding ethical practice and adjudication. In the history of mental health professions, ethical principles and standards frequently are at risk of being lost in attention to the negative reinforcers of law and legal rules for practice. In fact, there is healthy room for attention and adherence to law and ethics, and this chapter does both with some enlightening points of view and examples.

Probably the most vital aspect of ethics in counselor preparation is close and deliberate attention to, and discussion of, ethics, ethical issues, and ethical standards within the quiet calm of a noncrisis classroom environment. Though one might typically think of legal and ethical standards as negative reinforcers highlighting what to avoid, a closer look at ethical standards and principles might help one see the fuller context of ethics as inspiring and empowering. One might sense this uplifting aspect of ethics in the preamble to the American Counseling Association's Ethical Standards, noting counselors' dedication to human worth, dignity, uniqueness, and potential and similar perspectives at points in the Ethical Standards of the American Psychological Association. Finally, as one notes that standards are minimal, the least one must do, counselors and aspiring counselors can begin to ponder and commit to maxima, to aspirational standards focused on the most one can ethically do for one's client.

With these thoughts in mind, welcome to a chapter of considerable breadth and depth and welcome to what may be new perspectives in professional growth for readers of this text. Readers should find much to ponder and much potential for growth. Read, learn, ponder, and enjoy.

Dennis Engels, Ph.D., LPC, NCC, NCCC
Regents Professor
Counseling Program
University of North Texas

The authors of this text, like others who teach and work in the area of career counseling, often deal with questions or statements that suggest that career counseling is not "real" counseling and question whether professional concepts such as ethical standards apply to those who are involved in career development interventions. We believe that all career professionals are subject to ethical standards. Likewise, those who work for or who are employed or supervised by career professionals in providing career services must be aware of and in most instances adhere to the same standards. We have elected to follow the NCDA Code of Ethics (2007) and use the term "career professional" to refer to all those covered by that code. As you know by now, we also view career counseling as "real" counseling that is quite central to a person's life. This chapter is our attempt to provide an orientation to the ethical standards of the counseling profession with emphasis and examples relevant for career professionals. Ethical, professional behavior requires adherence to applicable laws and regulations, and in some instances we will suggest that those faced with certain dilemmas seek not only ethical consultation from a supervisor or respected colleague but also seek legal advice. Before we begin our exploration of ethical issues, however, we would like you to meet a counselee, José.

José, a 16-year-old student in the ninth grade, was asked to come into the school counselor's office to review his interest inventory results (the inventory had been administered to all ninth-grade students). José's academic record throughout his school years has been mixed. He had been held back twice in elementary school and was often absent from school. His absences were mostly the result of José working with his father in the fields during harvest season. Lately, he had shown some interest in developing his career plans.

A frequent computer user, José had gone online at the local library to explore career options in the computer field. He found a Web site that offered free "vocational aptitude testing." He took the test and was excited that the results seemed to suggest that he had the aptitude necessary for working as a computer programmer. He was eager to receive the information about becoming a computer programmer that the Web site offered to send everyone who took the online test. José was not sure what a computer programmer's job involved, but he knew that he loved playing computer games.

José's father was "dead set against" this type of work. A blue-collar worker all his life with no computer experience and only a ninth-grade education, José's father felt strongly that José should acquire training in a more traditional trade, such as carpentry. José's grandfather had been a carpenter in his home country, Guatemala. When the family relocated to the southeastern United States, the only work José's father could acquire was in agriculture. He thought that he had not been given serious consideration for a number of jobs for which he was qualified, due to being Guatemalan. His father thought that becoming a carpenter would be in line with the family tradition and would provide an income that would be sufficient for raising a family (something that was a constant struggle for José's father). José told his counselor that his father wanted to speak with the counselor about José attending vocational school. His father was also interested in exploring options that José might have in the military. In fact, he wanted José to meet with military recruiters when they visited José's school. José had no interest in becoming a carpenter and was not enthusiastic about the prospect of military service.

The counselor had several concerns about José's situation. For example, the counselor was concerned about the quality of the online test José had taken. The counselor was also uneasy about "bursting José's bubble" and deflating the interest he had shown in making career plans. However, the results of the interest inventory administered at school gave no indication that José had high interest in computer-related occupations. His interests were more focused on artistic and helping occupations. The counselor was also anxious about the strong, clear vision José's father had for what occupation and career path José would choose. The counselor wondered whether José's father's encounter with discriminatory hiring practices influenced the career goals he had identified for his son. Finally, the counselor was reluctant to encourage José to meet with the military recruiters but was not sure how to communicate this reluctance to José's father.

MyCounselingLab™

Visit the **MyCounselingLab**™ site for *Career Development Interventions in the 21st Century*, Fourth Edition to enhance your understanding of chapter concepts. You'll have the opportunity to practice your skills through video- and case-based Assignments and Activities as well as Building Counseling Skills units, and to prepare for your certification exam with Practice for Certification quizzes.

You may remember that when we introduced José, his counselor was introduced as a school counselor and not a career counselor. Yet his presenting concern was certainly career related if not career counseling per se. A number of ethical issues and concerns are apparent in the brief scenario. A positive outcome of an increased awareness of ethical and legal concerns that affect counseling practice is that professional counselors have become increasingly concerned with ethical issues in interventions. For example, José presents a variety of ethical issues that would probably never have been identified as ethical concerns 20 years ago. Counselors today would be concerned about some of the ethical questions embedded in José's case: the quality of the assessment he took online, and even whether the assessment instrument the counselor administered to José was appropriate for a person from José's background; the ethics of the online service suggesting a specific career option as if it were the result of career counseling rather than a blatant marketing ploy; the ethical dilemma confronting the school counselor regarding José's father's wishes and José's wishes; and the always-present ethical issue of the counselor's competence in dealing with the concerns and issues presented by José.

These are complex issues. To help career professionals practice ethically, professional columns, publications, and workshops on ethics abound. Despite the increased attention to ethical practice in career services delivery, there are no clear answers to many career practitioners' most difficult questions about proper practice. Given the frequency of litigation in the helping professions, it is perplexing that career development textbooks, at best, pay minimal attention to ethical issues confronting career practitioners. Thus, in this chapter we hope to heighten the awareness of career professionals to ethical issues and provide guidance for career development practitioners as they consider ethical issues. Because readers will have varied backgrounds in the ethical concepts that affect career counselors, we offer a primer on basic principles.

A good starting point for addressing ethical issues in career development interventions is to consider the following question: How can it be that career practitioners have multiple ethics codes to guide their practice and yet ethical violations continue? Even when practitioners are well trained and conscientious, situations can arise in which determining proper practice is a complex task. The following chart provides a useful framework for examining behaviors within the career counseling relationship.[1] This matrix can be used to classify career practitioners' behaviors into one of four categories.

Ethical and Legal	Unethical and Legal
Ethical and Illegal	Unethical and Illegal

Tips from the Field

At all times regarding ethical practice in career interventions, remember, "when in doubt, check it out!" If you are not sure whether ethical issues exist in your work with students and clients, refer to the ethical standards of practice and consult with other counseling professionals.

[1]Because we have seen this chart attributed to various authors, and thus its origin is somewhat ambiguous, we simply acknowledge that the concept of this 2×2 matrix is not ours.

The obvious goal for career professionals is to function ethically and legally and to avoid any activity that would be acknowledged as illegal and/or unethical. Although this goal seems straightforward, there are instances in which achieving this goal is not so simple. A career client might disclose his or her frustration with an unsuccessful job search by saying, "I was so upset over my layoff that when my daughter asked me a question I snapped and hit her. I have never done anything like that before." Some career counselors would suggest an ethical (and legal) obligation to report the possible child abuse. Others might cite the circumstances of one episode without evidence of harm and the primacy of client confidentiality as a reason to oppose reporting. Some career professionals would include a counselor's "Miranda warning" about the limits of confidentiality and required disclosures in the initial discussion of counseling expectations, as part of informed consent, which is off-putting at best and demeaning to clients at worst. However, without such an orientation to the limits of confidentiality, the counselor who received the information might be reluctant to even consider reporting it.

Ethical issues can arise in which practices common outside the career professional's helping relationship deviate from what is ethically appropriate. For example, a business relationship between a career professional and a client is considered unethical because it constitutes a dual relationship that could impair objectivity. A career professional helping a friend, relative, or the child of a friend might cause a strain on objectivity, which could also occur for any other professional, yet the recognition is not so apparent to the person who asks for "a small personal favor." For example, if, in the earlier scenario, José's father and José's counselor were friends, then how should the counselor proceed to help José in this instance? The situation could become even more complicated if José's counselor were the only counselor in José's high school.

Career professionals are also likely to face dilemmas that could be labeled as "business ethics." Examples of such dilemmas are when clients ask career counselors awkward questions, such as how much to tell potential employers about other job options they have, or how to deal with multiple offers. Likewise, potential employers can ask the career counselors about their clients. Those who work in settings that have a placement function often deal with inquiries from potential employers of their clients. The career professional, in ways not so common in other types of counseling, is often asked to assist clients in dealing with workplace issues such as unethical behavior on the part of supervisors, sexual harassment, and unfair hiring and promotion practices. Career professionals might have access to nonpublic information that could be used unethically. For example, should a placement counselor tell a client that he or she overheard a recruiter say the client was the top choice for a position? What about information that might lead to a financial gain to the professional, such as information about the plans of a business that might have implications for noncounseling-related investments of the counselor? Career professionals often need guidance in dealing with ethical situations that are not covered in current ethical codes.

Chapters and sections of chapters throughout this text recognize the role of school counselors in developmental career interventions for both individuals and groups. There is one area of ethical concern that troubles many secondary school counselors, and which we believe deserves special mention. That is the role of the secondary school counselor in assisting students with determining appropriate educational and/or training plans and the role of the same counselor as a provider of recommendations for their counselees to the institutions at which they might pursue postsecondary education. Many colleges have a specific expectation that secondary school counselors provide a recommendation for applicants. The simultaneous role of helping the students determine an appropriate institution and providing a recommendation to the institution could be considered a dual relationship. These issues are complicated by the role of parents who, in addition to sometimes expecting counselors to help them realize their hopes and dreams for their children's educational and career plans, often want to review recommendations written for college admission. There are complex ethical and legal issues involved in such activities, and we advise school counselors to become well versed in their school systems' policies pertaining to student records and recommendations, and to become familiar with the provisions of the Family Educational Rights and Privacy Act (1974). The National Association for College Admissions Counseling (NACAC) has produced a *Statement of Principles of Good Practice* (2007). We suggest that secondary school counselors who provide required recommendations for their students study the statement and consult with supervisors, and when necessary with the legal advisor for their school, when questions and issues arise.

Although studying the ACA's 2005 *Code of Ethics* and the NCDA's 2007a Standards is important and effective for career professionals who are career counselors, more is needed. That "more" is an understanding of the bases and intention of the standards. It is not possible for an ethical code or standard to provide an unambiguous answer to every potential ethical question. There will inevitably be occasions when career counselors and other career professionals will need the assistance of trusted professional colleagues to provide an assessment of the proper action in response to an ethical dilemma. Thus, a useful rule of thumb for career professionals is to consult with professional colleagues who understand career interventions whenever they are unsure about the proper action to take to resolve an ethical dilemma.

ETHICAL DILEMMAS VERSUS MORAL TEMPTATIONS

Clearly, resolving ethical dilemmas can be a complex task for career professionals. It is important to note, however, that not all issues involving ethics or proper behaviors deserve the title "dilemma." Kidder (1995) contends that an ethical dilemma occurs only in instances in which there are competing "rights" or there is a struggle to determine the "least bad" course of action. Instead of dilemmas, Kidder labels situations in which the struggle is between right and wrong as *moral temptations*. Unfortunately, some career professionals struggle with moral temptations and may take actions that most peers would categorize as unethical.

For example, a career professional might become interested in a noncounseling business or personal relationship with a client and be tempted to prematurely end a formal career counseling relationship to start the "clock" or deny that a relationship was counseling. The involved professional might not be the best judge of whether the relationship meets the ethical standards to change from career counseling to a personal relationship. Attempting to judge the propriety of one's own actions might be the ultimate dual relationship.

Sometimes the career practitioner faces choices between actions that may help the client but have some risk to the counselor. For example, the ACA (2005), NCDA (2007), and the American Psychological Association (APA) (2002) ethics statements address the topic of bartering (as a means of paying for services) as a specific of dual relationships, and they discourage the practice. Many bartering relationships begin innocently, and bartering may even be based on the career counselor's desire to provide a way for a client to invest in counseling and be motivated by clinical, rather than financial, reasons. However, if problems develop in either the counseling or the bartering aspect of the relationship, the potential for the client to raise ethical issues *ex post facto* exists.

To guide career professionals in resolving ethical dilemmas, we will review the principles on which ethical codes are based. We will then examine the basic ethical concepts included in all counseling ethical codes. It is important to note again, however, that no ethics code and certainly no book chapter can provide answers to all the questions that will arise in the delivery of career services. The following excerpt from the "Purpose" section of the National Association of Social Workers (NASW) *Code of Ethics* (1999) eloquently states and reinforces this point:

> A code of ethics cannot guarantee ethical behavior. Moreover, a code of ethics cannot resolve all ethical issues or disputes, or capture the richness and complexity involved in striving to make responsible choices within a moral community. Rather a code of ethics sets forth values, ethical principles, and ethical standards to which professionals aspire and by which their actions can be judged. (p. 2)

The NCDA *Code of Ethics* (2007) requires all career professionals who believe an ethical violation has occurred to take action, and the code cites the ACA *Code of Ethics* (2005) as a source of guidance. We hope that your exploration of the topic will heighten your awareness of potential ethical problems and the multiple considerations involved in addressing those problems.

USING PRINCIPLES TO RESOLVE ETHICAL DECISIONS

VanHoose (1986), a pioneer in the study of counseling ethics, observed that "ethical principles provide a more solid framework for decision making than do ethical codes or statutes" (p. 168). VanHoose recommended that counselors use the following five principles, which Herlihy and Corey (2006) continue to consider foundational and essential to counseling practice, and the basis of the ACA ethical standards.

1. *Autonomy* refers to independence and self-determination. Under this principle, counselors respect the freedom of clients to choose their own directions, make their own choices, and control their own lives. We have an ethical obligation to decrease client dependency and foster independent decision making. We refrain from setting imposing goals, avoid being judgmental, and are accepting of different values.
2. *Nonmaleficence* means do no harm. Counselors must take care that their actions do not risk hurting clients, even inadvertently. We have a responsibility to avoid engaging in practices that cause harm or have the potential to result in harm.

3. *Beneficence* means to promote good, or mental health and wellness. This principle mandates that counselors actively promote the growth and welfare of those they serve.
4. *Justice* is the foundation of our commitment to fairness in professional relationships. Justice includes consideration of such factors as quality of services, allocation of time and resources, establishment of fees, and access to counseling services. This principle also refers to the fair treatment of an individual when his or her interests need to be considered in the context of the rights and interests of others.
5. *Fidelity* means counselors make honest promises and honor their commitments to clients, students, and supervisees. This principle involves creating a trusting and therapeutic climate in which people can search for their own solutions and taking care not to deceive or exploit clients. (Herlihy & Corey, 2006, pp. 9–10)

The principles are similar to those suggested by Beauchamp and Childress (2001) in their classic text on medical ethics. They also identified the following additional principles as relevant for professional–patient relationships:

1. **Veracity:** Tell the truth and do not lie or deceive others.
2. **Privacy:** Allow individuals to limit access to information about themselves.
3. **Confidentiality:** Allow individuals to control access to information they have shared.

Collectively, the ACA principles and those offered by Beauchamp and Childress (2001), including their suggestions for professional–patient relationships, provide guidelines for ethical behavior in career services. The principles are the basis for mandatory ethical standards, those behaviors of the counselor that can be enforced, whereas aspirational ethics refer to the highest standards of conduct to which career professionals can aspire (Herlihy & Corey, 2006). Other writers (e.g., Herlihy & Watson, 2006) suggest that virtue ethics as contrasted with principle ethics are necessary to produce a culturally sensitive approach to making ethical decisions. Corey and Herlihy offer the following six as virtue ethics distilled from the literature on virtue ethics:

- Discernment or prudence
- Respectfulness
- Integrity
- Self-awareness
- Acknowledgement of the role of emotion
- Connectedness with the community

When questions arise pertaining to proper practice, these principles can be used to help career professionals identify appropriate behaviors. Career counselors should feel especially comfortable with the principles of autonomy and beneficence because they represent the hallmarks of counseling at its best. Finally, it is worth noting that despite the various purposes and audiences to which ethical codes and principles are addressed, ethical codes and statements for the major psychologically based helping professions (counseling, psychology, and clinical social work) are remarkably similar. However, some ethical questions and decisions related to career interventions cannot be easily resolved by reference to ethical codes that were written to address interventions that were likely to be therapeutic in nature. Some of those issues in career interventions have their basis in values that are often the basis of aspirational and virtue ethics.

THE ROLE OF VALUES IN DEFINING CAREER DEVELOPMENT INTERVENTIONS

Values assumptions underlie all questions (and answers) related to ethical behavior in career development interventions. Values assumptions are particularly relevant regarding the counselor's and client's understanding, and definition, of the career counseling relationship. Bergin (1985) suggests, "values are orienting beliefs about what is good for the clients and how that good should be achieved" (p. 99). As such, value issues permeate the career development intervention process. Any intervention in the life space or lifestyle of people carries with it values implications (London, 1964). The need for practitioners to clearly understand their own values represents an essential starting point for career services delivery and is an ethical issue within career services. Because value-free career interventions do not exist, career practitioners must be cognizant of how their personal values influence their work with clients.

Tjeltveit (1986, pp. 515–537) suggests the following strategies for minimizing the likelihood of counselors behaving in ways that are insensitive to clients' values:

1. Become informed about the variety of values held in society;
2. Be aware of your own values;
3. Present value options to clients in an unbiased manner;
4. Be committed to clients' freedom of choice;
5. Respect clients with values that differ from your own;
6. Consult with others when necessary;
7. Consider referring clients to another counselor when substantial moral, religious, or political value differences exist.

When career practitioners incorporate Tjeltveit's strategies into their daily practice, they go a long way toward ensuring that their interventions will be ethical. Career counselors must constantly monitor their own values and how those values affect their career interventions.

Tjeltveit's suggestions to consult with professional colleagues and to refer clients to more appropriate service providers when necessary also apply to instances in which the client's concerns extend beyond the traditional issues of clarifying, specifying, and implementing a career choice. For example, it is increasingly evident that adults in career transition experience ego dystonic emotions that must be addressed within the career counseling process (Anderson & Niles, 1995; Subich, 1993). When clients' concerns include depressive feelings, low self-esteem, low self-efficacy, and so on, career practitioners need to evaluate whether they are competent to address such issues. In this regard, Niles and Pate (1989) argue that a career practitioner must, at the minimum, be able to identify mental health issues presented by a client. Once such issues are identified, the career practitioner must determine whether it is appropriate to refer the client to a mental health practitioner (if the career practitioner does not feel competent to deal with these issues, then a referral is the ethical decision) or address the client's mental health issues within the context of career counseling.

The ACA *Code of Ethics* (2005) requires that counseling including career development interventions also requires counselors to be aware of the client's values and the values embedded in career development intervention models. Each of these value sets (i.e., the counselor's, the client's, and the values embedded in interventions) interacts. Personal values influence such dynamics as the client behaviors the practitioner attends to in the career counseling process and the intervention strategies selected by the practitioner. Career practitioners communicate personal values through nonverbal and verbal behavior. Thus, the counselor's values can inadvertently influence the client's behavior. For example, if a client seeks to earn the counselor's approval, the client may opt for career options that the client perceives will please the counselor and disregard other factors in the career decision-making process. In such instances, a career practitioner can unknowingly convert a client to the counselor's values.

Herr and Niles (1988) point out that beyond being sensitive to personal values, the client's values, and the values embedded within career interventions models, counselors need to be cognizant of the values being propagated at the national level. For example, in comparing the evolution of career development theories in Britain and the United States, Watts, Super, and Kidd (1981) observed the following:

> It is intriguing that theories of career development in the USA have been so heavily dominated by psychologists. . . . The dominant focus in the USA has been on the actions of individuals, while in Britain, indigenous theoretical work has been more preoccupied with the constraints of social structures. . . . From the beginning of its independent existence, the USA has been formally committed to the proposition that all people are created equal. As a result, there is the belief that the individual controls his or her own destiny; that with appropriate abilities and with the appropriate development of the appropriate abilities, one's fate lies in one's own hands. (p. 3)

Referring to counseling and psychotherapy, Herr and Niles (1988) noted that:

> Western therapies have a particular way of looking at and processing human behavior; Eastern therapies have a different way of defining such behavior and planning interventions. One is not a substitute for the other because value sets, assumptions, and cultural artifacts make some forms of counseling and psychotherapy unacceptable or ineffective in cultures different from those in which such interventions were invented. (p. 14)

Career intervention models based on European American values emphasizing individualism do not mesh with family expectations or traditions found in societies in which group decisions are the norm and the family is the principle arbiter of appropriate occupational choices. Thus, a career practitioner adhering to European American career intervention models steeped in individual action runs the risk of violating clients' values when those values reflect a collectivistic orientation. An illustration of this point is provided by the career counseling case of Kenji.

Having recently relocated to the United States from China, Kenji came to the guidance office during his senior year in high school with the concern of whether poor performance in his physics and math courses would prevent him from being able to major in engineering in college. In the course of meeting with Kenji, it became obvious to the counselor that, although his concerns were projected toward a college major in engineering, his interests and abilities pointed toward a program of study in a nonscience area. In fact, he had failed physics and just barely passed several math courses. He thoroughly enjoyed the social sciences and had performed well in classes related to this area. When asked to discuss his tentative decision to pursue a college major in engineering, it quickly became apparent that his decision was based on the plans his father had made for him. When asked about the appropriateness of this goal, given his prior academic performance and his interests, it was clear that Kenji was not about to enlarge the range of options under consideration.

A counselor who believes Kenji should adhere to the need for students to develop traditional European American career development values of individual action and an internal locus of control may decide to use a counseling strategy that would challenge Kenji's tendency to adhere to the wishes of others (his father in this case) in his career decision making. The projected treatment plan may even include assertiveness training with the goal of having Kenji confront his father about his career development goals. Unfortunately, this type of career counseling strategy is not sensitive to Kenji's culture of origin in which it is not uncommon for fathers to dominate the career decision making of their sons. Any attempts to influence Kenji's career direction would need to include sensitivity to this very important cultural dynamic. (Interestingly, after the case of Kenji was developed from a composite of the authors' experiences, one of the authors discovered a novel with a plot strikingly similar in many ways to the case [Lee, 1994]. We believe the case of Kenji is based on experiences that are, unfortunately, too common.)

The case of José, presented at the beginning of this chapter, also illustrates the potential for value conflicts between the counselor, José's family, and José. If José has become acculturated into European American values of individualistic action, but his father maintains a collectivistic orientation toward José's career development, then, as with Kenji, the counselor will need to be sensitive to these culturally based values interactions. Such value conflicts illustrate that career development practitioners must be sensitive to the interaction between their personal values, the values prized by the client, and the value sets embedded within specific career counseling models. The latter often reflect the values propagated at the national level.

Because career development interventions promote specific values, national governments vary in their support and expectations of career interventions. Super (1983) notes that countries that are relatively prosperous and free from the threat of outside interventions tend to view career development interventions as vehicles for fostering the individual's abilities, personal values, and interests. Conversely, countries experiencing economic hardships or the possible threat of outside intervention tend to view career development interventions as vehicles for channeling people into occupations deemed as being crucial for national survival. In the United States, *Sputnik* provides an example of the latter. Feeling threatened by the apparent superiority of Soviet space technology in the late 1950s, the U.S. government focused funding and legislative efforts on directing young people into science-related occupations. More recently, the shifting winds of the political climate in the United States have resulted in funding support at the national level moving from school-to-work initiatives to welfare-to-work programs. Often, career development programs, initiatives, and interventions "follow the money" or the financial support that government provides for such initiatives.

In summary, avoiding unethical practice in career development interventions requires career development practitioners to be sensitive to the assumptions underlying their personal values, their clients' values, career interventions models, and the values being propagated at the national level at any point in time (Herr & Niles, 1988). Practicing only within one's area of training and competence is an additional requirement for ethical practice in the career development intervention process. Again, we offer the suggestion of consultation with professional colleagues because counselors may need help to objectively judge their competence. When career practitioners possess value awareness, use ethical principles in their professional decision making, and adhere to the relevant ethical codes, they increase the likelihood that they will function ethically in providing career development interventions to their clients.

USING ETHICAL CODES

Many believe that there are too many ethical codes and that we should move toward a unified ethics code for the counseling profession (Herlihy & Remley, 1995). Most readers of this chapter are, or will be, subject to the ethical codes of the American Counseling Association (2005), the National Career Development Association (2007b), the American Psychological Association (2002), the International Association of Educational and Vocational Guidance (1996), and/or the National Board for Certified Counselors (2005).

We agree with the position that too many ethical codes exist and we hope that at some future time the counseling profession will move toward a model of a single ethics code with annotations or appendices for special situations and areas of practice. However, we doubt that the multiple codes themselves are the source of ethics violations. There are many situations that are unique to specialized areas of counseling practice, such as career counseling. The authors commend those responsible for the NCDA *Code of Ethics* (2007) and for structuring the code to be compatible with the ACA code while making the code profession specific for NCDA members. Likewise, the authors of the NCDA code recognized that many career professionals are associated with professionals associations in addition to or instead of ACA. This effort is an important step in addressing the problems of multiple codes identified by Herlihy and Remley.

In our previous edition we discussed three areas for which we found the then-current ethical codes inadequate to provide direction for career professionals: (1) the definition of a career counseling relationship, given the fact that not all career interventions constitute therapy; (2) ethical standards for the appropriate and proper role of those who provide career services but are not professionally trained counselors; and (3) the ethical use of the Internet to provide or enhance services. These three areas demand greater attention in professional training and workshops. They also presented important challenges to be addressed by the profession.

Progress on Ethical Challenges Facing Career Counselors

This section reviews and explores recent progress on the three challenges that we identified in our previous edition. The issues are: whether all career interventions are counseling relationships subject to the ethical standards of counseling; what the proper role is of those who have training and experience in career interventions but do not have the training, education, and experience that are accepted as essential for one to be a professional counselor; and how to determine the proper use of Internet technology in career interventions. We stated that we considered the existing ethical codes lacking in adequate guidance for career counselors in these areas, and we were bold enough to offer suggestions about needed clarifications. We are happy to report that progress has been made in each of the areas and we offer the following progress report. This report demonstrates that ethical codes are as they should be dynamic and responsive to current situations.

Are All Individual Career Interventions Governed by the Same Ethical Standards?

An area of continuing ethical concern is personal relationships with clients. Confidentiality, counseling relationships, professional responsibility, and relationships with other professionals consistently remain at the top of the list of inquiries received by the American Counseling Association (ACA) Ethics Committee (Glosoff & Freeman, 2007). Some ethical requirements are clear and unambiguous. For example, sexual relationships between career counselors and their clients are unethical. The ethical requirements are clear and unambiguous. However, situations exist in which the expected ethical behavior is not so clearly defined. For example, the psychologically based helping professions are not uniform in their view of how much time must elapse before a "helper" might make a case that an intimate relationship with a former client was not exploitative. Other ethical standards (e.g., the Ethical Standards for Global Career Development Facilitators, 1998) only note that Global Career Development Facilitators "will not be sexually, physically, or romantically intimate with their clients" and offer no time parameters beyond the current professional relationship. The authors of this chapter believe that career counselors are professional counselors with specialized education and experience in career interventions (Niles & Pate, 1989). However, there were many questions about the nature of helping relationships that focus on career issues. Career professionals in and outside educational settings provide services that are typically not considered therapy. For example, consider the case of a career professional in a university career center who reviews a resume for a graduate student of the same age. Some weeks later they meet at a social event and begin a social relationship. Is that relationship subject to the same ethical scrutiny as a relationship that involved multiple sessions of counseling in a university counseling center and complex career issues? Reasonable professionals might offer different answers.

Additional complications in determining proper action can arise because the specific requirements of many laws governing counselor behavior are far from clear, and the standards of practice incorporated in the regulations of many states are inconsistent with the ethical codes they resemble. For example, the regulations of the Commonwealth of Virginia Board of Counseling (2007) contain a standards of practice section. Included in that section is a statement about sexual relationships, which states:

Counselors shall not engage in any type of sexual intimacies with clients or those included in a collateral relationship with the client and not counsel persons with whom they have had a sexual relationship. Counselors shall not engage in sexual intimacies with former clients within a minimum of five years after terminating the counseling relationship. Counselors who engage in such relationship after five years following termination shall have the responsibility to examine and document thoroughly that such relations do not have an exploitive nature, based on factors such as duration of counseling, amount of time since counseling, termination circumstances, client's personal history and mental status, or adverse impact on the client. A client's consent to, initiation of or participation in sexual behavior or involvement with a counselor does not change the nature of the conduct nor lift the regulatory prohibition. (p.15)

The ACA *Code of Ethics* (2005) similarly address sexual relationships between counselors and clients:

A.5. Roles and Relationships With Clients
(See F.3., F.10., G.3.)

A.5.a. Current Clients
Sexual or romantic counselor–client interactions or relationships with current clients, their romantic partners, or their family members are prohibited.

A.5.b. Former Clients
Sexual or romantic counselor–client interactions or relationships with former clients, their romantic partners, or their family members are prohibited for a period of 5 years following the last professional contact.

Counselors, before engaging in sexual or romantic interactions or relationships with clients, their romantic partners, or client family members after 5 years following the last professional contact, demonstrate forethought and document (in written form) whether the interactions or relationship can be viewed as exploitive in some way and/or whether there is still potential to harm the former client; in cases of potential exploitation and/or harm, the counselor avoids entering such an interaction or relationship.

A.5.c. Nonprofessional Interactions or Relationships (Other Than Sexual or Romantic Interactions or Relationships)
Counselor–client nonprofessional relationships with clients, former clients, their romantic partners, or their family members should be avoided, except when the interaction is potentially beneficial to the client. *(See A.5.d.)*

A career professional might have previously believed or asserted that engaging in an intimate personal relationship with a former client was permissible because, as in the previous resume critique example, the professional service was not counseling. However, the same career counselor (who would be required to be licensed if he or she practiced privately in Virginia and called himself or herself a counselor) might be judged to have behaved unethically by those with different interpretations of the ethical requirements. Likewise, a career professional might have believed that the two-year (American Psychological Association [2002]) standard to begin to make a case that an intimate relationship was nonexploitive could apply.

The 2007 NCDA Ethical Code recognizes in section A.1.b. that career professionals provide different types of services. The responsibility of all career professionals to provide only those services within the scope of their competence and qualifications is made explicit. Although the discrepancy between the APA (2002) "two-year standard" and the ACA and NCDA five-year standard for sexual intimacy to even be defended as other than exploitive continues, section A.5.b of the NCDA code makes the five-year limitation applicable to all career professionals. The issue has been addressed clearly and explicitly. All career professionals are subject to the code in their professional activities.

Should Those Without Traditional Training and Credentials as Professional Counselors Provide Career Services?

The issue of the proper role of those providing career services (e.g., providing career information, career advising) without the customary training and credentials for professional counseling relates to managed care and third-party payers because many professional counselors depend on those sources for their livelihood. These counselors are understandably concerned about anything that would make the competence of those delivering counseling services subject to question. However, many consider prohibiting persons with appropriate talents and skills from providing the services for which they are qualified as itself an unethical and unnecessary restraint. Still others contend that having any person other than a fully qualified counselor provide any career services is a threat to client welfare and the reputation of the counseling profession. These are contentious issues within the profession. Regardless of one's opinion, the reality is that many individuals engage in providing career services with little or no formal training in career development theory and practice. Moreover, many of these individuals have no training in the helping professions. Counselor and psychology licensure laws typically do not prohibit unlicensed individuals from providing training in job-search skills, resume writing, and so on.

Section A.1.b. of the NCDA *Code of Ethics*, mentioned above, recognizes that career professionals provide different types of services. That same section makes it obligatory for career professionals to make explicit the limits of the services for which they are competent and qualified, and which they can offer. As explained above, the section that addresses sexual intimacy with former clients also makes explicit the obligation of all career professionals to follow the *Code of Ethics*. Likewise, section A.1.c. makes clear the obligation of all career professionals to engage only in nonprofessional interactions that are beneficial to their clients.

Great progress has been made. NCDA has recognized, by providing training and credentials for Career Development Facilitators (CDF), that there are persons who, although they not trained as professional counselors, can provide career services. The NCDA *Code of Ethics* (2007) has made those who are recognized as career professionals subject to the code. The basic question has been answered; but the challenge of the many who provide career services who are not subject to the NCDA, or any other ethical code, remains as a concern to all career professionals and a potential threat to the clients who are unaware of the distinctions among those offering career services.

How Should the Internet Be Used in Career Development Interventions?

The dimensions of the Internet counseling controversy are in many ways similar to the issues in endorsing career interventions by the untrained or undertrained professional counselor. Most counselors acknowledge the potential of the Internet as a source of information that can be accessed by people who might not have access to other sources of the information. They also recognize the superiority, breadth, depth, and currency of the information available through the Internet. Although there are some copyright issues about information and assessment provided through the Internet, ethical issues most often arise when the services are considered to be professional counseling. Many counselors define counseling as face-to-face contact and that ends the consideration. Others allow the possibility that some career counseling services (e.g., information) might be provided through the Internet, but wonder about regulation. How can service providers potentially thousands of miles from the person helped be accountable? The questions are many and the answers are not yet determined. Since NBCC's pioneer effort, which ironically drew criticism because it gave professional recognition to Internet services, ACA, NBCC, and NCDA have struggled with the ethical and professional issues related to the use of technology in counseling. NCDA developed guidelines for the use of the Internet for providing career information and planning services (NCDA, 1997). In addition, NCDA published a guide to using the Internet in career planning (Harris-Bowlsbey, Dikel, & Sampson, 1998). These guidelines acknowledge that the Internet can be used in four ways for the purpose of providing career services to clients:

1. To deliver occupational information;
2. To provide online searches of occupational databases for the purpose of identifying occupational options;
3. To deliver interactive career counseling and career planning services;
4. To provide online job searches.

These four purposes are subject to guidelines that address a variety of ethical issues. For example, the qualifications of the Web site developer or provider must be clearly stated on the site. Clients have the right to be informed about the expertise and experience of the counselor. Moreover, the counselor must not use a false e-mail identity when interacting with clients. The provider must clearly state the appropriate uses (and limitations) of the Web site. The counselor must appropriately screen clients to determine whether the client can benefit from using the online services provided. The counselor must also provide adequate support for the client via periodic telephone contact or videoconferencing.

Providing career services to clients in other geographical locations presents a variety of challenges to the service provider. For instance, the counselor has the obligation to be aware of local conditions, cultures, and events that may have an impact on the client using the online services. The counselor must also be able to refer clients to local practitioners when the client is in need of additional services. Internet providers of career services must also ensure that the content of the Web site is current and appropriate for use in electronic form. Current online information is especially critical when the service includes online job searching. The costs of all services provided must be clearly stated. When the services include assessment instruments, only assessments with adequate psychometric evidence of their reliability and validity may be used. The issues of confidentiality and storage of client data must be clearly addressed on the Web site.

The use of the Internet to provide career services increases each day. With its increased use, career practitioners are consistently presented with new ethical issues in services delivery. Adhering to guidelines offered by the NCDA, consulting with others, and having external consultants evaluate online services are some strategies career practitioners can use to ensure that their online services are ethical. Clearly, this mode of services delivery will continue to present practitioners with ethical dilemmas as its use increases in the future.

THE ETHICAL STANDARDS OF THE NCDA

Last, but certainly not least important, we focus directly on the ethical standards of NCDA and offer what we hope will be a summary of counseling ethics for students and those who have not yet studied counseling ethics, and a review for career professionals whose study of ethical standards preceded the 2007 major revision of the NCDA code. We have included the introduction to each of the nine main sections of the NCDA code and we **urge careful reading of the entire code included as Appendix A.**

Section A: The Professional Relationship

Career professionals encourage client growth and development in ways that foster the interest and welfare of clients and promote formation of healthy relationships. Career professionals actively attempt to understand the diverse cultural backgrounds of the individuals they serve. Career professionals also explore their own cultural identities and how one's cultural identity affects one's values and beliefs about the working relationship.

Career professionals are encouraged to contribute to society by devoting a portion of their professional activity to services for which there is little or no financial return (*pro bono publico*).

Section B: Confidentiality, Privileged Communication, and Privacy

Career professionals recognize that trust is a cornerstone of the professional relationship. Career professionals work to earn the trust of clients by creating an ongoing partnership, establishing and upholding appropriate boundaries, and maintaining confidentiality. Career professionals communicate the parameters of confidentiality in a culturally competent manner.

Section C: Professional Responsibility

Career professionals provide open, honest, and accurate communication in dealing with the public and other professionals. They practice in a nondiscriminatory manner within the boundaries of professional and personal competence and have a responsibility to abide by the NCDA *Code of Ethics*. Career professionals actively participate in local, state, and national associations that foster the development and improvement of the provision of career services. Career professionals promote changes at the individual, group, institutional, and societal levels that improve the quality of life for individuals and groups and remove potential barriers to the provision or access of appropriate services being offered. Career professionals have a responsibility to the public to engage in ethical practice. In addition, career professionals engage in self-care activities to maintain and promote their emotional, physical, mental, and spiritual well-being to best meet their professional responsibilities.

Section D: Relationships with Other Professionals

Career professionals recognize that the quality of their interactions with colleagues can influence the quality of services provided to clients. They work to become knowledgeable about colleagues within and outside the profession. Career professionals develop positive working relationships and systems of communication with colleagues to enhance services to clients.

Section E: Evaluation, Assessment, and Interpretation

Career professionals use assessment instruments as one component of the career services process, taking into account the client's personal and cultural context. Career professionals promote the well-being of individual clients or groups of clients by developing and using appropriate career, educational, and psychological assessment instruments.

Section F: Use of the Internet in Career Services

Career professionals have always been at the forefront in using new technologies to assist in serving clients. More and more, technology (and specifically the Internet) is being used to provide and/or support services offered by career professionals. However, the Internet should typically be only one component of the career services process and then its use must be evaluated based on the client's personal and cultural context. Above all, career professionals must practice ethically and continually promote the well-being of individual clients or groups of clients.

Section G: Supervision, Training, and Teaching

Career professionals foster meaningful and respectful professional relationships and maintain appropriate boundaries with supervisees and students. Career professionals have theoretical and pedagogical foundations for their work and aim to be fair, accurate, and honest in their assessments of students.

Section H: Research and Publication

Career professionals who conduct research are encouraged to contribute to the knowledge base of the profession and promote a clearer understanding of the conditions that lead to a healthy and more just society. Career professionals support efforts of researchers by participating fully and willingly whenever possible. Career professionals minimize bias and respect diversity in designing and implementing research programs.

Section I: Resolving Ethical Issues

Career professionals behave in a legal, ethical, and moral manner in the conduct of their professional work. They are aware that client protection and trust in the profession depend on a high level of professional conduct. They hold other career professionals to the same standards and are willing to take appropriate action to ensure that these standards are upheld. Career professionals work to resolve ethical dilemmas with direct and open communication among all parties involved and seek consultation with colleagues and supervisors when necessary. Career professionals incorporate ethical practice into their daily work. They engage in ongoing learning and development regarding current topics in ethical and legal issues in the profession.

If you have not read the NCDA *Code of Ethics* (2007), please stop now and read the code in Appendix A before you proceed. As you read this standard, it is important to be aware of the fact that ethical statements contain both mandatory and aspirational standards. The authors' reading of the NCDA, IAEVG, APA, ACA, and other ethical statements suggests variation primarily among the aspirational standards (i.e., standards that reflect the philosophy of the profession but are not easily enforceable). There is, in our interpretation, more consistency across ethical codes regarding the mandatory standards.

Based on our interpretation of multiple ethical codes, we offer seven standards that are central to ethical standards and ethical practice. These standards are each based on an overriding principle of concern for the welfare of the client. Maintaining an overriding concern for client welfare means that career counselors must constantly test all potential actions they take against the principles of promoting client autonomy, promoting client good and removing harm, never acting to harm a client, promoting equal treatment of those similarly situated and adapting services based on client needs, and keeping promises to clients. As a result of the enhanced emphasis on advocacy and social justice in the ACA and NCDA codes of ethics. We offer the following as critical ethical concepts for career professionals:

1. Career professionals offer only services they are competent to offer. Competence includes training, supervised experience, and some external validation of that competence. This includes all counseling techniques and strategies, assessment devices, and technology-assisted counseling.
2. Career professionals respect and value individual differences among clients and potential clients. To respect and value these differences, it is necessary for counselors to study ways to serve diverse populations.
3. Career professionals treat information received from and about clients as owned by the client and held in trust by the counselor. Such information is revealed only with the consent of the client, when required by law, or to protect the

client or others from harm. The basis of career professionals' relationships with clients is the assumption that their communications will be respected as confidential.

4. The career professional does not engage in any professional relationship in which the counselor's objectivity and ability to work solely for the welfare of the client might be impaired. This includes but is not limited to intimate emotional and physical relationships. Professionals must anticipate how potential nonprofessional relationships could possibly lead to future ethical conflicts and take action to avoid future problems.

5. Career professionals assume professional responsibility for clients, and if they are unable to assist, they help the client to obtain alternative services. This requirement extends to assisting clients who cannot, or do not, pay for services as agreed, and for providing services when the career counselor is not available.

6. Career professionals recognize that they have obligations to other members of the profession and to society to act in responsible ways and to consider the effects of their behavior on others. This requirement extends to research and publication, to online services, and to business relationships, so that counselors do not use their profession for inappropriate financial gain (e.g., diverting clients from a provided service to a private practice).

Career professionals are advocates for their clients and for social justice. The latest revisions of the ACA (2005) and NCDA (2007) ethical statements recognize career professionals' responsibility for advocacy on behalf of their clients and for social justice. The chapters of this book leave no doubt that that work is a vital component of the ability of people to achieve their potential to contribute to society. Advocacy for career professionals can range from appropriate advocacy for individual clients to advocacy for changes that expand the opportunities for all and remove barriers to employment. The ethical principle of justice suggests that career professionals have a special obligation to work to ensure that those who are equal on criteria related to any selection are treated equally, and that those who have potential that might not be recognized without encouragement and assistance receive the appropriate encouragement and assistance from career professionals. This is a statement of aspirational and virtue ethics that is difficult, if not impossible, to mandate for enforcement. However, we believe career professionals have not only the unique expertise to advocate for expanded and equal access to meaningful and rewarding work, but that they have an ethical obligation to do so.

Using an Ethical Decision-Making Model

The information we have provided in this chapter thus far provides useful information for you to use in understanding the various dilemmas that career practitioners often confront. Integrating this information into an ethical decision-making model will also guide you in determining a specific course of action to take when you encounter such dilemmas. Forester-Miller and Davis (1996) provide an ethical decision-making model for professional counselors that can be applied to career counseling. Specifically, they identify the following steps in ethical decision making:

1. Identify the problem
2. Apply the NCDA *Code of Ethics*
3. Determine the nature and dimensions of the dilemma
4. Generate possible courses of action
5. Consider the potential consequences of all options and choose a course of action
6. Evaluate the selected course of action
7. Implement the course of action selected

In identifying the problem, career practitioners should gather extensive information to clarify the ethical concern. Being specific, objective, and factual will help remove bias and opinion from the problem being identified. Forester-Miller and Davis (1996) recommend considering the following questions: "Is it an ethical, legal, professional, or clinical problem? Is it a combination of more than one of these? Is the issue related to me and what I am or am not doing? Is it related to a client and/or the client's significant others and what they are or are not doing? Is it related to the institution or agency and their policies and procedures?

After you have clarified the problem, refer to the NCDA *Code of Ethics* (NCDA, 2007) to see if the issue is addressed there. If so, then follow the course of action described by the standard. "If the problem is more complex and a resolution does not seem apparent, then you probably have a true ethical dilemma and need to proceed with further steps in the ethical decision making process" (Forester-Miller & Davis, 1996). In the latter case, consider the moral principles described earlier in this chapter (e.g., autonomy, nonmaleficence, etc.) to determine if any apply to the current dilemma. Draw upon the professional literature for guidance in deciding a course of action.

To determine the nature of the dilemma and to generate possible courses of action, it is helpful to consult with experienced professional colleagues and/or supervisors. They may be able to provide alternative viewpoints or they may identify additional dimensions regarding the situation. Consulting with the ethics professional within the relevant professional association (e.g., ACA, APA) is also an important consultative step.

Use the information gathered through this process to generate several potential courses of action. It may also be helpful to involve a colleague in this process. Brainstorm as many courses of action as possible and consider the potential consequences of each action. Evaluate each potential course of action relative to its impact on your client, you, and others. Consider whether the course of action creates any additional ethical concerns. Review whether the course of action is fair, whether it is the sort of action that you would recommend to others in a similar situation, and whether you would be comfortable if the public knew about the course of action should you take it (Forester-Miller & Davis, 1996).

Once an appropriate course of action has been identified, it should be implemented. Forester-Miller and Davis (1996) recommend that, after implementing your course of action, it is important to assess whether your actions had the anticipated effect and consequences.

Summary

The need for career professionals to be vigilant in providing interventions that are ethical is, perhaps, obvious. Unfortunately, ethical practice itself is not always obvious. Career development practitioners and, most importantly, their clients, will be best served when practitioners use multiple strategies to guide their ethical decision making. Using ethical principles, possessing values awareness, and adhering to the relevant ethical codes (e.g., those published by the NCDA, ACA, APA, and IAEVG) are strategies that career professionals can use to increase the probability that they will engage in proper practice. We recommend the use of the strategies for ethical practice that are discussed in this chapter. Whenever possible, we also encourage readers to discuss their questions and concerns with trusted and respected consultants. Discussion of these issues will provide multiple perspectives related to each issue presented. What do you think would be proper behavior of the career counselor faced with the following challenges?

a) A school counselor has reservations about military service. The father of the client, whom the counselor knows to be caring and concerned, asks the counselor about giving his child information about military service as a means to help the child become more mature and live up to his/her high potential. The counselor knows the child has high potential but lacks self-discipline. The counselor tends to agree with the father but questions the military as source of that discipline.

b) A small career services office counselor helps a second-year, 32-year-old college student write a resume and then has no further contact with the student until the counselor enrolls in a yoga class in which the student is also enrolled. The student asks the counselor to go for coffee after class.

c) A career counselor in private practice is counseling an executive about her career plans. She shares information about her excitement concerning an offer she will accept and tells the counselor about the IPO Corporation and her anticipation of a position with stock options. The client believes the stock options will multiply over a short term. The counseling is terminated and the counselor wonders about an investment in IPO. The counselor does not think there is a counseling dilemma because the gain or loss could not affect the terminated counseling relationship.

d) A high school counselor meets with a student who is excited about military service due to recent advertisements about the military service providing resources for higher education. The student has no resources for further study and no potential family support. The student has great potential but the counselor is concerned about recent press information about the military attitude toward gays and lesbians in military. Rumors about the young person's sexual orientation abound in the school, but the counselor has no information that the student has ever mentioned his/her sexuality.

e) An elementary school counselor is planning career-related activities and has arranged a class trip to a large, nearby dairy that has supported the school. A parent objects not only to his child's participation but also to any participation of the school because the parent believes dairy farming is an unethical exploitation of animals. The parent has written the local press and has been on "call-in radio" objecting to the school serving milk, in spite of meetings with officials that have demonstrated legal requirements for serving milk in lunch programs.

Case Study

Molly is an 18-year-old college freshman experiencing substantial stress related to her inability to identify a college major. Her father, a CEO of a large pharmaceutical company, has told her to major in business to prepare for working within his company when Molly graduates. Molly's mother, a painter, has been silent about her expectations for Molly. Molly feels that her father is overbearing and her mother is nonsupportive. Molly's struggles have resulted in her experienceing depression and a sense of urgency about how to resolve her dilemma. She lacks academic motivation and has been spending afternoons smoking pot and listening to music. Recently, she and her younger sister, Susan, have concocted a plan to leave school and home to travel throughout Europe. They have already saved money for this experience and plan on simply leaving without informing their parents. At the same time, you have recently received an e-mail from Molly's father, who would like to meet with you during the upcoming Parents' Weekend.

He wants to discuss Molly's career plans. Molly wants your advice about her trip to Europe. What potential ethical issues do you foresee?

Student Activities

1. Identify which of the following topics could present personal ethical/moral issues for you in your work as a career counselor:

   • A student who wants to explore a career in the military.

   • A client whose religious beliefs lead him to conclude that a "woman's place is in the home."

   • A parent who wants you to convince her child to pursue a career in engineering because the student is good at math.

   • An Asian student who firmly believes she should choose the occupation her parents have identified for her, despite the fact that she has no interest in this occupation.

- An acquaintance that is out of work but asks you to provide career counseling in exchange for him performing some light maintenance work around your home.

- A mother of a student for whom you are a school counselor who asks you to tell her which educational options her daughter is considering.

- An adult college student for whom you once provided a resume critique who (unbeknownst to you) has been asked to play on your YMCA volleyball team.

2. What are the similarities and differences between the ethical standards for the International Association for Educational and Vocational Guidance (iaevg.org/iaevg/nav.cfm?lang52&menu51&submenu52), and the ethical standards for the National Career Development Association (ncda.org/)?

References

American Counseling Association (ACA). (2005). *Code of Ethics*. Alexandria, VA: Author.

American Psychological Association (APA). (2002). *Ethical Principles of Psychologists and Code of Conduct*. Washington, DC: Author.

Anderson, W. P., Jr., & Niles, S. G. (1995). Career and personal concerns expressed by career counseling clients. *The Career Development Quarterly, 43*, 240–245.

Beauchamp, T. L., & Childress, J. F. (2001). *Principles of biomedical ethics* (5th ed.). New York: Oxford University Press.

Bergin, A. E. (1985). Proposed values for guiding and evaluating counseling and psychotherapy. *Counseling and Values, 29*, 99–115.

Center for Credentialing and Education (1998). *Ethical standards for global career development facilitators*. Greensboro, NC: Author.

Commonwealth of Virginia Board of Counseling. (2007). *Regulations Governing the Practice of Professional Counseling*. (18 VAC 115-20-10 et seg.)

Family Educational Rights and Privacy Act of 1974, 20 U. S. C. § 1232g; 34 CFR Part 99.

Forester-Miller, H. & Davis, T. (1996). *A practitioner's guide to ethical decision making*. Alexandria, VA: American Counseling Association.

Glosoff, H. L., & Freeman, L. T. (2007). Report of the ACA Ethics Committee: 2005–2006. *Journal of Counseling and Development, 85*, 251–254.

Harris-Bowlsbey, J., Dikel, M. R., & Sampson, J. P. (1998). *The Internet: A tool for career planning*. Columbus, OH: National Career Development Association.

Herlihy, B., & Corey, G. (2006). *ACA Ethical Standards Casebook* (6th ed.). Alexandria, VA: American Counseling Association.

Herlihy, B., & Remley, T. P. (1995). Unified ethical standards: A challenge for professionalism. *Journal of Counseling and Development, 74*, 130–133.

Herlihy, B. R., & Watson, Z. E. (2006.) Gender issues in career counseling. In D. Capuzzi & M. D. Stauffer (Eds.), *Career counseling: Foundations, perspectives, and applications* (pp. 363–385). Boston: Pearson Education.

Herr, E. L., & Niles, S. G. (1988). The values of counseling: Three domains. *Counseling and Values, 33*, 4–17.

International Association for Educational and Vocational Guidance. (1996). *IAEVG Ethical Standards*. Berlin, Germany: Author.

Kidder, R. M. (1995). *How good people make tough choices: Resolving the dilemmas of ethical living*. New York: Fireside.

Lee, G. (1994). *Honor and duty*. New York: Knopf.

London, P. (1964). *The modes and morals of psychotherapy*. New York: Holt, Rinehart, and Winston.

National Association for College Admissions Counseling. (2007). *Statement of Principles of Good Practice*. Alexandria, VA: Author.

National Association of Social Workers. (1999). *Code of Ethics of the National Association of Social Workers*. Washington, DC: Author.

National Board for Certified Counselors. (2005). *Code of Ethics*. Greensboro, NC: Author.

National Career Development Association. (1997). *NCDA Guidelines for the Use of the Internet for*

Provision of Career Information and Planning Services. Columbus, OH: Author.

National Career Development Association (2007a). *Code of ethics.* Broken Arrow, OK: Author.

National Career Development Association. (2007b). *Ethical Standards.* Columbus, OH: Author.

Niles, S. G., & Pate, R. H. (1989). Competency and training issues related to the integration of career counseling and mental health counseling. *Journal of Career Development, 16,* 63–71.

Subich, L. M. (1993). How personal is career counseling? *The Career Development Quarterly, 42,* 129–131.

Super, D. E. (1983). Assessment in career guidance: Toward truly developmental counseling. *Personnel and Guidance Journal, 61,* 555–562.

Tjelveit, A. C. (1986). The ethics of value conversion in psychotherapy: Appropriate and inappropriate therapist influence on client values. *Clinical Psychology Review, 6,* 515–537.

VanHoose, W. H. (1986). Ethical principles in counseling. *Journal of Counseling and Development, 65,* 168–169.

Watts, A. G., Super, D. E., & Kidd, J. M. (1981). *Career development in Britain.* Cambridge, England: Hobson's Press.

appendix **A**

National Career Development Association Ethical Standards

These Ethical Standards were developed by the National Board for Certified Counselors (NBCC), an independent, voluntary, not-for-profit organization incorporated in 1982. Titled "Code of Ethics" by NBCC and last amended in February 1987, the Ethical Standards were adopted by the National Career Development Association (NCDA) Board of Directors in 1987 and revised in 1991, with minor changes in wording (e.g., the addition of specific references to NCDA members).

PREAMBLE
NCDA is an educational, scientific, and professional organization dedicated to the enhancement of the worth, dignity, potential, and uniqueness of each individual and, thus, to the service of society. This code of ethics enables the NCDA to clarify the nature of ethical responsibilities for present and future professional career counselors.

SECTION A: GENERAL
1. NCDA members influence the development of the profession by continuous efforts to improve professional practices, services, and research. Professional growth is continuous through the career counselor's career and is exemplified by the development of a philosophy that explains why and how a career counselor functions in the helping relationship. Career counselors must gather data on their effectiveness and be guided by their findings.
2. NCDA members have a responsibility to the clients they are serving and to the institutions within which the services are being performed. Career counselors

also strive to assist the respective agency, organization, or institution in providing the highest caliber of professional services. The acceptance of employment in an institution implies that the career counselor is in agreement with the general policies and principles of the institution. Therefore, the professional activities of the career counselor are in accord with the objectives of the institution. If, despite concerted efforts, the career counselor cannot reach agreement with the employer as to acceptable standards of conduct that allow for changes in institutional policy that are conductive to the positive growth and development of clients, then terminating the affiliation should be seriously considered.
3. Ethical behavior among professional associates (e.g., career counselors) must be expected at all times. When accessible information raises doubt as to the ethical behavior of professional colleagues, the NCDA member must take action to attempt to rectify this condition. Such action uses the respective institution's channels first and then uses procedures established by the American Counseling Association, of which NCDA is a division.
4. NCDA members neither claim nor imply professional qualifications which exceed those possessed, and are responsible for correcting any misrepresentations of these qualifications by others.
5. NCDA members must refuse a private fee or other remuneration for consultation or counseling with persons who are entitled to their services through the career counselor's employing institution or agency. The policies of some agencies may make explicit

Source: From "Ethical Standards of the National Career Development Association" (revised 1991), Tulsa, OK.

provisions for staff members to engage in private practice with agency clients. However, should agency clients desire private counseling or consulting services, they must be apprised of other options available to them. Career counselors must not divert to their private practices, legitimate clients in their primary agencies or of the institutions with which they are affiliated.

6. In establishing fees for professional counseling services, NCDA members must consider the financial status of clients and the respective locality. In the event that the established fee status is inappropriate for the client, assistance must be provided in finding comparable services of acceptable cost.

7. NCDA members seek only those positions in the delivery of professional services for which they are professionally qualified.

8. NCDA members recognize their limitations and provide services or only use techniques for which they are qualified by training and/or experience. Career counselors recognize the need, and seek continuing education, to assure competent services.

9. NCDA members are aware of the intimacy in the counseling relationship, maintain respect for the client, and avoid engaging in activities that seek to meet their personal needs at the expense of the client.

10. NCDA members do not condone or engage in sexual harassment, which is defined as deliberate or repeated comments, gestures, or physical contacts of a sexual nature.

11. NCDA members avoid bringing their personal or professional issues into the counseling relationship. Through an awareness of the impact of stereotyping and discrimination (e.g., biases based on age, disability, ethnicity, gender, race, religion, or sexual preference), career counselors guard the individual rights and personal dignity of the client in the counseling relationship.

12. NCDA members are accountable at all times for their behavior. They must be aware that all actions and behaviors of a counselor reflect on professional integrity and, when inappropriate, can damage the public trust in the counseling profession. To protect public confidence in the counseling profession, career counselors avoid public behavior that is clearly in violation of accepted moral and legal standards.

13. NCDA members have a social responsibility because their recommendations and professional actions may alter the lives of others. Career counselors remain fully cognizant of their impact and are alert to personal, social, organizational, financial, or political situations or pressures which might lead to misuse of their influence.

14. Products or services provided by NCDA members by means of classroom instruction, public lectures, demonstrations, written articles, radio or television programs, or other types of media must meet the criteria cited in Sections A through F of these Ethical Standards.

SECTION B: COUNSELING RELATIONSHIP

1. The primary obligation of NCDA members is to respect the integrity and promote the welfare of the client, regardless of whether the client is assisted individually or in a group relationship. In a group setting, the career counselor is also responsible for taking reasonable precautions to protect individuals from physical and/or psychological trauma resulting from interaction within the group.

2. The counseling relationship and information resulting from it remains confidential, consistent with the legal obligations of the NCDA member. In a group counseling setting, the career counselor sets a norm of confidentiality regarding all group participants' disclosures.

3. NCDA members know and take into account the traditions and practices of other professional groups with whom they work, and they cooperate fully with such groups. If a person is receiving similar services from another professional, career counselors do not offer their own services directly to such a person. If a career counselor is contacted by a person who is already receiving similar services from another professional, the career counselor carefully considers that professional relationship and proceeds with caution and sensitivity to the therapeutic issues as well as the client's welfare. Career counselors discuss these issues with clients so as to minimize the risk of confusion and conflict.

4. When a client's condition indicates that there is a clear and imminent danger to the client or others, the NCDA member must take reasonable personal action or inform responsible authorities. Consultation with other professionals must be used where possible. The assumption of responsibility for the client's behavior must be taken only after careful deliberation, and the client must be involved in the resumption of responsibility as quickly as possible.

5. Records of the counseling relationship, including interview notes, test data, correspondence, audio or visual tape recordings, electronic data storage, and other documents are to be considered professional information for use in counseling. They should not be considered a part of the records of the institution or agency in which the NCDA member is employed unless specified by state statute or regulation. Revelation to others of counseling material must occur only upon the expressed consent of the client; career counselors must make provisions for maintaining confidentiality in the storage and disposal of records. Career

counselors providing information to the public or to subordinates, peers, or supervisors have a responsibility to ensure that the content is general; unidentified client information should be accurate and unbiased, and should consist of objective, factual data.

6. NCDA members must ensure that data maintained in electronic storage are secure. The data must be limited to information that is appropriate and necessary for the services being provided and accessible only to appropriate staff members involved in the provision of services by using the best computer security methods available. Career counselors must also ensure that electronically stored data are destroyed when the information is no longer of value in providing services.

7. Data derived from a counseling relationship for use in counselor training or research shall be confined to content that can be disguised to ensure full protection of the identity of the subject/client and shall be obtained with informed consent.

8. NCDA members must inform clients, before or at the time the counseling relationship commences, of the purposes, goals, techniques, rules and procedures, and limitations that may affect the relationship.

9. All methods of treatment by NCDA members must be clearly indicated to prospective recipients and safety precautions must be taken in their use.

10. NCDA members who have an administrative, supervisory, and/or evaluative relationship with individuals seeking counseling services must not serve as the counselor and should refer the individuals to other professionals. Exceptions are made only in instances where an individual's situation warrants counseling intervention and another alternative is unavailable. Dual relationships with clients that might impair the career counselor's objectivity and professional judgment must be avoided and/or the counseling relationship terminated through referral to another competent professional.

11. When NCDA members determine an inability to be of professional assistance to a potential or existing client, they must, respectively, not initiate the counseling relationship or immediately terminate the relationship. In either event, the career counselor must suggest appropriate alternatives. Career counselors must be knowledgeable about referral resources so that a satisfactory referral can be initiated. In the event that the client declines a suggested referral, the career counselor is not obligated to continue the relationship.

12. NCDA members may choose to consult with any other professionally competent person about a client and must notify clients of this right. Career counselors must avoid placing a consultant in a conflict-of-interest situation that would preclude the consultant's being a proper party to the career counselor's efforts to help the client.

13. NCDA members who counsel clients from cultures different from their own must gain knowledge, personal awareness, and sensitivity pertinent to the client populations served and must incorporate culturally relevant techniques into their practice.

14. When NCDA members engage in intensive counseling with a client, the client's counseling needs should be assessed. When needs exist outside the counselor's expertise, appropriate referrals should be made.

15. NCDA members must screen prospective group counseling participants, especially when the emphasis is on self-understanding and growth through self-disclosure. Career counselors must maintain an awareness of each group participant's welfare throughout the group process.

16. When electronic data and systems are used as a component of counseling services, NCDA members must ensure that the computer application, and any information it contains, is appropriate for the respective needs of clients and is nondiscriminatory. Career counselors must ensure that they themselves have acquired a facilitation level of knowledge with any system they use including hands-on application, search experience, and understanding of the uses of all aspects of the computer-based system. In selecting and/or maintaining computer-based systems that contain career information, career counselors must ensure that the systems provide current, accurate, and locally relevant information. Career counselors must also ensure that clients are intellectually, emotionally, and physically compatible with the use of the computer application and understand its purpose and operation. Client use of a computer application must be evaluated to correct possible problems and assess subsequent needs.

17. NCDA members who develop self-help, stand-alone computer software for use by the general public must first ensure that it is initially designed to function in a stand-alone manner, as opposed to modifying software that was originally designed to require support from a counselor. Secondly, the software must include program statements that provide the user with intended outcomes, suggestions for using the software, descriptions of inappropriately used applications, and descriptions of when and how counseling services might be beneficial. Finally, the manual must include the qualifications of the developer, the development process, validation data, and operating procedures.

SECTION C: MEASUREMENT AND EVALUATION

1. NCDA members must provide specific orientation or information to an examinee prior to and following the administration of assessment instruments or techniques so that the results may be placed in proper

perspective with other relevant factors. The purpose of testing and the explicit use of the results must be made known to an examinee prior to testing.

2. In selecting assessment instruments or techniques for use in a given situation or with a particular client, NCDA members must evaluate carefully the instrument's specific theoretical bases and characteristics, validity, reliability, and appropriateness. Career counselors are professionally responsible for using unvalidated information with special care.

3. When making statements to the public about assessment instruments or techniques, NCDA members must provide accurate information and avoid false claims or misconceptions concerning the meaning of psychometric terms. Special efforts are often required to avoid unwarranted connotations of terms such as IQ and grade-equivalent scores.

4. Because many types of assessment techniques exist, NCDA members must recognize the limits of their competence and perform only those functions for which they have received appropriate training.

5. NCDA members must note when tests are not administered under standard conditions or when unusual behavior or irregularities occur during a testing session and the results must be designated as invalid or of questionable validity. Unsupervised or inadequately supervised assessments, such as mail-in tests, are considered unethical. However, the use of standardized instruments that are designed to be self-administered and self-scored, such as interest inventories, is appropriate.

6. Because prior coaching or dissemination of test materials can invalidate test results, NCDA members are professionally obligated to maintain test security. In addition, conditions that produce most favorable test results must be made known to an examinee (e.g., penalty for guessing).

7. NCDA members must consider psychometric limitations when selecting and using an instrument, and must be cognizant of the limitations when interpreting the results. When tests are used to classify clients, career counselors must ensure that periodic review and/or retesting are conducted to prevent client stereotyping.

8. An examinee's welfare, explicit prior understanding, and agreement are the factors used when determining who receives the test results. NCDA members must see that appropriate interpretation accompanies any release of individual or group test data (e.g., limitations of instrument and norms).

9. NCDA members must ensure that computer-generated assessment administration and scoring programs function properly, thereby providing clients with accurate assessment results.

10. NCDA members who are responsible for making decisions based on assessment results must have appropriate training and skills in educational and psychological measurement including validation criteria, test research, and guidelines for test development and use.

11. NCDA members must be cautious when interpreting the results of instruments that possess insufficient technical data, and must explicitly state to examinees the specific purposes for the use of such instruments.

12. NCDA members must proceed with caution when attempting to evaluate and interpret performances of minority group members or other persons who are not represented in the norm group on which the instrument was standardized.

13. NCDA members who develop computer-based interpretations to support the assessment process must ensure that the validity of the interpretations is established prior to the commercial distribution of the computer application.

14. NCDA members recognize that test results may become obsolete, and avoid the misuse of obsolete data.

15. NCDA members must avoid the appropriation, reproduction, or modification of published tests or parts thereof without acknowledgment and permission from the publisher.

SECTION D: RESEARCH AND PUBLICATION

1. NCDA members will adhere to relevant guidelines on research with human subjects. These include:

a. Code of Federal Regulations, Title 45, Subtitle A, Part 46, as currently issued.

b. American Psychological Association. (1982). *Ethical principles in the conduct of research with human participants*. Washington, DC: Author.

c. American Psychological Association. (1981). Research with human participants. *American Psychologist, 36*, 633–638.

d. Family Educational Rights and Privacy Act. (Buckley Amendment to P. L. 93–380 of the Laws of 1974.)

e. Current federal regulations and various state privacy acts.

2. In planning research activities involving human subjects, NCDA members must be aware of and responsive to all pertinent ethical principles and ensure that the research problem, design, and execution, are in full compliance with the principles.

3. The ultimate responsibility for ethical research lies with the principal researcher, although others involved in research activities are ethically obligated and responsible for their own actions.

4. NCDA members who conduct research with human subjects are responsible for the subjects' welfare throughout the experiment and must take all

reasonable precautions to avoid causing injurious psychological, physical, or social effects on their subjects.

5. NCDA members who conduct research must abide by the following basic elements of informed consent:

a. a fair explanation of the procedures to be followed, including an identification of those which are experimental.

b. a description of the attendant discomforts and risks.

c. a description of the benefits to be expected.

d. a disclosure of appropriate alternative procedures that would be advantageous for subjects.

e. an offer to answer any inquiries concerning the procedures.

f. an instruction that subjects are free to withdraw their consent and to discontinue participation in the project or activity at any time.

6. When reporting research results, explicit mention must be made of all the variables and conditions known to the NCDA member that may have affected the outcome of the study or the interpretation of the data.

7. NCDA members who conduct and report research investigations must do so in a manner that minimizes the possibility that the results will be misleading.

8. NCDA members are obligated to make available sufficient original research data to qualified others who may wish to replicate the study.

9. NCDA members who supply data, aid in the research of another person, report research results, or make original data available must take due care to disguise the identity of respective subjects in the absence of specific authorization from the subject to do otherwise.

10. When conducting and reporting research, NCDA members must be familiar with, and give recognition to, previous work on the topic, must observe all copyright laws, and must follow the principles of giving full credit to those to whom credit is due.

11. NCDA members must give due credit through joint authorship, acknowledgment, footnote statements, or other appropriate means to those who have contributed significantly to the research and/or publication, in accordance with such contributions.

12. NCDA members should communicate to others the results of any research judged to be of professional value. Results that reflect unfavorably on institutions, programs, services, or vested interests must not be withheld.

13. NCDA members who agree to cooperate with another individual in research and/or publication incur an obligation to cooperate as promised in terms of punctuality of performance and with full regard to the completeness and accuracy of the information required.

14. NCDA members must not submit the same manuscript, or one essentially similar in content, for simultaneous publication consideration by two or more journals. In addition, manuscripts that are published in whole or substantial part in another journal or published work should not be submitted for publication without acknowledgment and permission from the previous publication.

SECTION E: CONSULTING

Consultation refers to a voluntary relationship between a professional helper and help-needing individual, group, or social unit in which the consultant is providing help to the client(s) in defining and solving a work-related problem or potential work-related problem with a client or client system.

1. NCDA members acting as consultants must have a high degree of self-awareness of their own values, knowledge, skills, limitations, and needs in entering a helping relationship that involves human and/or organizational change. The focus of the consulting relationship must be on the issues to be resolved and not on the person(s) presenting the problem.

2. In the consulting relationship, the NCDA member and client must understand and agree upon the problem definition, subsequent goals, and predicted consequences of interventions selected.

3. NCDA members must be reasonably certain that they, or the organization represented, have the necessary competencies and resources for giving the kind of help that is needed or that may develop later, and that appropriate referral resources are available to the consultant.

4. NCDA members in a consulting relationship must encourage and cultivate client adaptability and growth toward self-direction. NCDA members must maintain this role consistently and not become decision makers for clients or create a future dependency.

5. NCDA members conscientiously adhere to the NCDA Ethical Standards when announcing consultant availability for services.

SECTION F: PRIVATE PRACTICE

1. NCDA members should assist the profession by facilitating the availability of counseling services in private as well as public settings.

2. In advertising services as private practitioners, NCDA members must advertise in a manner that accurately informs the public of the professional services, expertise, and counseling techniques available.

3. NCDA members who assume an executive leadership role in a private practice organization do not permit their names to be used in professional notices during periods of time when they are not actively engaged in the private practice of counseling.

4. NCDA members may list their highest relevant degree, type, and level of certification and/or license, address, telephone number, office hours, type and/or description of services, and other relevant information. Listed information must not contain false, inaccurate misleading, partial, out-of-context, or otherwise deceptive material or statements.

5. NCDA members who are involved in partnership or corporation with other professionals must, in compliance with the regulations of the locality, clearly specify the separate specialties of each member of the partnership or corporation.

6. NCDA members have an obligation to withdraw from a private-practice counseling relationship if it violates the NCDA Ethical Standards, if the mental or physical condition of the NCDA member renders it difficult to carry out an effective professional relationship, or if the counseling relationship is no longer productive for the client.

PROCEDURES FOR PROCESSING ETHICAL COMPLAINTS

As a division of the American Counseling Association (ACA) the National Career Development Association (NCDA) adheres to the guidelines and procedures for processing ethical complaints and the disciplinary sanctions adopted by ACA. A complaint against an NCDA member may be filed by any individual or group of individuals ("complainant"), whether or not the complainant is a member of NCDA. Action will not be taken on anonymous complaints. For specifics on how to file ethical complaints and a description of the guidelines and procedures for processing complaints, contact:

ACA Ethics Committee
c/o Executive Director
American Counseling Association
5999 Stevenson Avenue
Alexandria, VA 22304
(800) 347–6647

Educational and Career Planning Portfolio

Name _____

_____ (Last)   _____ (First)   _____ (Middle)

Name of School/Division _____   Predominant Language Used at Home _____

Dates Contacts Made, Name, and Relationship to Student

Date of Contact	Name	Relationship to Student	Date of Contact	Name	Relationship to Student

Curriculum Emphasis:

☐ Apprenticeship   ☐ College Preparatory   ☐ Tech Prep   ☐ Occupational & Technical Education

☐ Technical Education   ☐ Youth Work-Study   ☐ Cooperative Education   ☐ Other (Please Specify) _____

Required and Elective Courses

(If this information is available elsewhere, please place a copy of the student's record of required and elective courses in the portfolio.)

School Year: _____

Required Courses	Grade	Credit
_____	____	____
_____	____	____
_____	____	____
_____	____	____

Elective Courses
_____	____	____
_____	____	____
_____	____	____

School Year: _____

Required Courses	Grade	Credit
_____	____	____
_____	____	____
_____	____	____
_____	____	____

Elective Courses
_____	____	____
_____	____	____
_____	____	____

School Year: _____

Required Courses	Grade	Credit
_____	____	____
_____	____	____
_____	____	____
_____	____	____

Elective Courses
_____	____	____
_____	____	____
_____	____	____

School Year: _____

Required Courses	Grade	Credit
_____	____	____
_____	____	____
_____	____	____
_____	____	____

Elective Courses
_____	____	____
_____	____	____
_____	____	____

Planning Future Assessments/Examinations

(Circle if needed and indicate anticipated dates of examinations)

Literacy Passport Test ____	Interest Inventory ____
ACT ____	PSAT ____
ASVAB ____	SAT ____
Achievement ____	Vocational Assessment ____
Aptitude ____	Virginia VIEW ____

Other ____

Counselor/Student Review of Assessment/Examinations

(Circle when completed and indicate date of review)

Literacy Passport Test ____	Interest Inventory ____
ACT ____	PSAT ____
ASVAB ____	SAT ____
Achievement ____	Vocational Assessment ____
Aptitude ____	Virginia VIEW ____

Other ____

Extracurricular or Cocurricular Activities

School Year: _____

Activity _____ Student's Role or Responsibility
_____
_____

School Year: _____

Activity _____ Student's Role or Responsibility
_____
_____

School Year: _____

Activity _____ Student's Role or Responsibility
_____
_____

School Year: _____

Activity _____ Student's Role or Responsibility
_____
_____

School Year: _____

Activity _____ Student's Role or Responsibility
_____
_____

School Year: _____

Activity _____ Student's Role or Responsibility
_____
_____

Career Exploration Activities

School Year: _____

Activity: (e.g., volunteering, job shadowing, work-study, cooperative education, other) Career(s) Explored
_____

School Year: _____

Activity: (e.g., volunteering, job shadowing, work-study, cooperative education, other) Career(s) Explored
_____

School Year: _____

Activity: (e.g., volunteering, job shadowing, work-study, cooperative education, other) Career(s) Explored
_____

School Year: _____

Activity: (e.g., volunteering, job shadowing, work-study, cooperative education, other) Career(s) Explored
_____

School Year: _____

Activity: (e.g., volunteering, job shadowing, work-study, cooperative education, other) Career(s) Explored
_____

School Year: _____

Activity: (e.g., volunteering, job shadowing, work-study, cooperative education, other) Career(s) Explored
_____

Transition Plan (Complete as appropriate)

Services Provided	Activity Completed	Date Completed
Vocational Assessment		
Career Counseling		
Employability Skills		
Work-Based Learning		
Social Skills		
Continuing Ed. Support		
Postsecondary Transition Plan		
Vocational Rehab.		
Employment Services		
Job Placement		
Ongoing Job Support		
Financial Aid Info		
Reference Letters		
Other		

Special Prizes, Honors, Offices, and Recognition

School Year: _____ _____

School Year: _____ _____

School Year: _____ _____

School Year: _____ _____

School Year: _____ _____

School Year: _____ _____

PART II

INDIVIDUAL CAREER PLAN (ICP)–ADOLESCENT EDUCATION

SCHOOL YEAR _____

(ICP to be completed annually)

NAME _____

Last   First   Middle

SCHOOL _____

1. My interests are:

_____

_____

2. My abilities are:

_____

_____

3. My hobby and recreational/leisure activities are as follows:

_____

_____

4. I do best in these school subjects:

_____

_____

5. I have explored the following careers:

_____

_____

_____

6. I have worked part-time or had some experience with the following jobs or works tasks:

_____

_____

_____

7. My tentative career goal(s) is (are) the following:

_____

_____

_____

8. In order to achieve my career goal(s):

a. I need to develop the following habits or behaviors: (Check the item when it has been successfully accomplished).

_____

_____

_____

b. I plan to develop the following knowledge, skills, or attitudes: (Check the item when it has been accomplished successfully).

_____

_____

_____

c. I plan to participate in the following home, school, and community activities to help me develop the knowledge, skills, and attitudes I want: (Check the item when accomplished successfully).

_____

_____

_____

d. I plan to pursue further education beyond high school in the following programs, schools, colleges, or military services:

_____

_____

_____

e. I plan to obtain work after high school in one of the following jobs:

_____

_____

_____

Signature _____ (Date) _____ (Date) _____ (Date)

Student   Parent   Counselor

Career Counseling Competencies of the National Career Development Association (NCDA)

INTRODUCTION TO CAREER COUNSELING COMPETENCY STATEMENTS

These competency statements are for those professionals interested and trained in the field of career counseling. For the purpose of these statements, career counseling is defined as the process of assisting individuals in the development of a life career with focus on the definition of the worker role and how that role interacts with other life roles.

NCDA's Career Counseling Competencies are intended to represent minimum competencies for those professionals at or above the master's degree level of education. These competencies are reviewed on an ongoing basis by the NCDA Professional Standards Committee, the NCDA Board, and other relevant associations. Professional competency statements provide guidance for the minimum competencies necessary to perform effectively a particular occupation or job within a particular field. Professional career counselors (master's degree or higher) or persons in career development positions must demonstrate the knowledge and skills for a specialty in career counseling that the generalist counselor might not possess. Skills and knowledge are represented by designated competency areas, which have been developed by professional career counselors and counselor educators. The Career Counseling Competency Statements can serve as a guide for career counseling training programs or as a checklist for persons wanting to acquire or to enhance their skills in career counseling.

CAREER DEVELOPMENT THEORY
(Chapters 1, 2, and 3)
Theory base and knowledge considered essential for professionals engaging in career counseling and development. Demonstration of knowledge of:

1. Counseling theories and associated techniques
2. Theories and models of career development
3. Individual differences related to gender, sexual orientation, race, ethnicity, and physical and mental capacities
4. Theoretical models for career development and associated counseling and information-delivery techniques and resources
5. Human growth and development throughout the life span
6. Role relationships that facilitate life-work planning
7. Information, techniques, and models related to career planning and placement

INDIVIDUAL AND GROUP COUNSELING SKILLS
(Chapter 8)
Individual and group counseling competencies considered essential to effective career counseling. Demonstration of ability to:

1. Establish and maintain productive personal relationships with individuals
2. Establish and maintain a productive group climate
3. Collaborate with clients in identifying personal goals

Source: From National Career Development Association, 1997, Career Counseling Competencies, Tulsa, OK: http://www.ncda.org/pdf/counselingcompetencies.pdf.

4. Identify and select techniques appropriate to client or group goals and client needs, psychological states, and developmental tasks
5. Identify and understand clients' personal characteristics related to career
6. Identify and understand social contextual conditions affecting clients' careers
7. Identify and understand familial, subcultural, and cultural structures and functions as they are related to clients' careers
8. Identify and understand clients' career decision-making processes
9. Identify and understand clients' attitudes toward work and workers
10. Identify and understand clients' biases toward work and workers based on gender, race, and cultural stereotypes
11. Challenge and encourage clients to take action to prepare for and initiate role transitions by locating sources of relevant information and experience, obtaining and interpreting information and experiences, and acquiring skills needed to make role transitions
12. Assist the client to acquire a set of employability and job search skills
13. Support and challenge clients to examine life-work roles, including the balance of work, leisure, family, and community in their careers

INDIVIDUAL/GROUP ASSESSMENT
(Chapter 5)
Individual/group assessment skills considered essential for professionals engaging in career counseling. Demonstration of ability to:

1. Assess personal characteristics such as aptitude, achievement, interests, values, and personality traits
2. Assess leisure interests, learning style, life roles, self-concept, career maturity, vocational identity, career indecision, work environment preference (e.g., work satisfaction), and other related life style/development issues
3. Assess conditions of the work environment (such as tasks, expectations, norms, and qualities of the physical and social settings)
4. Evaluate and select valid and reliable instruments appropriate to the client's gender, sexual orientation, race, ethnicity, and physical and mental capacities
5. Use computer-delivered assessment measures effectively and appropriately
6. Select assessment techniques appropriate for group administration and those appropriate for individual administration

7. Administer, score, and report findings from career assessment instruments appropriately
8. Interpret data from assessment instruments and present the results to clients and to others
9. Assist the client and others designated by the client to interpret data from assessment instruments
10. Write an accurate report of assessment results

INFORMATION/RESOURCES
(Chapter 6)
Information/resource base and knowledge essential for professionals engaging in career counseling. Demonstration of knowledge of:

1. Education, training, and employment trends; labor market information and resources that provide information about job tasks, functions, salaries, requirements, and future outlooks related to broad occupational fields and individual occupations
2. Resources and skills that clients utilize in life-work planning and management
3. Community/professional resources available to assist clients in career planning, including job search
4. Changing roles of women and men and the implications that this has for education, family, and leisure
5. Methods of good use of computer-based career information delivery systems (CIDS) and computer-assisted career guidance systems (CACGS) to assist with career planning

PROGRAM PROMOTION, MANAGEMENT, AND IMPLEMENTATION
(Chapters 9, 10, 11, 12, and 13)
Knowledge and skills necessary to develop, plan, implement, and manage comprehensive career development programs in a variety of settings. Demonstration of knowledge of:

1. Designs that can be used in the organization of career development programs
2. Needs assessment and evaluation techniques and practices
3. Organizational theories, including diagnosis, behavior, planning, organizational communication, and management useful in implementing and administering career development programs
4. Methods of forecasting, budgeting, planning, costing, policy analysis, resource allocation, and quality control
5. Leadership theories and approaches for evaluation and feedback, organizational change, decision making, and conflict resolution

6. Professional standards and criteria for career development programs
7. Societal trends and state and federal legislation that influence the development and implementation of career development programs
8. Implement individual and group programs in career development for specified populations
9. Train others about the appropriate use of computer-based systems for career information and planning
10. Plan, organize, and manage a comprehensive career resource center
11. Implement career development programs in collaboration with others
12. Identify and evaluate staff competencies
13. Mount a marketing and public relations campaign in behalf of career development activities and services

COACHING, CONSULTATION, AND PERFORMANCE IMPROVEMENT
(Chapters 8 and 9)
Knowledge and skills considered essential in relating to individuals and organizations that impact the career counseling and development process. Demonstration of ability to:

1. Use consultation theories, strategies, and models
2. Establish and maintain a productive consultative relationship with people who can influence a client's career
3. Help the general public and legislators to understand the importance of career counseling, career development, and life-work planning
4. Impact public policy as it relates to career development and workforce planning
5. Analyze future organizational needs and current level of employee skills and develop performance improvement training
6. Mentor and coach employees

DIVERSE POPULATIONS
(Chapter 4)
Knowledge and skills considered essential in relating to diverse populations that impact career counseling and development processes. Demonstration of ability to:

1. Identify development models and multicultural counseling competencies
2. Identify developmental needs unique to various diverse populations, including those of different gender, sexual orientation, ethnic group, race, and physical or mental capacity

3. Define career development programs to accommodate needs unique to various diverse populations
4. Find appropriate methods or resources to communicate with individuals who have a limited proficiency in English
5. Identify alternative approaches to meet career planning needs for individuals of various diverse populations
6. Identify community resources and establish linkages to assist clients with specific needs
7. Assist other staff members, professionals, and community members in understanding the unique needs/characteristics of diverse populations with regard to career exploration, employment expectations, and economic/social issues
8. Advocate for the career development and employment of diverse populations
9. Design and deliver career development programs and materials to hard-to-reach populations

SUPERVISION
(Chapter 9)
Knowledge and skills considered essential in critically evaluating counselor or career development facilitator performance, maintaining and improving professional skills. Demonstration of:

1. Ability to recognize own limitations as a career counselor and to seek supervision or refer clients when appropriate
2. Ability to utilize supervision on a regular basis to maintain and improve counselor skills
3. Ability to consult with supervisors and colleagues regarding client and counseling issues and related to one's own professional development as a career counselor
4. Knowledge of supervision models and theories
5. Ability to provide effective supervision to career counselors and career development facilitators at different levels of experience
6. Ability to provide effective supervision to career development facilitators at different levels of experience by knowledge of their roles, competencies, and ethical standards; determining their competence in each of the areas included in their certification; further training them in competencies, including interpretation of assessment instruments; monitoring and mentoring their activities in support of the professional career counselor; and scheduling regular consultations for the purpose of reviewing their activities

ETHICAL/LEGAL ISSUES
(Chapter 14)

Information base and knowledge essential for the ethical and legal practice of career counseling. Demonstration of knowledge of:

1. Adherence to ethical codes and standards relevant to the profession of career counseling (e.g.,, NBCC, NCDA, APA, and ACA)
2. Current ethical and legal issues which affect the practice of career counseling with all populations
3. Current ethical/legal issues with regard to the use of computer-assisted career guidance systems
4. Ethical standards relating to consultation issues
5. State and federal statutes relating to client confidentiality

RESEARCH/EVALUATION
(Chapter 9)

Knowledge and skills considered essential in understanding and conducting research and evaluation in career counseling and development. Demonstration of ability to:

1. Write a research proposal
2. Use types of research and research designs appropriate to career counseling and development research
3. Convey research findings related to the effectiveness of career counseling programs
4. Design, conduct, and use the results of evaluation programs

5. Design evaluation programs which take into account the need of various diverse populations, including persons of both genders, differing sexual orientations, different ethnic and racial backgrounds, and differing physical and mental capacities
6. Apply appropriate statistical procedures to career development research

TECHNOLOGY
(Chapter 7)

Knowledge and skills considered essential in using technology to assist individuals with career planning. Demonstration of knowledge of:

1. Various computer-based guidance and information systems as well as services available on the Internet
2. Standards by which such systems and services are evaluated (e.g., NCDA and ACSCI)
3. Ways in which to use computer-based systems and Internet services to assist individuals with career planning that are consistent with ethical standards
4. Characteristics of clients that make them profit more or less from use of technology-driven systems
5. Methods to evaluate and select a system to meet local needs

Reference

National Career Development Association Professional Standards Committee. (1997). *Career counseling competencies*. Alexandria, VA: National Career Development Association.

2009 CACREP Standards Related to Career Development

Career Development—studies that provide an understanding of career development and related life factors, including all of the following:

Book Chapter	CACREP Standard
2, 3	a. career development theories and decision-making models;
6, 7	b. career, avocational, educational, occupational and labor market information resources, visual and print media, and career information systems;
9, 15	c. career development program planning, organization, implementation, administration, and evaluation;
1, 2, 4	d. interrelationships among and between work, family, and other life roles and factors including the role of multicultural issues in career development;
8, 9, 15	e. career and educational planning, placement, follow-up, and evaluation;
5, 7	f. assessment instruments and techniques that are relevant to career planning and decision making;
4, 6–8, 10–14	g. career counseling processes, techniques, and resources, including those applicable to specific populations.

Source: From The 2009 CACREP Standards retrieved June 9, 2008. Retrieved from: http://www.cacrep.org/2009 standards.html.

E

National Career Development Guidelines (NCDG) Framework

UNDERSTANDING THE NCDG FRAMEWORK

Domains and Goals

Domains, goals, and indicators organize the NCDG framework. The **three domains**: Personal Social Development (PS), Educational Achievement and Lifelong Learning (ED), and Career Management (CM) describe content. Under each domain are **goals** (eleven in total). The goals define broad areas of career development competency.

Personal Social Development Domain

- GOAL PS1: Develop understanding of self to build and maintain a positive self-concept.
- GOAL PS2: Develop positive interpersonal skills including respect for diversity.
- GOAL PS3: Integrate growth and change into your career development.
- GOAL PS4: Balance personal, leisure, community, learner, family, and work roles.

Educational Achievement and Lifelong Learning Domain

- GOAL ED1: Attain educational achievement and performance levels needed to reach your personal and career goals.
- GOAL ED2: Participate in ongoing, lifelong learning experiences to enhance your ability to function effectively in a diverse and changing economy.

Career Management Domain

- GOAL CM1: Create and manage a career plan that meets your career goals.
- GOAL CM2: Use a process of decision making as one component of career development.
- GOAL CM3: Use accurate, current, and unbiased career information during career planning and management.
- GOAL CM4: Master academic, occupational, and general employability skills in order to obtain, create, maintain, and/or advance your employment.
- GOAL CM5: Integrate changing employment trends, societal needs, and economic conditions into your career plans.

Indicators and Learning Stages

Under each goal in the framework are indicators of mastery that highlight the knowledge and skills needed to achieve that goal. Each indicator is presented in **three learning stages** derived from *Bloom's Taxonomy*: knowledge acquisition, application, and reflection. The stages describe learning competency. They are not tied to an individual's age or level of education.

Knowledge Acquisition (K). Youth and adults at the knowledge acquisition stage expand knowledge awareness and build comprehension. They can recall, recognize, describe, identify, clarify, discuss, explain, summarize, query, investigate, and compile new information about the knowledge.

Application (A). Youth and adults at the application stage apply acquired knowledge to situations and to self. They seek out ways to use the knowledge. For example, they can demonstrate, employ, perform, illustrate, and solve problems related to the knowledge.

Reflection (R). Youth and adults at the reflection stage analyze, synthesize, judge, assess, and evaluate knowledge in accord with their own goals, values, and beliefs. They decide whether or not to integrate the acquired knowledge into their ongoing response to situations and adjust their behavior accordingly.

Coding System
The NCDG framework has a simple **coding system** to identify domains, goals, indicators, and learning stages. The coding system makes it easy for you to use the NCDG for program development and to track activities by goal, learning stage, and indicator. However, you do **not** need to know or include the codes to use the NCDG framework.

Domains
- PS—Personal Social Development
- ED—Educational Achievement and Lifelong Learning
- CM—Career Management

Goals
(Coded by domain and then numerically.)
For example, under the Personal Social Development domain:

- Goal PS1: Develop understanding of yourself to build and maintain a positive self-concept.

- Goal PS2: Develop positive interpersonal skills including respect for diversity.

Indicators and Learning Stages
(Coded by domain, goal, learning stage, and then numerically.)
Learning Stages:

- K—Knowledge Acquisition
- A—Application
- R—Reflection

For example, the second indicator under the first goal of the Personal Social Development domain:

- PS1.K2: Identify your abilities, strengths, skills, and talents.
- PS1.A2: Demonstrate use of your abilities, strengths, skills, and talents.
- PS1.R2: Assess the impact of your abilities, strengths, skills, and talents on your career development.

If you have questions about the NCDG framework, in general, or its technical development, please contact the National Training Support Center (703-416-1840).

THE FRAMEWORK
National Career Development Guidelines Revision 09/30/04

PERSONAL SOCIAL DEVELOPMENT DOMAIN	
Goal PS1	Develop understanding of yourself to build and maintain a positive self-concept.
PS1.K1	Identify your interests, likes, and dislikes.
PS1.A1	Demonstrate behavior and decisions that reflect your interests, likes, and dislikes.
PS1.R1	Assess how your interests and preferences are reflected in your career goals.
PS1.K2	Identify your abilities, strengths, skills, and talents.
PS1.A2	Demonstrate use of your abilities, strengths, skills, and talents.
PS1.R2	Assess the impact of your abilities, strengths, skills, and talents on your career development.
PS1.K3	Identify your positive personal characteristics (e.g., honesty, dependability, responsibility, integrity, and loyalty).
PS1.A3	Give examples of when you demonstrated positive personal characteristics (e.g., honesty, dependability, responsibility, integrity, and loyalty).
PS1.R3	Assess the impact of your positive personal characteristics (e.g., honesty, dependability, responsibility, integrity, and loyalty) on your career development.

(continued)

Goal PS1	Develop understanding of yourself to build and maintain a positive self-concept.
PS1.K4	Identify your work values/needs.
PS1.A4	Demonstrate behavior and decisions that reflect your work values/needs.
PS1.R4	Assess how your work values/needs are reflected in your career goals.
PS1.K5	Describe aspects of your self-concept.
PS1.A5	Demonstrate a positive self-concept through your behaviors and attitudes.
PS1.R5	Analyze the positive and negative aspects of your self-concept.
PS1.K6	Identify behaviors and experiences that help to build and maintain a positive self-concept.
PS1.A6	Show how you have adopted behaviors and sought experiences that build and maintain a positive self-concept.
PS1.R6	Evaluate the effect of your behaviors and experiences on building and maintaining a positive self-concept.
PS1.K7	Recognize that situations, attitudes, and the behaviors of others affect your self-concept.
PS1.A7	Give personal examples of specific situations, attitudes, and behaviors of others that affected your self-concept.
PS1.R7	Evaluate the effect of situations, attitudes, and the behaviors of others on your self-concept.
PS1.K8	Recognize that your behaviors and attitudes affect the self-concept of others.
PS1.A8	Show how you have adopted behaviors and attitudes to positively affect the self-concept of others.
PS1.R8	Analyze how your behaviors and attitudes might affect the self-concept of others.
PS1.K9	Recognize that your self-concept can affect educational achievement (i.e., performance) and/or success at work.
PS1.A9	Show how aspects of your self-concept could positively or negatively affect educational achievement (i.e., performance) and/or success at work.
PS1.R9	Assess how your self-concept affects your educational achievement (performance) and/or success at work.
PS1.K10	Recognize that educational achievement (performance) and/or success at work can affect your self-concept.
PS1.A10	Give personal examples of how educational achievement (performance) and/or success at work affected your self-concept.
PS1.R10	Assess how your educational achievement (performance) and/or success at work affect your self-concept.
Goal PS2	Develop positive interpersonal skills including respect for diversity.
PS2.K1	Identify effective communication skills.
PS2.A1	Demonstrate effective communication skills.
PS2.R1	Evaluate your use of effective communication skills.
PS2.K2	Recognize the benefits of interacting with others in a way that is honest, fair, helpful, and respectful.

Goal PS2	Develop positive interpersonal skills including respect for diversity.
PS2.A2	Demonstrate that you interact with others in a way that is honest, fair, helpful, and respectful.
PS2.R2	Assess the degree to which you interact with others in a way that is honest, fair, helpful, and respectful.
PS2.K3	Identify positive social skills (e.g., good manners and showing gratitude).
PS2.A3	Demonstrate the ability to use positive social skills (e.g., good manners and showing gratitude).
PS2.R3	Evaluate how your positive social skills (e.g., good manners and showing gratitude) contribute to effective interactions with others.
PS2.K4	Identify ways to get along well with others and work effectively with them in groups.
PS2.A4	Demonstrate the ability to get along well with others and work effectively with them in groups.
PS2.R4	Evaluate your ability to work effectively with others in groups.
PS2.K5	Describe conflict resolution skills.
PS2.A5	Demonstrate the ability to resolve conflicts and to negotiate acceptable solutions.
PS2.R5	Analyze the success of your conflict resolution skills.
PS2.K6	Recognize the difference between appropriate and inappropriate behavior in specific school, social, and work situations.
PS2.A6	Give examples of times when your behavior was appropriate and times when your behavior was inappropriate in specific school, social, and work situations.
PS2.R6	Assess the consequences of appropriate or inappropriate behavior in specific school, social, and work situations.
PS2.K7	Identify sources of outside pressure that affect you.
PS2.A7	Demonstrate the ability to handle outside pressure on you.
PS2.R7	Analyze the impact of outside pressure on your behavior.
PS2.K8	Recognize that you should accept responsibility for your behavior.
PS2.A8	Demonstrate that you accept responsibility for your behavior.
PS2.R8	Assess the degree to which you accept personal responsibility for your behavior.
PS2.K9	Recognize that you should have knowledge about, respect for, be open to, and appreciate all kinds of human diversity.
PS2.A9	Demonstrate knowledge about, respect for, openness to, and appreciation for all kinds of human diversity.
PS2.R9	Assess how you show respect for all kinds of human diversity.
PS2.K10	Recognize that the ability to interact positively with diverse groups of people may contribute to learning and academic achievement.
PS2.A10	Show how the ability to interact positively with diverse groups of people may contribute to learning and academic achievement.

(continued)

Goal PS2	Develop positive interpersonal skills including respect for diversity.
PS2.R10	Analyze the impact of your ability to interact positively with diverse groups of people on your learning and academic achievement.
PS2.K11	Recognize that the ability to interact positively with diverse groups of people is often essential to maintain employment.
PS2.A11	Explain how the ability to interact positively with diverse groups of people is often essential to maintain employment.
PS2.R11	Analyze the impact of your ability to interact positively with diverse groups of people on your employment.

Goal PS3	Integrate personal growth and change into your career development.
PS3.K1	Recognize that you will experience growth and changes in mind and body throughout life that will impact on your career development.
PS3.A1	Give examples of how you have grown and changed (e.g., physically, emotionally, socially, and intellectually).
PS3.R1	Analyze the results of your growth and changes throughout life to determine areas of growth for the future.
PS3.K2	Identify good health habits (e.g., good nutrition and constructive ways to manage stress).
PS3.A2	Demonstrate how you have adopted good health habits.
PS3.R2	Assess the impact of your health habits on your career development.
PS3.K3	Recognize that your motivations and aspirations are likely to change with time and circumstances.
PS3.A3	Give examples of how your personal motivations and aspirations have changed with time and circumstances.
PS3.R3	Assess how changes in your motivations and aspirations over time have affected your career development.
PS3.K4	Recognize that external events often cause life changes.
PS3.A4	Give examples of external events that have caused life changes for you.
PS3.R4	Assess your strategies for managing life changes caused by external events.
PS3.K5	Identify situations (e.g., problems at school or work) in which you might need assistance from people or other resources.
PS3.A5	Demonstrate the ability to seek assistance (e.g., with problems at school or work) from appropriate resources including other people.
PS3.R5	Assess the effectiveness of your strategies for getting assistance (e.g., with problems at school or work) from appropriate resources including other people.
PS3.K6	Recognize the importance of adaptability and flexibility when initiating or responding to change.
PS3.A6	Demonstrate adaptability and flexibility when initiating or responding to change.
PS3.R6	Analyze how effectively you respond to change and/or initiate change.

Goal PS4	Balance personal, leisure, community, learner, family, and work roles.
PS4.K1	Recognize that you have many life roles (e.g., personal, leisure, community, learner, family, and work roles).
PS4.A1	Give examples that demonstrate your life roles including personal, leisure, community, learner, family, and work roles.
PS4.R1	Assess the impact of your life roles on career goals.
PS4.K2	Recognize that you must balance life roles and that there are many ways to do it.
PS4.A2	Show how you are balancing your life roles.
PS4.R2	Analyze how specific life role changes would affect the attainment of your career goals.
PS4.K3	Describe the concept of lifestyle.
PS4.A3	Give examples of decisions, factors, and circumstances that affect your current lifestyle.
PS4.R3	Analyze how specific lifestyle changes would affect the attainment of your career goals.
PS4.K4	Recognize that your life roles and your lifestyle are connected.
PS4.A4	Show how your life roles and your lifestyle are connected.
PS4.R4	Assess how changes in your life roles would affect your lifestyle.

EDUCATIONAL ACHIEVEMENT AND LIFELONG LEARNING DOMAIN

Goal ED1	Attain educational achievement and performance levels needed to reach your personal and career goals.
ED1.K1	Recognize the importance of educational achievement and performance to the attainment of personal and career goals.
ED1.A1	Demonstrate educational achievement and performance levels needed to attain your personal and career goals.
ED1.R1	Evaluate how well you have attained educational achievement and performance levels needed to reach your personal and career goals.
ED1.K2	Identify strategies for improving educational achievement and performance.
ED1.A2	Demonstrate strategies you are using to improve educational achievement and performance.
ED1.R2	Analyze your educational achievement and performance strategies to create a plan for growth and improvement.
ED1.K3	Describe study skills and learning habits that promote educational achievement and performance.
ED1.A3	Demonstrate acquisition of study skills and learning habits that promote educational achievement and performance.
ED1.R3	Evaluate your study skills and learning habits to develop a plan for improving them.
ED1.K4	Identify your learning style.

(continued)

Goal ED1	Attain educational achievement and performance levels needed to reach your personal and career goals.
ED1.A4	Show how you are using learning-style information to improve educational achievement and performance.
ED1.R4	Analyze your learning style to develop behaviors to maximize educational achievement and performance.
ED1.K5	Describe the importance of having a plan to improve educational achievement and performance.
ED1.A5	Show that you have a plan to improve educational achievement and performance.
ED1.R5	Evaluate the results of your plan for improving educational achievement and performance.
ED1.K6	Describe how personal attitudes and behaviors can impact educational achievement and performance.
ED1.A6	Exhibit attitudes and behaviors that support educational achievement and performance.
ED1.R6	Assess how well your attitudes and behaviors promote educational achievement and performance.
ED1.K7	Recognize that your educational achievement and performance can lead to many workplace options.
ED1.A7	Show how your educational achievement and performance can expand your workplace options.
ED1.R7	Assess how well your educational achievement and performance will transfer to the workplace.
ED1.K8	Recognize that the ability to acquire and use information contributes to educational achievement and performance.
ED1.A8	Show how the ability to acquire and use information has affected your educational achievement and performance.
ED1.R8	Assess your ability to acquire and use information in order to improve educational achievement and performance.
Goal ED2	Participate in ongoing, lifelong learning experiences to enhance your ability to function effectively in a diverse and changing economy.
ED2.K1	Recognize that changes in the economy require you to acquire and update knowledge and skills throughout life.
ED2.A1	Show how lifelong learning is helping you function effectively in a diverse and changing economy.
ED2.R1	Judge whether or not you have the knowledge and skills necessary to function effectively in a diverse and changing economy.
ED2.K2	Recognize that viewing yourself as a learner affects your identity.
ED2.A2	Show how being a learner affects your identity.
ED2.R2	Analyze how specific learning experiences have affected your identity.

Goal ED2	Participate in ongoing, lifelong learning experiences to enhance your ability to function effectively in a diverse and changing economy.
ED2.K3	Recognize the importance of being an independent learner and taking responsibility for your learning.
ED2.A3	Demonstrate that you are an independent learner.
ED2.R3	Assess how well you function as an independent learner.
ED2.K4	Describe the requirements for transition from one learning level to the next (e.g., middle school to high school, high school to postsecondary).
ED2.A4	Demonstrate the knowledge and skills necessary for transition from one learning level to the next (e.g., middle to high school, high school to postsecondary).
ED2.R4	Analyze how your knowledge and skills affect your transition from one learning level to the next (e.g., middle school to high school, high school to postsecondary).
ED2.K5	Identify types of ongoing learning experiences available to you (e.g., two- and four-year colleges, technical schools, apprenticeships, the military, online courses, and on-the-job training).
ED2.A5	Show how you are preparing to participate in ongoing learning experiences (e.g., two- and four-year colleges, technical schools, apprenticeships, the military, online courses, and on-the-job training).
ED2.R5	Assess how participation in ongoing learning experiences (e.g., two- and four-year colleges, technical schools, apprenticeships, the military, online courses, and on-the-job training) affects your personal and career goals.
ED2.K6	Identify specific education/training programs (e.g., high school career paths and courses, college majors, and apprenticeship programs).
ED2.A6	Demonstrate participation in specific education/training programs (e.g., high school career paths and courses, college majors, and apprenticeship programs) that help you function effectively in a diverse and changing economy.
ED2.R6	Evaluate how participation in specific education/training programs (e.g., high school career paths and courses, college majors, and apprenticeship programs) affects your ability to function effectively in a diverse and changing economy.
ED2.K7	Describe informal learning experiences that contribute to lifelong learning.
ED2.A7	Demonstrate participation in informal learning experiences.
ED2.R7	Assess, throughout your life, how well you integrate both formal and informal learning experiences.

CAREER MANAGEMENT DOMAIN

Goal CM1	Create and manage a career plan that meets your career goals.
CM1.K1	Recognize that career planning to attain your career goals is a lifelong process.
CM1.A1	Give examples of how you use career planning strategies to attain your career goals.
CM1.R1	Assess how well your career planning strategies facilitate reaching your career goals.

(continued)

Goal CM1	Create and manage a career plan that meets your career goals.
CM1.K2	Describe how to develop a career plan (e.g., steps and content).
CM1.A2	Develop a career plan to meet your career goals.
CM1.R2	Analyze your career plan and make adjustments to reflect ongoing career management needs.
CM1.K3	Identify your short-term and long-term career goals (e.g., education, employment, and lifestyle goals).
CM1.A3	Demonstrate actions taken to attain your short-term and long-term career goals (e.g., education, employment, and lifestyle goals).
CM1.R3	Reexamine your career goals and adjust as needed.
CM1.K4	Identify skills and personal traits needed to manage your career (e.g., resiliency, self-efficacy, ability to identify trends and changes, and flexibility).
CM1.A4	Demonstrate career management skills and personal traits (e.g., resiliency, self-efficacy, ability to identify trends and changes, and flexibility).
CM1.R4	Evaluate your career management skills and personal traits (e.g., resiliency, self-efficacy, ability to identify trends and changes, and flexibility).
CM1.K5	Recognize that changes in you and the world-of-work can affect your career plans.
CM1.A5	Give examples of how changes in you and the world-of-work have caused you to adjust your career plans.
CM1.R5	Evaluate how well you integrate changes in you and the world-of-work into your career plans.
Goal CM2	Use a process of decision making as one component of career development.
CM2.K1	Describe your decision-making style (e.g., risk taker, cautious).
CM2.A1	Give examples of past decisions that demonstrate your decision-making style.
CM2.R1	Evaluate the effectiveness of your decision-making style.
CM2.K2	Identify the steps in one model of decision making.
CM2.A2	Demonstrate the use of a decision-making model.
CM2.R2	Assess what decision-making model(s) work best for you.
CM2.K3	Describe how information (e.g., about you, the economy, and education programs) can improve your decision making.
CM2.A3	Demonstrate use of information (e.g., about you, the economy, and education programs) in making decisions.
CM2.R3	Assess how well you use information (e.g., about you, the economy, and education programs) to make decisions.
CM2.K4	Identify alternative options and potential consequences for a specific decision.
CM2.A4	Show how exploring options affected a decision you made.
CM2.R4	Assess how well you explore options when making decisions.
CM2.K5	Recognize that your personal priorities, culture, beliefs, and work values can affect your decision making.

Goal CM2	Use a process of decision making as one component of career development.
CM2.A5	Show how personal priorities, culture, beliefs, and work values are reflected in your decisions.
CM2.R5	Evaluate the effect of personal priorities, culture, beliefs, and work values in your decision making.
CM2.K6	Describe how education, work, and family experiences might impact your decisions.
CM2.A6	Give specific examples of how your education, work, and family experiences have influenced your decisions.
CM2.R6	Assess the impact of your education, work, and family experiences on decisions.
CM2.K7	Describe how biases and stereotypes can limit decisions.
CM2.A7	Give specific examples of how biases and stereotypes affected your decisions.
CM2.R7	Analyze the ways you could manage biases and stereotypes when making decisions.
CM2.K8	Recognize that chance can play a role in decision making.
CM2.A8	Give examples of times when chance played a role in your decision making.
CM2.R8	Evaluate the impact of chance on past decisions.
CM2.K9	Recognize that decision making often involves compromise.
CM2.A9	Give examples of compromises you might have to make in career decision making.
CM2.R9	Analyze the effectiveness of your approach to making compromises.
Goal CM3	Use accurate, current, and unbiased career information during career planning and management.
CM3.K1	Describe the importance of career information to your career planning.
CM3.A1	Show how career information has been important in your plans and how it can be used in future plans.
CM3.R1	Assess the impact of career information on your plans and refine plans so that they reflect accurate, current, and unbiased career information.
CM3.K2	Recognize that career information includes occupational, education and training, employment, and economic information and that there is a range of career information resources available.
CM3.A2	Demonstrate the ability to use different types of career information resources (i.e., occupational, educational, economic, and employment) to support career planning.
CM3.R2	Evaluate how well you integrate occupational, educational, economic, and employment information into the management of your career.
CM3.K3	Recognize that the quality of career information resource content varies (e.g., accuracy, bias, and how up-to-date and complete it is).
CM3.A3	Show how selected examples of career information are biased, out-of-date, incomplete, or inaccurate.

(continued)

Goal CM3	Use accurate, current, and unbiased career information during career planning and management.
CM3.R3	Judge the quality of the career information resources you plan to use in terms of accuracy, bias, and how up-to-date and complete it is.
CM3.K4	Identify several ways to classify occupations.
CM3.A4	Give examples of how occupational classification systems can be used in career planning.
CM3.R4	Assess which occupational classification system is most helpful to your career planning.
CM3.K5	Identify occupations that you might consider without regard to your gender, race, culture, or ability.
CM3.A5	Demonstrate openness to considering occupations that you might view as nontraditional (i.e., relative to your gender, race, culture, or ability).
CM3.R5	Assess your openness to considering nontraditional occupations in your career management.
CM3.K6	Identify the advantages and disadvantages of being employed in a nontraditional occupation.
CM3.A6	Make decisions for yourself about being employed in a nontraditional occupation.
CM3.R6	Assess the impact of your decisions about being employed in a nontraditional occupation.
Goal CM4	Master academic, occupational, and general employability skills in order to obtain, create, maintain, and/or advance your employment.
CM4.K1	Describe academic, occupational, and general employability skills.
CM4.A1	Demonstrate the ability to use your academic, occupational, and general employability skills to obtain or create, maintain, and advance your employment.
CM4.R1	Assess your academic, occupational, and general employability skills and enhance them as needed for your employment.
CM4.K2	Identify job-seeking skills such as the ability to: write a resume and cover letter, complete a job application, interview for a job, and find and pursue employment leads.
CM4.A2	Demonstrate the following job-seeking skills: the ability to write a resume and cover letter, complete a job application, interview for a job, and find and pursue employment leads.
CM4.R2	Evaluate your ability to: write a resume and cover letter, complete a job application, interview for a job, and find and pursue employment leads.
CM4.K3	Recognize that a variety of general employability skills and personal qualities (e.g., critical thinking, problem solving, resource, information, and technology management, interpersonal skills, honesty, and dependability) are important to success in school and employment.
CM4.A3	Demonstrate attainment of general employability skills and personal qualities needed to be successful in school and employment (e.g., critical thinking, problem solving, resource, information, and technology management, interpersonal skills, honesty, and dependability).

Goal CM4	**Master academic, occupational, and general employability skills in order to obtain, create, maintain, and/or advance your employment.**
CM4.R3	Evaluate your general employability skills and personal qualities (e.g., critical thinking, problem solving, resource, information, and technology management, interpersonal skills, honesty, and dependability).
CM4.K4	Recognize that many skills are transferable from one occupation to another.
CM4.A4	Show how your skills are transferable from one occupation to another.
CM4.R4	Analyze the impact of your transferable skills on your career options.
CM4.K5	Recognize that your geographic mobility impacts on your employability.
CM4.A5	Make decisions for yourself regarding geographic mobility.
CM4.R5	Analyze the impact of your decisions about geographic mobility on your career goals.
CM4.K6	Identify the advantages and challenges of self-employment.
CM4.A6	Make decisions for yourself about self-employment.
CM4.R6	Assess the impact of your decision regarding self-employment on your career goals.
CM4.K7	Identify ways to be proactive in marketing yourself for a job.
CM4.A7	Demonstrate skills that show how you can market yourself in the workplace.
CM4.R7	Evaluate how well you have marketed yourself in the workplace.
Goal CM5	**Integrate changing employment trends, societal needs, and economic conditions into your career plans.**
CM5.K1	Identify societal needs that affect your career plans.
CM5.A1	Show how you are prepared to respond to changing societal needs in your career management.
CM5.R1	Evaluate the results of your career management relative to changing societal needs.
CM5.K2	Identify economic conditions that affect your career plans.
CM5.A2	Show how you are prepared to respond to changing economic conditions in your career management.
CM5.R2	Evaluate the results of your career management relative to changing economic conditions.
CM5.K3	Identify employment trends that affect your career plans.
CM5.A3	Show how you are prepared to respond to changing employment trends in your career management.
CM5.R3	Evaluate the results of your career management relative to changes in employment trends.

Reference

Bloom, B. S., Engelhart, M. D., Furst, E. J., Hill, W. H., & Krathwohl, D. R. (Eds.). (1956). *Taxonomy of educational objectives: Handbook I: Cognitive domain*. New York: David McKay.

Index